Mastering™
Microsoft® VBA
2nd Edition

Guy Hart-Davis

Wiley Publishing, Inc.

Wiley Publishing, Inc.

Acquisitions and Development Editor: Tom Cirtin

Technical Editor: John Mueller

Production Editor: Katherine Perry, Rachel Gunn

Copy Editor: Linda Recktenwald

Production Manager: Tim Tate

Vice President & Executive Group Publisher: Richard Swadley

Vice President and Executive Publisher: Joseph B. Wikert

Vice President and Publisher: Neil Edde

Book Designer: Maureen Forys, Happenstance Type-O-Rama; Judy Fung

Compositor: Craig Woods, Happenstance Type-O-Rama

Proofreader: Nancy Riddiough

Indexer: Nancy Guenther

Cover Design: Design Site

Cover Illustration: Jack T. Myers, Design Site

Acknowledgments

My thanks go to the following people for making this book happen:

- Tom Cirtin, Acquisitions and Developmental Editor, for getting the book approved, developing it, and keeping it moving along.

- Katherine Perry and Rachel Gunn, Project Editors, for guiding the book through the editing and production process.

- John Mueller for his intelligent and meticulous technical review.

- Linda Recktenwald, Copyeditor, for considerate and light editing.

- Craig Woods, Happenstance Type-O-Rama, Compositor, for laying out the pages.

- Nancy Riddiough, for proofreading the book

- Nancy Guenther, Indexer, for creating the index for the book.

Contents at a Glance

Contents

Introduction

Visual Basic for Applications (VBA) is a powerful tool that enables you to automate operations in the Microsoft Office applications and in all other applications that host VBA. By automating operations using VBA, you can save yourself and your colleagues huge amounts of time and effort. Getting more work done in less time is usually good for your humor and self-esteem and can do wonderful things for your job security and your career.

This book shows you how to program VBA, using the Microsoft Office 2003 applications for specific examples. You can apply the principles you learn in this book to any other VBA-enabled application as well, from AutoCAD to WordPerfect and the hundreds of other applications in between.

What Can I Do with VBA?

In a VBA-enabled application, you can use VBA to automate almost any action that you can perform interactively (manually) with the application. For example, in Word, you can create a document, add text to it, format it, and edit it; in Excel, you can integrate data from multiple workbooks into a single workbook; or in PowerPoint, you can automatically create a custom presentation including the latest data drawn from a variety of sources.

VBA performs actions faster, more accurately, more reliably, and far more cheaply than any human. As long as you can define firm conditions for making a decision, VBA can also make decisions for you. By adding decision-making structures and loops (conditional repetitions) to your code, you can take it far beyond the range of actions that the human user can perform.

Beyond automating actions you would otherwise perform manually, VBA also gives you the tools to create interfaces for your code—message boxes, input boxes, and *user forms*, graphical objects that you can use to create forms and custom dialog boxes. Using VBA, you can create a custom application that runs within the host application. For example, you could create within PowerPoint a custom application that automatically creates a presentation for you.

By using VBA, you can also access one application from another application. For example, when working with VBA from Word, you can use it to start an Excel session, perform some calculations, and then put the results into a Word document. Similarly, when using VBA from Excel, you can export particular objects to a new presentation that Excel created automatically in PowerPoint by using VBA.

Because VBA provides a standard set of tools that differ in capability according to the capabilities of the host application, once you've learned to use VBA in one application, you'll be able to apply that knowledge quickly to using VBA in another application. For example, you might start by learning VBA in order to manipulate Excel and then move on to using your VBA skills with

Outlook. You'll need to learn the components of the Outlook application, because they're different from the Excel components, but you'll be able to transition the framework of your VBA knowledge without a problem.

As with any programming language, getting started with VBA involves a considerable learning curve—but you can use the Macro Recorder tool built into some of the Microsoft Office applications (notably Word, Excel, and PowerPoint) to bend the curve downward. This book uses the Macro Recorder as the jumping-off point for you to start creating code. The book takes you through recording macros and then teaches you to edit recorded code before delving into the essentials of VBA syntax. From there, you work your way into more complex topics.

What's in This Book?

This book teaches you how to use VBA to automate your work in VBA-enabled applications. For its general examples, the book uses Word, Excel, and PowerPoint, because those are the Microsoft Office applications that you're most likely to have. The last part of the book discusses how to program these three applications and also Outlook and Access.

Part 1 of the book, "Recording Macros and Getting Started with VBA," comprises the following chapters:

◆ Chapter 1 shows you how to record a macro using the Macro Recorder in those applications that support it. You record macros in Word, Excel, PowerPoint, and Project. You also learn how to assign a way of running the macro and how to delete a macro.

◆ Chapter 2 introduces you to the Visual Basic Editor, the application in which you create VBA code (either by editing recorded code or by writing code from scratch) and user forms. The second half of this chapter discusses how you can customize the Visual Basic Editor so that you can work in it more quickly and efficiently.

◆ Chapter 3 shows you how to edit recorded macros, using the macros you recorded in Chapter 1. You learn how to step through and test a macro in the Visual Basic Editor.

◆ Chapter 4 teaches you how to start creating code from scratch in the Visual Basic Editor. You create a procedure for Word, one for Excel, and a third for PowerPoint.

Part 2, "Learning How to Work with VBA," contains the following chapters:

◆ Chapter 5 explains the essentials of VBA syntax, giving you a brief overview of the concepts you need to know. You also practice creating statements in the Visual Basic Editor.

◆ Chapter 6 shows you how to work with variables and constants, which you use to store information for your procedures to work on.

◆ Chapter 7 discusses how to use arrays. Arrays are like super-variables that can store multiple pieces of information at the same time.

◆ Chapter 8 teaches you how to find the objects you need to create your procedures. You learn how to use the Macro Recorder, the Object Browser, and the Help system to find objects; how to use object variables to represent objects; and understand what object models are and what they're for.

Part 3, "Making Decisions and Using Loops and Functions," consists of the following chapters:

◆ Chapter 9 describes how to use VBA's built-in functions—everything from string-conversion functions through mathematical and date functions to file-management functions.

◆ Chapter 10 shows you how to create functions of your own to supplement the built-in functions. You create functions that work in any VBA-enabled application, together with application-specific functions for Word, Excel, and PowerPoint.

◆ Chapter 11 shows you how to use conditional statements (such as If statements) to make decisions in your code. Conditional statements are key to making your code flexible.

◆ Chapter 12 covers how you can use loops to repeat actions in your procedures: fixed-iteration loops for fixed numbers of repetitions, and indefinite loops that match their number of repetitions to conditions you specify. You also learn how to avoid creating infinite loops, which cause your code to run either forever or until your computer crashes.

Part 4, "Using Message Boxes, Input Boxes, and Dialog Boxes," has the following chapters:

◆ Chapter 13 shows you how to use message boxes to communicate with the users of your procedures and let them make simple decisions about how the procedures run, and how to use input boxes to allow them to supply the information the procedures need.

◆ Chapter 14 discusses how to use VBA's user forms to create simple custom dialog boxes that enable the users to supply information, make choices, and direct the flow of your procedures.

◆ Chapter 15 discusses how to build more complex dialog boxes. These include dynamic dialog boxes that update themselves when the user clicks a button, dialog boxes with hidden depths that the user can reveal to access infrequently used options, dialog boxes with multiple pages of information, and dialog boxes with controls that respond to actions the user takes.

Part 5, "Creating Effective Code," contains the following chapters:

◆ Chapter 16 illustrates the benefits of building reusable modular code rather than monolithic procedures and then shows you how to build it.

◆ Chapter 17 explains the principles of debugging VBA code, examining the different kinds of errors that occur and discussing how to deal with them.

◆ Chapter 18 discusses how to build well-behaved code stable enough to withstand being run under the wrong circumstances and civilized enough to leave the user in the best possible state to continue their work after it finishes running.

◆ Chapter 19 discusses the security mechanism that VBA 6 provides for securing VBA code and ensuring that you or your users do not run malevolent code unintentionally. The chapter discusses digital certificates and digital signatures, how to choose an appropriate security setting for the application you're using, and how to make—and break—passwords.

Part 6, "Programming the Office Applications," consists of these 11 chapters:

◆ Chapter 20 explains the Word object model and shows you how to work with key objects in Word, including the Document object, the Selection object, and Range objects. You also learn how to set options in Word.

- Chapter 21 discusses how to work with widely used objects in Word, including the objects for Find and Replace; headers, footers, and page numbers; sections, page setup, windows, and views; and tables.

- Chapter 22 introduces you to the Excel object model and shows you how to work with key objects in Excel, including the `Workbook` object, the `Worksheet` object, the `ActiveCell` object, and `Range` objects. You also learn how to set options in Excel.

- Chapter 23 shows you how to work with charts, windows, and Find and Replace in Excel via VBA.

- Chapter 24 gets you started working with the PowerPoint object model and the key objects that it contains. You work with `Presentation` objects, `Window` objects, `Slide` objects, and `Master` objects.

- Chapter 25 teaches you how to go further with VBA in PowerPoint by working with shapes, headers and footers, and the VBA objects that enable you to set up and run a slide show automatically.

- Chapter 26 introduces you to the Outlook object model and the key objects that it contains. You meet Outlook's creatable objects and main interface items; learn general methods for working with Outlook objects; and work with messages, calendar items, tasks and task requests, and searches.

- Chapter 27 shows you how to work with events in Outlook. There are two types of events, application-level events and item-level events, which you can program to respond to both Outlook actions (such as new mail arriving) and user actions (such as creating a new contact).

- Chapter 28 shows you how to get around the Access object model and perform certain key actions with some of its main objects.

- Chapter 29 tells you how to manipulate the data in an Access database via VBA.

- Chapter 30 shows you how access one application from another application via VBA. You learn which tools are available, how to use Automation, how to use the `Shell` function, and how to use data objects, DDE, and `SendKeys`.

Finally, the Glossary contains a list of VBA-related terms and their definitions.

How Should I Use This Book?

This book tries to present material in a sensible and logical pattern. To avoid repeating information unnecessarily, the chapters build on each other, so the later chapters assume that you've read the earlier chapters.

The first five parts of this book present a variety of code samples using Word, Excel, and Power-Point. If you have these applications (or some of them), work through these examples as far as possible to get the most benefit from them. While you may be able to apply some of the examples directly to your work, mostly you'll find them illustrative of the techniques and principles discussed, and you'll need to create code of your own that follows those techniques and principles.

The sixth and last part of this book shows you some specifics of using VBA to program Word, Excel, PowerPoint, Outlook, and Access. Work through the chapters that cover the application or applications that you want to program with VBA. The final chapter shows you how to use one application to control another application; for example, you might use Word to control Excel.

Is This Book Suitable for Me?

Yes.

This book is for anyone who wants to learn to use VBA to automate their work in a VBA-enabled application. Automating your work could involve anything from creating a few simple procedures that would enable you to perform some complex and tedious operations in a single keystroke to building a custom application with a complete interface that looks nothing like the host application's regular interface.

This book attempts to present theoretical material in as practical a context as possible by giving examples of the theory in action. For example, when you learn about loops, you execute short procedures that illustrate the use of each kind of loop, so that you can see them at work right away.

Conventions Used in This Book

This book uses several conventions to convey information succinctly:

- ➢ designates choosing a command from a menu. For example, "choose File ➢ Open" means that you should pull down the File menu and choose the Open command from it.

- + signs indicate key combinations. For example, "press Ctrl+Shift+F9" means that you should hold down the Ctrl and Shift keys and then press the F9 key. Some of these key combinations are confusing (for example, "Ctrl++" means that you hold down Ctrl and press the + key—in other words, hold down Ctrl and Shift together and press the = key), so you may need to read them carefully.

- Likewise, "Shift+click" means that you should hold down the Shift key as you click with the mouse, and "Ctrl+click" means that you should hold down the Ctrl key as you click.

- ←, →, ↑, and ↓ represent the arrow keys that should appear in some form on your keyboard. The important thing to note is that ← is not the Backspace key (which on many keyboards bears a similar arrow). The Backspace key is represented by "Backspace" or "the Backspace key."

- **Boldface** indicates items that you may want to type in letter for letter.

- Program font indicates program items, or text derived from program lines. Complete program lines appear offset in separate paragraphs like the example below, while shorter expressions appear as part of the main text.

```
Sub Sample_Listing()
    'lines of program code look like this.
End Sub
```

- *Italics* usually indicate either new terms being introduced or variable information (such as a drive letter that will vary from computer to computer and that you'll need to establish on your own).

- ➥ (a continuation arrow) indicates that a single line of code has been broken onto a second or subsequent line in the book. Enter these lines of code as a single line when you use them. For example, the three lines below represent a single line of code:

```
MsgBox System.PrivateProfileString("",
➥"HKEY_CURRENT_USER\Software\Microsoft\
➥Office\11.0\Common\AutoCorrect", "Path")
```

You'll also see Notes, Tips, and Warnings throughout the book:

NOTE   A Note provides additional information about (or related to) the current topic.

TIP   A Tip provides useful information or a recommendation, usually related to the current topic.

WARNING   A Warning alerts you to potential problems related to the current topic.

Part 1

Recording Macros and Getting Started with VBA

- ◆ Chapter 1: Recording and Running Macros in the Office Applications
- ◆ Chapter 2: Getting Started with the Visual Basic Editor
- ◆ Chapter 3: Editing Recorded Macros
- ◆ Chapter 4: Creating Code from Scratch in the Visual Basic Editor

Chapter 1

Recording and Running Macros in the Microsoft Office Applications

- ◆ What is a macro?
- ◆ Recording a macro in Word
- ◆ Recording a macro in Excel
- ◆ Recording a macro in PowerPoint
- ◆ Running a macro
- ◆ Deleting a macro

In this chapter, you'll learn the easiest way to get started with Visual Basic for Applications (VBA): recording simple macros using the built-in Macro Recorder in the Office applications and then running them to repeat the actions they contain. By recording macros, you can automate straightforward but tediously repetitive tasks and speed up your regular work. You can also use the Macro Recorder to create VBA code that performs the actions you need and then edit the code to add flexibility and power.

What Is VBA and What Can You Do with It?

Visual Basic for Applications is a programming language created by Microsoft that can be built into applications. You use VBA to automate operations in applications that support it. All the main Office applications—Word, Excel, PowerPoint, Outlook, Access, FrontPage, and Project—support VBA, so you can automate operations through most Office applications. But Microsoft has also licensed VBA to other software companies (see `http://msdn.microsoft.com/isv/technology/vba/partners/default.aspx` for a list) and to corporate developers, so VBA is also used to program many other applications.

The previous paragraph said "automate operations in applications." That's vague because of the vast range of actions you can take using VBA. Here are some examples:

- ◆ You can record a macro that automatically performs a standard series of actions. For example, you might need to insert a picture in a Word document, format it to give it the right size and layout, and then add a caption under it, using the appropriate text style. Or you might need to insert an Excel chart on a PowerPoint slide, format it, and add descriptive text.

- You can write code that performs actions a certain number of times and that makes decisions depending on the situation in which it is running. For example, you could write code that takes a series of actions on every presentation that's open in PowerPoint.

- You can create *user forms*, or custom dialog boxes, that enable the user to make choices and specify settings for the code that's running.

- You can take actions via VBA that you can't take directly in the user interface. For example, when you're working interactively in most applications, you're limited to working with the active file—the active document in Word, the active workbook in Excel, and so on. By using VBA, you can manipulate files that aren't active.

- You can make one application manipulate another application. For example, you can make Word place a table from a document into an Excel worksheet.

The Difference between Visual Basic and Visual Basic for Applications

VBA is based on Visual Basic, a programming language derived from BASIC. *BASIC* stands for Beginner's All-Purpose Symbolic Instruction Code. BASIC is supposedly user-friendly, because it uses recognizable English words (or quasi-recognizable permutations of them) rather than abstruse and incomprehensible programming terms. Visual Basic is visual in that it supports the Windows GUI and provides tools for drag-and-drop programming and working with shared graphical elements.

Visual Basic for Applications consists of Visual Basic implementations that contain a common core of commands and application-specific objects. The set of objects available in each application is different because no two applications share the same features and commands.

For example, the set of VBA objects available in Word is different from the set of VBA objects available in Excel, because VBA implements features and commands that Word has but Excel does not. But because the commands and structure of VBA in Word and VBA in Excel are the same, you can quickly translate your knowledge of VBA in Word to VBA in Excel. For example, you'd use the Save method (a method is essentially a command) to save a file in Excel VBA, Word VBA, or PowerPoint VBA. In Excel VBA, the command would be `ActiveWorkbook.Save`, whereas in Word VBA, it would be `ActiveDocument.Save`, and in PowerPoint, it would be `ActivePresentation.Save`.

VBA always works with a host application (such as Word, Quattro Pro, or Visio). With the exception of some standalone projects that the Microsoft Office Developer Edition enables, a host application always needs to be open for VBA to run. This means that you can't build standalone applications with VBA the way you can with Visual Basic. If necessary, you can hide the host application from the user so that all they see is the interface (typically user forms) that you give to your VBA procedures. By doing this, you can create the illusion of a standalone application. Whether you need to create this effect will depend on the type of programming you do.

Macro Basics

A *macro* is a sequence of commands you can repeat at will. You can repeat the actions by using a single command to run the macro. In some applications, you can also set a macro to run itself automatically. For instance, you might create a macro in Word to automate basic formatting tasks on a type of document you regularly receive incorrectly formatted. You could run the macro either manually or automatically upon opening a document of that type.

A macro is a type of *subprocedure*, and a subprocedure is sometimes also called a *subroutine*. Generally, people tend to use the terms *procedure* and *routine* rather than the two *sub* words when speaking more loosely. A macro is sometimes understood to consist of recorded code rather than written code, but many people use the word in a wider sense, so it can include written code as well. For example, if you record a macro and then edit it until it's more compact and efficient, or add commands to make it take further actions, many people still consider it a macro.

In an application that supports the VBA Macro Recorder (such as Word, Excel, and PowerPoint), you can create macros in two ways:

- ◆ Turn on the Macro Recorder and perform the sequence of actions you want the macro to perform.

- ◆ Open the Visual Basic Editor and type the VBA commands into it.

You can also record the basic sequence of actions and then open the macro and edit out any unneeded commands. While editing the macro, you can add other commands; you can also add control structures and user-interface elements (such as message boxes and dialog boxes), so users of the macro can make decisions and choose options for how to run it.

Once you've created a macro, you can assign a way of running it. In most applications, you can assign a macro to a menu item, a key combination, or a toolbar button and run it at any time. You can also assign a way of running a macro when you record the macro, but in most cases it's best to move the macro from its default location before assigning a means of running it.

Recording a Macro

The easiest way to create VBA code is to record a macro using the Macro Recorder, but only some applications support the Macro Recorder. You switch on the Macro Recorder, optionally assign a method for running the macro (a toolbar button, a menu item, or a key combination), perform the actions you want in the macro, and then switch off the Macro Recorder. As you perform the actions, the Macro Recorder records them as instructions—*code*—in the VBA programming language.

Once you finish recording the macro, you can view the code in the Visual Basic Editor and change it if necessary. If the code works perfectly as you recorded it, you never have to look at it—you can just run the macro at any time by choosing the assigned toolbar button, menu item, or key combination or by running it directly from the Macros dialog box.

In the following sections, you'll look at the stages involved in recording a macro. The process is easy, but you need to be familiar with some background if you haven't recorded macros before. After the general explanations, you'll record example macros in Word, Excel, and PowerPoint. You'll examine and adapt those macros later in the book, after you learn how to use the Visual Basic Editor.

Planning the Macro

Before you even start the Macro Recorder, plan what you will do in the macro. In most cases, you should set up the application so that everything's ready for the sequence of commands you want to record. For example, if you want to create an editing macro in Word, make sure you have a document open with suitable text or other contents, and then activate the window containing the document.

In other cases, the setup will be part of the macro. In this case, you should make sure that the application is in the state that the macro expects before you start recording the macro. For example, if the macro will assume that the active workbook in Excel is blank, the macro should create a blank workbook rather than using whichever workbook happens to be active at the time.

NOTE Some applications (such as Word) let you pause the Macro Recorder when you need to take an action without recording it. This capability allows you to work around problems you hadn't anticipated when planning the macro—for example, having to open another file that should have been open when you started recording the macro. But usually you'll get better results from planning your macros carefully before you start recording.

Starting the Macro Recorder

Start the Macro Recorder by choosing Tools ➢ Macro ➢ Record New Macro. The Macro Recorder displays the Record Macro dialog box with a default macro name (Macro1, Macro2, and so on) and description that you can accept or change. Figure 1.1 shows the Record Macro dialog box for Word with a custom name and description entered.

TIP In Word, you can also start (and stop) the Macro Recorder by double-clicking the REC indicator on the status bar (if you have the status bar displayed, as it is by default). In Word for the Mac, click the REC indicator rather than double-clicking it.

NOTE If you're using Office's adaptive menus, the Macro item doesn't appear immediately on the Tools menu until you've used it at least once. So drop down the short menu and either wait a second for Word to display the lesser used items on the menu or click the down-arrow button at the foot of the menu to display them. (If you want to stop using adaptive menus, choose Tools ➢ Customize and select the Show Full Menus check box on the Options page. In the Office 2000 applications, clear the Menus Show Recently Used Commands First check box on the Options page. This setting affects all the Office applications at once.)

The appearance of the Record Macro dialog box varies somewhat from one application to another, because the dialog box must offer suitable options to accommodate particular needs that each application has. In each case, you get to name the macro and add a description for it. In most cases, you also get to specify where to save the macro—for example, in a particular template, presentation, or workbook. Most versions of the Record Macro dialog box let you specify a way of running the macro, providing either a text box for entering a shortcut key combination or a command button that takes you to a separate dialog box (such as the Customize dialog box that Word uses).

Most of the Microsoft applications that host VBA have a Visual Basic toolbar, from which you can take some actions with macros and the Visual Basic Editor. These Visual Basic toolbars also vary in the actions they support and, consequently, in the number of buttons they have. If the Visual Basic toolbar in the application you're using has a Record Macro button, you can click that button to display the Record Macro dialog box. Figure 1.2 shows Word's version of the Visual Basic toolbar.

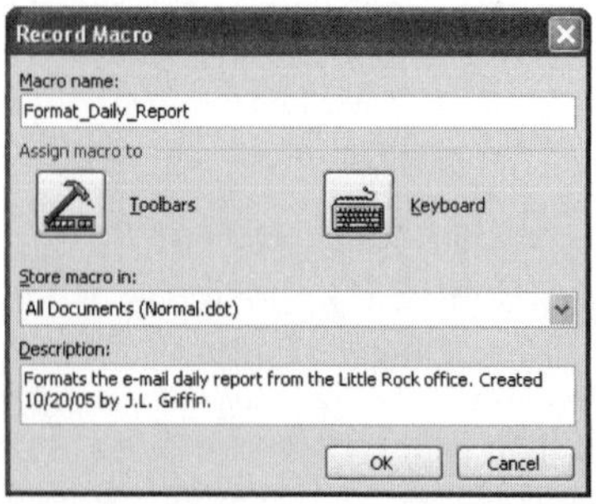

FIGURE 1.1

In the Record Macro dialog box, enter a name for the macro you're about to record. Type a concise but helpful description in the Description box. This is the Record Macro dialog box for Word.

FIGURE 1.2
You can use the Visual
Basic toolbar to work
with macros.

NOTE   Outlook and Access don't have the Visual Basic toolbar.

Here's what the Visual Basic toolbar buttons do:

Run Macro button   Displays the Macros dialog box, in which you can choose the macro to run. (You can also use this dialog box to start creating a macro in the Visual Basic Editor, if you choose.)

Record Macro button   Displays the Record Macro dialog box. When you're recording a macro and the Visual Basic toolbar is on screen, the Record Macro button appears pushed in; you can click it to stop recording the macro.

Security button   Displays the Security dialog box, which you'll examine in Chapter 19. The Security dialog box lets you choose which level of security the application should use for code. You can also specify trusted sources for code. (A *trusted source* is a person or organization designated as providing code that is trusted to be safe.)

Visual Basic Editor button   Starts or switches to the Visual Basic Editor. You'll start working in the Visual Basic Editor in Chapter 2 (and you'll spend most of the rest of the book working in it).

Control Toolbox button   Toggles the display of the Control Toolbox, which you use to add controls to documents. In some applications, you can also display the Control Toolbox from the context menu of toolbars (right-click the menu bar or any displayed toolbar to display this context menu) or from the View ➢ Toolbars submenu.

Design Mode button   Switches the current document to Design mode, displays the Control Toolbox if it isn't already displayed, and displays the Exit Design Mode toolbar (which you use to exit Design mode). The Design Mode button is a toggle button. However, when you use it to exit Design mode, it doesn't hide the Control Toolbox—even if it displayed the Control Toolbox when you entered Design mode.

Microsoft Script Editor button   Displays the Microsoft Script Editor, which you use to create web scripts.

Naming the Macro

Next, enter a name for the new macro in the Macro Name text box in the Record Macro dialog box. The name

◆   Must start with a letter; after that, it can contain both letters and numbers

◆   Can be up to 80 characters long

◆   Can contain underscores, which are useful for separating words

◆   Cannot contain spaces, punctuation, or special characters (such as ! or *)

See the sidebar for some suggestions on how to name your macros.

ALWAYS NAME AND DESCRIBE YOUR MACROS

If you create many macros, organize them carefully so you know which to keep and which to toss. Recording macros lets you create code so quickly that it's easy to get confused about which macro does what.

You may be tempted not to assign a macro description when you're in a hurry or when you're playing with different ways to approach a problem and you're not sure which (if any) of your test macros you'll keep. Even so, make sure you enter a few notes for each macro that you record. Otherwise, it's easy to end up with a mass of recorded macros that have cryptic names and no descriptions. To figure out what each macro does and which ones you can safely discard, you'll have to plow through the code—and a recorded macro's code can be surprisingly long, even if the macro does nothing more than adjust a few options in a couple of dialog boxes.

Use a macro-naming convention to indicate which recorded macros you can kill without remorse. Start the name with a constant part, then add numeric values sequentially to keep track of the versions: For example, Scratch (Scratch01, Scratch02, and so on), Temp (Temp01, Temp02, and so on), or even aaa (which keeps the macros at the top of the list in the Macros dialog box). Never use the default name that VBA assigns to a macro (Macro1, Macro2, and so on, using the next-higher unused number tacked onto the word *Macro*), unless you choose to use the automatic name as the designator for a scratch macro. With names this vague, chances are you will never be able to identify your macros later.

Because VBA code increases the size of the file that contains it, it's a good idea to clear out unwanted macros frequently. Doing so will prevent your files from ballooning to sizes large enough to slow down your applications.

FIGURE 1.3

If you enter an invalid macro name in the Record Macro dialog box, the application lets you know in its own way when you click the OK button. Word displays an unhelpful dialog box titled Microsoft Visual Basic. Excel and PowerPoint identify themselves correctly and give somewhat more helpful messages.

The Microsoft applications don't prevent you from entering an invalid name in the Macro Name text box in the Record Macro dialog box. Instead, they raise objections when you click the OK button to start recording the macro. Figure 1.3 shows how Word, Excel, and PowerPoint respond to an invalid macro name once it's entered.

Type a description for the macro in the Description text box. This description is to help you (and anyone you share the macro with) identify the macro and understand when to use it. If the macro runs successfully only under particular conditions, note them briefly in the Description text box. For example, if the user must make a selection in the document before running the macro in Word, note that requirement. If the macro formats the active presentation in PowerPoint, that's something the user needs to know too.

ANOTHER NAMING CONSIDERATION: HOW WILL THE SCREENTIP READ?

When you create a toolbar button for a macro in an Office application, the application automatically assigns to the button a ScreenTip that consists of the macro's name. This default ScreenTip seems designed to encourage you to name your macros consistently, or at least comprehensibly—if you use a capital letter to indicate the start of each word, and perhaps use an underscore between words, the ScreenTip will be much easier to read than if you just use all lowercase letters or all uppercase letters.

The exception here is Word, which creates its ScreenTips in a more sophisticated way than the other Office applications, automatically adding a space before each capital letter that it judges to be the start of a new word. For example, if you name a macro `FormatDailyReport` and create a toolbar button for it, Word gives the button the ScreenTip Format Daily Report. But if the name of the macro contains a clump of capital letters, Word breaks the macro name with a space before the first capital in the clump, but it won't divide the others. For example, if you create a macro named `FixTCPIPSettings`, Word creates the ScreenTip Fix TCPIPSettings rather than the Fix TCPIP Settings you might want. In this case, you'd do best to use an underscore in the macro name—`FixTCPIP_Settings`—to provide a readable division in the second half of the ScreenTip.

Choose where to store the macro. Your choices with Word, Excel, and PowerPoint are as follows:

- In Word, if you want to restrict availability of the macro to just the current template or document, choose that template or document from the Store Macro In drop-down list. If you want the macro to be available no matter which template you're working in, make sure the default setting—All Documents (Normal.dot)—appears in the Store Macro In combo box. (If you're not clear on what Word's templates are and what they do, see the sidebar "Understanding Word's Normal.dot, Templates, and Documents.")

- In Excel, you can choose to store the macro in This Workbook (the active workbook), New Workbook, or Personal Macro Workbook. The Personal Macro Workbook is a special workbook named `PERSONAL.XLS` and stored in your `%userprofile%\Application Data\ Microsoft\Excel\XLSTART\` folder. Excel creates the Personal Macro Workbook the first time you choose to store a macro in the Personal Macro Workbook. By keeping your macros and other customizations in the Personal Macro Workbook, you can make them available to any of your procedures—in that way, the Personal Macro Workbook is similar to Word's `Normal.dot`. If you choose New Workbook, Excel creates a new workbook for you and creates the macro in it.

NOTE `%userprofile%` is a Windows environment variable that stores the path to the folder that contains your user profile—folders and files with details of your preferences and settings for Windows and your applications. An *environment variable* is a container that holds a piece of information so that you can access it easily. For example, `%userprofile%` takes you to your user profile folder no matter which drive it's stored on.

- In PowerPoint, you can store the macro in the active presentation or in any other open presentation or template. PowerPoint does not provide a global macro storage container, although you can make your macros and code available to other presentations by using a presentation or template as global storage and keeping it open all the time (or opening it whenever you want to run a macro or code).

Word, Excel, and PowerPoint automatically store recorded macros in a default location in the specified document, template, workbook, or presentation:

◆ Word stores each recorded macro in a module named NewMacros in the selected template or document, so you'll always know where to find macros you've recorded. If the module doesn't exist, the Macro Recorder creates it. Because it receives each macro recorded into its document or template, a NewMacros module can soon grow large if you record many macros. The NewMacros module in the default global template, Normal.dot, is especially likely to grow bloated, because it receives each macro you record unless you specify another document or template. It's a good idea to clear out the NewMacros module frequently, putting those recorded macros you want to keep into other modules and disposing of any useless recorded macros.

◆ Excel and PowerPoint store each recorded macro for any given session in a new module named Module*n*, where *n* is the lowest unused number in ascending sequence (Module1, Module2, and so on). Any macros you create in the next session go into a new module with the next available number. If you record macros frequently with Excel and PowerPoint, you'll most likely need to consolidate the macros you want to keep so that they're not scattered in many modules like this.

UNDERSTANDING WORD'S NORMAL.DOT, TEMPLATES, AND DOCUMENTS

Storing macros and VBA code in Word is confusing because you must choose between several storage locations. To choose, it helps to understand how Word's Normal template (Normal.dot), templates, and documents interact.

Word has a four-layer architecture. Each of the four layers can affect how Word appears and how it behaves, but not all four layers have to be used at the same time.

The bottom layer, which is always used, is the Word application, which contains all the Word objects and built-in commands. The interface objects that the application contains include the Word menus, toolbars, and so on. This layer is the most difficult to picture, because usually you don't see it directly: Instead, you see it through Normal.dot, the global template, which forms the second layer and is also always used.

When you start Word, it loads Normal.dot automatically, and Normal.dot stays loaded until you exit Word. (There's a special switch you can use—winword /n—to prevent Normal.dot from being loaded if you need to troubleshoot it.) Normal.dot contains styles, AutoText entries, formatted AutoCorrect entries, and customizations. These customizations show up in the other layers unless specifically excluded.

Default blank documents (such as the document that Word normally creates when you start it and any document you create by clicking the New Blank Document button on the Standard toolbar) are based on Normal.dot. So when you're working in a default blank document, you see the Word interface as it is set in Normal.dot.

The current template sits on top of the Word application and Normal.dot. This template can contain styles, AutoText entries, macro modules, and customized toolbars and settings for the template, along with any boilerplate text needed for this particular type of document. This is the third layer, but it is used only if the current document (or *active document*) is attached to a template other than Normal.dot.

On top of the current template sits the current document, which contains the text and graphics in the document, the formatting, and the layout. Documents can also contain macro modules, custom toolbars, custom menus, and custom keyboard shortcuts, so the document itself can act as a fourth layer. This layer is always present when a document is open, but it has no effect on Word's interface or behavior unless the document contains customizations.

Customized settings work from the top layer downward. So customized settings in the active document take precedence over those in the active template, while customized settings in the current template take precedence over any global templates or add-ins other than Normal.dot. Customized settings in those global templates or add-ins take precedence over those in Normal.dot. So for example, if you remove the Table menu from the menu bar in Normal.dot, documents attached to other templates do not show it either—unless you restore it in one of those templates, in which case that setting take precedence over the setting in Normal.dot for documents based on that template.

As another example, say you have the keyboard combination Ctrl+Shift+K assigned to different procedures in Normal.dot, in a loaded global template, in a document's template, and in the document itself. When you press that keyboard combination, only the procedure assigned in the document runs, because that is the topmost layer. If you remove the keyboard combination from the document, the template is the topmost layer, so the procedure assigned in the template runs. If you remove the keyboard combination from the template as well, the procedure in the loaded global template runs. Finally, if you remove that keyboard combination too, the procedure in Normal.dot runs.

Word allows you to load two or more global templates other than Normal.dot. If you load multiple global templates, Word handles them in alphabetical order. So if you have the global templates Alpha Global.dot and Beta Global.dot loaded, the customizations in Beta Global.dot take precedence over those in Alpha Global.dot.

Assigning a Way to Run the Macro

At this point, when you've named the macro, typed a description, and chosen where to store it, Word and Excel also let you choose a way to run the macro: a keyboard shortcut (in either Word or Excel) or a command-bar item (in Word). This feature is handy for people who record very few macros and neither tinker with them nor move them from one module to another. It's less helpful for those who create many macros, edit them, and move them to other modules. This is because moving a macro from one module to another disconnects any way you've assigned for running the macro.

NOTE A *command bar* is a menu, a toolbar, or a context menu (the menu that appears when you right-click an object in an application). Depending on the application, you can customize all the command bars or only some of them.

This limitation means that it makes sense to assign a way of running a macro only if you're planning to use the macro in its recorded form (as opposed to, say, using part of it to create another macro) *and* from its default location. If you plan to move the macro or rename it, don't assign a way of running it now. Instead, wait until the macro is in its final form and location, and then assign the means of running it. See "Assigning a Way of Running the Macro," later in this chapter, for details.

TIP By moving your recorded macros into different modules, you can group related macros so you can compare the code, adjust them, or distribute them easily.

To assign a way to run the macro, follow the instructions in the next sections, which cover what you need to do in Word, Excel, and PowerPoint.

ASSIGNING A WAY TO RUN THE MACRO IN WORD

In Word, you use the Customize dialog box and the Customize Keyboard dialog box to assign a way of running a macro. Here's how to use the Customize dialog box to assign the macro to a toolbar button, a menu item, or a context menu item

1. Click the Toolbars button in the Record Macro dialog box to display the Customize dialog box.

2. If it isn't already displayed, select the Commands tab to display the Commands page, shown in Figure 1.4. In the Categories list box, only the category Macros should be listed, and it should be selected.

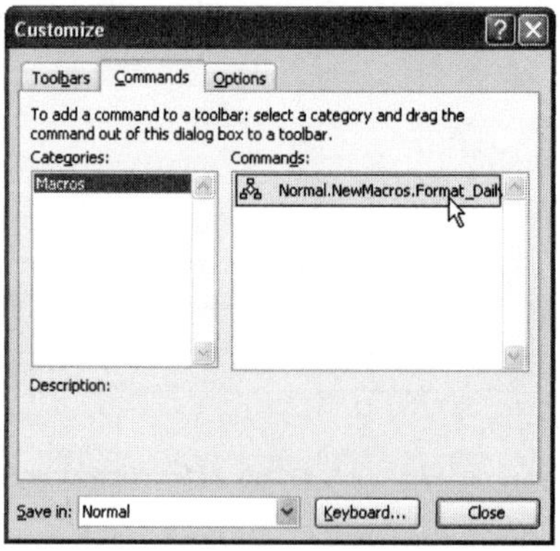

FIGURE 1.4

Choose a way to run the macro in the Customize dialog box.

3. Make sure Word has chosen the correct customization context (the scope that the customization affects) in the Save In drop-down list box at the bottom of the Customize dialog box. You can apply the customization to the default global template (Normal.dot), the active document, or the template attached to the active document. (If the active document is attached to Normal.dot, no other template is available in the Save In combo box.)

4. If you're going to assign the macro to a toolbar button or a context menu item, make sure the toolbar or the Shortcut Menus toolbar is displayed. To display a toolbar or the Shortcut Menus toolbar, click the Toolbars tab of the Customize dialog box to display the Toolbars page, and then select the check box for the toolbar or the Shortcut Menus toolbar to display it. Click the Commands tab to display the Commands page of the Customize dialog box again.

5. Click the macro's name in the Commands list box and drag the macro item to the toolbar, the context menu, or the menu, as appropriate, as shown in Figure 1.5.

6. Word adds a button or menu item for the macro giving it the macro's full name, such as Normal.NewMacros.CreateDailyReport. This name consists of the name of the template or document in which the macro is stored, the name of the module that contains the macro, and the macro's name, respectively.

7. To rename the button or menu item, right-click it (or click the Modify Selection button in the Customize dialog box) and enter your preferred name in the Name text box on the context menu that appears (see Figure 1.6).

FIGURE 1.5
To assign a macro to a context menu, select the Shortcut Menus check box on the Toolbars page of the Customize dialog box. Then drag the macro item from the Commands page to the relevant context menu.

2. Drag to the Shortcut Menus toolbar and hover over the category of shortcut menu.

1. Drag the item from the Commands list box.

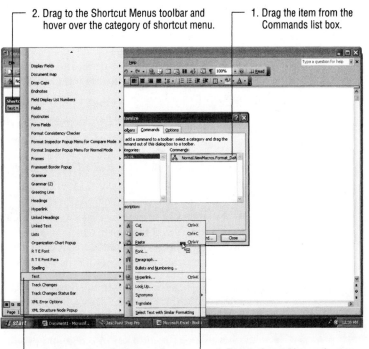

3. Drag to the subcategory of menu.

4. Drag to the position on the menu, and then drop the item.

FIGURE 1.6
Word gives the menu item or toolbar button the full name of the macro. Use the Modify Selection command to change the name to something shorter and better.

TIP   Keep two points in mind. First, a macro's menu-item name or button name doesn't have to bear any relation to the macro's name. Second, you can also create new toolbars and new menus as you need them.

8. To assign an access key to an item, put an ampersand (**&**) before the character that you want to use as the access key, and then press the Enter key.

TIP The access key doesn't have to be unique, but using it will be easiest if it is. If multiple menus or commands share the same access key, Word selects the first of them the first time you press the access key. You can then press the Enter key to display that menu or run that command, or you can press the access key again to access the next item associated with that key. For example, if you assign the access key T to the button for a macro named Transpose_Word, Word selects the Tools menu (unless you've removed it) the first time you press Alt+T and the Transpose_Word button the second time you press Alt+T.

9. Click the Close button to close the Customize dialog box.

To assign the macro to a keyboard combination

1. Click the Keyboard button in the Record Macro dialog box to display the Customize Keyboard dialog box.

NOTE As with the other ways of running a macro, you can assign a keyboard combination to run a macro either at the time you record the macro or at any point after you finish recording it. If you intend to move the macro from the NewMacros module to another module, don't assign the keyboard combination until the macro has reached its ultimate destination.

2. Click to place the insertion point in the Press New Shortcut Key box, and then press the key combination you want. Figure 1.7 shows the Customize Keyboard dialog box with a new shortcut key selected. A key combination can be

◆ Alt plus either a function key or a regular key not used as a menu access key

◆ Ctrl plus a function key or a regular key

◆ Shift plus a function key

◆ Ctrl+Alt, Ctrl+Shift, Alt+Shift, or even Ctrl+Alt+Shift plus a regular key or function key. Pressing Ctrl+Alt+Shift and another key tends to be too awkward for frequent use.

3. Check the Current Keys list box to make sure the key combination you've chosen isn't already in use. If it is, press the Backspace key to clear the current key combination (unless you want to reassign the key combination), and then press another combination.

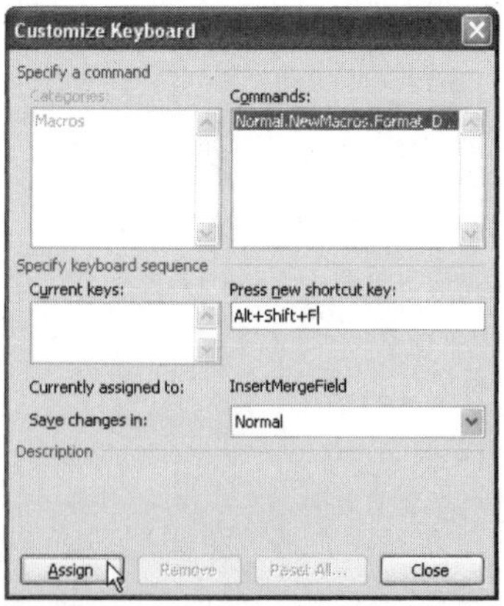

FIGURE 1.7
Set a shortcut key combination for the macro in the Customize Keyboard dialog box.

TIP   You can set up shortcut keys that have two steps—for example, Ctrl+Alt+F, 1 and Ctrl+Alt+F, 2—
by pressing the second key (in this case, the 1 or the 2) after pressing the key combination. However,
these shortcuts tend to be more trouble than they're worth, unless you're assigning literally hundreds of extra shortcut keys.

4. Click the Assign button to assign the key combination to the macro.

5. Click the Close button to close the Customize Keyboard dialog box.

ASSIGNING A WAY TO RUN THE MACRO IN EXCEL

When you're recording a macro, Excel lets you do no more than assign a Ctrl shortcut key to run it.
If you want to add a menu item or a toolbar button, you need to do so after recording the macro.
Because you may well want to move the macro to a different module than the one VBA automatically
stores it in, this may be no bad thing.

To assign a Ctrl shortcut key to run the macro you're recording

1. Enter the key in the Shortcut Key text box. Press the Shift key if you want to include Shift in the
shortcut key.

2. In the Store Macro In drop-down list, specify where you want the Macro Recorder to store the
macro. Your choices are as follows:

◆ This Workbook stores the macro in the active workbook. This option is useful for macros
that belong to a particular workbook and do not need to be used elsewhere.

◆ New Workbook causes Excel to create a new workbook for you and store the macro in it.
This option is useful for experimental macros that you'll need to edit before unleashing
them on actual work.

◆ Personal Macro Workbook stores the macro in the Personal Macro Workbook, a special
workbook named `PERSONAL.XLS` stored in your `\Application Data\Microsoft\Excel\`
`XLSTART\` folder. By keeping your macros and other customizations in the Personal Macro
Workbook, you can make them available to any of your procedures—in that way, the Personal
Macro Workbook is similar to Word's `Normal.dot`. If the Personal Macro Workbook does not
exist yet, the Macro Recorder creates it automatically.

3. Click the OK button to start recording the macro.

ASSIGNING A WAY TO RUN THE MACRO IN POWERPOINT

PowerPoint does not let you assign a way to run a macro when you record it, but you can assign a way
to run it afterward, as discussed in the section "Assigning a Way of Running the Macro," later in the
chapter. You can choose to store the macro in any open presentation or template.

RECORDING THE ACTIONS IN THE MACRO

When you dismiss the Customize dialog box, the Customize Keyboard dialog box, or the Record
Macro dialog box, the Macro Recorder is ready to start recording the macro. For most applications,
the Macro Recorder displays the Stop Recording toolbar (usually undocked in the upper-left corner
of the screen); for Word, the Macro Recorder also adds a cassette-tape icon to the mouse pointer and
turns the REC indicator in the status bar black from its default gray.

Now perform the sequence of actions you want to record. What exactly you can do varies from application to application, but in general, you can use the mouse to select items from menus and toolbars, to make choices in dialog boxes, and to select defined items (such as cells in spreadsheets or shapes in PowerPoint slides) in documents. You'll find a number of things that you can't do with the mouse, such as select items within a document window in Word. To select items in a document window, you have to use keyboard commands.

NOTE When you make choices in a dialog box and click the OK button, the Macro Recorder records the current settings for *all* the options on that page of the dialog box. So, for example, when you change the left indentation of a paragraph in the Paragraph dialog box in Word, the Macro Recorder records all the other settings on the Indents and Spacing page as well (Alignment, Before and After spacing, and so forth). You can edit out the code representing these settings later, if you don't want to use them.

In Word, if you need to perform any actions that you don't want recorded, pause the Macro Recorder by clicking the Pause Recording button on the Stop Recording toolbar. The Pause Recording button takes on a pushed-in look, and its ScreenTip identifies it as the Resume Recorder button. Click this button again to resume recording.

To stop recording, choose Tools ➢ Macro ➢ Stop Recording (or Stop Recorder, depending on the application), or click the Stop Recording button on the Stop Recording toolbar if it is displayed. In Word, you can also double-click the REC indicator on the status bar to stop recording.

The Macro Recorder has now recorded your macro and assigned it to the control you chose. If you didn't assign a control, you can do so afterward (as discussed later in this chapter).

Running a Macro

To run a macro you've recorded, use either of these methods:

◆ If you assigned a control for running the macro, use it: click the toolbar button, choose the menu item or context menu item, or press the key combination.

◆ If not, press Alt+F8 or choose Tools ➢ Macro ➢ Macros to display the Macros dialog box, select the macro, and then click the Run button. (Alternatively, double-click the macro name in the list box.)

NOTE You can also display the Macros dialog box by clicking the Run Macro button (the button with the "play" symbol) on the Visual Basic toolbar. You can also run a macro from the Visual Basic Editor, which is useful when you're working in it.

The macro runs, performing the actions in the sequence in which you recorded them. For example, suppose you create a macro in Excel that selects cell A2 in the current worksheet, boldfaces that cell, enters the text **Yearly Sales**, selects cell B2, and enters the number **100000** in it. The Macro Recorder registers five actions: selecting cell A2, applying the boldface, entering the text, selecting cell B2, and entering the second text. VBA then performs all five actions each time you run the macro.

TIP To stop a running macro, press Ctrl+Break (Break is usually written on the front face of the Pause key on the keyboard). VBA stops running the code and displays a dialog box telling you that code execution has been interrupted. Click the End button to dismiss this dialog box.

Some applications (such as Word) let you undo most actions executed via VBA after the macro stops running (by using the Edit ➢ Undo menu item or the Undo button on the Standard toolbar, undoing one command at a time); other applications do not.

NOTE If running the macro results in an error, chances are that the macro is trying to do something to a file or an object that isn't available. For example, if you record a macro in Excel that works on the active workbook, the macro causes an error if you run it when no workbook is open. Likewise, if you record a macro in PowerPoint that works with the third shape on the active slide, that macro fails if you run it on a slide that has no third shape. To get the macro to run properly, re-create the conditions it needs, and then try it again.

Recording a Sample Word Macro

In this section, you'll record a sample macro in Word that you can work with later. This macro selects the current word, cuts it, moves the insertion point one word to the right, and pastes the word back in. This is a straightforward sequence of actions that you'll later view and edit in the Visual Basic Editor.

Follow these steps to record the macro:

1. If you don't have a new document open (or a document you don't care about), create a new document. Click the New Blank Document button on the Standard toolbar.

2. Double-click the REC indicator on the status bar or choose Tools ➤ Macro ➤ Record Macro. Either way, Word displays the Record Macro dialog box.

3. In the Macro Name text box, enter `Transpose_Word_Right`.

4. In the Store Macro In drop-down list, make sure All Documents (Normal.dot) is selected, unless you want to assign the macro to a different template. (This example assumes that the macro is in `Normal.dot` and that you'll take care of any consequences if you've put it elsewhere.)

5. In the Description box, enter a description for the macro (see Figure 1.8). The Description box contains something like "Macro recorded 6/1/2006 by Joanna Bermudez," which is Word's best attempt to help you identify the macro later. Be more explicit and enter a description such as **"Transposes the current word with the word to its right. Created 6/1/2006 by Joanna Bermudez."**

TIP You can change the description for a macro later, either in the Macros dialog box or in the Visual Basic Editor, but it's a good idea to start by entering an appropriate description when you record the macro. If you put off describing the macro until after you create it, you're apt to forget. As a result, you may end up with dozens of macros bearing names that were clear as the midday sun when you created them but now give little clue as to the macros' function.

FIGURE 1.8
Creating the sample
macro in Word

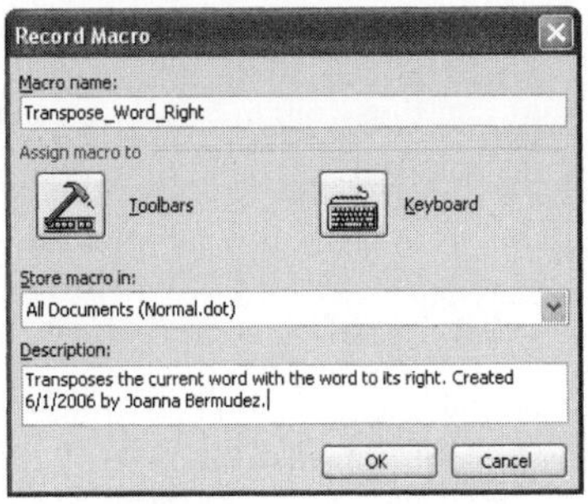

6. Assign a method of running the macro, as described in the previous section, if you want to. Create a toolbar button, a menu item, or a context menu item, or assign a keyboard shortcut. (The method or methods you choose is strictly a matter of personal preference.) If you'll need to move the macro to a different module (or a different template or document) later, don't assign a method of running the macro at this point.

7. Click the Close button to dismiss the Customize dialog box or the Customize Keyboard dialog box (or click the OK button to dismiss the Record Macro dialog box if you chose not to assign a way of running the macro). Now you're ready to record the macro. The Stop Recording toolbar appears on screen, and the mouse pointer has a cassette-tape icon attached to it.

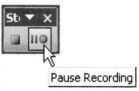

8. As a quick demonstration of how you can pause recording, click the Pause Recording button on the Stop Recording toolbar. The cassette-tape icon disappears from the mouse pointer, and the Pause Recording button changes into a Resume Recorder button. Enter a line of text in the document: **The quick brown dog jumped over a lazy fox.** Position the insertion point anywhere in the word *quick*, and then click the Resume Recorder button on the Stop Recording toolbar to reactivate the macro recorder.

9. Record the actions for the macro as follows:

   A. Use the Extend Selection feature to select the word *quick* by pressing the F8 key twice. The EXT indicator on the status bar darkens to show that Extend mode is active.

   B. Press the Escape key to cancel Extend mode. The EXT indicator on the status bar dims again. (This step isn't absolutely necessary for the macro, but perform it anyway so that the Macro Recorder records it.)

   C. Press Shift+Delete or Ctrl+X to cut the selected word to the Clipboard. (You can also click the Cut button or choose Edit ➤ Cut, if you prefer.)

   D. The insertion point is now at the beginning of the word *brown*. Press Ctrl+→ to move the insertion point right by one word so that it's at the beginning of the word *dog*.

   E. Press Shift+Insert or Ctrl+V to paste in the cut word from the Clipboard. (Again, you could click the Paste button instead, or you could choose Edit ➤ Paste.)

   F. Press Ctrl+← to move the insertion point one word to the left. (This is an extra instruction that you'll use when you edit the macro.)

10. Click the Stop Recording button on the Stop Recording toolbar to stop recording the macro (or double-click the REC indicator on the status bar or choose Tools ➤ Macros ➤ Stop Recording). Your sentence now reads, "The brown quick dog jumped over the lazy fox."

You can now run this macro by using the toolbar button, menu or context menu item, or keyboard shortcut that you assigned (if you chose to assign one). Alternatively, choose Tools ➤ Macro ➤ Macros and run the macro from the Macros dialog box. Try positioning the insertion point in the word *brown* and running the macro to restore the words in the sentence to their original order.

TIP   Holding down the Shift key as you click the File menu makes the Save All item appear in place of the Save item and the Close All command appear in place of the Close item. The Save All command is especially useful for forcing Word to save the changes to templates as well as changes to the active document.

At this point, Word has stored the macro in Normal.dot, but it has not saved the changes. If you don't save them until you exit Word, it prompts you to save them then. But to avoid losing the macro if Word or Windows crashes, it's best to save Normal now. To do so, hold down the Shift key, click the File menu, and then click the Save All item. If Word prompts you to save changes (see Figure 1.9), click the Yes button. The change in this case is the macro you've created in the Normal template.

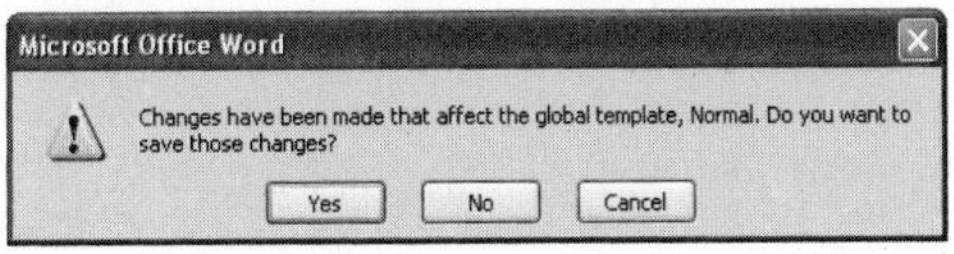

FIGURE 1.9
Word may prompt you to save changes to the Normal template after you create a macro in the template.

NOTE   If you prefer to have Word save changes to the Normal template automatically without prompting you, choose Tools ➢ Options to display the Options dialog box, click the Save tab, clear the Prompt To Save Normal Template check box, and then click the OK button.

Recording a Sample Excel Macro

In this section, you'll record a sample Excel macro. This macro creates a new workbook, enters a sequence of months into it, and then saves it. You'll work with this macro in Chapter 3.

Create a Personal Macro Workbook if You Don't Have One Yet

If you haven't already created a Personal Macro Workbook in Excel, you'll need to create one before you can create this procedure. Follow these steps:

1. Choose Tools ➢ Macro ➢ Record New Macro to display the Record Macro dialog box.

2. Accept the default name for the macro, because you'll be deleting it momentarily.

3. In the Store Macro In drop-down list, choose Personal Macro Workbook.

4. Click the OK button to dismiss the Record Macro dialog box and start recording the macro.

5. Type a single character in whichever cell is active, and press the Enter key.

6. Click the Stop Recording button on the Stop Recording toolbar to stop recording the macro.

7. Choose Window ➢ Unhide to display the Unhide dialog box. Select PERSONAL.XLS and click the OK button.

8. Choose Tools ➢ Macro ➢ Macros to display the Macros dialog box.

9. Select the macro you recorded and click the Delete button to delete it. Click the Yes button in the confirmation message box.

You'll now have a Personal Macro Workbook that you can use.

Record the Sample Excel Macro

To create the macro, start Excel and follow these steps:

1. Choose Tools ➤ Macro ➤ Record New Macro to display the Record Macro dialog box, shown in Figure 1.10 with information entered.

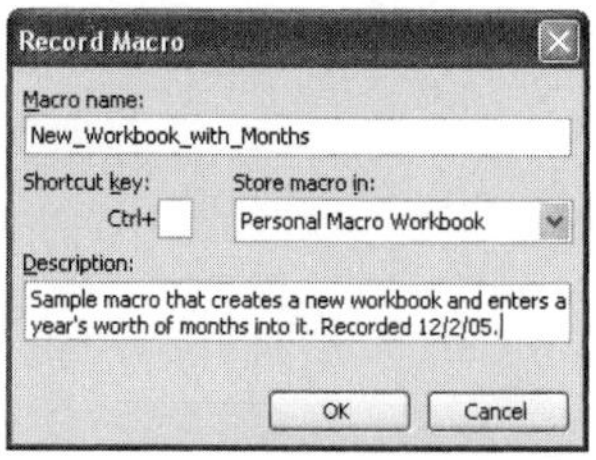

FIGURE 1.10
Display the Record Macro dialog box for Excel and make your choices in it.

2. Enter the name for the macro in the Macro Name text box: **New_Workbook_with_Months**.

3. In the Shortcut Key text box, enter a shortcut key if you want to. (You can change the shortcut key later, so there's no need to enter one at this point.)

4. In the Store Macro In drop-down list, choose whether to store the macro in the Personal Macro Workbook, in the active workbook, or in a new workbook. As discussed a little earlier in this chapter, storing the macro in the Personal Macro Workbook gives you the most flexibility. For this example, don't store the macro in the active workbook, because you're going to delete the active workbook almost immediately.

5. Type a description for the macro in the Description text box.

6. Click the OK button to dismiss the Record Macro dialog box and start recording the macro.

7. Choose File ➤ New to display the New Workbook task pane, and then click the On My Computer link to display the Templates dialog box. (On Excel 2000 and earlier versions, choose File ➤ New to display the New dialog box.)

8. Select the Workbook item on the General page of the dialog box, and then click the OK button. Excel creates a new workbook and selects the first sheet on it.

9. Click cell A1 to select it. (It may already be selected; click it anyway, because you need to record the instruction.)

10. Enter **January 2006** and press the → key to select cell B1. Excel automatically changes the date to your default date format. That's fine.

11. Enter **February 2006** and press the ← key to select cell A1 again.

12. Drag from cell A1 to cell B1 so that the two cells are selected.

13. Drag the fill handle from cell B1 to cell L1, so that Excel's AutoFill feature enters the months March 2006 through December 2006 in the cells.

14. Click the Save button on the Standard toolbar (or choose File ➢ Save) to display the Save As dialog box. Save the workbook in a convenient folder (for example, the My Documents folder) under a name such as **Sample Workbook.xls**.

15. Click the Stop Recording button on the Stop Recording toolbar to stop the Macro Recorder. (Alternatively, choose Tools ➢ Macro ➢ Stop Recording.)

Close the sample workbook, and use Windows Explorer to navigate to it and delete it. Then run the macro and watch what happens. (If you don't delete the workbook, Excel prompts you to decide whether to overwrite it when step 14 tries to save the new workbook using the same name as the existing workbook.)

Recording a Sample PowerPoint Macro

In this section, you'll record a sample PowerPoint macro. This macro creates a new slide, moves and resizes one of the shapes on it, enters text in the shape, and formats the text. You'll examine the macro in Chapter 3.

To create the macro, start PowerPoint and follow these steps:

1. Open a new presentation based on any template you choose. (If PowerPoint opened a new presentation automatically when you started it, use that presentation instead.) If the New Slide dialog box appears, dismiss it for the time being.

2. Choose Tools ➢ Macro ➢ Record New Macro to display the Record Macro dialog box, shown in Figure 1.11 with information filled in.

FIGURE 1.11
Display the Record Macro dialog box for PowerPoint and make your choices in it.

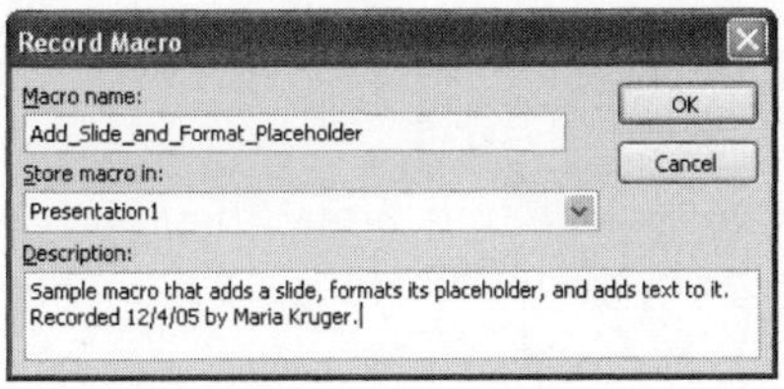

3. Type the name for the macro in the Macro Name text box: **Add_Slide_and_Format_ Placeholder**.

4. In the Store Macro In drop-down list, choose to store the macro in the active presentation rather than in another open presentation or template. The presentations in the Store Macro In drop-down list are identified by name rather than by a description such as This Presentation or Active Presentation. By default, PowerPoint selects the active presentation in the Store Macro In drop-down list, so you shouldn't need to change this setting.

5. In the Description text box, type a description for the macro.

6. Click the OK button to dismiss the Record Macro dialog box and start recording the macro.

7. Choose Insert ➢ New Slide to insert a new slide and display the Slide Layout task pane.

NOTE   In PowerPoint 2000 and earlier versions, choose Insert ➢ New Slide to display the New Slide dialog box. Click the Title Slide layout, and then click the OK button to insert the slide.

8. Click the Title Slide layout to apply it to the slide, and then click the close button to close the Slide Layout task pane.

9. Click the first placeholder on the slide to select it.

10. Click in the selected border of the placeholder and drag it up toward the top of the slide to move the placeholder.

11. Click the sizing handle in the middle of the bottom edge of the placeholder and drag it down toward the lower placeholder, deepening the placeholder.

12. Click in the placeholder (in the Click To Add Title area) and type the classic text: **The quick brown dog jumped over a lazy fox.**

13. Hold down Ctrl and Shift and press the Home key to select all the text in the placeholder.

14. Choose Format ➢ Font to display the Font dialog box.

15. Select font formatting, such as Impact font, Regular font style, and 54-point size. Click the Preview button to make sure that the result fits within the resized placeholder and looks legible.

16. Click the OK button to dismiss the Font dialog box.

17. Press the → key to deselect the selected text.

18. Click the Stop Recording button on the Stop Recording toolbar, or choose Tools ➢ Macro ➢ Stop Recording to stop recording the macro.

19. Save the presentation under a name such as `Sample Presentation.ppt`. (You'll need to save it so that you can work with the recorded macro later in the book.)

Now choose Tools ➢ Macro ➢ Macros to display the Macros dialog box, select the macro, and click the Run button. VBA runs through the actions again, adding a new slide, moving and resizing the first placeholder on it, and entering and formatting the text.

Once you're satisfied that the macro is running as it should, close the presentation without saving changes.

Assigning a Way of Running the Macro

If you didn't assign a way of running the macro when you recorded it, you can assign a way of running it as described here.

The procedures for assigning a macro to a toolbar button, a menu item, and a context menu item (in those applications that support customizing the context menus) are almost identical, so this section goes through them all together, noting variations as appropriate.

Assigning a Macro to a Toolbar Button or Menu Item

To assign a macro to a toolbar button, menu item, or a context menu item (in Word or PowerPoint), follow these steps:

1. Right-click any displayed toolbar or the menu bar and choose Customize from the context menu to display the Customize dialog box. Alternatively, choose Tools ➢ Customize to display the dialog box.

2. If the Toolbars page of the Customize dialog box isn't displayed, click the Toolbars tab to display it. Figure 1.12 shows the Toolbars page of the Customize dialog box for Word. The Toolbars pages of the Customize dialog box for Excel and PowerPoint are similar but do not have the Keyboard button.

3. Make sure the toolbar to which you want to assign the macro is displayed.

   ◆ To display a toolbar, select its check box in the Toolbars list box.

   ◆ To hide a toolbar, clear its check box.

   ◆ To add an item to a context menu in Word or PowerPoint, select the Shortcut Menus check box. The application displays a toolbar with buttons that lead to drop-down lists for the different categories of toolbars. Figure 1.13 shows the Shortcut Menu toolbar for Word on the left and the Shortcut Menus toolbar for PowerPoint on the right.

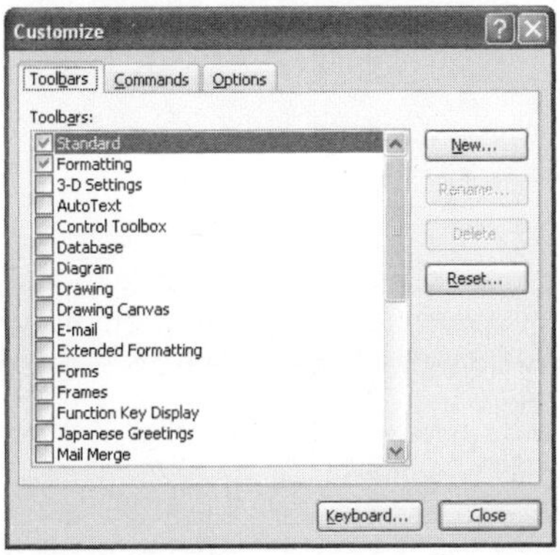

FIGURE 1.12

To add an item to a context menu in Word or PowerPoint, display the Shortcut Menus toolbar. Here you see Word's Shortcut Menu toolbar (on the left) and Power-Point's (on the right).

   ◆ To create a new toolbar, click the New button to display the New Toolbar dialog box (shown in Figure 1.14 with a name entered), enter the name for the button in the Toolbar Name text box, and click the OK button. In Word, you must also choose where to store the new toolbar: in Normal.dot, in the active document, or in the template attached to the active document. See step 5 of this list for a reminder of the implications of your choice.

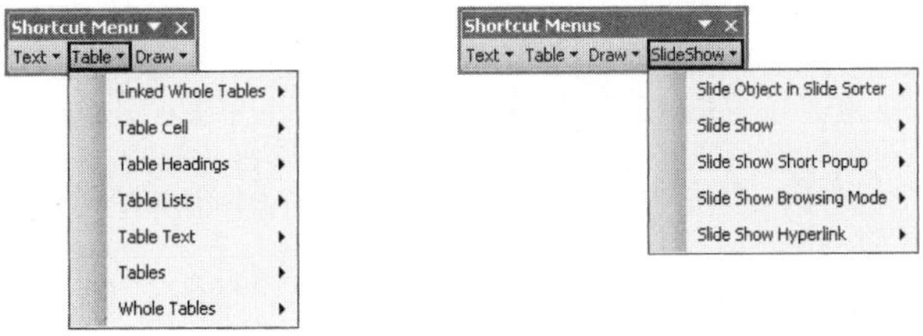

FIGURE 1.13

You can create a new toolbar to contain the button for your macro.

4. Click the Commands tab to display the Commands page. Figure 1.15 shows the Commands page of the Customize dialog box for Word, because again, Word's version of this dialog box is more complex than the other applications' versions: The other Office applications have neither the Save In drop-down list nor the Keyboard button.

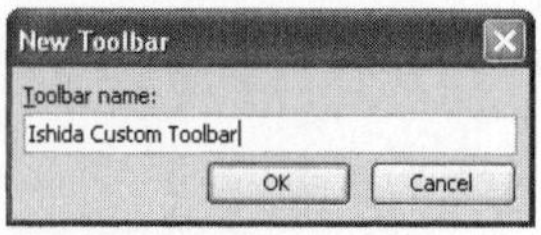

FIGURE 1.14
On the Toolbars page
of the Customize dialog
box, select the toolbar
you want to customize.

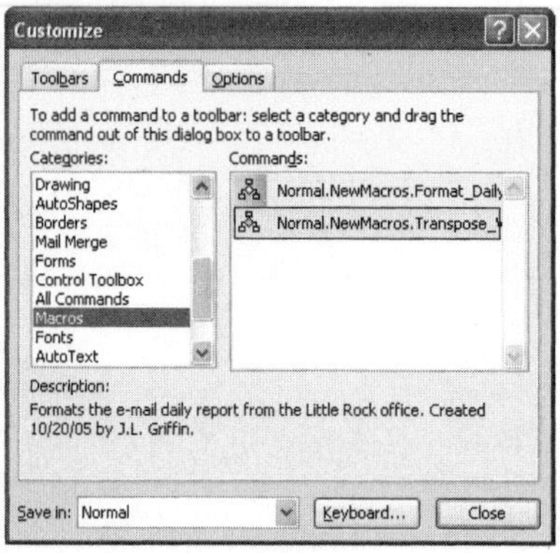

FIGURE 1.15
The Commands page of
the Customize dialog box

5. In Word, make sure that the Save In drop-down list is displaying the document or template in which you want to save this customization. If it's not, select the appropriate document or template from the drop-down list:

◆ If you save a customization in Normal.dot, the global template, it is available to all documents.

◆ If you save a customization in the template attached to the active document, the customization is available to all documents to which that template is attached. (If the active document has Normal.dot attached as its template, the Save In drop-down list does not show another template.)

◆ If you save a customization in the active document, it is available only to that document.

6. In any of the applications, scroll down and select the Macros item from the Categories list box, as shown in the figure. All the applications except Excel display a list of the available macros.

WARNING In some cases, Word lists its macros by their fully qualified names, which consist of the project (the template or document) and module that contain the macro plus the macro's name. For example, a macro named Example_Macro stored in the module named Demos in the Normal template may be listed as Normal.Demos.Example_Macro.

7. Select the macro in the Commands list box and drag the macro to the toolbar, menu, or submenu on which you want it to appear. Drop the macro at the appropriate position; the application creates a button or menu item for the macro and gives the button or menu item the macro's name. (Word gives the fully qualified name, which produces awkwardly long buttons.)

TIP To create a new menu, select the New Menu category in the Categories list box and drag the New Menu item to the menu bar or a toolbar.

◆ In Excel, drag the Custom Button icon to a suitable position on the appropriate toolbar or the Custom Menu Item icon to the appropriate menu. Excel creates a custom button with the Be Happy face on it or a custom menu item with the text "Custom Menu Item." At this point, the button or menu item has no connection with the macro. Right-click the button or menu item and choose Assign Macro from the context menu to display the Assign Macro dialog box (see Figure 1.16).

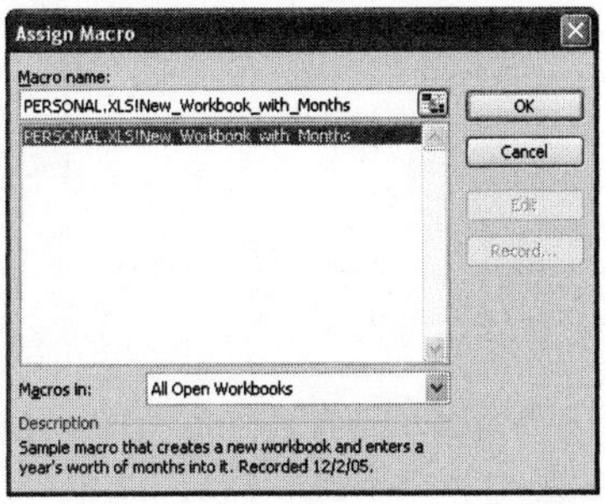

FIGURE 1.16

In Excel, use the Assign Macro dialog box to assign the macro to the button or menu item you created.

◆ To create a context menu item in Word and PowerPoint, drag the macro item to the button on the Shortcut Menus toolbar that represents the type of context menu to which you want to add the item. Then drag the item to the individual context menu to display the menu. Position the horizontal bar where you want the entry to appear, and then drop the entry.

8. Right-click the toolbar button, menu item, or context menu item you created to display the context menu. Then drag through the Name box to select its contents. Enter a suitable name for the new button or item. For a menu item or context menu item, put an ampersand (&) before the letter you want to use as an access key. Make sure this access key letter isn't already assigned to another menu item or context menu item—otherwise you'll have to press the access key twice to reach the second item, and you'll have to press the Enter key to execute the command.

9. Choose how you want the button or item to appear—as text, as an image, or as text with an image—by right-clicking the button or item and choosing Default Style, Text Only (Always), Text Only (In Menus), or Image And Text from the context menu. The default style for a toolbar button is an image; the default style for a menu item or a context menu item is text.

10. If you choose to use an image, you can manipulate it as follows:

◆ Use the Copy Button Image item on the context menu to copy an image from another button, and use the Paste Button Image item to paste the image onto your new button.

◆ Choose the Edit Button Image item to display the Button Editor dialog box (see Figure 1.17), in which you can draw a custom button pixel by pixel and then apply it to your button.

◆ Select the Change Button Image item to display a pop-up panel of built-in button images that you can quickly apply. (You can then edit these as described in the previous bullet to customize them a bit.)

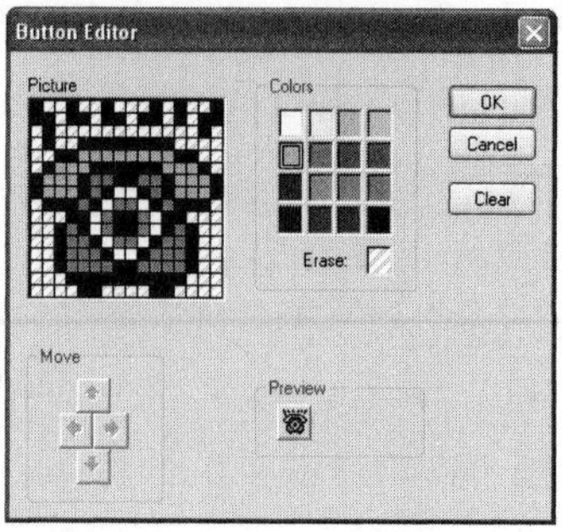

FIGURE 1.17
Use the Button Editor dialog box to create a custom button if you find that none of the predefined buttons is suitable.

11. When you've finished adding toolbar buttons and menu items, click the Close button to close the Customize dialog box.

Assigning a Macro to a Key Combination

In this section, you'll learn how to assign a macro to a key combination.

The section "Assigning a Way to Run the Macro in Word," earlier in this chapter, explained how to do this in Word. PowerPoint does not let you assign a macro to a key combination. Excel uses a different method from Word.

ASSIGNING A MACRO TO A KEY COMBINATION IN WORD

To assign a macro to a keyboard combination in Word, choose Tools ➢ Customize to display the Customize dialog box, and then click the Keyboard button to display the Customize Keyboard dialog box. Then proceed as discussed in the section "Assigning a Way to Run the Macro in Word," earlier in this chapter.

ASSIGNING A MACRO TO A KEY COMBINATION IN EXCEL

To assign a macro to a key combination in Excel, follow these steps:

1. Choose Tools ➢ Macro ➢ Macros to display the Macros dialog box.

2. Select the macro for which you want to assign a key combination.

3. Click the Options button to display the Macro Options dialog box (see Figure 1.18).

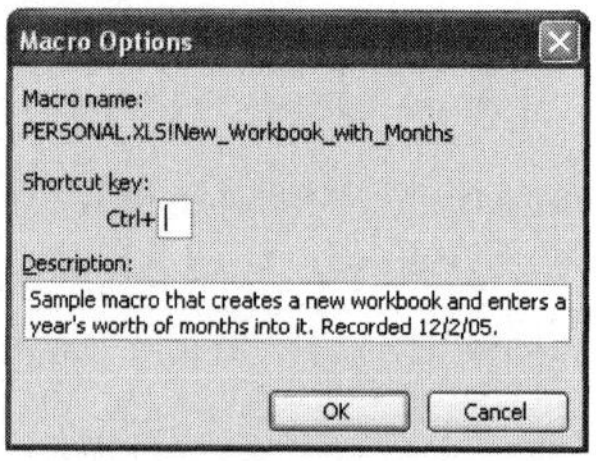

FIGURE 1.18
In Excel, use the Macro Options dialog box to assign a macro to a key combination.

4. Enter the key combination in the Shortcut Key text box. You can use only Ctrl key combinations (as opposed to, say, Ctrl+Alt key combinations), but you can add Shift to the key combination by pressing it as you press the letter.

TIP You can also change the description of the macro in the Macro Options dialog box if you need to.

5. Click the OK button to close the Macro Options dialog box.

6. Click the close button or the Cancel button to close the Macros dialog box.

Deleting a Macro

To delete a macro you no longer need, follow these steps:

1. Choose Tools ➢ Macro ➢ Macros to display the Macros dialog box.

2. Choose the macro in the Macro Name list box.

3. Click the Delete button.

4. In the warning message box that appears, click the Yes button. Figure 1.19 shows Excel's variation of this warning message box.

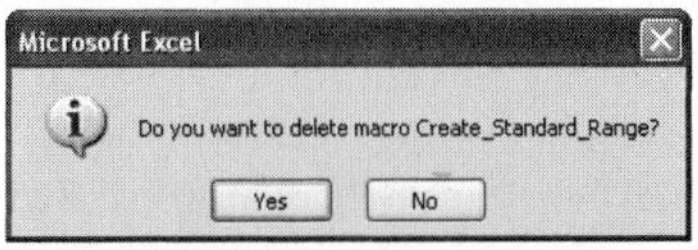

FIGURE 1.19

When you delete a macro, the application checks to make sure you mean to do so.

5. Click the Close button or the Cancel button to close the Macros dialog box.

ORGANIZING MACROS IN WORD WITH THE ORGANIZER DIALOG BOX

Most VBA-enabled applications require you to use the Visual Basic Editor (which is discussed in the next chapter) to move code modules, user forms, and other code items from one file to another file. (A *code module* is a virtual container used for storing macros. A *user form* is a custom dialog box.) But Word provides a useful tool called the Organizer dialog box that you can use to copy, move, rename, and delete code modules, user forms, and other code items directly from the Word interface.

To use the Organizer dialog box, follow these steps:

1. In Word, press Alt+F8 or choose Tools ➢ Macro ➢ Macros to display the Macros dialog box.

2. Click the Organizer button to display the Organizer dialog box, and click the Macro Project Items tab if the Macro Project Items page (shown here) isn't automatically displayed.

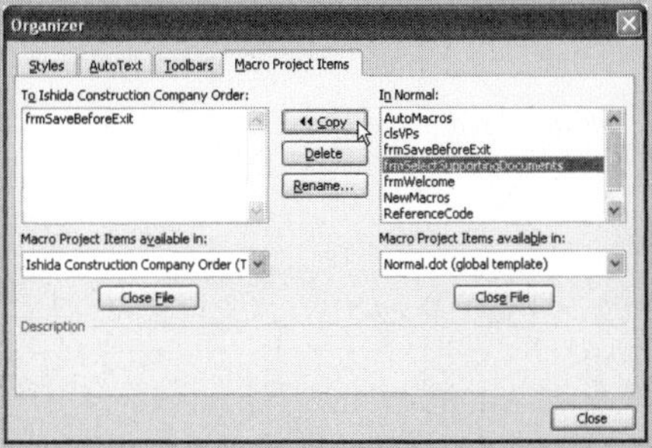

3. Look at the two documents or templates listed in the readouts above the two list boxes. Usually, the left list box shows the active document, and the right shows Normal.dot. Change these so that one list box shows the document or template that contains the code you want to copy or move and the other list box shows the destination document or template. (If you want only to delete or rename code items, you need only make the Organizer dialog box list only the document or template that contains the items.) To change the document or template listed, click the Close File button underneath the list box on that side. The Close File button changes to an Open File button. Click this button to display the Open dialog box, navigate to and select the document or template you want, and then click the Open button.

4. You can then delete, rename, copy, and move macro project items:

   ◆ To delete one or more macro project items from a template, choose the item or items from either panel of the Organizer dialog box and click the Delete button. Click the Yes button in the confirmation message box. Any copies of the items in other templates are unaffected.

   ◆ To rename a macro project item, select it from either panel and click the Rename button to open the Rename dialog box. Enter the new name and click the OK button. Any copies of the item in other templates are unaffected.

   ◆ To copy one or more macro project items from one template to another, open the templates in the Organizer dialog box. Select the item or items to copy in either panel of the dialog box (the arrows on the Copy button change direction to point to the other panel). Then click the Copy button. If the recipient template contains a macro project item of the same name as one you're copying, Word displays a warning message box telling you that it can't copy the item. If you still want to copy the item, rename either the item you're copying or the item with the same name in the destination template, and then perform the copy operation.

   ◆ To move a macro project item from one template to another, copy it as described in the previous paragraph, and then delete the macro project item from the source template.

5. Once you've deleted, renamed, copied, or moved macro project items, click the Close button to close the Organizer dialog box. If Word prompts you to save any changes to affected documents or templates that aren't open in your Word session, click the Yes button.

Chapter 2

Getting Started with the Visual Basic Editor

- ◆ Opening the Visual Basic Editor

- ◆ Opening a macro in the Visual Basic Editor

- ◆ Using the Visual Basic Editor's main windows

- ◆ Setting properties for a project

- ◆ Customizing the Visual Basic Editor

- ◆ Closing the Visual Basic Editor and returning to the host application

In this chapter, you'll start learning how to use the Visual Basic Editor, the tool that Microsoft provides for working with VBA code and user forms. All applications that host VBA use the Visual Basic Editor, so when you're working with VBA, the environment looks much the same no matter which application you're using.

The chapter shows you the basics of the Visual Basic Editor: its components, what they do, and how you use them. You'll learn more advanced maneuvers as you work with VBA later in this book.

This chapter also shows you how to customize the Visual Basic Editor to make your work more comfortable. This customization doesn't take long, and you'll find the resulting ease of use more than worth the amount of time you invest.

Opening the Visual Basic Editor

You open the Visual Basic Editor from the host application that you're using. For example, if you're working in Word, you open the Visual Basic Editor from Word. The instance of the Visual Basic Editor that you open is then associated with Word. You can open two or more instances of the Visual Basic Editor. For example, if you've already opened an instance of the Visual Basic Editor from Word, you could open another instance of the Visual Basic Editor from Excel, and then another from PowerPoint.

You can open the Visual Basic Editor in two ways:

- ◆ Specify the macro that you want to edit. The host application then opens the Visual Basic Editor and displays the macro, so that you're ready to work with it.

- ◆ Open it directly, and then navigate to the code you want to work with.

The next two sections demonstrate the two ways of opening the Visual Basic Editor, and the third section shows you how to navigate to a macro. The indirect way saves time when you want to work on a specific macro. The direct way is convenient for when you need to open the Visual Basic Editor and start work.

Opening the Visual Basic Editor with a Macro Selected

If you know which macro you want to work with, use this method to open the Visual Basic Editor and the macro at the same time. This example uses Word to open the `Transpose_Word_Right` macro that you recorded in Chapter 1.

1. Open Word if it's not already running, or activate Word if it is running.

2. Press Alt+F8 or choose Tools ➢ Macro ➢ Macros to display the Macros dialog box.

3. Select the `Transpose_Word_Right` macro and click the Edit button. Word opens the Visual Basic Editor with the macro displayed and ready for editing, as shown in Figure 2.1.

4. Choose File ➢ Close And Return To Microsoft Word to close the Visual Basic Editor for the moment, so that you can open it using the method described in the next section.

Opening the Visual Basic Editor

To open the Visual Basic Editor directly, follow these steps:

1. Open or activate the host application. In this case, open or activate Word.

2. Press Alt+F11 or choose Tools ➢ Macro ➢ Visual Basic Editor. The Visual Basic Editor opens.

FIGURE 2.1

The Visual Basic Editor with the Transpose_ Word_Right macro open in the Code window

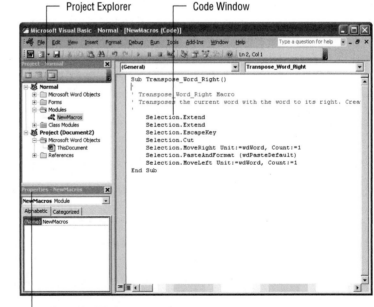

NOTE   Depending on the state of the Visual Basic Editor the last time it was closed, you may see one or more Code windows open. For example, if you left the Code window for the NewMacros module open in the previous section, the Visual Basic Editor will probably display this Code window again.

Navigating to a Macro

After opening the Visual Basic Editor directly, use the Project Explorer window to navigate to your macro. You also use the Project Explorer to navigate among open projects and modules when you're working in the Visual Basic Editor.

NOTE   The Project Explorer window works like a standard Windows Explorer tree. Depending on the application you're using, you'll see different projects in the tree (more on this later in the chapter).

To navigate to the Transpose_Word_Right macro, follow these steps:

1. In the Project Explorer window in the upper-left corner of the Visual Basic Editor, expand the entry for Normal (which represents Normal.dot, the Normal template) by clicking the + sign to the left of its name. (If the Normal entry is expanded, skip this step.)

2. Double-click the Modules object to expand it.

3. Double-click the NewMacros module. (This is the module in which Word automatically creates the macros you record.) The Visual Basic Editor displays the contents of the module in the Code window on the right side.

If the module contains more than one macro, you'll also need to select the macro you want to work with—in this case, the Transpose_Word_Right macro. (If you've recorded only the Transpose_Word_Right macro, only this macro appears in the Code window.) To do so, use one of these methods:

◆ In the Code window, select the macro from the Procedure drop-down list, as shown in Figure 2.2. (If you hover the mouse pointer over the list before dropping it down, you'll see a ScreenTip that gives its name: Procedure.)

◆ Use the scroll bar to scroll to the macro you want to edit, which is identified by the word *Sub*, the name you gave it, and a pair of parentheses—in this case, Sub Transpose_Word_Right().

Using the Visual Basic Editor's Main Windows

In this section, you'll learn how to use the main windows of the Visual Basic Editor to get your work done.

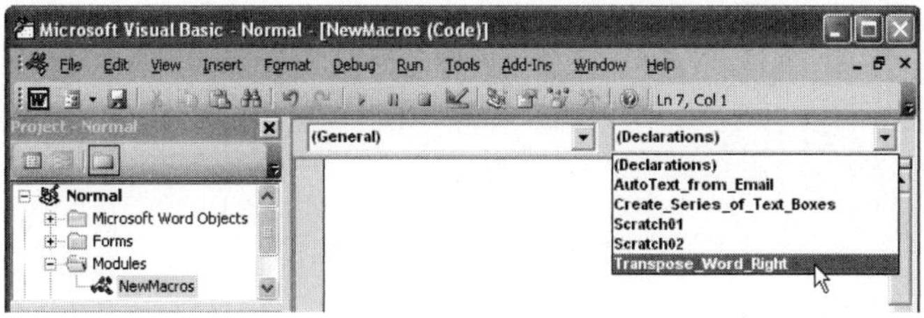

FIGURE 2.2

If the module contains two or more macros, scroll to the macro you want to edit, or select it from the Procedure drop-down list.

The Project Explorer

The Project Explorer is the tool for navigating among the various components in the Visual Basic Editor. Figure 2.3 shows the Project Explorer for a Visual Basic Editor session with Word as the host application.

Depending on the host application and its capabilities, each project can contain some or all of the following elements:

◆ User forms (forms that make up part of the application's user interface, such as a custom dialog box).

◆ Modules containing macros, procedures, and functions.

◆ Class modules (modules that define objects, their properties, and their values).

◆ References to other projects or to library files (such as DLLs—Dynamic Link Libraries).

◆ Objects related to the application. For example, each Word document and template contains a Microsoft Word Objects folder that holds a class object named ThisDocument. ThisDocument gives you access to the properties and events for the document or template. Each Excel workbook contains a class object named ThisWorkbook that gives you access to the properties and events for the workbook, and a Sheet object (named Sheet1, Sheet2, and so on) for each worksheet.

For most host applications, each open document and template is considered a project and is displayed as a root in the project tree. The project tree also contains any global macro storage—such as the Normal.dot template in Word or the Personal Macro Workbook in Excel—and any add-ins that are loaded.

As an example, in Figure 2.3, Normal.dot is identified as Normal, and the active document is identified as Project (Document2): a document named Document2 (one that hasn't been saved yet). The template attached to the active document is identified as TemplateProject(Sales Memo)—in other words, a template named Sales Memo.dot. A global template named TemplateProject(Sales Global Template) is also loaded; this is a template named Sales Global Template.dot. You can't tell that this is a global template from the listing (other than by its descriptive name), but if you click its + sign to expand it, a message box tells you that the template is locked.

FIGURE 2.3
Use the Project Explorer to navigate to the module you want to work with.

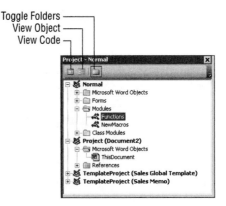

TIP You can change the name of a project by using the Project Properties dialog box (discussed later in this chapter) or by selecting the project and entering a new name in the Properties window. Once you change the name, the project is identified by that name in the Project Explorer, followed by the name of the document or template. For example, if you change the project name of the document Document2 to **Testing**, the document project is identified as Testing(Document2) in the Project Explorer rather than Project(Document2).

You navigate the Project Explorer in the same way that you navigate the Windows Explorer tree: Click the boxed plus sign to the left of a project item to expand the view and display the items contained within the project, and click the resulting boxed minus sign to collapse the view and hide the items again. Double-click a module to display its code in the Code window. Double-click a user form to display it in the Code window (a user form is considered to be code because it is an object created using code).

The Visual Basic Editor displays the Project Explorer by default, and because the Project Explorer provides fast and efficient navigation among the various elements of your VBA projects, it's usually easiest to keep it displayed unless you're short of screen space or you're working for long periods in the Code window and don't need to switch to other elements. To close the Project Explorer, click its close button (the × button in its title bar). To display the Project Explorer again, press Ctrl+R or choose View ➤ Project Explorer. As you'll see later in this chapter, you can also undock the Project Explorer. This lets you push it aside when you need more room.

In Figure 2.3, three buttons appear on a toolbar at the top of the Project Explorer:

View Code   Displays the Code window for the selected object. For example, if you select a user form in the Project Explorer and click the View Code button, the Visual Basic Editor displays a Code window containing the code attached to the user form. If you select a module or a class module in the Project Explorer and click the View Code button, the Visual Basic Editor displays a Code window containing the code in the module. You can also right-click the object and choose View Code from the shortcut menu.

TIP For a module or a class module, you can also double-click the object to view its code. This is usually faster than selecting it and then clicking the View Code button. For a user form or a file, however, double-clicking issues the View Object command (discussed next) rather than the View Code command.

View Object   Displays a window containing the selected object. The View Object button remains dimmed and unavailable until you select an object (such as a user form or a file or object within a file) that can be displayed. If the selected object is a user form, clicking the View Object button displays the user form; if the selected object is a file or an object within a file, clicking the View Object button displays that object in the host application's window. For example, selecting the ThisDocument object for a Word document and clicking the View Object button displays the Word document in the Word window. Selecting the Sheet1 object in an Excel workbook and clicking the View Object button displays that worksheet in the Excel workbook in the Excel window.

TIP You can also issue the View Object command by right-clicking an object and choosing View Object from the shortcut menu or by double-clicking an object that supports the View Object command. (If the object doesn't support the View Object command, double-clicking it issues the View Code command instead.)

Toggle Folders Toggles the view of the objects in the Project Explorer between *folder view* (a view that shows the objects separated into their folders beneath the document projects or template projects that contain them) and *folder contents view* (which displays the objects within the projects that contain them). The left part of Figure 2.4 shows the Project Explorer for an application session sorted by folder view, and the right part shows the Project Explorer for the same situation in folder contents view. Whether you spend more time in folder view or folder contents view will depend on the size of your screen, the number of objects you put in any given project, and the way your mind works, not necessarily in that order. For many purposes, you'll want to toggle between folder view and folder contents view to locate objects most easily.

Apart from navigating to the items you need to work with, you can perform the following tasks with the Project Explorer:

◆ Add components to or remove them from a project. For example, you can use the Project Explorer to add a module or a user form to a project.

◆ Compare the components of one project to the components of another project. Such a comparison can be useful when you need to establish the differences between two or more projects quickly (for example, your reference copy of a company template and the copies users have been adding to).

◆ Move or copy items from one project to another. You can drag a code module, class module, or user form from one project to another in the Project Explorer to copy it, or from the Project Explorer in one instance of the Visual Basic Editor to a project in the Project Explorer in another instance. For example, you could drag a user form from a Visual Basic Editor instance hosted by Excel to a Visual Basic Editor session hosted by PowerPoint to copy the user form.

◆ Import or export a code module or a user form to or from a project.

NOTE Many actions that you can perform through the Project Explorer you can also perform through the Visual Basic Editor's menu items, which is useful when the Project Explorer isn't displayed. In general, though, the Project Explorer provides the easiest way to navigate from module to module in the Visual Basic Editor, especially when you have several complex projects open at the same time. You can access the most commonly used commands for an object by right-clicking it in the Project Explorer to display the shortcut menu.

FIGURE 2.4
Folder view (left) displays the objects separated into folders beneath the projects that contain them. Folder contents view (right) displays the objects within the projects that contain them.

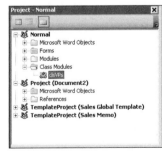

The Object Browser

The Visual Basic Editor provides a full Object Browser for working with objects in VBA. You'll look at the Object Browser in detail in Chapter 8 and when you examine the object models for the various applications in the final part of the book. But, in the meantime, take a quick look at Figure 2.5, which shows the Object Browser for a Word VBA session. The Document object is selected in the left-hand panel, and its list of properties appears in the right-hand panel.

You'll find that a number of these properties immediately make sense from your knowledge of Word documents. For example, the AttachedTemplate property tells you which template the document is currently attached to. Likewise, the Bookmarks property contains information on all the bookmarks in the document. The property information is displayed at the bottom of the Object Browser.

The Code Window

You'll do most of the actual work of creating and editing your macros in the Visual Basic Editor's Code window. The Visual Basic Editor provides a Code window for each open project, for each document section within the project that can contain code, and for each code module and user form in the project. Each Code window is identified by the project name, the name of the module within the project, and the word *Code* in parentheses. Figure 2.6 shows the Visual Basic Editor Code window with the Transpose_Word_Right macro open in it.

As you can see from the figure, two drop-down list boxes appear just below the title bar of the Code window:

◆ The Object drop-down list box at the upper-left corner of the Code window provides a quick way of navigating between different objects.

◆ The Procedure drop-down list box at the upper-right corner of the Code window lets you move quickly from procedure to procedure within the current module. Click the down-arrow button to display the drop-down list of procedures. You'll see that the first procedure is (Declarations). This takes you to the Declarations area at the top of the current code sheet, which is where you declare public variables and other VBA information that multiple procedures need to know.

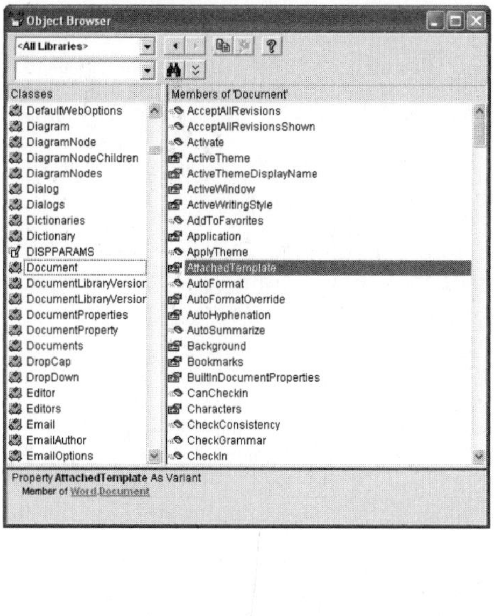

FIGURE 2.5
The Object Browser provides a quick way to look up objects and their properties. Here, you can see the properties contained in the Document object.

FIGURE 2.6
You create and edit macros in the Code window.

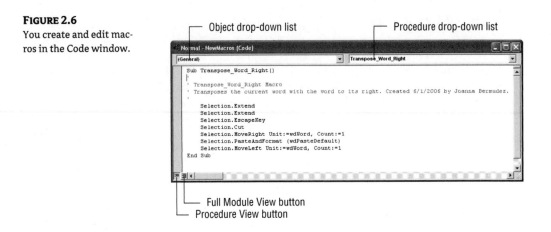

Object drop-down list   Procedure drop-down list

Full Module View button
Procedure View button

TIP   Because the Declarations area is located at the beginning of the code sheet, choosing (Declarations) from the Procedure drop-down list box is an alternative way of moving the insertion point to the beginning of the code sheet. (Usually it's easier to use the scrollbar or a keyboard shortcut such as Ctrl+Home to move to the beginning of the code sheet.)

The Visual Basic Editor Code window provides a half-dozen features for helping you create code efficiently and accurately, as discussed in the following sections.

COMPLETE WORD

The Complete Word feature completes the word you're typing, once you've typed enough letters to distinguish that word from any other. If you haven't typed enough letters to distinguish the word, the Visual Basic Editor gives you the closest possibilities (see Figure 2.7). You can either "type down" (continue typing to narrow the selection) or scroll through them to find the one you want.

FIGURE 2.7
The Complete Word feature automatically completes a term when you've typed enough to identify it. If you haven't typed enough, you can choose from a short list.

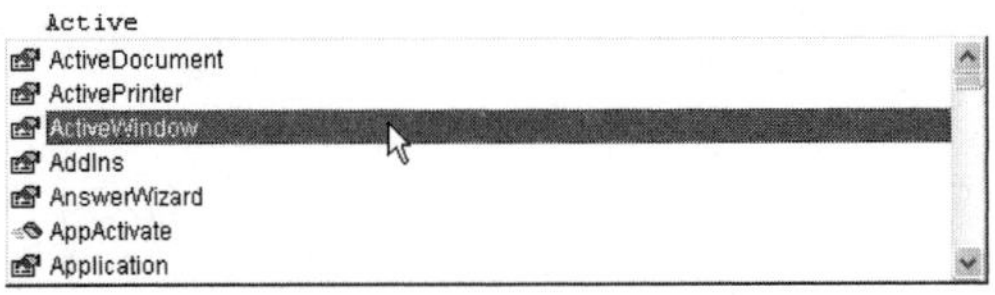

The easiest way to activate Complete Word when you're typing code is to press Ctrl+spacebar. You can also choose Edit ➢ Complete Word or click the Complete Word button on the Edit toolbar (see Figure 2.8).

QUICK INFO

The Quick Info command displays a ScreenTip showing syntax information on the current variable, function, method, statement, or procedure. Figure 2.9 shows an example of a Quick Info ScreenTip.

FIGURE 2.8

The Edit toolbar contains commands for working in the Code window.

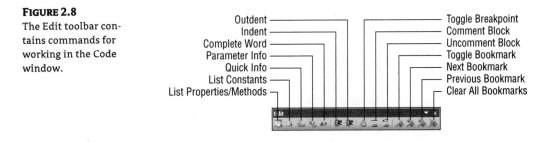

Outdent — Toggle Breakpoint
Indent — Comment Block
Complete Word — Uncomment Block
Parameter Info — Toggle Bookmark
Quick Info — Next Bookmark
List Constants — Previous Bookmark
List Properties/Methods — Clear All Bookmarks

FIGURE 2.9

Use the Quick Info command to get a quick reminder of syntax or a quick readout of status.

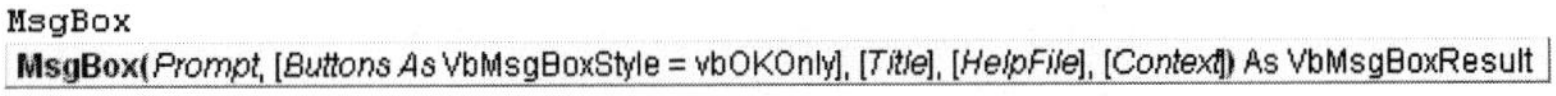

MsgBox
MsgBox(*Prompt*, [*Buttons As* VbMsgBoxStyle = vbOKOnly], [*Title*], [*HelpFile*], [*Context*]**)** As VbMsgBoxResult

To issue the Quick Info command, use one of these methods:

◆ Right-click the term and choose Quick Info from the shortcut menu.

◆ Position the insertion point in the term and press Ctrl+I.

◆ Position the insertion point in the term and choose Edit ➢ Quick Info.

LIST PROPERTIES/METHODS

The List Properties/Methods command displays a pop-up list box containing properties and methods for the object you've just typed so that you can quickly complete the expression. List Properties/Methods is switched on by default and automatically pops up the list box when you type a period within an expression. Alternatively, you can display the list box by clicking the List Properties/Methods button on the Edit toolbar.

To use List Properties/Methods, follow these steps:

1. Press ↓ to scroll down to the property or method, or scroll down with the mouse (see Figure 2.10). You can also type the first few letters of the property or method's name to jump to it.

2. Enter the property or method into the code:

   ◆ Press Tab, or double-click the property or method, if you want to continue working on the same line after entering the property or method.

   ◆ Press Enter if you want to start a new line after entering the property or method.

FIGURE 2.10

Use the List Properties/ Methods command to enter code items quickly and accurately.

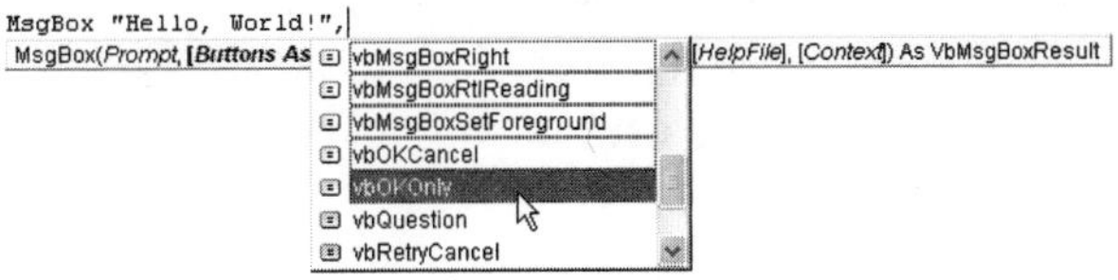

MsgBox "Hello, World!",
MsgBox(*Prompt*, [*Buttons As* | vbMsgBoxRight | [*HelpFile*], [*Context*]) As VbMsgBoxResult
vbMsgBoxRtlReading
vbMsgBoxSetForeground
vbOKCancel
vbOKOnly
vbQuestion
vbRetryCancel

LIST CONSTANTS

The List Constants command displays a pop-up list box containing constants for a property you've typed, so that you can quickly complete the expression. List Constants is switched on by default. Alternatively, you can display the list box by clicking the List Constants button on the Edit toolbar.

To use List Constants (see Figure 2.11), follow these steps:

1. Press ↓ to scroll down to the constant, type its first letter (or first few letters), or scroll down with the mouse.

2. Enter the constant in the code:

   ◆ Press Tab, or double-click the constant, if you want to continue working on the same line after entering the constant.

   ◆ Press Enter if you want to start a new line after entering the constant.

FIGURE 2.11
The List Constants feature saves you time and effort, especially when typing complex constant names.

DATA TIPS

The Data Tips feature displays a ScreenTip containing the value of a variable the mouse pointer moves over when the Visual Basic Editor is in Break mode (a mode you use for testing and debugging macros). Figure 2.12 shows an example. The Data Tips feature is switched on by default.

FIGURE 2.12
Use the Data Tips feature to check the value of a variable when you're running code.

```
strFirstName = "Lexi"
strLastName = "Brown"

strUserName = strFirstName & " " & strLastName
                strFirstName = "Lexi"
```

MARGIN INDICATORS

The Margin Indicators feature lets you quickly set a breakpoint, the next statement, or a bookmark by clicking in the margin of the Code window. You'll look at setting breakpoints, setting the next statement, and setting bookmarks later in this book.

OTHER EDITING FEATURES

Apart from these features, the Code window includes standard Office editing features such as copy and move, cut and paste, and drag and drop. Drag and drop is particularly useful, because you can drag code from one procedure or module to another.

The Properties Window

The Visual Basic Editor provides a Properties window you can use to view and modify the properties of an object in VBA, such as a project, a module or class module, a user form, or a control (for example, a button or check box in a dialog box). The drop-down list at the top of the Properties window lets you pick the object whose properties you want to view or modify. The Alphabetic page presents an alphabetical list of the properties in the item, and the Categorized page presents a list of the properties broken down into categories.

Figure 2.13 shows the Alphabetic page with the properties for an Excel workbook on the left, and the Categorized page for a user form (a custom dialog box) on the right. (Showing the Categorized page for the Excel workbook isn't very helpful, as all of the properties belong to a Misc. category—miscellaneous.) Many of the workbook properties are easy to grasp. For example, the `HasRoutingSlip` property is set to `False`, indicating that the workbook does not have an e-mail routing slip attached to it; and the `Saved` property is set to `True`, indicating that the workbook does not contain any unsaved changes. You'll meet the properties for user forms in Chapters 14 and 15, but for now, look at properties such as `Caption` (which is listed in the Appearance category and sets the text in the user form's title bar) and `Height` (which appears in the Position category and specifies the height of the user form in points).

UNDERSTANDING DESIGN MODE, RUN MODE, AND BREAK MODE

The Visual Basic Editor uses three modes:

Design mode   Also known as *design time*. Any time you're working in the Visual Basic Editor on your code, you're in Design mode. You don't have to be actively designing anything (although you often will be).

Run mode   Also known as *runtime*. When code is running, you're in Run mode.

Break mode   When code is running but execution is temporarily suspended, you're in Break mode. Break mode lets you step through your code one command or one procedure at a time (rather than running all the commands at once). You use it to debug or otherwise critique your code. You'll spend a lot of time in Break mode.

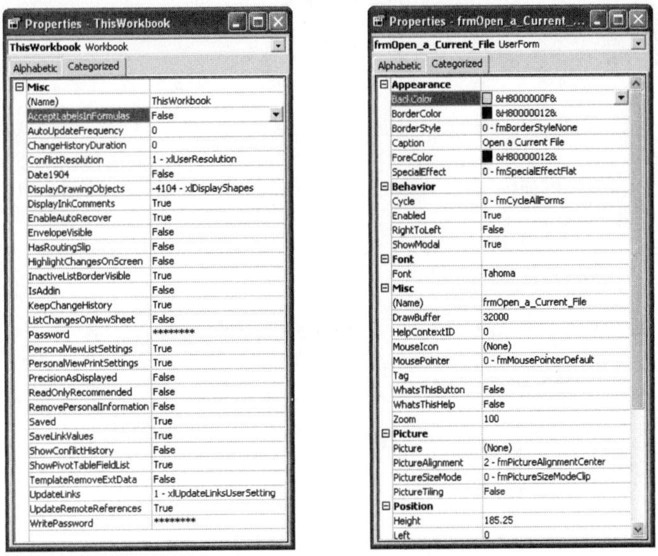

FIGURE 2.13

Use the Properties window to view the properties of a project, a user form, module, class module, or a control.

The Visual Basic Editor displays the Properties window by default, but you can close it by clicking its close button (the × button). To display the Properties window again, press F4 or choose View ➤ Properties Window.

To change a property, click the cell containing the property name (if you want to select a different value for the property) or in the value cell (if you want to edit the value), and then change the value. You'll be able to choose different values depending on the type of property: For a True/False property, you'll be limited to those two choices in the drop-down list; for a text property such as Name, you can enter any valid VBA name.

By default, the Properties window is docked below the Project Explorer. You can resize the Properties window or the Project Explorer by dragging the border between them, or you can resize both at once by dragging the border to their right. If you undock the Properties window, you can resize it by dragging its borders or corners to display more properties or to shrink the window so it takes up less space in the Visual Basic Editor.

The Immediate Window

Beyond the Project Explorer, the Code window, and the Properties window, the Visual Basic Editor includes a number of other windows that it doesn't display by default. Two of the key windows are the Object Browser (which you met earlier in this chapter) and the Immediate window, which you'll use during the discussion of the VBA language in Chapter 5.

The Immediate window, shown in Figure 2.14, is a small, unadorned window you can use as a virtual scratch pad to enter lines of code you want to test without entering them in the macro itself. When you type a line of code into the Immediate window and press the Enter key, the Visual Basic Editor executes that code.

FIGURE 2.14
Use the Immediate window for on-the-fly work and information.

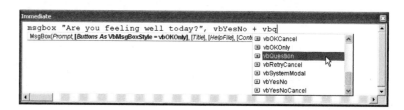

To display the Immediate window, press Ctrl+G or choose View ➤ Immediate Window. If the Immediate window is docked to one side of the Visual Basic Editor window, you can undock it by double-clicking its title bar. To return the Immediate window to its docked position, double-click its title bar again.

To close the Immediate window, click its close button (the × button). Pressing Ctrl+G or choosing View ➤ Immediate Window again doesn't close the Immediate window.

NOTE You can also use the Immediate window to display information to help you check the values of variables and expressions while code is executing.

Setting Properties for a Project

Each VBA project has several properties that you can set, including its project name, its description, and whether it is locked against viewing. To examine or set the properties for a project, right-click the project or one of its components in the Project Explorer and choose the Properties item from the context menu to display the Project Properties dialog box. Both the menu item and the resulting dialog box are identified by the description of the project—for example, the properties dialog box for a template in Word is identified as TemplateProject - Project Properties, and the properties dialog box for an Excel workbook is identified as VBAProject - Project Properties. Figure 2.15 shows the Project Properties dialog box for an Excel workbook project.

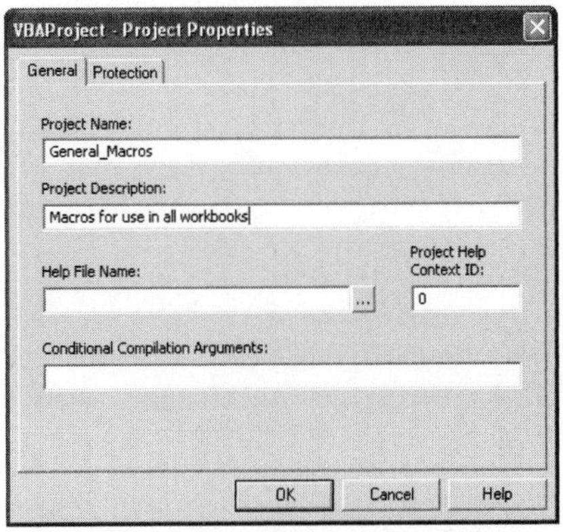

FIGURE 2.15

Use the Project Properties dialog box to view and set the properties for a project and to lock a project against change.

Here's what you can do on the General page of the Project Properties dialog box:

◆ Set the project name in the Project Name text box. This name identifies the project in the Object Browser and, when necessary, in the Windows Registry. Make sure the name is unique to avoid confusion with any other project. Technically, the project name is the name of the type library for the project (the *type library* describes the objects—such as modules and user forms—that the project contains); it is used to build the fully qualified class name of classes in the project (more on this later in the book). The project name can contain underscores but cannot contain spaces.

◆ Enter a description of the project in the Project Description text box. This description appears in the Description pane in the Object Browser to help the user understand what the project is. So be as concise, yet descriptive, as possible.

◆ Designate the Help file for the project by entering the name and path of the Help file in the Help File Name text box. Click the button marked with the ellipsis (…) to the right of the Help File Name text box to display the Help File dialog box. Then select the file and click the Open button to enter the Help filename in the text box. (Alternatively, you can type or paste in the name and path.)

◆ Specify the Help context for the project in the Project Help Context ID text box. The Help context refers to a location in the Help file. The default Help context is 0, which causes the Help file to display the opening screen of the Help file (the same screen you'll see if you run the Help file from the Run dialog box or by double-clicking the file in Explorer). You can specify a different Help context to take the user to a particular topic—for example, one relevant to the project on which they're seeking Help.

◆ Specify any conditional compilation arguments needed for the project.

Here's what you can do on the Protection page of the Project Properties dialog box, shown in Figure 2.16:

FIGURE 2.16

The Protection page of the Project Properties dialog box lets you lock your project with a password so that nobody can view or edit it.

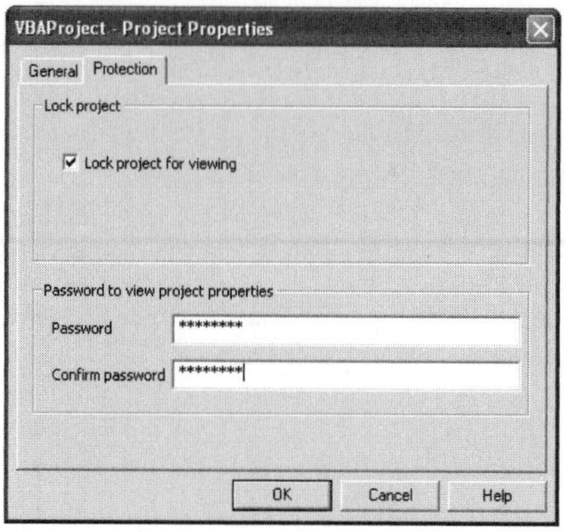

◆ Select the Lock Project For Viewing check box to prevent other people from opening the project, viewing it, and changing it without knowing the password.

◆ In the Password To View Project Properties group box, enter a password for the project in the Password text box, and then enter the same password in the Confirm Password text box. Click the OK button and close the project. Now nobody can open and view (let alone change) the project if they don't know the password. That said, Office's security is weak and can easily be cracked. More on this in Chapter 19.

TIP If you enter a password in the Password text box and the Confirm Password text box, but you don't select the Lock Project For Viewing check box, the Visual Basic Editor will prompt you for the password the next time you try to display the Project Properties dialog box. However, you'll be able to open and view the project and its contents without supplying the password.

Customizing the Visual Basic Editor

Given how much time you're likely to spend in the Visual Basic Editor, you ought to customize it so you can work as quickly and comfortably as possible. You can

◆ Choose editor and view preference settings in the Visual Basic Editor to control how it interacts with you

◆ Choose which windows to display in the Visual Basic Editor, and lay them out to use your workspace as effectively as possible

◆ Customize the toolbar and menus in the Visual Basic Editor so the commands you need are at hand (without cluttering up your workspace)

◆ Customize the Toolbox so it contains the tools you need to build your user forms

The following sections explain your options.

WARNING Any customization you make applies across all hosts using that version of VBA. For example, if you change the font in an instance of the Visual Basic Editor hosted by Excel 2003, the font changes for Visual Basic Editor instances hosted by Word, PowerPoint, Outlook, and so on.

Choosing Editor and View Preferences

To begin choosing editor and view preferences, choose Tools ➢ Options to open the Options dialog box (see Figure 2.17).

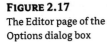

FIGURE 2.17
The Editor page of the Options dialog box

EDITOR PAGE OPTIONS

The Editor page of the Options dialog box includes the following settings:

Auto Syntax Check   Controls whether VBA displays warning message boxes when it discovers errors while automatically checking your syntax as you type expressions This feature is usually helpful because VBA can instantly point out errors that would otherwise remain unseen until you tried to run or debug your code. But if your style is to move from one unfinished line of code to another (and ultimately finish all the lines at your convenience), you may want to turn off this feature to prevent the Visual Basic Editor from bombarding you with message boxes for errors you're aware of but can't yet fix.

NOTE   Even if you turn off Auto Syntax Check, the Visual Basic Editor still turns the offending lines of code red to draw your attention to them.

Require Variable Declaration   Governs whether you must declare variables explicitly. Declaring variables explicitly is a little more work than declaring them implicitly, but it's good practice and will save you time down the road—so make sure that this check box is selected. (Chapter 6 discusses how to work with variables.)

Auto List Members   Controls whether the List Properties/Methods and List Constants features automatically suggest properties, methods, and constants as you work in the Code window. Most people find these features helpful, but some experienced programmers turn these features off because they know all the properties, methods, and constants they need and prefer not to be distracted by a busy interface.

NOTE   You may also want to turn off features such as Auto List Members, Auto Quick Info, and Auto Data Tips because they take up memory and processing power and may slow your computer. The speed difference is relatively small, but it can make all the difference on an older computer.

Auto Quick Info   Controls whether the Quick Info feature automatically displays information about functions and their parameters as you work with functions in the Code window.

Auto Data Tips   Controls whether the Visual Basic Editor displays ScreenTips when you hover the mouse pointer over a variable or expression in Break mode, enabling you to check the value of a variable or expression quickly. (Alternatively, you can use the Locals window or the Watch window, but these take up more space.)

Auto Indent   Controls whether the Visual Basic Editor automatically indents subsequent lines of code after you've indented a line. When Auto Indent is switched on, the Visual Basic Editor starts each new line of code indented to the same level (the same number of tabs or spaces or the same combination of the two) as the previous line. When Auto Indent is switched off, the Visual Basic Editor starts each new line of code at the left margin of the Code window. Usually, automatic indentation is a time-saver, although it means that each time you need to decrease a new line's level of indentation, you must press Shift+Tab, click the Outdent button on the Edit toolbar, or delete the tabs or spaces.

Tab Width   Sets the number of spaces in a tab. You can adjust this setting from 1 to 32 spaces. The default setting is four spaces, which works well for the default font. If you choose to use a proportional font (such as Times or Arial) rather than a monospaced font (such as Courier) for your code, you may want to increase the number of spaces a tab represents in order to clarify the levels of indentation in your code.

Drag-And-Drop Text Editing   Controls whether the Visual Basic Editor supports drag-and-drop. Most people find this feature helpful. You can drag portions of your code around the Code window or from one Code window to another. You can also drag code into the Immediate window or drag an expression into the Watch window.

Default To Full Module View   Controls whether the Visual Basic Editor displays all the procedures in a module in one list (Full Module view) or displays them one at a time (Procedure view). If you're working with short procedures, you may find Full Module view useful; for most other purposes, the individual view provides a less cluttered and more workable effect. When working in Procedure view, you open the procedure you want to work with by choosing it from the Procedure drop-down list at the top of the Code window. To toggle between Full Module view and Procedure view, click the Full Module View button or the Procedure View button in the lower-left corner of any Code window.

NOTE   You can also use the Procedures drop-down list when working in Full Module view to quickly move to a procedure by name.

Procedure Separator   Controls whether the Visual Basic Editor displays horizontal lines to separate the procedures within a module shown in Full Module view in the Code window. Usually these lines are helpful, providing a quick reference as to where one procedure ends and the next begins. (If you're using Procedure view, this check box isn't relevant.)

EDITOR FORMAT PAGE OPTIONS

The Editor Format page of the Options dialog box, shown in Figure 2.18, controls how code appears in the Visual Basic Editor.

FIGURE 2.18
The Editor Format page
of the Options dialog box

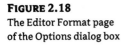

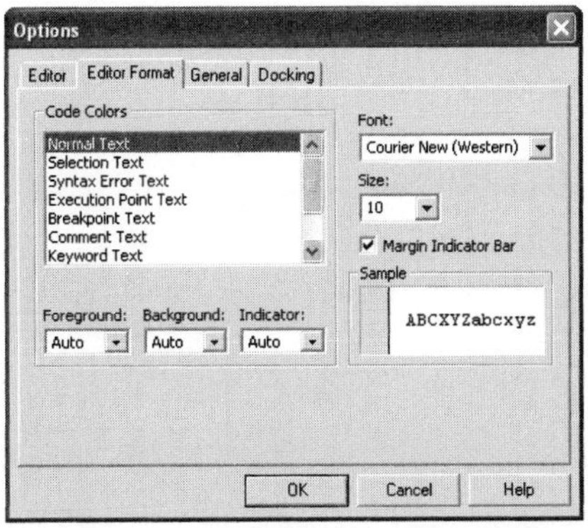

You can change the default colors for various types of text used in procedures by choosing a type of text in the Code Colors list box and selecting colors from the Foreground, Background, and Indicator drop-down lists. Here's what the Code Colors choices mean:

Normal Text   Takes care of much of the text in a typical procedure. You'll probably want to make this a conventional color (such as black, the default).

Selection Text   Affects the color of selected (highlighted) text.

Syntax Error Text   Affects the color VBA uses for offending lines. The default color is red.

Execution Point Text   Affects the color VBA uses for the line currently being executed in Break mode. You'll usually want to make this a highlighter color (like the fluorescent yellow the Visual Basic Editor uses as the default) so you can immediately see the current line.

Breakpoint Text   Affects the color in which VBA displays breakpoints (points where execution of the procedure stops).

Comment Text   Affects the color of comment lines. The default color is dark green.

Keyword Text   Affects the color of keywords (words recognized as part of the VBA language). Such text accounts for a sizable portion of each procedure. Display keywords in a different color than normal text, because it's helpful to be able to distinguish keywords without needing to read the code. The default color is dark blue.

Identifier Text   Affects the color VBA uses for identifiers. Identifiers include the names of variables, constants, and procedures you define.

Bookmark Text   Affects the color VBA uses for the bookmarks in your code.

Call Return Text   Affects the color VBA uses for calls to other procedures. By default, the Visual Basic Editor uses lime green for call return text.

You can change the font and size of all the text in the Code window by using the Font and Size drop-down lists on the Editor Format tab. You can also prevent the display of the margin indicator bar (in which items such as the Next Statement and Breakpoint icons appear) by clearing the Margin Indicator Bar check box. (Usually, these icons are helpful, but removing this bar slightly increases the code area on screen.)

GENERAL PAGE OPTIONS

The General page of the Options dialog box, shown in Figure 2.19, contains several categories of settings. The following sections discussed them in groups.

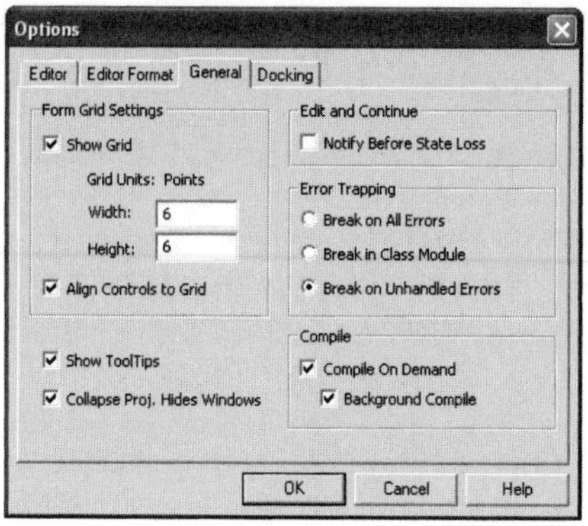

FIGURE 2.19
The General page of the
Options dialog box

Form Grid Settings Group Box

The Form Grid Settings control how the Visual Basic Editor handles user forms:

◆ The Show Grid check box controls whether the Visual Basic Editor displays a grid pattern of dots on the user form in Design mode to help you place and align controls. This check box is selected by default.

◆ The Width and Height text boxes set the spacing of the dots that make up the grid. You can set any value from 2 points to 60 points (the default setting is 6 points). If you display the grid on screen, you'll see the dots; if you don't display the grid, it still affects the Align Controls To Grid feature, discussed next. Experiment and find the coarseness of grid that you can most easily work with.

◆ The Align Controls To Grid check box governs whether the Visual Basic Editor automatically snaps the edges of controls you place or move to the nearest grid line. This option lets you place controls in approximately the right positions rapidly and easily, but it can be frustrating when you're trying to improve the layout of controls you've already placed on a user form. (If so, one option is to clear the Align Controls To Grid check box; another is to leave it selected but to decrease the size of the grid.)

The Edit And Continue Group Box

The Edit And Continue group box contains only one control—the Notify Before State Loss check box. This check box controls whether the Visual Basic Editor warns you, when you're running code, if you try to take an action that requires VBA to reset the values of all variables in the module.

Error Trapping Group Box

The Error Trapping group box contains three option buttons you use to specify how VBA handles errors that occur when you're running code:

Break On All Errors   Tells VBA to enter Break mode when it encounters any error, no matter whether an error handler (a section of code designed to handle errors) is active or whether the code is in a class module. Break On All Errors is useful for pinpointing where errors occur, which helps you track them down and remove them. If you've included an error handler in your code, you probably won't need this option.

Break In Class Module Arguably the most useful option for general use. When VBA encounters an unhandled error in a class module (a module that defines a type of object), VBA enters Break mode at the offending line of code.

Break On Unhandled Errors The default setting, this is useful when you've constructed an error handler to handle predictable errors in the current module. If there is an error handler, VBA allows the handler to trap the error and doesn't enter Break mode; but if there is no handler for the error generated, VBA enters Break mode on the offending line of code. An unhandled error in a class module, however, causes the project to enter Break mode on the line of code that invoked the offending procedure of the class, thus enabling you to identify (and alter) the line that caused the problem.

Compile Group Box

The Compile group box controls when VBA compiles the code for a project into executable code. Before any code can be executed, it needs to be compiled; but not all the code in a project must necessarily be compiled before the Visual Basic Editor can start executing the first parts of the code.

You can select the Compile On Demand check box if you want VBA to compile the code only as needed. VBA compiles the code in the procedure you're running before starting to execute that procedure, but it doesn't compile code in other procedures in the same module unless the procedure you're running calls them. As a result, execution of the procedure you run first in a module can begin as soon as VBA finishes compiling the code for that procedure. If the procedure then calls another procedure in the module, VBA compiles the code for the second procedure when the first procedure calls it, not when you begin running the first procedure.

Compile On Demand is usually a good option. It's especially useful when you're building a number of procedures in a module and have semi-completed code lying around in some of them. In contrast, if you clear the Compile On Demand check box, VBA compiles all the code in all the procedures in the module before starting to execute the procedure you want to run. This means that not only does the procedure start a little later (more code takes more time to compile), but any language error or compile error in any procedure in the module prevents you from running the current procedure, even if the code in that procedure contains no errors.

Suppose you have a module named Compilation that contains two procedures, GoodCode and BadCode, which look like this:

```
Sub GoodCode()
    MsgBox "This code is working."
End Sub

Sub BadCode()
    Application.Delete
End Sub
```

GoodCode simply displays a message box to indicate that it's working, whereas BadCode contains an invalid statement (Application objects don't have a Delete method). GoodCode runs without causing a problem, but BadCode causes an error every time.

If you try to run GoodCode with Compile On Demand switched on, the procedure runs fine: VBA compiles the code in GoodCode, finds no errors, and runs it. But if you try to run GoodCode with Compile On Demand switched off, VBA compiles the code in BadCode as well before starting to run GoodCode—and it stops with a compile error at the bogus Application.Delete statement. This thorough checking before running any code is good for finished modules that work together, but it can cause problems when you're experimenting with code in a module.

On the other hand, you can see the advantage of compiling all the code in the module when GoodCode calls BadCode, as in the third line of this version of the procedure:

```
Sub GoodCode()
   MsgBox "This code is working."
   BadCode
End Sub
```

Here, compiling the code in BadCode before starting to run GoodCode is a good idea, because doing so prevents GoodCode from running if BadCode contains an error. If you run this version of GoodCode with Compile On Demand switched on, VBA compiles GoodCode and starts to run it, displaying the message box in the second line. The BadCode call in the third line then causes VBA to compile BadCode, at which point VBA stops with the compile error. You don't want this to happen in the middle of a complex procedure; in such a case, you'd want Compile On Demand switched off.

The Background Compile check box, which is available when the Compile On Demand check box is selected, controls whether the Visual Basic Editor uses idle CPU time to compile further code while it's running the code that it has already compiled. Keep Background Compile switched on unless you suspect that it's slowing the execution of your code.

Show ToolTips and Collapse Proj. Hides Windows

The final two options on the General page of the Options dialog box are Show ToolTips and Collapse Proj. Hides Windows. The Show ToolTips check box controls whether the Visual Basic Editor displays ToolTips (aka ScreenTips) for its toolbar buttons. ToolTips tend to be useful unless you're desperate to save the memory and processor cycles they consume.

The Collapse Proj. Hides Windows check box controls whether the Visual Basic Editor hides the Code window and other project windows that you collapse in the Project Explorer's tree. This check box is selected by default, and in general it's a useful feature. When you collapse a project in the Project Explorer, the Visual Basic Editor hides any Code windows or user form windows belonging to that project and removes them from the list that appears on the Window menu. When you expand the project again, the Visual Basic Editor displays the windows in their previous positions and restores them to the Window menu's list.

DOCKING PAGE OPTIONS

The Docking page of the Options dialog box, shown in Figure 2.20, controls whether the various windows in the Visual Basic Editor are dockable—that is, whether they attach automatically to a side of the window when you move them there. Keeping windows dockable usually makes for a more organized interface. However, you may want to make the windows undockable so you can drag them off the edge of the screen as necessary and arrange them as you like.

Choosing and Laying Out the Editor Windows

Next, you can choose how to lay out the windows in the Visual Basic Editor. Your layout depends largely on the size and resolution of your screen and your personal preferences, but here are a couple of suggestions:

◆ Always maximize the Code window. If you write long lines of code and break them to a reasonable length only under duress once everything is working, you'll want to free as much space in the Visual Basic Editor window as possible.

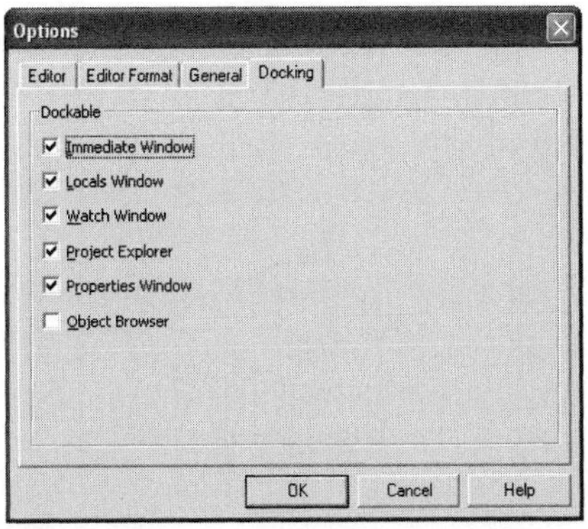

FIGURE 2.20
The Docking page of the
Options dialog box

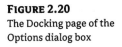

- ◆ Much of the time that you're actively writing code, you can dispense with the Project Explorer, invoking it only when you need it. As a handy way of getting it back, put the Project Explorer command on the Code Window, Code Window Break, Watch Window, Immediate Window, and Locals Window context menus. (You'll learn how to do this in the next section.)

- ◆ If you undock some of the windows, you can collapse them to icons at the bottom of the Visual Basic Editor window.

- ◆ If you're using a multi-monitor arrangement, you'll wish you could drag the child windows outside the Visual Basic Editor parent window and onto the second monitor. Unfortunately, they won't go far beyond the boundaries of the parent window. But you can achieve a similar effect by expanding the Visual Basic Editor window from the right-hand monitor onto the left-hand monitor, and then docking the Properties window and the Project Explorer on the left-hand monitor. The appearance of the menu bar and toolbar will suffer, but you'll have more space for the Code window, and all three windows will be available.

Customizing the Toolbar and Menu Bar

The Visual Basic Editor supports the same toolbar and menu bar customizations as the Office applications, enabling you to customize the interface of the Visual Basic Editor so that all the commands you need are at hand.

To customize the Visual Basic Editor, choose View ➢ Toolbars ➢ Customize (or right-click a displayed toolbar or the menu bar and choose Customize from the context menu) to display the Customize dialog box, shown in Figure 2.21.

NOTE Unlike the Office applications, the Visual Basic Editor doesn't let you create new menus or customize keyboard shortcuts.

You can now customize the toolbars, menus, and context menus to suit the way you work. Above all, if you use the context menus, be sure to customize them so they provide the commands you need.

FIGURE 2.21
Use the Customize dialog box to customize the Visual Basic Editor's menu bar, toolbar, and context menus.

In particular, you may want to add two key commands to the context menus: Comment Block and Uncomment Block. The Comment Block command adds a comment apostrophe (') to the beginning of each line of code in the selected block, making the line into a comment that VBA won't execute. The Uncomment Block command removes the first comment apostrophe from each command in the selected block, activating those lines that don't have further comment apostrophes. (Any line that's commented before you run the Comment Block command remains commented after you run the Uncomment Block command. You can run the Uncomment Block command again to remove further commenting.) These commands are available from the Edit toolbar in the normal configuration of the Visual Basic Editor, but it's much easier to make them available at all times in the Code window from the context menu.

The Visual Basic Editor provides the context menus listed in Table 2.1. To customize a context menu, select the Shortcut Menus check box in the Toolbars list on the Toolbars page of the Customize dialog box, and then drag the command you want from the Commands page to the context menu (see Figure 2.22).

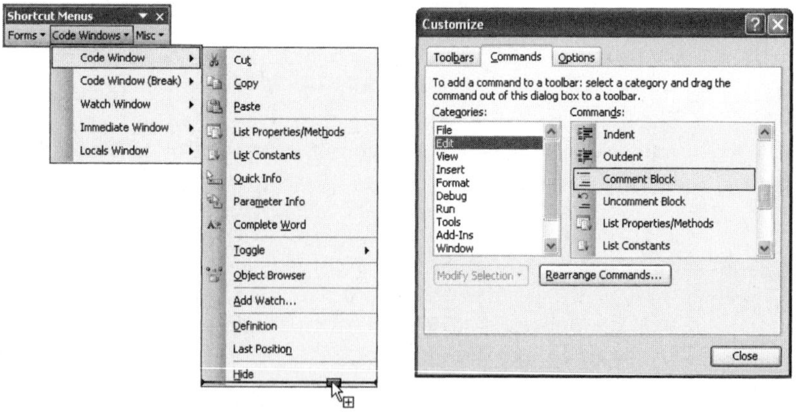

FIGURE 2.22
Use the Shortcut Menus toolbar to put key commands on the context menus in the Visual Basic Editor.

TABLE 2.1: Context Menus in the Visual Basic Editor

CONTEXT MENU	APPEARS WHEN YOU RIGHT-CLICK IN OR ON
MSForms	A user form
MSForms Control	A control on a user form
MSForms Control Group	A group of controls on a user form
MSForms MPC	A multipage control on a user form
Code Window	The Code window in Design mode
Code Window (Break)	The Code window in Break mode
Watch Window	The Watch window
Immediate Window	The Immediate window
Locals Window	The Locals window
Project Window	The Project window in Design mode
Project Window (Break)	The Project window in Break mode
Object Browser	The Object Browser
MSForms Palette	The clear space on a page in the Toolbox
MSForms Toolbox	The tab on a page in the Toolbox.
MSForms DragDrop	An item on a user form: drag it and drop it elsewhere on the user form
Property Browser	A property in the Properties window
Docked Window	A docked window (for example, the Project Explorer)

Here are a couple of suggestions for customizing the Visual Basic Editor:

◆ If you use the Locals window often to track the value of variables when stepping through your code, place a button for it on a toolbar that you always keep displayed (the standard button is on the Debug toolbar), or place an item for it on the context menus for the Code window (both in Design mode and in Break mode), Watch window, and Immediate window.

◆ Put the Watch window and the Immediate window on the context menus for the windows from which you'll invoke them.

◆ If you have a medium-sized monitor, consider grouping all the toolbar buttons you use on one toolbar, so that you don't waste space by displaying multiple toolbars.

Customizing the Toolbox

You can also customize the Toolbox, a special toolbar that contains controls for building user forms and is available only when a user form is selected. (Chapters 14 and 15 show you how to build user forms.)

You can customize the Toolbox by adding controls, removing controls, and adding new Toolbox pages of your own. You'll typically do this to put your most-used controls on the Toolbox, probably all on one page, to save yourself time. These controls will include customized variations on the regular Toolbox controls; by putting them on the Toolbox, you can avoid having to customize them again.

For example, many dialog boxes you create need an OK button that dismisses the dialog box, implements some code, and then continues execution of the procedure. Each OK button needs its `Name` property set to `cmdOK`, its `Caption` property set to `OK`, its `Default` property set to `True`, and its `Height` and `Width` properties set to a size smaller than the clunky dimensions the Visual Basic Editor assigns by default. Once you've customized a command button, you can place a copy of the customized button on the Toolbox and reuse it for subsequent forms.

Another reason to customize the Toolbox is to add advanced controls that extend the things you can do with dialog boxes and user forms.

ADDING CONTROLS TO THE TOOLBOX

The first way you'll probably want to add controls to the Toolbox is directly from a user form. For example, once you've created custom OK and Cancel buttons, you can copy them from the user form to the Toolbox so you can reuse them in any user forms you subsequently create.

To copy a control from a displayed user form to the Toolbox, just drag it and drop it, as shown in Figure 2.23. (Chapter 14 shows you how to put controls on to user forms you create yourself.)

To add controls to the Toolbox, right-click in the page to which you want to add controls (you'll learn how to add pages to the Toolbox in "Adding Pages to the Toolbox," a little later in this chapter), and choose Additional Controls from the context menu to display the Additional Controls dialog box shown in Figure 2.24. In the Available Controls list box, select the check boxes for the controls you want to add to the Toolbox, and then click the OK button. (To collapse the list to only the currently selected items, select the Selected Items Only check box in the Show group box.)

You can move a control from one page of the Toolbox to another by dragging it from the page it's on, moving the mouse pointer (still dragging) over the tab of the destination page to display that page. Then, move the mouse pointer down (again, still dragging) into the body of that page and drop the control.

RENAMING A TOOLBOX CONTROL

When you move the mouse pointer over a control in the Toolbox, a ScreenTip appears, showing the name of that control. To rename a control, right-click it in the Toolbox and choose the Customize item from the context menu to display the Customize Control dialog box. (The menu item is identified by the name of the control—for example, if the control is identified as New Label, the menu item is called Customize New Label.)

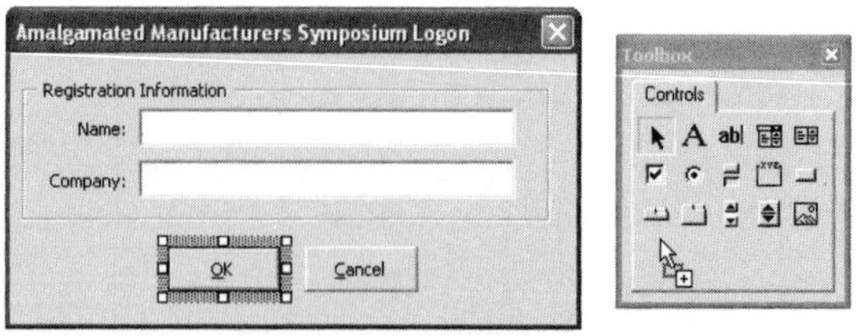

FIGURE 2.23
The quickest way to add a control to the Toolbox is to drag it there from a user form.

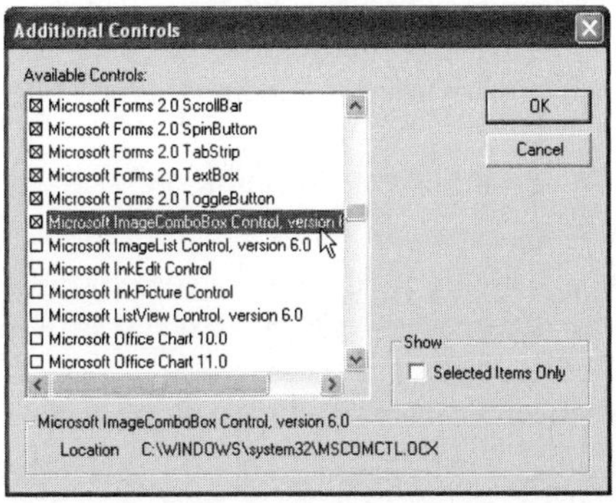

FIGURE 2.24
In the Additional Controls dialog box, select the check boxes for the controls you want to add, and then click the OK button.

Type the name for the control in the Tool Tip Text text box (delete or change the existing name as necessary); this name appears as a ScreenTip when the user moves the mouse pointer over the control in the Toolbox. Then, if you wish, assign a different picture to the control's Toolbox icon, as described in the next section. Otherwise, click the OK button to close the Customize Control dialog box.

ASSIGNING A PICTURE TO A CONTROL'S TOOLBOX ICON

Each control in the Toolbox is identified by a picture. You can assign a new picture to the control by displaying the Customize Control dialog box, clicking the Load Picture button, and selecting the picture or icon in the resulting dialog box.

TIP You can create your own icons by using a special-purpose icon editor (such as the freeware IconEdit32, available from www.pcmag.com).

For some controls, you can edit the picture assigned to the control by displaying the Customize Control dialog box, clicking the Edit Picture button, and using the Edit Image dialog box to color the pixels that make up the picture.

REMOVING CONTROLS FROM THE TOOLBOX

To remove a control from the Toolbox, right-click it and choose the Delete item from the context menu. The item is identified by the name of the control—for example, if you right-click a control named Company Name Combo Box, the menu item is named Delete Company Name Combo Box.

If the item is a custom control, this action gets rid of the control, and you can't restore it (unless you have a copy elsewhere). If the item is one of the Microsoft-supplied controls that come with the Microsoft Forms 2.0 package (which is part of VBA), you can restore it from the Additional Controls dialog box by selecting the check box for the appropriate object (for example, Microsoft Forms 2.0 CommandButton).

You can also remove controls from the Toolbox by deleting the entire page they're on. See "Removing Pages from the Toolbox," later in this chapter.

ADDING PAGES TO THE TOOLBOX

To add a page to the Toolbox, right-click the tab at the top of a page (or the label on the tab) and choose New Page from the context menu. The Visual Basic Editor adds a new page named New Page, to which it adds the Select Objects control. This control appears on every page in the Toolbox (so that it's always at hand), and you can't remove it.

You'll probably want to rename the new page immediately.

RENAMING PAGES IN THE TOOLBOX

To change the name of a Toolbox page, right-click its tab or label and choose Rename from the context menu to display the Rename dialog box. Type the name in the Caption text box, type any control tip text in the Control Tip Text text box, and click the OK button to close the dialog box.

REMOVING PAGES FROM THE TOOLBOX

To remove a page from the Toolbox, right-click its tab or label and choose Delete Page from the context menu. The Visual Basic Editor removes the page from the Toolbox without any confirmation, regardless of whether the page contains controls.

IMPORTING AND EXPORTING TOOLBOX PAGES

If you need to share Toolbox pages, you can save them as separate files and distribute them to your colleagues. Toolbox pages have a .pag file extension.

To import a Toolbox page, right-click the tab or label on an existing page in the Toolbox and choose Import Page from the context menu to display the Import Page dialog box. Select the page you want to import and choose the Open button. The Visual Basic Editor adds the new page after the last page currently in the Toolbox and names it New Page. Right-click the page's tab or label, choose Rename, type the new name and description, and then click the OK button.

Likewise, you can export a Toolbox page by right-clicking its tab or label and choosing Export Page from the context menu to display the Export Page dialog box. Type a name for the page, choose the folder in which to save it, and then click the Save button to save it. Now anyone can import the page as just described.

MOVING PAGES IN THE TOOLBOX

To move a page in the Toolbox, right-click its tab or label and choose Move from the context menu to display the Page Order dialog box. In the Page Order list box, select the page or pages you want to move (Shift+click to select multiple contiguous pages, Ctrl+click to select multiple pages individually) and use the Move Up and Move Down buttons to rearrange the pages as desired. Click the OK button to close the Page Order dialog box when you've finished.

Closing the Visual Basic Editor and Returning to the Host Application

When you finish an editing session in the Visual Basic Editor, you can either close the Visual Basic Editor or leave it running but switch to another window:

◆ To close the Visual Basic Editor, choose File ➢ Close And Return To <*Application*>, press Alt+Q, or click the close button on the Visual Basic Editor window.

◆ To leave the Visual Basic Editor running and work in another application, switch to the other application by using the Taskbar or pressing Alt+Tab.

Chapter 3

Editing Recorded Macros

- ◆ Testing a macro in the Visual Basic Editor
- ◆ Setting breakpoints and using comments
- ◆ Editing the recorded Word macro
- ◆ Editing the recorded Excel macro
- ◆ Editing the recorded PowerPoint macro

In this chapter, you'll use the Visual Basic Editor to edit the macros you recorded in Chapter 1 in Word, Excel, and PowerPoint using the Macro Recorder.

There are three reasons for working with macros in the Visual Basic Editor:

- ◆ First, to fix any problems in the way a macro you recorded is executing. For example, if you made a misstep when recording the macro, the macro will keep performing that wrong instruction every time you run it, unless you remove or change the instruction.

- ◆ Second, to add further instructions to the macro to make it behave differently (as mentioned earlier). This is a great way to get started with VBA, because by making relatively simple changes to a recorded macro, you can greatly increase its power and flexibility.

- ◆ Third, to create new macros by writing them in the Visual Basic Editor instead of recording them. You can write a new macro from scratch or cull parts of an existing macro, as appropriate.

NOTE   Even if you don't have an application that supports the Macro Recorder, you may still want to read through this chapter, because it shows you how to use some of the key editing features of the Visual Basic Editor.

Testing a Macro in the Visual Basic Editor

If a macro fails when you try to run it from the host application, the quickest way to find out what's going wrong is to open the macro in the Visual Basic Editor, run it, and see where it fails.

1. In the host application, press Alt+F8 or choose Tools ➢ Macro ➢ Macros to display the Macro dialog box.

2. Select the macro, and then click the Edit button. The host application opens an instance of the Visual Basic Editor and displays the macro for editing.

3. Start the macro running by pressing F5, choosing Run, or clicking the Run Sub/UserForm button on the Standard toolbar in the Visual Basic Editor (see Figure 3.1).

FIGURE 3.1
Click the Run Sub/
UserForm button on the
Standard toolbar to start
running the code.

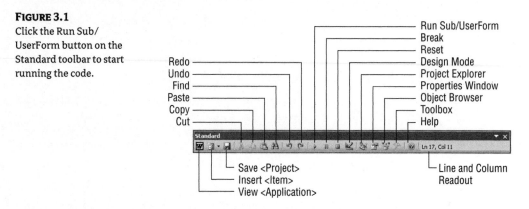

4. If the macro encounters an error and crashes, VBA displays an error message box on screen and selects the offending statement in the Code window. You can then edit the statement to fix the problem. Once you've done so, step through the macro as described in the next section.

WARNING Always test your macros on files (or copies of files) that you don't care about. There are many better ways to lose valuable work than to unleash untested macros on it. Store your code in a central location (such as Normal.dot in Word, the Personal Macro Workbook in Excel, or a code-only presentation in PowerPoint) so that it's accessible to all your files rather than only the file that contains it. If you create a macro in the wrong file, export it from that file and import it in your centralized storage. To export the macro, right-click its module in the Project Explorer, choose Export File from the shortcut menu, use the Export File dialog box to specify the folder and file name, and then click the Save button. To import the module, right-click the destination project in the Project Explorer, choose Import File, select the file in the Import File dialog box, and then click the Open button.

Stepping Through a Macro

To see exactly what a macro does (and what it does wrong), you can *step through* the macro—go through the macro, executing one command at a time—so that you can see the effect of each command. Stepping through a macro can be time consuming, but it enables you to identify problems and fix them.

To step through a macro, follow these steps:

1. Open the host application, and then open the macro for editing: press Alt+F8 or choose Tools ➢ Macro ➢ Macros, select the macro, and then click the Edit button.

2. Arrange the Visual Basic Editor window and the host application's window so that you can see them both. Either arrange the windows manually or use a Windows command to do so. For example, if the Visual Basic Editor window and the host application's window are the only two open windows that are not minimized, right-click in open space on the Windows Taskbar and choose Tile Windows Horizontally or Tile Windows Vertically from the context menu.

3. Position the insertion point in a suitable place in the application window for the macro's requirements. (For example, you might need to position the insertion point in a particular place or select an object for the macro to run properly.)

4. Click the Visual Basic Editor window to activate it, and then position the insertion point in the macro you want to run.

5. Press F8 to step through the macro command-by-command. Each time you press F8, one line of your VBA code will be executed. The Visual Basic Editor highlights each command as it's executed, and you can watch the effect in the application window to catch errors.

TIP You can also step into a macro by choosing Debug ➤ Step Into or clicking the Step Into button on the Debug toolbar, but usually the F8 key is easiest to use.

Figure 3.2 provides an example of stepping through a macro recorded in Word.

You'll learn about debugging macros in detail in Chapter 17. In the meantime, here are two straightforward techniques to try to resolve problems quickly in your macros: setting breakpoints and commenting out lines.

FIGURE 3.2

To catch what a macro is doing wrong, arrange the application window and the Visual Basic Editor window so that you can see them both. Then step through the macro by pressing the F8 key or using the Step Into command.

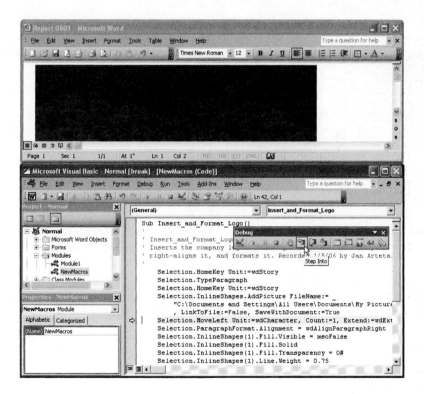

Setting Breakpoints

A *breakpoint* is a toggle switch you set on a line of code to tell VBA to stop executing the macro there. By using a breakpoint, you can run through functional parts of a macro at full speed and then stop where you want to begin watching the code execute statement-by-statement.

To toggle a breakpoint on or off, right-click in a line of executable code (not a comment line) and choose Toggle ➢ Breakpoint from the context menu or click the Toggle Breakpoint button on the Edit toolbar. Alternatively, click in the margin indicator bar next to the line of code. A line on which you set a breakpoint is shaded brown by default. The breakpoint itself is designated by a brown circle in the margin indicator bar (see Figure 3.3).

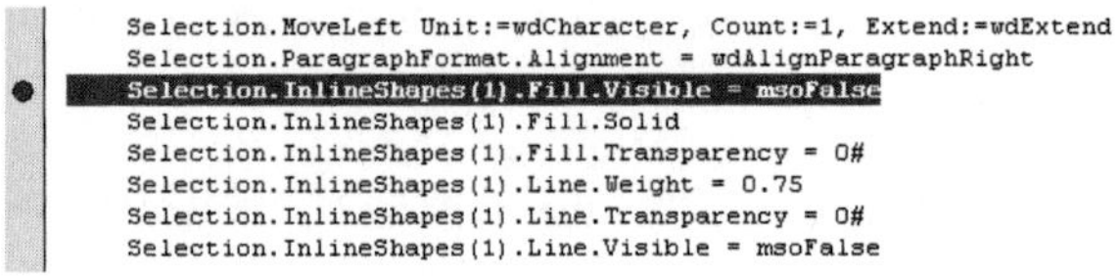

FIGURE 3.3

Use a breakpoint (the brown circle that appears in the margin indicator bar) to stop code execution at a line of your choice.

```
Selection.MoveLeft Unit:=wdCharacter, Count:=1, Extend:=wdExtend
Selection.ParagraphFormat.Alignment = wdAlignParagraphRight
Selection.InlineShapes(1).Fill.Visible = msoFalse
Selection.InlineShapes(1).Fill.Solid
Selection.InlineShapes(1).Fill.Transparency = 0#
Selection.InlineShapes(1).Line.Weight = 0.75
Selection.InlineShapes(1).Line.Transparency = 0#
Selection.InlineShapes(1).Line.Visible = msoFalse
```

NOTE Breakpoints are temporary— the Visual Basic Editor doesn't save them with your code. You must place them for each editing session.

Commenting Out Lines

Like most programming languages, VBA lets you add comments to your code so that it's easier to understand. Comments can be invaluable both when you're creating code and when you're revisiting your own code after long enough to forget what it does—or, worse, trying to figure out what someone else's code does.

You can also comment out lines of code to prevent the Visual Basic Editor from executing them. Commenting can be a useful technique for excluding suspect lines of code without actually removing them from the macro.

To comment out a line manually, type an apostrophe (') before any code on the line. Putting the apostrophe at the very beginning of a line is usually easiest. You can also use Rem instead of the apostrophe. (*Rem* is short for "remark," and comment lines are sometimes called "remark lines.") To uncomment the line manually, delete the apostrophe or Rem.

The Visual Basic Editor provides the Comment Block and Uncomment Block commands for commenting out lines automatically. Select the lines of code (or click in the single line you want to affect), and then click the Comment Block button on the Edit toolbar to place an apostrophe at the beginning of each line; to uncomment a line or selected lines, click the Uncomment Block button, and the Visual Basic Editor removes an apostrophe from each line.

The Comment Block and Uncomment Block commands work only with apostrophes, not with Rem lines. If you prefer Rem, you must comment and uncomment lines manually.

NOTE The Comment Block command adds an apostrophe to the beginning of each line in the selected block, even for lines that are already commented off. Likewise, the Uncomment Block command removes apostrophes one at a time from each line in the selected block, rather than removing all apostrophes at once. This behavior helps preserve comment lines and enables you to use different levels of commenting.

Stepping Out of a Macro

Once you've identified and fixed the problem with a macro, you probably won't want to step through the rest of the macro command-by-command. To run the rest of the macro and the rest of any macro that called it, you can press the F5 key, click the Continue button on the Standard toolbar or the Debug toolbar (see Figure 3.4), or choose Run ➢ Continue. If you just want to run the rest of this macro, and then return to stepping through the macro that called this one, use the Step Out command. The Step Out command finishes executing the current macro or procedure at full speed, but if the code then continues with another procedure, the Visual Basic Editor reverts to Break mode so you can examine that procedure's code.

FIGURE 3.4

The Debug toolbar contains commands for running code, stepping into it and out of it, and displaying key windows for debugging.

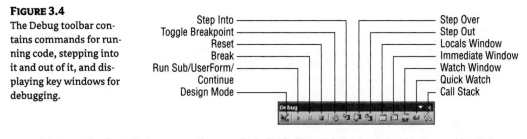

To issue the Step Out command, press Ctrl+Shift+F8, click the Step Out button on the Debug toolbar, or choose Debug ➢ Step Out.

Editing the Word Macro

Now, edit the Transpose_Word_Right macro that you created in Word and use it to build another macro. To begin, open the macro in the Visual Basic Editor:

1. Start Word if it's not already running, or activate it.

2. Press Alt+F8 or choose Tools ➢ Macro ➢ Macros to display the Macros dialog box.

3. Select the Transpose_Word_Right macro, and then click the Edit button.

In the Code window, you should see code similar to Listing 3.1, except for the line numbers, which the book uses to identify the lines of code.

LISTING 3.1:

```
1.   Sub Transpose_Word_Right()
2.   '
3.   ' Transpose_Word_Right Macro
4.   ' Transposes the current word with the word to its right. _
5.   ' Created 6/1/2006 by Joanna Bermudez.
6.   '
7.       Selection.Extend
8.       Selection.Extend
9.       Selection.EscapeKey
10.      Selection.Cut
```

```
11.     Selection.MoveRight Unit:=wdWord, Count:=1
12.     Selection.Paste
13.     Selection.MoveLeft Unit:=wdWord, Count:=1
14.  End Sub
```

Here's what the macro does:

◆ Line 1 starts the macro with the Sub Transpose_Word_Right() statement, and line 14 ends the macro with the End Sub statement. The Sub and End Sub lines mark the beginning and end of the macro (as they do any subprocedure).

◆ Lines 2 and 6 are blank comment lines the Macro Recorder inserts to make your macro easier to read. You can use any number of blank lines or blank comment lines in a macro to help separate statements into groups. (A blank line doesn't have to be commented out—it can just be blank—but the Macro Recorder has added commenting to these blank lines to make it clear what they are.)

◆ Lines 3 through 5 are comment lines that contain the name of the macro and its description. The Macro Recorder entered these lines from the information in the Record Macro dialog box.

◆ Line 7 records the first keypress of the F8 key, which starts Extend mode.

◆ Line 8 records the second keypress of the F8 key, which continues Extend mode and selects the current word.

◆ Line 9 records the keypress of the Escape key, which cancels Extend mode.

◆ Line 10 records the Cut command, which cuts the selection (in this case, the selected word) to the Clipboard.

◆ Line 11 records the Ctrl+→ command, which moves the insertion point one word to the right.

◆ Line 12 records the Paste command, which pastes the selection into the document at the current position of the insertion point.

◆ Line 13 records the Ctrl+← command, which moves the insertion point one word to the left.

First, comment out line 13, which you recorded so you could build a Transpose_Word_Left macro from this one. Enter an apostrophe at the beginning of the line—anywhere before the start of the instruction is fine, but you may find it easiest to enter the apostrophe in the leftmost column, where it's clearly visible:

```
'   Selection.MoveLeft Unit:=wdWord, Count:=1
```

Alternatively, click anywhere in line 13 and click the Comment Block button to have the Visual Basic Editor enter the apostrophe for you.

When you move the insertion point out of line 13, VBA checks the line, identifies it as a comment line, and changes its color to the color currently set for comment text. When you run the macro, VBA ignores this line, and doesn't execute the command, so the insertion point in the Word window doesn't move one word to the left as it did previously.

Stepping Through the Transpose_Word_Right Macro

Try stepping through this macro in Break mode using the Step Into command:

1. Arrange your screen so you can see both the active Word window and the Visual Basic Editor window (for example, by right-clicking the Taskbar and choosing Tile Windows Horizontally or Tile Windows Vertically from the context menu).

2. Click in the Visual Basic Editor, and then click to place the insertion point in the Transpose_Word_Right macro in the Code window.

3. Press F8 to step through the code one active line at a time. You'll notice that VBA skips the blank lines and the comment lines, because they're not active. VBA highlights the current statement when you press F8, and you see the actions taking place in the Word window.

The Visual Basic Editor switches off Break mode when it reaches the end of the macro (in this case, when it executes the End Sub statement in line 14). You can also exit Break mode at any time by clicking the Reset button on the Standard toolbar or the Debug toolbar, or by choosing Run ➢ Reset.

Running the Transpose_Word_Right Macro

If the macro works fine when you step through it, you may also want to run it from the Visual Basic Editor by clicking the Run Sub/UserForm button on the Edit toolbar or the Debug toolbar. You can also click this button (which will then be identified as Continue rather than Run Sub/UserForm) from Break mode to run a macro beginning from the current instruction.

Creating a Transpose_Word_Left Macro

Now, create a Transpose_Word_Left macro by making minor adjustments to the Transpose_Word_Right macro:

1. In the Code window, select all the code for the Transpose_Word_Right macro, from the Sub Transpose_Word_Right() line to the End Sub line. You can select by dragging with the mouse, by holding down Shift and using the arrow keys to extend the selection, or by positioning the insertion point at one end of the macro and then Shift-clicking the other end.

2. Copy the code by issuing a Copy command (for example, by right-clicking and choosing Copy from the context menu or by pressing Ctrl+C or Ctrl+Insert).

3. Move the insertion point to the line below the End Sub statement for the Transpose_Word_Right macro in the Code window.

4. Paste the code by issuing a Paste command (for example, by right-clicking and choosing Paste from the context menu or by pressing Ctrl+V or Shift+Insert). The Visual Basic Editor automatically enters a horizontal line between the End Sub statement for the Transpose_Word_Right macro and the new macro you've pasted.

5. Change the name of the second Transpose_Word_Right macro to Transpose_Word_Left by editing the Sub line:

```
Sub Transpose_Word_Left()
```

6. Edit the comment lines at the beginning of the macro accordingly—for example:

```
'Transpose_Word_Left Macro
'Transposes the current word with the word to its left. _
'Created 6/1/2006 by Joanna Bermudez.
```

7. Now all you need to do is replace the MoveRight method with the MoveLeft method to move the insertion point one word to the left instead of one word to the right. While you could do that by typing the correction or by using Cut and Paste to replace the Selection.MoveRight line with the commented-out Selection.MoveLeft line, try using the List Properties/Methods feature instead:

   ◆ Click to place the insertion point in the MoveRight method.

   ◆ Click the List Properties/Methods button on the Edit toolbar to display the list of properties and methods.

   ◆ Double-click the MoveLeft method to make it replace the MoveRight method.

8. Now that you no longer need it even for reference, delete the commented Selection .MoveLeft line from the end of the macro.

You should end up with a macro that looks like Listing 3.2.

LISTING 3.2:

```
Sub Transpose_Word_Left()
'
' Transpose_Word_Left Macro
' Transposes the current word with the word to its left. _
' Created 6/1/2006 by Joanna Bermudez.
'
    Selection.Extend
    Selection.Extend
    Selection.EscapeKey
    Selection.Cut
    Selection.MoveLeft Unit:=wdWord, Count:=1
    Selection.Paste
End Sub
```

Try stepping through this macro to make sure it works. If it does, you're ready to save it—and perhaps to create a toolbar button, menu item, context menu item, or keyboard shortcut for it in Word.

Save Your Work

When you finish working with this or any other macro, choose File ➤ Save from the Visual Basic Editor to save the document or template that contains the macro and the changes you've made to it. Then press Alt+Q or choose File ➢ Close And Return To Microsoft Word to close the Visual Basic Editor and return to Word.

Editing the Excel Macro

In this section, you edit the Excel macro that you recorded in Chapter 1. This time, you don't create a new macro—instead, you add to the existing one.

Unhiding the Personal Macro Workbook

Before you can edit the Excel macro, you'll need to unhide the Personal Macro Workbook if it's currently hidden:

1. Choose Window ➢ Unhide to display the Unhide dialog box

2. Select PERSONAL.XLS, and click the OK button.

NOTE   If you stored the macro in another workbook rather than in the Personal Macro Workbook, open that workbook before trying to proceed. To hide the Personal Macro Workbook again after editing the macro, choose Window ➢ Hide when the Personal Macro Workbook is active.

Opening the Macro for Editing

Now take the following steps to open up the macro for viewing and editing:

1. Choose Tools ➢ Macro ➢ Macros (or press Alt+F8) to display the Macros dialog box.

2. Select the macro named New_Workbook_with_Months. (If you gave the macro a different name, select that name instead.)

3. Click the Edit button to display the macro for editing in the Visual Basic Editor. Listing 3.3 shows code similar to what you should be seeing.

LISTING 3.3:

```
1.  Sub New_Workbook_with_Months()
2.  '
3.  ' New_Workbook_with_Months Macro
4.  ' Sample macro that creates a new workbook and enters a year's worth of months
into it. Recorded 12/2/05.
5.  '
6.  '
7.      Workbooks.Add
8.      Range("A1").Select
9.      ActiveCell.FormulaR1C1 = "Jan-2006"
10.     Range("B1").Select
11.     ActiveCell.FormulaR1C1 = "Feb-2006"
12.     Range("A1:B1").Select
13.     Selection.AutoFill Destination:=Range("A1:L1"), Type:=xlFillDefault
```

```
14.        Range("A1:L1").Select
15.        ActiveWorkbook.SaveAs Filename:= _
           "C:\Documents and Settings\Jack Ishida\My Documents\Sample Workbook.xls", _
           FileFormat:=xlNormal, Password:="", WriteResPassword:="", _
           ReadOnlyRecommended:=False, CreateBackup:=False
16.  End Sub
```

Here's what happens in the macro in Listing 3.3:

◆ Line 1 starts the macro with the Sub New_Workbook_with_Months() statement, and line 16 ends the macro with the End Sub statement.

◆ Lines 2, 5, and 6 are comment lines that the Macro Recorder automatically adds. (The comment line in line 6 seems superfluous. It's there because Excel allows you to enter two lines in the Description text box in the Record Macro dialog box, but this macro uses only one line.)

◆ Line 3 is a comment line that gives the macro's name and describes it as a macro, and line 4 contains the description from the Record Macro dialog box.

◆ Line 7 creates a new blank workbook by using the Add method on the Workbooks collection object (a *collection object*, or more concisely a *collection*, is an object that contains objects of a given type).

◆ Line 8 selects the Range object A1, making cell A1 active.

◆ Line 9 enters Jan-2006 in the active cell. Notice that the Macro Recorder has stored the parsed date value rather than the text that was entered (January 2006). Also, keep in mind that the date displayed in the cell may be in a different format than MMM-YYYY.

◆ Line 10 selects the Range object B1, making cell B1 active, and line 11 enters Feb-2006 in that cell.

◆ Line 12 selects the range A1:B1.

◆ Line 13 performs a default AutoFill operation on the range A1:L1, and line 14 selects that range. Note how the Macro Recorder has recorded two separate actions, although in the Excel interface you performed only one action.

◆ Line 15 saves the workbook under the name and folder given. Note that the Macro Recorder has automatically broken this long statement onto four lines by using the continuation character, an underscore preceded by a space. You can break statements anywhere between keywords to make the lines of code a comfortable length for working with.

Editing the Macro

Now extend the macro by following these steps:

1. Select lines 8 through 13.

2. Issue a Copy command by pressing Ctrl+C, clicking the Copy button on the Standard toolbar, choosing Edit ➢ Copy, or right-clicking in the selection and choosing Copy from the context menu.

3. Press the → key to collapse the selection and move the insertion point to after its end, so that the insertion point is at the beginning of line 14.

4. Issue a Paste command by pressing Ctrl+V, clicking the Paste button on the Standard toolbar, choosing Edit ➢ Paste, or right-clicking at the insertion point and choosing Paste from the context menu.

Your new macro should look like Listing 3.4.

LISTING 3.4:

```
1.  Sub New_Workbook_with_Months()
2.  '
3.  ' New_Workbook_with_Months Macro
4.  ' Sample macro that creates a new workbook and enters a year's worth _
        of months into it. Recorded 12/2/05.
5.  '
6.  '
7.      Workbooks.Add
8.      Range("A1").Select
9.      ActiveCell.FormulaR1C1 = "Jan-2006"
10.     Range("B1").Select
11.     ActiveCell.FormulaR1C1 = "Feb-2006"
12.     Range("A1:B1").Select
13.     Selection.AutoFill Destination:=Range("A1:L1"), Type:=xlFillDefault
14.     Range("A1").Select
15.     ActiveCell.FormulaR1C1 = "Jan-2006"
16.     Range("B1").Select
17.     ActiveCell.FormulaR1C1 = "Feb-2006"
18.     Range("A1:B1").Select
19.     Selection.AutoFill Destination:=Range("A1:L1"), Type:=xlFillDefault
20.     Range("A1:L1").Select
21.     ActiveWorkbook.SaveAs Filename:= _
        "C:\Documents and Settings\Jack\My Documents\Sample Workbook.xls", _
        FileFormat:=xlNormal, Password:="", WriteResPassword:="", _
        ReadOnlyRecommended:=False, CreateBackup:=False
22. End Sub
```

Now, change the macro by taking the following steps:

1. Delete line 6. It's not doing any good, and it's taking up space in the Code window.

2. Delete line 20. It's not necessary for what the macro does—you don't need the macro to select the range, because the AutoFill instruction in line 13 is enough to perform the AutoFill operation without selecting the range.

3. Change line 14 to select cell A2 instead of cell A1:

```
Range("A2").Select
```

4. Change line 15 so that it enters the value 100 instead of Jan-2006:

```
ActiveCell.FormulaR1C1 = 100
```

5. Change line 16 to select cell B2 instead of cell B1:

```
Range("B2").Select
```

6. Change line 17 so that it enters the value 200 instead of Feb-2006:

```
ActiveCell.FormulaR1C1 = 200
```

7. Change line 18 so that it selects the range A2:B2:

```
Range("A2:B2").Select
```

8. Change line 19 so that it performs the AutoFill operation on the range A2:L2:

```
Selection.AutoFill Destination:=Range("A2:L2"), Type:=xlFillDefault
```

9. Break line 13 with a space, underscore, and carriage return before the Type argument, as shown below. Indent the second line by one tab.

```
Selection.AutoFill Destination:=Range("A1:L1"), _
    Type:=xlFillDefault
```

10. Similarly, break line 19 with a space, underscore, carriage return, and tab before the Type argument.

11. Click the Save button or choose File ➤ Save to save the changes you made.

The macro should now read like Listing 3.5.

LISTING 3.5:

```
1.   Sub New_Workbook_with_Months()
2.   '
3.   ' New_Workbook_with_Months Macro
4.   ' Sample macro that creates a new workbook and enters a year's worth _
         of months into it. Recorded 12/2/05.
5.   '
6.       Workbooks.Add
7.       Range("A1").Select
8.       ActiveCell.FormulaR1C1 = "Jan-2006"
9.       Range("B1").Select
10.      ActiveCell.FormulaR1C1 = "Feb-2006"
11.      Range("A1:B1").Select
```

```
12.        Selection.AutoFill Destination:=Range("A1:L1"), _
               Type:=xlFillDefault
13.        Range("A2").Select
14.        ActiveCell.FormulaR1C1 = "100"
15.        Range("B2").Select
16.        ActiveCell.FormulaR1C1 = "200"
17.        Range("A2:B2").Select
18.        Selection.AutoFill Destination:=Range("A2:L2"), _
               Type:=xlFillDefault
19.        ActiveWorkbook.SaveAs Filename:= _
               "C:\Documents and Settings\Jack\My Documents\Sample Workbook.xls", _
               FileFormat:=xlNormal, Password:="", WriteResPassword:="", _
               ReadOnlyRecommended:=False, CreateBackup:=False
20.    End Sub
```

Now step through the macro and watch what happens: It creates the new workbook as before and enters the months, but then it enters the values 100 through 1200 in the second row of cells. At the end, it saves the workbook as before, prompting you to overwrite the previous workbook (unless you've already deleted it).

Saving Your Work

When you finish working with this macro, choose File ➢ Save from the Visual Basic Editor to save the workbook that contains the macro and the changes you've made to it. Then press Alt+Q or choose File ➢ Close And Return To Microsoft Excel to close the Visual Basic Editor and return to Excel.

Editing the PowerPoint Macro

In this section, you'll edit the PowerPoint macro that you recorded in Chapter 1. Start by opening up the macro as follows:

1. Open the PowerPoint presentation containing the macro.

2. Choose Tools ➢ Macro ➢ Macros to display the Macros dialog box.

3. Select the Add_Slide_and_Format_Placeholder macro.

4. Click the Edit button.

Listing 3.6 shows the macro almost exactly as it was recorded, except that some long lines of code have been broken into shorter lines using the underscore continuation character.

LISTING 3.6:

```
1.    Sub Add_Slide_and_Format_Placeholder()
2.    '
3.    ' Sample macro that adds a slide, formats its placeholder, and adds text _
          to it. Recorded 12/4/05 by Maria Kruger.
```

```
4.   '
5.        ActiveWindow.View.GotoSlide Index:= _
              ActivePresentation.Slides.Add(Index:=2, _
              Layout:=ppLayoutText).SlideIndex
6.        ActiveWindow.Selection.SlideRange.Layout = ppLayoutTitle
7.        ActiveWindow.Selection.SlideRange.Shapes("Rectangle 4").Select
8.        With ActiveWindow.Selection.ShapeRange
9.            .IncrementLeft -6#
10.           .IncrementTop -125.75
11.       End With
12.       ActiveWindow.Selection.ShapeRange.ScaleHeight 1.56, msoFalse, _
              msoScaleFromTopLeft
13.       ActiveWindow.Selection.SlideRange.Shapes("Rectangle 4").Select
14.       ActiveWindow.Selection.ShapeRange.TextFrame.TextRange.Select
15.       ActiveWindow.Selection.ShapeRange.TextFrame.TextRange.Characters _
              (Start:=1, Length:=0).Select
16.       With ActiveWindow.Selection.TextRange
17.           .Text = "The quick brown dog jumped over a lazy fox"
18.           With .Font
19.               .Name = "Arial"
20.               .Size = 44
21.               .Bold = msoFalse
22.               .Italic = msoFalse
23.               .Underline = msoFalse
24.               .Shadow = msoFalse
25.               .Emboss = msoFalse
26.               .BaselineOffset = 0
27.               .AutoRotateNumbers = msoFalse
28.               .Color.SchemeColor = ppTitle
29.           End With
30.       End With
31.       ActiveWindow.Selection.ShapeRange.TextFrame.TextRange.Characters _
              (Start:=1, Length:=42).Select
32.       With ActiveWindow.Selection.TextRange.Font
33.           .Name = "Impact"
34.           .Size = 54
35.           .Bold = msoFalse
36.           .Italic = msoFalse
37.           .Underline = msoFalse
38.           .Shadow = msoFalse
39.           .Emboss = msoFalse
40.           .BaselineOffset = 0
41.           .AutoRotateNumbers = msoFalse
42.           .Color.SchemeColor = ppTitle
43.       End With
44.   End Sub
```

Here's what happens in the macro:

◆ Line 1 starts the macro, and line 44 ends it.

◆ Lines 2 and 4 are blank comment lines used to set off the description of the macro, which appears in line 3.

◆ Line 5 adds the slide to the presentation. This statement is a little complicated, but don't worry about it too much just yet. For now, note two things: First, the statement uses the Add method with the Slides collection object to add a slide to the collection (in other words, to create a new slide), just as the Excel macro used the Add method to add a workbook to the Workbooks collection. Second, the layout of the slide is ppLayoutText, the VBA constant for the Text slide layout that PowerPoint uses for a default new slide.

NOTE If you're using PowerPoint 2000, lines 5 and 6 will be a single statement that creates a new slide and assigns the slide layout to it.

◆ Line 6 applies the Title layout (ppLayoutTitle) that you chose when recording the macro. (If you chose a different slide layout, you'll see a different constant than ppLayoutTitle.)

◆ Line 7 selects the shape named Rectangle 4 in the Shapes collection on the active slide. (For the moment, don't worry about how you get to the active slide.)

◆ Lines 8 to 11 contain a With statement that works with the shape that has been selected (ActiveWindow.Selection.ShapeRange). A With statement is a way of simplifying object references, and everything between the With statement and the End With statement refers to the objects that the With statement mentions. In this case, line 9 uses the IncrementLeft method with a negative value to move the shape to the left, and line 10 uses the IncrementTop method with a negative value to move the shape up the slide.

TIP With statements have two benefits: they simplify code (because you don't need to specify the object in each of the lines between the With and End With lines) and make code run faster.

◆ Line 13 selects the shape named Rectangle 4, and line 14 selects the TextRange object in the TextFrame object in the shape. When you're working interactively, PowerPoint makes this selection process seamless: You click in a shape displaying the legend "Click to add title" (or whatever), and PowerPoint selects the text range in the text frame in the shape—but all you see is that the text in the shape becomes selected. In VBA, you have to go through a couple of unseen layers in the object model before getting to the text.

◆ When you select the placeholder text, PowerPoint gets rid of it. The same thing happens when you select the placeholder text via VBA. So line 15 makes a new selection at the beginning of the first character in the text range. The Length of the selection is 0, meaning that the selection is collapsed to an insertion point rather than containing any characters.

◆ Line 16 starts a With statement that continues until line 30. The With ActiveWindow .Selection.TextRange statement in line 16 lets line 17 reference the Text property of the TextRange object in the Selection object in the ActiveWindow object much more simply (instead of ActiveWindow.Selection.TextRange.Text), and it lets line 18 reference the Font property of the TextRange object in the Selection object in the ActiveWindow object easily (instead of ActiveWindow.Selection.TextRange.Font).

- Line 17 sets the `Text` property of the `ActiveWindow.Selection.TextRange` object to the text typed.

- Line 18 then begins a nested `With` statement that sets the properties of the `Font` object for the `TextRange` object. Line 19 sets the `Name` property of the `Font` object to `Arial`; line 20 sets the `Size` property of the `Font` object to `44`; line 21 sets the `Bold` property of the `Font` object to `msoFalse`, the Microsoft Office (`mso`) constant for `False`; and so on. The Macro Recorder created all these separate statements to record the font formatting used when the text was typed, and it's not necessary to the macro. Line 29 ends the nested `With` statement.

TIP A *nested* `With` statement is one that is placed within another `With` statement and specifies an object within the object specified in the outer `With` statement. You can nest multiple-level `With` statements when necessary.

- Line 31 uses the `Select` method to select characters 1 through 42 in the text range. This is the result of pressing the Ctrl+Shift+Home key combination. Because this statement specifies the characters to select, you'll need to change it if you change the text that the macro inserts. (If you run the statement on a text range that has fewer than 42 characters, it will return an error. If you run it on a text range that has more than 42 characters, it will select only the first 42 characters in the text range—not what you want.)

- Line 32 begins another `With` statement that works with the `Font` object of the `TextRange` object—but this `With` statement records the actions you took in the Font dialog box, so you want to keep it.

- Line 43 ends the `With` statement, and line 44 ends the macro.

Edit this macro by slimming it down a little and changing the text it inserts:

1. Delete the unnecessary `With` statement in lines 18 through 29.

2. Delete line 30.

3. Change lines 16 and 17 into a single statement without `With`:

```
ActiveWindow.Selection.TextRange.Text = _
    "The quick brown dog jumped over a lazy fox"
```

4. Now change the text that the new line 16 inserts. Type text of your choice between the double quotation marks.

5. Change line 31 to use the `Select` method on the text range rather than specifying which characters to select. Delete `Characters(Start:=1, Length:=42)` to leave this statement:

```
ActiveWindow.Selection.ShapeRange.TextFrame.TextRange.Select
```

6. Click the Save button on the Standard toolbar or choose File ➢ Save to save the changes you've made to the presentation.

You should now have code that reads like Listing 3.7.

LISTING 3.7:

```
1.   Sub Add_Slide_and_Format_Placeholder()
2.   '
3.   ' Sample macro that adds a slide, formats its placeholder, and adds text to it. _
         Recorded 12/4/05 by Maria Kruger.
4.   '
5.       ActiveWindow.View.GotoSlide Index:= _
             ActivePresentation.Slides.Add(Index:=2, _
             Layout:=ppLayoutText).SlideIndex
6.       ActiveWindow.Selection.SlideRange.Layout = ppLayoutTitle
7.       ActiveWindow.Selection.SlideRange.Shapes("Rectangle 4").Select
8.       With ActiveWindow.Selection.ShapeRange
9.           .IncrementLeft -6#
10.          .IncrementTop -125.75
11.      End With
12.      ActiveWindow.Selection.ShapeRange.ScaleHeight 1.56, msoFalse, _
             msoScaleFromTopLeft
13.      ActiveWindow.Selection.SlideRange.Shapes("Rectangle 4").Select
14.      ActiveWindow.Selection.ShapeRange.TextFrame.TextRange.Select
15.      ActiveWindow.Selection.ShapeRange.TextFrame.TextRange.Characters _
             (Start:=1, Length:=0).Select
16.      ActiveWindow.Selection.TextRange.Text = "Welcome to Acme Industries"
17.      ActiveWindow.Selection.ShapeRange.TextFrame.TextRange.Select
18.      With ActiveWindow.Selection.TextRange.Font
19.          .Name = "Impact"
20.          .Size = 54
21.          .Bold = msoFalse
22.          .Italic = msoFalse
23.          .Underline = msoFalse
24.          .Shadow = msoFalse
25.          .Emboss = msoFalse
26.          .BaselineOffset = 0
27.          .AutoRotateNumbers = msoFalse
28.          .Color.SchemeColor = ppTitle
29.      End With
30.  End Sub
```

Now step through the changed macro and make sure it works as you expect it to.

Save Your Work

When you finish working with this macro, choose File ➤ Save from the Visual Basic Editor to save the presentation that contains the macro and the changes you've made to it. Then press Alt+Q or choose File ➤ Close And Return To Microsoft PowerPoint to close the Visual Basic Editor and return to PowerPoint.

WHEN SHOULD YOU USE THE MACRO RECORDER?

As you've seen so far in this book, you can create VBA code either by using the Macro Recorder (in the applications that provide it) to record a series of actions when working interactively in the application or by entering VBA statements into the Code window in the Visual Basic Editor. You're probably wondering when you should record a macro and when you should create code from scratch. Writing a procedure is more difficult and more advanced than recording a procedure—so is it wrong to record a procedure when you could write it instead?

Using the Macro Recorder has advantages and disadvantages. The advantages are

◆ The Macro Recorder creates usable code every time (provided you run the macro under suitable conditions).

◆ The Macro Recorder is quick and easy to use.

◆ The Macro Recorder can help you discover which VBA objects, methods, and properties correspond to which part of an application's interface.

The disadvantages of using the Macro Recorder are

◆ Code created in the Macro Recorder may contain unnecessary statements, because the Macro Recorder records *everything* you do in the application—including all the options in every built-in dialog box you use when recording the macro. For example, if you start the Macro Recorder from Word, choose Tools ➢ Options to display the View page of the Options dialog box, click the Edit tab to display the Edit page, and change the Auto-Keyboard Switching setting, the Macro Recorder will record all the settings on the Edit page as well as all those on the View page. The result is about 40 lines of unnecessary code. (If you visit any other pages in the Options dialog box on the way to the Edit page, the Macro Recorder will record all the settings in those pages as well.) If you create the code manually in the Visual Basic Editor, you can achieve the same effect by using one statement.

◆ Code created by the Macro Recorder can work only in the active document rather than using other documents, because whichever document you're working with interactively becomes the active document. Later in this book, you'll learn how to use objects in the applications' object models to work with documents other than the active document. Working with other documents can have advantages; for example, you can hide the manipulations you're performing from the user and make your code run faster.

◆ The Macro Recorder can create VBA code for only *some* of the actions you perform in the host application. For example, if you want to display a dialog box or a user form in the course of a procedure, you need to write the appropriate statement manually—you can't record it. The subset of VBA actions available through the Macro Recorder is similar to the set of actions you can take in the host application when working interactively, so you can get a lot done with it. Still, you'll find it's limited compared to the full range of actions you can perform through VBA.

However expert you become with VBA, consider the Macro Recorder a useful tool for creating either rough-and-ready macros or the basis of more complex procedures. You'll often find it makes sense to have the Macro Recorder handle as much of the strain of creating a procedure as possible. If you can save time by using the Macro Recorder to quickly identify the VBA object or property that you need, then do so.

Chapter 4

Creating Code from Scratch in the Visual Basic Editor

- ◆ Setting up the Visual Basic Editor for creating the procedures
- ◆ Creating a procedure for Word
- ◆ Creating a procedure for Excel
- ◆ Creating a procedure for PowerPoint

In this chapter, you'll practice creating procedures from scratch in the Visual Basic Editor. The chapter assumes that you have the Visual Basic Editor arranged in a default configuration and (for good practice) set to require explicit declarations of variables, so the chapter starts by making sure you have it set up like this. The examples then walk you through creating a procedure in Word, Excel, and PowerPoint.

The purpose of this chapter is to give you a feel for creating code in the Visual Basic Editor before you study the details of the language. In this chapter, you'll work quickly with VBA elements (such as objects, properties, methods, variables, and constants) that you'll learn about more fully later in this book. Along the way, you'll meet several of the many forms of assistance that the Visual Basic Editor provides, including the Macro Recorder, the Object Browser, and the Help system. You'll explore these forms of assistance later in this book as well.

Setting Up the Visual Basic Editor for Creating the Procedures

You'll find it easiest to follow the instructions in the following procedures if you have the Visual Basic Editor set up in a default configuration (like that you'll see the first time you display the Visual Basic Editor from a VBA host). For good practice, you should also require explicit variable declarations. The following steps describe how to set up the Visual Basic Editor. Each of the procedures tells you when to make sure the Visual Basic Editor is set up correctly.

1. If the Project Explorer isn't displayed, choose View ➢ Project Explorer or press Ctrl+R to display it.

2. If the Properties window isn't displayed, choose View ➢ Properties Window or press the F4 key to display it.

3. Unless you really prefer things otherwise, dock the Project Explorer in its conventional position at the upper-left corner of the main Visual Basic Editor area. Dock the Properties window below the Project Explorer, again in its default position. (To change docking, choose Tools ➤ Options, click the Docking tab, and work on the Docking page of the Options dialog box.)

4. Close any Code windows or user form windows that are open.

5. Set the Visual Basic Editor up to require variables to be declared explicitly, so that you must declare each variable formally before you use it. Choose Tools ➤ Options to display the Options dialog box, select the Require Variable Declaration check box on the Editor page, and then click the OK button. This setting makes the Visual Basic Editor automatically enter the `Option Explicit` statement for all modules and user forms you create from now on.

NOTE   It's best to work through all these procedures if you have all three applications available.

Creating a Procedure for Word

The procedure you'll create for Word causes the Track Changes feature to toggle the way deleted text is displayed between Strikethrough and Hidden. You'll be able to switch instantly between having the deleted text remain on screen with a line through it and having it simply disappear.

Follow these steps to create the procedure:

1. Start Word. If Word is already running, exit it and restart it.

2. Record a macro to get to the object, property, and settings you need. (Recording may feel like cheating, but the Macro Recorder is truly a gift when it comes to finding objects.) Follow these sub-steps:

   A. Choose Tools ➤ Macro ➤ Record New Macro to display the Record Macro dialog box.

   B. Either accept the macro name that the Macro Recorder automatically assigns (`Macro1`, `Macro2`, and so on) or create a scratch name of your own that will remind you to delete the macro if you omit to do so. This example uses the name `Macro_to_Delete_1`.

   C. Leave the Store Macro In drop-down list set to All Documents (Normal .dot). Leave the description alone unless you think you'll forget to delete the macro at the end of this section.

   D. Click the OK button to start recording the macro.

   E. Choose Tools ➤ Options to display the Options dialog box. By default, Word displays the View page first. Click the Track Changes tab to display the Track Changes page (see Figure 4.1), select Strikethrough in the Deletions drop-down list, and then click the OK button to close the Options dialog box.

   F. Choose Tools ➤ Options to display the Options dialog box again. This time, the Track Changes page should come up on top of the stack of pages. Now, select Hidden in the Deletions drop-down list, and again click the OK button to close the Options dialog box.

   G. Double-click the REC indicator on the status bar, or click the Stop Recording button on the Stop Recording toolbar, or choose Tools ➤ Macro ➤ Stop Recording to stop recording the macro.

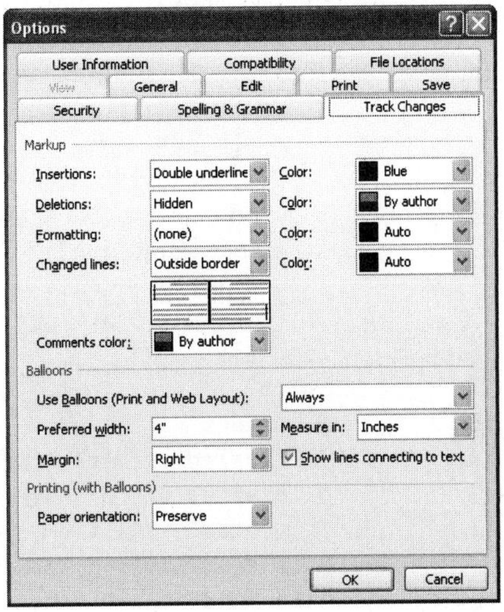

FIGURE 4.1

The Track Changes page of the Options dialog box in Word

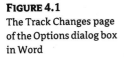

3. Choose Tools ➢ Macros ➢ Macros to display the Macros dialog box. Select the macro you just recorded and click the Edit button to open it for editing in the Visual Basic Editor. Your code should look like this (apart from the user name and date):

```
1.  Sub Macro_to_Delete_1()
2.  '
3.  ' Macro_to_Delete_1 Macro
4.  ' Macro recorded 1/7/2006 by Jack Ishida
5.  '
6.      Application.DisplayStatusBar = True
7.      Application.ShowWindowsInTaskbar = True
8.      Application.ShowStartupDialog = True
9.      With ActiveWindow
10.         .DisplayHorizontalScrollBar = True
11.         .DisplayVerticalScrollBar = True
12.         .DisplayLeftScrollBar = False
13.         .StyleAreaWidth = InchesToPoints(0)
14.         .DisplayRightRuler = False
15.         .DisplayScreenTips = True
16.         With .View
17.             .ShowAnimation = True
18.             .Draft = False
19.             .WrapToWindow = False
20.             .ShowPicturePlaceHolders = False
21.             .ShowFieldCodes = False
22.             .ShowBookmarks = False
23.             .FieldShading = wdFieldShadingWhenSelected
24.             .ShowTabs = False
25.             .ShowSpaces = False
```

```
26.                    .ShowParagraphs = False
27.                    .ShowHyphens = False
28.                    .ShowHiddenText = False
29.                    .ShowAll = False
30.                    .ShowDrawings = True
31.                    .ShowObjectAnchors = False
32.                    .ShowTextBoundaries = False
33.                    .ShowHighlight = True
34.                    .DisplayPageBoundaries = True
35.                    .DisplaySmartTags = True
36.                End With
37.            End With
38.            With Options
39.                .InsertedTextMark = wdInsertedTextMarkUnderline
40.                .InsertedTextColor = wdByAuthor
41.                .DeletedTextMark = wdDeletedTextMarkStrikeThrough
42.                .DeletedTextColor = wdByAuthor
43.                .RevisedPropertiesMark = wdRevisedPropertiesMarkNone
44.                .RevisedPropertiesColor = wdByAuthor
45.                .RevisedLinesMark = wdRevisedLinesMarkOutsideBorder
46.                .RevisedLinesColor = wdAuto
47.                .CommentsColor = wdByAuthor
48.                .RevisionsBalloonPrintOrientation = _
                       wdBalloonPrintOrientationPreserve
49.            End With
50.            With ActiveWindow.View
51.                .RevisionsMode = wdBalloonRevisions
52.                .RevisionsBalloonShowConnectingLines = True
53.                .RevisionsBalloonSide = wdRightMargin
54.                .RevisionsBalloonWidthType = wdBalloonWidthPoints
55.                .RevisionsBalloonWidth = InchesToPoints(2.5)
56.            End With
57.            With Options
58.                .InsertedTextMark = wdInsertedTextMarkUnderline
59.                .InsertedTextColor = wdByAuthor
60.                .DeletedTextMark = wdDeletedTextMarkHidden
61.                .DeletedTextColor = wdByAuthor
62.                .RevisedPropertiesMark = wdRevisedPropertiesMarkNone
63.                .RevisedPropertiesColor = wdByAuthor
64.                .RevisedLinesMark = wdRevisedLinesMarkOutsideBorder
65.                .RevisedLinesColor = wdAuto
66.                .CommentsColor = wdByAuthor
67.                .RevisionsBalloonPrintOrientation = _
                       wdBalloonPrintOrientationPreserve
68.            End With
69.            With ActiveWindow.View
70.                .RevisionsMode = wdBalloonRevisions
71.                .RevisionsBalloonShowConnectingLines = True
```

```
72.            .RevisionsBalloonSide = wdRightMargin
73.            .RevisionsBalloonWidthType = wdBalloonWidthPoints
74.            .RevisionsBalloonWidth = InchesToPoints(2.5)
75.        End With
76.  End Sub
```

4. That's a daunting amount of code for the actions you took. This is because the Macro Recorder records the settings for all of the options on the Options dialog box page that you visited. Look quickly at the code for the many settings:

   ◆ Lines 6 through 37 record the settings on the View page (see Figure 4.2). You didn't change any of these settings, so they're irrelevant to the macro, but if you look at the figure, you can see how the code reflects the settings. For example, the `Application`
   `.DisplayStatusBar = True` statement means that the Status Bar check box is selected; the `Application.ShowWindowsInTaskbar = True` statement shows that the Windows In Taskbar check box is selected; and the `Application.ShowStartupDialog = True` statement shows that the Startup Task Pane check box is selected. (A selected check box is `True`, and a cleared check box is `False`.)

FIGURE 4.2
The View page of the Options dialog box in Word

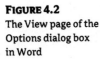

   ◆ Lines 38 through 49 record the settings on the Track Changes page of the Options dialog box on your first visit. These statements are divided into two sections: first, the settings for the Markup area and the Printing (With Balloons) area of the page (which appear within the `With Options` structure); and second, the settings for the Balloons area (which appear within the `With ActiveWindow.View` structure).

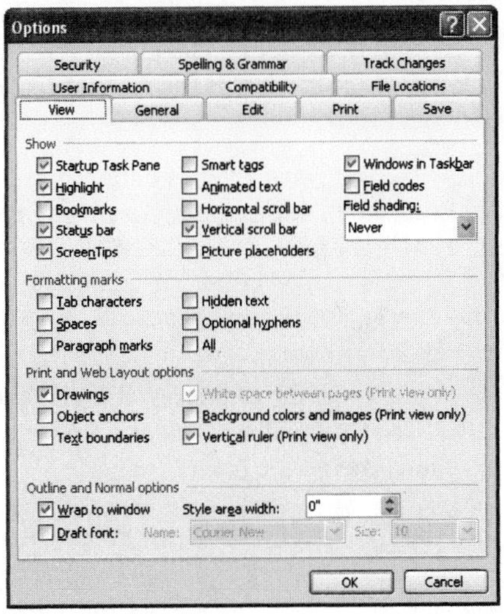

   ◆ Lines 50 through 75 record the settings on the Track Changes page of the Options dialog box on your second visit.

5. Identify the command needed—the `DeletedTextMark` property for the `Options` object—and the value you need for it: `wdDeletedTextMarkStrikeThrough` (when you set the Deletions drop-down list to Strikethrough) and `wdDeletedTextMarkHidden` (when you set it to Hidden).

6. Select the whole of the recorded macro, from the Sub statement down to the End Sub statement, and press the Delete key to get rid of it.

7. Make sure the Visual Basic Editor is set up as described in the section, "Setting Up the Visual Basic Editor for Creating the Procedures," earlier in this chapter.

8. In the Project Explorer window, right-click anywhere in the `Normal` item and choose Insert ➤ Module from the context menu. The Visual Basic Editor inserts a new module in the `Normal.dot` global template, displays a Code window for it, and expands the `Normal` tree if it was collapsed.

9. Press the F4 key to activate the Properties window for the new module. The Visual Basic Editor selects the `(Name)` property, the only property available. (Confusingly, the property's name includes the parentheses.)

10. Type the name for the new module in the Properties window. This example uses the name `Procedures_to_Keep_1`.

11. Press the F7 key or click in the Code window to activate it.

12. Verify that the Visual Basic Editor has entered the `Option Explicit` statement in the declarations area at the top of the code sheet (the code area) in the Code window. If not, type the statement now.

13. Below the `Option Explicit` statement, type the Sub statement for the procedure and press the Enter key. Name the procedure `Toggle_Track_Changes_between_Hidden_and_Strikethrough`:

    Sub Toggle_Track_Changes_between_Hidden_and_Strikethrough

14. When you press the Enter key, the Visual Basic Editor enters for you the parentheses at the end of the Sub statement, a blank line, and the End Sub statement, and places the insertion point on the blank line:

    ```
    Sub Toggle_Track_Changes_between_Hidden_and_Strikethrough()

    End Sub
    ```

15. Press the Tab key to indent the first line below the Sub statement.

16. Type **if options.** (in lowercase and including the period) to display the List Properties/ Methods drop-down list.

17. Type down (**d-e-l**) and use the ↓ key, or simply scroll with the ↓ key or the mouse, to select the `DeletedTextMark` entry.

18. Type **=**. The Visual Basic Editor enters the `DeletedTextMark` keyword for you, followed by the equal sign, and then displays the List Properties/Methods list of constants for the `DeletedTextMark` property (see Figure 4.3).

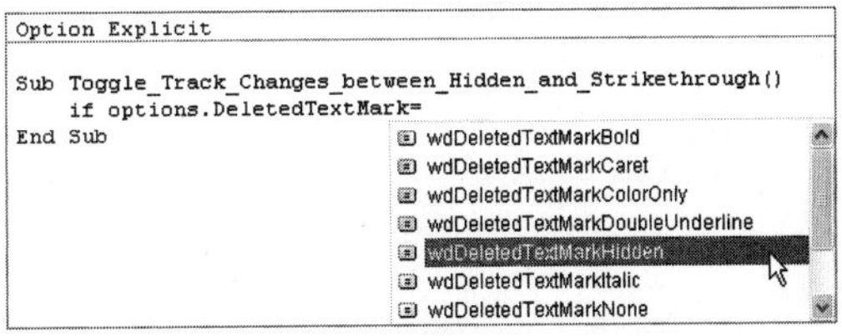

FIGURE 4.3

The Visual Basic Editor's List Properties/Methods list provides the constants available for the Deleted-TextMark property.

19. Select the wdDeletedTextMarkHidden item and enter it by pressing the Tab key or by double-clicking it.

20. Type **Then** and press the Enter key. Note that when you start the next line of code (by pressing the Enter key), the Visual Basic Editor checks the line of code for errors. If you used lowercase for the If Options part of the statement, the Visual Basic Editor applies the correct capitalization. If there is no space on either side of the equal sign, the Visual Basic Editor adds them too.

21. Enter **Options.DeletedTextMark=wdDeletedTextMarkStrikethrough**, using the assistance that the Visual Basic Editor's features offer you, and then press the Enter key.

22. Press the Backspace key or Shift+Tab to unindent the new line of code by one tab stop.

23. Type the **ElseIf** keyword, and then enter the rest of the procedure as follows:

```
ElseIf Options.DeletedTextMark = wdDeletedTextMarkStrikeThrough Then
    Options.DeletedTextMark = wdDeletedTextMarkHidden
End If
```

24. Make sure your procedure looks like this:

```
Sub Toggle_Track_Changes_between_Hidden_and_Strikethrough()
    If Options.DeletedTextMark = wdDeletedTextMarkHidden Then
        Options.DeletedTextMark = wdDeletedTextMarkStrikeThrough
    ElseIf Options.DeletedTextMark = wdDeletedTextMarkStrikeThrough Then
        Options.DeletedTextMark = wdDeletedTextMarkHidden
    End If
End Sub
```

25. Press Alt+F11 to switch to Word, and then create a short document that uses Track Changes marks including deleted text.

26. Arrange the Word window and the Visual Basic Editor window side by side. In Word, choose Tools ➢ Options, check the current setting for the Deletions drop-down list on the Track Changes tab of the Options dialog box, and then click the OK button. In the Visual Basic Editor, press the F5 key or click the Run Sub/UserForm button on the Standard toolbar or the Debug toolbar to run the macro. Back in Word, choose Tools ➢ Options, and verify that the Deletions setting has changed.

27. Click the Save button on the Standard toolbar in the Visual Basic Editor.

Note that you can also set up this procedure as a With statement using the Options object, so that it looks like this:

```
Sub Toggle_Track_Changes_between_Hidden_and_Strikethrough_2()
    With Options
        If .DeletedTextMark = wdDeletedTextMarkHidden Then
            .DeletedTextMark = wdDeletedTextMarkStrikeThrough
        ElseIf .DeletedTextMark = wdDeletedTextMarkStrikeThrough Then
            .DeletedTextMark = wdDeletedTextMarkHidden
        End If
    End With
End Sub
```

Creating a Procedure for Excel

The procedure you'll create for Excel is short but helpful: When the user runs Excel, the procedure maximizes the Excel window and opens the last file worked on. The procedure provides an example of working with events in Excel and of using the Object Browser to find the objects, methods, and properties you need.

Follow these steps to create the procedure:

1. Start Excel if it's not already running.

2. If your Personal Macro Workbook is currently hidden, choose Window ➢ Unhide to display the Unhide dialog box, select PERSONAL.XLS in the Unhide Workbook list box, and then click the OK button.

3. Press Alt+F11 or choose Tools ➢ Macros ➢ Visual Basic Editor to open the Visual Basic Editor.

4. Make sure the Visual Basic Editor is set up as described in the section "Setting Up the Visual Basic Editor for Creating the Procedures," earlier in this chapter.

5. In the Project Explorer window, expand VBAProject (PERSONAL.XLS) if it's collapsed. Either double-click its name or click the + sign to its left.

6. Expand the Microsoft Excel Objects folder.

7. Double-click the ThisWorkbook item to open its code sheet in a Code window. The ThisWorkbook object represents the workbook.

8. Verify that the Visual Basic Editor has entered the Option Explicit statement in the declarations area at the top of the code sheet. If not, type the statement now.

9. In the Object drop-down list at the upper-left corner of the Code window, select Workbook. The Visual Basic Editor automatically creates the stub of an Open event for the Workbook object and places the insertion point on the blank line:

```
Private Sub Workbook_Open()

End Sub
```

NOTE   The Private keyword limits the *scope* of the macro—the area in which it can operate. Private scope makes the macro available to all procedures in the module that contains it, but not to procedures in other modules. Chapter 6 explains scope in more detail.

10.   Press the F2 key, choose View ➤ Object Browser, or click the Object Browser button on the Standard toolbar to display the Object Browser window (see Figure 4.4).

FIGURE 4.4

Use the Object Browser to find the objects, methods, and properties you need for a procedure.

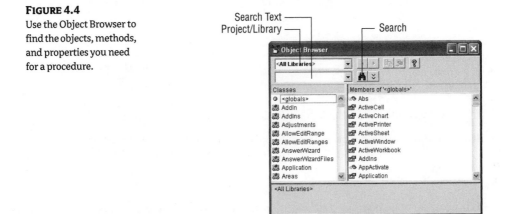

11.   The first action you want to take in the macro is to maximize the application window. As in any application, VBA uses the Application object to represent the Excel application, but you need to find the property to work with. Select Excel in the Project/Library drop-down list, type **maximize** in the Search Text box, and either click the Search button or press the Enter key. The Object Browser displays the result of the search (see Figure 4.5) in its Search Results pane (which was collapsed and not visible in Figure 4.4): The constant xlMaximized is a member of the class XlWindowState.

FIGURE 4.5

The result of the search for "maximize" in the Object Browser

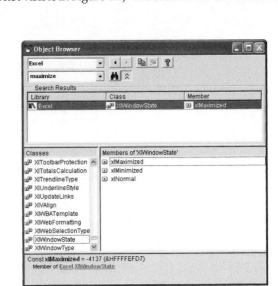

12. Press the F7 key to activate the Code window. (Alternatively, click the Code window, choose View ➤ Code, or choose the Code window from the Window menu.)

13. Type **application.** (in lowercase and including the period) so that the Visual Basic Editor displays the drop-down list, type **w** to jump to the items beginning with *W*, and select the WindowState item.

14. Type = to enter the WindowState item in your code and to display the list of constants available for WindowState (see Figure 4.6).

FIGURE 4.6

Use the list of constants to enter the constant quickly and easily.

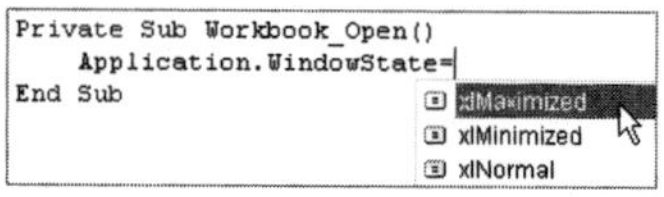

15. Select the xlMaximized item and press Enter to start a new statement.

16. The second action for the macro is to open the last file used—file 1 on the recently used files list (this is the list that appears at the foot of the File menu if the Recently Used File List check box on the General tab of Excel's Options dialog box is selected). Press the F2 key to activate the Object Browser again.

17. Leave Excel selected in the Project/Library drop-down list, type **recent**, and either press the Enter key or click the Search button. The Object Browser displays the results of the search (see Figure 4.7). The item you need is the RecentFiles property of the Application object. The RecentFiles property returns the RecentFiles collection, an object that contains details of the files in the recently used files list.

FIGURE 4.7

The result of the search for "recent" in the Object Browser

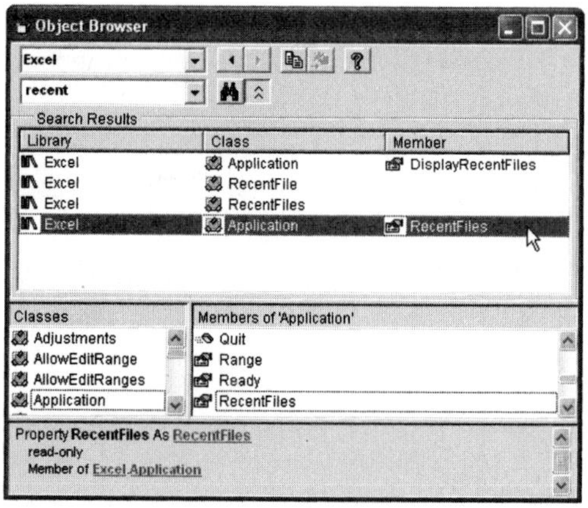

18. Press the F7 key to activate the Code window. Type **application.** and select RecentFiles from the List Properties/Methods drop-down list. Then type **(1).** to indicate the first item in the RecentFiles collection), and select the Open method from the List Properties/Methods list.

```
Application.RecentFiles(1).Open
```

19. That's it. Your procedure should look like this:

```
Private Sub Workbook_Open()
    Application.WindowState = xlMaximized
    Application.RecentFiles(1).Open
End Sub
```

20. Press Alt+Q or chose File ➢ Close And Return To Microsoft Excel to return to Excel.

21. Choose File ➢ Save to save the Personal Macro Workbook.

22. Choose Window ➢ Hide to hide the Personal Macro Workbook.

23. Open a sample document, make a change to it, save it, and close it.

24. Choose File ➢ Exit to exit Excel.

25. Restart Excel. Excel maximizes the application window and opens the most recently used file.

Creating a Procedure for PowerPoint

The procedure you'll create for PowerPoint is short and straightforward, but it can save the user enough effort over the long run to make it worthwhile. It adds a title slide to the active presentation, inserting a canned title that includes the current date and the company's name as the presenter.

Follow these steps to create the procedure:

1. Start PowerPoint. If PowerPoint is already running, close it and restart it. If PowerPoint creates a default presentation on startup, close the presentation.

2. Create a new presentation based on a template of your choosing. Make sure the default slide on the presentation has the Title Slide layout. If not, choose Format ➢ Slide Layout, and then click the Title Slide layout to apply it to the default slide.

3. Choose Tools ➢ Macros ➢ Visual Basic Editor, or press Alt+F11, to open the Visual Basic Editor.

4. Make sure the Visual Basic Editor is set up as described in the section, "Setting Up the Visual Basic Editor for Creating the Procedures," earlier in this chapter.

5. In the Project Explorer window, right-click anywhere in the VBAProject(Presentation1) item and choose Insert ➢ Module from the context menu. The Visual Basic Editor inserts a new module in the project, displays a Code window containing the code sheet for the module, and expands the project tree.

6. Verify that the Visual Basic Editor has entered the Option Explicit statement in the declarations area at the top of the code sheet. If not, type the statement now.

7. Press the F4 key to activate the Properties window for the new module. Alternatively, click in the Properties window.

8. Type the name for the new module in the Properties window: **General_ Procedures**.

9. Press the F7 key or click in the Code window to activate it.

10. Below the `Option Explicit` statement, type the Sub statement for the procedure and press the Enter key:

```
Sub Add_Title_Slide
```

11. The Visual Basic Editor enters the parentheses at the end of the Sub statement, a blank line, and the End Sub statement for you, and places the insertion point on the blank line.

```
Sub Sub Add_Title_Slide()

End Sub
```

12. Press the Tab key to indent the first line below the Sub statement.

13. Now identify the objects you need by using the Help system. You'll be working with the active presentation, which is represented by the `ActivePresentation` object. So type **activepresentation**, place the insertion point anywhere in the word, and press the F1 key to launch Microsoft Visual Basic Help. It'll give you the ActivePresentation Property screen shown in Figure 4.8.

> **NOTE** If pressing the F1 key with the insertion point in the word *activepresentation* doesn't work, choose Help ➤ Microsoft Visual Basic Help to display the Visual Basic Help task pane. Type **active-presentation** in the Search box and press the Enter key or click the Start Searching button. In the Search Results window, click the ActivePresentation Property link.

FIGURE 4.8

The ActivePresentation Property screen

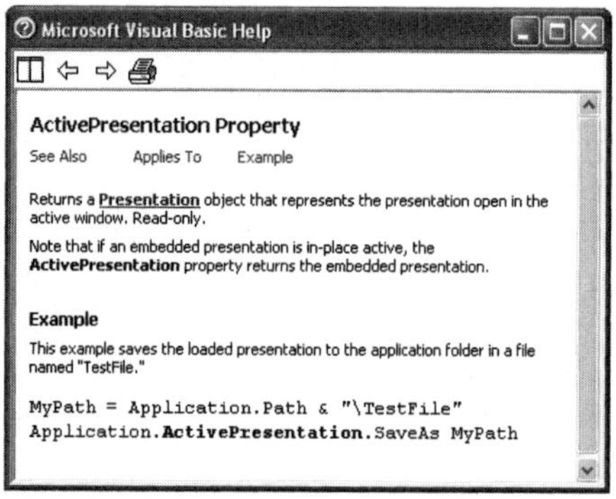

14. Click the link to the `Presentation` object on the ActivePresentation Property screen to display its Help screen.

15. Click the lower Multiple Objects box in the partial object hierarchy towards the top of the Presentation Object Help screen, and then click the Slides object in the pop-up menu (see Figure 4.9) to display the Slides Collection Object screen (see Figure 4.10).

16. From this screen, take two pieces of information: First, that a slide is represented by a `Slide` object (organized into the `Slides` collection), and second, that you use the `Add` method to create a new slide.

FIGURE 4.9
Click the lower of the two Multiple Objects boxes on the Presentation Object screen and choose Slides Object from the pop-up menu.

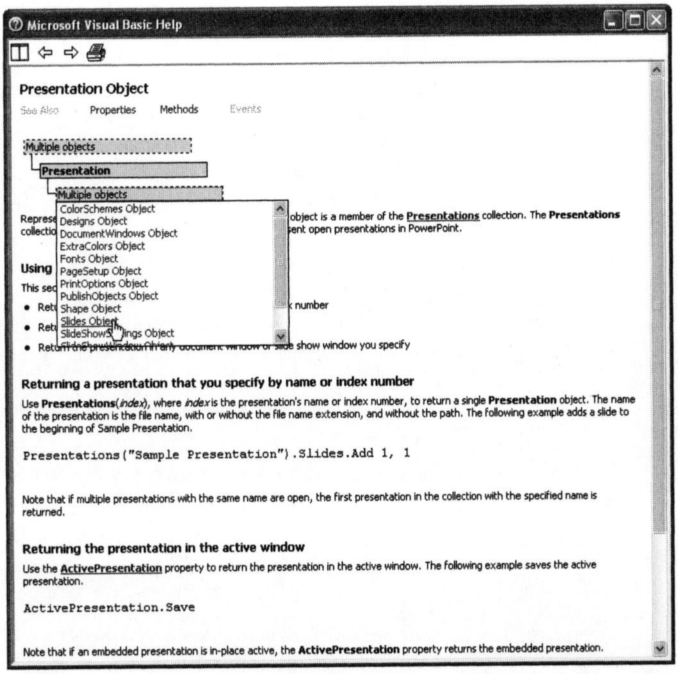

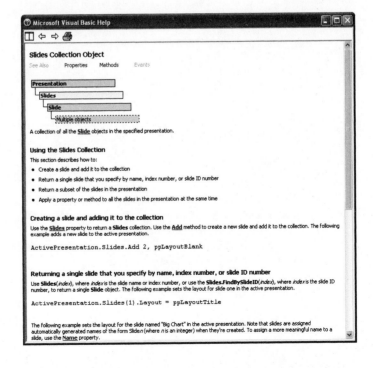

FIGURE 4.10
The Slides Collection Object screen

17. Return to the Visual Basic Editor and delete that `activepresentation` you added.

18. Type a declaration for an object variable of the `Slide` object type to represent the slide the procedure creates. Notice that after you type **as** and a space, the Visual Basic Editor displays the list of available keywords. Type down through the list (type **s** and **l**) until you have selected `Slide`, and then press the Enter key to complete the term and start a new line of code:

```
Dim sldTitleSlide As Slide
```

19. Then use a `Set` statement to assign to the `sldTitleSlide` object a new slide you create by using the Add method. Type **set sld** and then press Ctrl+spacebar to make the Complete Word feature enter `sldTitleSlide` for you. Then type **activepresentation.slides.add(**, using the Visual Basic Editor's assistance, so that the line reads as shown here:

```
Set sldTitleSlide = ActivePresentation.Slides.Add(
```

20. When you type the parenthesis, the Auto Quick Info feature displays for you the syntax for the Add method, as shown in Figure 4.11.

FIGURE 4.11
The Auto Quick Info feature displays the syntax for the Add method when you type the parenthesis after the Add method.

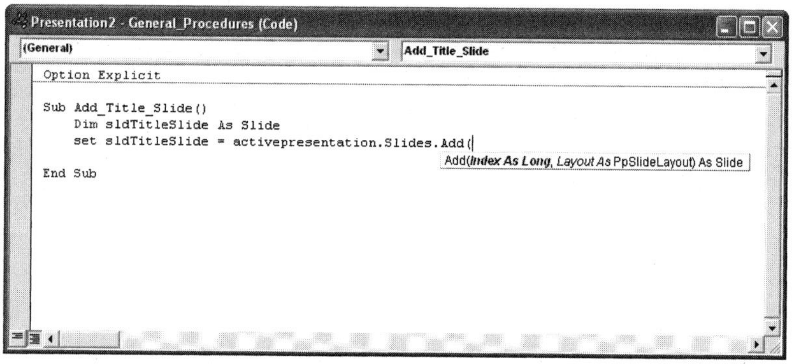

21. Type the **Index** argument, a colon, an equal sign, the value **1** (because the title slide is to be the first slide in the presentation), and a comma:

```
Set sldTitleSlide = ActivePresentation.Slides.Add(Index:=1,
```

NOTE When a method uses arguments, as the Add method does here, you can choose between specifying the argument names and omitting them and letting VBA infer the arguments from the order of the values or constants. For example, in this case, you can either specify Add(Index:=1, Layout:=ppLayoutTitle) or Add(1, ppLayoutTitle). The latter is more concise and easier to enter, but the former is much clearer to read.

22. Break the statement to the next line with a line-continuation character (an underscore preceded by a space). Then type a tab to indent the new line, type the **Layout** argument, a colon, and an equal sign, and pick the `ppLayoutTitle` constant from the List Properties/Methods dropdown list, as shown in Figure 4.12.

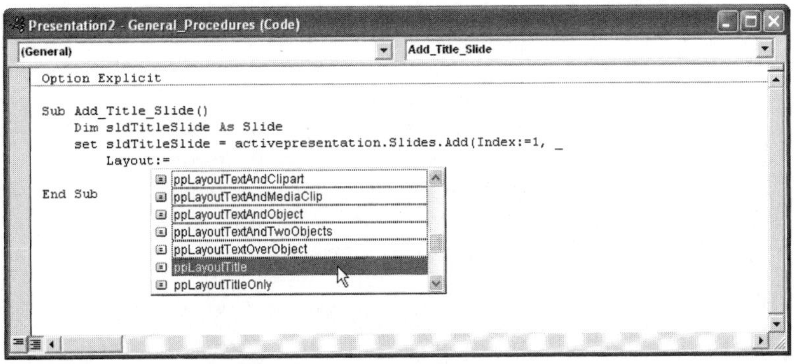

FIGURE 4.12

Choose the ppLayoutTitle constant for the Layout argument.

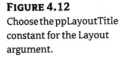

23. Type the parenthesis to end the statement:

```
Set sldTitleSlide = ActivePresentation.Slides.Add(Index:=1, _
    Layout:=ppLayoutTitle)
```

24. Press the Enter key to start a new line, and then press either the Backspace key or Shift+Tab to unindent the new line by one tab stop.

25. You'll be working with the sldTitleSlide from here on, so create a With statement using it, and place the insertion point on the line between the With statement and the End With statement:

```
With sldTitleSlide

End With.
```

26. Next, the macro will manipulate the two items on the slide. To make it do so, you need to know the objects that represent them. You could use the Macro Recorder to find out, but this time, try a more direct method: Place the insertion point on the line within the With statement and type . (a period) to display the List Properties/Methods drop-down list of available properties and methods for the Slide object.

27. Sometimes the List Properties/Methods drop-down list is of little help, because you'll find so many possibly relevant properties and methods that you can't identify the property you need. But if you scan the list in this case, you'll see that the Shapes property (which returns the Shapes collection) is the only promising item.

28. Press Ctrl+G, choose View ➤ Immediate, or click the Immediate Window button on the Debug toolbar to display the Immediate window for a bit of testing.

29. Type the exploratory statement below into the Immediate window and press the Enter key. Press Alt+F11 or click the View Microsoft PowerPoint button on the Standard toolbar to display the PowerPoint window to verify that VBA has selected the first Shape object on the slide:

```
ActivePresentation.Slides(1).Shapes(1).Select
```

30. This is the right object to start with, but you need to find out how to add text to the shape. Go back to the Code window (click in the Code window or press the F7 key). Press the Backspace key to delete the period, and then type it again to display the list. Type **te** to jump down to the items in the list whose names start with *text*. Select the TextFrame item in the list, and then type a period to enter the term and display the next list. Scroll down the list, select the TextRange object, and type a period to enter the term and display the next list. In the next list, select the Text property. Type an equal sign to enter the term. Then type double quotation marks followed by the text to assign to the text property: **Pollution Update:** (with a space after it), double quotation marks, an ampersand, and the date (supplied by the Date function):

```
Shapes(1).TextFrame.TextRange.Text = "Pollution Update: " & Date
```

31. Assign information to the second Shape in the same way:

```
.Shapes(2).TextFrame.TextRange.Text = "JMP Industrials."
```

32. The whole procedure should look like this:

```
Sub Add_Title_Slide()
    Dim sldTitleSlide As Slide
    Set sldTitleSlide = ActivePresentation.Slides.Add(Index:=1, _
        Layout:=ppLayoutTitle)
    With sldTitleSlide
        .Shapes(1).TextFrame.TextRange.Text = _
            "Pollution Update: " & Date
        .Shapes(2).TextFrame.TextRange.Text = _
            "JMP Industrials"
    End With
End Sub
```

33. Test the procedure; then delete all slides from the presentation. Choose Tools ➢ Customize and add a toolbar button or menu item for the Add_Title_Slide procedure.

34. Save the presentation under a name such as Procedures.ppt.

35. Create a new presentation; then test the toolbar button or menu item for the procedure. Close the presentation without saving changes.

Part 2

Learning How to Work with VBA

- ◆ Chapter 5: Understanding the Essentials of VBA Syntax
- ◆ Chapter 6: Working with Variables and Constants
- ◆ Chapter 7: Using Array Variables
- ◆ Chapter 8: Finding the Objects, Methods, and Properties You Need

Chapter 5

Understanding the Essentials of VBA Syntax

- ◆ Understanding the basics of VBA
- ◆ Understanding procedures and functions
- ◆ Using the Immediate window to execute statements
- ◆ Understanding objects, properties, methods, and events

In this chapter, you'll learn the essentials of VBA syntax, building on what you learned via practical examples in the previous chapters. This chapter defines the key terms that you need to know about VBA to get going with it, and you'll practice using some of the elements in the Visual Basic Editor.

NOTE   You'll find lots of definitions for programming terms as you work your way through the chapter. If you come across something that doesn't yet make sense to you, skip ahead, and you'll most likely find it in the next few pages.

Getting Ready

To work through this section, get set up for working in the Visual Basic Editor with Word by following the steps shown below. This chapter uses Word because it's probably the most widely distributed of the VBA-enabled applications. If you don't have it, read along anyway without performing the actions on the computer; the examples are easy to follow. (Much of this will work on any VBA host, though many of the commands shown here are specific to Word.)

1. Start Word as usual.
2. Launch the Visual Basic Editor by pressing Alt+F11 or choosing Tools ➢ Macro ➢ Visual Basic Editor.
3. Arrange the Word window and the Visual Basic Editor window so that you can see both of them at once. For example, if these are the only two open windows that are not minimized, right-click the Taskbar and choose Tile Windows Horizontally or Tile Windows Vertically from the context menu to arrange the windows.
4. Display the Immediate window in the Visual Basic Editor by pressing Ctrl+G, choosing View ➢ Immediate Window, or clicking the Immediate Window button on the Debug toolbar.

TIP If you're using a multi-monitor setup, you can dedicate one monitor to Word and another to the Visual Basic Editor.

Procedures

A *procedure* in VBA is a named unit of code that contains a sequence of statements to be executed as a group. For example, VBA contains a function (a type of procedure) named `Left`, which returns the left portion of a text string that you specify. For example, `hello` is a string of text five characters long. The statement `Left("hello", 4)` returns the leftmost four characters of the string: `hell`. (You could then display this four-character string in a message box or use it in code.) The name assigned to the procedure gives you a way to refer to the procedure.

All executable code in VBA must be contained in a procedure—if it isn't, VBA can't execute it, and an error occurs. (The exception is statements you execute in the Immediate window, which take place outside a procedure. However, the contents of the Immediate window exist only during the current VBA session.) Procedures are contained within modules, which in turn are contained within project files, templates, or other VBA host objects, such as user forms.

There are two types of procedures: functions and subprocedures.

Functions

A *function* in VBA is one of two types of procedures. A function is a type of complete procedure designed to perform a specific task. For example, the `Left` function returns the left part of a text string, and the `Right` function, its counterpart, returns the right part of a text string. Each function has a clear task that you use it for, and it doesn't do anything else. To take a ridiculous example, you can't use the `Left` function to print a document in Word or make characters boldface—for those tasks, you need to use the appropriate functions, methods, and properties.

VBA comes with many built-in functions, but you can also create your own. You'll create your own functions later in the book. They will begin with a `Function` statement and end with an `End Function` statement.

Each function returns a value. For example, the `Left` function returns the left part of the string. Other functions test a condition and return `True` if the condition is met and `False` if it is not met.

Subprocedures

A *subprocedure* is a self-contained unit of code that doesn't return a value. All the macros you record using the Macro Recorder are subprocedures, as are many of the procedures you'll look at in the rest of this book.

Each subprocedure begins with a `Sub` statement and ends with an `End Sub` statement. Subprocedures are also called *subroutines*.

NOTE Only subprocedures appear in the Macros dialog box. Functions don't appear there.

Statements

A *statement* is a unit of code that describes an action, defines an item, or gives the value of a variable. VBA usually has one statement per line of code, although you can put more than one statement on a line by separating them with colons. (This isn't usually a good idea, as it makes your code harder to read.)

You can also break a line of code onto a second line or a subsequent line to make it easier to read by using a line-continuation character: an underscore (_) preceded by a space (and followed by a carriage return). You do so strictly for visual convenience; VBA still reads both lines, or all the lines, as a single line of code.

WARNING You can't break a string enclosed in quotations by using a line-continuation character. If you need to break a line that involves a long string in quotes, break the string into shorter strings and concatenate them using the & operator.

VBA statements vary widely in length and complexity. A statement can be a single word (such as Beep, which makes the computer beep, or Stop, which halts the execution of VBA code) to very long and complicated lines involving many components. That said, let's examine the makeup of several sample VBA statements in Word. Most of them use the ActiveDocument object, which represents the active document in the current session of Word; a couple use the Documents collection, which represents all open documents (including the active document); and one uses the Selection object, which represents the current selection. Don't worry if some of these statements aren't immediately comprehensible—you'll understand them soon enough.

Here are the example statements:

```
Documents.Open "c:\temp\Sample Document.doc"
MsgBox ActiveDocument.Name
ActiveDocument.Words(1).Text = "Industry"
ActiveDocument.Close SaveChanges:=wdDoNotSaveChanges
Documents.Add
Selection.TypeText "The quick brown fox jumped over the lazy dog."
ActiveDocument.Save
Documents.Close SaveChanges:=wdDoNotSaveChanges
Application.Quit
```

Let's look at each of these statements in turn.

```
Documents.Open "c:\temp\Sample Document.doc"
```

This statement uses the Open method on the Documents collection to open the specified document—in this case, Sample Document.doc. Enter this statement in the Immediate window, using a path and filename of a document that exists on your computer. Press the Enter key, and VBA opens the document in the Word window. As when you open a document while working interactively in Word, the document becomes the active document (the document whose window is currently selected).

```
MsgBox ActiveDocument.Name
```

This statement uses the MsgBox function to display the Name property of the ActiveDocument object (in this example, Sample Document.doc). Enter this statement in the Immediate window (type in lowercase, and use VBA's help features as you choose) and press the Enter key. VBA displays a message box over the Word window. Click the OK button to dismiss the message box.

```
ActiveDocument.Words(1).Text = "Industry"
```

This statement uses the *assignment operator* (the equal [=] sign) to assign the value *Industry* to the Text property of the first item in the Words collection in the ActiveDocument object. Enter this statement in the Immediate window and press the Enter key. You'll see Word enter **Industry** (in the current typeface, and probably without the boldface) at the beginning of the document you opened. Note that the insertion point is at the beginning of the word, rather than at the end of the word, where it would be if you'd typed the word. This happens because VBA manipulates the properties of the document rather than "typing" into it.

```
ActiveDocument.Close SaveChanges:=wdDoNotSaveChanges
```

This statement uses the `Close` method to close the `ActiveDocument` object. It uses one argument, `SaveChanges`, which controls whether Word saves the document that's being closed (if the document contains unsaved changes). In this case, the statement uses the constant wdDoNotSaveChanges to specify that Word shouldn't save changes when closing the document. Enter this statement in the Immediate window and press the Enter key, and you'll see VBA make Word close the document.

Now try entering these statements in the Immediate window:

```
Documents.Add
```

This statement uses the `Add` method on the `Documents` collection to add a new `Document` object to the `Documents` collection. In other words, it creates a new document. Because the statement doesn't specify which template to use, the new document is based on the default template (`Normal.dot`). Enter this statement in the Immediate window and press Enter, and Word creates a new document. As usual, this new document becomes the active document.

```
Selection.TypeText "The quick brown fox jumped over the lazy dog."
```

This statement uses the `TypeText` method of the `Selection` object to type text into the active document at the position of the insertion point or current selection. (The `Selection` object represents the current selection, which can be either a collapsed selection—an insertion point with nothing actually selected—or one or more selected objects.) If text is selected in the active document, that selection is overwritten as usual (unless you've cleared the Typing Replaces Selection check box on the Edit tab of the Options dialog box, in which case the selection is collapsed to its beginning, and the new text is inserted before the previously selected text). Because you just created a new document, nothing is selected. Enter this statement in the Immediate window and press the Enter key, and Word enters the text. Note that this time the insertion point ends up after the text; the `TypeText` method of the `Selection` object is analogous to typing interactively.

```
ActiveDocument.Save
```

This statement uses the `Save` method (command) to save the `ActiveDocument` object. This statement is the VBA equivalent of choosing File ➢ Save while working interactively in Word. If you enter this statement into the Immediate window and press Enter, Word displays the Save As dialog box so you can save the document as usual. For now, however, click the Cancel button to dismiss the Save As dialog box. Word displays the Microsoft Visual Basic error message box (see Figure 5.1). Click the OK button to dismiss it; you'll learn how to handle errors such as this in your code in Chapter 17.

```
Documents.Close SaveChanges:=wdDoNotSaveChanges
```

This statement is similar to the previous `ActiveDocument.Close SaveChanges:` `=wdDoNotSaveChanges` statement, except that it works on the `Documents` collection rather than the `ActiveDocument` object. The `Documents` collection represents all open documents in the current Word session. This statement closes all open documents without saving any unsaved changes in them. Enter this statement into the Immediate window and press Enter, and Word closes all the open documents.

```
Application.Quit
```

FIGURE 5.1

The Visual Basic Editor displays a Microsoft Visual Basic error message box when it encounters an unhandled error in a command.

This statement uses the `Quit` method on the `Application` object to close the Word application. Enter the statement in the Immediate window and press the Enter key. Word closes itself, closing the Visual Basic Editor in the process, because Word is the host for the Visual Basic Editor.

GETTING HELP ON VISUAL BASIC FOR APPLICATIONS

The Visual Basic Editor offers comprehensive help on the Visual Basic for Applications programming language. To view it, choose Help ➤ Microsoft Visual Basic Help from the Visual Basic Editor. Most of the statements and functions have examples, which can be particularly helpful when you're creating and troubleshooting code.

The Visual Basic Help files use a couple of conventions you should know about before you try to use them:

◆ Italics denote variables or values you'll need to change yourself.

◆ Brackets ([and]) denote optional arguments.

This book uses the same conventions, so you'll see them in use soon.

If your computer doesn't offer you any help on VBA, whoever installed the application in question may not have installed the relevant files (perhaps to save space). Install the files, and all should be well.

Keywords

A *keyword* is a word defined as part of the VBA language. Here are some examples:

◆ The Sub keyword indicates the beginning of a subprocedure, and the End Sub keywords mark the end of a subprocedure.

◆ The Function keyword indicates the beginning of a function, and the End Function keywords mark the end of a function.

◆ The Dim keyword starts a declaration (for example, of a variable) and the As keyword links the item declared to its type, which is also a keyword. For example, in the declaration Dim strExample As String, there are three keywords: Dim, As, and String.

The names of functions and subprocedures are not keywords.

TIP The Visual Basic Editor displays all keywords in the color specified for Keyword Text on the Editor Format tab of the Options dialog box (choose Tools ➤ Options from the Visual Basic Editor). The default color for keywords is dark blue. If you're not sure if an item is a keyword or not, check if the color the Visual Basic Editor gives the item is the same color as keywords such as Sub.

Expressions

An *expression* consists of keywords, operators, variables, and constants combined to produce a string, number, or object. For example, you could use an expression to run a calculation or to compare one variable against another.

Operators

An *operator* is an item you use to compare, combine, or otherwise work with values in an expression. VBA has four kinds of operators:

- ◆ *Arithmetic operators* (such as + and −) perform mathematical calculations.

- ◆ *Comparison operators* (such as < and >, less than and greater than, respectively) compare values.

- ◆ *Concatenation operators* (& and +) join two strings together.

- ◆ *Logical operators* (such as And, Not, and Or) build logical structures.

You'll look at the different kinds of operators and how they work in Chapter 6.

Variables

A *variable* is a location in memory set aside for storing a piece of information that can be changed while a procedure is running. (Think of it as a resizable compartment within the memory area.) For example, if you need the user to input their name via an input box or a dialog box, you'll typically store the name in a variable so you can work with it in the procedure.

VBA uses several types of variables, including these:

- ◆ *Strings* store text characters or groups of characters.

- ◆ *Integers* store whole numbers (numbers without fractions).

- ◆ *Objects* store objects.

- ◆ *Variants* can store any type of data. Variant is the default type of variable.

You can either let VBA create Variant variables in which to store your information, or you can specify which type any given variable can be. Specifying the types of variable has certain advantages that you'll learn about in due course.

For the moment, try creating a variable in the Immediate window. Type the following line and press Enter:

```
myVariable = "Sample variable text"
```

Nothing visible happens, but VBA has created the myVariable variable. Now, type the following line and press Enter:

```
MsgBox myVariable
```

This time, you can see the result: A message box appears containing the text you entered in the variable.

You can declare variables either explicitly or implicitly. An *explicit* declaration sets the variable's name, and usually its type, before you use it. An *implicit* declaration occurs when you tell VBA to store data in a variable that you have not explicitly declared. VBA then stores the data in a Variant variable.

In the next few chapters, you'll use a few implicit variable declarations to keep things simple—you don't have to type anything for implicit variable declarations, because VBA will make them up when it needs them. After that, you'll start using explicit variable declarations to make your code faster and easier to read.

Constants

A *constant* is a named item that keeps a constant value while a program is executing. The constant's meaning doesn't change at different times of program execution.

VBA uses two types of constant: *intrinsic constants*, which are built into an application; and *user-defined constants*, which you create. For example, the built-in constant vbOKCancel is used with the MsgBox function to create a message box that contains an OK button and a Cancel button. You might define a constant to store a piece of information that doesn't change, such as the name of a procedure.

Arguments

An *argument* is a piece of information—supplied by a constant, a variable, or an expression—that you pass to a procedure, a function, or a method. Some arguments are required; others are optional. As you saw earlier, the following statement uses the optional argument SaveChanges to specify whether Word should save any unsaved changes while closing the active document:

```
ActiveDocument.Close SaveChanges:=wdDoNotSaveChanges
```

The Visual Basic Editor's helpful prompts and the Visual Basic Help file show the list of arguments for a function, a procedure, or a method in parentheses, with any optional arguments enclosed in brackets. If you're using the Auto Quick Info feature, the Visual Basic Editor displays the argument list for a function, procedure, or method after you type its name followed by a space.

Figure 5.2 shows the argument list for the Open method. The FileName argument is required, so it isn't surrounded by brackets. All the other arguments (ConfirmConversions, ReadOnly, AddToRecentFiles, and so on) are optional, and so are surrounded by brackets. If you don't supply a value for an optional argument, VBA uses the default value for the argument. (To find out the default value for an argument, consult the VBA Help file.) The Visual Basic Editor uses boldface to indicate the current argument in the list; as you enter each argument, the next argument in the list becomes bold.

FIGURE 5.2

You can tell whether an argument is required or optional by the way the Visual Basic Editor displays information about it. Optional arguments are listed within brackets.

```
Documents.Open
Open(FileName, [ConfirmConversions], [ReadOnly], [AddToRecentFiles], [PasswordDocument],
[PasswordTemplate], [Revert], [WritePasswordDocument], [WritePasswordTemplate], [Format], [Encoding],
[Visible], [OpenAndRepair], [DocumentDirection], [NoEncodingDialog], [XMLTransform]) As Document
```

Specifying Argument Names vs. Omitting Argument Names

You can use arguments in either of two ways:

◆ Enter the name of the argument (for example, ConfirmConversions) followed by a colon and an equal sign (ConfirmConversions:=) and the constant or value you want to set for it (ConfirmConversions:=True). For example, the start of the statement might look like this:

```
Documents.Open FileName:="c:\temp\Example.doc", _
    ConfirmConversions:=True, ReadOnly:=False
```

◆ Enter the constant or value in the appropriate position in the argument list for the method, without entering the name of the argument. The previous statement would look like this:

```
Documents.Open "c:\Temp\Example.doc", True, False
```

When you use the names of the arguments, you don't need to put them in order, because VBA uses the names to identify them. The following statements are functionally equivalent:

```
Documents.Open ReadOnly:=False, FileName:="c:\temp\Example.doc", _
    ReadOnly:=False, ConfirmConversions:=True
```

```
Documents.Open FileName:="c:\temp\Example.doc", _
    ConfirmConversions:=True, ReadOnly:=False
```

You also don't need to indicate to VBA which arguments you're omitting. By contrast, when you omit the argument names and specify the arguments positionally, the arguments must be in the correct order for VBA to recognize them correctly. If you choose not to use an optional argument, but instead to use another optional argument that follows it, enter a comma to denote the omitted argument. For example, the following statement omits the ConfirmConversions argument and uses a comma to denote that the False value refers to the ReadOnly argument rather than the ConfirmConversions argument:

```
Documents.Open "c:\temp\Example.doc",, False
```

When you type the comma in the Code window or the Immediate window, Auto Quick Info moves the boldface to the next argument in the argument list to indicate that it's next in line for your attention.

NOTE　Typically, required arguments are listed before optional arguments, so you don't have to specify the omission of optional arguments in order to enter the required arguments.

When to Include the Parentheses around the Argument List

When you're assigning the result of a function to a variable or other object, you enclose the whole argument list in parentheses. For example, to assign to the variable objMyDocument the result of opening the document c:\temp\Example.doc, use the following statement.

```
objMyDocument = Documents.Open(FileName:="c:\temp\Example.doc", _
    ConfirmConversions:=True, ReadOnly:=False)
```

When you aren't assigning the result of an operation to a variable or an object, you don't use the parentheses around the argument list.

Objects

To VBA, each application consists of a series of *objects*. Here are a few examples:

◆ In Word, a document is an object (the `Document` object), as is a paragraph (the `Paragraph` object) or a table (the `Table` object). Even a single character is an object (the `Character` object).

◆ In Excel, a workbook is an object (the `Workbook` object), as are the worksheets (the `Worksheet` object) and charts (the `Chart` object).

◆ In PowerPoint, a presentation is an object (the `Presentation` object), as are its slides (the `Slide` object) and the shapes (the `Shape` object) they contain.

Most of the actions you can take in VBA involve manipulating objects. For example, as you saw earlier, you can close the active document in Word by using the `Close` method on the `ActiveDocument` object:

```
ActiveDocument.Close
```

Collections

A *collection* is an object that contains several other objects. Collections provide a way to access all their members at the same time. For example, the `Documents` collection contains all the open documents, each of which is an object. Instead of closing `Document` objects one by one, you can close all open documents by using the `Close` method on the `Documents` collection:

```
Documents.Close
```

Likewise, you can use a collection to change the properties of all the members of a collection simultaneously.

Properties

Each object has a number of *properties*. For example, a document in Word has properties such as its title, its subject, and its author. You can set these properties through the Properties dialog box (File ➤ Properties). Likewise, a single character has various properties, such as its font, font size, and various types of emphasis (bold, italic, strikethrough, and so on).

Methods

A *method* is an action you can perform with an object. Loosely speaking, a method is a command. Different objects have different methods associated with them—actions you can take with them or commands you can specify that they perform. For example, the following methods are associated with the `Document` object in Word (and with other objects such as the `Workbook` object in Excel and the `Presentation` object in PowerPoint):

Activate   Activates the document (the equivalent of selecting the document's window with the keyboard or mouse)

Close   Closes the document (the equivalent of choosing File ➤ Close)

Save   Saves the document (the equivalent of choosing File ➤ Save)

SaveAs   Saves the document under a specified name (the equivalent of choosing File ➤ Save As and specifying a name and path in the Save As dialog box)

Events

An *event* is an occurrence that VBA recognizes as having happened. For example, the opening of a file (either by a user or by a procedure) typically generates an event. The user's clicking a button in a user form generates an event.

By attaching code to an event, you can cause VBA to take actions when an event occurs. For example, in a user form, the code might check that all necessary settings were chosen in the user form when the user clicked the OK button to dismiss the user form and apply the settings.

Chapter 6

Working with Variables, Constants, and Enumerations

◆ Understanding what variables are and what you use them for

◆ Creating and using variables

◆ Specifying the scope and lifetime for a variable

◆ Working with constants

◆ Working with enumerations

This chapter covers the basics of working with variables, constants, and enumerations. *Variables* provide a way of storing and manipulating information derived from a procedure and include String variables for storing text, various numeric data types for storing numbers (for example, Integer variables for storing integer values), Date variables for storing dates and times, Boolean variables for storing True/False values, and Object variables for storing objects. A *constant* is a named item that keeps a constant value while a program is executing. An *enumeration* is a predefined list of unique integers that have individual names and meanings in a particular context—essentially, a list of constants.

The one type of variable that this chapter doesn't discuss is the Array variable, which is used to store multiple pieces of information at the same time (keeping them separate). Chapter 7 shows you how to use arrays.

Working with Variables

A variable is a named area in memory that you use for storing data while a procedure is running. For example, in Chapter 5, you created a variable that stored a simple string of text that you then displayed in a message box:

```
myVariable = "Sample variable text"
MsgBox myVariable
```

The first statement sets aside an area in memory, names it myVariable, and assigns the string Sample variable text to it. The second statement retrieves the contents of myVariable from memory and uses the MsgBox function to display it in a message box. The contents of myVariable remains in memory, so you can use it again if necessary.

Choosing Names for Variables

VBA imposes several constraints on variable names:

- Variable names must start with a letter and can be up to 255 characters in length. Usually, you'll want to keep them much shorter than this so that you can easily type them into your code and so that your lines of code don't rapidly reach awkward lengths.

TIP   The Visual Basic Editor's AutoComplete feature helps make long variable names a little more manageable: Type enough of the variable's name to distinguish it from any keywords and other variable names, and press Ctrl+spacebar. If you've typed enough to uniquely identify the variable, the Visual Basic Editor inserts its name; if not, the Visual Basic Editor displays the drop-down list of keywords and names starting with those letters.

- Variable names can't contain characters such as periods, exclamation points, mathematical operators (+, −, /, *), or comparison operators (=, <>, >, >=, <, <=); nor can they internally contain type-declaration characters (@, &, $, #). (You'll learn about the type-declaration characters later in this chapter.)

- Variable names can't contain spaces but can contain underscores, which you can use to make the variable names more readable.

In other words, you're pretty safe if you stick with straightforward alphanumerics enlivened with the occasional underscore.

For example, all of the following variable names are fine, although the last is awkwardly long to use:

```
i
John
MyVariable
MissionParameters
The_String_That_the_User_Entered_in_the_Input_Box
```

On the other hand, these variable names are not usable:

Variable Name	Problem
My Variable	Contains a space
My!Variable	Contains an exclamation point
Time@Tide	Contains a type-declaration character (@)
1_String	Does not start with a letter

Each variable name must be unique within the scope in which it's operating (to prevent VBA from confusing it with any other variable). Typically, the scope within which a variable operates is a procedure, but if you declare the variable as public or module-level private (discussed later in the chapter), its scope is wider.

The other constraint on variable names is that you should avoid assigning to a variable a name that VBA already uses as the name of a function, a statement, or a method. Doing so is called *shadowing* a VBA keyword. It doesn't necessarily cause problems, but it may prevent you from using that function, statement, or method without specifically identifying it to VBA by prefacing its name with **VBA.** For example, instead of Date, you'd have to use VBA.Date—no big deal, but worth avoiding in the first place.

There's no reason to shadow a VBA keyword, but VBA has so many keywords that it's surprisingly easy to do so.

Declaring a Variable

VBA lets you declare variables either implicitly or explicitly. As you'll see shortly, each method has pros and cons. Explicit declarations are almost always a good idea, and when you've been working with VBA for even a little while, you'll probably use them all the time. For this reason, it's best to declare your variables explicitly right from the beginning. But this chapter also teaches you to use implicit declarations so that you know how to do so.

DECLARING A VARIABLE IMPLICITLY

Declaring a variable implicitly means that you use it in your code without declaring it explicitly. When you declare a variable implicitly, VBA checks to make sure that there isn't already an existing variable with that name. It then automatically creates a variable with that name for you and assigns it the Variant data type, which can contain any type of data except a fixed-length string.

For example, in the previous chapter, you declared the variable myVariable by using the following implicit declaration:

```
myVariable = "Sample variable text"
```

Here, myVariable is implicitly declared as a variable. VBA assigns it the Variant data type, which has a dozen or so subtypes. In this case, the variable's subtype is a string because it contains text. VBA usually assigns the variable the value Empty (a special value used to indicate Variant variables that have never been used) when it creates it, but in this case the variable receives a value immediately (because the string of text is assigned to it).

The advantage of declaring a variable implicitly is that you don't have to code it ahead of time. If you want a variable, you can simply declare it on the spot. But declaring a variable implicitly also has a couple of disadvantages:

◆ It's easier to make a mistake when re-entering the name of an implicitly declared variable later in the procedure. For example, suppose you implicitly declare the variable FilesToCreate and then later type FllesToCreate instead. VBA doesn't query the latter spelling with its typo but creates another variable with that name, and the new variable has a different value than the old one. When you're working with a number of variables, it can be difficult and time-consuming to catch little mistakes like these, which can cause problems in your code.

◆ The Variant variable type takes up more memory than other types of variable, because it has to be able to store various types of data. This difference is negligible under most normal circumstances, particularly if you're using only a few variables or writing only short procedures; but if you're using many variables on a computer with limited memory, the extra memory used by Variant variables might slow down a procedure or even run the computer out of memory. What's more important on an underpowered computer is that manipulating Variants takes longer than manipulating the other data types. This is because VBA has to keep checking to see what sort of data is in the variable.

You can get around this second disadvantage in a couple of ways: by using a type-declaration character to specify the data type when you declare a variable implicitly or, as you will see in the next section, by telling VBA to force you to declare variables explicitly.

A *type-declaration character* is a character that you add to the end of a variable's name in an implicit declaration to tell VBA which data type to use for the variable. Table 6.1 lists the type-declaration characters.

TABLE 6.1:   Type-Declaration Characters

CHARACTER	DATA TYPE OF VARIABLE	EXAMPLE
%	Integer	Quantity%
&	Long	China&
@	Currency	Profits@
!	Single	temperature!
#	Double	Differential#
$	String (variable length)	myMessage$

So you could implicitly declare the String variable UserName with the following statement, which assigns the value Jane Magnolia to the variable:

```
UserName$ = "Jane Magnolia"
```

And you could implicitly declare the currency variable Price by using this statement:

```
Price@ = Cost * Margin
```

You use the type-declaration character only when declaring the variable. Thereafter, you can refer to the variable by its name—UserName and Price in the previous examples.

DECLARING A VARIABLE EXPLICITLY

Declaring a variable explicitly means telling VBA that the variable exists before you use it. VBA then allocates memory space to that variable and registers it as a known quantity. You can also declare the variable type at the same time—a good idea but not obligatory.

You can declare a variable explicitly at any point in code before you use it, but custom and good sense recommend declaring all your variables at the beginning of the procedure that uses them. Doing so makes them easy to find, which helps anyone reading the code.

Declaring variables explicitly offers the following advantages:

♦ Your code is easier to read and to debug, both for you yourself and for other programmers. When you write complex code, this is an important consideration.

♦ When you use the Option Explicit statement to force explicit variable declarations, it is more difficult for you to create new variables unintentionally by mistyping the names of existing variables.

◆ It is also more difficult for you to wipe out the contents of an existing variable unintentionally when trying to create a new variable.

◆ VBA can catch some data-typing errors at design time or compile time that with implicit declarations wouldn't surface until runtime.

NOTE   A *data-typing error* occurs when you assign the wrong type of information to a variable. For example, if you declare an Integer variable and then assign a string of text to it, VBA gives an error, because it can't store string information in an Integer variable.

◆ Your code runs a fraction faster because VBA won't need to determine each variable's type while the code is running.

The disadvantage of declaring variables explicitly is that doing so takes a little more time, effort, and thought. For most code, however, this disadvantage is far outweighed by the advantages.

To declare a variable explicitly, you use one of the following keywords: `Dim`, `Private`, `Public`, or `Static`.

For example, the following statement declares the variable `MyValue`:

```
Dim MyValue
```

`Dim` is the regular keyword to use for declaring a variable, and you'll probably want to use it for most of your variable declarations. You use the other keywords to specify a different scope, lifetime, and data type for the variable in the declaration. In the previous example, the `MyValue` variable receives the default scope and lifetime and the Variant data type, which makes it suitable for general-purpose use.

You can also declare multiple variables on the same line by separating the variable statements with commas:

```
Dim Supervisor As String, ControllerCode As Long
```

This can help you keep down the number of declaration lines in your code, but it makes the declarations harder to read, so it's not usually a good idea.

Be warned that when you declare multiple variables on the same line, you need to specify the data type for each, as in the previous example. You might be tempted to try a little abbreviation, like this, hoping for a couple of String variables:

```
Dim strManager, strReportingEmployee As String
```

This statement doesn't create two String variables: `strReportingEmployee` is a String variable, but `strManager` is a Variant, because the `As String` part of the code applies only to `strReportingEmployee`.

Choosing the Scope and Lifetime of a Variable

The *scope* of a variable is the area in VBA within which it can operate. Typically, you'll want to use a variable with its default scope: within the procedure that declares the variable (either implicitly or explicitly). For example, suppose you have a module named `Financial_Procedures` that contains the procedures `Breakeven_Table` and `Profit_Analysis_Table`, each of which uses a variable named `Gross_Revenue` and another named `Expenses`. The variables in each procedure are distinct from the variables in the other procedure, and there is no danger of VBA confusing the two. (For the human reader, though, using the same variable names in different procedures rapidly becomes confusing when debugging. In general, it's a good idea to use unique variable names, even at the default procedure level.)

REQUIRING EXPLICIT DECLARATIONS FOR VARIABLES

You can set VBA to require you to declare variables explicitly, either globally (for all modules you work with) or on a module-by-module basis. Most people find this feature useful, because you can use it to prevent yourself from declaring any variables implicitly, whether intentionally or otherwise.

To require variable declarations globally, choose Tools ➤ Options in the Visual Basic Editor to display the Options dialog box, click the Editor tab to display the Editor page, select the Require Variable Declaration check box in the Code Settings area, and then click the OK button. (The Require Variable Declaration check box is cleared by default, enabling you to declare variables implicitly, which is usually the easiest way to start working with variables.) The Visual Basic Editor then adds an Option Explicit statement to each new module that you create. This statement requires explicit variable declarations for the module it's in.

When you select the Require Variable Declaration check box, the Visual Basic Editor doesn't add the Option Explicit statement to your existing modules. You must add the Option Explicit statement to your existing modules manually if you want to force explicit declarations in them too.

To require variable declarations only for specified modules, put an Option Explicit statement at the beginning of each module for which you want to require declarations. The Option Explicit statement must go before the Sub or Function statement for the first procedure in the module—if you put it inside a procedure, or between procedures, VBA gives an error when you try to run any of the code in the module.

If you've set Option Explicit either globally or for a module, VBA tests the procedure before running it. More precisely, VBA protests when it tries to compile the code and discovers that you haven't declared one or more of the variables, and it warns you if a variable isn't explicitly declared, as shown here. VBA also highlights the variable in your code.

If you get this message box, you can solve the problem either by declaring the variable or by turning off the requirement of variable declarations for the module. To turn off the requirement, remove the Option Explicit statement from the module by selecting and deleting the line that contains it or by commenting out this line.

The *lifetime* of a variable is the period during which VBA remembers the value of the variable. You need different lifetimes for your variables for different purposes. A variable's lifetime is tied to its scope.

Sometimes you need to access a variable from outside the procedure in which it's declared. In these cases, you need to declare a different scope for the variable.

A variable can have three types of scope:

◆ procedure

◆ private

◆ public

PROCEDURE SCOPE

A variable with *procedure scope* (also known as *procedure-level scope* or *local scope*) is available only to the procedure that contains it. As a result, the lifetime of a local variable is limited to the duration of the procedure that declares it: As soon as the procedure stops running, VBA removes all local variables from memory and reclaims the memory that held them.

Procedure scope is all you'll need for variables that operate only in the procedure in which they're declared. For example, say you implicitly declare a Variant variable named Supervisor like this:

```
Supervisor = "Paul Smith"
```

You can then use the Supervisor variable in the rest of that procedure—for example, retrieving the text stored in it or changing that text. When the procedure stops running, VBA removes the variable and reclaims the memory it occupied.

NOTE   When you declare a variable implicitly, it's automatically assigned procedure scope.

To explicitly declare a local variable, use the Dim keyword and place the declaration inside the procedure like this:

```
Sub Create_Weekly_Report()
    Dim strSupervisor As String
    Dim lngController As Long
...
End Sub
```

Here, the second line declares the variable strSupervisor as the String data type, the third line declares the variable lngController as the Long data type, and the fourth line declares the variable intReportNumber as the Integer data type. (The section "Specifying the Data Type for a Variable," in a few pages' time, goes through the variable types.)

On the other hand, if you need to pass any of these variables to another procedure that you call from the current procedure, procedure scope isn't sufficient—you need to use either private scope or public scope.

PRIVATE SCOPE

A variable with private scope is available to all procedures in the module that contains it but not to procedures in other modules. Using private variables enables you to pass the value of a variable from one procedure to another. Unlike local variables, which retain their value only as long as the procedure that contains them is running, private variables retain their value as long as the project that contains them is open.

To declare a variable with private scope, you can use either the Dim keyword or the Private keyword at the beginning of a module, placing it before the Sub statement for the first procedure in the module:

```
Dim strSupervisor As String
Private blnConsultantAssigned As Boolean
Sub Assign_Personnel()
```

The Visual Basic Editor displays the private declarations above the dividing line that appears between the declarations area and the code (see Figure 6.1).

FIGURE 6.1
Private variable declarations appear in the declarations area.

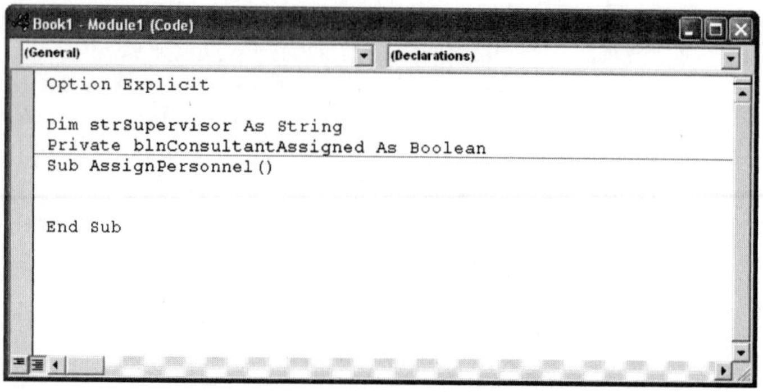

You'll notice that the `Dim` statement here uses exactly the same syntax as the earlier declaration for the local variable. The difference is that to declare a private variable, you place the statement in the declarations area rather than within a procedure. Because the `Private` statement has the same effect as the `Dim` statement for declaring private variables and can't be used within a procedure, it's clearer to use the `Private` statement rather than the `Dim` statement for declaring private variables.

WARNING   After you edit a procedure in the Visual Basic Editor, private variables and public variables are reset (their values are erased) when the Visual Basic Editor recompiles the code. If you're testing a project that uses private or public variables, you need to reinitialize (reassign values to) them after each edit you make.

PUBLIC SCOPE

A variable with public scope is available to all procedures in all modules in the project that contains it.

To declare a public variable, you use the `Public` keyword in the declarations area at the beginning of a module, before the `Sub` statement for the first procedure in the module—for example:

```
Option Explicit
Public intMyVar As Integer
```

The second statement declares the public variable `intMyVar` as the Integer type.

NOTE   The declarations area appears at the beginning of each module that contains declarations. For example, if you choose to use explicit variable declarations (by selecting the Require Variable Declaration check box on the Editor page of the Options dialog box), the Visual Basic Editor enters the `Option Explicit` declaration at the start of each new module you create. If not, the Visual Basic Editor creates the declarations area when you first enter a statement there manually.

Like private variables, public variables retain their value as long as the project that contains them is open. For example, if you wanted to track the user's name through a series of operations in Word, you could create an `AutoExec` procedure that prompted the user to enter their name when they started Word. (`AutoExec` is the built-in name for a procedure that runs automatically when Word starts.) By storing the result of their input in a public variable, you could then retrieve the value for use later in the same Word session. Listing 6.1 shows an example of using a public variable with an `AutoExec` procedure like this.

Public variables are reset when the Visual Basic Editor recompiles code, so you'll need to reinitialize them after editing your code.

LISTING 6.1:

```
1.  Public strCurrentUser As String
2.
3.  Sub AutoExec()
4.      strCurrentUser = InputBox("Please enter your name.", _
            "Current User Identity")
5.  End Sub
6.
7.  Sub Identify_Current_User()
8.      MsgBox "The current user is " & strCurrentUser, _
            vbOKOnly + vbInformation, "Current User"
9.  End Sub
```

This code consists of three different parts:

◆ Line 1 declares the public String variable strCurrentUser.

◆ Lines 3 through 5 contain the AutoExec procedure. This procedure runs each time the user starts Word. Line 4 displays an input box that prompts the user to enter their name and stores their response in the public variable strCurrentUser.

◆ Lines 7 through 9 contain the Identify_Current_User procedure, which simply displays a message box that gives the name of the user, along with lead-in text and an information icon and title bar for completeness.

Test these procedures by stepping first through the AutoExec procedure and then through the Identify_Current_User procedure in the Visual Basic Editor by using the F8 key, but to see their effect, create the procedures and then exit Word. When you restart Word, the AutoExec procedure displays the input box for you to enter your name. At any point thereafter (until you exit Word), you can run the Identify_Current_User procedure, and VBA displays a message box with the name you entered.

WARNING Because public variables retain their value when no procedure is running, they continue to take up space in memory. If you use large numbers of public variables, you might run short of memory or cause increased swap-file use on a computer with limited quantities of memory available.

USING STATIC VARIABLES

Beside Dim, Private, and Public, there's also the Static keyword, which you can use for declaring *static* variables—variables whose values you want to preserve between calls to the procedure in which they are declared. Static variables are similar to public variables in that their lifetime is not limited to the duration of the procedure that declares them. The difference is that static variables, once declared, are available only to the procedure that declared them, whereas public variables are available to all procedures once they've been declared.

Static variables are useful for maintaining information on a process that you need to run a number of times during a session of the application, either to maintain a running total (for example, a count of the times you performed a procedure) or to keep at hand a piece of information that may prove useful when you run a procedure a second or subsequent time.

The following statement declares the static String variable `strSearchTerm1`:

```
Static strSearchTerm1 As String
```

NOTE Like public variables, static variables take up memory once you've created them, so don't use them unnecessarily.

Specifying the Data Type for a Variable

Table 6.2 explains the data types that VBA supports and the amount of memory each variable type requires.

TABLE 6.2:

VARIABLE	SHORT DESCRIPTION	MEMORY REQUIRED
Boolean	`True` or `False`	2 bytes
Byte	An integer from 0 to 255	1 byte
Currency	A positive or negative number with up to 15 digits to the left of the decimal point and 4 digits to the right of it	8 bytes
Date	A floating-point number with the date to the left of the decimal point and the time to the right of it	8 bytes
Decimal	An unsigned integer scaled by a power of 10	12 bytes
Double	A floating-point number with a negative value from -1.79769313486232^{308} to -4.94065645841247^{-324} or a positive value from 4.94065645841247^{-324} to 1.79769313486232^{308}	8 bytes
Integer	An integer from −32,768 to 32,767	2 bytes
Long	An integer from −2,147,483,648 to 2,147,483,647	4 bytes
Object	A reference to an object	4 bytes
Single	A floating-point number with a negative value from -3.40282^{338} to -1.401298^{-45} or a positive value from 1.401298^{-45} to 3.402823^{38}	4 bytes
String	A string of text, either variable length or fixed length	Variable-length String: 10 bytes plus the storage for the string. Fixed-length String: the storage for the string
Variant	Any type of data except a fixed-length string in a subtype of the Variant	Variants containing numbers: 16 bytes. Variants containing characters: 22 bytes plus the storage for the characters

The next few pages discuss these data types in detail.

DO YOU NEED TO SPECIFY THE DATA TYPE?

Specifying the data type for each variable you create is a good idea, but it's not compulsory. You can almost always use the default Variant data type (as you've done a couple of times so far) and let VBA figure out which subtype to assign to the Variant.

There are three disadvantages to using the Variant data type like this:

◆ First, the Variant data type takes up more memory than any of the other data types except long strings.

◆ Second, using the Variant data type causes your code to run more slowly. However, with short procedures (or long procedures involving relatively few variables), memory and speed are rarely an issue.

◆ Third, your code is harder for humans to read and to debug. This is more of a concern.

Chapter 18, which discusses how to optimize your code, explains the pros and cons of specifying data types for your variables.

BOOLEAN

A Boolean variable can be set only to `True` or `False`. You can use the keywords `True` and `False` to set the value of a Boolean variable, as in the second line below (the first declares the Boolean variable `blnProduct_Available`):

```
Dim blnProduct_Available As Boolean
blnProduct_Available = True
```

You can then retrieve the result of the Boolean variable and take action accordingly:

```
If blnProduct_Available = True Then
    MsgBox "The product is available."
Else                'blnProduct_Available = False
    MsgBox "The product is not available."
End If
```

When you convert a Boolean variable to another data type (such as a numeric value), `True` returns −1 and `False` returns 0. When you convert a numeric value to a Boolean value, 0 returns `False` and all other numbers (whether positive or negative) return `True`.

Boolean variables are a good place to start declaring the data types of your variables, simply because they're so easy to use. Boolean variables take up two bytes each.

BYTE

A Byte variable takes up the least memory of any data type—just one byte—and can store a number from 0 to 255.

CURRENCY

The Currency data type is designed for use with money. It allows for positive and negative numbers with up to 15 digits to the left of the decimal point and 4 digits to the right of it. Unlike the Single and Double data types, the Currency data type is exact, not rounded.

To implicitly declare a currency variable, use the type-declaration character @. For example, you could work out your weekly salary with a little simple math:

```
Sub Calculate_Weekly_Salary()
    Salary@ = InputBox("Enter your salary.", _
        "Calculate Weekly Salary")
    WeeklySalary@ = Salary / 52
    MsgBox WeeklySalary
End Sub
```

Currency variables take up eight bytes each.

DATE

The Date data type is relatively complex. VBA works with dates and times as floating-point numbers, with the date displayed to the left of the decimal point and the time to the right. VBA can handle dates from 1 January 100 to 31 December 9999 and times from 0:00:00 to 23:59:59.

NOTE   Computer programming typically stores a number in either of two ways: as a floating-point number or as a fixed-point number. A *floating-point number* is a number in which the quantity is given by one number multiplied by a power of the number base (for example, 10): the decimal point "floats" to different locations. A *fixed-point number* is one in which the decimal place remains in the same location.

You can enter date variables as literal date values—such as **6/30/36** or **June 30, 1936**—by placing a # sign before and after the literal date value:

```
#June 30, 1936#
```

When you move the insertion point from the line in the code window in which you've entered a literal date value between # signs, VBA converts the data to a number and changes the display to the date format set in your computer. For example, if you enter **June 30, 1936**, VBA will probably display it as 6/30/36. Likewise, you can enter a literal time value (for example, **#10:15PM#**) and VBA converts it to a number and displays it according to the current time format (for example, 10:15:00 PM).

WARNING   Always specify the century of the dates you use, because VBA may supply the wrong century if you don't. Earlier versions of VBA (for example, in Office 2000 and Office 97) used to assign any year from 1 through 29 to the twentieth century and any year from 30 through 00 to the twenty-first century.

Date variables take up eight bytes each.

DECIMAL

The Decimal data type stores unsigned integers scaled by powers of 10. *Unsigned* means that the integers carry no plus or minus designation.

NOTE You can't declare a Decimal variable directly: You can use the Decimal data type only within a Variant data type (discussed later in this section).

Decimal variables take up 12 bytes each.

DOUBLE

The Double data type is for floating-point numbers and can handle negative values from -1.79769313486232^{308} to -4.94065645841247^{-324} and positive numbers from 4.94065645841247^{-324} to 1.79769313486232^{308}. Some numbers in this range cannot be represented exactly in binary, so VBA rounds them.

NOTE *Double* here stands for double-precision floating point—the way in which the number is handled by the computer. *Single* (discussed later in this list) stands for single-precision floating point.

You can use the # type-declaration character to declare a Double variable implicitly. Double variables take up eight bytes each.

INTEGER

The Integer data type is the most efficient way of handling numbers from –32,768 to 32,767, a range that makes it useful for many procedures. For example, if you wanted to repeat an action 300 times, you could use an Integer variable for the counter, as in the following lines:

```
Dim intMyVar As Integer
For intMyVar = 1 to 300
    'repeat actions
Next intMyVar
```

Integer variables take up two bytes each.

LONG

The Long data type is for integer numeric values larger or smaller than those the Integer data type can handle: Long variables can handle numbers from –2,147,483,648 to 2,147,483,647. (For numbers even larger or smaller than these, use the Double data type, but beware of its rounding.)

Long variables use the type-declaration character & for implicit declarations and take up four bytes each.

OBJECT

The Object data type is for storing addresses that reference objects (for example, objects in an application's object model), providing an easy way to refer to an object.

Object variables take up four bytes each.

SINGLE

The Single data type, like the Double data type, is for working with floating-point numbers. Single can handle negative values from -3.40282^{338} to -1.401298^{-45} and positive values from 1.401298^{-45} to 3.402823^{38}. Some numbers in this range cannot be represented exactly in binary, so VBA rounds them.

Use the exclamation point type-declaration character to declare a Single variable implicitly (if you must use implicit declarations). Single variables take up four bytes each.

STRING

The String data type is for handling text:

◆ Variable-length strings can contain up to about two billion characters. They take up 10 bytes plus the storage required for the string.

◆ Fixed-length strings can contain from 1 to about 64,000 characters. They take up only the storage required for the string. If the data assigned to the string is shorter than the fixed length, VBA pads the data with trailing spaces to make up the full complement of characters. If the data assigned to the string is longer than the fixed length, VBA truncates the data after the relevant character. VBA counts the characters from the left end of the string: For example, if you assign the string Output to a fixed-length string that's four characters long, VBA stores Outp.

◆ Strings can contain letters, numbers, spaces, and punctuation, not to mention special characters.

◆ You can use the $ type-declaration character to declare a string implicitly, but (as usual) you'll do best to declare your strings explicitly, along with all your other variables.

VARIANT

The Variant data type, as mentioned earlier in this chapter, is assigned by VBA to all variables whose data type isn't declared—so a declaration such as Dim myUntypedVariable creates a Variant. (You can also declare a Variant variable explicitly: Dim myVariant As Variant, for example.) Variants can handle most of the different types of data, but there are a couple characteristics of Variants to keep in mind:

◆ Variants can't contain fixed-length string data. If you need to use a fixed-length string, you need to specify a fixed-length string.

◆ Variant variables can also contain four special values: Empty (which means the variable hasn't yet been initialized), Error (a special value used for tracking errors in a procedure), Nothing (a special value used for disassociating a variable from the object it was associated with), and Null (which you use to indicate that the variable deliberately contains no data).

Variant variables take up more memory than other types. Variant variables that contain numbers take up 16 bytes, and Variant variables that contain characters take up 22 bytes plus the storage required for the characters.

DECIDING AMONG TYPES FOR VARIABLES

If you found the details of the different types of variables confusing, relax. First, you can usually avoid the whole issue of choosing a variable type by declaring the variable either implicitly or explicitly and letting VBA assign the Variant data type with the appropriate subtype. Second, if you do choose to specify data types for some of your variables, you can apply a few straightforward rules to direct your choices:

◆ If the variable will contain only the values True and False, declare it as the Boolean data type.

◆ If the variable will always contain an integer (if it will never contain a fraction), declare it as the Integer data type. (If the number may be too big for the Integer data type, declare it as the Long data type instead.)

- ◆ If the variable will be used for calculating money, or if you require no-rounding fractions, use the Currency data type.

- ◆ If the variable may sometimes contain a fraction, declare it as the Single or Double data type.

- ◆ If the variable will always contain a string, declare it as the String data type.

TIP If you aren't sure what type of variable will best contain the information you're planning to use, start by declaring the variable as a Variant. Then step through the procedure in Break mode with the Locals window displayed (View ➤ Locals) and see what Variant subtype VBA assigns to the variable: You'll see a listing such as Variant/Double or Variant/String in the Type column. Test the procedure a couple more times to make sure this subtype is consistent, and then try declaring the variable as the data type indicated by the subtype. Run the code a few times to make sure that the new data type works.

Working with Constants

A constant is a named item that keeps a constant value during execution of a program. VBA provides many built-in constants, but you can also declare your own constants to help you work with information that stays constant through a procedure.

Declaring Your Own Constants

To declare your own constants, use the Const statement. By declaring a constant, you can simplify your code when you need to reuse a set value a number of times in your procedures.

SYNTAX

The syntax for the Const statement is as follows:

```
[Public/Private] Const constant [As type] = expression
```

Here, Public and Private are optional keywords used for declaring public or private scope for a constant. You'll learn how they work in a moment. *constant* is the name of the constant, which follows the normal rules for naming variables. *type* is an optional argument that specifies the data type of the constant. *expression* is a literal (a value written into your code), another constant, or a combination of the two.

As with variables, you can declare multiple constants in the same line by separating the statements with a comma:

```
Const conPerformer As String = "Carmen Singer", _
    conTicketPrice As String = "$34.99"
```

EXAMPLE

Declaring a constant in VBA works in a similar way to declaring a variable explicitly, but you declare the value of the constant when you declare the constant (rather than at a later point of your choosing). You can't change its value afterward.

As an example, take a look at the statements below:

```
Const conVenue As String = "Davies Hall"
Const conDate As Date = #December 31, 2005#
MsgBox "The concert is at " & conVenue & " on " _& conDate & "."
```

The first line declares the constant conVenue as a String data type and assigns it the data Davies Hall. The second line declares the constant conDate as a Date string type and assigns it the date December 31, 2005. (When you finish creating this line of code and move the insertion point to another line, VBA changes the date to the date format set in your computer's clock—#12/31/2005#, for example.) The third line displays a message box containing a string concatenated from the three text items in double quotation marks, the conVenue string constant, and the conDate date constant.

Choosing the Scope and Lifetime for Your Constants

The default scope for a constant declared in a procedure is local—that is, its scope is the procedure that declares it. Consequently, its lifetime is the time for which the procedure runs. But you can set a different scope and lifetime for your constants by using the Public or Private keywords.

◆ To declare a private constant, place the declaration at the beginning of the module in which you want the constant to be available. A private constant's lifetime isn't limited, but it's available only to procedures in the module in which it's declared:

```
Private Const conPerformer As String = "Carmen Singer"
```

◆ To declare a public constant, place the declaration at the beginning of a module. A public constant's lifetime isn't limited, and it's available to all procedures in all modules in the project in which it's declared:

```
Public Const conTicketPrice As String = "$34.99"
```

Working with Enumerations

An *enumeration* is a predefined list of unique integers that have individual names and meanings in a particular context. An enumeration is typically used to set a property of an object. Each integer in the enumeration has a meaning to VBA and a name that allows you to refer to it easily. The names that correspond to the integers in the enumeration are called *enumerated constants*.

For example, when you use the MsgBox function to display a message box using VBA, you can use the enumerated constants in the VbMsgBoxStyle enumeration to specify the type of message box required. If you require an icon in the message box, you can specify the enumerated constant vbCritical or the integer 16 to get a Stop icon, the enumerated constant vbQuestion or the integer 32 to get a question-mark icon, the enumerated constant vbExclamation or the integer 48 to get an exclamation-point icon, or the enumerated constant vbInformation or the integer 64 to get an information icon. The enumerated constants are far easier for humans to grasp and remember than the values to which they are mapped.

VBA includes many built-in enumerations, and the Visual Basic Editor displays the list of available enumerated constants to help you select the appropriate integer value when you're creating code.

You can also define your own enumerations in custom objects that you create.

Chapter 7

Using Array Variables

◆ Understanding what arrays are and what you use them for

◆ Creating and using arrays

◆ Redimensioning an array

◆ Erasing an array

◆ Finding out whether a variable is an array

◆ Sorting an array

◆ Searching an array

In this chapter, you learn how to use array variables—variables that can each store multiple values at the same time. You start by examining what arrays are and what you use them for. You then examine how to create them, populate them, and erase them. Along the way, you look at how to resize an array to make it contain more (or fewer) values, how to specify the scope for an array, and how to find out whether a variable is an array or a regular, single-value variable.

What Is an Array?

An *array* is a variable on steroids—a variable that can contain a number of values that have the same data type. VBA treats an array as a single variable that can store multiple values. You can refer to the array itself to work with all the values it contains, or you can refer to the individual values stored within the array by using their index numbers, which indicate their positions within the array. If you're having difficulty visualizing what this means, try picturing an array as a list. Each item in the list is located in its own row and is identified by an index number, so you can access the value of the item by specifying the index number. You'll see visual examples of arrays later in this chapter.

NOTE An array with the Variant data type can store multiple types of data.

That's a simple array, one that has only one dimension. You can also declare multidimensional arrays, as discussed later in this chapter.

An array is *delimited* (or bounded) by a lower bound and an upper bound. By default, the lower bound is zero, so the first item in an array is indexed as zero. This can be confusing, because you're always working with an index number that's one lower than the item's position in the array. But VBA also lets you make the default index number of the first item in an array 1 by using an `Option Base 1` statement at the beginning of the module that contains the array. This makes the index number for each item in the array the same as the item's position in the array, so the array is easier to work with.

```
Option Base 1
```

Declaring an Array

An array is a kind of variable, so you would declare it by using the regular keywords: `Dim`, `Private`, `Public`, or `Static`. To indicate that it's an array, you add a pair of parentheses after the array's name. For example, the following statement declares an array named `curMonthProfit`:

```
Dim curMonthProfit()
```

That example creates a Variant array. VBA then assigns the appropriate subtype or subtypes when you store data in the array.

You can specify the data type of the array just as for a variable. For example, the following statement declares the array named `curMonthProfit` and assigns the Currency data type:

```
Dim curMonthProfit() As Currency
```

You can also declare the number of items in the array by using an *array subscript*. For example, the following statement declares the array named `curMonthProfit`, assigns the Currency data type, and specifies that the array contains 12 items:

```
Dim curMonthProfit(11) As Currency
```

NOTE The array subscript in the `Dim curMonthProfit(11) As Currency` statement is 11 rather than 12 because counting starts at 0 rather than 1. The first item is `curMonthProfit(0)`, the second is `curMonthProfit(1)`, and the twelfth is `curMonthProfit(11)`.

Figure 7.1 shows a simple representation of the single-dimensional array created by the `Dim curMonthProfit(11) As Currency` statement.

To make numbering start at 1, add an `Option Base` statement to the declarations area at the beginning of the module in which you declare the array. Here is an example:

```
Option Base 1    'at the beginning of the code sheet

Dim curMonthProfit(12) As Currency
```

Figure 7.2 shows a simple representation of how this array would look.

NOTE Omitting the data type and making VBA automatically use the Variant data type causes slightly increased memory usage, which could (under extreme circumstances) slow the performance of the computer: Because an array needs storage for each item it contains, a large array can consume a significant amount of memory. This is particularly true with multidimensional arrays.

You can also specify both bounds of an array explicitly:

```
Option Base 1    'at the beginning of the code sheet

Dim curMonthProfit(1 To 12) As Currency
```

FIGURE 7.1
The single-dimensional array created by the statement Dim curMonthProfit(11) As Currency can be thought of as looking like this.

Element #	Name	Contents
0	curMonthProfit(0)	—
1	curMonthProfit(1)	—
2	curMonthProfit(2)	—
3	curMonthProfit(3)	—
4	curMonthProfit(4)	—
5	curMonthProfit(5)	—
6	curMonthProfit(6)	—
7	curMonthProfit(7)	—
8	curMonthProfit(8)	—
9	curMonthProfit(9)	—
10	curMonthProfit(10)	—
11	curMonthProfit(11)	—

FIGURE 7.2
The single-dimensional array created by the statement Dim curMonthProfit(12) As Currency with the Option Base 1 statement

Element #	Name	Contents
1	curMonthProfit(1)	—
2	curMonthProfit(2)	—
3	curMonthProfit(3)	—
4	curMonthProfit(4)	—
5	curMonthProfit(5)	—
6	curMonthProfit(6)	—
7	curMonthProfit(7)	—
8	curMonthProfit(8)	—
9	curMonthProfit(9)	—
10	curMonthProfit(10)	—
11	curMonthProfit(11)	—
12	curMonthProfit(12)	—

NOTE Because working with arrays is much easier if you use an Option Base 1 statement, the examples in the rest of this chapter use Option Base 1 statements.

Storing Values in an Array

To assign a value to an item in an array, you use the index number to identify the item. For example, the following statements assign the values London, Hong Kong, and Taipei to the first three items in the array strLocations:

```
Option Base 1

Dim strLocations(6) As String
strLocations(1) = "London"
strLocations(2) = "Hong Kong"
strLocations(3) = "Taipei"
```

Figure 7.3 shows how this array can be envisioned.

FIGURE 7.3

A simple String array with three values assigned

Element #	Name	Contents
1	strLocations(1)	London
2	strLocations(2)	Hong Kong
3	strLocations(3)	Taipei
4	strLocations(4)	—
5	strLocations(5)	—
6	strLocations(6)	—

Multidimensional Arrays

The curMonthProfit example in the previous section is a one-dimensional array, which is the easiest kind of array to use. But VBA supports arrays with up to 60 dimensions—enough to tax the visualization skills of anyone without a Ph.D. in multidimensional modeling. You probably won't want to get this complicated with arrays—two, three, or four dimensions are enough for most purposes.

To declare a multidimensional array, you separate the dimensions with commas. For example, the following statements declare a two-dimensional array named MyArray with three items in each dimension:

```
Option Base 1
Dim MyArray(3, 3)
```

Figure 7.4 shows how you might represent the resulting array.

FIGURE 7.4

You can think of a two-dimensional array as consisting of rows and columns.

Column 1	Column 2	Column 3
1,1	2,1	3,1
1,2	2,2	3,2
1,3	2,3	3,3

Multidimensional arrays sound forbidding, but a two-dimensional array is quite straightforward if you think of it basically as a table that consists of rows and columns. Here, the first series of 10 elements would appear in the first column of the table, and the second series of 10 elements would appear in the second column. The information in any series doesn't need to be related to information in the other series, although it does need to be the same data type. For example, you could assign 10 folder names to the first dimension of a String variable array, 10 filenames to the second dimension (more strings), the names of your 10 cats to the third, the list of assassinated or impeached U.S. presidents to the fourth, and so on. You could then access the information in the array by specifying the position of the item you want to access—for instance, the second item in the first column of the table. You'll learn how to do this in just a minute.

Similarly, you could picture a three-dimensional array as being something like a workbook of spreadsheets—rows and columns, with further rows and columns in the third dimension (down, or away from you). But that's about the range of easily pictureable arrays—four-dimensional and larger arrays start to tax the imagination.

Declaring a Dynamic Array

You can declare both *fixed-size* arrays and *dynamic* arrays. The examples you've seen so far were fixed-size arrays. For instance, the size of the `curMonthProfit` array was specified as 12 items.

Dynamic arrays are useful when you need to store a variable number of items. For example, for a procedure that arranges two windows side by side, you might create an array to contain the name of each open window. Because you won't know how many windows will be open when you run the procedure, you may want to use a dynamic array to contain the information.

To declare a dynamic array, you use a declaration statement without specifying the number of items, by including the parentheses but leaving them empty. For example, the following statement declares the dynamic array `arrTestArray` and causes VBA to assign it the Variant data type:

```
Dim arrTestArray()
```

Redimensioning an Array

You can change the size of, or *redimension*, a dynamic array by using the `ReDim` statement. For example, to redimension the dynamic array `arrTestArray` declared in the previous example and assign it a size of five items, you could use the following statement:

```
ReDim arrTestArray(5)
```

When you use `ReDim` to redimension an array like this, you lose the values currently in the array. If so far you've only declared the array as a dynamic array, and it contains nothing, losing its contents won't bother you; but at other times, you'll want to increase the size of an array while keeping its current contents. To preserve the existing values in an array when you raise its upper bound, use a `ReDim Preserve` statement instead of a straight `ReDim` statement:

```
ReDim Preserve arrTestArray(5)
```

If you use `ReDim Preserve` to lower the upper bound of the array, you lose the information stored in any subscripts not included in the redimensioned array. For example, if you have a five-subscript array with information in each slot, and you redimension it using `ReDim Preserve` so that it has only three subscripts, you lose the information in the fourth and fifth subscripts.

NOTE   ReDim Preserve works only for the last dimension of the array. You can't preserve the data in other dimensions in a multidimensional array.

Returning Information from an Array

To return information from an array, you use the index number to specify the position of the information you want to return. For example, the following statement returns the fourth item in the array named arrMyArray and displays it in a message box:

```
Option Base 1

MsgBox arrMyArray(4)
```

The following statement returns the fifth item in the second dimension of a two-dimensional array named arrMy2DArray and displays it in a message box:

```
Option Base 1

MsgBox arrMy2DArray(2,5)
```

NOTE   To return multiple items from an array, specify each item individually.

Erasing an Array

To erase the contents of an array, use the Erase statement with the name of the array. This statement reinitializes the items in a fixed-size array and frees the memory taken by items in dynamic arrays (completely erasing the array). For example, the following statement erases the contents of the fixed-size array named arrMyArray:

```
Erase arrMyArray
```

Finding Out Whether a Variable Is an Array

Because an array is a type of variable, you may occasionally need to check whether a particular variable name denotes an array or a *scalar variable* (a variable that isn't an array). To find out whether a variable is an array, use the IsArray function with the variable's name. For example, the following statements check the variable MyVariable and display the results in a message box:

```
If IsArray(MyVariable) = True Then
    Msg = "MyVariable" & " is an array."
Else
    Msg = "MyVariable" & " is not an array."
End If
MsgBox Msg, vbOKOnly + vbInformation, "Array Check"
```

Finding the Bounds of an Array

To find the bounds of an array, use the LBound function and the UBound function. LBound returns the *lower bound,* the index number of the first item; UBound returns the upper bound, the index number of the last item.

The LBound function and the UBound function take the following syntax:

```
LBound(array [, dimension])
UBound(array [, dimension])
```

Here, *array* is a required argument specifying the name of the array, and *dimension* is an optional variant specifying the dimension whose bound you want to return—1 for the first dimension, 2 for the second, and so on. (If you omit the *dimension* argument, VBA assumes you mean the first dimension.)

For example, the following statement returns the upper bound of the second dimension in the array named `arrMyArray` and displays it in a message box:

```
MsgBox UBound(arrMyArray, 2)
```

Sorting an Array

You'll often need to sort an array, especially when you load information into the array from an external source rather than assigning values one by one in your code.

Sorting is easy to understand conceptually: You simply put things into the desired order. For example, you could sort the strings in one array into alphabetical order or reverse alphabetical order, or the integers in another array into ascending order or descending order. But executing sorting programmatically is much more difficult.

This section shows you a simple form of sorting—the bubble sort, so called because the items being sorted to the earlier positions in the array gradually bubble up to the top. The bubble sort consists of two loops that compare two items in the array; if the second item belongs further up the list than the first item, the sort reverses their positions, and the comparisons continue until the whole list is sorted into order. The bubble sort is a relatively inefficient method of sorting items, but it's easy to grasp, and processor cycles are comparatively cheap these days.

NOTE   Chapter 12 shows you how to work with loops.

Listing 7.1 contains the code for the bubble sort.

LISTING 7.1:

```
1.  Option Explicit
2.  Option Base 1
3.
4.  Sub Sort_an_Array()
5.
6.      'declare the array and other variables
7.      Dim strArray(12) As String
8.      Dim strTemp As String
9.      Dim strMsg As String
10.     Dim X As Integer, Y As Integer, i As Integer
11.
12.     'assign strings to the array
13.     strArray(1) = "nihilism"
14.     strArray(2) = "defeatism"
```

```
15.        strArray(3) = "hope"
16.        strArray(4) = "gloom"
17.        strArray(5) = "euphoria"
18.        strArray(6) = "despondency"
19.        strArray(7) = "optimism"
20.        strArray(8) = "pessimism"
21.        strArray(9) = "misery"
22.        strArray(10) = "happiness"
23.        strArray(11) = "bliss"
24.        strArray(12) = "mania"
25.
26.        strMsg = "Current items in array:" & vbCr & vbCr
27.        For i = 1 To UBound(strArray)
28.            strMsg = strMsg & i & ":" & vbTab & strArray(i) & vbCr
29.        Next i
30.        MsgBox strMsg, vbOKOnly + vbInformation, "Array Sorting: 1"
31.
32.        For X = LBound(strArray) To (UBound(strArray) - 1)
33.            For Y = (X + 1) To UBound(strArray)
34.                If strArray(X) > strArray(Y) Then
35.                    strTemp = strArray(X)
36.                    strArray(X) = strArray(Y)
37.                    strArray(Y) = strTemp
38.                    strTemp = ""
39.                End If
40.            Next Y
41.        Next X
42.
43.        strMsg = "Items in sorted array:" & vbCr & vbCr
44.        For i = 1 To UBound(strArray)
45.            strMsg = strMsg & i & ":" & vbTab & strArray(i) & vbCr
46.        Next i
47.        MsgBox strMsg, vbOKOnly + vbInformation, "Array Sorting: 2"
48.
49. End Sub
```

Here's what happens in Listing 7.1:

◆ Line 1 contains an `Option Explicit` statement to force explicit declarations of variables, and line 2 contains an `Option Base 1` statement to make the numbering of arrays start at 1 rather than 0. These two statements appear in the declarations part of the code sheet, before any other procedure. Line 3 is a spacer—a blank line inserted to make the code easier to read.

◆ Line 4 begins the `Sort_an_Array` procedure. Line 5 is a spacer.

◆ Line 6 is a comment line prefacing the declaration of the array and the variables. Line 7 declares the String array `strArray` with 12 subscripts. Line 8 declares the String variable `strTemp`. Line 9 declares the String variable `strMsg`. Line 10 declares the Integer variables X, Y, and i. Line 11 is a spacer.

◆ Line 12 is a comment line explaining that the next 12 statements (lines 13 through 24) assign strings to the array. The strings used are single words loosely associated with moods. Line 25 is a spacer.

◆ Lines 26 through 30 build a string out of the strings assigned to the array and then display it in a message box. This section of code is included to help the user easily see what's going on if they run the procedure rather than stepping through it. Line 26 assigns introductory text and two carriage returns (two vbCr characters) to the String variable strMsg. Line 27 starts a For… Next loop that runs from i = 1 to i = UBound(strArray)—in other words, once for each item in the array. (The loop could also have run to i = 12 because the upper bound of the array is set, but using the upper bound is more flexible than hard-coding values.) Line 28 adds to strMsg the value of the counter variable i, a colon, a tab (vbTab), the contents of the array item currently referenced (strArray(i)), and a carriage return (vbCr). Line 29 concludes the loop, and line 30 displays a message box containing strMsg, as shown in Figure 7.5. Line 31 is a spacer.

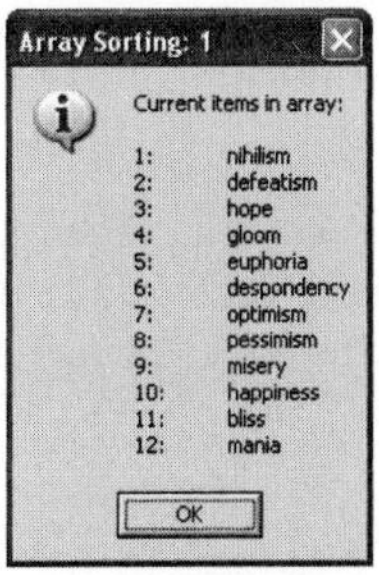

FIGURE 7.5

The Sort_an_Array procedure displays a message box of the unsorted terms so that the user can see what's going on.

Array Sorting: 1

Current items in array:

1:	nihilism
2:	defeatism
3:	hope
4:	gloom
5:	euphoria
6:	despondency
7:	optimism
8:	pessimism
9:	misery
10:	happiness
11:	bliss
12:	mania

OK

◆ The sorting part of the procedure takes place in lines 32–41. Here are the details:

  ◆ Line 32 begins the outer For… Next loop, which ends in line 41. This loop runs from X = LBound(strArray) (in other words, X = 1) to X = (UBound(strArray) - 1) (in other words, X = 11—the upper bound of the array minus 1).

  ◆ Line 33 begins the inner (nested) For… Next loop, which runs from Y = (X + 1) to Y = UBound(strArray). Line 40 ends this loop.

  ◆ Line 34 compares strArray(X) to strArray(Y). If strArray(X) is greater than strArray(Y)—in other words, if strArray(X) should appear after strArray(Y) in the sorted array—line 35 assigns strArray(X) to strTemp, line 36 assigns strArray(Y) to strArray(X), and line 37 assigns strTemp to strArray(Y), thus switching the values. Line 38 restores strTemp to an empty string. Line 39 ends the If statement. Line 40 ends the inner loop; line 41 ends the outer loop; and line 42 is a spacer.

◆ Lines 43 through 47 essentially repeat lines 26 through 30, displaying a message box (shown in Figure 7.6) of the sorted array—again, so that the user can see that the sort has worked.

◆ Line 48 is a spacer, and line 49 ends the procedure.

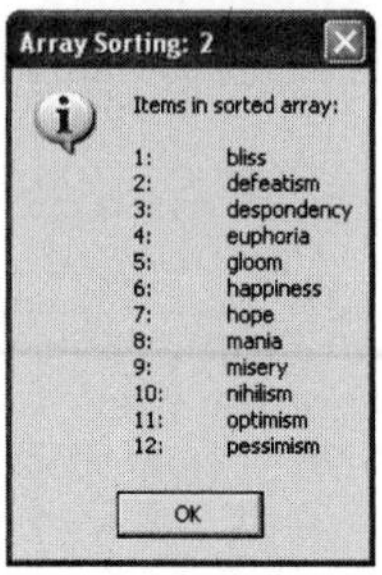

FIGURE 7.6
When the Sort_an_
Array procedure has
finished sorting, it dis-
plays the sorted list in
another message box.

Searching through an Array

Another action you'll often need to perform with an array is searching to find a particular value in it. This section shows you two methods of sorting—a linear search, which you can perform on either a sorted array or an unsorted array, and a binary search, which you can perform only on a sorted array.

Performing a Linear Search through an Array

A *linear* search is a very simple form of search: You start at the beginning of the array and continue until you find your target, or until you reach the end of the array.

Before starting the code, display the Immediate window by pressing Ctrl+G or choosing View ➢ Immediate Window. This procedure prints information to the Immediate window so that you can see what's going on—and whether the code is running as intended.

Listing 7.2 contains the code for a simple linear search through a one-dimensional array.

LISTING 7.2:

```
1.   Option Explicit
2.   Option Base 1
3.
4.   Sub Linear_Search_of_Array()
5.
6.       'declare the array and the variables
7.       Dim intArray(10) As Integer
8.       Dim i As Integer
9.       Dim varUserNumber As Variant
10.      Dim strMsg As String
11.
12.      'add random numbers between 0 and 10 to the array
13.      'and print them to the Immediate window for reference
14.      For i = 1 To 10
15.          intArray(i) = Int(Rnd * 10)
16.          Debug.Print intArray(i)
17.      Next i
18.
```

```
19.  Loopback:
20.      varUserNumber = InputBox _
             ("Enter a number between 1 and 10 to search for:", _
             "Linear Search Demonstrator")
21.      If varUserNumber = "" Then End
22.      If Not IsNumeric(varUserNumber) Then GoTo Loopback
23.      If varUserNumber < 0 Or varUserNumber > 10 Then GoTo Loopback
24.
25.      strMsg = "Your value, " & varUserNumber & _
             ", was not found in the array."
26.
27.      For i = 1 To UBound(intArray)
28.          If intArray(i) = varUserNumber Then
29.              strMsg = "Your value, " & varUserNumber & _
                     ", was found at position " & i & " in the array."
30.              Exit For
31.          End If
32.      Next i
33.
34.      MsgBox strMsg, vbOKOnly + vbInformation, "Linear Search Result"
35.
36.  End Sub
```

Here's what happens in Listing 7.2:

◆ As in the previous listing, line 1 contains an Option Explicit statement to force explicit declarations of variables, and line 2 contains an Option Base 1 statement to make the numbering of arrays start at 1 rather than 0. These two statements appear in the declarations part of the code sheet, before any other procedure. Line 3 is a spacer.

◆ Line 4 begins the Linear_Search_of_Array procedure. Line 5 is a spacer.

◆ Line 6 is a comment line prefacing the declaration of the array and the other variables that the code uses. Line 7 declares the Integer array intArray with 10 subscripts. Line 8 declares the Integer variable i, which is often used as a counter variable. Line 9 declares the Variant variable varUserNumber, which the code uses to store the user's input from an input box. (More on this in a moment.) Line 10 declares the String variable strMsg. Line 11 is a spacer.

NOTE The procedure declares the variable varUserNumber as a Variant rather than an Integer so that Visual Basic doesn't automatically stop with an error if the user enters something other than an integer (for example, text) in the input box.

◆ Lines 12 and 13 contain an extended comment line on the code in lines 14 through 17. (These two lines could be combined into one logical line by adding a continuation character at the end of the first line and omitting the apostrophe at the beginning of the second line, but the code is easier to read when the second line begins with the comment character as well.)

◆ Line 14 begins a For... Next loop that runs from i = 1 to 1 = 10. Line 15 assigns to the current item in the intArray array the integer result of a random number multiplied by 10: intArray(i) = Int(Rnd * 10). (The Rnd function generates a random number between 0 and 1 with a decent number of decimal places. So the procedure multiplies that random number by 10 to get a number between 0 and 10 and then takes the integer portion of the number.) Line 16 then uses the Print method of the Debug object to print the current item in intArray to the Immediate window, producing an easy way of keeping track of the values that the array contains. Line 17 ends the loop with the Next i statement. Line 18 is a spacer.

◆ Line 19 contains a label, Loopback, used to return execution to this point in the code if the user does not meet required conditions.

◆ Line 20 assigns to the Variant variable varUserNumber the result of an input box (shown in Figure 7.7) prompting the user to enter a number between 0 and 10.

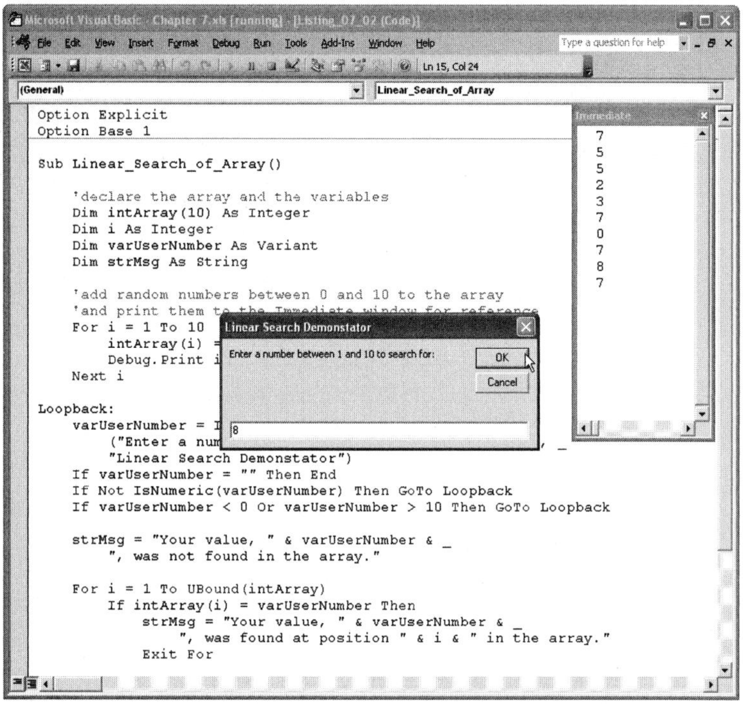

FIGURE 7.7
The Linear_Search_ of_Array procedure displays an input box prompting the user to enter a number between 0 and 10. Enter one of the numbers that the procedure has printed to the Immediate window to get a positive result.

◆ Line 21 then compares the contents of varUserNumber to an empty string—the result you get if the user clicks the Cancel button in the input box or clicks the OK button without entering anything in the text box. If varUserNumber is an empty string, the End statement ends execution of the procedure.

◆ Line 22 uses the IsNumeric function to see whether the contents of varUserNumber are numeric. If they're not, the GoTo Loopback statement returns execution to the Loopback label, after which the input box is displayed again for the user to try their luck once more. Line 23 checks to see if `varUserNumber` is less than 0 or greater than 10. If either is the case, another `GoTo Loopback` statement returns execution to the `Loopback` label, and the input makes another appearance. Line 24 is a spacer.

NOTE   Note the flexibility of VBA here: The code solicits user input and makes sure that it's a number between 0 and 10 (inclusive). Though that number is still stored in a Variant rather than explicitly converted to an Integer, VBA still performs the comparison needed.

◆ Line 25 assigns to the String variable `strMsg` a preliminary message stating that the value (which it specifies) was not found in the array. (If the code finds the value in the array, it changes the message before displaying it.) Line 26 is a spacer.

◆ Lines 27 through 32 contain the searching part of the procedure. Line 27 begins a `For... Next` loop that runs from `i = 1` to `i = UBound(intArray)`—once for each subscript in the array. Line 28 compares `intArray(i)` to `varUserNumber`; if there's a match, line 28 assigns to `strMsg` a string telling the user at which position in the array the value was found, and line 29 uses an `Exit For` statement to exit the `For... Next` loop. (If line 28 does not match, the `Next i` statement in line 32 causes the code to loop.)

◆ Line 33 is a spacer. Line 34 displays a message box containing `strMsg` to convey to the user the result of the linear search operation. Figure 7.8 shows the result of a successful search. Line 35 is a spacer, and line 36 ends the procedure.

FIGURE 7.8
Line 34 of Listing 7.2 displays a message box telling the user the result of the linear search operation.

Performing a Binary Search through an Array

As you saw in the previous section, a linear search is easy to perform, but it's pretty dumb—it starts looking at the beginning of the array and then looks through everything else in turn. This approach works fine for small searches, such as the 10-subscript array you searched in the last example, but you wouldn't want to try it on anything the size of a phone book—even for a small town. For even moderately heavy-duty searching, you need a smarter approach.

For conventional purposes, a *binary search* is a good way to approach searching a sorted array. A binary search formalizes the technique you probably use when searching for something that you expect to be in a given location—you focus down on the relevant area and search it thoroughly.

The binary search determines the relevant area by dividing the sorted array in half, establishing which half will contain the search item, and then repeating the divide-and-interrogate procedure until it either finds the search item or reaches the last subdivisible unit of the array without finding it. For example, say a binary search is searching for the value 789,789 in a million-subscript array that contains the numbers 1 through 1,000,000 in ascending order. It divides the array into two halves, each of which contains a half million subscripts. It establishes whether the search item is in the first half or the second half and then narrows the search to the appropriate half and divides it into new halves. It establishes whether the search item is in the first of these halves or the second and then focuses on that half, dividing *it* into halves—and so on until it finds the term or has gotten down to a single subscript.

This is a simple example, but a million's still a hefty number. Listing 7.3 makes things even simpler by using an array of a thousand subscripts that contains the numbers 1 through 1000 in order: The first subscript contains the number 1, the second subscript contains the number 2, and so on up to 1000. The example is unrealistic, but it makes it easy to see what's happening in the code.

LISTING 7.3:

```
1.   Option Explicit
2.   Option Base 1
3.
4.   Sub Binary_Search_of_Array()
5.
6.       'declare the array and the variables
7.       Dim intThousand(1000) As Integer
8.       Dim i As Integer
9.       Dim intTop As Integer
10.      Dim intMiddle As Integer
11.      Dim intBottom As Integer
12.      Dim varUserNumber As Variant
13.      Dim strMsg As String
14.
15.      'populate the array with numbers 1 to 1000, in order
16.      For i = 1 To 1000
17.          intThousand(i) = i
18.      Next i
19.
20.      'prompt the user for the search item
21.  Loopback:
```

```
22.          varUserNumber = InputBox _
                 ("Enter a number between 1 and 1000 to search for:", _
                 "Binary Search Demonstrator")
23.          If varUserNumber = "" Then End
24.          If Not IsNumeric(varUserNumber) Then GoTo Loopback
25.
26.          'search for the search item
27.          intTop = UBound(intThousand)
28.          intBottom = LBound(intThousand)
29.
30.          Do
31.              intMiddle = (intTop + intBottom) / 2
32.              If varUserNumber > intThousand(intMiddle) Then
33.                  intBottom = intMiddle + 1
34.              Else
35.                  intTop = intMiddle - 1
36.              End If
37.          Loop Until (varUserNumber = intThousand(intMiddle)) _
                 Or (intBottom > intTop)
38.
39.          'establish whether the search discovered the search item _
                 or not and add the appropriate information to strMsg
40.          If varUserNumber = intThousand(intMiddle) Then
41.              strMsg = "The search found the search item, " _
                     & varUserNumber & ", at position " & intMiddle _
                     & " in the array."
42.          Else
43.              strMsg = "The search did not find the search item, " _
                     & varUserNumber & "."
44.          End If
45.
46.          MsgBox strMsg, vbOKOnly & vbInformation, "Binary Search Result"
47.
48.  End Sub
```

Here's what happens in Listing 7.3:

◆ Line 1 contains an Option Explicit statement to force explicit declarations of variables, and line 2 contains an Option Base 1 statement to make the numbering of arrays start at 1 rather than 0. These two statements appear in the declarations part of the code sheet, before any procedure.

◆ Line 3 is a spacer. Line 4 declares the Binary_Search_of_Array procedure, and line 5 is another spacer.

◆ Line 6 is a comment line prefacing the declaration of the array (the thousand-subscript Integer array intThousand, declared in line 7) and the other variables that the procedure uses: the Integer variables i (line 8), intTop (line 9), intMiddle (line 10), and intBottom (line 11); the Variant variable varUserNumber (line 12); and the String variable strMsg (line 13). Line 14 is yet another spacer.

◆ Line 15 is a comment line announcing that lines 16 through 18 populate the array with the numbers 1 to 1000 in order. To do so, these lines use a For… Next loop that runs from i = 1 to i = 1000, assigning the current value of i to the subscript in the array referenced by i—in other words, assigning to each subscript the number that corresponds to its position in the array. Line 19 is a spacer.

◆ Line 20 is a comment line introducing the section of code (lines 21 through 24) that uses an input box (shown in Figure 7.9) to prompt the user to enter a number to search for and checks that they do so. As in the previous listing, this section of code checks to make sure that the user didn't enter an empty string in the input box (line 23) and terminates execution of the procedure if they did. It also uses a label named Loopback (in line 21) to which the code returns if what the user entered in the input box (in line 22) turns out not to be numeric when line 24 checks. Because this time you know which numbers the array will contain, you don't need to check to make sure that the user enters a suitable value. If they want to enter a value that doesn't appear in the array, so be it.

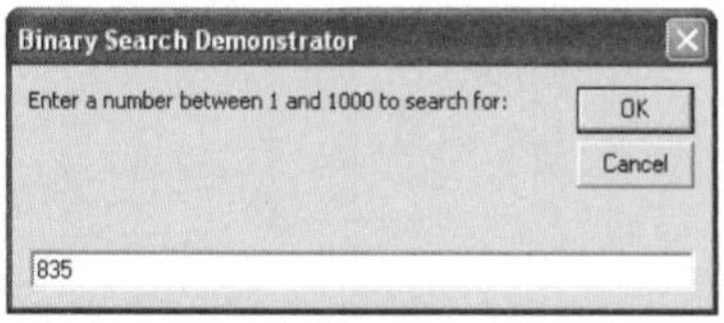

FIGURE 7.9

The Binary_Search_ of_Array procedure prompts the user to enter a number between 1 and 1000.

◆ Line 25 is a spacer, and line 26 is a comment that introduces the section of code that searches for the search item the user entered. Line 27 assigns to the intTop variable the upper bound of the array, and line 28 assigns to intBottom the lower bound. Line 29 is a spacer.

◆ Lines 30 through 37 contain a Do… Loop Until loop that performs the bulk of the binary searching. Here are the details:

◆ Line 30 starts the Do… Loop Until loop with the Do keyword, and line 37 ends it with the Loop Until keywords and the condition ((varUserNumber = intThousand(intMiddle)) Or (intBottom > intTop)). You'll look at loops in detail in Chapter 12; for now, all you need to know is that a Do… Loop Until runs once and then evaluates the condition in the Loop Until statement to determine whether it should end or run again. The condition here specifies that the loop continue until either the value of the subscript in the array identified by intMiddle (intThousand(intMiddle)) matches the value in varUserNumber or the value of intBottom is greater than the value of intTop (intBottom > intTop).

◆ Line 31 sets the value of the Integer variable intMiddle to the sum of intTop and intBottom divided by two: (intTop + IntBottom) / 2. Doing so gives the midpoint for dividing the array. For example, in the thousand-subscript array, intTop has a value of 1000 on the first iteration of the loop, and intBottom has a value of 0, so intMiddle receives the value 500 (1000 divided by 2).

◆ Line 32 tests whether varUserNumber is greater than the value stored in the subscript identified by intMiddle—intThousand(intMiddle), the midpoint of the current section of the array. If it is, the search needs to work on the top half of the array, so line 33 resets intBottom to intMiddle + 1. If it's not, the Else statement in line 34 kicks in, and line 35 resets intTop to intMiddle-1, so that the search works on the lower half of the array.

- ◆ Line 36 ends the `If` statement, and line 37 tests the condition and continues or terminates the loop, as appropriate.

- ◆ Line 38 is a spacer. Line 39 contains a two-line comment introducing the code in lines 40 through 44, which establish whether the search found the search item and assign suitable information to the `strMsg` String variable. Line 40 compares `varUserNumber` to `intThousand(intMiddle)`; if it matches, line 41 assigns to `strMsg` a string telling the user where the search item was found in the array. If it doesn't match, line 43 assigns a string telling the user that the search did not find the search item. Line 45 is a spacer, and line 46 displays a message box telling the user the result of the search. Figure 7.10 shows examples—one successful, one otherwise—of the message box.

- ◆ Line 47 is another spacer, and line 48 ends the procedure.

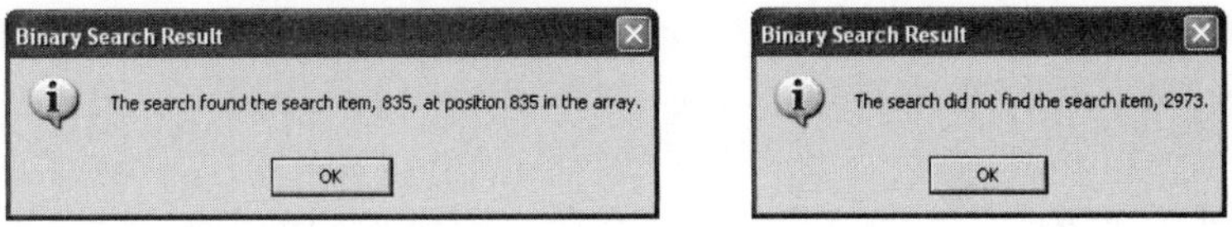

FIGURE 7.10

The `Binary_Search_of_Array` procedure tells the user whether the search was successful (top) or not (bottom).

The most complex part of the procedure is what happens in the loop. Download the code from the Sybex website, open it, and paste it into the Visual Basic Editor (it'll work in any VBA-enabled application). Then open up the module and follow these steps:

1. Display the Locals window (View ➢ Locals) so that you can track the values of the variables `intTop`, `intMiddle`, and `intBottom`. Figure 7.11 shows the Locals window while the procedure is running.

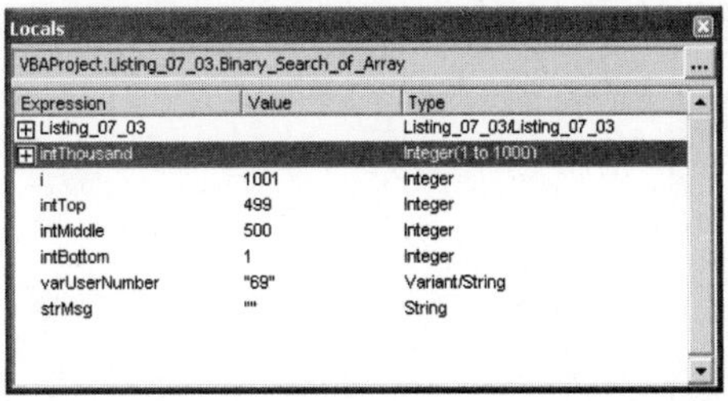

FIGURE 7.11

Use the Locals window to track the values of the `intTop`, `intMiddle`, and `intBottom` variables as the procedure runs.

2. Set a breakpoint in the procedure on line 22 by clicking in the margin indicator bar next to the statement that begins `varUserNumber = InputBox`. (Because the statement is broken onto two lines, the Visual Basic Editor displays two brown dots rather than one in the margin indicator bar.)

3. Press the F5 key (or choose Run ➢ Run Sub/UserForm) to run the code up to the breakpoint. VBA creates and populates the array and then stops at line 22.

4. Press the F8 key to step through the next statements. The first press displays the input box. Enter the value **69** for this example and click the OK button.

5. As the code enters the Do loop and cycles through it, watch the values of the variables intTop, intMiddle, and intBottom in the Locals window. You'll see them change, as shown in the list below.

Iteration	intTop	intMiddle	intBottom
0	1000	—	1
1	499	500	1
2	249	250	1
3	124	125	1
4	124	62	63
5	93	94	63
6	77	78	63
7	69	70	63
8	69	66	67
9	69	68	69
10	68	69	69

At the end of the tenth iteration of the loop, intThousand(intMiddle) is equal to varUserNumber, so the loop ends.

Chapter 8

Finding the Objects, Methods, and Properties You Need

◆ Understanding and using objects, properties, and methods

◆ Using collections of objects

◆ Finding objects, properties, and methods

◆ Using object variables to represent objects

In this chapter, you learn how to find the objects you need in the applications you're using. To learn the material in this chapter, you build on what you learned in the earlier chapters. You start by examining the concepts involved: what objects and collections are, what properties are, and what methods are. You then learn how to find the objects, collections, properties, and methods you need to make your code work. To identify these items, you use a number of tools you've already read about, including the Object Browser (which you used briefly in Chapter 4) and the Help files for VBA.

Along the way, this chapter explains how to use object variables to represent objects in your code.

What Is an Object?

VBA-enabled applications (and many other modern applications) consist of a number of discrete objects, each with its own characteristics and capabilities.

Building an application out of objects is called *object-oriented programming*, which is abbreviated to OOP. In theory, object-oriented programming has a number of benefits, including the code being easier to build and maintain, because you break down the code into objects of a manageable size.

Object-oriented programs should also be easier to understand than monolithic programs, because it's easier for most people to grasp the concept of individual objects with associated characteristics and actions than to remember a far longer list of capabilities for the application. It's also easier to get to the commands you need. For example, a table in Word is represented by a `Table` object, and a column is represented by a `Column` object. The `Column` object has a `Width` property that sets and returns its width. It's easier to know this information when it's broken down into small and easy-to-understand pieces than to deal with some complex command such as `WordTableSetColumnWidth` or `WordTableGetColumnWidth`.

A third benefit of object-oriented programs is that they can be extensible: The user can build custom objects to implement functionality that the application doesn't contain. For example, you can use VBA to build your own objects that do things that the applications themselves can't do.

Objects can—and frequently do—contain other objects. Typically, the objects in an object-oriented application are arranged into a logical hierarchy called the *object model* of the application.

This hierarchy gives the logical relationship of the objects to each other, through which you access them via VBA.

NOTE   This chapter discusses object models only a little, at the conceptual level: You need to know what an object model *is* in order to make sense of what you'll be learning in the following chapters, but you don't need to know the specifics of each object model to manipulate the objects used in the examples. Part 5 of this book examines the object models of each of the applications covered in this book in enough detail to get you started on exploring the depths of each object model on your own.

Most VBA host applications, including all the major Office applications, have an `Application` object that represents the application as a whole. The `Application` object has properties and methods for things that apply to the application as a whole. For example, many applications have a `Quit` method that exits the application and a `Visible` property that controls whether the application is visible or hidden.

In a typical object model, the `Application` object essentially contains all the other objects (and collections—groups—of objects) that make up the application. For example, Excel has an `Application` object that represents the Excel application, a `Workbook` object (grouped into the `Workbooks` collection) that represents a workbook, and a `Worksheet` object (grouped into the `Sheets` collection) that represents a worksheet. The `Workbook` object is contained within the `Application` object, because you normally need to have the Excel application open to work with an Excel workbook.

In turn, the `Worksheet` object is contained within the `Workbook` object, because you need to have an Excel workbook open to work with a worksheet. Walking further down the object model, the `Worksheet` object contains assorted other objects, including `Row` objects that represent rows in the worksheet, `Column` objects that represent columns in the worksheet, and `Range` objects (which represent ranges of cells)—and these in turn contain further objects.

To get to an object, you typically walk down through the hierarchy of the object model until you reach the object. For example, to get to a `Range` object in Excel, you would go through the `Application` object to the `Workbook` object, through the `Workbook` object to the appropriate `Sheet` object, and then to the `Range` object. The following statement shows an example using the range A1 in the first worksheet in the first open workbook (more on this in a minute):

```
Application.Workbooks(1).Sheets(1).Range("A1").Select
```

Because you'd have to go through the `Application` object to get to pretty much anything in the application, most applications expose a number of *creatable* objects—objects that you can access without referring explicitly to the `Application` object. These creatable objects are usually the most-used objects for the application, and by going through them, you can access most of the other objects without referring to the `Application` object. For example, Excel exposes the `Workbooks` collection as a creatable object, so you can use the following statement, which doesn't use the `Application` object, instead of the previous statement:

```
Workbooks(1).Sheets(1).Range("A1").Select
```

Any object can have properties and methods. The next sections discuss these items in detail.

Properties

In VBA, a *property* is an attribute or characteristic of an object—a way of describing it or part of it. Most objects have multiple properties that describe each relevant aspect of the object. Each property has a specific data type for the information it stores. For example, the objects that represent files (such as documents, workbooks, or presentations) typically have a Boolean property named `Saved` that stores a value denoting whether all changes in the object have been saved (a value of True) or not (a value of False). These two values encompass the range of possibilities for the object: It can either contain unsaved changes or not contain unsaved changes, but there is no third state.

Similarly, most objects that represent files have a Name property that contains the name of the file in question. The Name property is a String property because it needs to contain text, and that text can be set to just about anything (limited by the 255-character path that Windows can support and certain characters—such as colons and pipe characters—that it cannot).

To work with a property, you *return* (get) it to find out its current value or *set* it to a value of your choosing. Many properties are *read/write*, meaning that you can both *get* (return) and set their values, but some properties are *read-only*, meaning that you can return their values but not set them.

The Saved property is read/write for most applications, so you can set it. This means that you can tell the application that a file contains unsaved changes when it really doesn't or that it contains no unsaved changes when it actually has some. (Changing the Saved property can be useful when you're manipulating a file without the user's explicit knowledge.) But the Name property of a file object is read-only—you'll typically set the name by issuing a Save As command, after which you cannot change the name from within the application while the file is open. So you can return the Name property but not set it. You'll also encounter some write-only properties, properties that you can set but that you cannot get.

When an object contains another object, or a collection, it typically has a property that you call to return the object or the collection. For example, the Word Document object includes a PageSetup property that returns the PageSetup object for the document (the PageSetup object contains settings such as paper size, orientation, and margins for the document) and a Tables property that you call to return the Tables collection.

Each object of the same type has the same set of properties but stores its own values for them. For example, if you're running PowerPoint and have three Presentation objects open, each can have a different Name property. The setting for a property in one object has nothing to do with the setting for that property in another object: Each object is independent of the other objects.

Methods

A *method*—an action that an object can perform—is shared (so to speak) among the objects of that type. For example, the Document object in various applications has a Save method that saves the document. You can use the Save method on different Document objects—Documents(1).Save saves the first Document object in the Documents collection, and Documents(2).Save saves the second Document object—but it does the same thing in each case. An object can have one or more methods associated with it. Some objects have several dozen methods to implement all the functionality they need.

The Save method appears in many applications, as do other methods such as SaveAs (which saves the file with a different name, location, or both) and Close (which closes the file), but other methods are unique to an application. For example, the Presentation object in PowerPoint has an AddBaseline method that applies a baseline (consisting either of the active presentation or of a specified presentation file) that enables you to track changes for a merge. The Document object in Word has no AddBaseline method, but it has an AcceptAllRevisions method that accepts all revisions in the document. PowerPoint doesn't have an AcceptAllRevisions method.

Some methods are associated with more than one object. For example, the Delete method is associated with many different objects. As its name suggests, the Delete method usually deletes the specified object. But other methods perform somewhat different actions depending on the object they're working with—so even if you're familiar with a method from using it with one object, you need to make sure that it'll have the effect you expect when you use it with another object.

Some methods take one or more arguments that supply information. Some arguments are required, while others are optional. Other methods take no arguments. When a method applies to multiple objects, it may have different syntax for different objects. Again, even if you're familiar with a method, you need to know exactly what it does with the object for which you're planning to use it.

To use a method, you access it through the object involved. For example, to close the `ActivePresentation` object, which represents the active presentation in PowerPoint, you use the `Close` method:

```
ActivePresentation.Close
```

OBJECTIFYING OBJECTS, METHODS, AND PROPERTIES

If you have a hard time getting a grip on objects, methods, and properties, you can draw a somewhat strained comparison between logical objects, properties, and methods in VBA and physical objects, properties, and actions in the real world. Try this example.

Let's say you have a massive dog—a Pyrenean mountain dog; white; 200 lb.; male, not, uh, *fixed*; four years old; named Max (after Max Frisch).

Max performs all the usual dog actions—sleep, run, eat, bark, growl, chew things, various unmentionable actions that we'll skip over, and so on—and has a couple of unusual (for dogs) actions built in, such as slobbering on command, knocking down people, and intimidating bailiffs.

If Max were implemented in VBA, he'd be a Dog object in a Dogs collection. The Dog object for Max would have properties such as these:

Property	Property Type	Value
Name	Read-only String	Max
Sex	Read-only String	Male
Fixed	Read/write Boolean	False
Height	Read/write Long	36
Weight	Read/write Long	200
Age	Read/write Integer	4
Type	Read/write String	Pyrenean Mountain
Color	Read/write String	White

Max would have methods such as Slobber, Bark, KnockDown, Intimidate, Chew, Run, and so on. Some of these methods would require arguments. The Slobber method would definitely need arguments like this, probably using Dog-specific constants that start with the dog designation:

```
Dogs("Max").Slobber OnWhat:="MyKnee", How:=dogSlobberDisgustingly
```

The Dog object would contain objects representing the many component pieces of the dog—ears, eyes, tongue, brain (probably), stomach, legs, tail, and so on. Each of these objects would have its own properties and methods as appropriate. For example, the Tail object would need a Wag method, which you would probably invoke something like this:

```
Dogs("Max").Tail.Wag Direction:=dogWagHorizontal, Frequency:=200
```

Working with Collections

When an object contains more than one object of the same type, the objects are grouped into a *collection*. For example, Word uses Document objects, which are grouped into the Documents collection; PowerPoint has a Presentations collection for Presentation objects, and Excel has the Workbooks collection.

As in these examples, the names of most collections are the plural of the object in question. There are a number of exceptions, such as the Sheets collection in Excel that contains the Worksheet objects; but by-and-large the names of most collections are easy to derive from the name of the objects they contain—and vice versa.

A collection is an object too and can have its own properties and methods. Most collections have fewer properties and methods than the objects. Most collections have an Add method for adding another object to the collection and an Item property (the default property) for accessing an item within the collection. Some collections are read-only and do not have an Add method.

Most collections in VBA have the core group of properties listed in Table 8.1.

TABLE 8.1:   Core Properties for Collections in VBA

PROPERTY	EXPLANATION
Application	A read-only property that returns the application associated with the object or collection—the root of the hierarchy for the document. For example, the Application property for objects in PowerPoint returns Microsoft PowerPoint.
Count	A read-only Long property that returns the number of items in the collection—for example, the number of Shape objects in the Shapes collection in a PowerPoint slide.
Creator	In Microsoft applications, a read-only Long property that returns a 32-bit integer indicating the application used to create the object or collection.
Item	A read-only property that returns the specified member of the collection. Item is the default property of every collection, which means that you seldom need to specify it.
Parent	In Microsoft applications, a read-only String property that returns the parent object for the object or collection. The *parent* object is the object that contains the object in question; the contained object is the *child* object.

Working with an Object in a Collection

To work with an object in a collection, you identify the object within the collection either by its name or its position in the collection. For example, the following statement returns the first Document object in the Documents collection and displays its Name property in a message box:

```
MsgBox Documents(1).Name
```

You can use the Item property to return an object from the collection; but because Item is the default property of a collection, you don't need to use it. The following two statements have the same effect, and there's no advantage to using the Item method.

```
strName = Documents(1).Name
strName = Documents.Item(1).Name
```

NOTE In most collections, numbering starts at 1, which makes it easy to identify the object you need. For example, Documents(1) gives you the first document, Workbooks(2) gives you the second workbook, and so on. Most of the collections in Office applications are one-based (the numbering starts at 1). Be warned that some collections in VBA implementations are *zero-based*—their numbering starts at 0 (zero) rather than 1. Collections in Access are zero-based. If you're not sure whether a particular collection is one-based or zero-based, consult the Help topic for that collection.

Adding an Object to a Collection

To create a new object in a collection, you add an object to the collection. In many cases, you use the Add method to do so. For example, the following statement creates a new Document object in Word:

```
Documents.Add
```

Finding the Objects You Need

The Visual Basic Editor provides a number of tools for finding the objects you need:

- (Microsoft applications only) The Macro Recorder, which you used to record macros in the Microsoft Office applications in Chapter 1

- The Object Browser, which you used briefly in Chapter 4

- The online Help system, which should provide detailed help on the objects in the application (though this depends on how much effort the software manufacturer put into the Help system)

- The List Properties/Methods feature

The following sections show you how to use these tools to find objects.

Using the Macro Recorder to Record the Objects You Need

If you're using a Microsoft application, chances are that the easiest way to find the objects you need is to use the Macro Recorder to record a quick macro using the objects you're interested in. By recording the actions you perform, the Macro Recorder creates code that you can then open in the Visual Basic Editor, examine, and modify.

Along with its advantages, the Macro Recorder has two problems:

- First, you can't record all the actions that you might want. Let's say you're working in Excel and want to create a statement that performs an action on a specified workbook in the Workbooks collection rather than on the active workbook. With the Macro Recorder, you can record only actions performed on the active workbook. (This is the case because the Macro Recorder can record only those actions you can perform interactively in Excel, and you can't work interactively with any workbook other than the active one.)

- Second, the Macro Recorder is apt to record statements that you don't strictly need, particularly when you're trying to record a setting in a dialog box.

You saw an example of the second problem in Chapter 4. Here's another example, this time recording a macro to create an AutoCorrect entry:

1. Start Word or activate it if it's already running.

2. Double-click the REC indicator on the status bar, or choose Tools ➤ Macro ➤ Record New Macro, to display the Record Macro dialog box. Type **Add_Item_to_AutoCorrect** in the Macro Name text

box, and type a description in the Description text box. Make sure that All Documents (Normal.dot) is selected in the Store Macro In drop-down list, and then click the OK button to start recording.

3. Choose Tools ➢ AutoCorrect Options to display the AutoCorrect dialog box. Type **reffs** in the Replace box and **references** in the With box, and then click the OK button to close the Auto-Correct dialog box.

4. Click the Stop Recording button on the Stop Recording toolbar, double-click the REC indicator on the status bar, or choose Tools ➢ Macro ➢ Stop Recording to stop the Macro Recorder.

Now press Alt+F8 or choose Tools ➢ Macro ➢ Macros to display the Macros dialog box, select the Add_Item_to_AutoCorrect entry, and then click the Edit button to open the macro in the Visual Basic Editor. The code should look like this:

```
Sub Add_Item_to_AutoCorrect()
'
' Add_Item_to_AutoCorrect Macro
' Creates an AutoCorrect item (recorded macro)
'
    AutoCorrect.Entries.Add Name:="reffs", Value:="references"
    With AutoCorrect
        .CorrectInitialCaps = True
        .CorrectSentenceCaps = True
        .CorrectDays = True
        .CorrectCapsLock = True
        .ReplaceText = True
        .ReplaceTextFromSpellingChecker = True
        .CorrectKeyboardSetting = False
        .DisplayAutoCorrectOptions = True
        .CorrectTableCells = True
    End With
End Sub
```

Here, you get 13 lines of padding around the one line you need:

```
AutoCorrect.Entries.Add Name:="reffs", Value:="references"
```

This line shows you that to add an AutoCorrect entry, you need to work with the Entries collection object in the AutoCorrect object. You use the Add method on the Entries collection to add an AutoCorrect entry to the list.

By removing the nine lines containing the With… End With statement from this recorded macro, you can reduce it to just the line it needs to contain (together with the comment lines, which you can also remove if you want):

```
Sub Add_Item_to_AutoCorrect()
'
' Add_Item_to_AutoCorrect Macro
' Creates an AutoCorrect item (recorded macro)
'
    AutoCorrect.Entries.Add Name:="reffs",Value:="references"
End Sub
```

In spite of its limitations, the Macro Recorder does provide quick access to the objects you need to work with, and you can always adjust the resulting code in the Visual Basic Editor.

Using the Object Browser

The primary tool for finding the objects you need is the Object Browser, which you used briefly in Chapter 4. In this section, you get to know the Object Browser better and learn to use it to find the information you need about objects.

COMPONENTS OF THE OBJECT BROWSER

The Object Browser provides the following information about both built-in objects and custom objects you create:

◆ Classes (formal definitions of objects)

◆ Properties (the attributes of objects or aspects of their behavior)

◆ Methods (actions you can perform on objects)

◆ Events (for example, the opening or closing of a document)

◆ Constants (named items that keep a constant value while a program is executing)

Figure 8.1 shows the components of the Object Browser. Here's what the different elements of the Object Browser do:

◆ The Project/Library drop-down list provides a list of object libraries available to the current project. (An *object library* is a reference file containing information on a collection of objects available to programs.) Use the drop-down list to choose the object libraries you want to view. For example, you might choose to view only objects in Outlook by choosing Outlook in the Project/ Library drop-down list. Alternatively, you could stay with the default choice of <All Libraries>.

◆ In the Search Text box, enter the string you want to search for: Either type it in or choose a previous string in the current project session from the drop-down list. Then either press Enter or click the Search button to find members containing the search string.

TIP To make your searches less specific, you can use wildcards such as **?** (representing any one character) and ***** (representing any group of characters). You can also choose to search for a whole word only (rather than matching your search string with part of another word) by right-clicking anywhere in the Object Browser (except in the Project/Library drop-down list or in the Search Text box) and choosing Find Whole Word Only from the context menu. The Find Whole Word Only choice has a check mark next to it in the context menu when it's active; to deactivate it, choose Find Whole Word Only again on the context menu.

◆ Click the Go Back button to retrace one by one your previous selections in the Classes list and the Members Of list. Click the Go Forward button to go forward through your previous selections one by one. The Go Back button becomes available when you go to a class or member in the Object Browser; the Go Forward button becomes available only when you've used the Go Back button to go back to a previous selection.

FIGURE 8.1

The Object Browser provides information on built-in objects and custom objects. Here, the application is AutoCAD.

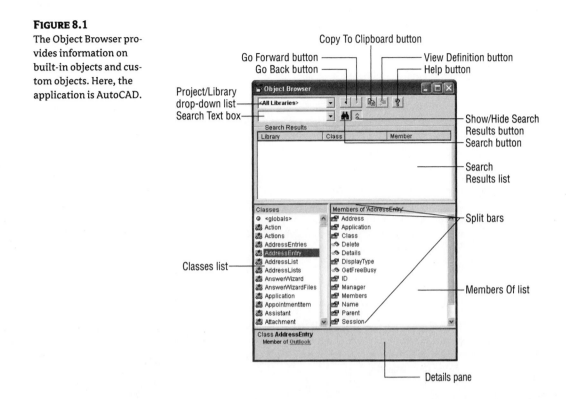

◆ Click the Copy To Clipboard button to copy the selected item from the Search Results list, the Classes list, the Members Of list, or the Details pane to the Clipboard so that you can paste it into your code.

◆ Click the View Definition button to display a code window containing the code for the object selected in the Classes list or the Members Of list. The View Definition button is available (undimmed) only for objects that contain code, such as procedures and user forms that you've created.

◆ Click the Help button to display any available Help for the currently selected item. Alternatively, press the F1 key.

◆ Click the Search button to search for the term entered in the Search Text box. If the Search Results pane isn't open, VBA opens it at this point.

◆ Click the Show/Hide Search Results button to toggle the display of the Search Results pane on and off.

◆ The Search Results list in the Search Results pane contains the results of the latest search you've conducted for a term entered in the Search Text box. If you've performed a search, the Object Browser updates the Search Results list when you use the Project/Library drop-down list to switch to a different library. Choosing a different library in the Project/Library drop-down list is a handy way of narrowing, expanding, or changing the focus of your search.

- The Classes list shows the available classes in the library or project specified in the Project/ Library drop-down list.

- The Members Of list displays the available elements of the class selected in the Classes list. A method, constant, event, property, or procedure that has code written for it appears in bold-face. The Members Of list can display the members either grouped into their different categories (methods, properties, events, and so on) or ungrouped as an alphabetical list of all the members available. To toggle between grouped and ungrouped, right-click in the Members Of list and choose Group Members from the context menu; click either to place a check mark (to group the members) or to remove the check mark (to ungroup the members).

- The Details pane displays the definition of the member selected in the Classes list or in the Members Of list. For example, if you select a procedure in the Members Of list, the Details pane displays its name, the name of the module and template or document in which it's stored, and any comment lines you inserted at the beginning of the procedure. The module name and project name contain hyperlinks (jumps) so that you can quickly move to them. You can copy information from the Details pane to the Code window by using either copy and paste or drag and drop.

- Drag the three split bars to resize the panes of the Object Browser to suit you. (You can also resize the Object Browser window to suit you or maximize it so that it docks itself in the Code window.)

The Object Browser uses different icons to indicate the various types of object that it lists. Figure 8.1 shows several icons; Table 8.2 shows the full range of icons and what they represent.

A blue dot in the upper-left corner of a Property icon or a Method icon indicates that that property or method is the default.

TABLE 8.2:   Object Browser Icons

Icon	Meaning	Icon	Meaning
	Property		User-defined type
	Method		Global
	Constant		Library
	Module		Project
	Event		Built-in keyword or type
	Class		Enum (enumeration)

ADDING AND REMOVING OBJECT LIBRARIES

You can add and remove object libraries by choosing Tools ≻ References and using the References dialog box:

◆ By adding object libraries, you can make available additional objects to work with.

◆ By removing object libraries that you don't need to view or use, you can reduce the number of object references that VBA needs to resolve when it is compiling the code in a project. This allows the code to run faster.

When you start the Visual Basic Editor, it automatically loads the object libraries required for using VBA and user forms with the host application. You don't need to change this set of object libraries until you need to access objects contained in other libraries. For example, if you create a procedure in Word that draws on Excel's functionality, you'll usually add to Word a reference to Excel to make its objects available.

You can adjust the priority of different references by adjusting the order in which the references appear in the References dialog box. The priority of references matters when you use in your code an object whose name appears in more than one reference: VBA checks the References list to determine the order of the references that contain that object name and uses the first of them, unless specifically told to do otherwise by use of a disambiguated name.

To add or remove object libraries, follow these steps:

1. In the Visual Basic Editor, choose Tools ≻ References to display the References dialog box (see Figure 8.2).

TIP You can also display the References dialog box by right-clicking in the Object Browser and choosing References from the shortcut menu. (You can right-click almost anywhere in the Object Browser: in the Project/Library drop-down list, in the Search Results area, in the Classes list, in the Members Of list, or in the Details pane.)

2. In the Available References list box, select the check boxes for the references you want to have available and clear the check boxes for the references you want to remove. You should find a reference for an object library for each application that supports Automation and is installed on your computer. The references that are in use appear together at the top of the Available References list box, not in alphabetical order.

FIGURE 8.2
You add and remove object libraries by using the References dialog box. The title bar of the dialog box includes "Normal" because the current project is the Normal template in Word.

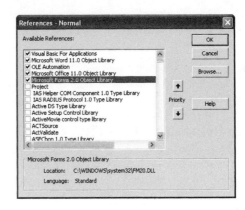

3. Adjust the priority of the references if necessary by selecting a reference and using the up- and down-arrow Priority buttons to move it up or down the list. Usually, you'll want to keep Visual Basic for Applications and the application's Object Library at the top of your list.

TIP You can add further reference libraries by clicking the Browse button to display the Add Reference dialog box, selecting the library file, and then clicking the Open button.

4. Click the OK button to close the References dialog box and return to the Object Browser.

NAVIGATING WITH THE OBJECT BROWSER

To browse the objects available to a project, follow these steps:

1. First, activate a code module by double-clicking it in the Project Explorer.

2. Display the Object Browser by choosing View ➢ Object Browser, by pressing the F2 button, or by clicking the Object Browser button on the Standard toolbar. (If the Object Browser is already displayed, make it active by clicking it or by selecting it from the list at the bottom of the Window menu.)

3. In the Project/Library drop-down list, select the name of the project or the library that you want to view. The Object Browser displays the available classes in the Classes list.

4. In the Classes list, select the class you want to work with. For example, if you chose a project in step 3, select the module you want to work with in the Classes list.

5. If you want to work with a particular member of the class or project, select it in the Members Of list. For example, if you're working with a template project, you might want to choose a specific procedure or user form to work with.

Once you've selected the class, member, or project, you can perform the following actions on it:

◆ View information about it in the Details pane at the bottom of the Object Browser window.

◆ View the definition of an object by clicking the View Definition button. Alternatively, right-click the object in the Members Of list and choose View Definition from the context menu. The View Definition button and the View Definition command are available (undimmed) only for objects that contain code, such as procedures and user forms that you've created.

NOTE The definition of a procedure is the code that it contains. The definition of a module is all the code in all the procedures that it contains. The definition of a user form is the code in all the procedures attached to it.

◆ Copy the text for the selected class, project, or member to the Clipboard by clicking the Copy To Clipboard button or by issuing a standard Copy command (such as pressing Ctrl+C or Ctrl+Insert).

Using Help to Find the Object You Need

VBA's Help system provides another easy way to access the details of the objects you want to work with. The Help files provide a hyperlinked reference to all the objects, methods, and properties in VBA, including graphics that show how the objects are related to each other.

The quickest way to access VBA Help is to activate the Visual Basic Editor and then press the F1 key. VBA displays the Visual Basic Help task pane, shown in Figure 8.3 with some topics expanded to reveal their contents. If you're using an Office application and you've disabled the Office Assistant, you can also choose Help ➢ Microsoft Visual Basic Help; if you haven't disabled the Office Assistant, choosing Help ➢ Microsoft Visual Basic Help displays the Office Assistant.

TIP To get help on a specific item referenced in your code, place the insertion point somewhere in the appropriate word before pressing the F1 key. This makes VBA display the Help topics for that item.

Once you've opened the Help task pane, you can search for help by typing keywords into the Search box and clicking the Start Searching button or by browsing the topics. Click the topic you want to see, and it opens in the Microsoft Visual Basic Help window. Figure 8.4 shows an example of the Help you see if you display the topic for the Document object in Word.

Apart from the regular Help information you'll find in the Help window, a few items deserve comment here:

♦ The graphic at the top of the Help listing shows the relationship of the current object (in this case, Document) to the object or objects that contain it and to the objects it contains. You can click on either of these objects to display a pop-up list showing the relevant objects, as shown in Figure 8.5.

FIGURE 8.3
The Visual Basic Help task pane

♦ If a See Also hyperlink appears at the top of the window, you can click it to display a list of associated topics. For example, as you'd discover if you clicked on the hyperlink, one of the See Also topics from the Document Object Help screen is Help on the Template object.

♦ Click the Properties hyperlink at the top of the window to display a list of the Help available for the properties of the object, and then click the topic you want to display.

♦ Click the Methods hyperlink at the top of the window to display a list of the Help available on the object's methods, and then click the topic you want to display.

♦ Some objects also have one or more events associated with them. If the object has any events associated with it (as the Document object does here), click the Events hyperlink at the top of the window to display a list of the Help available for the events, and then click the topic you want to display.

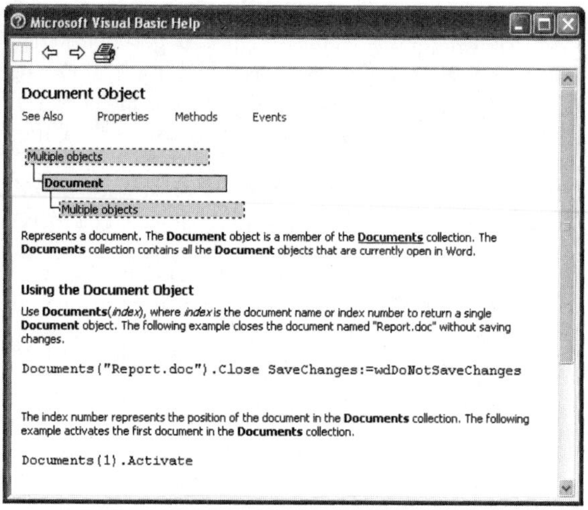

FIGURE 8.4

Here's what you'll get if you display Help on the Document object in Word.

FIGURE 8.5

Click on one of the objects in the graphic to display the list of objects it contains. Here, you can see that the Document object contains a plethora of other objects, including Bookmarks and Characters.

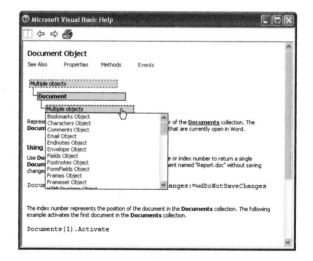

Using the List Properties/Methods Feature

You've already used the List Properties/Methods feature a couple of times in the previous chapters. To recap, when you're entering a statement in the Visual Basic Editor and you type the period at the end of the current object, the List Properties/Methods feature displays a list of properties and methods appropriate to the statement you've entered so far.

The List Properties/Methods feature provides a quick way of entering statements, but you need to know the object from which to start. Sometimes using this feature is a bit like finding your way through a maze and being given detailed directions that end with the phrase, "But you can't get there from here."

Once you know the object from which to start, though, you can easily find the property or method you need. For example, to put together the statement `Application.Documents(1).Close` to close the first document in the `Documents` collection in Word, you could work as follows:

1. Place the insertion point on a fresh line in an empty procedure (between the `Sub` and `End Sub` statements). Create a new procedure if necessary.

2. Type the word **application**, or type **appl** and press Ctrl+spacebar to have the Complete Word feature complete the word for you.

3. Type the period (.) after **Application**. The List Properties/Methods feature displays the list of properties and methods available to the `Application` object.

4. Choose the `Documents` item in the List Properties/Methods list. You can either scroll to it using the mouse and then double-click it to enter it in the code window, scroll to it by using the ↑ and ↓ keys and enter it by pressing Tab, or scroll to it by typing the first few letters of its name and then enter it by pressing Tab. The latter method is shown in Figure 8.6, which uses Word.

FIGURE 8.6

Using the List Properties/Methods feature to enter code

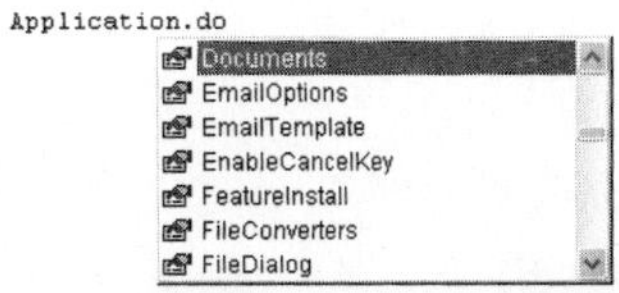

5. Type **(1).** after **Documents**. When you type the period, the List Properties/Methods feature displays the list of properties and methods available to the `Documents` collection.

6. Choose the `Close` method in the List Properties/Methods list by scrolling to it with the mouse or with the ↓ key. Because this is the end of the statement, press the Enter key to enter the method and start a new line, rather than pressing the Tab key (which enters the method and continues the same line).

TIP For most people, the quickest way to enter statements in the Code window is to keep their hands on the keyboard. To help you do this, the Visual Basic Editor automatically selects the current item in the List Properties/Methods list when you type a period or an opening parenthesis. In the previous example, you can type **Application.** to display the list, **Do** to select the Documents item, and **(** to enter the Documents item.

Using Object Variables to Represent Objects

As you learned in Chapter 6, one of the data types available for variables in VBA is *Object*. You use an object variable to represent an object in your code: Instead of referring to the object, you can refer to the object variable to access or manipulate the object it represents.

Using object variables makes it simpler to know which object a section of code is working with, especially when you're working with multiple objects in the same section of code. For example, say you create a procedure that manipulates the three open workbooks in Excel, copying a range of cells from one to the two others. If you have only those three workbooks open, you'll be able to refer to them as `Workbooks(1)`, `Workbooks(2)`, and `Workbooks(3)`, respectively, because they'll occupy the first (and only) three slots in the `Workbooks` collection.

But if your procedure changes the order of the workbooks, closes one or more workbooks, or creates one or more new workbooks, things rapidly get confusing. If, however, you've created Object variables (named, say, `xlWorkbook1`, `xlWorkbook2`, and `xlWorkbook3`) to refer to those workbooks, it'll be much easier to keep them straight. This is because no matter which workbook is first in the `Workbooks` collection, you'll be able to refer to the object represented by the Object variable `xlWorkbook1` and know that you'll be getting the workbook you intend.

To create an object variable, you declare it in almost exactly the same way as you declare any other variable, using a `Dim`, `Private`, or `Public` statement. For example, the following statement declares the object variable `objMyObject`:

```
Dim objMyObject As Object
```

As normal for the `Dim` statement, if you use this declaration within a procedure, it creates a variable with local scope. If you use it in the declarations section of a code sheet, it creates a variable with module-level private scope. Similarly, the `Private` and `Public` keywords create module-level private and public object variables, respectively.

Once you've declared the object variable, you can assign an object to it. To do so, use a `Set` statement. The syntax for a `Set` statement is as follows:

```
Set objectvariable = {[New] expression|Nothing}
```

Here's how that syntax breaks down:

- ◆ *objectvariable* is the name of the object variable to which you're assigning the object.

- ◆ `New` is an optional keyword that you can use to implicitly create a new object of the specified class. Usually it's better to create objects explicitly and then assign them to object variables rather than use `New` to create them implicitly.

- ◆ *expression* is a required expression that specifies or returns the object you want to assign to the object variable.

- ◆ `Nothing` is an optional keyword that you assign to an existing object variable to obliterate its contents and release the memory they occupied.

For example, the following statements declare the object variable `objMyObject` and assign to it the active workbook in Excel:

```
Dim objMyObject As Object
Set objMyObject = ActiveWorkbook
```

The following statement uses the `Nothing` keyword to release the memory occupied by the `objMyObject` object variable:

```
Set objMyObject = Nothing
```

What's different about declaring an object variable versus declaring other types of variable is that not only can you declare the object variable as being of the type `Object`, but you can specify which type of object it is. For example, if an object variable will always represent a `Workbook` object, you can declare it as being of the Workbook data type. The following statement declares the object variable x1Workbook1 as being of the Workbook data type:

```
Dim xlWorkbook1 As Workbook
```

Strongly associating a type with an object variable like this has a couple of advantages. First, once you've strongly typed the object variable, the Visual Basic Editor provides you with full assistance for the object variable, just as if you were dealing with the object directly. For example, once you've created that object variable x1Workbook1 of the Workbook object type, the Visual Basic Editor displays the List Properties/Methods drop-down list when you type the object variable's name followed by a period, as shown in Figure 8.7.

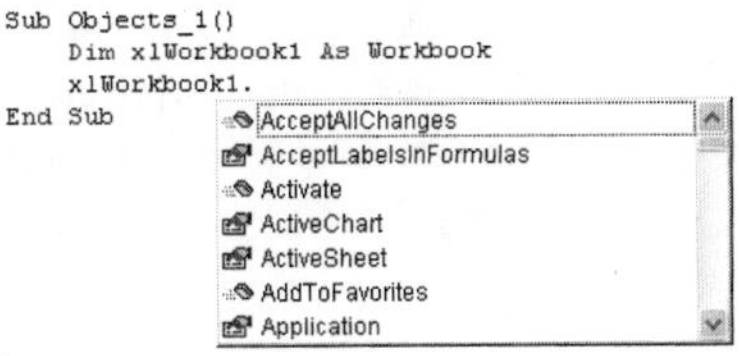

FIGURE 8.7

When you strongly type your object variables, you get the full benefit of the Visual Basic Editor's code-completion features for the object variables.

```
Sub Objects_1()
    Dim xlWorkbook1 As Workbook
    xlWorkbook1.
End Sub
```

AcceptAllChanges
AcceptLabelsInFormulas
Activate
ActiveChart
ActiveSheet
AddToFavorites
Application

Second, when you strongly type an object variable, you make it a bit harder to get things wrong in your code. If you try to assign the wrong type of object to a strongly typed object variable, VBA gives an error. For example, if you create a Worksheet object variable in Excel, as in the first of the following statements, and assign to it a Workbook object, as in the second statement, VBA gives a Type Mismatch error—as well it should:

```
Dim wksSheet1 As Worksheet
Set wksSheet1 = ActiveWorkbook
```

Finding out at this stage that you've created a problem is usually preferable to finding out later (for example, when you go to manipulate the wksSheet1 object and discover it doesn't behave as you expect it to).

The main reason for *not* strongly typing an object variable is that you're not sure what kind of object it will store, or if the kind of object it will store may vary from one execution of the code to another. (If either is the case, your code will need to be flexible enough to accommodate objects of different types showing up for the object variable.) Usually, though, you'll want to strongly type all your object variables.

If you're not sure which object type to use for an object variable, start by declaring the object variable as being of the Object data type. Then run through the code a couple of times with the Locals window (View ➢ Locals) displayed, and note the data type that VBA assigns to the object variable. For example, if you step through the following statements in a Visual Basic Editor session hosted by Excel, the readout in the Locals window at first identifies the object variable wks only as Object (as shown on the left in Figure 8.8), but then as Object/Sheet1 (as shown on the right in Figure 8.8) when the second statement assigns the first sheet in the active workbook to it:

```
Dim wks As Object
Set wks = ActiveWorkbook.Sheets(1)
```

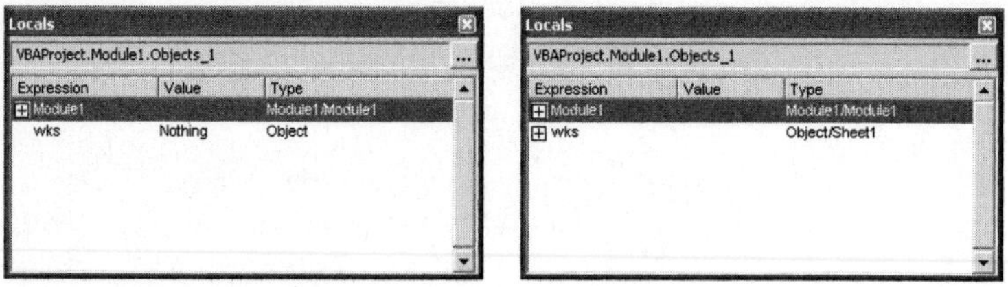

FIGURE 8.8
You can use the Locals window to help identify the object type that an object variable will contain.

NOTE As you learned earlier in the book, you can avoid specifying data types altogether. For example, the statement `Dim varMyVariant` creates a Variant variable because the statement does not specify a data type. Variant variables can contain objects as well as other data types—but as before, using Variants requires VBA to do a little more work each time it encounters the variable (because VBA has to determine what data type the variable currently is) and denies you the benefits of strongly typing your variables. Weak typing also makes your code harder to read.

Part 3

Making Decisions and Using Loops and Functions

Chapter 9

Using Functions

◆ What functions are and what they do

◆ How to use functions

◆ Using key VBA functions

◆ Converting data from one type to another

◆ Manipulating strings and dates

VBA comes with a large number of built-in functions to perform commonly needed operations—everything from determining whether a file exists, to returning the current date, to converting data from one format to another. (For example, you can use a function to convert numeric data into a text string.) This chapter shows you what functions are and what they do, and shows you how to use functions. Along the way, you'll meet some of the key functions that VBA provides, including functions for converting data from one data type to another, file-operation functions, date functions, and mathematical functions.

You can also create custom functions of your own to supplement VBA's functions. The next chapter tells you how to do that when VBA's functions don't meet your needs.

What Is a Function?

A *function* is a type of procedure. A function differs from a subprocedure in that a function always returns a value (which a subprocedure doesn't) and almost always takes one or more arguments. Some functions take no arguments, and subprocedures can take arguments if they're designed to do so. Typically, you feed information into the function, which processes it and returns a value for you to use. But you can also create your own functions in VBA that simply perform one or more tasks and return only a null value.

Functions are so essential to VBA that you've already used several in this book before introducing them properly here. For example, in Chapter 7 you used the Rnd function to generate random numbers to fill an array named intArray and the Int function to turn the random numbers into integers:

```
intArray(i) = Int(Rnd * 10)
```

Rnd is one of the rare functions that does not have to take one or more arguments. (Rnd takes one optional argument, but the previous example doesn't use it.) Int, on the other hand, requires an argument—the number or expression that it's to turn into an integer—which here is supplied by the expression

Rnd * 10. Here the Rnd function returns a value that the Int function uses; the Int function then returns a value to the procedure, which uses it to populate a subscript in the array.

An *argument* is a piece of information that VBA uses with a function, method, or command. You can tell when arguments are optional because they're enclosed within brackets. You can include or omit the arguments displayed in the brackets. For example, the syntax for the Rnd function looks like this:

```
Rnd([number]) As Single
```

The brackets indicate that the *number* argument is optional, and the As Single part of the syntax denotes that the value returned is of the Single data type. Different functions return different data types suited to their contents: Many functions return a Variant, but yes/no functions, such as the IsNumeric function used in Chapter 7, return a Boolean value, either True or False. When necessary, VBA may convert the result of a function to a different data type needed by another function in the expression.

If any pair of brackets contains two arguments, you have to use both of them at once. For example, the MsgBox function displays a message box. The syntax for the MsgBox function is as follows

```
MsgBox(prompt[, buttons] [, title][, helpfile, context])
```

Here, *prompt* is the only required argument: *buttons, title, helpfile,* and *context* are all optional. But *helpfile* and *context* are enclosed within a single set of brackets instead of each having its own pair. You need to use either both of these arguments or neither of them; you cannot use one without the other.

NOTE   Chapter 13 shows you how to use the MsgBox function in your code.

Using Functions

To use a function, you *call* it (or *invoke* it) from a subprocedure or from another function. To call a function, you use a Call statement, either with the Call keyword or just the name of the function. Using the Call keyword can make your code clearer and easier to read. It also allows you to search for all calls by searching for "call " (*call* followed by a space). However, using the Call keyword may seem like overkill for everyday functions.

NOTE   As you'll see later in the book, you call a procedure in the same way as you call a function.

The syntax for the Call statement is as follows:

```
[Call] name[, argumentlist]
```

Here, *name* is a required String argument giving the name of the function or procedure to call; and *argumentlist* is an optional argument providing a comma-delimited list of the variables, arrays, or expressions to pass to the function or procedure. When calling a function, you'll almost always need to pass arguments (except for those few functions that take no arguments); when calling a procedure, you use the *argumentlist* argument only for procedures that require arguments.

The brackets around the Call keyword indicate that it is optional. If you use this keyword, you need to enclose the *argumentlist* argument in parentheses. In most cases, it's clearer *not* to use the Call keyword when calling a function.

For example, the following statement calls the MsgBox function, supplying the required argument *prompt* (the string Hello, World!):

```
MsgBox "Hello, World!"
```

You could use the `Call` keyword (and enclose the argument list in parentheses) instead, as shown in the following statement, but there's little advantage in doing so:

```
Call MsgBox("Hello, World!")
```

NOTE To run a function from the Visual Basic Editor, you must call it from a procedure. You can also execute a function call from the Immediate window, but since the Immediate window runs only one statement at a time, it's useful only for testing.

You can assign the result of a function to a variable. For example, consider the following code fragment. The first two of the following statements declare the String variables `strExample` and `strLeft10`. The third statement assigns a string of text to `strExample`. The fourth statement uses the `Left` function to return the left-most 10 characters from `strExample` and assign them to `strLeft10`, which the fifth statement then displays in a message box (see Figure 9.1).

```
Dim strExample As String
Dim strLeft10 As String
strExample = "Technology is interesting."
strLeft10 = Left(strExample, 10)
MsgBox strLeft10
```

FIGURE 9.1

Using the Left function to take the left part of a string—in this case, the first 10 characters of the string

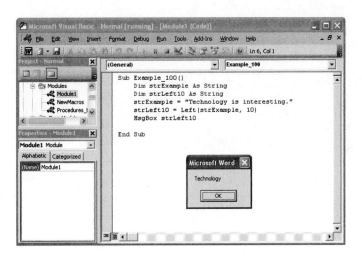

Instead of assigning the result of a function to a variable, you can insert it directly in your code or pass it to another function. Take a look at the following statement:

```
MsgBox Right(Left("This is Pride and Patriotism", 13), 5)
```

This statement uses three functions: the `MsgBox` function, the `Left` function, and the `Right` function. The `Right` function is the conservative counterpart of the `Left` function and returns the specified number of characters from the right wing of the specified string.

When you have multiple sets of parentheses in a VBA statement, things happen from the inside, just as in math. So, in this example the `Left` function is evaluated first, returning the leftmost 13 characters from the string: This is Pride (the spaces are characters too). VBA passes this new string to the Right function, which in this case returns the rightmost five characters from it: Pride. VBA passes this second new string to the MsgBox function, which displays it in a message box.

NOTE   You can nest functions to many levels without giving VBA much trouble, but for most practical purposes, it's a good idea to limit nesting to only a few levels. This makes your code easier to read and to troubleshoot for both you and others.

Passing Arguments to a Function

When a function takes more than one argument, you can pass the arguments to it in any of three ways:

◆ By supplying the arguments, without their names, positionally (in the order in which the function expects them)

◆ By supplying the arguments, with their names, in the order in which the function expects them

◆ By supplying the arguments, with their names, in any order you choose

The first method, supplying the arguments positionally without using their names, is usually the quickest way to proceed. The only disadvantage to doing so is that anyone reading your code may not know immediately which value corresponds to which argument—though they can look this up without trouble. To omit an optional argument, you place a comma where it would appear in the sequence of arguments.

Using argument names takes longer (and makes your code more verbose) but makes your code easier to read. When you omit an argument, you don't need to use the comma to indicate that you're skipping it.

There's no advantage to using named arguments out of order over using them in order unless you happen to find doing so easier.

For example, the DateSerial function returns a Variant/Date containing the date for the given year, month, and day. The syntax for DateSerial is as follows:

```
DateSerial(year, month, day)
```

Here, *year* is a required Integer argument supplying the year; *month* is a required Integer argument supplying the month; and *day* is a required Integer argument supplying the day.

The following statement supplies the arguments positionally without their names:

```
MsgBox DateSerial(2006, 12, 31)
```

The following statement supplies the arguments positionally with their names:

```
MsgBox DateSerial(Year:=2006, Month:=12, Day:=31)
```

The following statement supplies the arguments, with their names, out of order:

```
MsgBox DateSerial(Day:=31, Year:=2006, Month:=12)
```

All three of these statements work fine. You'll get a problem only if you list out-of-order arguments that you're supplying without names (positionally), if you name some arguments and don't name others, or if your omit required arguments. Figure 9.2 shows two of the errors you may encounter.

FIGURE 9.2
An "Expected: named parameter" error occurs when you name some arguments but not others. An "Argument not optional" error occurs when you omit a required argument.

Using Functions to Convert Data from One Type to Another

VBA provides a full set of functions for converting data from one data type to another. These functions fall into two distinct groups: simple data conversion and more complex data conversion.

Table 9.1 lists VBA's functions for simple data conversion.

TABLE 9.1: VBA's Functions for Simple Data Conversion

FUNCTION(ARGUMENTS)	DATA TYPE RETURNED
CBool(*number*)	Boolean
CByte(*expression*)	Byte
CCur(*expression*)	Currency
CDate(*expression*)	Date
CDbl(*expression*)	Double
CInt(*expression*)	Integer
CLng(*expression*)	Long
CSng(*expression*)	Single
CStr(*expression*)	String
CVar(*expression*)	Variant

For example, the following statements declare the untyped variable varMyInput and the Integer variable intMyVar and then display an input box prompting the user to enter an integer. In the third statement, the user's input is assigned to varMyInput, which automatically becomes a Variant/String. The fourth statement uses the CInt function to convert varMyInput to an integer, assigning the result to intMyVar. The fifth statement compares intMyVar to 10, converts the result to Boolean by using the CBool function, and displays the result (True or False) in a message box.

```
Dim varMyInput
Dim intMyVar As Integer
```

```
varMyInput = InputBox("Enter an integer:", "10 Is True, Other Numbers Are False")
intMyVar = CInt(varMyInput)
MsgBox CBool(intMyVar = 10)
```

Table 9.2 lists VBA's functions for more complex data conversion.

TABLE 9.2: VBA's Functions for Complex Data Conversion

FUNCTION(ARGUMENTS)	RETURNS
Asc(*string*)	The ANSI character code for the first character in the string.
Chr(*number*)	The string for the specified character code (a number between 0 and 255).
Format(*expression*, *format*)	A variant containing *expression* formatted as specified by *format*. (You'll see how Format works in "Using the *Format* Function to Format an Expression," later in the chapter.)
Hex(*number*)	A string containing the hexadecimal value of *number*.
Oct(*number*)	A string containing the octal value of *number*.
RGB(*number1*, *number2*, *number3*)	A Long integer representing the color value specified by *number1*, *number2*, and *number3*.
QBColor(*number*)	A Long containing the RGB value for the specified color.
Str(*number*)	A Variant/String containing a string representation of *number*.
Val(*string*)	The numeric portion of *string*; if *string* does not have a numeric portion, Val returns 0.

Using the *Asc* Function to Return a Character Code

The Asc function returns the character code for the first character of a string. *Character codes* are the numbers by which computers refer to letters. For example, the character code for a capital *A* is 65 and for a capital *B* is 66; a lowercase *a* is 97, and a lowercase *b* is 98.

NOTE Asc stands for ASCII, the acronym for American Standard Code for Information Interchange. But in fact the Asc function returns the ANSI—American National Standards Institute—number for a character

The syntax for the Asc function is straightforward:

```
Asc(string)
```

Here, *string* is any string expression. For example, Asc("A") returns 65.

The following statements use the Asc function to return the character code for the first character of the current selection in the active document and display that code in a message box:

```
strThisCharacter = Asc(Selection.Text)
MsgBox strThisCharacter, vbOKOnly, "Character Code"
```

Using the *Val* Function to Extract a Number from the Start of a String

The Val function converts the numbers contained in a string into a numeric value. Val follows these rules:

- ◆ It reads only numbers in a string.
- ◆ It starts at the beginning of the string and reads only as far as the string contains characters that it recognizes as numbers.
- ◆ It ignores tabs, line-feeds, and blank spaces.
- ◆ It recognizes the period as a decimal separator but not the comma.

This means that if you feed Val a string consisting of tabbed columns of numbers, such as the second line below, it will read them as a single number (in this case, 445634.994711):

```
Item#   Price   Available   On Order   Ordered
4456    34.99   4           7          11
```

If, however, you feed it something containing a mix of numbers and letters, Val will read only the numbers and strings recognized as numeric expressions (for example, Val("4E5") returns 400000, because it reads the expression as exponentiation). For example, if fed the address shown below, Val returns 8661, ignoring the other numbers in the string (because it stops at the *L* of *Laurel*, the first character that isn't a number, a tab, a line-feed, or a space):

```
8661 Laurel Avenue Suite 3806, Oakland, CA 94610
```

The syntax for Val is straightforward:

```
Val(string)
```

Here, *string* is a required argument consisting of any string expression.

The following statement uses Val to return the numeric variable StreetNumber from the string Address1:

```
StreetNumber = Val(Address1)
```

Using the *Str* Function to Convert a Value to a String

Just as you can convert a string to a value, you can also convert a value to a string. You'll need to do this when you want to concatenate the information contained in a value with a string—if you try to do this simply by using the + operator, VBA attempts to perform a mathematical operation rather than concatenation.

For example, suppose you've declared a String variable named strYourAge and a numeric variable named intAge. You can't use a strYourAge + intAge statement to concatenate them, because they're different types; you first need to create a string from the intAge variable and then concatenate that string with the strYourAge string. (Alternatively, you can use the & operator to concatenate the two variables.)

To convert a value to a string, use the Str function. The syntax for the Str function is this:

```
Str(number)
```

Here, *number* is a variable containing a numeric expression (such as an Integer data type, a Long data type, or a Double data type).

The following short procedure provides an example of converting a value to a string:

```
Sub Age
    Dim intAge As Integer, strYourAge As String
    intAge = InputBox("Enter your age:", "Age")
    strYourAge = "Your age is" & Str(intAge) & "."
    MsgBox YourAge, vbOKOnly + vbInformation, "Age"
End Sub
```

Using the *Format* Function to Format an Expression

The Format function is a powerful tool for changing numbers, dates and times, and strings into the shape in which you need them.

The syntax for the Format function is as follows:

```
Format(expression[, format[, firstdayofweek[, firstweekofyear]]])
```

These are the components of the syntax:

◆ *expression* is any valid expression.

◆ *format* is an optional argument specifying a named format expression or a user-defined format expression. More on this in a moment.

◆ *firstdayofweek* is an optional constant specifying the day that starts the week (for date information): The default setting is vbSunday (1), but you can also set vbMonday (2), vbTuesday (3), vbWednesday (4), vbThursday (5), vbFriday (6), vbSaturday (7), or vbUseSystem (0; uses the system setting).

◆ *firstweekofyear* is an optional constant specifying the week considered first in the year (again, for date information):

Constant	Value	Year Starts with Week
vbUseSystem	0	Use the system setting.
vbFirstJan1	1	The week in which January 1 falls (the default setting).
vbFirstFourDays	2	The first week with a minimum of four days in the year.
vbFirstFullWeek	3	The first full week (7 days) of the year.

You can define your own formats for the Format function as described in the following sections if none of the predefined numeric formats (described next) suits your needs.

USING PREDEFINED NUMERIC FORMATS

Table 9.3 lists the following predefined numeric formats that you can use with the Format function.

TABLE 9.3:   Predefined Numeric Formats

FORMAT NAME	EXPLANATION	EXAMPLE
General Number	The number is displayed with no thousand separator.	124589
Currency	The number is displayed with two decimal places, a thousand separator, and the currency symbol appropriate to the system locale.	$1,234.56
Fixed	The number is displayed with two decimal places and at least one integer place.	5.00
Standard	The number is displayed with two decimal places, at least one integer place, and a thousand separator (when needed).	1,225.00
Percent	The number is displayed multiplied by 100, with two decimal places, and with a percent sign.	78.00%
Scientific	The number is displayed in scientific notation.	5.00E+00
Yes/No	A non-zero number is displayed as Yes; a zero number is displayed as No.	Yes
True/False	A non-zero number is displayed as True; a zero number is displayed as False.	False
On/Off	A non-zero number is displayed as On; a zero number is displayed as Off.	Off

For example, the following statement returns $123.45:

```
Format("12345", "Currency")
```

CREATING A NUMERIC FORMAT

If none of the predefined numeric formats suits your needs, you can create your own numeric formats by using your choice of combination of the characters listed in Table 9.4.

TABLE 9.4:   Characters for Creating Your Own Number Formats

CHARACTER	EXPLANATION
[None]	Displays the number without any formatting. (You won't usually want to use this option.)
0	Placeholder for a digit. If there's no digit, VBA displays a zero. If the number has fewer digits than you use zeroes, VBA displays leading or trailing zeroes as appropriate.
#	Placeholder for a digit. If there's no digit, VBA displays nothing.

TABLE 9.4: Characters for Creating Your Own Number Formats *(CONTINUED)*

CHARACTER	EXPLANATION
.	Placeholder for a decimal. Indicates where the decimal separator should fall. The decimal separator varies by locale (for example, a decimal point in the U.S., a comma in Germany).
%	Placeholder for a percent character. VBA inserts the percent character and multiplies the expression by 100.
,	Thousand separator (depending on locale, a comma or a period).
:	Time separator (typically a colon, but again this depends on the locale).
/	Date separator. (Again, what you'll see depends on the locale.)
E- E+ e- e+	Scientific format: E- or e- places a minus sign next to negative exponents. E+ or e+ places a minus sign next to negative exponents and places a plus sign next to positive exponents.
- + $ ( )	Displays a literal character.
\[character]	Displays the literal character.
"[string]"	Displays the literal character. Use Chr(34) (the character code for double quotation marks) to provide the double quotation marks.

For example, the following statement returns a currency formatted with four decimal places:

```
Format("123456", "$00.0000")
```

CREATING A DATE OR TIME FORMAT

Similarly, you can create your own date and time formats by mixing and matching the characters listed in Table 9.5.

TABLE 9.5: Characters for Creating Your Own Date and Time Formats

CHARACTER	EXPLANATION
:	Time separator (typically a colon, but this depends on the locale).
/	Date separator (also locale-dependent).
c	Displays the date (if there is a date or an integer value) in the system's short date format and the time (if there is a date or a fractional value) in the system's default time format.
d	Displays the date (1 to 31) without a leading zero for single-digit numbers.
dd	Displays the date with a leading zero for single-digit numbers (01 to 31).

TABLE 9.5:   Characters for Creating Your Own Date and Time Formats *(CONTINUED)*

CHARACTER	EXPLANATION
ddd	Displays the day as a three-letter abbreviation (Sun, Mon, Tue, Wed, Thu, Fri, Sat) with no period.
dddd	Displays the full name of the day.
ddddd	Displays the complete date (day, month, and year) in the system's short date format.
dddddd	Displays the complete date (day, month, and year) in the system's long date format.
aaaa	Displays the full, localized name of the day.
w	Displays an integer from 1 (Sunday) to 7 (Monday) containing the day of the week.
ww	Displays an integer from 1 to 54 giving the number of the week in the year. The number of weeks is 54 rather than 52 because most years start and end with partial weeks rather than having 52 start-to-finish weeks.
m	Displays an integer from 1 to 12 giving the number of the month without a leading zero on single-digit months. When used after h, returns minutes instead of months.
mm	Displays a number from 01 to 12 giving the two-digit number of the month. When used after h, returns minutes instead of months.
mmm	Displays the month as a three-letter abbreviation (except for May) without a period.
mmmm	Displays the full name of the month.
oooo	Displays the full localized name of the month.
q	Displays a number from 1 to 4 giving the quarter of the year.
y	Displays an integer from 1 to 366 giving the day of the year.
yy	Displays a number from 00 to 99 giving the two-digit year.
yyyy	Displays a number from 0100 to 9999 giving the four-digit year.
h	Displays a number from 0 to 23 giving the hour.
Hh	Displays a number from 00 to 23 giving the two-digit hour.
N	Displays a number from 0 to 60 giving the minute.
Nn	Displays a number from 00 to 60 giving the two-digit minute.
S	Displays a number from 0 to 60 giving the second.
Ss	Displays a number from 00 to 60 giving the two-digit second.

TABLE 9.5:   Characters for Creating Your Own Date and Time Formats *(CONTINUED)*

CHARACTER	EXPLANATION
ttttt	Displays the full time (hour, minute, and second) in the system's default time format.
AM/PM	Uses the 12-hour clock and displays AM or PM as appropriate.
am/pm	Uses the 12-hour clock and displays am or pm as appropriate.
A/P	Uses the 12-hour clock and displays A or P as appropriate.
a/p	Uses the 12-hour clock and displays a or p as appropriate.
AMPM	Uses the 12-hour clock and displays the AM or PM string literal defined for the system.

For example, the following statement returns Saturday, April 01, 2006:

```
Format(#4/1/2006#, "dddddd")
```

CREATING A STRING FORMAT

Format also lets you create custom string formats using the options shown in Table 9.6.

TABLE 9.6:   Characters for Creating Your Own String Formats

CHARACTER	EXPLANATION
@	Placeholder for a character. Displays a character if there is one and a space if there is none.
&	Placeholder for a character. Displays a character if there is one and nothing if there is none.
<	Displays the string in lowercase.
>	Displays the string in uppercase.
!	Causes VBA to fill placeholders from left to right instead of from right to left (the default direction).

For example, the following statement assigns to strUser a string consisting of four spaces if there is no input in the input box:

```
strUser = Format(InputBox("Enter your name:"), "@@@@")
```

Using the *Chr* Function and Constants to Enter Special Characters in a String

To add special characters (such as a carriage return or a tab) to a string, specify the built-in constant (for those special characters that have built-in constants defined) or enter the appropriate character code using the Chr function. The syntax for the Chr function is straightforward:

Chr(*charactercode*)

Here, *charactercode* is a number that identifies the character to add.
Table 9.7 lists the most useful character codes and character constants.

TABLE 9.7:   VBA Character Codes and Character Constants

CODE	BUILT-IN CHARACTER CONSTANT	CHARACTER
Chr(9)	vbTab	Tab
Chr(10)	vbLf	Line-feed
Chr(11)	vbVerticalTab	Soft return (Shift+Enter)
Chr(12)	vbFormFeed	Page break
Chr(13)	vbCr	Carriage return
Chr(13) + Chr(10)	vbCrLf	Carriage return/line-feed combination
Chr(14)	—	Column break
Chr(34)	—	Double straight quotation marks (")
Chr(39)	—	Single straight quote mark/apostrophe (')
Chr(145)	—	Opening single smart quotation mark (')
Chr(146)	—	Closing single smart quotation mark/ apostrophe (')
Chr(147)	—	Opening double smart quotation mark (")
Chr(148)	—	Closing double smart quotation mark (")
Chr(149)	—	Bullet
Chr(150)	—	En dash
Chr(151)	—	Em dash

Say that you wanted to build a string containing a person's name and address from individual strings containing items of that information, and that you also wanted the individual items separated by tabs in the resulting string so that you could insert the string into a document and then convert it into a table. To do this, you could use a statement like the one below. Here, VBA uses a For...Next loop to repeat the action until the counter i reaches the number stored in the variable intNumRecords:

```
For i = 1 to intNumRecords
    AllInfo = FirstName & vbTab & MiddleInitial & vbTab _
    & LastName & vbTab & Address1 & vbTab & Address2 _
        & vbTab & City & vbTab & State & vbTab & Zip _
        & vbTab & BusinessPhone & vbTab & HomePhone & _
        & vbTab & BusinessEMail & vbTab & HomeEMail & vbCr
    Selection.TypeText AllInfo
Next i
```

The second line (split here over five physical lines) assigns data to the string AllInfo by concatenating the strings FirstName, MiddleInitial, LastName, and so on with tabs—vbTab characters—between them. The final character added to the string is vbCr (a carriage-return character), which creates a new paragraph.

The third line enters the AllInfo string into the current document, thus building a tab-delimited list containing the names and addresses. This list can then be easily converted into a table whose columns each contain one item of information: the first column contains the FirstName string, the second column the MiddleInitial string, and so on.

Using Functions to Manipulate Strings

String variables are widely useful for manipulating text. You can use them to store any quantity of text, from a character or two up to a large number of pages from a Word document or other text document; you can also use them to store filenames and folder names. Once you've stored the data in a string, you can manipulate it and change it according to your needs.

Table 9.8 lists VBA's built-in functions for manipulating strings. Because some of these functions are more complex than other functions you've seen in the chapter, and because they're frequently useful, there are detailed examples after the table.

TABLE 9.8: VBA's String-Manipulation Functions

FUNCTION(ARGUMENTS)	RETURNS
InStr(*start*, *string1*, *string2*, *compare*)	A Variant/Long giving the position of the first instance of the search string (*string2*) inside the target string (*string1*), starting from the beginning of the target string
InStrRev(*stringcheck*, *stringmatch*, *start*, *compare*)	A Variant/Long giving the position of the first instance of the search string (*stringmatch*) inside the target string (*stringcheck*), starting from the end of the target string
LCase(*string*)	A String containing the lowercased *string*
Left(*string*, *number*)	A Variant/String containing the specified number of characters from the left end of *string*
Len(*string*)	A Long containing the number of characters in *string*

TABLE 9.8:   VBA's String-Manipulation Functions *(CONTINUED)*

FUNCTION(ARGUMENTS)	RETURNS
LTrim(*string*)	A Variant/String containing *string* with any leading spaces trimmed off it
Mid(*string*, *start*, *length*)	A Variant/String containing the specified number of characters from the specified starting point within *string*
Right(*string*, *number*)	A Variant/String containing the specified number of characters from the right end of *string*
RTrim(*string*)	A Variant/String containing *string* with any trailing spaces trimmed off it
Space(*number*)	A Variant/String containing *number* of spaces.
StrComp(*string1*, *string2*, *compare*)	A Variant/Integer containing the result of comparing *string1* and *string2*
StrConv(*string*, *conversion*, *LCID*)	A Variant/String containing *string* converted as specified by *conversion* for the (optional) specified Locale ID (*LCID*)
String(*number*, *character*)	A Variant/String containing *number* of instances of *character*
StrReverse(*expression*)	A String containing the characters of *expression* in reverse order
Trim(*string*)	A Variant/String containing *string* with any leading spaces or trailing spaces trimmed off it
UCase(*string*)	A String containing the uppercased *string*

Using the *Left, Right,* and *Mid* Functions to Return Part of a String

Frequently, you'll need to use only part of a string in your procedures. For example, you might want to take only the first three characters of the name of a city to create the code for a location.

VBA provides several functions for returning from strings the characters you need:

◆ The Left function returns the specified number of characters from the left end of the string.

◆ The Right function returns the specified number of characters from the right end of the string.

◆ The Mid function returns the specified number of characters from the specified location inside a string.

NOTE   VBA provides two versions of a number of string functions, including the Left, Right, and Mid functions: the versions shown here, which return String-type Variant values, and versions whose names end with $ (Left$, Right$, Mid$, and so on), which return String values. The functions that return the Strings run faster (though you're not likely to notice any difference with normal use) but return an error if you use them on a Null value. The functions that return the String-type Variants can deal with Null values with no problem.

USING THE *LEFT* FUNCTION

The Left function returns the specified number of characters from the left end of a string. The syntax for the Left function is as follows:

```
Left(string, length)
```

Here, the *string* argument is any string expression—that is, any expression that returns a sequence of contiguous characters. Left returns Null if *string* contains no data. The *length* argument is a numeric expression specifying the number of characters to return. *length* can be a straightforward number (such as 4, or 7, or 11) or an expression that results in a number. For example, if the length of a word were stored in the variable named LenWord, and you wanted to return two characters fewer than LenWord, you could specify LenWord - 2 as the *length* argument; to return three characters more than LenWord, you could specify LenWord + 3 as the *length* argument.

For example, you could use the Left function to separate the area code from a telephone number that was provided as an unseparated 10-digit number by your mainframe. In the following statements, the telephone number is stored in the String variable strPhone, which the code assumes was created earlier:

```
Dim strArea As String
strArea = Left(strPhone, 3)
```

This statement creates the variable Area and fills it with the leftmost three characters of the variable strPhone.

USING THE *RIGHT* FUNCTION

The Right function is the mirror image of the Left function and returns a specified number of characters from the right end of a string. The syntax for the Right function is as follows:

```
Right(string, length)
```

Again, the *string* argument is any string expression, and *length* is a numeric expression specifying the number of characters to return. Again, Right returns Null if *string* contains no data, and *length* can be a number or an expression that results in a number.

To continue the previous example, you could use the Right function to separate the last seven digits of the phone number stored in the string strPhone from the area code:

```
Dim strLocalNumber As String
strLocalNumber = Right(strPhone, 7)
```

This statement creates the variable strLocalNumber and fills it with the rightmost seven characters from the variable strPhone.

USING THE *MID* FUNCTION

The Mid function returns the specified number of characters from inside the given string. You specify a starting position in the string and the number of characters (to the right of the starting position) to return.

The syntax for the Mid function is as follows:

```
Mid(string, start[, length])
```

As in `Left` and `Right`, the *string* argument is any string expression. `Mid` returns `Null` if *string* contains no data.

start is a numeric value specifying the character position in *string* at which to start the *length* selection. If *start* is larger than the number of characters in *string*, VBA returns a zero-length string.

length is a numeric expression specifying the number of characters to return. If you omit *length* or use a *length* argument greater than the number of characters in *string*, VBA returns all characters from the *start* position to the end of *string*. Once more, *length* can be a straightforward number or an expression that results in a number.

Still using the phone-number example, you could use `Mid` to return the local exchange code from a 10-digit phone number (for instance, 555 from 5105551212). Here, the telephone number is stored in the variable `strPhone`:

```
Dim strLocalExchange As String
strLocalExchange = Mid(strPhone, 4, 3)
```

This statement creates the variable `strLocalExchange` and fills it with the three characters of the variable `strPhone` starting at the fourth character.

NOTE   If the phone number were supplied in a different format, such as (510) 555-1212 or 510-555-1212, you'd need to adjust the *start* value to allow for the extra characters. For example, if the area code were in parentheses and followed by a space, as in the first instance here, you'd need a *start* value of 7. If the area code were divided from the rest of the phone number only by a hyphen, as in the second instance here, you'd need a *start* value of 5.

You can use `Mid` to find the location of a character within a string. In the following snippet, the `Do Until…` Loop walks backward through the string `strFilename` (which contains the `FullName` property of the template attached to the active document in Word) until it reaches the first backslash (\), storing the resulting character position in the Integer variable `intLen`. The message box then displays that part of `strFilename` to the right of the backslash (determined by subtracting `intLen` from the length of `strFilename`)—the name of the attached template without its path:

```
Dim strFilename As String, intLen As Integer
strFilename = ActiveDocument.AttachedTemplate.FullName
intLen = Len(strFilename)
Do Until Mid(strFilename, intLen, 1) = "\"
    intLen = intLen - 1
Loop
MsgBox Right(strFilename, Len(strFilename) - intLen)
```

This example is more illustrative than realistic for two reasons: First, you can get the name of the template more easily by using the `Name` property rather than the `FullName` property; and second, there's a function called `InStrRev` (discussed next) that returns the position of one string within another by walking backwards through it.

Using *InStr* and *InStrRev* to Find a String within Another String

The `InStr` function allows you to find one string within another string. For example, you could check a string derived from, say, the current paragraph to see if it contained a particular word. If it did, you could take action accordingly—for instance, replacing that word with another word or selecting the paragraph for inclusion in another document.

The InStrRev function is the counterpart of the InStr function, working in a similar way but in the reverse direction.

The syntax for InStr is as follows:

```
InStr([start, ]string1, string2[, compare])
```

The arguments are as follows:

♦ *start* is an optional argument specifying the starting position in the first string, *string1*. If you omit *start*, VBA starts the search at the first character in *string1* (which is usually where you want to start). However, you do need to use *start* when you use the *compare* argument to specify the type of string comparison to perform.

♦ *string1* is a required argument specifying the string expression in which to search for *string2*.

♦ *string2* is a required argument specifying the string expression for which to search in *string1*.

♦ *compare* is an optional argument specifying the type of string comparison you want to perform: a *binary comparison*, which is case sensitive, or a *textual comparison*, which is non–case sensitive. The default is a binary comparison, which you can specify by using the constant vbBinaryCompare or the value 0 for compare; while specifying this value isn't necessary (because it's the default), you might want to use it to make your code ultra-clear. To specify a textual comparison, use the constant vbTextCompare or the value 1 for *compare*.

TIP A textual comparison is a useful weapon when you're dealing with data that may arrive in a variety of cases. For example, if you wanted to search a selection for instances of a name, you'd probably want to find instances of the name in uppercase and lowercase as well as in title case—otherwise you'll find only the name with exactly the same case (for example, title case) as you specified the name.

You could use InStr to find the location of a certain string within another string so that you could then change that inner string. You might want to do this if you needed to move a file from its current position in a particular folder or subfolder to another folder that had a similar subfolder structure. For instance, suppose you work with documents stored in a variety of subfolders beneath a folder named In (such as z:\Documents\In\), and after you're finished with them, you save them in corresponding subfolders beneath a folder named Out (z:\Documents\Out\). The short procedure shown in Listing 9.1 automatically saves the documents in the Out subfolder.

LISTING 9.1:

```
1.  Sub Save_in_Out_Folder()
2.      Dim strOName As String, strNName As String, _
            intToChange As Integer
3.      strOName = ActiveDocument.FullName
4.      intToChange = InStr(strOName, "\In\")
5.      strNName = Left(strOName, intToChange - 1) & "\Out\" _
            & Right(strOName, Len(strOName) - intToChange - 3)
6.      ActiveDocument.SaveAs strNName
7.  End Sub
```

The code in Listing 9.1 works as follows:

◆ Line 1 begins the procedure, and line 7 ends it.

◆ Line 2 declares the String variable strOName (as in *original name*), the String variable strNName (as in *new name*), and the Integer variable intToChange. Line 3 then assigns strOName the FullName property of the ActiveDocument object: the full name of the active document, including the path to the document (for example, z:\Documents\In\ Letters\My Letter.doc).

◆ Line 4 assigns to the variable intToChange the value of the InStr function that finds the string \In\ in the variable strOName. Using the example path from the previous paragraph, intToChange will be assigned the value 13, because the first character of the \In\ string is the thirteenth character in the strOName string.

◆ Line 5 assigns to the variable strNName the new filename created in the main part of the statement. This breaks down as follows:

  ◆ Left(strOName, intToChange - 1) takes the left section of the strOName string, returning the number of characters specified by intToChange - 1—the number stored in intToChange minus one.

  ◆ & "\Out\" adds to the partial string specified in the previous bullet (to continue the previous example, z:\Documents) the characters \Out\, which effectively replace the \In\ characters, thus changing the directory name (z:\Documents\Out\).

  ◆ & Right(strOName, Len(strOName) - intToChange - 3) completes the partial string by adding the right section of the strOName string, starting from after the \In\ string (Letters\My Letter.doc), giving z:\Documents\Out\Letters\My Letter.doc. The number of characters to take from the right section is determined by subtracting the value stored in intToChange from the length of strOName and then subtracting 3 from the result. Here, the value 3 comes from the length of the string \In\; because the intToChange value stores the character number of the first backslash, you need count only the *I*, the *n*, and the second backslash to reach its end.

◆ Line 6 saves the document using the name in the strNName variable.

The syntax for InStrRev is similar to that of InStr:

```
InStrRev(stringcheck, stringmatch[, start[, compare]])
```

These are the arguments:

◆ *stringcheck* is a required String argument specifying the string in which to search for *stringmatch*.

◆ *stringmatch* is a required String argument specifying the string for which to search.

◆ *start* is an optional numeric argument specifying the starting position for the search. If you omit *start*, VBA starts at the last character of *stringcheck*.

◆ *compare* (as for InStr) is an optional argument specifying how to search: vbTextCompare for text, vbBinaryCompare for a binary comparison.

Using *LTrim*, *RTrim*, and *Trim* to Trim Spaces from a String

Often you'll need to trim strings before concatenating them to avoid ending up with extra spaces in inappropriate places, such as in the middle of eight-character filenames.

As you saw in Table 9.8, VBA provides three functions specifically for trimming leading spaces and trailing spaces from strings:

◆ LTrim removes leading spaces from the specified string.

◆ RTrim removes trailing spaces from the specified string.

◆ Trim removes both leading and trailing spaces from the specified string.

TIP In many cases, you can simply use Trim instead of figuring out whether LTrim or RTrim is appropriate for what you expect a variable to contain. At other times, you'll need to remove either leading or trailing spaces while retaining their counterparts, in which case you'll need either LTrim or RTrim. RTrim is especially useful for working with fixed-length String variables, which will contain trailing spaces if the data assigned to them is shorter than their fixed length.

The syntax for the LTrim, RTrim, and Trim functions is straightforward:

```
LTrim(string)
RTrim(string)
Trim(string)
```

In each case, *string* is any string expression.

You could use the Trim function to remove both leading and trailing spaces from a string derived from the current selection in the active document in Word. The first line in the code below declares strUntrimmed and strTrimmed as String variables. The second line assigns the data in the current selection to the strUntrimmed string. The third line assigns the trimmed version of the strUntrimmed string to the strTrimmed string:

```
Dim strUntrimmed As String, strTrimmed As String
strUntrimmed = Selection.Text
strTrimmed = Trim(strUntrimmed)
```

Using *Len* to Check the Length of a String

To check how long a string is, use the Len function. The syntax for the Len function is straightforward:

```
Len(string)
```

Here, *string* is any valid string expression. (If *string* is Null, Len also returns Null.)

You can use Len to make sure that a user's entry in an input box or in a text box of a dialog box is of a suitable length. For example, the CheckPassword procedure shown in Listing 9.2 uses Len to make sure that the password the user enters is of a suitable length.

LISTING 9.2:

```
1.  Sub CheckPassword()
2.      Dim strPassword As String
```

```
3.  BadPassword:
4.      strPassword = InputBox _
            ("Enter the password to protect this item from changes:" _
            , "Enter Password")
5.      If Len(strPassword) = 0 Then
6.          End
7.      ElseIf Len(strPassword) < 6 Then
8.          MsgBox "The password you chose is too short." _
                & vbCr & vbCr & _
                "Choose a password between 6 and 15 characters in length.", _
                vbOKOnly + vbCritical, "Unsuitable Password"
9.          GoTo BadPassword
10      ElseIf Len(strPassword) > 15 Then
11.         MsgBox "The password you chose is too long." _
                & vbCr & vbCr & _
                "Choose a password between 6 and 15 characters in length.", _
                vbOKOnly + vbCritical, "Unsuitable Password"
12.         GoTo BadPassword
13.     End If
14.  End Sub
```

Listing 9.2 provides a relatively crude check of a password, making sure that it contains between 6 and 15 characters (inclusive). Here's how the code works:

◆ Line 2 declares a String variable named strPassword.

◆ Line 3 contains the label BadPassword, to which the GoTo statements in line 9 and line 12 redirect execution if the password fails either of the checks.

◆ Line 4 assigns to strPassword the result of an input box that invites the user to enter the password for the item.

◆ Lines 5 through 13 then use an If statement to check that the password is an appropriate length. First, line 5 checks strPassword for zero length, which would mean that the user either clicked the Cancel button or the close button on the input box, or clicked the OK button with no text entered in the input box. If the length of strPassword is zero, the End statement in line 6 terminates the procedure. If the password passes that test, line 7 checks to find out if its length is less than six characters; if so, the procedure displays a message box alerting the user to the problem and then redirects execution to the BadPassword label. If the password is 6 or more characters long, line 10 checks to see if it's more than 15 characters long; if it is, the user gets another message box and another trip back to the BadPassword label.

Using *StrConv*, *LCase*, and *UCase* to Change the Case of a String

For changing the case of a string, VBA provides the StrConv (whose name comes from *string conversion*), LCase, and UCase functions. Of these, the easiest to use is StrConv, which can convert a string to a number of different formats varying from straightforward uppercase, lowercase, or *propercase* (as VBA refers to initial capitals) to the Japanese *hiragana* and *katakana* phonetic characters.

USING *STRCONV*

The StrConv function has the following syntax:

```
StrConv(string, conversion)
```

Here, the *string* argument is any string expression, and the *conversion* argument is a constant or value specifying the type of conversion required. The most useful conversion constants and values are these:

Constant	Value	Effect
vbUpperCase	1	Converts the given string to uppercase characters.
vbLowerCase	2	Converts the given string to lowercase characters.
vbProperCase	3	Converts the given string to propercase (aka title case—the first letter of every word is capitalized).
vbUnicode	64	Converts the given string to Unicode using the system's default code page.
vbFromUnicode	128	Converts the given string from Unicode to the system's default code page.

For example, suppose you received from a database program a string called strCustomerName containing a person's name. You could use StrConv to make sure that it was in title case by using a statement such as this:

```
strProperCustomerName = StrConv(strCustomerName, vbProperCase)
```

NOTE   StrConv doesn't care about the case of the string you feed it—it simply returns the case you asked for. For example, feeding StrConv uppercase and asking it to return uppercase doesn't give any problem.

USING *LCASE* AND *UCASE*

If you don't feel like using StrConv, you can also use the LCase and UCase functions, which convert a string to lowercase and uppercase, respectively.

LCase and UCase have the following syntax:

```
LCase(string)
UCase(string)
```

Here, *string* is any string expression.

For example, the following statement lowercases the string MyString and assigns it to MyLowerString:

```
MyLowerString = LCase(MyString)
```

Using the *StrComp* Function to Compare Apples to Apples

As you've seen already, you can compare one item to another item by simply using the = operator:

```
If 1 = 1 Then MsgBox "One is one."
```

This straightforward comparison with the = operator also works with two strings, as shown in the second line below:

```
strPet = InputBox("What is your pet?", "Pet")
If strPet = "Dog" Then MsgBox "We do not accept dogs."
```

The problem with this code as written is that the strings need to match exactly in capitalization for VBA to consider them equal: If strPet is dog or DOG (not to mention dOG, doG, dOg, or DoG) rather than Dog, the condition isn't met.

To get around this, you can use the Or operator to hedge your bets:

```
If Pet = "Dog" Or Pet = "dog" Or Pet = "DOG" Or Pet = "dogs" _
    Or Pet = "Dogs" or Pet = "DOGS" Then MsgBox _
    "We do not accept dogs."
```

As you can see, such code rapidly becomes clumsy, even omitting dOG and its miscapitalized canines. You could change the case of one or both strings involved to make sure their case matched, but it's simpler to use the StrComp function, which is designed for this job. The syntax for StrComp is as follows:

```
StrComp(string1, string2 [, compare])
```

Here, *string1* and *string2* are required String arguments specifying the strings to compare, and *compare* is an optional argument specifying textual comparison (vbTextCompare) or binary comparison (vbBinaryCompare).

The following statement uses StrComp to settle the pet question once and for all:

```
If StrComp(Pet, "dog", vbTextCompare) = True Then _
    MsgBox "We do not accept dogs."
```

Using VBA's Mathematical Functions

VBA provides a solid suite of functions for standard mathematical operations. Table 9.9 lists these functions with examples.

TABLE 9.9:   VBA's Mathematical Functions

FUNCTION(ARGUMENT)	RETURNS	EXAMPLE
Abs(*number*)	The absolute value of *number*—the unsigned magnitude of the number.	Abs(-100) returns 100
Atn(*number*)	The arctangent of *number* in radians.	Atn(dblMyAngle)
Cos(*number*)	The cosine of angle *number*.	Cos(dblMyAngle)
Exp(*number*)	e, the base of natural logarithms, raised to the power of *number*.	Exp(5) returns 148.413159102577

TABLE 9.9:   VBA's Mathematical Functions *(CONTINUED)*

FUNCTION(ARGUMENT)	RETURNS	EXAMPLE
Fix(*number*)	The integer portion of *number* (without rounding). If *number* is negative, returns the negative number greater than or equal to *number*.	Fix(3.14159) returns 3 Fix(-3.14159) returns -3
Int(*number*)	The integer portion of *number* (again, without rounding). If *number* is negative, returns the negative number less than or equal to *number*.	Int(3.14159) returns 3 Int(-3.14159) returns -4
Log(*number*)	The natural logarithm of *number*.	Log(dblMyAngle)
Rnd([*number*])	A random number (with no argument) or a number based on the given initial seed.	Rnd(1) returns a random number
Sgn(*number*)	-1 if *number* is negative, 0 if *number* is 0, 1 if *number* is positive.	Sgn(7) returns 1 Sgn(-7) returns -1 Sgn(0) returns 0
Sin(*number*)	The sine of the angle specified by *number* (measured in radians).	Sin(dblMyAngle)
Sqr(*number*)	The square root of *number*. If *number* is negative, VBA gives a runtime error.	Sqr(9) returns 3
Tan(*number*)	The tangent of the angle specified by *number* (measured in radians).	Tan(dblMyAngle)

Using VBA's Date and Time Functions

VBA provides a full complement of date and time functions, as listed in Table 9.10. The table provides brief examples of working with the functions. The sections after the table provide longer examples of working with some of the more complex functions.

TABLE 9.10:   VBA's Date and Time Functions

FUNCTION(ARGUMENTS)	RETURNS	EXAMPLE
Date	A Variant/Date containing the current date according to your computer	MsgBox Date might display 04/01/2006 (the format depends on your Windows date settings).
DateAdd(*interval*, *number*, *date*)	A Variant/Date containing the date of the specified interval after the specified date	DateAdd("m", 1, "6/3/06") returns 7/3/2006.

TABLE 9.10: VBA's Date and Time Functions *(CONTINUED)*

FUNCTION(ARGUMENTS)	RETURNS	EXAMPLE
DatePart(*interval*, *date*)	The part (specified by *interval*) of the specified date	See the example below in the next section.
DateSerial(*year*, *month*, *day*)	A Variant/Date containing the date for the specified year, month, and day	`dteCompanyFounded = DateSerial(1997, 7, 4)`
DateValue(*date*)	A Variant/Date containing the specified date	`dteDeath = "July 2, 1971"`
Day(*date*)	A Variant/Integer between 1 and 31, inclusive, representing the day of the month for *date*	`If Day(Date) = 1 And Month(Date) = 1 Then MsgBox "Happy new year!"`
Hour(*time*)	A Variant/Integer between 0 and 23, inclusive, representing the hour for *time*	`dteHour = Hour(dteLoggedIn)`
Minute(*time*)	A Variant/Integer between 0 and 59, inclusive, representing the minute for *time*	`dteMinute = Minute(dteLoggedIn)`
Month(*date*)	A Variant/Integer between 1 and 12, inclusive, representing the month for *date*	`strThisDate = Month(Date) & "/" & Day(Date)`
MonthName(*month*)	A String containing the name of the month represented by *month*	`MsgBox MonthName(Month(Date))` displays a message box containing the current month.
Now	A Variant/Date containing the current date and time according to your computer	`MsgBox Now` might display 04/01/2006 9:25:15PM. (The format of date and time will depend on your Windows date settings.)
Second(*time*)	A Variant/Integer between 0 and 59, inclusive, representing the second for *time*	`dteSecond = Second(dteLoggedIn)`
Time	A Variant/Date containing the current time according to your computer	`MsgBox Time` might display 9:25:15PM. (The time format and time will depend on your Windows date settings.)
Timer	A Single giving the number of seconds that have elapsed since midnight	`If Timer > 43200 Then MsgBox _ "This code only works in the morning.": End`

TABLE 9.10: VBA's Date and Time Functions *(CONTINUED)*

FUNCTION(ARGUMENTS)	RETURNS	EXAMPLE
TimeSerial(*hour*, *minute*, *second*)	A Variant/Date containing the time for the specified hour, minute, and second	TimeSerial(11, 12, 13) returns 11:12:13AM. (The format will depend on your Windows date settings.)
TimeValue(*time*)	A Variant/Date containing the time for *time*	TimeValue(Now)
Weekday(*date*)	A Variant/Integer containing the day of the week represented by *date*	See the next entry.
WeekdayName (*weekday*)	A String containing the weekday denoted by *weekday*	WeekdayName(Weekday (#4/1/2006#)) returns Saturday, the day of the week for April Fool's Day 2006.

Using the *DatePart* Function to Parse Dates

The DatePart function lets you take a date and separate it into its components. You can often achieve the same effect as DatePart by using other date functions, but DatePart is a great tool to have in your VBA toolbox.

The syntax for DatePart is as follows:

```
DatePart(interval, date[,firstdayofweek[, firstweekofyear]])
```

The components of the syntax are as follows:

◆ *interval* is a required String expression giving the unit in which you want to measure the interval: yyyy for year, q for quarter, m for month, y for the day of the year, d for day, w for weekday, ww for week, h for hour, n for minute (because m is for month), and s for second.

◆ *date* is a required Variant/Date giving the date you want to examine.

◆ *firstdayofweek* is an optional constant specifying the day that starts the week (for date information): The default setting is vbSunday (1), but you can also set vbMonday (2), vbTuesday (3), vbWednesday (4), vbThursday (5), vbFriday (6), vbSaturday (7), or vbUseSystem (0; this uses the system setting).

◆ *firstweekofyear* is an optional constant specifying the week considered first in the year:

Constant	Value	Year Starts with Week
vbUseSystem	0	Use the system setting.
vbFirstJan1	1	The week in which January 1 falls (the default setting).

Constant	Value	Year Starts with Week
vbFirstFourDays	2	The first week with a minimum of four days in the year.
vbFirstFullWeek	3	The first full week (7 days) of the year.

For example, the following statement assigns the current year to the variable dteThisYear:

```
dteThisYear = DatePart("yyyy", Date)
```

Using the *DateDiff* Function to Return an Interval

The DateDiff function returns the interval between two specified dates. The syntax for DateDiff is as follows:

```
DateDiff(interval, date1, date2[, firstdayofweek[, firstweekofyear]])
```

The components of the syntax are as follows:

♦ *interval* is a required String expression giving the unit in which you want to measure the interval: yyyy for year, q for quarter, m for month, y for the day of the year, d for day, w for weekday, ww for week, h for hour, n for minute (because m is for month), and s for second.

♦ *date1* and *date2* are the dates between which you're calculating the interval.

♦ *firstdayofweek* is an optional constant specifying the day that starts the week (for date information). The default setting is vbSunday (1), but you can also set vbMonday (2), vbTuesday (3), vbWednesday (4), vbThursday (5), vbFriday (6), vbSaturday (7), or vbUseSystem (0; uses the system setting).

♦ *firstweekofyear* is an optional constant specifying the week considered first in the year:

Constant	Value	Year Starts with Week
vbUseSystem	0	Use the system setting.
vbFirstJan1	1	The week in which January 1 falls (the default setting).
vbFirstFourDays	2	The first week with a minimum of four days in the year.
vbFirstFullWeek	3	The first full week (7 days) of the year.

For example, the following statement returns the number of weeks between June 3, 2006 and September 30, 2006:

```
MsgBox DateDiff("ww", "6/3/2006", "9/30/2006")
```

Using the *DateAdd* Function to Add to a Date

The DateAdd function lets you easily add an interval of time to, or subtract an interval of time from, a specified date, returning the resulting date. The syntax for DateAdd is as follows:

```
DateAdd(interval, number, date)
```

The components of the syntax are as follows:

- *interval* is a required String expression giving the unit of measurement for the interval: yyyy for year, q for quarter, m for month, y for the day of the year, d for day, w for weekday, ww for week, h for hour, n for minute, and s for second.

- *number* is a required numeric expression giving the number of intervals to add (a positive number) or to subtract (a negative number). If *number* isn't already of the data type Long, VBA rounds it to the nearest whole number before evaluating the function.

- *date* is a required Variant/Date or literal date giving the starting date.

For example, the following statement returns the date 10 weeks from May 27, 2006:

```
DateAdd("ww", 10, #5/27/2006#)
```

Using File-Management Functions

This section shows you a couple of key file-management functions that VBA provides: the Dir function, which you use to find out whether a file exists, and the CurDir function, which returns the current path.

Using the *Dir* Function to Check Whether a File Exists

Before performing many file operations, you'll want to check whether a particular file exists. If you're about to save a new file automatically with a procedure, you may want to make sure that the save operation won't overwrite an existing file. If you're going to open a file automatically, you may want to check that the file exists in its supposed location before you use the Open method; otherwise, VBA will give an error.

To test whether a file exists, you can use a straightforward procedure such as the one shown in Listing 9.3.

LISTING 9.3:

```
1.  Sub Does_File_Exist()
2.      Dim strTestFile As String, strNameToTest As String, _
            strMsg As String
3.      strNameToTest = InputBox("Enter the file name and path:")
4.      If strNameToTest = "" Then End
5.      strTestFile = Dir(strNameToTest)
6.      If Len(strTestFile) = 0 Then
7.          strMsg = "The file " & strNameToTest & _
                " does not exist."
8.      Else
```

```
 9.             strMsg = "The file " & strNameToTest & " exists."
10.         End If
11.         MsgBox strMsg, vbOKOnly + vbInformation, _
                "File-Existence Check"
12.     End Sub
```

This procedure in Listing 9.3 uses the `Dir` function to check whether a file exists and displays a message box indicating whether it does or doesn't. Figure 9.3 shows examples of the message box. This message box is for demonstration purposes only—in most cases, you'll use the result of the test to direct the flow of the procedure according to whether the file exists. Here's how the code works:

◆ Line 2 declares the string variables `strTestFile`, `strNameToTest`, and `strMsg`.

FIGURE 9.3
You can use the Dir function to check whether a file exists so that you don't accidentally overwrite it or cause an error by trying to open a nonexistent file.

◆ Line 3 then displays an input box prompting the user to enter a filename and path; VBA assigns the result of the input box to `strNameToTest`.

◆ Line 4 compares `strNameToTest` to a blank string (which means the user clicked the Cancel button in the input box or clicked the OK button without entering any text in the text box) and uses an `End` statement to end the procedure if it gets a match.

◆ Line 5 assigns to `strTestFile` the result of running the `Dir` function on the `strNameToTest` string. If `Dir` finds a match for `strNameToTest`, `strTestFile` will contain the name of the matching file; otherwise, it will contain an empty string.

◆ Line 6 begins an `If…` `Then` statement by testing the length of the `strTestFile` string. If the length is 0, the statement in line 7 assigns to `strMsg` text saying that the file doesn't exist; otherwise, VBA branches to the `Else` statement in line 8 and runs the statement in line 9, assigning text to `strMsg` saying that the file does exist. Line 10 ends the `If` statement.

◆ Line 11 displays a message box containing `strMsg`. Line 12 ends the procedure.

WARNING   The code shown in Listing 9.3 isn't bulletproof, because `Dir` is designed to work with wildcards as well as regular characters. As long as you have a textual filename in `strNameToTest`, you'll be fine, because `Dir` compares that text to the filenames, and the result lets you know whether you have a match. But if `strNameToTest` contains suitable wildcards (say it's `c:\temp\*.*`), `Dir` tells you that the file exists—but of course there's no file by that name, just one or more files that match the wildcards. You can check on line 5 whether the name returned by `Dir` is exactly the same as the input name, but then you need to make sure you do a case-insensitive comparison. This literalness of `Dir` is a nice illustration of GIGO (garbage in, garbage out)—from the computer's (and VBA's) point of view, it's doing what you asked it to, but the result is far from what you intended.

Returning the Current Path

You can return the current path (the path to which the host application is currently set) on either the current drive or on a specified drive by using the CurDir function. Often, you'll need to change the current path to make sure the user is saving files in, or opening files from, a suitable location.

To return the current path, use CurDir without an argument:

```
CurDir
```

To return the current path for a specified drive, enter the drive letter as an argument. For example, to return the current path on drive D, use this statement:

```
CurDir("D")
```

Chapter 10

Creating Your Own Functions

- ◆ Components of a function statement
- ◆ Creating a function
- ◆ Creating a function for Word
- ◆ Creating a function for Excel
- ◆ Creating a function for PowerPoint

In this chapter, you'll learn how to create your own functions. You create a function just like you create a procedure, by working in the Code window for the module in which you want to store the function. (You can't record a function, even if the application you're using hosts the Macro Recorder—you have to write it.)

This chapter starts by explaining the components of a function and showing you how to put them together. You then create some functions that work in any VBA host and some functions that are specific to Word, Excel, and PowerPoint.

Components of a Function

To create a function, you use a Function statement. The syntax for the Function statement is as follows:

```
[Public | Private] [Static] Function function_name [(argument_list)] [As type]
    [statements]
    [function_name = expression]
    [Exit Function]
    [statements]
    [function_name = expression]
End Function
```

The syntax breaks down like this:

- ◆ Public is an optional keyword that you can use to make the function publicly accessible—accessible to all other procedures in all loaded modules. (If you need to limit the function's scope to the project that contains it, you can override this public availability by putting an Option Private Module statement in the module that contains the function.)

- ◆ Private is an optional keyword that you can use to make the function accessible to the other procedures in the module that contains it. The function is hidden from procedures in any other module.

♦ `Static` is an optional keyword that you can use to make local variables in the function retain their value between calls to the function.

♦ *function_name* is a required argument that gives the name of the function. Functions follow the same naming rules as other VBA items: Alphanumerics and underscores are fine, but no spaces, symbols, or punctuation.

♦ *argument_list* is an optional argument supplying the list of variables that represent arguments passed to the function. *argument_list* takes the syntax shown below:

```
[Optional] [ByRef | ByVal] [ParamArray] variable_name[( )] [As type]
[= default_value]
```

♦ `Optional` is an optional keyword that you can use to denote that an argument is optional—in other words, that it is not required. Once you've used `Optional` to declare an optional argument, all the other arguments in *argument_list* have to be optional. That means you have to put the required arguments before the optional arguments, just the same way VBA does. It's a good idea to give optional arguments a default value.

♦ `ByRef` is an optional keyword that you can use to specify that an argument be passed *by reference*; `ByVal` is an optional keyword that you can use to specify that an argument be passed *by value*. Briefly, you can pass an argument either by reference or by value. See the next Note for an explanation of these terms.

NOTE   When a procedure (either a function or a subprocedure) passes an argument to another procedure *by reference*, the recipient procedure gets access to the memory location where the original variable is stored and can change the original variable. By contrast, when an argument is passed *by value*, the recipient procedure or function gets only a copy of the information in the variable and can't change the information in the original variable. By reference is the default way to pass an argument, but you can also use the ByRef keyword to state explicitly that you want to pass an argument by reference.

♦ `ParamArray` is an optional keyword you can use as the last argument in *argument_list* to denote an optional array of Variants. You can't use `ParamArray` with `ByVal`, `ByRef`, or `Optional`.

♦ *variable_name* is the name of the variable that represents the argument.

♦ *type* is an optional keyword giving the data type of the argument (Byte, Boolean, Currency, Date, Decimal, Double, Integer, Long, Object, Single, variable-length String, or Variant. For non-optional arguments, you can also specify an object type (for example, a `Worksheet` object) or a custom object (one you've created).

♦ *default_value* is an optional constant or constant expression that you use to specify a default value for optional parameters.

♦ *type* is an optional argument specifying the data type of value that the function returns: Byte, Boolean, Currency, Date, Decimal, Double, Integer, Long, Object, Single, variable-length String, Variant, or a custom type.

- *statements* represents the statement or statements in the function. In theory, *statements* is optional, but in practice, most functions will need one or more statements.

- *expression* represents the value the function returns. *expression* is also optional.

Creating a Function

This section walks you through the process of creating a function.

Starting a Function Manually

The easiest way to start creating a function is to type **Function**, the name you want to give to the function, and the necessary arguments in parentheses, and then press Enter. VBA automatically enters a blank line and an End Function statement for you and places the insertion point on the blank line ready for you to create the function. For example, if you type the following line and press Enter, the Visual Basic Editor gives you what you see in Figure 10.1.

```
Function MyFunction(MaxTemp, MinTemp)
```

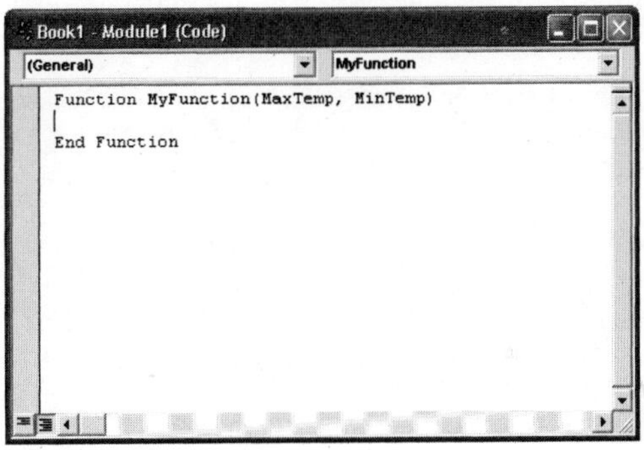

FIGURE 10.1

When you type a Function statement and press Enter, the Visual Basic Editor automatically inserts a blank line and an End Function statement for you.

Starting a Function by Using the Add Procedure Dialog Box

If you like to make the Visual Basic Editor work *for* you as much as possible, you can also start creating a new function by using the Add Procedure dialog box:

1. Choose Insert ➤ Procedure to display the Add Procedure dialog box (see Figure 10.2).

2. Type the name for the procedure in the Name text box.

3. Select the Function option button in the Type group box.

4. Select the Public option button or the Private option button (as appropriate) in the Scope group box.

5. If you want all local variables to be statics (which you usually won't), select the All Local Variables As Statics check box.

6. Click the OK button to enter the stub for the function, and then enter its arguments in the parentheses manually.

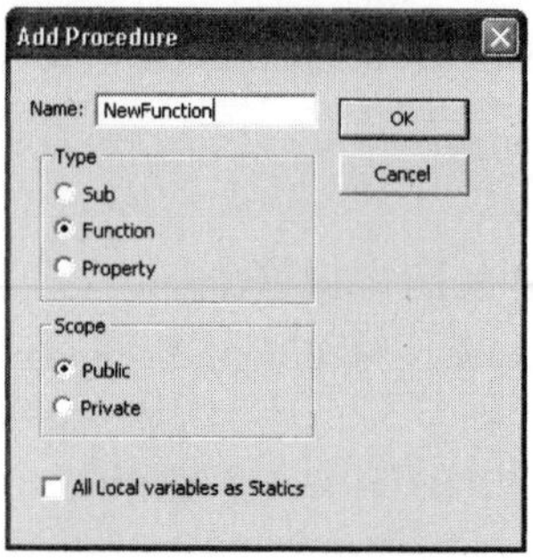

FIGURE 10.2
You can also use the Add
Procedure dialog box to
specify the parameters
for a new function.

Passing Arguments to the Function

The Function statement assigns to the given function name (in the example above, MyFunction) the value
that the function returns. In parentheses, separated by a comma, are the arguments that will be passed to
the Function statement. In our example, the function will work with an argument named MaxTemp and an
argument named MinTemp to return its result. You can define the data type of the arguments if you want
by including an As statement with the data type after the argument's name. For example, you could use
the following statement to set the MaxTemp and MinTemp arguments to the Double data type:

```
Function MyFunction(MaxTemp As Double, MinTemp As Double)
```

Passing an argument by reference is useful when you want to manipulate the variable in the recipient
procedure and then return the variable to the procedure from which it originated. Alternatively, passing
an argument by value is useful when you want to use the information stored in the variable in the recipient
procedure and at the same time ensure that the original information in the variable doesn't change.

As mentioned above, by reference is the default way of passing an argument, so both of the
following statements pass the argument MyArg by reference:

```
Function PassByReference(MyArg)
Function PassByReference(ByRef MyArg)
```

To pass an argument by value, you must use the ByVal keyword. The following statement passes
the ValArg argument by value:

```
Function PassByValue(ByVal ValArg)
```

If necessary, you can pass some arguments for a procedure by reference and others by value. The
following statement passes the MyArg argument by reference and the ValArg argument by value:

```
Function PassBoth(ByRef MyArg, ByVal ValArg)
```

Declaring the Data Types of Arguments

You can explicitly declare the data type of arguments you pass in order to take up less memory and
ensure that your procedures are passing the type of information you intend them to. But when passing an argument by reference, make sure that the data type of the argument you're passing matches
the data type expected in the procedure. For example, if you declare a String and try to pass it as an
argument when the receiving procedure is expecting a Variant, VBA gives an error.

To declare the data type of an argument, include a data-type declaration in the argument list. The following statement declares `MyArg` as a string to be passed by reference and `ValArg` as a variant to be passed by value:

```
Function PassBoth(ByRef MyArg As String, ByVal ValArg As Variant)
```

Specifying an Optional Argument

You can specify an optional argument by using the `Optional` keyword. Place the `Optional` keyword before the `ByRef` or `ByVal` keyword if you need to use `ByRef` or `ByVal`:

```
Function PassBoth(ByRef MyArg As String, ByVal ValArg As Variant, _
    Optional ByVal strName As String)
```

When you specify an optional argument, it's a good idea to assign a default value to it. Doing so makes the code less susceptible to errors. To assign the default value, type an equal sign after the variable's definition and then the default value (use double quotation marks for a String value). For example, the following function statement declares the strName optional argument and assigns the default value if no value is passed:

```
Function PassBoth(ByRef MyArg As String, ByVal ValArg As Variant, _
    Optional ByVal strName As String = "Sacramento")
```

Controlling the Scope of a Function

Like a procedure, a function can have private or public scope. Private scope makes the function available only to procedures in the module that contains it, and public scope makes the function available to all open modules. If you don't specify whether a function is private or public, VBA makes it public by default, so you don't need to specify the scope of a function unless you need it to have private scope. However, if you do use explicit `Public` declarations on those functions you intend to be public, your code will be somewhat easier to read than if you don't:

```
Private Function MyFunction(MaxTemp, MinTemp)
Public Function AnotherFunction(Industry, Average)
```

TIP   You can restrict all the functions and procedures in a module to private scope by using an `Option Private Module` statement in the declarations area of the module.

Examples of Functions for Any VBA-Enabled Application

This section contains two examples of functions that will work in any application that hosts VBA. Later in this chapter, you'll see examples of functions that are specific to certain applications.

To start, first declare the function and its arguments. The following statement declares a function named `NetProfit`:

```
Function NetProfit(Gross As Double, Expenses As Double) As Double
```

`NetProfit` uses two arguments, `Gross` and `Expenses`, declaring each as the Double data type. Likewise, it explicitly types its return value as a Double. Explicitly typing the arguments and the return value can help you avoid unpleasant surprises in your code, because VBA catches any attempt to pass the wrong data type to the function and alerts you if the function is asked to return a data type other than its declared type.

Armed with the arguments (and their type, if they're explicitly typed), you call NetProfit as you would a built-in function, by using its name and supplying the two arguments it needs:

```
MyProfit = NetProfit(44000, 34000)
```

Here, the variable MyProfit is assigned the value of the NetProfit function run with a Gross argument of 44000 and an Expenses argument of 34000.

Once you've created a function, the Visual Basic Editor displays its argument list when you type the name of the function in a procedure in the Code window, as shown in Figure 10.3.

FIGURE 10.3

The Visual Basic Editor displays a ScreenTip of Quick Info on functions you create, as well as on its built-in functions.

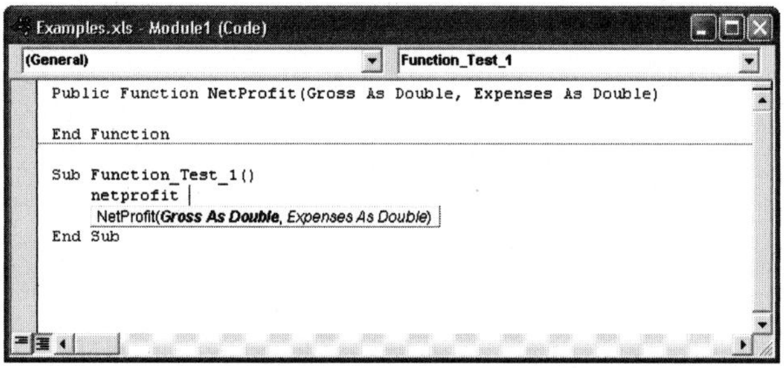

Listing 10.1 contains an example of calling a function: The ShowProfit procedure calls the NetProfit function and displays the result in a message box.

LISTING 10.1:

```
1.  Sub ShowProfit()
2.      MsgBox (NetProfit(44000, 34000)),, "Net Profit"
3.   End Sub
4.
5.  Function NetProfit(Gross As Double, Expenses As Double) As Double
6.      NetProfit = (Gross - Expenses) * 0.9
7.  End Function
```

In Listing 10.1, lines 1 to 3 contain the ShowProfit procedure, which simply calls the NetProfit function in line 2, passes it the arguments 44000 for Gross and 34000 for Expenses, and displays the result in a message box titled Net Profit.

Lines 5 to 7 contain the NetProfit function. Line 5 declares the function as working with two Double arguments, Gross and Expenses, telling VBA what to do with the two arguments that line 2 has passed to the function. Line 6 sets NetProfit to be 90 percent (0.9) of the value of Gross minus Expenses. Line 7 ends the function, at which point the value of NetProfit is passed back to line 2, which displays the message box containing the result.

Listing 10.2 contains a function that returns a String argument.

LISTING 10.2:

```
1.  Sub TestForSmog()
2.      Dim intCYear As Integer, strThisCar As String
3.  BadValueLoop:
4.      On Error GoTo Bye
5.      intCYear = InputBox("Enter the year of your car.", _
            "Do I Need a Smog Check?")
6.      strThisCar = NeedsSmog(intCYear)
7.      If strThisCar = "Yes" Then
8.          MsgBox "Your car needs a smog check.", _
                vbOKOnly + vbExclamation, "Smog Check"
9.      ElseIf strThisCar = "BadValue" Then
10.         MsgBox "The year you entered is in the future.", _
                vbOKOnly + vbCritical, "Smog Check"
11.         GoTo BadValueLoop
12.     Else
13.         MsgBox "Your car does not need a smog check.", _
                vbOKOnly + vbInformation, "Smog Check"
14.     End If
15. Bye:
16. End Sub
17.
18. Function NeedsSmog(CarYear As Integer) As String
19.     If CarYear > Year(Now) Then
20.         NeedsSmog = "BadValue"
21.     ElseIf CarYear <= Year(Now) - 3 Then
22.         NeedsSmog = "Yes"
23.     Else
24.         NeedsSmog = "No"
25.     End If
26. End Function
```

Listing 10.2 contains the procedure TestForSmog (lines 1 to 16) and the NeedsSmog function (lines 18 to 26). The TestForSmog procedure calls the NeedsSmog function, which returns a value indicating whether the user's car needs a smog check. TestForSmog uses this value to display a message box (see Figure 10.4) informing the user whether or not their car needs a smog check.

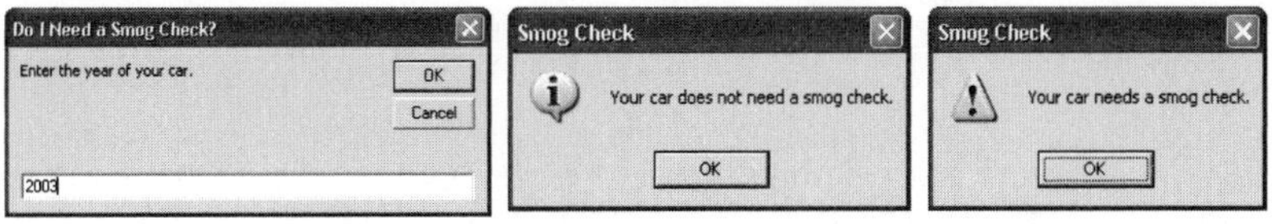

FIGURE 10.4
The TestForSmog procedure prompts for the car's year and then displays a message box stating whether the car needs a smog test.

Here's how the code works:

◆ `TestForSmog` starts by declaring the Integer variable `intCYear` and the String variable `strThisCar` in line 2.

◆ Line 3 contains the `BadValueLoop` label, to which execution returns from line 11 if the user has entered an unsuitable value for the year of their car.

◆ Line 4 contains an `On Error` statement to direct execution to the `Bye` label in line 15 if an error occurs. An error occurs if the user cancels the upcoming input box or chooses its OK button with no value entered in its text box.

◆ Line 5 displays an input box prompting the user to enter the year of their car. This line assigns to the `intCYear` variable the value the user enters in the input box.

◆ Line 6 then sets the value of the String variable `strThisCar` to the result of the `NeedsSmog` function running on the `intCYear` integer variable.

◆ Execution now shifts to the `NeedsSmog` function (line 18), which evaluates `intCYear` and returns the value for `strThisCar`. Line 18 declares the function, assigning its value to `NeedsSmog`. The function takes one argument, `CarYear`, which is declared as the Integer data type.

◆ Line 19 checks to see whether `CarYear` is greater than the value of the current year (`Year(Now)`). If so, line 20 sets the value of `NeedsSmog` to `BadValue`, which is used to indicate that the user has entered a date in the future. If not, the `ElseIf` statement in line 21 runs, checking if the value of `CarYear` is less than or equal to `Year(Now) - 3`, the current year minus three. If so, line 22 sets the value of `NeedsSmog` to `Yes`; if not, the `Else` statement in line 23 runs, and line 24 sets the value of `NeedsSmog` to `No`. Line 25 ends the `If` statement, and line 26 ends the function.

◆ Execution then returns to the calling line (line 6) in the `TestForSmog` procedure, to which the `NeedsSmog` function returns the value it has assigned to the `strThisCar` variable.

◆ The rest of the `TestForSmog` procedure then works with the `strThisCar` variable. Line 7 compares `strThisCar` to `Yes`; if it matches, line 8 displays a message box stating that the car needs a smog check. If `strThisCar` doesn't match `Yes`, line 9 compares `ThisCar` to `BadValue`. If it matches, line 10 displays an alert message box, and line 11 returns execution to the `BadValueLoop` label in line 3. If `strThisCar` doesn't match `BadValue`, the `Else` statement in line 12 runs, and line 13 displays a message box stating that the car doesn't need a smog check.

◆ Line 14 ends the `If` statement; line 15 contains the `Bye` label; and line 16 ends the procedure.

You don't have to use a function as simply as the examples shown here: You can also include a function as part of a larger expression. For example, you could add the results of the functions `NetProfit` and `CurrentBalance` (which takes a single argument) by using a statement such as this:

```
CurrentEstimate = NetProfit(44000, 33000) + CurrentBalance(MainAccount)
```

Creating a Function for Word

Functions such as those shown in the previous section work in any VBA-hosting application because they do not call any application-specific features. This section and the following two sections show you examples of functions that are specific to applications.

TIP Keep your functions that aren't application-specific in separate modules so that you can export the module as a BAS file and import it into whichever application needs the functions. For example, you might maintain separate modules that contained your math equations, your string-manipulation functions, and other custom functions that would work in any VBA host.

The function shown in Listing 10.3 is for Word and—unusually for a function—returns a null value. The function's main purpose is to perform several operations on the specified document.

TIP When you don't need to return a value, it's technically better to use a subprocedure rather than a function, because a subprocedure uses slightly fewer resources. However, the difference is seldom worth worrying about.

LISTING 10.3:

```
1.   Option Explicit
2.
3.   Function Strip_Hyperlinks_Bookmarks_Fields()
4.       Dim myLink As Hyperlink
5.       Dim myBookmark As Bookmark
6.       Dim myField As Field
7.       With ActiveDocument
8.           For Each myLink In .Hyperlinks
9.               myLink.Delete
10.          Next myLink
11.          For Each myBookmark In .Bookmarks
12.              myBookmark.Delete
13.          Next myBookmark
14.          For Each myField In .Fields
15.              myField.Unlink
16.          Next myField
17.      End With
18.  End Function
19.
20.  Sub Clean_Up_Document_for_Conversion()
21.      Call Strip_Hyperlinks_Bookmarks_Fields
22.      'other cleanup functions here
23.  End Sub
```

Here's how the code works:

◆ Line 1 contains the `Option Explicit` statement for the module to force explicit declarations of all variables. Line 2 is a spacer.

◆ Line 3 starts the function named `Strip_Hyperlinks_Bookmarks_Fields`, which removes all hyperlinks, bookmarks, and fields from the active document. The function continues until the `End Function` statement in line 18.

◆ Line 4 declares a variable named myLink as being of the Hyperlink type. Line 5 declares a variable named myBookmark as being of the Bookmark type. Line 6 declares a variable named myField as being of the Field type.

◆ Line 7 begins a With statement that works with the ActiveDocument object and continues until the End With statement in line 17. This With statement contains three For Each... Next loops.

◆ The first For Each... Next loop, in lines 8 through 10, goes through each myLink object in the Hyperlinks collection. Line 9 uses the Delete method to delete each of the links in turn. Deleting a hyperlink removes the link from the document but leaves the text that was displayed for the hyperlink.

◆ The second For Each... Next loop, in lines 11 through 13, works with each myBookmark object in the Bookmarks collection. Line 12 uses the Delete method to delete each of the bookmarks in turn. Deleting a bookmark removes the marker from the document but leaves any text or other object that the bookmark contained.

◆ The third For Each... Next loop, in lines 14 through 16, works with each myField object in the Fields collection. Line 15 uses the Unlink method to unlink each of the fields in turn. Unlinking a field leaves the field's contents in the document as text or as an object but removes the field link.

◆ Line 17 contains the End With statement that ends the With statement, and line 18 contains the End Function statement that ends the function. Line 19 is a spacer.

◆ Lines 20 through 23 contain a short subprocedure that simply calls the Strip_Hyperlinks_ Bookmarks_Fields function. Line 22 contains a comment stating that the subprocedure would call other cleanup functions.

Creating a Function for Excel

This section shows you a function for Excel. The function in Listing 10.4 checks whether a workbook contains any unused sheets.

LISTING 10.4:

```
1.  Option Explicit
2.
3.  Function BlankSheetsInWorkbook(ByRef WorkbookToTest As Workbook) As Boolean
4.      Dim objWorksheet As Worksheet
5.      BlankSheetsInWorkbook = False
6.      For Each objWorksheet In WorkbookToTest.Worksheets
7.          If Application.WorksheetFunction.CountBlank _
                (objWorksheet.Range("A1:IV65536")) = 16777216 Then
8.              BlankSheetsInWorkbook = True
9.              Exit Function
10.         End If
11.     Next objWorksheet
```

```
12.   End Function
13.
14.   Sub Check_Workbook_for_Blank_Worksheets()
15.       If BlankSheetsInWorkbook(ActiveWorkbook) = True Then
16.           MsgBox "This workbook contains one or more blank worksheets." & _
                  vbCr & vbCr & "Please remove all blank worksheets before" & _
                  " submitting the workbook.", vbOKOnly & vbExclamation, _
                  "Check Workbook for Blank Worksheets"
17.       End If
18.   End Sub
```

Here's how the code works:

◆ Line 1 contains the `Option Explicit` statement for the module to force explicit declarations of all variables. Line 2 is a spacer.

◆ Line 3 starts the function named `BlankSheetsInWorkbook`, which it declares as a Boolean function. The function works on an object named `WorkbookToTest`, which has the type `Workbook`—in other words, it's a workbook.

◆ Line 4 declares a variable named `objWorksheet` that is of the `Worksheet` type.

◆ Line 5 sets the value of the `BlankSheetsInWorkbook` function to `False`.

◆ Line 6 starts a `For Each... Next` loop that runs for each `objWorksheet` object (each worksheet) in the `Worksheets` collection in the `WorkbookToTest` object—that is, with each worksheet in the workbook that is passed to the function.

◆ Line 7 uses the COUNTBLANK worksheet function to count the number of blank cells in the range A1:IV65536 in the worksheet being tested by the loop. If the number of blank cells is 16777216, the worksheet is blank, because this is the number of cells in a worksheet. Line 8 then sets the value of the `BlankSheetsInWorkbook` function to `True`, and line 9 uses an `Exit Function` statement to exit the function. This is because there is no need to test any more worksheets once the function has found that one worksheet is blank.

◆ Line 10 contains the `End If` statement that ends the `If` statement. Line 11 contains the `Next objWorksheet` statement that ends the `For Each... Next` loop. And line 12 contains the `End Function` statement that ends the function. Line 13 is a spacer.

◆ Line 14 begins a short subprocedure named `Check_Workbook_for_Blank_Worksheets`. Line 15 runs the `BlankSheetsInWorkbook` function on the `ActiveWorkbook` object, which represents the active workbook in the Excel session. If the `BlankSheetsInWorkbook` function returns `True`, line 16 displays a message box (shown below) that points out to the user that the workbook contains one or more blank worksheets and tells the user to remove them.

Creating a Function for PowerPoint

This section shows an example function for PowerPoint. The function in Listing 10.5 checks that all the text on a slide is at least the minimum font size specified and displays a error message box if any font is too small.

LISTING 10.5:

```
1.   Option Explicit
2.
3.   Function CheckMinFontSize(objPresentation As Presentation) As Boolean
4.
5.       Dim objSlide As Slide
6.       Dim objShape As Shape
7.
8.       CheckMinFontSize = True
9.
10.      For Each objSlide In objPresentation.Slides
11.          objSlide.Select
12.          objSlide.Shapes.SelectAll
13.          For Each objShape In Windows(1).Selection.ShapeRange
14.              If objShape.Type = msoPlaceholder Then
15.                  If objShape.TextFrame.TextRange.Font.Size < 14 Then
16.                      CheckMinFontSize = False
17.                      Exit Function
18.                  End If
19.              End If
20.          Next objShape
21.      Next objSlide
22.  End Function
23.
24.  Sub Font_Check()
25.      If CheckMinFontSize(ActivePresentation) = False Then
26.          MsgBox "Some of the fonts in this presentation are too small." _
             & vbCr & vbCr & "Please change all fonts to 14 points or larger.", _
             vbCritical + vbOKOnly, "Font Size Check"
27.      End If
28.  End Sub
```

Here's how the code works:

◆ Line 1 contains the `Option Explicit` statement for the module to force explicit declarations of all variables. Line 2 is a spacer.

◆ Line 3 declares the function named `CheckMinFontSize` as Boolean and specifies that it works on a variable named `objPresentation`, which is of the `Presentation` type. Line 4 is a spacer.

◆ Line 5 declares a variable named `objSlide` that is of the `Slide` type. Line 6 declares a variable named `objShape` that is of the `Shape` type. Line 7 is a spacer.

◆ Line 8 sets the value of the `CheckMinFontSize` function to `True`. This indicates that the font sizes are the minimum size or larger. Line 9 is a spacer.

◆ Line 10 starts a `For Each... Next` loop that continues until line 21 and works with each `objSlide` object in the `Slides` collection in the `objPresentation` object. This loop makes the function examine each of the `Slide` objects in the presentation that is passed to the function.

◆ Line 11 selects the current `objSlide` object, and line 12 uses the `SelectAll` method of the `Slides` collection.

◆ Line 13 starts a nested `For Each... Next` loop that runs once for each of the `objShape` objects in the `ShapeRange` object in the `Selection` object in the first window (`Windows(1)`). The `ShapeRange` object contains all of the `Shape` objects within the selection. Here, the `Shape` objects are represented by the `objShape` variable.

◆ Line 14 uses an `If` statement to see if the `Type` property of the current `Shape` object is `msoPlaceholder`, the type that indicates a placeholder used for text. If the shape is a placeholder, line 15 checks if the font size used in the `TextRange` object within the `TextFrame` object within the `Shape` object is smaller than 14 points. If so, line 16 assigns the value `False` to the `CheckMinFontSize` function, and line 17 uses an `Exit Function` statement to stop execution of the function. This is because, once a font smaller than the minimum permitted size has been found, there is no need to check further.

◆ Line 18 contains the `End If` statement that ends the nested `If` structure, and line 19 contains the `End If` statement that ends the outer `If` structure.

◆ Line 20 contains the `Next objShape` statement that ends the nested `For Each... Next` loop, and line 21 contains the `Next objSlide` statement that ends the outer `For Each... Next` loop.

◆ Line 22 contains the `End Function` statement that ends the function. Line 23 is a spacer.

◆ Lines 24 through 28 contain a brief subprocedure named `Font_Check` that runs the `CheckMinFontSize` function on the `ActivePresentation` object. If the function returns `False`, the subprocedure displays a message box (shown here) alerting the user to the problem.

Chapter 11

Making Decisions in Your Code

- ◆ Comparison operators
- ◆ Comparing one item with another
- ◆ Testing multiple conditions
- ◆ *If* statements
- ◆ *Select Case* statements

This chapter shows you the conditional expressions that VBA provides for creating decision structures to direct the flow of your procedures. By using decision structures, you can cause your procedures to branch to different sections of code depending on such things as the value of a variable or expression, or which button the user chooses in a message box or dialog box.

VBA provides several types of If statements suitable for making simple or complex decisions, as well as the heavy-duty Select Case statement for simplifying the coding of truly involved decisions.

The chapter starts by introducing you to the comparison operators and logical operators you can use when building conditional expressions and logical expressions. Then it covers the different types of If statements, which take up the bulk of the chapter. At the end of the chapter, you'll learn about Select Case statements.

How Do You Compare Things in VBA?

To compare things in VBA, you use *comparison operators* to specify what type of comparison you want to apply: Is one variable or expression equal to another; is one greater than another; is one less than or equal to another; and so on.

VBA supports the comparison operators shown in Table 11.1.

TABLE 11.1: VBA's Comparison Operators

OPERATOR	MEANING	EXAMPLE
=	Equal to	`If strMyString = "Hello" Then`
<>	Not equal to	`If x <> 5 Then`
<	Less than	`If y < 100 Then`

TABLE 11.1: VBA's Comparison Operators *(CONTINUED)*

OPERATOR	MEANING	EXAMPLE
>	Greater than	`If strMyString > "handle" Then`
<=	Less than or equal to	`If intMyCash <= 10 Then`

>=	Greater than or equal to	`If Time >= 12:00 PM Then`
		`    MsgBox "It's afternoon"`
		`Else`
		`    MsgBox "It's morning."`
		`End If`

Is	Is the same object variable as	`If Object1 Is Object2 Then`

The first six comparison operators shown in Table 11.1 are straightforward, particularly if you recall your math. Numeric expressions are evaluated as normal. Alphabetical expressions are evaluated in alphabetical order: for example, because *ax* comes before *handle* in alphabetical order, it's considered "less than" *handle*. Mixed expressions (numbers and letters) are evaluated in alphabetical order as well: *Office 97* is "greater than" *Office 2003* because 9 is greater than 2.

The seventh comparison operator, `Is`, is more complex. You use `Is` to establish whether two object variables represent the same object—a named object, not an object such as a document or a range. For example, the following statements declare two objects—`objTest1` and `objTest2`—and assign to each `ActiveDocument.Paragraphs(1).Range`, the range consisting of the first paragraph in the active document in Word. The next statement then compares the two objects to each other, returning `False` in the message box because the two objects are different even though their contents are the same:

```
Dim objTest1 As Object
Dim objTest2 As Object
Set objTest1 = ActiveDocument.Paragraphs(1).Range
Set objTest2 = ActiveDocument.Paragraphs(1).Range
'the next statement returns False because the objects are different
MsgBox objTest1 Is objTest2
```

However, if both object variables refer to the same object, the `Is` comparison returns `True`, as in the following example, in which both `objTest1` and `objTest2` refer to the object variable `objTest3`:

```
Dim objTest1 As Object
Dim objTest2 As Object
Dim objTest3 As Object
Set objTest3 = ActiveDocument.Paragraphs(1).Range
Set objTest1 = objTest3
Set objTest2 = objTest3
'the next statement returns True because
'objTest1 and objTest2 refer to the same object
MsgBox objTest1 Is objTest2
```

When using `Is`, keep in mind that it isn't the contents of the object variables that are being compared, but what they refer to.

Testing Multiple Conditions by Using Logical Operators

Often, you'll need to test two or more conditions before taking an action: If statement X is `True` and statement Y is `True`, then do this; if statement X is `True` or statement Y is `True`, then do the other; if statement X is `True` and statement Y isn't `True`, then find something else to do; and so on.

To test multiple conditions, you use VBA's logical operators to link the conditions together. Table 11.2 lists the logical operators that VBA supports, with short examples and comments.

TABLE 11.2: VBA's Logical Operators

OPERATOR	MEANING	EXAMPLE	COMMENTS
And	Conjunction	`If ActiveWorkbook.FullName= "c:\temp\Example.xls" And Year(Date) >= 2005 Then`	If both conditions are `True`, the result is `True`. If either condition is `False`, the result is `False`.
Not	Negation	`ActivePresentation.Saved = Not ActivePresentation.Saved`	`Not` reverses the value of x (`True` becomes `False`; `False` becomes `True`). The `Saved` property used in this example is Boolean.
Or	Disjunction	`If ActiveWindow.View= wdPageView Or ActiveWindow.View= wdOutlineView Then`	If either the first condition or the second is `True`, or if both conditions are `True`, the result is `True`.
XOr	Exclusion	`If Salary > 55000 XOr Experienced = True Then`	Tests for different results from the conditions: Returns `True` if one condition is `False` and the other is `True`; returns `False` if both conditions are `True` or both conditions are `False`.
Eqv	Equivalence	`If blnMyVar1 Eqv blnMyVar2 Then`	Tests for logical equivalence between the two conditions: If both values are `True`, or if both values are `False`, `Eqv` returns `True`. If one condition is logically different from the other (that is, if one condition is `True` and the other is `False`), `Eqv` returns `False`.
Imp	Implication	`If blnMyVar1 Imp blnMyVar2 Then`	Tests for logical implication. Returns `True` if both conditions are `True`, both conditions are `False`, or the second condition is `True`. Returns `Null` if both conditions are `Null` or if the second condition is `Null`. Otherwise, returns `False`.

Of these six logical operators, you'll probably use the conjunction (And), disjunction (Or), and negation (Not) operators the most, with the other three thrown in on special occasions. (If the Imp logical operator doesn't make sense to you at this point, you probably don't need to use it.)

WARNING: VBA DOESN'T DO SHORT-CIRCUIT EVALUATION

Here's something to beware of when evaluating multiple conditions: VBA doesn't do short-circuit evaluation in logical expressions, unlike other programming languages such as C and C++.

Short-circuit evaluation is the formal term for a simple logical technique most people use several times a day when making decisions in their daily lives: If the first of two or more complementary conditions is false, you typically don't waste time evaluating any other conditions contingent upon it. For example, suppose your most attractive coworker says they'll take you to lunch if you get the product out on time *and* get a promotion. If you don't get the product out on time, you've blown your chances—it doesn't much matter if you get the promotion, because even if you do, your lunch will still be that brown bag you forgot to put in the department fridge. There's no point in evaluating the second condition because it depends on the first, and the first condition wasn't met.

VBA doesn't think that way. It evaluates the second condition (and any subsequent conditions) whether or not it needs to. Evaluating the conditions takes a little more time (which isn't usually an issue) and can introduce unexpected complications in your code (which can be an issue). For example, the following snippet produces an error when the selection is only one character long. The error occurs because the code ends up running the Mid function on a zero-length string (the one-character selection minus one character)—even though you wouldn't expect this condition to be evaluated when the first condition is not met (because the length of the selection is not greater than 1):

```
Dim strShort As String
strShort = Selection.Text
If Len(strShort) > 1 And _
    Mid(strShort, Len(strShort) - 1, 1) = "T" Then
    MsgBox "The second-last character is T."
End If
```

To avoid problems such as this, use nested If statements. Because the first condition isn't met (again, for a one-character selection), the second condition isn't evaluated:

```
If Len(strShort) > 1 Then
    If Mid(strShort, Len(strShort) - 1, 1) = "T" Then
        MsgBox "The second-last character is T."
    End If
End If
```

If Statements

As in most programming languages, If statements are among the most immediately useful and versatile statements for making decisions in VBA.

In this section, you'll look at the following types of If statements:

◆ If... Then

◆ If... Then... Else

◆ If... Then... ElseIf... Else

If... Then

If... Then statements tell VBA to make the simplest of decisions: If the condition is met, execute the following statement (or statements); if the condition isn't met, skip to the line immediately following the conditional statement.

SYNTAX

If... Then statements can be laid out either on one line or on multiple lines. A one-line If... Then statement looks like this:

```
If condition Then statement[s]
```

If the condition is met, VBA executes the statement or statements that follow. If the condition isn't met, VBA doesn't execute the statement or statements.

A multiple-line If... Then statement (more properly known as a *block* If statement) looks like this:

```
If condition Then
    statement
    [statements]
End If
```

If the condition is met, VBA executes the statement or statements. Otherwise, VBA moves execution to the line after the End If statement.

NOTE The single-line If... Then statement has no End If to end it, whereas the block If statement requires an End If. VBA knows that a single-line If condition will end on the same line on which it starts, whereas a block If statement needs to have its end clearly specified. Block If statements tend to be easier for humans to read.

EXAMPLES

In the past chapters, you've already encountered a number of If statements—they're so necessary in VBA that it's hard to get anything done without them. This section shows you some further examples.

One-Line If Statements

Here's an example of a one-line If statement in context:

```
Dim bytAge As Byte
bytAge = InputBox("Enter your age.", "Age")
If bytAge < 21 Then MsgBox "You may not purchase alcohol.",, "Underage"
```

The first line declares the Byte variable bytAge. The second line prompts the user to enter their age in an input box, which stores it in the variable. The third line checks bytAge and displays an Underage message box if bytAge is less than 21.

A block If statement can be a good candidate for including multiple statements in the same line of code by separating them with a colon. For example, if you wanted to end the procedure after displaying the Underage message box, you could include the End statement after a colon on the same line, as shown here:

```
If bytAge < 21 Then MsgBox "You may not purchase alcohol.",, "Underage": End
```

VBA executes this as follows:

1. First, it evaluates the condition.

2. If the condition is met, it executes the first statement after Then—in this case, it displays the Underage message box.

3. Once the user has dismissed the Underage message box (by clicking the OK button, the only button it has), VBA executes the statement after the colon: End.

If you wanted, you could add several other statements on the same logical line, separated by colons. (End would have to be the last one, because it ends the procedure.) You could even add another If statement if you felt like it:

```
If bytAge < 21 Then If bytAge > 18 Then MsgBox _
    "You may vote but you may not drink.",, "Underage": End
```

As you'll see if you're looking at the Visual Basic Editor, there are a couple of problems with this approach:

◆ First, you need to break long lines of code with the line-continuation character, or else they go off the edge of the Code window in the Visual Basic Editor, so that you have to scroll horizontally to read the ends of each line. You *could* hide all windows but the Code window, use a minute font size for your code, or buy a larger monitor, but you're probably still not going to have any fun working with long lines of code.

◆ Second, long lines of code (broken or unbroken) that involve a number of statements tend to become visually confusing. Even if everything is obvious to you when you're entering the code, you may find the code hard to read when you have to debug it a few months later. Usually it's better to use block If statements rather than complex one-line If statements.

Block If Statements

Block If statements work the same way as one-line If statements, except that they're laid out on multiple lines—typically with one command to each line—and they require an End If statement at the end. For example, the one-line If statement from the previous section could also be constructed as a block If:

```
If bytAge < 21 Then
    MsgBox "You may not purchase alcohol.",, "Underage"
    End
End If
```

If the condition in the first line is True, VBA executes the statements within the block If, first displaying the message box and then executing the End statement.

As you can see from this example, block If statements are much easier to read (and so easier to debug) than one-line If statements. This is especially true when you nest If statements within one another, which you'll often need to do.

To make block If statements easier to read, the convention is to indent the lines of block If statements after the first line (VBA ignores the indentation). With short If statements, like the ones shown in this section, the indentation doesn't make a great deal of difference. But with complex If statements, it can make all the difference between clarity and incomprehensibility, as you'll see in "Nesting If Statements," later in this chapter.

If... Then... *Else* Statements

If... Then statements are good for taking a single action based on a condition, but often you'll need to decide between two courses of action. To do so, you use the If... Then... Else statement. By using an If... Then... Else statement, you can take one course of action if a condition is True and another course of action if it's False. For example, If... Then... Else statements are a great way to deal with two-button message boxes.

NOTE The If... Then... Else statement is best used with clear-cut binary conditions—those that lend themselves to a True/False analysis. (A binary condition is like a two-position switch—if it's not switched on, it must be switched off.) For more complex conditions, such as those that can have three or more positions, you need to use a more complex logical statement, such as If... Then... ElseIf... Else or Select Case. Note also that you need to set up the If... Then... Else statement to evaluate the conditions in the appropriate order: Each condition to be evaluated must exclude all the conditions that follow it.

SYNTAX

The syntax for the If... Then... Else statement is as follows:

```
If condition Then
    statements1
```

```
    Else
        statements2
    End If
```

If the condition is True, VBA executes *statements1*, the first group of statements. If the condition is False, VBA moves execution to the Else line and executes *statements2*, the second group of statements.

Again, you have the option of creating one-line If... Then... Else statements or block If... Then... Else statements. In almost all circumstances, it makes more sense to create block If... Then... Else statements, because they're much easier to read and debug, and because the If... Then... Else statement is inherently longer than the If... Then statement and thus more likely to produce an awkwardly long line.

EXAMPLE

As a straightforward example of an If... Then... Else statement, consider the Electronic_Book_ Critic procedure shown in Listing 11.1.

LISTING 11.1:

```
1.   Sub Electronic_Book_Critic()
2.
3.       Dim intBookPages As Integer
4.
5.       intBookPages = InputBox _
             ("Enter the number of pages in the last book you read.", _
             "The Electronic Book Critic")
6.       If intBookPages > 1000 Then
7.           MsgBox "That book is seriously long.", vbOKOnly _
                 + vbExclamation, "The Electronic Book Critic"
8.       Else
9.           MsgBox "That book is not so long.", vbOKOnly _
                 + vbInformation, "The Electronic Book Critic"
10.      End If
11.
12.  End Sub
```

Here's what happens in Listing 11.1:

◆ Line 1 starts the procedure, and line 12 ends it. Lines 2, 4, and 11 are spacers.

◆ Line 3 declares the Integer variable intBookPages. Line 5 then assigns to intBookPages the result of an input box prompting the user to enter the number of pages in the last book they read.

◆ Line 6 checks to see if intBookPages is greater than 1000. If it is, the statement in line 7 runs, displaying a message box that states that the book is long.

◆ If intBookPages is not greater than 1000, VBA branches to the Else statement in line 8 and executes the statement following it, which displays a message box telling the user that the book wasn't so long.

◆ Line 10 ends the If condition.

If... Then... ElseIf... Else Statements

The last If statement you'll look at here is If... Then... ElseIf... Else, which you can use to help VBA decide between multiple courses of action. You can use any number of ElseIf lines, depending on how complex the condition is that you need to check.

Again, you can create either one-line If... Then... ElseIf... Else statements or block If... Then... ElseIf... Else statements. In almost all cases, block If... Then... ElseIf... Else statements are easier to construct, to read, and to debug. As with the other If statements, one-line If... Then... ElseIf... Else statements don't need an End If statement, but block If... Then... ElseIf... Else statements do need one.

SYNTAX

The syntax for If... Then... ElseIf... Else is as follows:

```
If condition1 Then
    statements1
ElseIf condition2 Then
    statements2
[ElseIf condition3 Then
    statements3]
[Else
    statements4]
End If
```

If the condition expressed in *condition1* is True, VBA executes *statements1*, the first block of statements, and then resumes execution at the line after the End If clause. If *condition1* is False, VBA branches to the first ElseIf clause and evaluates the condition expressed in *condition2*. If this is True, VBA executes *statements2* and then moves to the line after the End If line; if it's False, VBA moves to the next ElseIf clause (if there is one) and evaluates its condition (here, *condition3*) in turn.

If all the conditions in the ElseIf statements prove False, VBA branches to the Else statement (if there is one) and executes the statements after it (here, *statements4*). The End If statement then terminates the conditional statement, and execution resumes with the line after the End If.

You can have any number of ElseIf clauses in a block If statement, each with its own condition. But if you find yourself needing to use If statements with large numbers of ElseIf clauses (say, more than five or ten), you may want to try using the Select Case statement instead, which you'll look at toward the end of the chapter.

The Else clause is optional, although in many cases it's a good idea to include it to let VBA take a different course of action if none of the conditions specified in the If and ElseIf clauses turns out to be True.

EXAMPLES

This section shows you two examples of If... Then... ElseIf... Else statements:

◆ A simple If... Then... ElseIf... Else statement for taking action from a three-button message box

◆ An If... Then... ElseIf statement without an Else clause

A Simple If... Then... ElseIf... Else Statement

A simple If... Then... ElseIf... Else statement, as used in Listing 11.2, is perfect for dealing with a three-button message box.

LISTING 11.2:

```
1.   Sub Creating_a_Document()
2.
3.       Dim lngButton As Long
4.       Dim strMessage As String
5.
6.       strMessage = "Create a new document based on the " & _
             "VP Report project?" & vbCr & vbCr & _
             "Click Yes to use the VP Report template." & vbCr & _
             "Click No to use a blank document." & vbCr & _
             "Click Cancel to stop creating a new document."
7.
8.       lngButton = MsgBox _
             (strMessage, vbYesNoCancel + vbQuestion, "Create New Document")
9.
10.      If lngButton = vbYes Then
11.          Documents.Add Template:="z:\public\template\vpreport.dot"
12.      ElseIf lngButton = vbNo Then
13.          Documents.Add
14.      Else     'lngButton is vbCancel
15.          End
16.      End If
17.
18.  End Sub
```

The Creating_a_Document procedure in Listing 11.2 displays a Yes/No/Cancel message box (shown here) inviting the user to create a new document based on the VP Report project. The user can choose the Yes button to create such a document, the No button to create a blank document, or the Cancel button to cancel out of the procedure without creating a document at all.

Here's what happens:

◆ Line 1 starts the procedure, and line 18 ends it.

◆ Line 2 is a spacer, after which line 3 declares the Long variable lngButton and line 4 declares the String variable strMessage. Line 5 is another spacer.

◆ Line 6 assigns to the String variable strMessage a long string that contains all the text for the message box. Line 7 is another spacer.

◆ Line 8 displays the message box, using `strMessage` as the prompt, specifying the `vbYesNoCancel` constant to produce a Yes/No/Cancel message box, and applying a suitable title (Create New Document). It assigns the result of the message box to the Long variable `lngButton`. Line 9 is a spacer.

◆ Line 10 starts the `If… Then… ElseIf… Else` statement, comparing the value of `lngButton` to `vbYes`.

◆ If line 10 matches, line 11 uses the `Add` method of the `Documents` object to create a new document based on the `vpreport.dot` template. If not, the `ElseIf` condition in line 12 is evaluated, comparing the value of `lngButton` to `vbNo`.

NOTE   If you run this procedure and choose the Yes button in the message box, you will need to have a template named `vpreport.dot` in the folder `z:\public\template\` for line 11 to run. If you don't have the template, you'll get an error. Given that you're unlikely to have this template, you might want to change the path and filename to a template that you do have.

◆ If this second comparison matches, line 13 uses the `Add` method of the `Documents` object to create a new blank document. If not, the `Else` statement in line 14 is activated, because the user must have chosen the Cancel button in the message box. The `End` statement in line 15 ends execution of the procedure.

◆ Line 16 ends the `If` statement. Line 17 is a spacer.

NOTE   This example is a little unusual in that the `Else` statement is limited by the number of possible responses from the message box—Yes, No, and Cancel. Because the `If` statement checks for the `vbYes` response and the `ElseIf` statement checks for the `vbNo` response, only the `vbCancel` response will trigger the `Else` statement. In other circumstances, the `Else` statement can serve as a catchall for anything not caught by the `If` and `ElseIf` statements, so you need to make sure that the `If` and `ElseIf` statements cover all the contingencies you want evaluated before the `Else` statement kicks in.

An If… Then… ElseIf Statement without an Else Clause

You can use an `If… Then… ElseIf` statement without an `Else` clause when you don't need to take an action if none of the conditions in the `If` statement proves `True`. In the previous example, the situation had three clearly defined outcomes: the user could choose the Yes button, the No button, or the Cancel button in the message box. So you were able to use an `If` clause to test for the user's having chosen the Yes button, an `ElseIf` clause to test for the user's having chosen the No button, and an `Else` clause to take action if neither was chosen, meaning that the Cancel button was chosen.

NOTE   Clicking the close button (the × button) on the title bar of a message box is the equivalent of choosing the Cancel button in the message box.

As an example of a situation where you don't need to take action if no condition is `True`, consider the `If` statement in the `Check_Password` procedure in Listing 11.3. This procedure checks to ensure that the password a user enters to protect an item is of a suitable length.

LISTING 11.3:

```
1.   Sub Check_Password()
2.
3.       Dim strPassword As String
4.
5.   BadPassword:
6.
7.       strPassword = InputBox _
            ("Enter the password to protect this item from changes:", _
            "Enter Password")
8.
9.       If Len(strPassword) = 0 Then
10.          End
11.      ElseIf Len(strPassword) < 6 Then
12.          MsgBox "The password you chose is too short." & vbCr _
                & vbCr & "Please choose a password between " & _
                "6 and 15 characters in length.", _
                vbOKOnly + vbCritical, "Unsuitable Password"
13.          GoTo BadPassword
14.      ElseIf Len(strPassword) > 15 Then
15.          MsgBox "The password you chose is too long." & vbCr _
                & vbCr & "Please choose a password between " & _
                "6 and 15 characters in length.",
                vbOKOnly + vbCritical, "Unsuitable Password"
16.          GoTo BadPassword
17.      End If
18.
19.  End Sub
```

This procedure forces the user to enter a suitable password for the item they're supposed to protect. (The procedure doesn't actually protect the item.) Here's what happens:

♦ Line 1 starts the procedure, and line 19 ends it.

♦ Line 2 is a spacer, after which line 3 declares the String variable strPassword.

♦ Line 4 is a spacer. Line 5 contains a label, BadPassword, to which VBA will loop if the password the user enters proves to be unsuitable. Line 6 is another spacer.

♦ Line 7 displays an input box (shown here) prompting the user to enter a password, which VBA stores in the variable strPassword. Line 8 is a spacer.

◆ Line 9 checks `strPassword` to see if its length is zero, which means it's an empty string. This could mean either that the user clicked the Cancel button in the input box or that they clicked the OK button without entering any text in the text box of the input box. Either of these actions causes VBA to branch to line 10, where it executes the `End` statement that ends execution of the procedure.

◆ If the length of `strPassword` isn't zero (that is, the user has entered text into the text box of the input box and clicked the OK button), the `If` clause in line 9 is `False`, and VBA moves to line 11, where it checks to see if the length of `strPassword` is less than 6 characters.

◆ If the length of `strPassword` is zero, VBA executes the code in lines 12 and 13. Line 12 displays a message box telling the user that the password is too short and specifying the length criteria for the password. This message box contains only an OK button, so when the user clicks it to continue, VBA continues with line 13, which returns execution to the `BadPassword` label on line 5. From there the procedure repeats itself, redisplaying the input box so that the user can try again.

◆ If the length of `strPassword` isn't more than 15 characters, execution passes from line 11 to the second `ElseIf` clause in line 14, where VBA checks to see if the length of `strPassword` is more than 15 characters.

◆ If the length of `strPassword` is more than 15 characters, VBA executes the code in lines 15 and 16: Line 15 displays a message box (again, with only an OK button) telling the user that the password is too long, and line 16 returns execution to the `BadPassword` label, again displaying the input box.

There's no need for an `Else` statement in this case, because once the user has supplied a password that doesn't trigger the `If` clause or either of the `ElseIf` clauses, execution continues at the line after the `End If` statement.

Creating Loops with *If* and *GoTo*

So far in this book, you've seen several examples of `For… Next` loops and `For Each… Next` loops in the context of performing other tasks. (Chapter 12 shows you how to construct these types of loops and other types, such as `Do` loops.) You can also create loops with `If` statements and the `GoTo` statement, as you did in the last example.

Many programmers frown upon creating loops with `If` and `GoTo`, because there are neater ways to create loops and because If…GoTo loops can create "spaghetti code" that is not only grotesque to contemplate but a nightmare to debug. But loops using `If` and `GoTo` work perfectly well; so even if you choose not to use this technique yourself, you should know how such loops work.

SYNTAX

The `GoTo` statement is straightforward, and it's so useful that it's already come up a number of times in the examples you've looked at so far in this book. The syntax is

```
GoTo line
```

Here, the *line* argument can be either a line number or a line label within the current procedure.

A line number is simply a number placed at the beginning of a line to identify it. For example, consider this demonstration of GoTo:

```
Sub Demo_of_GoTo()
1
    If MsgBox("Go to line 1?", vbYesNo) = vbYes Then
        GoTo 1
    End If
End Sub
```

The second line contains only the line number 1, which identifies the line. The third line displays a message box offering the choice of going back to line 1; if the user chooses the Yes button, VBA executes the GoTo 1 statement and returns to the line labeled 1, after which it displays the message box again. (If the user chooses the No button, the If statement ends.)

It's usually easier to use a line label than a line number. A line label is a name for a line. A label starts with a letter and ends with a colon; between the letter and the colon, it can consist of any combination of characters. For example, earlier in this chapter you saw the label BadPassword: used to loop back to an earlier stage in a procedure when certain conditions were met. Perhaps the quintessential example of a label is the Bye: label traditionally placed at the end of a procedure for use with this GoTo statement:

```
GoTo Bye
```

GoTo is usually used with a condition—if you use it without one to go back to a line earlier in the code than the GoTo statement, you're apt to create an infinite loop. And if you were to use the GoTo Bye statement without a condition, you would guarantee that your procedure would end at this statement: no statement after this line would ever be executed.

EXAMPLE

As an example of a GoTo statement with a condition, you might use the GoTo Bye statement together with a message box that makes sure that the user wants to run a certain procedure:

```
Response = MsgBox("Do you want to create a daily report for " & _
    "the head office from the current document?", _
    vbYesNo + vbQuestion, "Create Daily Report")
If Response = vbNo Then GoTo Bye
```

If the user chooses the No button in the message box that the first line displays, VBA executes the GoTo Bye statement, branching to the Bye: label located at the end of the subprocedure.

Nesting *If* Statements

You can nest If statements as necessary to produce the logical contortions you need in your code. Each nested If statement must be complete in and of itself. For example, if you nest one block If statement within another block If statement and forget the End If line for the nested If, VBA assumes that the End If line for the outer If belongs to the nested If.

To make your block If statements easy to read, indent them to different levels. This is particularly important with nesting If statements, when you need to make it clear which If line is paired with each End If line. To see how this is done, check out the following nested If statements:

```
1.   If condition1 Then            'start of first If
2.       If condition2 Then        'start of second If
3.           If condition3 Then    'start of third If
4.               statements1
5.           ElseIf condition4 Then 'ElseIf for third If
6.               statements2
7.           Else                  'Else for third If
8.               statements3
9.           End If                'End If for third If
10.      Else                      'Else for second If
11.          If condition5 Then    'start of fourth If
12.              statements4
13.          End If                'End If for fourth If
14.      End If                    'End If for second If
15.  Else                          'Else for first If
16.      statements5
17.  End If                        'End If for first If
```

By following the layout, you can easily trace the flow of execution. For example, if condition1 in line 1 is False, VBA branches to the Else statement in line 15 and continues execution from there. If *condition1* in line 1 is True, VBA evaluates *condition2* in line 2, and so on.

The indentation is for visual clarity only—it makes no difference to VBA—but it can be a great help to the human reader. The previous nested If statement is annotated so that you can see which Else, ElseIf, and End If line belongs with which If line, although with the indentation, doing so is unnecessary. On the other hand, check out the unindented version of this nested statement shown below. This version is hard for the human eye to follow—and is much harder when it's buried in a morass of other code:

```
1.   If condition1 Then            'start of first If
2.   If condition2 Then            'start of second If
3.   If condition3 Then            'start of third If
4.   statements1
5.   ElseIf condition4 Then        'ElseIf for third If
6.   statements2
7.   Else                          'Else for third If
8.   statements3
9.   End If                        'End If for third If
10.  Else                          'Else for second If
11.  If cond2ition5 Then           'start of fourth If
12.  statements4
13.  End If                        'End If for fourth If
14.  End If                        'End If for second If
15.  Else                          'Else for first If
16.  statements5
17.  End If                        'End If for first If
```

There's seldom a pressing need to nest many levels of If statements. Often, you'll need only to nest a simple If... Then statement within an If... Then... Else statement or within an If... Then... ElseIf... Else statement. Listing 11.4 shows an example using Word.

LISTING 11.4:

```
1.   Selection.HomeKey Unit:=wdStory
2.   Selection.Find.ClearFormatting
3.   Selection.Find.Style = ActiveDocument.Styles("Heading 5")
4.   Selection.Find.Text = ""
5.   Selection.Find.Execute
6.   If Selection.Find.Found Then
7.       lngResponse = MsgBox("Make this into a special note?", _
             vbOKCancel, "Make Special Note")
8.       If lngResponse = vbOK Then
9.           Selection.Style = "Special Note"
10.      End If
11.  End If
```

The code in Listing 11.4 searches through the active document for the Heading 5 style and, if it finds the style, displays a message box offering to make it into a special note by applying the Special Note style. Here's what happens:

◆ Line 1 starts by returning the insertion point to the beginning of the document.

◆ Line 2 clears formatting from the Find command (to make sure that it isn't searching for inappropriate formatting).

◆ Line 3 sets Heading 5 as the style for which the Find command is searching, and Line 4 sets the search string as an empty string ("").

◆ Line 5 then runs the Find operation.

◆ Lines 6 through 11 contain the outer If... Then loop. Line 6 checks to see if the Find operation in line 5 found a paragraph in Heading 5 style. If it did, VBA runs the code in lines 7 through 10.

◆ Line 7 displays a message box asking if the user wants to make the paragraph into a special note.

◆ Line 8 begins the nested If... Then statement and checks the user's response to the message box.

◆ If the user's response is a vbOK—if the user chose the OK button—VBA executes the statement in line 9, which applies the Special Note style (which I'll assume is included in the document or template) to the paragraph.

◆ Line 10 contains the End If statement for the nested If... Then statement, and line 11 contains the End If statement for the outer If... Then statement.

TIP If you expect a document to contain more than one instance of the Heading 5 style, use a Do While... Loop loop to search for each instance. See Chapter 12 for details on Do While... Loop loops.

Select Case Statements

The Select Case statement provides an effective alternative to multiple ElseIf statements, combining the same decision-making capability with tighter and more efficient code.

Use the Select Case statement when the decision you need to make in the code depends on one variable or expression that has more than three or four different values that you need to evaluate. This variable or expression is known as the *test case*.

Select Case statements are easier to read than complex If… Then statements, mostly because there's less code. This also makes them easier to change: when you need to adjust one or more of the values used, you have less code to wade through.

Syntax

The syntax for Select Case is as follows:

```
Select Case TestExpression
    Case Expression1
        Statements1
    [Case Expression2
        Statements2]
    [Case Else
        StatementsElse]
End Select
```

Here's how the syntax breaks down:

◆ Select Case starts the statement, and End Select ends it.

◆ *TestExpression* is the expression that determines which of the Case statements runs.

◆ *Expression1, Expression2,* and so on are the expressions against which VBA matches TestExpression.

For example, you might test to see which of a number of buttons in a user form the user chose. The *TestExpression* would be tied to a button having been chosen; if it were the first button, VBA would match that to *Expression1* and would run the statements in the lines following Case *Expression1*; if it were the second button, VBA would match that to *Expression2* and would run the statements in the lines following Case *Expression2*; and so on for the rest of the Case statements.

Case Else is similar to the Else clause in an If statement. Case Else is an optional clause that (if it's included) runs if none of the given expressions is matched.

Example

As an example of a Select Case statement, consider Listing 11.5, which prompts the user to enter their typing speed and then displays an appropriate response.

LISTING 11.5:

```
1.  Sub Check_Typing_Speed()
2.
3.      Dim varTypingSpeed As Variant
```

```
4.        Dim strMsg As String
5.
6.        varTypingSpeed = InputBox _
             ("How many words can you type per minute?", "Typing Speed")
7.        Select Case varTypingSpeed
8.            Case ""
9.                End
10.           Case Is < 0, 0, 1 To 50
11.               strMsg = "Please learn to type properly before " & _
                     "applying for a job."
12.           Case 50 To 60
13.               strMsg = "Your typing could do with a little brushing up."
14.           Case 60 To 75
15.               strMsg = "We are satisfied with your typing speed."
16.           Case 75 To 99
17.               strMsg = "Your typing is more than adequate."
18.           Case 100 To 200
19.               strMsg = "You wear out keyboards with your blinding speed."
20.           Case Is > 200
21.               strMsg = "I doubt that's true."
22.       End Select
23.
24.       MsgBox strMsg, vbOKOnly, "Typing Speed"
25.
26.   End Sub
```

Here's what happens in the Check_Typing_Speed procedure in Listing 11.5:

◆ Line 1 starts the procedure, and line 26 ends it.

◆ Line 2 is a spacer. Line 3 declares the Variant variable varTypingSpeed, and line 4 the String variable strMsg. Line 5 is another spacer.

◆ Line 6 displays an input box prompting the user to enter their typing speed. It stores this value in the variable varTypingSpeed.

◆ Line 7 begins the Select Case statement, predicating it on the variable varTypingSpeed.

◆ Next, VBA evaluates each of the Case clauses in turn until it finds one that proves True. The first Case clause, in line 8, compares varTypingSpeed to an empty string ("") to see if the user chose the Cancel button in the input box or clicked the OK button without entering a value in the text box. If Case "" is True, VBA executes the End statement in line 9, ending the procedure.

◆ If Case " " is False, VBA moves execution to the next Case clause—line 10 in this example— where it compares varTypingSpeed to three items: less than 0 (Is < 0), 0, and the range 1 to 50 words per minute. Notice three things here:

1. You can include multiple comparison items in the same Case statement by separating them from each other with commas.

2. Using the Is keyword with the comparison operator (here, less than) checks the relation of two numbers to each other.

3. The To keyword denotes the range of values.

◆ If varTypingSpeed matches one of the comparison items in line 10, VBA assigns to the String variable strMsg the text on line 11 and then continues execution at the line after the End Select statement.

◆ If varTypingSpeed isn't within this range, VBA moves to the next Case clause and evaluates it in turn. When VBA finds a Case clause that's True, it executes the statement following that clause (in this case, assigning a text string to the strMsg variable) and then continues execution at the line after the End Select statement.

◆ For any case other than that in line 8 (which ends the procedure), line 24 displays a message box containing the text stored in the statement strMsg.

A Select Case statement can be a good way of taking action on the user's choice in a list box or combo box, particularly if the list box or combo box contains many different items. For example, you could check the Value property of the ListBox control or ComboBox control as the test case and take action accordingly.

Chapter 12

Using Loops to Repeat Actions

- ◆ When to use loops
- ◆ Using *For...* loops for fixed repetitions
- ◆ Using *Do...* loops for variable numbers of repetitions
- ◆ Nesting one loop within another loop
- ◆ Avoiding infinite loops

As in life, so in VBA: At times, you may want to repeat an action to achieve a certain effect. Sometimes, you'll want to repeat an action a predetermined number of times: Break six eggs to make an omelet, or create six new documents based on a certain template. More often, you'll want to repeat an action until a certain condition is met: Buy two lottery tickets a week until you win more than $2,000 on the lottery, or repeat an action for every instance of a value that appears in an Excel spreadsheet. In these cases, you won't know when you'll triumph against the wretched odds of the lottery, and you won't know how many instances of the value will appear in the spreadsheet—you'll just carry on until the condition is met.

In VBA, you use *loops* to repeat actions. By using loops, you can transform a simple recorded macro into one that repeats itself as appropriate for the material it's working on. VBA provides a number of expressions for creating loops in your code. In this chapter, you'll learn about the different types of loops and typical uses for each.

When Should You Use a Loop?

To repeat an action or a series of actions in VBA, you can either record that repetition into a macro by using the Macro Recorder (if the application you're using supports the Macro Recorder) or edit a procedure containing the relevant commands and use Copy and Paste to repeat them. For example, you could record a macro containing the code for creating a new presentation based on the default template, open the macro in the Visual Basic Editor, and then copy that statement to five other lines to create a procedure that created six new presentations. But almost invariably, it's much better to use a loop structure to repeat the commands as necessary.

Loops have several straightforward advantages over simple repetition of code:

- ◆ Your procedures are shorter—they contain less code and fewer instructions—and easier to maintain.

◆ Your procedures are more flexible: Instead of hard-coding the number of repetitions, you can to control the number as necessary. (*Hard-coding* means writing fixed code as opposed to variable code.)

◆ Your procedures are easier to test and debug, particularly for people other than you.

That said, if you just need to repeat one or more actions two or three times in a procedure, and that procedure will always need to repeat the action the same number of times, there's nothing wrong with hard-coding the procedure by repeating the code. It'll work fine, it's easy to do, and you won't have to spend time with the logic of loops. The code will likely be longer and a tad harder to maintain, but that's no big deal as long as it works.

Understanding the Basics of Loops

In VBA, a loop is a structure that repeats a number of statements, looping back to the beginning of the structure once it has finished executing them. Each cycle of execution of a loop is called an *iteration*.

There are two basic categories of loops:

◆ *Fixed-iteration loops* repeat a set number of times.

◆ *Indefinite loops* repeat a flexible number of times.

The running of either type of loop is controlled by the *loop invariant*, also called the *loop determinant*. This can be either a numeric expression or a logical expression. Fixed-iteration loops typically use numeric expressions, whereas indefinite loops typically use logical expressions. For example, a fixed-iteration loop might need to run through five iterations of a loop, while an indefinite loop might need to continue taking an action until the end of the presentation is reached.

Table 12.1 explains the types of loops that VBA provides.

TABLE 12.1:   VBA's Loop Types

LOOP	TYPE	EXPLANATION
For… Next	Fixed	Repeats an action or a sequence of actions a given number of times.
For Each… Next	Fixed	Repeats an action or a sequence of actions once for each object in a VBA collection.
Do While… Loop	Indefinite	Performs an action or a sequence of actions if a condition is True and continues to perform it until the condition becomes False.
While… Wend	Indefinite	Performs an action or a sequence of actions if a condition is True and continues to perform it until the condition becomes False. Like Do… Loop While but almost obsolete.
Do Until… Loop	Indefinite	Performs an action or sequence of actions while a condition is false and continues to perform it until the condition becomes True.

TABLE 12.1: VBA's Loop Types *(CONTINUED)*

LOOP	TYPE	EXPLANATION
Do... Loop While	Indefinite	Performs an action or a sequence of actions once and then repeats it while a condition is True until it becomes False
Do... Loop Until	Indefinite	Performs an action or a sequence of actions once and repeats it while a condition is False until it becomes True.

Using *For*... Loops for Fixed Repetitions

For... loops execute for a fixed number of times. For... Next loops repeat for a number of times of your choosing, while For Each... Next loops execute once for each element in the specified VBA collection.

For... *Next* Loops

For... Next loops repeat an action or a sequence of actions a given number of times, specified by a counter variable. The counter variable can be hard-coded into the procedure, passed from an input box or dialog box, or passed from a value generated either by a different part of the procedure or by a different procedure.

SYNTAX

The syntax for For... Next loops is as follows:

```
For counter = start To end [Step stepsize]
    [statements]
[Exit For]
    [statements]
Next [counter]
```

Table 12.2 explains the components of the syntax. As usual, the brackets show optional items and the italics show placeholders.

TABLE 12.2: Components of the Syntax for a For... Next loop

COMPONENT	DESCRIPTION
counter	A numeric variable or an expression that produces a number. By default, VBA increases the *counter* value by an increment of 1 with each iteration of the loop, but you can change this increment by using the optional Step keyword and *stepsize* argument. *counter* is required in the For statement and is optional in the Next statement, but it's a good idea to include *counter* in the Next statement to make your code easy to read. This is particularly important when you're using multiple For... Next statements in the same procedure or nesting one For... Next statement within another.

TABLE 12.2:   Components of the Syntax for a For... Next loop *(CONTINUED)*

COMPONENT	DESCRIPTION
start	A numeric variable or numeric expression giving the starting value for *counter*.
end	A numeric variable or numeric expression giving the ending value for *counter*.
stepsize	A numeric variable or numeric expression specifying how much to increase or decrease the value of *counter*. To use *stepsize*, use the Step keyword and specify the *stepsize* variable. *stepsize* is 1 by default, but you can use any positive value or negative value.
Exit For	A statement for exiting a For loop.
Next	The keyword indicating the end of the loop. Again, you can specify the optional *counter* here to make your code clear.

Here's what happens in a For... Next loop:

1. When VBA enters the loop at the For statement, it assigns the *start* value to *counter*. It then executes the statements in the loop. When it reaches the Next statement, it increments *counter* by 1 or by the specified *stepsize* and loops back to the For statement.

2. VBA then checks the *counter* variable against the *end* variable. When *stepsize* is positive, if *counter* is greater than *end*, VBA terminates the loop and continues execution of the procedure with the statement immediately after the Next statement (which could be any action or the end of the procedure). If *counter* is less than or equal to *end*, VBA repeats the statements in the loop, increases *counter* by 1 or by *stepsize*, and loops back to the For statement again. (For a loop in which *stepsize* is negative, the loop continues while *counter* is greater than or equal to *end* and ends when *counter* is equal to or less than *end*.)

3. The Exit For statement exits the For loop early. You'll look at how to use the Exit For statement, and examples of the different uses of For... Next loops, later in this chapter.

STRAIGHTFORWARD *FOR... NEXT* LOOPS

In a straightforward For... Next loop, you first specify a counter variable and the starting and ending values for it:

```
Dim i As Integer
For i = 1 to 200
```

Here, i is the counter variable, 1 is the starting value, and 200 is the ending value. By default, VBA increases the counter variable by 1 with each iteration of the loop. Here, it will be 1, 2, 3, and so on up to 200; a value of 201 (or greater—although in this example, it can't reach a greater value than 201 because the *stepsize* is 1) terminates the loop. You can also use the Step keyword to specify a different increment, either positive or negative; more on this in the next section.

NOTE   i is the archetypal integer counter variable used in a For... Next loop; after using i, the convention is to use j, k, l, m, and n for subsequent counter variables. The short names derive from the days of key cards, when longer names represented a significant inconvenience. These days, VBA makes using longer names easy. Use i and these other letters for your loops if you prefer compactness. Otherwise, use more descriptive variable names, such as LoopCounter or intLoopCounter, if you want to make your code easier to decipher.

After the two statements shown above, you specify the actions to perform in the loop, followed by the Next keyword to end the loop:

```
Application.StatusBar = _
    "Please wait while Excel checks for nonuniform prices: " & i & "..."
Next i
```

This code produces a status bar readout indicating Excel's progress in checking your spreadsheet for improbable values.

As another example, say you need to check every paragraph in Word documents you receive from contributors to make sure there's no unsuitable formatting. By using a loop that runs from 1 to the number of paragraphs in the active document (which is stored in the Count property of the Paragraphs collection in the ActiveDocument object), you can check each paragraph in turn and provide a reference point for the user in the status bar display:

```
Dim i As Integer
For i = 1 To ActiveDocument.Paragraphs.Count
    CheckParagraphForIllegalFormatting
    Application.StatusBar = _
        "Please wait while Word checks the formatting in " _
        & " this document: Paragraph " & i & " out of " _
        & ActiveDocument.Paragraphs.Count & "..."
    Selection.MoveDown Unit:=wdParagraph, _
        Count:=1, Extend:=wdMove
Next i
```

This code snippet should be started at the beginning of the document. It runs the CheckParagraphForIllegalFormatting procedure on the current paragraph, displays a message in the status bar indicating which paragraph out of the total number it's working on, and then moves down a paragraph. When VBA reaches the Next statement, it increases the i counter by the default value, 1 (because no *stepsize* variable is specified), and loops back to the For statement, where it compares the value of i to the value of ActiveDocument.Paragraphs.Count. The procedure continues to loop until i has reached the value of ActiveDocument.Paragraphs.Count, which is the final iteration of the loop.

Likewise, you could use a simple For... Next loop to quickly build the structure of a timesheet or work log in Excel. The following statements use a For... Next loop to insert the labels 1.00 through 24:00 in the current column in the active sheet of the active workbook:

```
Dim i As Integer
For i = 1 To 24
    ActiveCell.FormulaR1C1 = i & ":00"
    ActiveCell.Offset(RowOffset:=1, ColumnOffset:=0).Select
Next i
```

Here, the `ActiveCell.FormulaR1Ci` statement inserts the automatically increased string for the counter—i—together with a colon and two zeroes (to create a time format). The `ActiveCell.Offset (RowOffset:=1, ColumnOffset:=0).Select` statement selects the cell in the next row and the same column. The loop runs from i = 1 to i = 24 and stops when the automatic increase takes i to 25.

FOR... NEXT LOOPS WITH STEP VALUES

If increasing the counter variable by the default 1 doesn't suit your purpose, you can use the `Step` keyword to specify a different increment or decrement. For example, the following statement increases the counter variable by 20, so the sequence is 0, 20, 40, 60, 80, 100:

```
For i = 0 to 100 Step 20
```

You can also use a decrement by specifying a negative `Step` value:

```
For i = 1000 to 0 Step -100
```

This statement produces the sequence 1000, 900, 800, and so on, down to 0.

Instead of the "x out of y" countdown example given in the previous section, you could produce a countdown running from `ActiveDocument.Paragraphs.Count` to zero:

```
Dim i As Integer
For i = ActiveDocument.Paragraphs.Count To 0 Step -1
    CheckParagraphForIllegalFormatting
    Application.StatusBar = _
        "Please wait while Word checks the formatting in this document: " & i
    Selection.MoveDown Unit:=wdParagraph, Count:=1, Extend:=wdMove
Next i
```

USING AN INPUT BOX TO DRIVE A FOR... NEXT LOOP

Sometimes you'll be able to hard-code the number of iterations into a For... Next loop. Other times, you'll take a number from another operation, such as the `ActiveDocument.Paragraphs.Count` property in the example above. But often you'll need to use input from the user to drive the loop. The easiest way of doing this is to have the user enter the value into an input box.

For example, Listing 12.1 contains a simple procedure named `CreatePresentations` that displays an input box prompting the user to enter the number of presentations they want to create. It then uses a For... Next loop to create the documents in PowerPoint.

LISTING 12.1:

```
1.  Sub CreatePresentations()
2.      Dim intPresentations As Integer
3.      Dim i As Integer
4.      intPresentations = InputBox _
            ("Enter the number of presentations to create:", _
            "Create Presentations")
5.      For i = 1 To intPresentations
6.          Presentations.Add
7.      Next i
8.  End Sub
```

Here's what happens in the `CreatePresentations` procedure in Listing 12.1:

- ◆ Line 2 declares the Integer variable `intPresentations`, and line 3 declares the Integer variable `i`.

- ◆ Line 4 displays an input box prompting the user to enter the number of presentations they want to create.

- ◆ Lines 5 through 7 contain a `For`... `Next` loop that runs from `i = 1` to `i = intPresentations` with the default increment of 1 per iteration. Each iteration of the loop executes the `Presentations.Add` statement in line 6, creating a new presentation based on the default template.

USING A DIALOG BOX CONTROL TO DRIVE A *FOR*... *NEXT* LOOP

For those occasions when an input box won't suffice, you can easily use a value from a dialog box to drive a `For`... `Next` loop. This book hasn't yet shown you how to create dialog boxes, but in this section you'll get a sneak preview by looking at a `Create_Folders` procedure designed to reduce the tedium of creating multiple folders with predictable names, such as for the sections of a multipart project.

For example, say that you're using a four-digit number to identify the project, the letter *s* for *section*, and a two-digit number to identify the section. So you'd end up with folders named *1234s01*, *1234s02*, *1234s03*, and so on—simple enough to create manually, but very boring if you needed more than a dozen or so.

In its simplest form, this dialog box would provide a text box for the number of folders to be created (though you could also use a drop-down list for this, or even a spinner) and a text box for the project number. Figure 12.1 shows an example of how the dialog box might look.

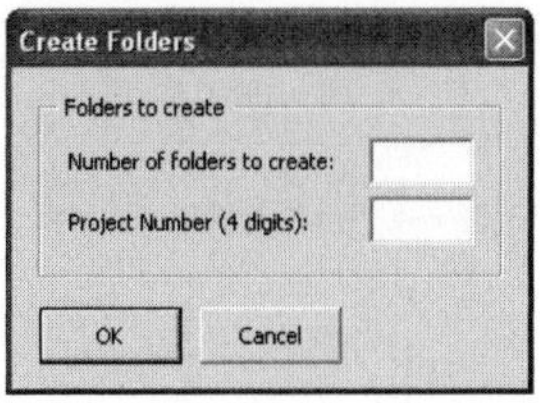

FIGURE 12.1
When you need more information than an input box can supply, use a custom dialog box to drive a For... Next loop.

You display the dialog box by using the Show method, perhaps with a Load statement first, like this:

```
Load frmCreateFolders
frmCreateFolders.Show
```

The example dialog box is called `frmCreateFolders`; any valid VBA name will work. The first text box—identified with the Number Of Folders To Create label—is named `txtFolders`; the second text box is named `txtProjectNumber`.

The Cancel button here has an End statement attached to its `Click` event, so that if the user clicks it, VBA ends the procedure:

```
Private Sub cmdCancel_Click()
    End
End Sub
```

The OK button in the dialog box has the code shown in Listing 12.2 attached to its `Click` event.

LISTING 12.2:

```
1.   Private Sub cmdOK_Click()
2.
3.       Dim strMsg As String
4.       Dim strFolder As String
5.       Dim i As Integer
6.
7.       frmCreateFolders.Hide
8.       Unload frmCreateFolders
9.       strMsg = "The Create_Folders procedure has created " _
             & "the following folders: " & vbCr & vbCr
10.
11.      For i = 1 To txtFolders.Value
12.          strFolder = txtProjectNumber.Value & "p" & Format(i, "0#")
13.          MkDir strFolder
14.          strMsg = strMsg & "     " & strFolder & vbCr
15.      Next i
16.
17.      MsgBox strMsg, vbOKOnly + vbInformation, _
             "Create Folders"
18.
19.  End Sub
```

The cmdOK_Click procedure in Listing 12.2 runs when the user clicks the OK button in the dialog box:

◆ Line 1 declares the cmdOK_Click subprocedure, and line 19 ends it. Line 2 is a spacer.

◆ Line 3 declares the String variable strMsg, which is used to contain a string to display in a message box at the end of the procedure.

◆ Line 4 declares the String variable strFolder, which will contain the name of the current folder to create in each iteration of the loop.

◆ Line 5 declares the Integer variable i, which will be the counter variable for the For... Next loop.

◆ Line 6 is a spacer.

◆ Line 7 hides frmCreateFolders.

◆ Line 8 unloads frmCreateFolders.

◆ Line 9 assigns some introductory text to strMsg, ending it with a colon and two vbCr carriage-return characters to make the start of a list.

◆ Line 10 is a spacer.

◆ Lines 11 through 15 contain the For... Next loop that creates the folders. Line 11 causes the loop to run from i = 1 to i = txtFolders.Value, the value supplied by the user in the Number Of Folders To Create text box. Line 12 assigns to the strFolder String variable the Value property of the txtProjectNumber text box, the letter *p*, and the value of i formatted via the

Format function to include a leading zero if it's a single digit (so that 1 will appear as 01, and so on). Line 13 uses the MkDir command with strFolder to create a folder (that is, make a directory—the old DOS command mkdir lives on in VBA) of that name. Line 14 adds some spaces (for an indent), the contents of strFolder, and a vbCr character to strMsg. Line 15 then loops back to the For statement, incrementing the i counter. VBA then compares the i counter to txtFolders.Value and repeats the loop as necessary.

NOTE   This procedure creates the new folders in the current folder, without giving the user a choice of location. Chances are you won't want to do this in real-life situations. You might want to change a folder to a set location (so as to keep all the project files together); but more likely you'll want to let the user choose a suitable location—for example, by displaying a common dialog box, such as the Save As dialog box used by most Windows applications.

For Each... Next Loops

The For Each... Next loop, which is unique to Visual Basic, has the same basic premise as the For... Next loop, namely that you're working with a known number of repetitions. In this case, though, the known number is the number of objects in a collection, such as the Slides collection in a presentation or the Documents collection of Word documents. For example, you can choose to take an action for each Slide object in a presentation—you don't need to know how many slides are in the collection, provided there is at least one. (If there are none, nothing happens.)

SYNTAX

The syntax for the For Each... Next statement is straightforward:

```
For Each object In collection
    [statements]
    [Exit For]
    [statements]
Next [object]
```

VBA starts by evaluating the number of objects in the specified collection. It then executes the statements in the loop for the first of those objects. When it reaches the Next keyword, it loops back to the For Each line, reevaluates the number of objects, and performs further iterations as appropriate.

Here's an example: The Documents collection contains the open documents in Word. So you could create a straightforward procedure to close all the open documents by using a For Each... Next loop like this:

```
Dim Doc As Document
For Each Doc in Documents
    Doc.Close SaveChanges:=wdSaveChanges
Next
```

VBA closes each open document in turn by using the Close method. The statement uses the wdSaveChanges constant for the SaveChanges argument to specify that any unsaved changes in the document be saved when the document is closed. As long as there are open documents in the Documents collection, VBA repeats the loop, so it closes all open documents and then terminates the procedure.

TIP   This example provides a straightforward millustration of how a For Each... Next loop works, but you probably wouldn't want to use the example in practice; instead, you'd probably use the Close method with the Documents collection (which contains all the open documents) to close all the open documents more simply. However, you might use a For Each... Next loop to check each document for certain characteristics before closing it.

Using an *Exit For* Statement

As you saw earlier in this chapter when looking at the syntax for For statements, you can use one or more Exit For statements to exit a For loop if a certain condition is met. Exit For statements are optional and are seldom necessary. If you find yourself needing to use Exit For statements in all your procedures, there's probably something wrong with the loops you're constructing. That said, you may sometimes find Exit For statements useful—for example, for when an error occurs in a procedure or when the user chooses to cancel a procedure.

On those occasions when you do need Exit For statements to exit a loop early, you'll typically use them with straightforward conditions. For example, in Word, if you wanted to close open windows until you reached a certain document that you knew to be open, you could use an Exit For statement like this:

```
Dim Doc As Document
For Each Doc in Documents
    If Doc.Name = "Document1" Then Exit For
    Doc.Close
Next Doc
```

This For Each... Next statement checks the Name property of the document to see if it's Document1; if it is, the Exit For statement causes VBA to exit the loop. Otherwise, VBA closes the document and returns to the start of the loop.

NOTE   You can also use multiple Exit For statements if you need to. For example, you might need to check two or more conditions during the actions performed in the loop.

Using *Do...* Loops for Variable Numbers of Repetitions

Do loops give you more flexibility than For loops in that you can test for conditions in them and direct the flow of the procedure accordingly. VBA includes several types of Do loops:

◆ Do While... Loop

◆ Do... Loop While

◆ Do Until... Loop

◆ Do... Loop Until

These loops break down into two categories:

◆ Loops that test a condition before performing any action. Do While... Loop and Do Until... Loop loops fall into this category.

◆ Loops that perform an action before testing a condition. Do... Loop While and Do... Loop Until fall into this category.

The difference between the two types of loop in each category is that each While loop repeats itself *while* a condition is True (until the condition becomes False), whereas each Until loop repeats itself *until* a condition becomes True (while the condition is False). This means that you can get by to some extent using only the While loops or only the Until loops—you'll just need to set up some of your conditions the other way around. For example, you could use a Do While... Loop loop with a condition of x < 100 or a Do Until... Loop loop with a condition of x = 100 to achieve the same effect.

This discussion assumes that you want to learn about all the different kinds of loops so that you can use each when it's most appropriate.

Do While... Loop **Loops**

In a Do While... Loop loop, you specify a condition that has to be True for the actions in the loop to be executed. If the condition isn't True, the actions aren't executed and the loop ends. For example, you might want to search a document for an instance of a particular word or phrase and take action once you find it. Figure 12.2 shows a Do While... Loop loop.

SYNTAX

The syntax for the Do While... Loop loop is straightforward:

```
Do While condition
    [statements]
    [Exit Do]
    [statements]
Loop
```

While the *condition* is met (Do While), the statements in the loop are executed. The Loop keyword returns execution to the Do While line, which is then reevaluated. If the *condition* remains True, the loop continues. If the *condition* is False, execution continues with the statement on the line after the Loop keyword. You can use one or more Exit Do statements to break out of the loop as necessary.

FIGURE 12.2
A Do While... Loop loop tests for a condition before performing the actions contained in the loop.

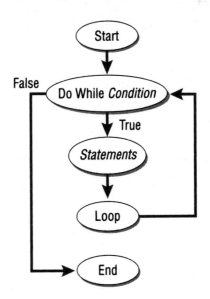

Say you wanted to construct a glossary from a long Word document that used italics to explain main terms in the body text and list paragraphs (which both used Times New Roman font) without picking up italics used for other elements (such as headings or captions). You could command Word to search for Times New Roman text with the italic attribute. If Word found instances of the text, it would take the appropriate actions, such as selecting the sentence containing the term, together with the next sentence (or the rest of the paragraph), and copying it to the end of another document. Then it would continue the search, performing the loop until it found no more instances of italic Times New Roman text.

Listing 12.3 shows an example of how such a procedure might be constructed with a Do While... Loop loop. This listing includes a number of commands that you haven't met yet, but you should be able to see easily how the loop works.

LISTING 12.3:

```
1.   Sub GenerateGlossary()
2.
3.       Dim strSource As String
4.       Dim strDestination As String
5.       Dim strGlossaryName As String
6.
7.       strSource = ActiveWindow.Caption
8.       strGlossaryName = InputBox _
             ("Enter the name for the glossary document.", _
             "Create Glossary")
9.       If strGlossaryName = "" Then End
10.
11.      Documents.Add
12.      ActiveDocument.SaveAs FileName:=strGlossaryName, _
             FileFormat:=wdFormatDocument
13.      strDestination = ActiveWindow.Caption
14.      Windows(strSource).Activate
15.
16.      Selection.HomeKey Unit:=wdStory
17.      Selection.Find.ClearFormatting
18.      Selection.Find.Font.Italic = True
19.      Selection.Find.Font.Name = "Times New Roman"
20.      Selection.Find.Text = ""
21.      Selection.Find.Execute
22.
23.      Do While Selection.Find.Found
24.          Selection.Copy
25.          Selection.MoveRight Unit:=wdCharacter, _
                 Count:=1, Extend:=wdMove
26.          Windows(strDestination).Activate
27.          Selection.EndKey Unit:=wdStory
28.          Selection.Paste
29.          Selection.TypeParagraph
30.          Windows(strSource).Activate
```

```
31.          Selection.Find.Execute
32.      Loop
33.
34.      Windows(strDestination).Activate
35.      ActiveDocument.Save
36.      ActiveDocument.Close
37.
38.  End Sub
```

The GenerateGlossary procedure in Listing 12.3 pulls italic items in the Times New Roman font from the current document and inserts them in a new document that it creates and saves. Here's what happens:

◆ Line 1 begins the procedure, and line 2 is a spacer.

◆ Lines 3, 4, and 5 declare the String variables strSource, strDestination, and strGlossaryName, respectively. Line 6 is a spacer.

◆ Line 7 assigns to the String variable strSource the Caption property of the active window. The procedure uses this variable to activate the document when it needs to work with it.

◆ Line 8 displays an input box requesting the user to enter a name for the document that will contain the glossary entries pulled from the current document. It stores the string the user enters in the String variable strGlossaryName.

◆ Line 9 then compares strGlossaryName to an empty string (" ") to make sure that the user hasn't clicked the Cancel button to cancel the procedure or clicked the OK button in the input box without entering a name in the text box. If GlossaryName is an empty string, line 9 uses an End statement to terminate execution of the procedure.

◆ Provided line 9 hasn't stopped the procedure in its tracks, the procedure rolls on. Line 10 is a spacer. Line 11 then creates a new blank document. (This document is based on the Normal.dot global template because no Template argument is used to specify a different template.) This document will become the glossary document.

◆ Line 12 saves the document with the name the user specified in the input box.

◆ Line 13 stores the Caption property of this document in the strDestination variable, again making it available to activate this document as necessary throughout the procedure. You now have the source document identified by the strSource variable and the destination document identified by the strDestination variable.)

◆ Line 14 uses the Activate method to activate the strSource window. Line 15 is a spacer.

◆ Line 16 uses the HomeKey method of the Selection object with the wdStory unit to move the insertion point to the beginning of the document, which is where the procedure needs to start working to catch all the italicized words in Times New Roman.

◆ Lines 17 through 20 detail the Find operation the procedure needs to perform: Line 17 removes any formatting applied to the current Find item; line 18 sets the Find feature to find italic formatting; line 19 sets Find to find Times New Roman text; and line 20 specifies the search string, which is an empty string (" ") that causes Find to search only for the specified formatting.

◆ Line 21 then performs the Find operation by using the `Execute` method. Line 22 is a spacer.

◆ Lines 23 through 32 implement the `Do While... Loop` loop. Line 23 expresses the condition for the loop: `While Selection.Find.Found` (while the Find operation is able to find an instance of the italic Times New Roman text specified in the previous lines). While this condition is met (is `True`), the commands contained in the loop will execute.

◆ Line 24 copies the selection (the item found with italic Times New Roman formatting).

◆ Line 25 moves the insertion point one character to the right, effectively deselecting the selection and getting the procedure ready to search for the next instance in the document. You need to move the insertion point off the selection to the right so that the next Find operation doesn't find the same instance. (If the procedure were searching up through the document instead of down through it, you'd need to move the insertion point off the selection to the left instead by using a `Selection.MoveLeft` statement.)

◆ Line 26 activates the `strDestination` window, putting Word's focus in it.

◆ Line 27 then moves the insertion point to the end of the glossary document, and line 28 pastes the copied item in at the position of the insertion point. Moving to the end of the document isn't strictly necessary here, provided that the `Normal.dot` global template doesn't contain any text—if `Normal.dot` is empty, the new document created in line 11 will be empty too, and the start and end of the document will be in the same position. And after each paste operation, Word positions the insertion point after the pasted item. However, if `Normal.dot` contains text, this step is necessary.

◆ Line 29 uses the `TypeParagraph` method of the `Selection` object to enter a paragraph after the text inserted by the paste operation.

◆ Line 30 activates the `strSource` document once more, and line 31 repeats the Find operation.

◆ The `Loop` statement in line 32 then loops execution of the procedure back to line 23, where the `Do While Selection.Find.Found` condition evaluates whether this latest Find operation was successful (`True`).

◆ If it was successful, the loop continues; if it wasn't, execution of the procedure continues at line 34, which activates the glossary document again. Line 35 saves the active document (the glossary document, because it was just activated), and line 36 closes it.

◆ Line 37 is a spacer, and line 38 ends the procedure.

Do... Loop While Loops

A `Do... Loop While` loop is similar to a `Do While... Loop` loop, except that in the `Do... Loop While` loop, the actions in the loop are run at least once, whether the condition is `True` or `False`. If the condition is `True`, the loop continues to run until the condition becomes `False`. Figure 12.3 shows a `Do... Loop While` loop.

If `Do While... Loop` loops make immediate sense to you, `Do... Loop While` loops may seem odd—you're going to take an action *before* checking a condition? But you'll probably find that `Do... Loop While` loops can be very useful, but they lend themselves to different situations than `Do While... Loop` loops.

Consider the lottery example from the beginning of the chapter. In that situation, you execute the action before you check the condition that controls the loop: First, you buy a lottery ticket, and then you check to see if you've won. If you haven't won, or you've won only a small sum, you loop back and buy more tickets for the next lottery. (Actually, this is logically a Do... Loop Until loop rather than a Do... Loop While loop, because you continue the loop while the condition is False; when you win a suitably large amount, the condition becomes True.) Likewise, in a procedure, you may want to take an action and then check whether you need to repeat it. For example, you might want to apply special formatting to a paragraph and then check to see if other paragraphs need the same treatment.

FIGURE 12.3

In a Do... Loop While loop, the actions in the loop run once before the condition is tested.

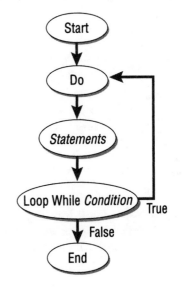

SYNTAX

The syntax for a Do... Loop While loop is as follows:

```
Do
    [statements]
    [Exit Do]
    [statements]
Loop While condition
```

VBA performs the statements included in the loop, after which the Loop While line evaluates the condition. If it's True, VBA returns execution to the Do line, and the loop continues to execute; if it's False, execution continues at the line after the Loop While line.

As an example of a Do... Loop While loop, consider this crude password checker that you could use to prevent someone from running a procedure without supplying the correct password:

```
Dim varPassword As Variant
Do
    varPassword = InputBox _
        ("Enter the password to start the procedure:", _
        "Check Password 1.0")
Loop While varPassword <> "CorrectPassword"
```

Here the Do... Loop While loop displays an input box for the user to enter the password. The Loop While line compares the value from the input box, stored in varPassword, against the correct password (here, CorrectPassword). If the two aren't equal (varPassword <> "CorrectPassword"), the loop continues, displaying the input box again.

This loop is just an example—you wouldn't want to use it as it is in real life. Here's why: Choosing the Cancel button in the input box causes it to return a blank string, which also doesn't match the correct password, causing the loop to run again. The security is perfect; the problem is that the only way to end the loop is for the user to supply the correct password. If they're unable to do so, they will see the input box again and again. If you wanted to build a password-checking procedure along these lines, you might specify a number of incorrect passwords that the user could enter (perhaps three) before the procedure terminated itself, or you could simply use an End statement to terminate the procedure if the user entered a blank string:

```
Do
    varPassword = InputBox _
        ("Enter the password to start the procedure:", _
        "Check Password 1.0")
    If varPassword = "" Then End
Loop While varPassword <> "CorrectPassword"
```

Do Until... Loop Loops

A Do Until... Loop loop is similar to a Do While... Loop loop, except that in a Do Until... Loop loop, the loop runs while the condition is False and stops running when it's True. Figure 12.4 shows a Do Until... Loop loop.

FIGURE 12.4
A Do Until... Loop loop runs while the condition is False and stops running when the condition becomes True.

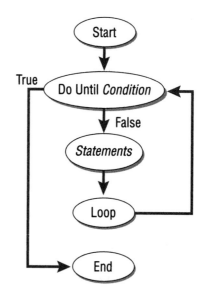

NOTE Do Until... Loop loops are useful if you prefer to work with a condition that's True and keep it looping until the condition becomes False. Otherwise, you can achieve the same effects using Do While... Loop loops and inverting the relative condition.

SYNTAX

The syntax for Do Until... Loop loops is as follows:

```
Do Until condition
    statements
    [Exit Do]
    [statements]
Loop
```

When VBA enters the loop, it checks the *condition*. If the *condition* is False, VBA executes the statements in the loop, encounters the Loop keyword, and loops back to the beginning of the loop, reevaluating the *condition* as it goes. If the *condition* is True, VBA terminates the loop and continues execution at the statement after the Loop line.

For example, consider the lottery experience redefined as a procedure in Listing 12.4.

LISTING 12.4:

```
1.  Sub Lottery_1()
2.      Dim sngWin As Single
3.      Do Until sngWin > 2000
4.          sngWin = Rnd * 2100
5.          MsgBox sngWin, , "Lottery"
6.      Loop
7.  End Sub
```

Here's how Listing 12.4 works:

◆ Line 2 declares the Single variable sngWin. Line 3 then starts a Do Until loop with the condition that sngWin > 2000—the value of sngWin variable must be larger than 2000 for the loop to end. Until then, the loop will continue to run.

◆ Line 4 assigns to sngWin the result of 2100 multiplied by a random number produced by the Rnd function, which generates random numbers between 0 and 1. (This means that the loop needs to receive a random number of a little more than .95 to end—a chance of a little less than one in 20, or considerably better than most lotteries.)

◆ Line 5 displays a simple message box containing the current value of the Win variable so that you can see how lucky you are.

◆ Line 6 contains the Loop keyword that completes the loop.

◆ Line 7 ends the procedure.

Listing 12.5 shows a more useful example of a Do Until loop in Word.

LISTING 12.5:

```
1.  Sub FindNextHeading()
2.      Do Until Left(Selection.Paragraphs(1).Style, 7) = "Heading"
3.          Selection.MoveDown Unit:=wdParagraph, _
                Count:=1, Extend:=wdMove
4.      Loop
5.  End Sub
```

Listing 12.5 contains a short procedure that moves the insertion point to the next heading in the active document in Word. Here's how it works:

◆ Line 2 starts a Do Until loop that ends with the Loop keyword in line 4. The condition for the loop is that the seven left-most characters in the name of the style for the first paragraph in the current selection—Left(Selection.Paragraphs(1).Style, 7)—match the string Heading. This will match any of the Heading styles (the built-in styles Heading 1 through 9, or any style the user has defined whose name starts with *Heading*).

◆ Until the condition is met, VBA executes the statement in line 3, which moves the selection down by one paragraph.

Do... Loop Until Loops

The Do... Loop Until loop is similar to the Do Until... Loop loop, except that in the Do... Loop Until loop, the actions in the loop are run at least once, whether the condition is True or False. If the condition is False, the loop continues to run until the condition becomes True. Figure 12.5 shows a Do... Loop Until loop.

FIGURE 12.5

In a Do... Loop Until loop, the actions in the loop are run once before the condition is tested.

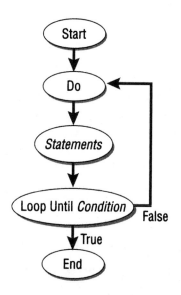

SYNTAX

The syntax for Do... `Loop Until` loops is as follows:

```
Do
    [statements]
    [Exit Do]
    [statements]
Loop Until condition
```

VBA enters the loop at the Do line and executes the *statements* in the loop. When it encounters the `Loop Until` line, it checks the *condition*. If the condition is `False`, VBA loops back to the Do line and again executes the *statements*. If the condition is `True`, VBA terminates the loop and continues execution at the line after the `Loop Until` line.

As an example, say you wanted to continue displaying an input box for adding new worksheets quickly to a workbook until the user chose the Cancel button or entered an empty string in the text box. You could use code such as that shown in Listing 12.6.

LISTING 12.6:

```
1.   Sub Create_Worksheets()
2.       Dim strNewSheet As String
3.       Do
4.           strNewSheet = InputBox _
                 ("Enter the name for the new worksheet " _
                 & "(31 characters max.):", "Add Worksheets")
5.           If strNewSheet <> "" Then
6.               ActiveWorkbook.Worksheets.Add
7.               ActiveSheet.Name = strNewSheet
8.           End If
9.       Loop Until strNewSheet = ""
10.  End Sub
```

Here's what happens in the `Create_Worksheets` procedure:

◆ Line 2 declares the String variable `strNewSheet`.

◆ Line 3 begins a Do... `Loop Until` loop.

◆ Line 4 displays an input box asking the user to enter the name for the new worksheet.

◆ Line 5 uses an If statement to make sure that `strNewSheet` is not an empty string. If it's not, line 6 adds a new worksheet to the active workbook, and line 7 assigns to the active sheet (the new sheet) the value of `strNewSheet`. Line 8 ends the If statement.

◆ Line 9 contains a `Loop Until strNewSheet = ""` statement that causes the procedure to loop back to the Do line until the user enters an empty string in the input box. The user can enter an empty string either by leaving the text box in the input box blank and clicking the OK button or by clicking the Cancel button.

◆ Line 10 ends the procedure.

Using an *Exit Do* Statement

As with an `Exit For` statement in a `For` loop, you can use an `Exit Do` statement to exit a `Do` loop without executing the rest of the statements in it. The `Exit Do` statement is optional, and you'll probably want to use `Exit Do` statements relatively seldom in your loops—at least if the loops are properly designed.

When you do need an `Exit Do` statement, you'll generally use it with a condition. The example shown in Listing 12.7 makes the lottery a little more interesting by adding an `If` condition with an `Exit Do` statement to take effect if the win is less than $500.

LISTING 12.7:

```
1.  Sub Lottery_2()
2.      Dim sngWin As Single
3.      Do Until sngWin > 2000
4.          sngWin = Rnd * 2100
5.          If sngWin < 500 Then
6.              MsgBox "Tough luck. You have been disqualified.", _
                    vbOKOnly + vbCritical, "Lottery"
7.              Exit Do
8.          End If
9.          MsgBox sngWin, , "Lottery"
10.     Loop
11. End Sub
```

The procedure in Listing 12.7 works in the same way as the example in Listing 12.4, except that line 5 introduces a new `If` condition. If the variable `sngWin` is less than 500, the statements in lines 6 and 7 run. Line 6 displays a message box announcing that the player has been disqualified from the lottery, and line 7 exits the `Do` loop.

IS USING *EXIT DO* AN INDICATION OF POOR PROGRAMMING TECHNIQUE?

Some programmers consider using an `Exit Do` statement to exit a `Do` loop a method of last resort, or at least clumsy programming. Others disagree. Many reckon that it's always acceptable to use an `Exit Do` statement to respond to an error or to the user choosing to cancel a procedure.

VBA executes `Exit Do` statements with no problem, so there's no harm in using an `Exit Do` statement. However, you can often create code that avoids using an `Exit Do` statement but has the same effect. For example, a condition that you check in the middle of the loop to decide whether to exit the loop can often be built into the main condition of the loop by using an operator such as And, Or, or Not.

If this code is simple, you might be better off using it. But if it's difficult to create and maintain, there's no good reason to force yourself to use it when an `Exit Do` statement will do the trick instead.

While... Wend Loops

In addition to the For... Next loop, the For Each... Next loop, and the four flavors of Do loops examined so far in this chapter, VBA supports the While... Wend loop. While... Wend is VBA's version of the While... Wend looping structure used by earlier programming languages, such as the WordBasic programming language used with versions of Word up to and including Word 95. VBA includes While... Wend more for compatibility with those earlier versions than as a recommended tool in its own right, but you can use it if you choose to. To some extent, the Do loops supersede While... Wend, but While... Wend still works fine.

The syntax of a While... Wend loop is as follows:

```
While condition
    [statements]
Wend
```

While the *condition* is True, VBA executes the *statements* in the loop. When it reaches the Wend keyword (which is a contraction of While End, it returns to the While statement and evaluates the *condition* again. When the *condition* evaluates as False, the statements in the loop are no longer executed, and execution moves to the statement after the Wend statement.

The following statements create a simple While... Wend loop for Word:

```
While Documents.Count < 10
    Documents.Add
Wend
```

While the number of documents in the Documents collection (measured here by the Count property of the Documents collection) is smaller than 10, the loop runs. Each time through, the Documents.Add statement in the second line creates a new document based on the Normal template (because no other template is specified). After the new document is created, the Wend statement in the third line returns execution to the first line, where the While condition is evaluated again.

WARNING When using a While... Wend loop, make sure the only way for execution to enter the loop is by passing through the gate of the While condition. Branching into the middle of a While... Wend loop (for example, by using a label and a GoTo statement) can cause errors.

Nesting Loops

You can nest one or more loops within another loop to create the pattern of repetition you need: You can nest one For loop inside another For loop, a For loop inside a Do loop, a Do loop inside a For loop, or a Do loop inside a Do loop.

NOTE You can nest up to 16 levels of loops in VBA, but you'll be hard pressed to read even half that number of levels. If you find your code becoming this complicated, consider whether you can take a less tortuous approach to solve the problem more simply.

For example, if you need to create a number of folders, each of which contains a number of subfolders, you could use a variation of the Create_Folders procedure you looked at earlier in the chapter.

The dialog box for the procedure will need another text box to contain the number of subfolders to create within each folder. The new dialog box is named frmCreateFoldersAndSubFolders and the text box for the number of subfolders is named txtHowManySubFolders. Figure 12.6 shows the dialog box.

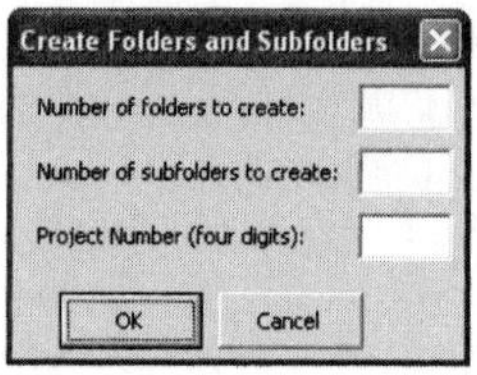

FIGURE 12.6
The Create Folders And
Subfolders dialog box

Listing 12.8 shows the code attached to the Click event on the cmdOK button of the form.

LISTING 12.8:

```
1.   Private Sub cmdOK_Click()
2.
3.       Dim strStartingFolder As String
4.       Dim strFolderName As String
5.       Dim strSubfolderName As String
6.       Dim intSubfolder As Integer
7.       Dim intLoopCounter As Integer
8.
9.       frmCreateFoldersAndSubfolders.Hide
10.      Unload frmCreateFoldersAndSubfolders
11.
12.      strStartingFolder = CurDir
13.
14.      For intLoopCounter = 1 To txtHowManyFolders.Value
15.          strFolderName = txtProjectNumber.Value & "s" & _
                 Format(intLoopCounter, "0#")
16.          MkDir strFolderName
17.          ChDir strFolderName
18.          For intSubfolder = 1 To txtHowManySubfolders.Value
19.              strSubfolderName = "Subsection" & intSubfolder
20.              MkDir strSubfolderName
21.          Next intSubfolder
22.          ChDir strStartingFolder
23.      Next intLoopCounter
24.
25.  End Sub
```

Here's what the code in Listing 12.8 does:

◆ Line 1 begins the procedure, and line 25 ends it. Line 2 is a spacer.

◆ Lines 3 through 5 declare three String variables, strStartingFolder, strFolderName, and strSubfolderName, respectively.

◆ Line 6 declares the Integer variable intSubfolder, and line 7 declares the Integer variable i. Line 8 is a spacer.

♦ Line 9 hides the user form, and line 10 unloads it. Line 11 is a spacer.

♦ Line 12 stores the name of the current folder in the String variable `strStartingFolder`. You'll need this variable to make sure everything happens in the appropriate folder later in the procedure. Line 13 is another spacer.

♦ Lines 14 through 16 and line 23 are essentially the same as in the previous procedure. They build the folder name out of the `Value` property of the `txtProjectNumber` text box, the letter *s*, a two-digit number, and the `i` variable, and then use the `MkDir` statement to create the folder.

♦ Line 17 uses a `ChDir` statement to change folders to the folder that was just created, `strFolderName`.

♦ In line 18, the nested `For...Next` loop starts. This loop is controlled by the loop invariant `intSubfolder` and will run from `intSubfolder = 1` to `intSubfolder = txtHowManySubFolders .Value`, which is the value entered by the user in the Number Of Subfolders To Create text box in the dialog box.

♦ Line 19 builds the String variable `strSubfolderName` out of the word *Subsection* and the value of the `intSubfolder` counter variable. For this procedure, you can assume that there will be fewer than 10 subsections for each of the sections, so single-digit numbering is adequate.

♦ Line 20 creates the subfolder by using a `MkDir` statement with the `strSubfolderName` String variable.

♦ Line 21 uses the `Next Subfolder` statement to loop back to the beginning of the nested `For...Next` loop. VBA reevaluates the condition and repeats the loop as necessary.

♦ Line 22 changes folders back to `strStartingFolder` for the next iteration of the outside loop. (Otherwise, the next folder would be created within the current folder, `strFolderName`.)

♦ Line 23 then loops back to the beginning of the outer loop.

TIP When nesting `For` loops, make sure that you use the *counter* argument to identify the loop that's ending. Using this argument makes your procedures much easier to read and may prevent VBA from springing any unpleasant surprises on you. Your nested loops must end in the exact reverse order of their starting, and the counters need to match.

Avoiding Infinite Loops

If you create an infinite loop in a procedure, it will happily run either forever or until your computer crashes. For example, one type of loop you haven't yet met is the Do... Loop loop. As you can see in the example in Listing 12.9, without a condition attached to it, this structure creates an infinite loop.

LISTING 12.9:

```
1.  Sub InfiniteLoop()
2.      Dim x
3.      x = 1
4.      Do
```

```
5.          Application.StatusBar = _
                "Your computer is stuck in an endless loop: " & x
6.          x = x + 1
7.      Loop
8.  End Sub
```

In Listing 12.9, Line 2 declares the variable x, and line 3 assigns it the value 1. Line 4 begins the Do loop, which displays a status-bar message and increases the value of x by 1. The effect of this loop is to display a message and an ever-increasing number on the status bar until you press Ctrl+Break to stop the procedure or until the value overflows the variable. This is all thoroughly pointless (except perhaps as part of a procedure for burning in a new computer), and is perhaps a good reason not to use the Do... Loop structure—at least not without a condition attached to one end of it.

No matter what type of loop you use, to avoid creating an infinite loop, you need to make sure the condition that will terminate the loop will be met at some point. For example, for an editing or cleanup procedure, you'll often want to perform an action until the end of the document is reached and then stop. Often, you'll want to include some form of counting mechanism to make sure that a Do loop doesn't exceed a certain number of iterations.

Part 4

Using Message Boxes, Input Boxes, and Dialog Boxes

Chapter 13

Getting User Input with Message Boxes and Input Boxes

◆ Displaying messages on the status bar

◆ Displaying message boxes

◆ Displaying input boxes

◆ Understanding the limitations of message boxes and input boxes

This chapter shows you how to start adding a user interface to recorded or written code in order to increase the code's power and functionality. You'll learn the three easiest ways of communicating with the user of your code, the two easiest ways of enabling the user to make decisions in a procedure, and the easiest way of soliciting input from the user. Along the way, you'll see how to decide what is the best way to communicate with the user in any given set of circumstances. This will set the scene for starting an examination of more complex interactions with the user via custom dialog boxes, later in the book.

In most applications, VBA offers up to five ways of communicating with the user of a procedure:

◆ Displaying messages on the status bar at the bottom of the window (if the application provides a status bar). This is a bit limited, but it can be an effective way of communicating with the user.

◆ Displaying a message box (usually in the middle of the screen). Message boxes are useful both for communicating with the user and for providing them with the means to make a single choice based on the information you give them. You'll spend the bulk of this chapter working with message boxes.

◆ Displaying an input box (again, usually in the middle of the screen). You can use input boxes to communicate with the user, but their primary purpose is to solicit one item of information. Input boxes also provide the user with the means of making a single choice to direct the flow of a procedure, although the mechanism for presenting this choice is much more limited than that in a message box. You'll look at input boxes toward the end of this chapter.

◆ Displaying a dialog box (once again, usually in the middle of a screen). You can use dialog boxes both to communicate with the user and to let them make a number of choices. Dialog boxes are best reserved for those times when other forms of communication won't suffice; in other words, there's no point in using a dialog box when a simple message box or input box will do. You'll look at creating custom dialog boxes by using VBA user forms later in the book.

◆ Communicating directly through the document or the application's interface. For example, the user can fill out a form, click a button on the screen, and wait for a reaction. Similarly, you can use toolbars or menus to provide interaction.

Open a Procedure to Work On

Make sure you're all set for editing in the Code window in the Visual Basic Editor:

1. Start the application for which you're creating code.

2. Launch the Visual Basic Editor from the host application by pressing Alt+F11 or by choosing Tools ➢ Macro ➢ Visual Basic Editor.

3. Open a procedure for editing in the Code window: Use the Project Explorer to navigate to the module that holds the procedure, and then either scroll to the procedure in the Code window or choose it from the Procedures drop-down list in the Code window.

TIP   Alternatively, choose Tools ➢ Macro ➢ Macros to display the Macro dialog box, select a procedure you've created in the Macro Name list box, and click the Edit button to display the Visual Basic Editor with the procedure open in the Code window.

If you want to work in a new procedure rather than in an existing one—which is probably a good idea, because it'll help prevent you from doing any damage—you can create a new procedure by entering the Sub keyword and the procedure's name on a blank line in a module and then pressing Enter. VBA adds the parentheses and End Sub statement. For example, you could type the following and press the Enter key:

```
Sub Experimentation_Zone
```

VBA adds the parentheses and End Sub statement, together with a separator line to separate the procedure from any adjacent procedures in the Code window:

```
Sub Experimentation_Zone()

End Sub
```

If you've opened a procedure, test it by using the F8 key to step through it in Break mode or by clicking the Run Sub/UserForm button to run it without highlighting each statement in turn. (You can also run it by typing the procedure's name into the Immediate window and pressing the Enter key.)

Displaying Status Bar Messages in Word and Excel

Word and Excel let you display information on the status bar, giving you an easy way to tell the user what's happening in a procedure without halting execution of the code. By displaying status information on the status bar as the procedure works, you can indicate to the user not only what the procedure is doing but also that it's still running.

NOTE A problem you'll sometimes encounter is that the user thinks the procedure has crashed or failed to work because no changes are visible on screen, whereas in fact the procedure is working properly in the background. In this case, an update on the status bar lets the user see that the procedure is working.

The main disadvantage of displaying messages on the status bar is that the user may miss them if they're not paying attention or if they're not expecting to see messages there. If the application in question uses the status bar extensively to give the user information (as Word and Excel do), this shouldn't be a problem. But if there's any doubt, notify the user that information will be displayed on the status bar. For example, you might display a message box at the beginning of a procedure to tell the user to watch the status bar for updates.

To display a message on the status bar in Word or Excel, you set the StatusBar property of the Application object to an appropriate string of text. The following example displays the status bar information shown in Figure 13.1.

```
Application.StatusBar = "Word is formatting the report. Please wait..."
```

FIGURE 13.1

In some applications, you can display information on the status bar.

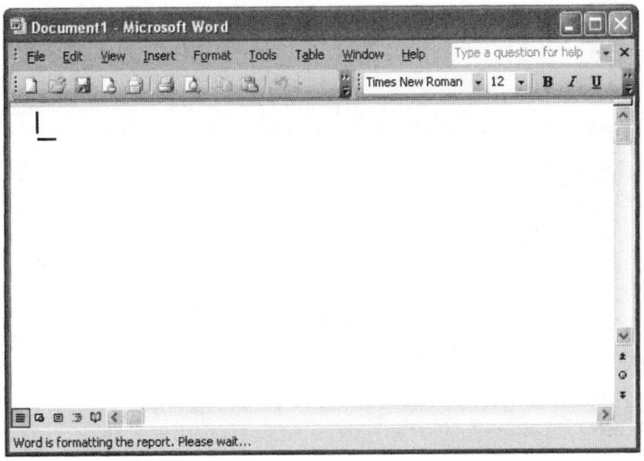

Typically, any information you display on the status bar remains displayed there until you change it or until the application displays a message there itself. For example, if you display a message on the status bar and then invoke the Copy command in Excel, Excel displays its normal Copy message, *Select destination and press ENTER or choose Paste*, on the status bar, wiping out your message. Application messages trump user-created messages.

If you display a message on the status bar in the course of a procedure, you usually need to update it later in the procedure so as to avoid leaving a misleading message on the status bar after the procedure has finished running. For example, you might display another message saying that the procedure has finished or clear the status bar by displaying a blank string on it.

To clear the status bar, assign an empty string to it, as in the following statement:

```
Application.StatusBar = ""
```

To see the effect of this statement, run it from the Visual Basic Editor with the Word or Excel window (or at least its status bar) visible. You'll see the effect best if you run a statement that displays information on the status bar (such as `Application.StatusBar = "Hello, World!"`) first so that the status bar has information for the `Application.StatusBar = ""` statement to clear:

```
Application.StatusBar = "Hello, World!"
Application.StatusBar = ""
```

TIP   It's especially helpful to display a progress indicator on the status bar during longer processes so that the user can tell that they're still running and that they're making progress. For example, you might display a readout of the progress, such as "Excel is working on sheet 9 out of 150." Even more simply, adding periods to the end of the status message gives an indication of progress, although it doesn't give an idea of how far or how long is left to go.

Message Boxes

Your second tool for providing information to the user is the message box, of which you've probably seen examples in almost every Windows application you've used. Message boxes are simple and limited, but they can play an important role in almost any procedure or module.

Typical uses of message boxes include the following:

◆ Telling the user what a procedure is about to do (and giving them the chance to cancel running the procedure if it isn't what they thought it was).

◆ Presenting the user with an explanation of what a procedure will do next and asking them to make a simple decision (usually, to let it proceed or to send it on a different course).

◆ Warning the user of an error that the procedure encountered and allowing them to take action on it.

◆ Informing the user that a procedure ran successfully and that it has finished. This message is particularly useful for procedures that turn off screen updating or otherwise hide from the user what they are doing, because such procedures may leave the user unsure whether the procedure is still running or has finished. You can also use the message box to report what the procedure has done—for example, that it changed particular items or that it discovered problems in the document that require attention.

This chapter shows you how to create a message box suitable for each of these tasks. In later chapters, you'll create specific message boxes to enhance various procedures.

The Pros and Cons of Message Boxes

These are the advantages of using a message box:

◆ The user can't miss seeing the message box. (If you want, you can even display a message box that the user can't escape by *coolswitching*—pressing Alt+Tab—to another application. You'll look at this a little later in the chapter.)

◆ You can present the user with a simple choice among two or three options.

These are the disadvantages of using a message box:

◆ A message box can present only one, two, or three buttons, which means it can offer only a limited set of options to the user.

◆ The buttons in message boxes are predefined in sets—you can't put a custom button in a message box. (For that, you have to use a dialog box.)

◆ You can't use features such as text boxes, group boxes, or list boxes in message boxes.

Message Box Syntax

The basic syntax for message boxes is as follows:

```
MsgBox(prompt[, buttons] [, title][, helpfile, context])
```

Here's what the elements of this syntax mean:

MsgBox The function that VBA uses to display a message box. You typically use it with a number of arguments enclosed in parentheses after it.

prompt A required argument for the MsgBox function that controls the text displayed in the message box. *prompt* is a String argument, meaning you need to type in text of your choice; it can be up to 1023 characters long, although it's usually a good idea to be more concise than this. (Any *prompt* longer than 1023 characters is truncated to 1023 characters without warning.)

buttons An optional argument that controls the type of message box that VBA displays by specifying which buttons it contains. For example, as you'll see in a couple of pages, you can display a message box with just an OK button; with OK and Cancel buttons; with Abort, Retry, and Ignore buttons; and so on. You can also add arguments to the *buttons* argument that control the icon in the message box and the modality of the message box. You'll also look at these options later in this chapter.

title An optional argument that controls the title bar of the message box. This too is a string argument. If you don't specify *title*, VBA uses the application's title—Microsoft Word for Word, Microsoft Excel for Excel, Microsoft PowerPoint for PowerPoint, and so on. Usually, it's best to specify the title, because the application name on its own isn't helpful (unless the user has become confused as to which application is running the procedure).

helpfile An optional argument that controls which Help file VBA displays when the user presses F1 within the message box to get help (or clicks the Help button in a message box that contains a Help button).

context An optional argument that controls which topic in the Help file VBA jumps to. If you specify the *helpfile* argument, you must specify the *context* argument as well.

In the following sections, you'll look first at how you can build the simplest of message boxes and then at how you can add the other arguments to it to make it more complex.

Displaying a Simple Message Box

You can display a straightforward message box by specifying only the prompt as a text string enclosed in double quotation marks:

```
MsgBox "This is a simple message box."
```

Run from Excel, this statement produces the simple message box shown in Figure 13.2. With *prompt* as the only argument supplied, VBA produces a message box with only an OK button and with the application's name in the title bar. This message box does nothing except display information.

You can enter this `MsgBox` statement on any blank line within a procedure. After you type the `MsgBox` keyword, VBA's Auto List Members feature prompts you with the syntax of the function, as shown in Figure 13.3.

NOTE   If you look at the Help listing for the `MsgBox` function, you'll see that the syntax appears a little differently than in the Auto List Members ScreenTip: The `helpfile` and `context` arguments share a bracket—[, `helpfile`, `context`]—rather than each having its own bracket. This is because you can use both of them or neither of them, but you can't use either on its own. The ScreenTip isn't able to convey this distinction. Because codependent optional arguments are relatively rare, this limitation of the ScreenTip seldom causes much of a problem; but if you find VBA balking at a statement that apparently carries the arguments shown in the ScreenTip, check the Help file.

Once you've entered the `MsgBox` statement with its required argument (*prompt*), you can display the message box by stepping through the code (by pressing the F8 key or clicking the Step Into button on the Debug toolbar) or by running the procedure (by clicking the Run Sub/UserForm button, by choosing Run ➤ Run Sub/UserForm, or by pressing the F5 key).

Instead of entering a text string for the *prompt* argument, you can use a String variable. The following example uses a String variable named `strMsg`:

```
Dim strMsg As String
strMsg = "This is a simple message box."
MsgBox strMsg
```

FIGURE 13.2

When you use only the prompt argument to display a simple message box, VBA uses the application's name as the title.

FIGURE 13.3

VBA's Auto List Members feature prompts you with the syntax for the message box.

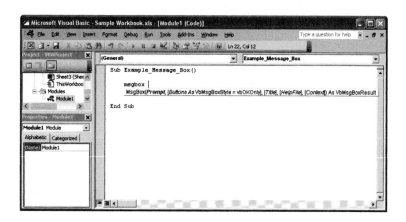

This method can be useful when you're working with long strings or when you need to display a string that has been defined earlier in the procedure or a string dynamically created by the procedure.

Displaying a Multiline Message Box

By default, VBA displays short message strings as a single line in a message box and wraps longer strings onto two or more lines as necessary, up to the limit of 1024 characters in a string.

You can deliberately break a string over more than one line by including line-feed and carriage-return characters in the string as follows:

◆ Chr(13) or vbCr represents a carriage return.

◆ Chr(10) or vbLf represents a line-feed.

◆ Chr(10) + Chr(13) or vbCrLf represents a line-feed–carriage return combination.

In message boxes, these three characters all have the same effect. Your code is easier to read if you use a constant (vbCr, vbLf, or vbCrLf) rather than the corresponding Chr() construction; it's also quicker to type. Usually, it's clearest to use the vbCr constant.

You can add a tab to a string by using Chr(9) or vbTab. Again, vbTab is easier to read and to type.

For example, the following code displays the Word message box illustrated in Figure 13.4. Note that each part of the text string is enclosed in double quotation marks (to tell VBA that they're part of the string). The Chr(149) characters are bullets, so the text after them starts with a couple of spaces to give the bullets some room:

```
Dim strMsg As String
strMsg = "Word has finished formatting the report you requested." _
    & vbCr & vbCr & "You can now run the following procedures:" & vbCr _
    & vbCr & Chr(149) & " Distribute_Report will e-mail the report to " _
    & "the head office." & vbCr & vbCr & Chr(149) & _
    " Store_Report will copy the report to the holding directory." _
    & vbCr & vbCr & Chr(149) & " Backup_Report will create a backup " _
    & "of the report on the file server."
MsgBox strMsg
```

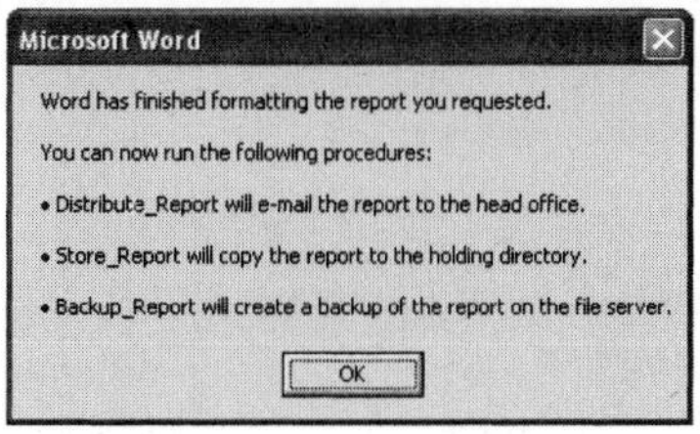

FIGURE 13.4
You can display a multi-line message box by using line-feed and carriage-return characters within the prompt string.

TIP   You'll notice that in this example, a space appears on either side of each of the ampersands (&) and the equal sign. You can enter these spaces yourself or have VBA enter them for you when you move the insertion point to another line. (Moving the insertion point to another line causes VBA to check the line you've just been working on.)

Choosing Buttons for a Message Box

The *buttons* argument controls which buttons a message box contains. VBA offers the types of message boxes shown in Table 13.1, controlled by the *buttons* argument.

TABLE 13.1: Message Box Types, Controlled by the *buttons* Argument

VALUE	CONSTANT	BUTTONS
0	vbOKOnly	OK
1	vbOKCancel	OK, Cancel
2	vbAbortRetryIgnore	Abort, Retry, Ignore
3	vbYesNoCancel	Yes, No, Cancel
4	vbYesNo	Yes, No
5	vbRetryCancel	Retry, Cancel

You can refer to these message box types by using either the value or the constant. For example, you can specify either 1 or vbOKCancel to produce a message box with OK and Cancel buttons. The value is easier to type; the constant is easier to read. Either of the following statements produces the message box shown in Figure 13.5 when run from PowerPoint:

```
Dim lngR As Long
lngR = MsgBox("Apply standard formatting to the slide?", vbYesNo)
lngR = MsgBox("Apply standard formatting to the slide?", 4)
```

From VBA's point of view, it doesn't matter whether you use values or constants in the message boxes for your procedures. For the human, though, the constants are far preferable. Even if you're the only person who ever sees your code, the code is much easier to read if you use the constants.

Choosing an Icon for a Message Box

You can also add an icon to a message box by including the appropriate value or constant argument. Table 13.2 shows the options.

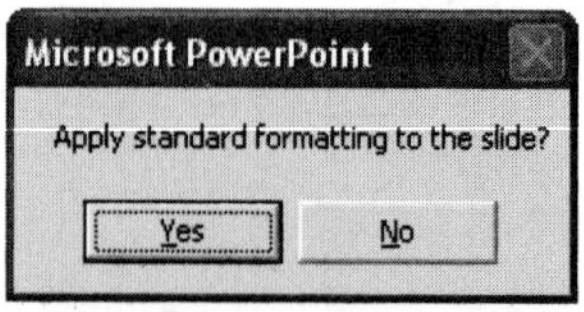

FIGURE 13.5
The vbYesNo constant produces a message box with Yes and No buttons.

Again, you can refer to these icons by using either the value or the constant: either **48** or vbExclamation will produce an exclamation point icon. Again, the constant is much easier to read.

TABLE 13.2: Arguments for Message Box Icons

VALUE	CONSTANT	DISPLAYS
16	vbCritical	Stop icon
32	vbQuestion	Question mark icon
48	vbExclamation	Exclamation point icon
64	vbInformation	Information icon

To link the value or constant for the message box with the value or constant for the icon, use a plus sign (**+**). For example, to produce a message box containing Yes and No buttons together with a question mark icon (see Figure 13.6), you could enter **vbYesNo + vbQuestion** (or **4 + 32**, **vbYesNo + 32**, or **4 + vbQuestion**):

```
lngR = MsgBox("Apply standard formatting to the slide?", _
    vbYesNo + vbQuestion)
```

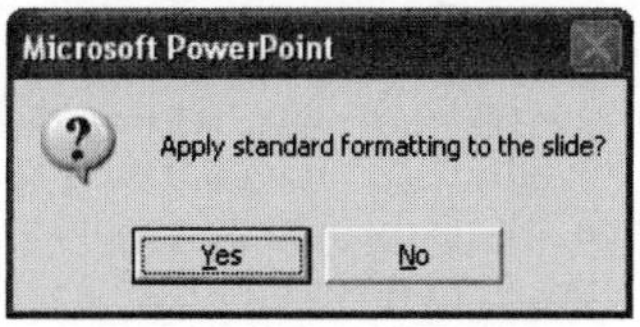

FIGURE 13.6
Adding an icon gives a message box greater visual impact.

Setting a Default Button for a Message Box

You can set a default button for a message box by specifying the button in the MsgBox statement. Specifying a default button can be a wise move when you distribute procedures that take drastic action.

For example, consider a procedure that deletes the current document without having to close it and then switch to a file-management program (such as Windows Explorer) or mess around in one of the common dialog boxes (such as the Open dialog box or the Save dialog box). Because this procedure can destroy someone's work if they run it inadvertently, you'd probably want to set a default button of No or Cancel in a confirmation message box so that the user has to actively choose to run the rest of the procedure.

As usual in the Windows interface, the default button in a message box is selected visually with a black border around its outside and a dotted line around its text area. You can move the selection to another button by using Tab or Shift+Tab or the →, ←, ↑, or ↓ keys.

NOTE Because the user can choose the default button by simply pressing Enter, having the appropriate default button on a message box or dialog box can help the user deal with the message box or dialog box more quickly. VBA automatically sets the first button in a message box to be the default button, so you need to specify the default button only when you need it to be a button other than the first.

Table 13.3 lists the arguments for default buttons.

TABLE 13.3:   Arguments for Default Message-Box Buttons

VALUE	CONSTANT	EFFECT
0	vbDefaultButton1	The first button is the default button.
256	vbDefaultButton2	The second button is the default button.
512	vbDefaultButton3	The third button is the default button.
768	vbDefaultButton4	The fourth button is the default button.

All the message boxes mentioned so far have only one, two, or three buttons, but you can add a Help button to any of the message boxes, making for a fourth button on those boxes that already have three buttons (such as vbYesNoCancel). You'll see how to add the Help button the section "Adding a Help Button to a Message Box," a little further along in the chapter.

In VBA, unless you specify otherwise, the first button on each of the message boxes is automatically the default button: for example, the OK button in a vbOKCancel message box, the Abort button in a vbAbortRetryIgnore message box, the Yes button in a vbYesNoCancel message box, the Yes button in a vbYesNo message box, and the Retry button in a vbRetryCancel message box. VBA counts the buttons in the order they're presented in the constant for the type of message box (which in turn is the left-to-right order in which they appear in the message box on screen). So in a vbYesNoCancel message box, Yes is the first button, No is the second button, and Cancel is the third button.

To set a different default button, specify the value or constant as part of the *buttons* argument. When run in PowerPoint, this statement produces the message box shown in Figure 13.7.

```
Dim lngQuery As Long
lngQuery = MsgBox("Do you want to delete this presentation?", _
    vbYesNo + vbCritical + vbDefaultButton2)
```

Controlling the Modality of a Message Box

VBA can display both application-modal message boxes and system-modal message boxes—at least in theory. *Application-modal* message boxes stop you from doing anything in the current application until you dismiss them, whereas *system-modal* message boxes stop you from doing anything *on your computer* until you dismiss them.

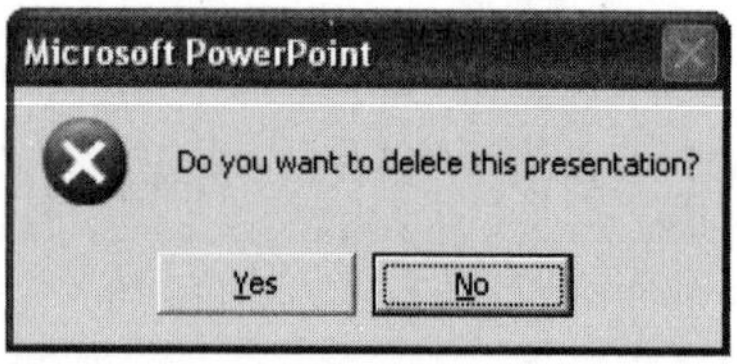

FIGURE 13.7
Specify a default button to steer the user toward a particular button in a message box.

Most message boxes are application modal, allowing you to "coolswitch" via pressing Alt+Tab (or switch via the Taskbar) to another application and work in it before you get rid of the message box, which gives you a reasonable amount of flexibility. In contrast, some installation message boxes are system modal, insisting that you concentrate your attention on them and them alone. Windows' critical system errors and "you must restart your computer now" messages are system modal to prevent you from avoiding them.

You probably know from your own experience how frustrating system-modal message boxes can be. So when designing procedures, use system-modal message boxes only when absolutely necessary—for example, when an action might result in data loss or system instability. For most conventional purposes, application-modal message boxes will do everything you need them to—and won't confuse or vex users of your procedures.

In theory, you can control the modality of a message box by using the two *buttons* arguments shown in Table 13.4.

TABLE 13.4:   Arguments for Message-Box Modality

VALUE	CONSTANT	RESULT
0	vbApplicationModal	The message box is application modal.
4096	vbSystemModal	The message box is system modal.

In practice, even if you use the vbSystemModal argument, the user can switch to another application (provided that one is running) and continue working. However, the message box stays "on top," remaining displayed—enough to annoy the user but not to prevent them from accessing another application.

By default, message boxes are application modal, so you need to specify modality only on those rare occasions when you need a system-modal message box. When you do, add the vbSystemModal constant or 4096 value to the *buttons* argument:

```
Response = MsgBox("Do you want to delete this document?", _
    vbYesNo + vbCritical + vbDefaultButton2 + vbSystemModal)
```

NOTE   System-modal message boxes look the same as application-modal message boxes.

Specifying a Title for a Message Box

The next component of the message box is its title bar, which is controlled by the optional *title* argument. If you omit *title*, VBA supplies the application's name as the title, but users of your procedures will benefit from your providing a more helpful title.

title is a string expression and can be up to 1024 characters in length in theory (longer strings are truncated with no warning or error message), but in practice, any title longer than about 75 characters gets truncated with an ellipsis. If you actually want people to read the title bars of your message boxes, 25 characters or so is a reasonable maximum.

TIP   The title bar is usually the first part of a message box that the user notices, so make your title bars as helpful as possible. Conventional etiquette is to put the name of the procedure in the title bar of a message box and then use the prompt to explain what choices the buttons in the message box will implement. In addition, if you expect to revise your procedures, you may find it helpful to include their version number in the title so that users can easily check which version of the procedure they're using (and update to a more current version as appropriate). For instance, the Delete Workbook procedure is identified as version 12.39 in the message box shown in Figure 13.8.

Specify the *title* argument after the *buttons* argument like this:

```
lngQ = MsgBox("Do you want to delete this workbook?", vbYesNo _
    + vbCritical + vbDefaultButton2, "Delete Workbook 12.39")
```

As with the *prompt* argument, you can use a string variable as the *title* argument. For example, you could declare a single string variable and use it to supply the title for each message box that a procedure calls. Or you might need to display in the title of the message box a string created or stored in the procedure.

NOTE   Don't try putting line-feed, carriage-return, or tab characters in the *title* argument. VBA accepts them but displays them as square boxes in the title bar rather than creating a two-line title bar. If you include one vbCr character, VBA does shift the text in the title bar up a bit, and if you include two vbCr characters, the text disappears off the top of the title bar with XP's default Windows scheme.

Adding a Help Button to a Message Box

To add a Help button to a message box, use the vbMsgBoxHelpButton constant. You add this argument to whichever buttons you're specifying for the message box:

```
lngQ = MsgBox("Do you want to delete this workbook?", vbYesNo _
    + vbCritical + vbDefaultButton2 + vbMsgBoxHelpButton, _
    "Delete Workbook")
```

Adding the vbMsgBoxHelpButton argument simply places the Help button in the message box—it doesn't make the Help button display a Help file until you specify which Help file and topic it should use (see the next section for details). Figure 13.9 shows the message box that this statement produces.

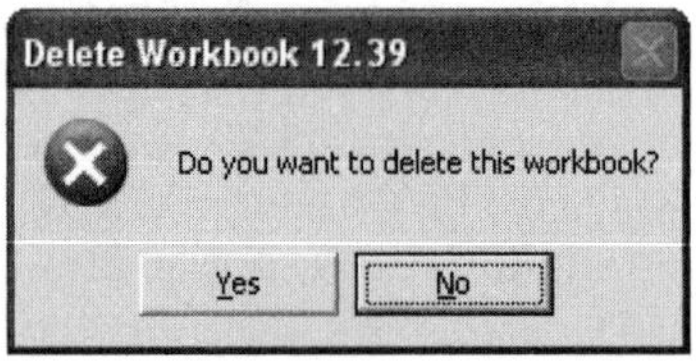

FIGURE 13.8
Usually, you'll want to specify the title argument for your message boxes. You may also want to include the version number of your code.

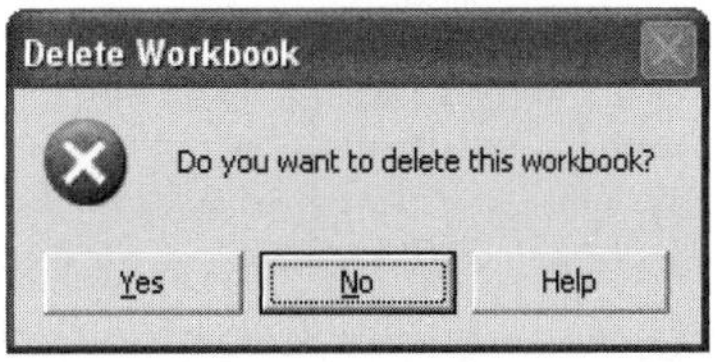

FIGURE 13.9
Use the vbMsgBoxHelp-
Button constant to add
a Help button to a mes-
sage box.

Specifying a Help File for a Message Box

The final arguments you can use for a message box are the *helpfile* and *context* arguments:

◆ The *helpfile* argument is a string argument specifying the name and location of the Help file that VBA displays when the user summons help from the message box.

◆ The *context* argument is a Help context number within the Help file. The Help context number controls which Help file topic is displayed.

The *helpfile* and *context* arguments are primarily useful if you're writing your own Help files, because otherwise it's difficult to access the Help context numbers, which are buried in the Help files. If you're writing your own Help files, the syntax for specifying the *helpfile* and *context* arguments is simple:

```
Dim lngQ As Long
lngQ = MsgBox("Do you want to delete this workbook?", vbYesNo _
    + vbCritical + vbDefaultButton2 + vbMsgBoxHelpButton, _
    "Delete Workbook", "c:\Windows\Help\My_Help.chm", 1012)
```

In this case, the Help file is specified as My_Help.chm in the \Windows\Help\ folder. VBA displays the help topic numbered 1012.

When the user clicks the Help button in the message box, VBA displays the preordained topic in the Help file. The message box stays on screen, so that when the user has finished consulting the Help file, they can make their choice in the message box.

TIP   The Help context number for the opening screen of a Help file is 0. Use 0 when you need to display a Help file for which you don't know the Help context numbers. The user must then find the information they need on their own.

THREE UNUSUAL CONSTANTS FOR SPECIAL EFFECTS

VBA provides three special constants for message boxes. You probably won't need to use these often, but if you do, they'll come in handy. Specify them in the *buttons* argument:

vbMsgBoxSetForeground   Tells VBA to make the message box the foreground window. You shouldn't need to use this constant often, because message boxes are displayed in the foreground by default (so that you can see them).

vbMsgBoxRight   Tells VBA to right-align the text in the message box.

vbMsgBoxRtlReading   Tells VBA to arrange the text from right to left on Hebrew and Arabic systems. It has no effect on non-BiDi (bidirectional) systems.

Using Some Arguments without Others

When displaying a message box, you can either specify or omit optional arguments. If you want to specify later arguments for a function without specifying the ones before them, use a comma to indicate each unused optional argument. For example, if you wanted to display the message box shown in the previous example without specifying *buttons* and *title* arguments, you could use the following statement:

```
Response = MsgBox("Do you want to format the report?",,, _
    "c:\Windows\Help\Procedure Help.chm", 1012
```

Here, the triple comma indicates that the *buttons* and *title* arguments are omitted (which will cause VBA to display a vbOKOnly message box with a title bar containing the application's name), preventing VBA from confusing the *helpfile* argument with the *buttons* argument. Alternatively, you could use named arguments, which makes for less-concise but easier-to-read code:

```
Response = MsgBox("Do you want to format the report?", _
    HelpFile:="c:\Windows\Help\Procedure Help.chm", Context:=1012)
```

Retrieving a Value from a Message Box

If you display a vbOKOnly message box, you know which button the user clicks, because the message box contains only an OK button. But when you use one of the other message boxes, which have two, three, or four buttons, you must retrieve a value from them that tells you which button the user clicked. You can then point the procedure in the appropriate direction.

To retrieve a value from a message box, declare a variable for it. You can do so quite simply by telling VBA that the variable name is equal to the message box (so to speak):

```
Response = MsgBox("Do you want to create the daily report?", _
    vbYesNo + vbQuestion, "Create Daily Report")
```

But typically you'll want to declare a variable of the appropriate type (a Long variable) to contain the user's choice, as in the examples throughout this chapter:

```
Dim lngResponse As Long
lngResponse = MsgBox("Do you want to create the daily report?", _
    vbYesNo + vbQuestion, "Create Daily Report")
```

When you run the code, VBA stores the user's choice of button as a value. You can then check the value and take action accordingly. Table 13.5 shows the full list of buttons the user may choose. You can refer to the buttons by either the constant or the value. As usual, the constant is easier to read than the value.

TABLE 13.5: Constants for Selected Buttons

VALUE	CONSTANT	BUTTON SELECTED
1	vbOK	OK
2	vbCancel	Cancel

TABLE 13.5: Constants for Selected Buttons *(CONTINUED)*

VALUE	CONSTANT	BUTTON SELECTED
3	vbAbort	Abort
4	vbRetry	Retry
5	vbIgnore	Ignore
6	vbYes	Yes
7	vbNo	No

For example, to check a vbYesNo message box to see which button the user chose, you can use a straightforward If... Then... Else statement:

```
Dim lngUserChoice As Long
lngUserChoice = MsgBox("Do you want to create the daily report?", _
    vbYesNo + vbQuestion, "Create Daily Report")
If lngUserChoice = vbYes Then
    Goto CreateDailyReport
Else
    Goto Bye
EndIf
```

Here, if the user chooses the Yes button, VBA goes to the line of code identified by the CreateDailyReport label and continues running the procedure from there; if not, it terminates the procedure by going to the Bye label at the end. The If condition checks the response generated by the choice the user made in the message box to see if it's a vbYes (generated by clicking the Yes button or pressing Enter with the Yes button selected). The Else statement runs if the response was not vbYes—that is, if the user chose the No button or pressed Escape, there being only the Yes button and the No button in this message box.

Input Boxes

When you want to retrieve one simple piece of textual information from the user, use an input box. You'll be familiar with input boxes by sight if not by name: They usually look something like the example shown in Figure 13.10.

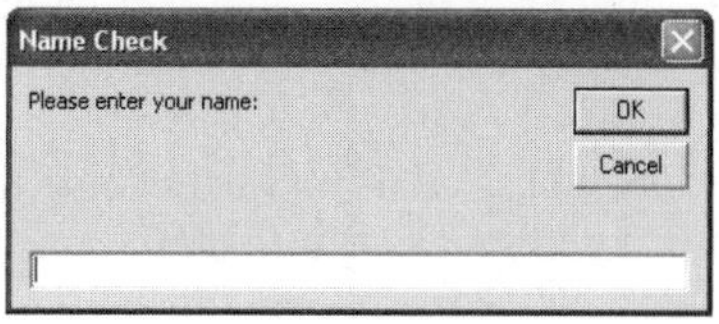

FIGURE 13.10
Use an input box to retrieve a single piece of information from the user.

TIP To retrieve two or more pieces of information from the user, you could use two or more input boxes in succession, but usually a custom dialog box is a better idea. You'll start looking at custom dialog boxes in Chapter 14.

Input Box Syntax

The syntax for displaying an input box is straightforward and similar to the syntax for a message box:

```
InputBox(prompt[, title] [, default] [, xpos] [, ypos] [, helpfile, context])
```

Here's what the arguments mean:

prompt   A required string that specifies the prompt that appears in the input box. As with MsgBox, *prompt* can be up to about 1024 characters long, and you can use line-feed and carriage-return characters to force separate lines. However, unlike the MsgBox prompt argument, the InputBox prompt doesn't automatically wrap, so you must use these characters to make it wrap if it's longer than about 35 characters.

title   A string that specifies the text in the title bar of the input box. If you don't specify a *title* argument, VBA enters the application's name for you.

default   A string that you can use to specify default text in the text box. Entering a *default* argument can be a good idea both for cases when the default text is likely to be suitable and when you need to display sample text so that the user can understand what type of response you're looking for. Here's an example of default text being suitable: If you display an input box asking for the user's name, you could enter the Name value from the User Information tab of the Options dialog box as a suggestion.

xpos and *ypos*   Optional numeric values for specifying the on-screen position of the input box. *xpos* governs the horizontal position of the left edge of the input box from the left edge of the screen (not of the Word window), whereas *ypos* governs the vertical position of the top edge of the input box from the top of the screen. Each measurement is in twips (see the next Note). If you omit these two arguments, VBA displays the input box at the default position of halfway across the screen and one-third of the way down it.

NOTE   A *twip* is $\frac{1}{1440}$ inch. An average computer screen uses 96 dots per inch (dpi), so there are 15 twips per pixel, and a computer screen at 800x600 resolution is 12,000x9,000 twips. If you need to position your input boxes and dialog boxes precisely, experiment with twips at different screen resolutions until you achieve satisfactory results. Generally, it's most effective to display an input box in the default position.

helpfile and *context*   Optional arguments for specifying the Help file and context in the Help file to jump to if the user summons help from the input box. If you use *helpfile*, you must also use *context*.

You can omit any of the optional arguments. But if you want to use an optional argument later in the syntax sequence than one you've omitted, you need to indicate the omission with a comma or use named arguments.

Unlike message boxes, input boxes come with a predefined set of buttons—OK and Cancel, plus a Help button if you specify the *helpfile* and *context* arguments—so there's no need for specifying the main buttons for an input box. The following example declares the String variable strWhichOffice and assigns to it the result of the input box shown in Figure 13.11.

```
Dim strWhichOffice As String
strWhichOffice = InputBox( _
    "Enter the name of the office that you visited:", _
    "Expense Assistant", "Madrid", , , _
    "c:\Windows\Help\Procedure Help.chm", 0)
```

FIGURE 13.11

The input box comes with a predefined set of buttons.

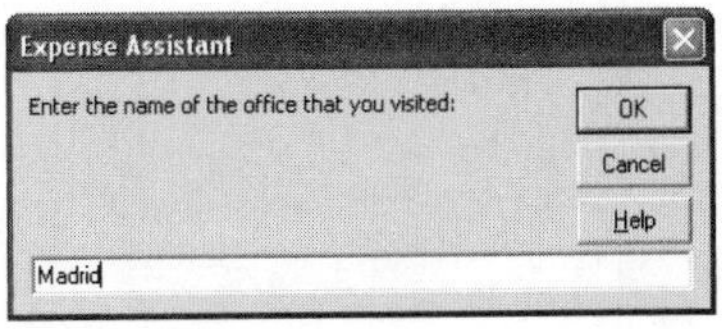

Retrieving Input from an Input Box

To retrieve input from an input box, declare the numeric variable or String variable that will contain it. Here, the variable strWhichOffice will contain what the user enters in the input box:

```
Dim strWhichOffice
strWhichOffice = _
    InputBox("Enter the name of the office that you visited:", _
    "Expense Assistant 2000", "Madrid", , , _
    "c:\Windows\Help\Procedure Help.chm", 0)
```

Once you've done that, and the user has entered a value or a string and chosen the OK button, you can use the value or string as usual in VBA. To make sure that the user has chosen the OK button, check that the input box hasn't returned a zero-length string (which it also returns if the user chooses the OK button with the text box empty) and take action accordingly:

```
strWhichOffice = InputBox _
    ("Enter the name of the office that you visited:", _
    "Expense Assistant 2000", "Madrid", , , _
    "c:\Windows\Help\Procedure Help.chm", 0)
If strWhichOffice = "" Then End
```

When Message Boxes and Input Boxes Won't Suffice

As you've seen in this chapter, a message box can greatly enhance a procedure by enabling the user to make a choice at a turning point or by presenting the user with important information. But once you've used message boxes for a while, you're apt to start noticing their limitations:

◆ You can present only a certain amount of information, and you're limited in the way you can display it (to whatever layout you can conjure up with new paragraphs, line breaks, tabs, and spaces).

◆ You can use only seven sets of buttons, which limit the possibilities of message boxes.

While you *can* get creative and enter complex messages in message boxes to make the most use of the buttons they offer, you'll usually do better to use a custom dialog box instead. As you'll see in Chapters 14 and 15, custom dialog boxes are relatively simple to create, and they give you far more power and flexibility than message boxes do.

You'll generally want to avoid writing procedures that present the user with a number of choices via a sequence of message boxes. Similarly, input boxes are useful for retrieving a single piece of information from the user, but beyond that, their limitations quickly become apparent. If you find yourself planning to use two or more input boxes in immediate succession, use a dialog box instead.

Chapter 14

Creating Simple Custom Dialog Boxes

- ◆ What you can do with a custom dialog box
- ◆ Creating a custom dialog box
- ◆ Adding controls to the dialog box
- ◆ Linking dialog boxes to procedures
- ◆ Retrieving the user's choices from a dialog box

In this chapter, you'll start looking at the capabilities that Visual Basic for Applications provides for creating custom dialog boxes that interact with the user. Dialog boxes are one of the most powerful and complex features of VBA. This chapter covers the more straightforward dialog box elements and how to manipulate them. The next chapter shows you how to create more complex dialog boxes, such as those that contain a number of tabbed pages and those that update themselves when the user clicks a control.

When Should You Use a Custom Dialog Box?

You'll often want to use a custom dialog box when simpler methods of interacting with the user fall short—for example, when you can't present the user with a reasonable choice using the limited selection of buttons provided in message boxes, or when you need to retrieve from the user information more involved than a straightforward input box can convey.

You'll also need to use a custom dialog box when a procedure requires that the user choose non-exclusive options by selecting or clearing check boxes, when you need to present mutually exclusive choices via option buttons, or when you need to provide the user with a list box from which to make a selection. Likewise, if you need to show the user a picture or have them choose one or more items from a list box or a combo box, you'll need to use a custom dialog box.

Custom dialog boxes provide the full range of interface elements with which the user is probably familiar from working with Windows applications. You can create custom dialog boxes that look and function almost exactly like built-in dialog boxes.

Typically, you'll use custom dialog boxes to drive your procedures, so they usually will appear in response to an action taken by the user. For example, when the user starts a procedure, you can have the procedure display a dialog box presenting options—such as choosing the files for the procedure to manipulate—that determine what the procedure will do. You can also create dialog boxes that VBA triggers in response to events in the computer system: for example, an event that runs at a specific time or when the user takes a specific action (such as creating, opening, or closing a document).

Because creating dialog boxes is relatively complex and can be time-consuming, it's wise to consider any practical alternatives to using them. You've already looked at message boxes and input boxes, which provide a simple alternative for some of the easier tasks for which you might want to create a custom dialog box. Some applications, such as Word and Excel, even let you borrow their built-in dialog boxes for your own purposes. If the user is familiar with the application, they're probably familiar with the dialog box and can immediately use it to perform standard actions—for example, to open or save files.

Creating a Custom Dialog Box

VBA uses visual objects called *user forms* to implement dialog boxes. A user form (also sometimes referred to as a *form*) is a blank sheet on which you can place controls (such as check boxes and buttons) to create a dialog box.

The user form contains a code sheet that holds code attached to the controls in the form: You can attach code to any of the controls and to the user form itself; and that code is stored in the user form's code sheet. You can display the user form's code sheet in the Code window of the Visual Basic Editor and work with it as you would any other code. You can run the user form as you would a procedure (for example, by pressing F5 with the user form selected), and the Visual Basic Editor will execute the code behind it.

Each user form becomes part of the application's user interface. In practical terms, this means that you can display a user form (a dialog box) for the user to interact with, and you can then retrieve information from the user form and manipulate it with VBA.

NOTE   You can also create user forms that aren't dialog boxes. The distinction between a dialog box and a window is arguable, but it's usually easiest to assume that a window is resizable (you can resize it by dragging its borders or by clicking its Maximize button), while a dialog box isn't. Some dialog boxes, such as the Find And Replace dialog box in Word, have an initially hidden part that you can display (in the case of the Find And Replace dialog box, by clicking the More button). But apart from this extension, the bounds of the dialog box are fixed—you can't grab the corner of the dialog box with the mouse and drag to enlarge the dialog box.

Each user form is itself one object and contains a number of other objects that you can manipulate separately. For example, you could create a simple dialog box with two option buttons, an OK button, and a Cancel button. Each option button would be an object; the OK button would be a third object; and the Cancel button would be a fourth object. You could set properties for each object—such as the action to take when the Cancel button was clicked, or the ScreenTip to display when the user moved the mouse pointer over one of the option buttons—to make the dialog box as comprehensible, straightforward, and useful as possible.

NOTE   ScreenTips are also called ToolTips.

You can set most properties for an object either at design time (when you're creating the user form) or at runtime (before or when you display the user form). For example, you can set the Value property of a check box control to True to display the check box in its selected state or to False to display the check box in its cleared state. You can set the Value property either when creating the user form (so that it will be set each time you run the user form) or when preparing to display the user form.

The next sections explain the process of creating a dialog box. At the end of the chapter, you'll find examples that step through creating a procedure and linking a dialog box to it.

Designing the Dialog Box

It's possible to whip together a half-decent dialog box that uses just a few controls without much planning. But usually, when you're creating a dialog box, you should adopt a more methodical approach and plan what you need to include in the dialog box before you start creating it. State the intended function of the dialog box and list the elements it will need in order to perform this function. Then sketch a rough diagram of the dialog box to get an approximate idea of where you'll fit in each of the elements.

TIP   Another option is to base the design for a custom dialog box on an existing dialog box—either a built-in dialog box or a custom dialog box that your company or organization has already implemented. Leveraging previous development efforts can not only save you from reinventing the wheel but also produce a custom dialog box that users find familiar and "intuitive." (It won't be intuitive at all—almost nothing about computers really is—but no matter. Perception is key.)

Inserting a User Form

Once you have a design in mind, the first step in creating a custom dialog box is to insert a user form in the appropriate template or document:

1. Display the Visual Basic Editor if it's not already open.

2. In the Project Explorer window, right-click the appropriate project and choose Insert ➢ User-Form from the shortcut menu.

NOTE   You can also insert a user form by clicking the project in the Project Explorer, clicking the Insert button on the Standard toolbar, and then choosing UserForm from the drop-down list. (If the button is already displaying its Insert UserForm face, just click the button rather than bothering with the drop-down list.) Alternatively, click the project, and then choose Insert ➢ UserForm.

The Visual Basic Editor opens a new user form like that shown in Figure 14.1, named UserForm1 (or the next available number if the project already contains a user form named UserForm1). The Visual Basic Editor also displays the Toolbox. (If you've previously hidden the Toolbox while working on a user form, the Visual Basic Editor doesn't display it. Choose View ➢ Toolbox or click the Toolbox button on the Standard toolbar to display the Toolbox.)

VBA inserts the user form in the Forms object (the collection of forms) for the project. If the project you chose didn't already contain a Forms object, VBA adds one to contain the new user form. You'll see the Forms object displayed in the Project Explorer.

CHOOSING USER FORM GRID SETTINGS

The Visual Basic Editor displays a grid in each user form to help you place controls relative to the dialog box and to align controls relative to each other. To switch off the display of this grid or to switch off the Visual Basic Editor's automatic alignment of controls to the grid, follow these steps:

1. Choose Tools ➢ Options to display the Options dialog box.

2. Click the General tab to display the General page (see Figure 14.2).

FIGURE 14.1

The first step in creating a new dialog box is to start a new user form. The Visual Basic Editor display the Toolbox when a user form is the active window.

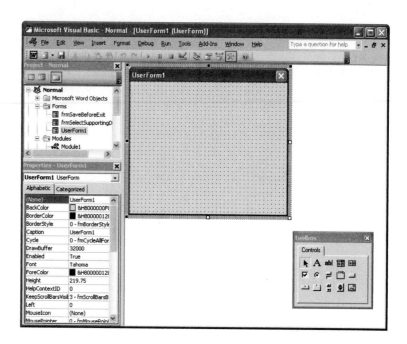

FIGURE 14.2

The General page of the Options dialog box includes options for toggling the display of the grid, resizing the grid, and toggling whether VBA aligns the controls to the grid.

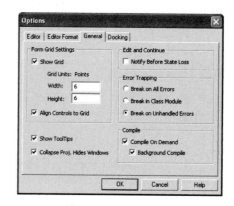

3. Choose the settings you want:

   A. Clear the Show Grid check box if you want to turn off the display of the grid. (The grid continues to function, but the dots are not displayed.)

   B. Clear the Align Controls To Grid check box if you want to stop using the grid whether it's aligned or not. This feature is usually a timesaver, but if the grid is too coarse for the placement you're trying to create, adjust the sizing of the grid.

   C. Change the number of points in the Width and Height text boxes to adjust the sizing of the grid's units. By default, each unit is 6 points.

4. Click the OK button to close the Options dialog box and apply your choices.

NAMING CONVENTIONS IN VISUAL BASIC FOR APPLICATIONS

Names for objects in VBA can be up to 40 characters long, must begin with a letter, and after that can be any combination of letters, numbers, and underscores. You can't use spaces or symbols in the names, and each name must be unique in its context—for example, each user form must have a unique name within a project, but within any user form or dialog box, an object can have the same name as an object in another dialog box.

Those are the rules; you can also use conventions to make the names of your VBA objects as consistent and easy to understand as possible. For example, by using the convention of starting a user form name with the letters frm, you can be sure that anyone else reading your code will immediately identify the name as belonging to a user form—and that you yourself will identify the name when you revisit old code you've written after a long interval. You should also add comments wherever necessary to make your code clear.

Some popular naming conventions for the most-used VBA objects are shown in the following list. You'll encounter the naming conventions for other VBA objects in due course later in the book.

Object	Prefix	Example
Check box	chk	chkReturnToPreviousPosition
Command button	cmd	cmdOK
Form (user form)	frm	frmMoveParagraph
Frame	fra	fraMovement
List box	lst	lstConferenceAttendees
Combo box	cmb	cmbColor
Menu	mnu	mnuProcedures
Option button	opt	optSpecialDelivery
Label	lbl	lblUserName
Text box	txt	txtUserDescription

The naming convention is to begin the prefix for each object with lowercase letters and then start the rest of the object's name with a capital to make it a little easier to read. You can also use underscores in VBA names to separate names into more discrete chunks, but you can't use spaces in any name.

Naming conventions tend to seem awkwardly formal at first, and there's a strong temptation to use any name that suits you for the objects in your VBA user forms. But if you plan to distribute your VBA modules or have others work with them, it's usually worth the time, effort, and formality to follow the naming conventions—or to create your own conventions and document them so that others can understand them.

Renaming the User Form

Next, change the user form's name from the default (UserForm1) to a more descriptive name:

TIP For advice on choosing names, refer to the sidebar "Naming Conventions in Visual Basic for Applications," earlier in this chapter.

1. If the Properties window isn't displayed, press F4 to display it. Figure 14.3 shows the two pages of the Properties window: Alphabetic and Categorized. Alphabetic contains an alphabetical listing of the properties of the currently selected object; Categorized contains a listing broken down into categories, such as Appearance, Behavior, Font, Misc., Picture, and Position. (Some controls have more categories than those listed here.) You can expand a category by clicking the plus (+) sign beside it to display the properties it contains and collapse it by clicking the resulting minus (–) sign. If the Alphabetic tab isn't selected, click it to select it.

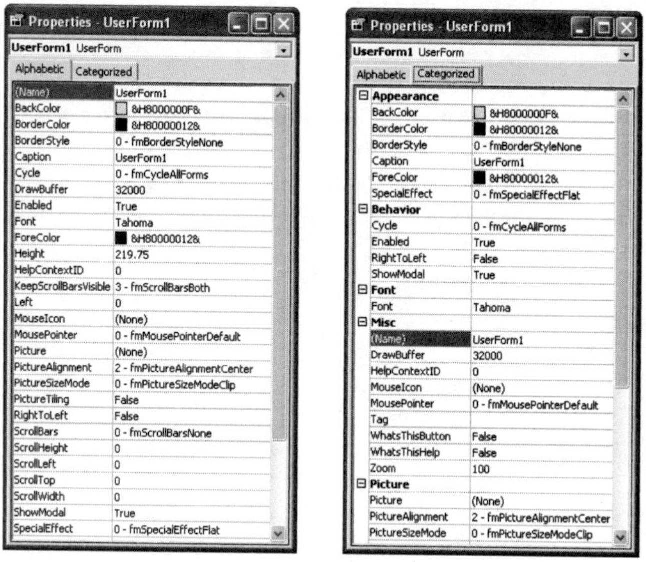

FIGURE 14.3

You can work on either the Alphabetic tab or the Categorized tab of the Properties window.

You can enter the user form's name and caption on the Categorized tab of the Properties window if you want—you just have to look a little harder to find the right places. The Caption property is contained in the Appearance collection, and the (Name) property is contained in the Misc. collection.

2. Make sure the drop-down list is displaying the default name of the user form. If it isn't, select the user form from the drop-down list.

3. Select the user form's default name (such as UserForm1 or UserForm2) in the cell to the right of the Name cell, and type a new name for the user form. This name can be anything you want, with the standard VBA limitations:

    ◆ It must start with a letter.

    ◆ It can contain letters, numbers, and underscores but no spaces or symbols.

    ◆ It can be up to 40 characters long.

4. Click the Caption cell to select the user form's default name and type the caption for the user form—that is, the text label that you want to appear in the title bar of the dialog box. This name has no restrictions beyond the constraints imposed by the length of the title bar. You can enter

a name longer than will fit in the title bar, but VBA truncates it with an ellipsis at its maximum displayable length. As you type, the name appears in the user form title bar as well, so it's easy to see what's an appropriate length—at least, for the current size of the user form.

5. Press Enter or click elsewhere in the Properties window (or elsewhere in the Visual Basic Editor) to enter the user form's name.

TIP Naming other objects works the same way as described here.

DEALING WITH THE "NAME CONFLICTS WITH EXISTING MODULE" ERROR

If you run into the "Name conflicts with existing module, project, or object library" error (shown here), chances are that you've just tried to give a user from the same name that you've already assigned to a procedure. This is surprisingly easy to do when you don't use a formal naming convention.

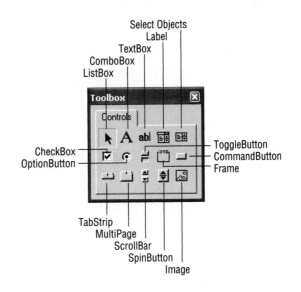

This error may also mean that you've reused the name of a VBA project or object library, but you're less likely to do this than to use a name that you yourself have already assigned.

Adding Controls to the User Form

Now that you've renamed the user form, you're ready to add controls to it from the Toolbox, shown in Figure 14.4. VBA automatically displays the Toolbox when a user form is active, but you can also display the Toolbox when no user form is active by choosing View ➤ Toolbox.

FIGURE 14.4
Use the Toolbox to add controls to the user form.

Here's what the buttons on the Toolbox do:

Button	Action
Select Objects	Restores the mouse pointer to selection mode. The mouse pointer automatically returns to selection mode once you've placed an object, so usually you'll need to click the Select Objects button only when you've selected another button and then decided not to use it or when you've double-clicked on a control to place multiple instances of it.
Label	Creates a *label*—text used to identify a part of the dialog box or to explain information the user needs to know in order to use the dialog box effectively.
TextBox	Creates a text box (also known as an *edit box*), a box into which the user can type text. You can also use a text box to display text to the user or to provide text for the user to copy and paste elsewhere. A text box can contain either one line (the default) or multiple lines and can display a horizontal scroll bar, a vertical scroll bar, or both horizontal and vertical scroll bars.
ComboBox	Creates a combo box, a control that combines a text box with a list box. The user can either choose a value from the list box or enter a new value in the text box.
ListBox	Creates a list box, a control that lists a number of values. The user can pick one value from the list, but can't enter a new value of their own (unlike a combo box). The list box is good for presenting closed sets of data.
CheckBox	Creates a check box and an accompanying label. The user can select or clear the check box to turn the associated action on or off.
OptionButton	Creates an option button (also known as a *radio button*) and an accompanying label. This button is usually a circle that contains a black dot when the option is selected. The user can select only one option button out of any group of option buttons. (The name "radio button" comes from radios with push buttons for stations, because you can select only one button at a time.)
ToggleButton	Creates a toggle button, a button that shows whether or not an item is selected. A toggle button can be defined with any two settings, such as On/Off or Yes/No. You can add a picture to a toggle button, which provides a graphical way of letting a user choose between options.
Frame	Creates a frame, an area of a user form or dialog box surrounded by a thin line, and an accompanying label. Use a frame (also known as a *group box*) to group related elements in your dialog boxes. As well as cordoning off elements visually, frames can separate them logically. For example, VBA treats a group of option buttons contained within a frame as separate from option buttons in other frames or option buttons loose in the dialog box. This separation makes it easier to use multiple sets of option buttons in a custom dialog box.

Button	Action
CommandButton	Creates a command button, a button used for issuing a command in a dialog box. Most dialog boxes contain command buttons such as OK and Cancel, or Open and Cancel, or Save, or Apply and Close.
TabStrip	Creates a tab strip for displaying multiple sets of data in the same set of controls. Tab strips are especially useful for presenting records in a database for review or modification: Each record in the database contains the same fields for information, so they can be displayed in the same group of controls. The tab strip provides an easy way of navigating between records.
MultiPage	Creates a multipage control for displaying multipage dialog boxes that have different layouts on each of their tabs. An example of a multipage dialog box is the Options dialog box (Tools ➤ Options), which has multiple pages (often referred to incorrectly as tabs) in most of the Office applications.
ScrollBar	Creates a stand-alone scroll bar. Stand-alone scroll bars are of relatively little use in dialog boxes. Combo boxes and list boxes have built-in scroll bars.
SpinButton	Creates a spin button control for attaching to another control. Spin buttons (also known as *spinners*) are typically small, rectangular buttons with one arrow pointing up and one down (or one arrow pointing left and the other pointing right). Spin buttons are useful for presenting sequential values with consistent intervals within an understood range, such as times or dates. For example, if you want the user to increment or decrement a price in a text box in 25-cent steps, you could use a spinner to adjust the price rather than letting them type directly into the text box.
Image	Creates an image control for displaying a picture within the user form. For example, you might use an image control to place a corporate logo or a picture in a dialog box.

NOTE The Toolbox shown in this chapter contains the basic set of tools provided by VBA. As discussed in "Customizing the Toolbox" in Chapter 2, you can customize the Toolbox in various ways: by adding other existing controls to it, creating additional pages for the controls, moving controls from page to page, and creating customized controls of your own making so that you can quickly place the elements you need most often.

Click in the user form to add a standard-size version of the selected control, as illustrated in Figure 14.5. VBA places the top-left corner of the control where you click. As you place a control, it snaps to the grid on the user form (unless you've turned off the Align Controls To Grid feature as described in "Choosing User Form Grid Settings," earlier in this chapter).

FIGURE 14.5
When you click in the user form, VBA places a standard-size control of the type you chose. If the Align Controls To Grid feature is switched on (as it is by default), VBA automatically aligns the control with the grid on the user form.

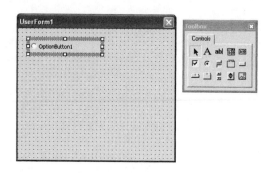

TIP To place multiple instances of the same control, double-click the control's button on the Toolbox. The Visual Basic Editor then doesn't revert to the selection pointer after you place the first control but rather remains at the ready for placing more instances of that control. When you've finished with that control, click the Select Objects button to restore the mouse pointer, or click any other Toolbox button so that you can place a control of that type.

You can resize the standard-size control as necessary by selecting it and then clicking and dragging one of the selection handles (the white squares) that appear around it, as shown in Figure 14.6. When you drag a corner handle, VBA resizes the control on both sides of the corner; when you drag the handle at the midpoint of one of the control's sides, VBA resizes the control only in that dimension. In either case, VBA displays a dotted outline indicating the size that the control will be when you release the mouse button.

FIGURE 14.6
Once you've placed a control, you can resize it as necessary by dragging one of its selection handles.

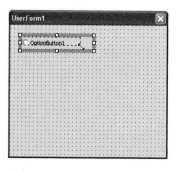

You can also create a custom-size version of the control by clicking and dragging when you place the control in the user form (as opposed to clicking to place a standard-size control and then dragging it to the size you want). Usually, however, it's easiest to place a standard-size version of the control and then resize it as necessary.

TIP To resize the user form itself, click its title bar (or in any blank space in the form—not in a control) to select it, and then click and drag one of the selection handles that appear around it.

To delete a control, right-click it in the user form and choose Delete from the context menu. Alternatively, click it to select it and then press the Delete key or choose Edit ➢ Delete.

To delete multiple controls, select them first as follows and then delete them by using the methods described in the previous paragraph:

◆ To select multiple contiguous controls, select the first control, hold down Shift, and then select the last control in the sequence.

◆ To select multiple noncontiguous controls—or to select further controls after you've selected multiple contiguous controls by using the Shift key—hold down the Ctrl key as you select each control after the first.

◆ To select multiple controls in the same area of the user form, click in the form outside the controls and drag the resulting selection box until it encompasses at least part of each control. When you release the mouse button, the Visual Basic Editor selects the controls.

Renaming Controls

As with user forms, VBA gives each control that you add a default name consisting of the type of control and a sequential number for the type of control. When you create the first text box in a user form, VBA names it TextBox1; when you create another text box, VBA names it TextBox2; and so on. Each control in a dialog box must have a unique name so that you can refer to it in code.

You'll usually want to change the controls' default names to names that describe their functions so you can remember what they do. For example, if TextBox2 is used for entering the user's organization name, you might want to rename it txtOrganizationName, txtOrgName, txtO_Name, or something similar.

To rename a control, follow these steps:

1. Click the control in the user form to select it and display its properties in the Properties window.

   ◆ When selecting a control, make sure the Select Objects button is selected in the Toolbox. (Unless you're performing another operation in the Toolbox—such as placing another control—the Select Objects button should be selected anyway.)

   ◆ If the Properties window is already displayed, you can select the control from the drop-down list instead of selecting it in the user form. VBA then selects the control in the user form, which helps you make sure that you've selected the control you want to affect.

   ◆ If the Properties window isn't displayed, you can quickly display it with the properties for the appropriate control by right-clicking the control in the user form and choosing Properties from the context menu.

2. On either the Alphabetic page or the Categorized page, select the default name in the cell to the right of the Name property.

3. Type the new name for the control. The name for a control (which is an object, like the user form) must start with a letter, can contain letters, numbers, and underscores (but no spaces or symbols), and can be up to 40 characters long.

4. Press Enter to set the control name, or click elsewhere in the Properties window or in the user form.

NOTE You can rename a control again at any point. But if you do, you must also change any references to it in the code that drives the user form. This gives you a strong incentive to choose suitable names for your controls before you write the code.

Moving a Control

To move a control that isn't currently selected, click anywhere in it to select it, and then drag it to where you want it to appear, as shown in Figure 14.7.

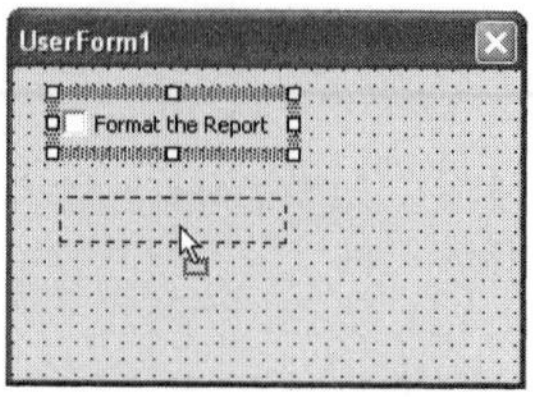

FIGURE 14.7

If a control isn't currently selected, you can move it by clicking it and dragging it.

To move a selected control, move the mouse pointer over the selection border around it so that the mouse pointer turns into a four-headed arrow (as shown in Figure 14.8), and then click and drag the control to where you want it to appear.

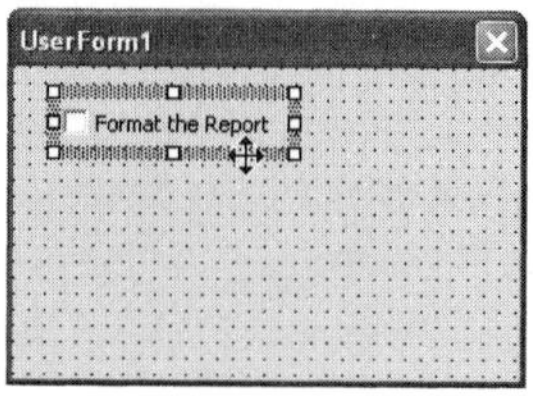

FIGURE 14.8

If a control is selected, move the mouse pointer over its selection border, and then click and drag the control.

NOTE You can use the Cut and Paste commands (either from the Standard toolbar, the Edit menu, the context menu, or the keyboard) to move a control, but it isn't a great way of proceeding: The Paste command places the control right in the middle of the user form or container (for example, a frame), so you have to drag it to its new position anyway.

Copying and Pasting Controls

You can use the Copy and Paste commands to copy and paste controls that you've already added to a user form. You can paste them either to the same user form or to another user form. The Paste command drops the copy of the control in the middle of the user form or container; from there you have to drag it to where you want it. The advantage of using Copy and Paste for creating new controls—versus using Cut and Paste to move existing controls—is that the new controls take on the characteristics of the original controls, so you can save time by creating a control, setting its properties, and then cloning it.

All you need to do then is move each cloned copy to a suitable location, change its name from the default name VBA has given it to something descriptive and memorable, and set any properties that differ from those of the control's siblings. For copies you paste to another user form, you don't even need to change the names of the copies you paste—they just need to be named suitably for the code with which they work.

TIP Add customized copies of controls that you use frequently to the Toolbox. From the Toolbox, you can quickly add multiple copies of the control to a user form. You'll need to set the name for each copy of the control after the first, but all the other properties will remain as you set them for the copy of the control on the Toolbox.

If you need to set all the properties separately for each control of the same type, you'll probably find it quicker to insert a new control by using the Toolbox buttons rather than Copy and Paste.

As an alternative to using the Copy and Paste commands, you can also copy a control by holding down the Ctrl key as you click and drag the control. VBA displays a + sign attached to the mouse pointer, as shown in Figure 14.9, to indicate that you're copying the control rather than moving it. Drop the copy where you want it to appear on the user form.

FIGURE 14.9
VBA displays a + sign attached to the mouse pointer when you Ctrl+drag to copy a control.

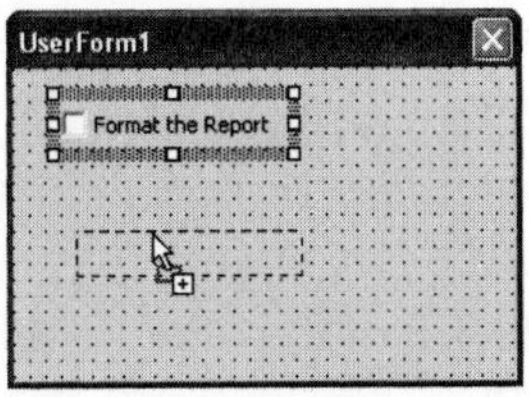

Changing the Label on a Control

When a control has a displayed label, you can change the label like this:

1. Click the control to select it.

2. Click once in the label to select it. VBA displays a faint dotted border around the label, as shown in Figure 14.10.

WARNING When you click a label to select it, and click again to position the insertion point, make sure that the two clicks are distinct enough that Windows doesn't interpret them as a double-click. A double-click displays the code sheet for the user form and adds a procedure for the Click event of the label. If this happens, press Shift+F7 or choose View ➢ Object to view the form again. Then start again with step 1.

FIGURE 14.10
To change the label on a control, select the control, and then click in the label so that it displays a faint dotted border.

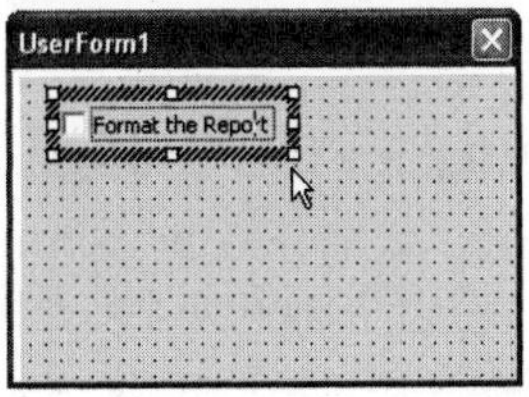

3. Click in the label to position the insertion point for editing it, or drag through the label to select all of it.

4. Edit the text of the label as desired.

5. Press Enter or click elsewhere in the user form to effect the change to the label.

TIP You can also change the label by changing its Caption property in the Properties window.

WHEN SHOULD YOU SET PROPERTIES FOR A CONTROL?

You can set many properties for a control either at design time or at runtime. There's a time and a place for each—and a time when either is a reasonable course of action.

Generally speaking, the more static the property, the more often you'll want to set it at design time. Some properties, such as the Name property of a user form, *have* to be set at design time—you can't set such properties at runtime for a user form. You'll also usually want to name your controls at design time, though you can add controls at runtime and set their Name properties.

In most cases, you'll want to set the properties that govern the position and size of the user form itself and its controls at design time. The advantages are straightforward: You can make sure that the user form looks as you intend it to, that it's legible, and so on.

Occasionally, you may need to adjust the properties of a user form or the size or position of some of the controls on it at runtime. For example, you might need to add a couple of option buttons to the form to take care of eventualities not included in the basic design of the form. Alternatively, you might create a form that had two groups of option buttons sharing the same space—one group, in effect, positioned on top of the other. At runtime, you could establish which group of option buttons was needed, make that group visible, and hide the other group. If each group contained the same number of option buttons, you could make do with one group of option buttons, assigning the appropriate properties to each at runtime.

Given the flexibility that the many properties of controls provide, you can often design your user forms to handle several circumstances by displaying and hiding different groups of controls at runtime, rather than having to add or remove controls at runtime. Creating the complete set of controls for a user form at design time avoids most of the difficulties that can arise from adding extra controls at runtime. That said, you may sometimes need to create a user form on-the-fly to present information about the situation in which users have placed themselves.

As you'll see as you continue to work with controls, you have to set information for some controls at runtime. For example, you can't assign the list of items to a list box or combo box at design time: You have to assign the list of items at runtime. (Typically, you assign the list of items during a `UserForm_Initialize` procedure that runs as the user form is being initialized for display.)

Key Properties for the Toolbox Controls

This section discusses the key properties for the controls in the default Toolbox.

First, it explains the common properties used to manipulate many of the controls effectively. After that, it goes through the controls one by one, listing the properties peculiar to each control.

NOTE If you're new to VBA and find this section heavy going, skip it for the time being and return to it when you need to reference information about the properties of the controls.

COMMON PROPERTIES

Table 14.1 lists the properties shared by all or most controls, grouped by category.

TABLE 14.1:   Properties Common to Most or All Controls

PROPERTY	APPLIES TO	EXPLANATION
Information		
BoundValue	All controls except Frame, Image, and Label	Contains the value of the control when the control receives the focus in the user form.
HelpContextID	All controls except Image and Label	Returns the context identifier of the Help file topic associated with the control.
Name	All controls	Contains the name for the control.
Object	All controls	Enables you to assign to a control a custom property or method that uses the same name as a standard property or method.
Parent	All controls	Returns the name of the user form that contains the control.
Tag	All controls	Used for assigning extra information to the control.
Value	CheckBox, ComboBox, CommandButton, ListBox, MultiPage, OptionButton, ScrollBar, SpinButton, TabStrip, TextBox, ToggleButton	One of the most varied properties, Value specifies the state or value of the control. A CheckBox, OptionButton, or ToggleButton can have an integer value of –1 (True), indicating that the item is selected, or a value of 0 (False), indicating that the item is cleared. A ScrollBar or SpinButton returns a Value containing the current value for the control. A ComboBox or ListBox returns the currently selected row's (or rows') BoundColumn value. A MultiPage returns an integer indicating the active page, and a TextBox returns the text in the text box. The Value of a CommandButton is False, because choosing the command button triggers a Click event. However, you can set the value of a CommandButton to True, which has the same effect as clicking it.
Size and Position		
Height	All controls	The height of the control, measured in points.
LayoutEffect	All controls except Image	Indicates whether a control was moved when the layout of the form was changed.
Left	All controls	The distance of the left border of the control in pixels from the left edge of the form or frame that contains it.
OldHeight	All controls	The previous height of the control, measured in pixels.

TABLE 14.1: Properties Common to Most or All Controls *(CONTINUED)*

PROPERTY	APPLIES TO	EXPLANATION
OldLeft	All controls	The previous position of the left border of the control, measured in pixels.
OldTop	All controls	The previous position of the top border of the control, measured in pixels.
OldWidth	All controls	The previous width of the control, measured in points.
Top	All controls	The distance of the top border of the control in pixels from the top edge of the form or frame that contains it.
Width	All controls	The width of the control, measured in points.
Appearance		
Alignment	CheckBox, OptionButton, ToggleButton	Specifies how the caption is aligned to the control.
AutoSize	CheckBox, ComboBox, CommandButton, Image, Label, OptionButton, TextBox, ToggleButton	A Boolean property that controls whether the object resizes itself automatically to accommodate its contents. The default setting is False, which means that the control doesn't automatically resize itself.
BackColor	All controls	The background color of the control. This property contains a number representing the color.
BackStyle	CheckBox, ComboBox, CommandButton, Frame, Image, Label, OptionButton, TextBox, ToggleButton	Specifies whether the background of the object is transparent (fmBackStyleTransparent) or opaque (fmBackStyleOpaque, the default). You can see through a transparent control—anything behind it on the form will show through. You can use transparent controls to achieve interesting effects—for example, by placing a transparent command button on top of an image or another control.
BorderColor	ComboBox, Image, Label, TextBox, ListBox	Specifies the color of the control's border. You can choose a border color from the System drop-down list or the palette, or enter BorderColor as an eight-digit integer value (such as 16711680 for mid-blue). VBA stores the BorderColor property as a hexadecimal value (for instance, 00FF0000). For BorderColor to take effect, BorderStyle must be set to fmBorderStyleSingle.

TABLE 14.1:   Properties Common to Most or All Controls *(CONTINUED)*

PROPERTY	APPLIES TO	EXPLANATION
BorderStyle	ComboBox, Frame, Image, Label, ListBox, TextBox, UserForm	Specifies the style of border on the control or user form. Use BorderStyle with the BorderColor property to set the color of a border.
Caption	CheckBox, CommandButton, Label, OptionButton, ToggleButton	A text string containing the description that appears for a control—the text that appears in a label, on a command button or toggle button, or next to a check box or option button.
Font (object)	All controls except Image, SpinButton, and ScrollBar	Font—an object rather than a property—controls the font in which the label for the object is displayed. For TextBox, ComboBox, and ListBox controls, Font controls the font in which the text in the control is displayed.
ForeColor	All controls except Image	The foreground color of the control (often the text on the control). This property contains a number representing the color.
Locked	CheckBox, ComboBox, CommandButton, ListBox, OptionButton, TextBox, ToggleButton	A Boolean property that specifies whether the user can change the control. When Locked is set to True, the user can't change the control, though the control can still receive the focus (that is, be selected) and trigger events. When Locked is False (the default value), the control is open for editing.
MouseIcon	All controls except MultiPage	Specifies the image to display when the user moves the mouse pointer over the control. To use the MouseIcon property, the MousePointer property must be set to 99, fmMousePointerCustom.
MousePointer	All controls except MultiPage	Specifies the type of mouse pointer to display when the user moves the mouse pointer over the control.
Picture	CheckBox, CommandButton, Frame, Image, Label, OptionButton, Page, ToggleButton, UserForm	Specifies the picture to display on the control. By using the Picture property, you can add a picture to a normally text-based control, such as a command button.
PicturePosition	CheckBox, CommandButton, Label, OptionButton, ToggleButton	Specifies how the picture is aligned with its caption.

TABLE 14.1: Properties Common to Most or All Controls *(CONTINUED)*

PROPERTY	APPLIES TO	EXPLANATION
SpecialEffect	CheckBox, ComboBox, Frame, Image, Label, ListBox, OptionButton, TextBox, ToggleButton	Specifies the visual effect to use for the control. For a CheckBox, OptionButton, or ToggleButton, the visual effect can be flat (fmButtonEffectFlat) or sunken (fmButtonEffectSunken). For the other controls, the visual effect can be flat (fmSpecialEffectFlat), raised (fmSpecialEffectRaised), sunken (fmSpecialEffectSunken), etched (fmSpecialEffectEtched), or a bump (fmSpecialEffectBump).
Visible	All controls	Indicates whether the control is visible; expressed as a Boolean value.
WordWrap	CheckBox, CommandButton, Label, OptionButton, TextBox, ToggleButton	A Boolean property that specifies whether the text in or on a control wraps at the end of a line. For most controls, WordWrap is set to True by default; you'll often want to change this property to False to prevent the text from wrapping inappropriately. If the control is a TextBox and its MultiLine property is set to True, VBA ignores the WordWrap property.
Behavior		
Accelerator	CheckBox, CommandButton, Label, OptionButton, Page, Tab, ToggleButton	The accelerator key (or *access key*, or *mnemonic*) for the control—the key you press (typically in combination with Alt) to access the control. For example, in many dialog boxes, you can access the Cancel button by pressing Alt+C. The accelerator key for a label applies to the next control in the tab order rather than to the label itself.
ControlSource	CheckBox, ComboBox, ListBox, OptionButton, ScrollBar, SpinButton, TextBox, ToggleButton	The cell or field used to set or store the Value of the control. The default value is an empty string (" "), indicating that there is no control source for the control.
ControlTipText	All controls	The text of the ScreenTip displayed when the user holds the mouse pointer over the control. The default value of ControlTipText is a blank string, which means that no ScreenTip is displayed.
Enabled	All controls	A Boolean value that controls whether the control can be accessed (either interactively or programmatically).

TABLE 14.1:   Properties Common to Most or All Controls *(CONTINUED)*

PROPERTY	APPLIES TO	EXPLANATION
TabIndex	All controls except Image	The position of the control in the tab order of the user form, expressed as an integer from 0 (the first position) through the number of controls on the user form.
TabStop	All controls except Image and Label	A Boolean value establishing whether the user can select the control by pressing the Tab key. If TabStop is set to False, the user can select the control only with the mouse. The TabStop setting doesn't change the tab order of the dialog box.

LABEL

The Label control simply displays text on screen. Use the positional properties to place the label and the Caption property to assign the text that you want the label to display. Use the TextAlign property as shown in Table 14.2 to align the text of the label with the borders of the label control.

TABLE 14.2:   *TextAlign* Property Values for the Label Control

fmTextAlign CONSTANT	VALUE	TEXT ALIGNMENT
fmTextAlignLeft	1	With the left border of the control
fmTextAlignCenter	2	Centered on the control's area
fmTextAlignRight	3	With the right border of the control

TEXTBOX

Table 14.3 lists the key properties for the TextBox control.

TABLE 14.3:   Key Properties for the TextBox Control

PROPERTY	DESCRIPTION
AutoTab	A Boolean property that determines whether VBA automatically moves to the next field when the user has entered the maximum number of characters in the text box or combo box. (Pressing Tab moves manually to the next field.)
AutoWordSelect	A Boolean property that determines whether VBA automatically selects a whole word when the user drags the mouse through text in a text box or a combo box.

TABLE 14.3:   Key Properties for the TextBox Control *(CONTINUED)*

PROPERTY	DESCRIPTION
DragBehavior	Enables or disables drag-and-drop for a text box or combo box: fmDragBehaviorDisabled (0) disables drag-and-drop; fmDragBehaviorEnabled (1) enables drag-and-drop.
EnterFieldBehavior	Determines whether VBA selects the contents of the edit area of the text box or combo box when the user moves the focus to the text box or combo box: fmEnterFieldBehaviorSelectAll (0) selects the contents of the text box or current row of the combo box; fmEnterFieldBehaviorRecallSelection (1) doesn't change the previous selection.
EnterKeyBehavior	A Boolean property that determines what VBA does when the user presses Enter with the focus on a text box. If EnterKeyBehavior is True, VBA creates a new line when the user presses Enter; if EnterKeyBehavior is False, VBA moves the focus to the next control on the user form. If MultiLine is False, VBA ignores the EnterKeyBehavior setting.
HideSelection	A Boolean property that determines whether VBA displays any selected text in a text box or combo box. If HideSelection is True, VBA displays the text without indicating the selection when the control doesn't have the focus. If HideSelection is False, VBA indicates the selection both when the control has the focus and when it doesn't.
IMEMode	Determines the default runtime mode of the Input Method Editor (IME). This property is used only in Far Eastern applications (for example, those using Japanese hiragana or katakana, or Korean hangul).
IntegralHeight	A Boolean property that determines whether a list box or a text box resizes itself vertically to display any rows that are too tall to fit into it at its current height (True) or not (False).
MultiLine	A Boolean property that determines whether the text box can contain multiple lines of text (True) or only one line (False). When MultiLine is True, the text box adds a vertical scroll bar when the content becomes more than will fit within the current dimensions of the text box.
PasswordChar	Specifies the placeholder character to use in place of text entered in a text box. When you specify the character for PasswordChar, VBA displays one instance of that character in place of each letter in the text box. This property is normally used for entering passwords and other information that needs to be obscured so that it cannot be read.
ScrollBars	Specifies which scroll bars to display on the text box. Usually, you'll do best to set the WordWrap property to True and let VBA add the vertical scroll bar to the text box as needed rather than using the ScrollBars property.
SelectionMargin	A Boolean property that determines whether the user can select a line of text in the text box or combo box by clicking in the selection bar to the left of the line.

TABLE 14.3: Key Properties for the TextBox Control *(CONTINUED)*

PROPERTY	DESCRIPTION
ShowDropButtonWhen	Determines when to display the drop-down button for a combo box or a text box. fmShowDropButtonWhenNever (0) never displays the drop-down button and is the default for a text box. fmShowDropButtonWhenFocus (1) displays the drop-down button when the text box or combo box has the focus. fmShowDropButtonWhenAlways (2) always displays the drop-down button and is the default for a combo box.
TabKeyBehavior	A Boolean property that specifies whether the user can enter tabs in the text box. If TabKeyBehavior is True and MultiLine is True, pressing Tab enters a tab in the text box. If MultiLine is False, VBA ignores a TabKeyBehavior setting of True. If TabKeyBehavior is False, pressing Tab moves the focus to the next control in the tab order.

COMBOBOX AND LISTBOX

Table 14.4 shows the key properties for the ComboBox control and the ListBox control. These two controls are similar and share many properties.

TABLE 14.4: Key Properties for the ComboBox Control and ListBox Control

PROPERTY	DESCRIPTION
AutoTab	See Table 14.3.
AutoWordSelect	See Table 14.3.
BoundColumn	A Variant property that determines the source of data in a combo box or a list box that has multiple columns. The default setting is 1 (the first column). To assign another column, specify the number of the column (columns are numbered from 1, the leftmost column). To assign the value of ListIndex to BoundColumn, use 0.
ColumnCount	A Long property that sets or returns the number of columns displayed in the combo box or list box. If the data source is unbound, you can specify up to 10 columns. To display all available columns in the data source, set ColumnCount to −1.
ColumnHeads	A Boolean property that determines whether the combo box or list box displays headings on the columns (True) or not (False).
ColumnWidths	A String property that sets or returns the width of each column in a multi-column combo box or list box.
ListRows	(Combo box only.) A Long property that sets or returns the number of rows displayed in the combo box. If the number of items in the list is greater than the value of ListRows, the combo box displays a scroll bar so that the user can scroll to the unseen items.

TABLE 14.4: Key Properties for the ComboBox Control and ListBox Control *(CONTINUED)*

PROPERTY	DESCRIPTION
ListStyle	Determines the visual effect the list uses. For both a combo box and a list box, fmListStylePlain displays a regular, unadorned list. For a combo box, fmListStyleOption displays an option button to the left of each entry, allowing the user to select one item from the list. For a list box, fmListStyleOption displays option buttons for a single-select list and check boxes for a multi-select list.
ListWidth	(Combo box only.) A Variant property that sets or returns the width of the list in a combo box. The default value is 0, which makes the list the same width as the text area of the combo box.
MatchEntry	Determines which type of matching the combo box or list box uses when the user types characters with the focus on the combo box or list box. fmMatchEntryFirstLetter (0) matches the next entry that starts with the letter or character typed: If the user types *t* twice, VBA selects the first entry beginning with *t* and then the second entry beginning with *t*. fmMatchEntryComplete (1) matches each letter the user types: If the user types *te*, VBA selects the entry that starts with *te*. fmEntryMatchNone (2) specifies no matching: The user can't select an item by typing in the list box or combo box but must use the mouse or the arrow keys instead. The default MatchEntry setting for a combo box is fmMatchEntryComplete. The default setting for a list box is fmMatchEntryFirstLetter.
MatchRequired	(Combo box only.) A Boolean property determining whether the user must select an entry from the combo box before leaving the control (True) or not (False). This property is useful for making sure that the user doesn't type a partial entry into the text box area of the combo box but forget to complete the selection in the drop-down list area. If MatchRequired is True and the user tries to leave the combo box without making a selection, VBA displays an *Invalid Property Value* message box.
MultiSelect	(List box only.) Controls whether the user can make a single selection in the list or multiple selections. fmMultiSelectSingle (0) lets the user select only one item. fmMultiSelectMulti (1) lets the user select multiple items by clicking with the mouse or by pressing the spacebar. fmMultiSelectExtended (2) lets the user use Shift+click, Ctrl+click, and Shift with the arrow keys to extend or reduce the selection.
RowSource	A String property that specifies the source of a list for a combo box or a list box.
SelectionMargin	See Table 14.3.
ShowDropButtonWhen	See Table 14.3.

CHECKBOX

Most of the properties for the CheckBox control have been discussed already. The key property of the CheckBox that you haven't examined yet is TripleState, which applies to the OptionButton and ToggleButton controls as well.

TripleState is a Boolean property that determines whether the check box, option button, or toggle button can have a null state as well as True and False states. When the check box is in the null state, it appears with its box selected but grayed out. For example, you get this effect in the Font dialog box in Word when one of the check box–controlled properties—such as the Shadow check box in Figure 14.11—is on for part of the current selection but not for the whole selection.

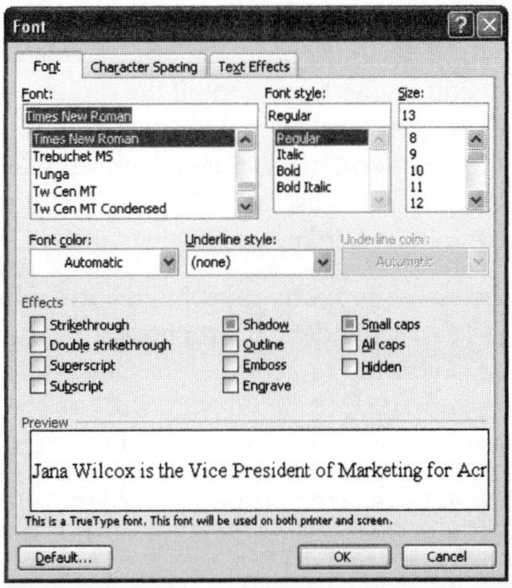

FIGURE 14.11
By setting the TripleState property of a check box to True, you can display a check box in a null state. Word's Font dialog box shows check boxes in a null state (with a square green dot) when they apply to part of the current selection but not to the whole of the current selection.

A couple of properties described briefly in the context of other controls deserve more detail here:

◆ The SpecialEffect property controls the visual appearance of the check box. The default value is fmButtonEffectSunken (2), which displays a sunken box—the norm for 3-D Windows dialog boxes. You can also choose fmButtonEffectFlat (0) to display a box with a flat effect. Figure 14.12 shows a sunken check box and a flat check box.

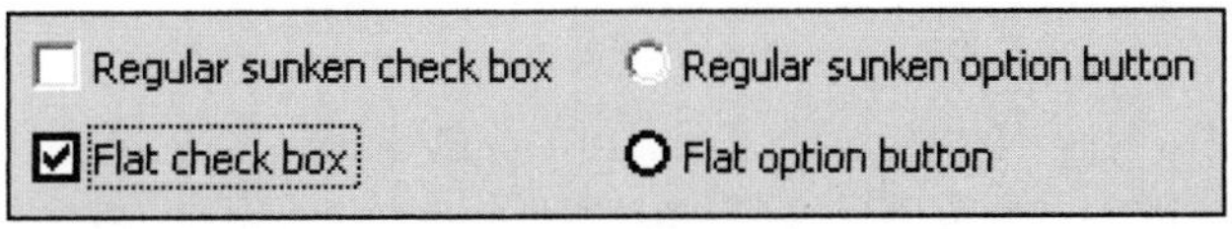

FIGURE 14.12
Use the SpecialEffect property to display a flat check box or option button (bottom line) rather than the normal sunken check box or option button.

◆ The Value property, which indicates whether the check box is selected (True) or cleared (False), is the default property of the check box. The following three statements have the same effect:

```
If CheckBox1.Value = True Then
If CheckBox1 = True Then
If CheckBox1 Then
```

◆ The Accelerator property provides quick access to the check box. Assign a unique accelerator key to check boxes so that the user can swiftly toggle them on and off from the keyboard.

OPTIONBUTTON

Like the CheckBox, the OptionButton control has a straightforward set of properties, almost all of which you've seen already in this chapter. This section shows you the GroupName property, which is unique to the OptionButton, and some of the key properties for working with option buttons.

The GroupName property is a string property that assigns the option button to a group of option buttons. The default setting for GroupName is a blank string (" "), which means that an option button isn't assigned to a group until you explicitly assign it. When you enter the group name, the group is created. By using the GroupName property, you can have multiple groups of option buttons on the same form without using frames to cordon off the groups, but you must distinguish the logical groups of option buttons from each other so that the user can immediately tell which option buttons constitute a group. In practice, a frame often provides the easiest way of segregating groups of option buttons both visually and logically—but it's useful to have the flexibility that GroupName provides when you need it.

These are the other key properties for the OptionButton control:

◆ The Value property, which indicates whether the option button is selected (True) or cleared (False), is the default property of the option button. So you can set or return the state of the option button by setting either the OptionButton object or its Value to True or False, as appropriate. Setting the Value of one OptionButton to True sets the Value of all other Option-Button controls in the same group or frame to False.

◆ The Accelerator property provides quick access to the option button. Assign a unique accelerator key to each option button so that the user can toggle it on and off from the keyboard.

◆ The SpecialEffect property controls the visual appearance of the option button. The default value of fmButtonEffectSunken (2) displays a sunken button, while fmButtonEffectFlat (0) displays a flattened button. Figure 14.12 shows a sunken option button and a flat option button.

◆ The TripleState property (discussed in the previous section, "CheckBox") lets you create an option button that has three states: selected (True), cleared (False), and null (which appears selected but grayed out). The TripleState property is disabled so that the user can't set the null state interactively, but you can set it programmatically as needed.

TOGGLEBUTTON

The ToggleButton control creates a toggle button. A *toggle button* is a button that, when not selected, appears raised, but whose appearance changes so that it appears pushed in when it's selected. The key properties for the ToggleButton control are the same as those for the CheckBox and CommandButton:

◆ The Value property is the default property of the ToggleButton.

◆ The TripleState property lets you create a ToggleButton that has three states: selected (True), cleared (False), and null (which appears selected but grayed out). The user can set a triple-state ToggleButton to its null state by clicking it. In its null state, a ToggleButton appears grayed out.

◆ The Accelerator property provides quick access to the toggle button.

FRAME

The Frame control is relatively straightforward, but it has several properties worth mentioning; they're shown in Table 14.5. The Frame control shares a couple of these properties with the Page object.

TABLE 14.5:   Properties of the Frame Control

PROPERTY	DESCRIPTION
Cycle	Determines the action taken when the user leaves the last control in the frame or on the page. fmCycleAllForms (0) moves the focus to the next control in the tab order for the user form or page, whereas fmCycleCurrentForm(2) keeps the focus within the frame or on the page until the focus is explicitly moved to a control in a different frame or on a different page. This property applies to the Page object as well.
InsideHeight	A read-only property that returns the height in points of the area inside the frame, not including the height of any horizontal scroll bar displayed. This property applies to the Page object as well.
InsideWidth	A read-only property that returns the width in points of the area inside the frame, not including the width of any vertical scroll bar displayed. This property applies to the Page object as well.
KeepScrollBarsVisible	A property that determines whether the frame or page displays horizontal and vertical scroll bars when they aren't required for the user to be able to navigate the frame or the page. fmScrollBarsNone (0) displays no scroll bars unless they're required. fmScrollBarsHorizontal (1) displays a horizontal scroll bar all the time. fmScrollBarsVertical (2) displays a vertical scroll bar all the time. fmScrollBarsBoth (3) displays a horizontal scroll bar and a vertical scroll bar all the time. fmScrollBarsNone is the default for the Frame object, and fmScrollBarsBoth is the default for the Page object. This property applies to the Page object as well.
PictureTiling	A Boolean property that determines whether a picture displayed on the control is tiled (True) so that it takes up the whole area covered by the control or not (False). To set the tiling pattern, you use the PictureAlignment and PictureSizeMode properties. This property applies to the Page object and the Image control as well.
PictureSizeMode	Determines how to display the background picture. fmPictureSizeModeClip (0), the default setting, crops off any part of the picture too big to fit in the page, frame, or image control. Use this setting to show the picture at its original dimensions and in its original proportions. fmPictureSizeModeStretch (1) stretches the picture horizontally or vertically to fill the page, frame, or image control. This setting is good for colored backgrounds and decorative effects but tends to be disastrous for pictures that need to be recognizable; it also overrides the PictureAlignment property setting. fmPictureSizeModeZoom (3) zooms the picture proportionately until the horizontal dimension or the vertical dimension reaches the edge of the control but doesn't stretch the picture so that the other dimension is maximized as well. This is good for maximizing the size of a picture while retaining its proportions, but you'll need to resize the non-maximized dimension to remove blank space. This property applies to the Page object and the Image control as well.

TABLE 14.5: Properties of the Frame Control *(CONTINUED)*

PROPERTY	DESCRIPTION
PictureAlignment	Determines where a picture is located. fmPictureAlignmentTopLeft (0) aligns the picture with the upper-left corner of the control. fmPictureAlignmentTopRight (1) aligns the picture with the upper-right corner of the control. fmPictureAlignmentCenter (2), the default setting, centers the picture in the control (both horizontally and vertically). fmPictureAlignmentBottomLeft (3) aligns the picture with the lower-left corner of the control. fmPictureAlignmentBottomRight (4) aligns the picture with the lower-right corner of the control. This property applies to the Page object and the Image control as well.

COMMANDBUTTON

The CommandButton control has three unique properties, listed in Table 14.6.

TABLE 14.6: Unique Properties of the CommandButton Control

PROPERTY	DESCRIPTION
Cancel	A Boolean property that determines whether the command button is the Cancel button for the user form (True) or not (False). The Cancel button for a user form can bear any name; what distinguishes it is that its Cancel property is set to True. The Cancel button is activated by the user's pressing Esc, or clicking the button, or putting the focus on the button and pressing Enter. Only one command button on a form can be the Cancel button at any given time. Setting the Cancel property for a command button to True causes VBA to set the Cancel property to False for any button for which it was previously set to True.
Default	A Boolean property that determines whether the command button is the default button for the user form (True) or not (False). Only one command button on a form can be the default button at any given time. Setting the Default property for a command button to True causes VBA to set the Default property to False for any button for which it was previously set to True. The default button is activated by the user's pressing Enter when the focus isn't on any other command button.
TakeFocusOnClick	A Boolean property that determines whether the command button takes the focus when the user clicks it (True) or not (False). The default setting for this property is True, but you may want to set it to False when you need the focus to remain on another control in the user form even when the user clicks the command button. However, if the user uses the Tab key or the arrow keys to move to the command button, the command button will take the focus even if the TakeFocusOnClick property is set to False.

TIP Set the Accelerator property for each command button on a form other than the default command button, so that the user can quickly access it from the keyboard.

NOTE The default button on a form can also be the Cancel button. This offers an obvious benefit for forms that offer irreversible actions, such as deleting text or deleting a file, but it can confuse accessibility aids (such as screen readers) and make it difficult for users with cognitive difficulties to work with the form. For these reasons, it's usually best to make the default button on a form a different button than the Cancel button.

TABSTRIP AND MULTIPAGE

The TabStrip control has several unique properties and a number of properties that it shares with the MultiPage control. Table 14.7 lists these properties.

TABLE 14.7: Properties of the TabStrip and MultiPage Controls

PROPERTY	DESCRIPTION
ClientHeight	(Tab strip only.) A Single property that sets or returns the height of the display area of the tab strip, measured in points.
ClientLeft	(Tab strip only.) A Single property that returns the distance, measured in points, between the left border of the tab strip and the left border of the control inside it.
ClientTop	(Tab strip only.) A Single property that returns the distance, measured in points, between the top border of the tab strip and the top border of the control inside it.
ClientWidth	(Tab strip only.) A Single property that sets or returns the width of the display area of the tab strip, measured in points.
SelectedItem	Sets or returns the tab currently selected in a tab strip or the page currently selected in a MultiPage control.
TabFixedHeight	A Single property that sets or returns the fixed height of the tabs, measured in points. Set TabFixedHeight to 0 to have the tabs automatically size themselves to fit their contents.
TabFixedWidth	A Single property that sets or returns the fixed width of the tabs, measured in points. Set TabFixedWidth to 0 to have the tabs automatically size themselves to fit their contents.
TabOrientation	Determines the location of the tabs in the tab strip or multipage. fmTabOrientationTop (0), the default, displays the tabs at the top of the tab strip or multipage. fmTabOrientationBottom (1) displays the tabs at the bottom of the tab strip or multipage. fmTabOrientationLeft (2) displays the tabs at the left of the tab strip or multipage, and fmTabOrientationRight displays the tabs at the right of the tab strip or multipage.

SCROLLBAR AND SPINBUTTON

The ScrollBar and SpinButton share a number of properties that you haven't yet met. Table 14.8 lists these properties.

TABLE 14.8: Properties of the ScrollBar and SpinButton Controls

PROPERTY	DESCRIPTION
Delay	A Long property that sets the delay in milliseconds between clicks registered on the control when the user clicks and holds down the mouse button. The default delay is 50 milliseconds. The control registers the first click immediately, the second click after Delay × 5 (the extra delay is to assist the user in clicking only once), and the third and subsequent clicks after Delay.
LargeChange	(Scroll bar only.) A Long property that determines how much the item is scrolled when the user clicks in the scroll bar between the thumb (the scroll box) and the scroll bar's arrow. Set the LargeChange property after setting the Max and Min properties of the scroll bar.
SmallChange	A Long property that determines how much movement occurs when the user clicks a scroll arrow in a scroll bar or spin button. SmallChange needs to be an integer value; the default value is 1.
Max	A Long property that specifies the maximum value for the Value property of the scroll bar or spin button. Max must be an integer. The default value is 1.
Min	A Long property that specifies the minimum value for the Value property of the scroll bar or spin button. Min must be an integer. The default value is 1.
ProportionalThumb	(Scroll bar only.) A Boolean property that determines whether the thumb (the scroll box) is a fixed size (False) or is proportional to the size of the scrolling region (True), giving the user an approximate idea of how much of the scrolling region is currently visible. The default setting is True.

IMAGE

By now, you've met all the properties of the Image control. For most of the Image controls you use in your user forms, you'll want to set the positional properties, the size properties, and the following properties:

◆ Use the Picture property to assign the picture file you want to appear in the Image control. Click in the Picture row in the Properties window, and then click the ellipsis button (…) that the text box displays. In the Load Picture dialog box, select the picture and click the OK button to add it. The Image control can display .BMP, .CUR (cursor), .GIF, .ICO (icon), .JPG, and .WMF files, but not graphics files such as .TIF or .PCX.

TIP The easiest way to display part of a Windows screen in an Image control is to capture it by using the PrintScreen key (to capture the full screen) or the Alt+PrintScreen key combination (to capture the active window). Then paste it into an application such as Paint, trim it there as necessary, and save it as a .BMP file.

- ◆ Use the `PictureAlignment` property to set the alignment of the picture.

- ◆ Use the `PictureSizeMode` property to set whether the picture is clipped, stretched, or zoomed to fill the Image control. Adjust the height and width of the Image control as necessary.

- ◆ Use the `PictureTiling` property if you need to tile the image to take up the full space in the control.

PAGE

The `Page` object is one of the pages contained within a `MultiPage` object. You've already met all its properties in the context of other controls except for the `Index` property, which it shares with the `Tab` object.

The `Index` property is an Integer property that determines the position of the `Page` object in the Pages collection in a MultiPage control or the position of a `Tab` object in the Tabs collection in a Tab-Strip. The first `Page` object or `Tab` object is numbered 0 (zero); the second `Page` or `Tab` object is numbered 1; and so on. You can change the `Index` property of a tab or page to change the position in which the tab or page appears in the collection.

TAB

The `Tab` object is one of the tabs contained within a `TabStrip` object. You've already met all its properties in the context of other controls.

Working with Groups of Controls

By grouping two or more controls, you can work with them as a single unit to size them, format them, or delete them.

GROUPING CONTROLS

To group controls, select them by Shift+clicking, Ctrl+clicking, or dragging around them, and then right-click and choose Group from the context menu. Alternatively, select the controls, and then click the Group button on the UserForm toolbar (you'll need to display this toolbar—it's not displayed by default) or choose Format ➢ Group. VBA creates a new group containing the controls and places a shaded border with handles around the whole group, as shown on the right in Figure 14.13.

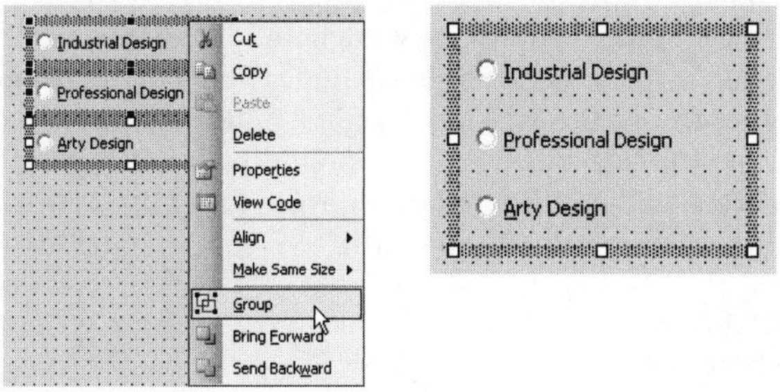

FIGURE 14.13
You can work with multiple controls simultaneously by grouping them. VBA indicates a group of controls by placing a border around it.

UNGROUPING CONTROLS

To ungroup controls, right-click any of the controls contained in the group and then choose Ungroup from the context menu. Alternatively, select the group of controls by clicking in any control in the group and then click the Ungroup button on the UserForm toolbar, or choose Format ➢ Ungroup. VBA removes the shaded border with handles from around the group and displays a border and handles around each individual control that was formerly in the group.

SIZING GROUPED CONTROLS

You can quickly size all controls in a group by selecting the group and then dragging the sizing handles on the surrounding border. For example, you could select the middle handle on the right side and drag it inward to shorten the controls, as shown in Figure 14.14. The controls will be resized proportionately to the change in the group outline.

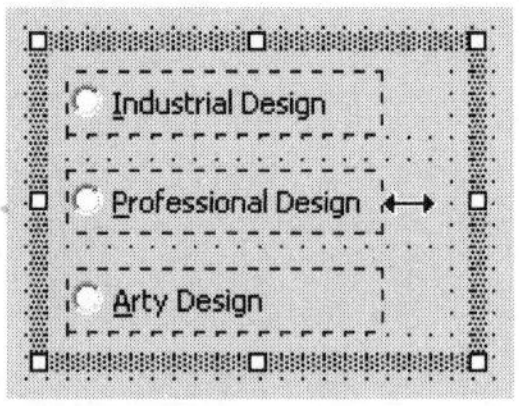

FIGURE 14.14
You can resize all the controls in a group by dragging a sizing handle on the surrounding border.

Generally speaking, this action works best when you group a number of controls of the same type, as in the illustration. For example, sizing a group that consists of several text boxes or several option buttons works well, whereas sizing a group that consists of a text box, a command button, and a combo box is seldom a good idea.

DELETING GROUPED CONTROLS

You can quickly delete a whole group of controls by right-clicking any of them and choosing Delete from the context menu or by selecting the group and pressing the Delete key.

WORKING WITH ONE CONTROL IN A GROUP

Even after you've grouped a number of controls, you can still work with them individually if necessary. To do so, first click any control in the group to select the group, as shown on the left in Figure 14.15. Then click the control you want to work with. As shown on the right in Figure 14.15, VBA displays a darker shaded border around the group (indicating that the group still exists) and displays the lighter shaded border around the individual control, indicating that that control is selected.

You can then work with the individual control as if it were not grouped. When you've finished working with it, click another control in the group to work with it, or click elsewhere in the user form to deselect the individual control.

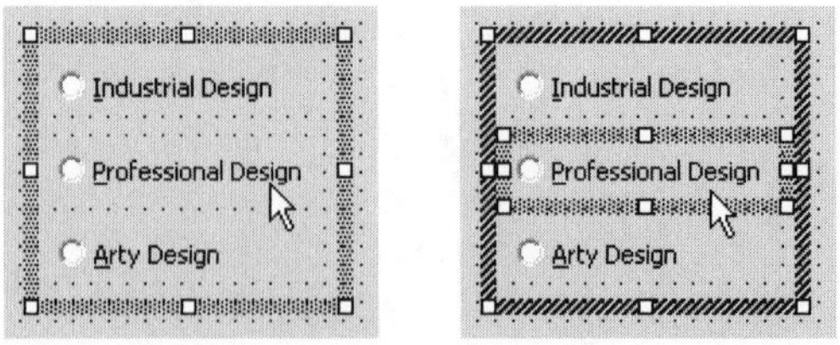

FIGURE 14.15
To work with one control in a group, start by selecting the group (as shown on the left) and then select the control (as shown on the right).

Aligning Controls

Even if you use the Snap To Grid feature, you'll often need to align controls manually. The easiest way to align selected controls is to right-click in any one of them and choose an option from the Align submenu: Lefts, Centers, Rights, Tops, Middles, Bottoms, or To Grid. These options work as follows:

Lefts	Aligns the left borders of the controls
Centers	Aligns the horizontal midpoints of the controls
Rights	Aligns the right borders of the controls
Tops	Aligns the tops of the controls
Middles	Aligns the vertical midpoints of the controls
Bottoms	Aligns the bottoms of the controls
To Grid	Aligns the controls to the grid

VBA aligns the borders or midpoints to the current position of that border or midpoint on the dominant control—the control that has white sizing handles around it rather than black sizing handles. After selecting the controls you want to align manually, make dominant the one that is already in the correct position by clicking it so that it takes on the white sizing handles. Then choose the alignment option you want.

WARNING   Make sure the alignment option you choose makes sense for the controls you've selected. VBA will happily align controls in an inappropriate way if you tell it to. For example, if you select a number of option buttons or text boxes and choose Tops from the Align submenu, VBA will obligingly stack all the controls on top of each other, rendering them all but unusable. (Use Undo to recover from such minor mishaps.)

Placing Controls

VBA offers several placement commands on the Format menu:

◆ On the Format ➢ Make Same Size submenu, use the Width, Height, and Both commands to make two or more controls the same size in one or both dimensions.

◆ Use the Format ➢ Size To Fit command to have VBA decide on a suitable size for an element, based on the size of its label. This works well for, say, a toggle button with a medium-length label, but VBA will shrink an OK button to an unusably small size.

◆ Use the Format ➢ Size To Grid command to increase or decrease the size of a control to the nearest gridpoints.

◆ On the Format ➢ Horizontal Spacing and Format ➢ Vertical Spacing submenus, use the Make Equal, Increase, Decrease, and Remove commands to set the horizontal spacing and vertical spacing of two or more controls. The Remove option removes extra space from between controls, which works well for, say, a vertical series of option buttons (which look good close together) but isn't a good idea for command buttons (which need a little space between them).

◆ On the Format ➢ Center In Form submenu, use the Horizontally and Vertically commands to center a control or a group of controls in the form. Centering controls vertically is seldom a good idea, but you'll often want to center a frame or a group of command buttons horizontally.

◆ On the Format ➢ Arrange Buttons submenu, use the Bottom and Right commands to rearrange command buttons in a dialog box quickly.

Adjusting the Tab Order of the Dialog Box

The *tab order* of a dialog box or a frame within a dialog box is the order in which VBA selects controls in the dialog box or frame when you move through them by pressing the Tab key (to move forward) or the Shift+Tab key combination (to move backward). Each frame in a user form has a separate tab order for the controls it contains: The frame appears in the tab order for the dialog box, and the controls within the frame appear in the tab order for the frame.

Set the tab order for a dialog box or a frame to make it as easy as possible to use. Generally, it's best to arrange the tab order from left to right and from top to bottom of the dialog box or frame for English-speaking users. For international users, you may want to arrange the tab order from right to left. You may also need to arrange the tab order to move from one control to a related control that would not normally be next in the tab order.

VBA assigns the tab order to the controls in a dialog box or frame on a first-come, first-served basis as you add them. Unless you add all the controls in perfect order, this order will seldom produce the optimal tab order for a dialog box, so usually you'll want to adjust the tab order—or at least check that it's right. For a frame, you're likely to place fewer controls, so you have a better chance of adding them in a suitable order; but you should check this too before unleashing the dialog box on users.

To change the tab order in a dialog box or frame:

1. Right-click in the open space in the user form or frame and choose Tab Order from the context menu to display the Tab Order dialog box, as shown in Figure 14.16. (Alternatively, select the user form or frame and choose View ➢ Tab Order.)

FIGURE 14.16
Use the Tab Order dialog box to arrange the controls in your user form or frame into a logical order for the user.

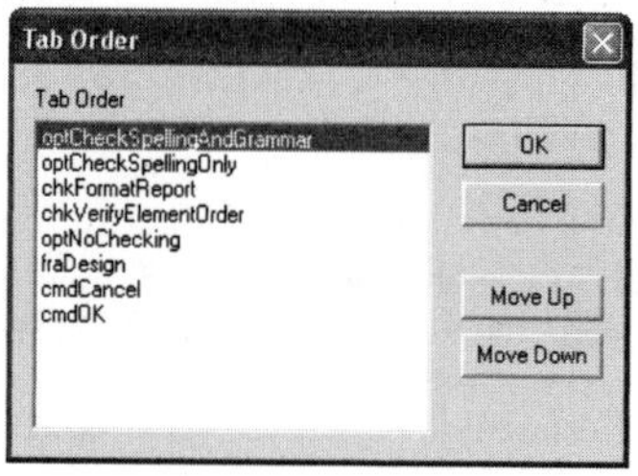

2. Rearrange the controls into the order in which you want them to appear by selecting them in the Tab Order list box and clicking the Move Up button or Move Down button as appropriate. You can Shift+click or drag to select a range of controls or Ctrl+click to select two or more noncontiguous controls.

3. Click the OK button to close the Tab Order dialog box.

Linking a Dialog Box to a Procedure

Designing a custom dialog box is only the first step in getting it to work in a procedure. The other step is writing the code to display the dialog box and make it perform its functions.

Typically, the code for a dialog box consists of the following:

◆ A procedure that displays the dialog box by loading it and using the Show method. Usually, this procedure is assigned to a menu item, a toolbar button, or a key combination so that the user can invoke it. However, a procedure can also run automatically in response to a system event (such as running at a specified time).

◆ The user form that contains the dialog box and its controls.

◆ The code attached to the user form. This code consists of procedures for designated controls. For example, for a simple dialog box containing two option buttons and two command buttons (an OK button and a Cancel button), you'd typically create one procedure for the OK button and one for the Cancel button. The procedure for the OK button, triggered by a Click event on the OK button (either a click on the OK button or a press of the Enter key with the focus on the OK button), would ascertain which option button was selected and then take action accordingly. The procedure for the Cancel button would cancel the procedure.

NOTE You could also assign a procedure to the Click event for an option button—or to another event; more on this in the next chapter—but usually it makes more sense to trap the command buttons in a static dialog box. In a dynamic dialog box, you may often want to trap the click on an option button and display further controls as appropriate.

Once the code attached to a button has run, execution returns to the dialog box (if it's still displayed) or to the procedure that called the dialog box.

NOTE Code that runs directly in response to an event is called an *event procedure*. An event procedure can call other procedures as necessary, so multiple procedures can be run indirectly by a single event.

Loading and Unloading a Dialog Box

You load a dialog box by using the Load statement and unload it by using the Unload statement. The Load statement loads the dialog box into memory so that it's available to the program, but doesn't display the dialog box; for that you use the Show method (discussed in the next section). The Unload statement unloads the dialog box from memory and reclaims any memory associated with that object. If the dialog box is displayed when the Unload statement runs, VBA removes the dialog box from the screen.

The syntax for the Load and Unload statements is straightforward:

```
Load Dialog_Box
Unload Dialog_Box
```

Here, Dialog_Box is the name of the user form or dialog box. For example, the following statement loads the dialog box named frmMyDialog:

```
Load frmMyDialog
```

Displaying and Hiding a Dialog Box

To display a dialog box, you use the Show method; to hide a dialog box, you use the Hide method. For example, the following statement displays the dialog box named frmMyDialog:

```
frmMyDialog.Show
```

Run a procedure containing this line, and the frmMyDialog dialog box appears on screen, where you can enter text in its text boxes, select or clear its check boxes, use its drop-down lists, and click its buttons as you wish. When you close the dialog box (by clicking the Close button on its title bar or by clicking a command button that dismisses the dialog box), the dialog box disappears from the screen and the procedure continues to run. But until you retrieve settings from the dialog box and take action on them, the dialog box has no effect beyond its graphical display.

You can display a dialog box by using the Show method without explicitly loading the dialog box with a Load command first; VBA takes care of the implied Load command for you. There's no particular advantage to including the Load command, but it makes your code easier to read and to debug. For example, the two procedures shown here have the same effect:

```
Sub Display_Dialog()
    Load frmMyDialog      'loads the dialog box into memory
    frmMyDialog.Show      'displays the dialog box
End Sub

Sub Display_Dialog()
    frmMyDialog.Show      'loads the dialog box into memory and displays it
End Sub
```

NOTE If you run a Hide method without having loaded the dialog box into memory by using the Load statement or the Show method, VBA loads the dialog box but does not display it on screen.

Once you've displayed the dialog box, take a moment to check its tab order by moving through it using the Tab key. When you open the dialog box, is the focus on the appropriate control? When you move forward from that control, is the next control that is selected the next control that the user will typically need to use? Adjust the tab order as necessary, as described in "Adjusting the Tab Order of the Dialog Box," earlier in this chapter.

Setting a Default Command Button

To set a default command button in a dialog box, set that command button's Default property to True. VBA selects the default button when it displays the dialog box, so that if the user simply presses the Enter key to dismiss the dialog box, this button receives the keystroke.

Only one button can be the default button at any given time. If you set the Default property of any button to True, VBA automatically changes to False the Default property of any other button previously set to True.

Retrieving the User's Choices from a Dialog Box

To make a dialog box take an action, you retrieve the user's choices from it. This section first shows you the VBA commands for retrieving information from a dialog box. It then goes through an example of retrieving the user's choices from a relatively simple dialog box and then from a more complex one.

Returning a String from a Text Box

To *return* (retrieve) a string from a text box, check its `Value` property or `Text` property after the user has dismissed the dialog box. For example, if you have a text box named `txtMyText`, you could return its value and display it in a message box by using the following line:

```
MsgBox txtMyText.Value
```

NOTE   For a text box, the `Value` property and the `Text` property return the same information; for most other VBA objects, the `Value` property and the `Text` property return different information.

VBA supports both one-line and multi-line text boxes. To create a multi-line text box, select the text box in the user form or in the drop-down list in the Properties window and set its `MultiLine` property to `True`. The user can then enter multiple lines in the text box and start new lines by pressing Shift+Enter.

To add a horizontal or vertical scroll bar to a text box, set its `ScrollBars` property to `1 - fmScrollBarsHorizontal` (for a horizontal scroll bar), `2 - fmScrollBarsVertical` (for a vertical scroll bar, which is usually more useful), or `3 - fmScrollBarsBoth` (for both).

Returning a Value from an Option Button

A regular option button is a Boolean control, so it can have only two values: `True` and `False`. `True` indicates that the button is selected, `False` that it's unselected. You can check an option button's value with a simple `If... Then` condition. For example, if you have two option buttons named `optSearchForFile` and `optUseThisFile`, you can check their values and find out which was selected by using the following condition:

```
If optSearchForFile = True Then
  'optSearchForFile was selected; take action on this
Else    'optSearchForFile was not selected, so optUseThisFile was
  'take action for optUseThisFile
End If
```

NOTE   `Value` is the default property of the OptionButton control. The previous code actually checks the value of the default property of the control. The first line of code could be written out more fully as `If optSearchForFile.Value = True Then`. It could also be written more succinctly, with `= True` implied: `If optSearchForFile Then`.

With more than two option buttons, use an `If... Then... ElseIf` condition or a `Select Case` statement to determine which option button is selected.

NOTE   As you saw earlier in this chapter, an option button or a check box can also have a null value if its `TripleState` property is set to `True`. If you allow your option buttons or check boxes to have a null state, you'll need to check for that as well in your procedures. You can't directly check for the control's value being `Null` (for example, `If opt1.Value = Null` causes an error), so use an `If` statement or `Select Case` statement to test `True` and `False` first. If the `Value` of the control is neither `True` nor `False`, it must be `Null`.

Returning a Value from a Check Box

Like an option button, a regular check box can only be either True or False, so you can use an If...
Then condition to check its value. For example:

```
If chkDisplayProgress = True Then
    'take actions for chkDisplayProgress
End If
```

Again, you're checking the default property of the control here—the Value property. The first line
of code could also be written as If chkDisplayProgress.Value = True Then.

NOTE Sometimes you'll need to take an action if the check box was cleared rather than selected. For
example, if the user clears the check box, you may need to turn off a configuration option.

Returning a Value from a List Box

Before you can return a value from a list box, you must tell VBA which choices to display in the list
box. To do so, you create a procedure to *initialize* (prepare) the user form and add the items to the
list box before displaying it:

1. Right-click the name of the user form in the Project Explorer and choose View Code from
   the context menu to display (in the Code window) the code for the controls assigned to the
   dialog box.

2. In the Object drop-down list, make sure that UserForm is selected.

3. Choose Initialize from the Procedure drop-down list. The Visual Basic Editor creates a new
   procedure named Private Sub UserForm_Initialize for you at the end of the procedures
   currently contained on the code sheet:

```
Private Sub UserForm_Initialize()

End Sub
```

NOTE VBA runs a UserForm_Initialize procedure every time the user form is invoked. This
procedure is a good way to add items to a list box or combo box or to set properties for other controls
on the user form.

4. To add items to the list box, use the AddItem method for the list box object (here, lstBatteries)
   with a text string in double quotation marks to specify each item in the list box:

```
lstBatteries.AddItem "Battery #A4601"
lstBatteries.AddItem "Battery #A4602"
lstBatteries.AddItem "Battery #A4603"
lstBatteries.AddItem "Battery #A4604"
```

TIP By adding items when you initialize the form, you can add different numbers of items as appropriate. For example, if you wanted the user to pick a document from a particular folder, you could
create a list of the documents in that folder on-the-fly and then use them to fill the list box.

To retrieve the result from a single-select list box, return the Value property. For example:

```
MsgBox "You chose this entry from the list box: " & lstBattery.Value
```

When you use the MultiSelect property to create a list box capable of multiple selections, you can no longer use the Value property to return the items selected in the list box: When MultiSelect is True, Value always returns a null value. Instead, you use the Selected property to determine which rows in the list box were selected and the List array to return the contents of each selected row. The following statements use a For... Next loop to build a string named strMsg containing the entries selected from a multi-select list box:

```
strMsg = "You chose the following entries from the list box: " & vbCr
For i = 1 To lstBatteries.ListCount
  If lstBatteries.Selected(i - 1) = True Then
    strMsg = strMsg & lstBatteries.List(i - 1) & vbCr
  End If
Next i
MsgBox strMsg
```

Returning a Value from a Combo Box

To return a value from a combo box (a combination list box and text box), you add items to the combo box list in an Initialize procedure and then check the Value of the combo box after the user has dismissed the dialog box. (The combo box control doesn't offer multiple-selection capabilities, so Value is the property to check.)

For example, to add items to a combo box named cmbColor:

```
Private Sub UserForm_Initialize()
  cmbColor.AddItem "Red"
  cmbColor.AddItem "Blue"
  cmbColor.AddItem "Yellow"
End Sub
```

To return the item the user chose in the combo box, retrieve the Value property:

```
Result = cmbColor.Value
```

The item retrieved from the combo box can be either one of the items assigned in the Initialize procedure or one that the user has typed into the text-box portion of the combo box.

Examples of Connecting Dialog Boxes to Procedures

This section shows you two examples of how you can create a procedure and then build a dialog box into it to make it more useful and powerful. In the first example, you'll record a macro in Word (if you have Word) and link a dialog box to it. In the second example, which will work with any VBA-enabled application, you'll create a user form and its code from scratch.

Word Example: The Move-Paragraph Procedure

The first procedure, in Word, moves the current paragraph up or down within the document by one or two paragraphs.

RECORDING THE PROCEDURE

Start by recording a procedure in Word to move the current paragraph. In the procedure, you need to record the commands for

- Selecting the current paragraph

- Cutting the selection and then pasting it

- Moving the insertion point up and down the document

- Inserting a bookmark, moving the insertion point to it, and then deleting the bookmark

The finished procedure displays a dialog box with option buttons for moving the current paragraph up one paragraph, up two paragraphs, down one paragraph, or down two paragraphs. The dialog box also includes a check box for returning the insertion point to its original position at the end of the procedure. Because this is presumably desirable behavior for the procedure, this check box is selected by default; the user can clear the check box if they don't want to return the insertion point to its original position.

First, start Word and create a scratch document, and enter three or four paragraphs of text—just about anything will do, but it'll be easier to have recognizable text so that you can make sure the procedure is moving paragraphs as it should. Then place the insertion point in one of the paragraphs you've just entered and start recording a macro as discussed in Chapter 1:

1. Double-click the REC indicator on the status bar, or choose Tools ➢ Macro ➢ Record New Macro, to display the Record Macro dialog box.

2. Type the name for the macro in the Macro Name text box, **Move_Paragraph**, and a description in the Description text box.

3. Choose a template or document if necessary in the Store Macro In drop-down list.

4. If you want, use the Toolbars button or Keyboard button to create a toolbar button, menu option, or keyboard shortcut for the macro.

5. Click the OK button to start recording the macro.

Record the following actions in the macro:

1. Insert a bookmark at the current position of the insertion point by using the Insert ➢ Bookmark command to display the Bookmarks dialog box, entering a name for the bookmark, and clicking the Add button. In this example, the bookmark is named Move_Paragraph_Temp to indicate that it's a temporary bookmark used for the Move_Paragraph procedure.

2. Select the current paragraph by pressing F8 four times. The first press of F8 activates Extend mode (toggling on the EXT indicator on the status bar), the second selects the current word, the third selects the current sentence, and the fourth selects the current paragraph. Press the Escape key to turn off Extend mode once the paragraph is selected. (The EXT indicator on the status bar toggles off again.)

3. Cut the selected paragraph by using some form of the Cut command (for example, click the Cut button or press either Ctrl+X or Shift+Delete).

4. Move the insertion point up one paragraph by pressing Ctrl+↑.

5. Paste the cut paragraph back in by using a Paste command (for example, click the Paste button or press Shift+Insert).

6. Move the insertion point down one paragraph by pressing Ctrl+↓.

7. Move the insertion point up two paragraphs by pressing Ctrl+↑ twice.

NOTE   If you started with the insertion point at the beginning of the first paragraph in the document, you'll only be able to move the insertion point up one paragraph. This doesn't matter—press the keystroke anyway to record it. If Word beeps at you, ignore it.

8. Move the insertion point down two paragraphs by pressing Ctrl+↓ twice. (If in doing so you hit the end of the document after the first keystroke, don't worry—perform the second keystroke anyway to record it. Again, Word may beep.)

9. Open the Bookmarks dialog box (choose Insert ➢ Bookmark), select the Move_Paragraph_Temp bookmark, and click the Go To button to go to it. Then click the Delete button to delete the Move_Paragraph_Temp bookmark. Click the Close button to close the Bookmarks dialog box.

10. Stop the Macro Recorder by clicking the Stop Recording button on the Stop Recording toolbar or by double-clicking the REC indicator on the status bar.

Open the recorded macro in the Visual Basic Editor by choosing Tools ➢ Macro ➢ Macros, selecting the macro's name in the Macros dialog box, and clicking the Edit button.

You should see a macro that looks something like this:

```
1.   Sub Move_Paragraph()
2.   '
3.   ' Move_Paragraph Macro
4.   ' Macro recorded 5/1/2006 by Jack Ishida
5.   '
6.       With ActiveDocument.Bookmarks
7.           .Add Range:=Selection.Range, Name:="Move_Paragraph_Temp"
8.           .DefaultSorting = wdSortByName
9.           .ShowHidden = False
10.      End With
11.      Selection.Extend
12.      Selection.Extend
13.      Selection.Extend
14.      Selection.Extend
15.      Selection.EscapeKey
16.      Selection.Cut
17.      Selection.MoveUp Unit:=wdParagraph, Count:=1
18.      Selection.PasteAndFormat (wdPasteDefault)
19.      Selection.MoveDown Unit:=wdParagraph, Count:=1
20.      Selection.MoveUp Unit:=wdParagraph, Count:=2
21.      Selection.MoveDown Unit:=wdParagraph, Count:=2
22.      Selection.GoTo What:=wdGoToBookmark, Name:="Move_Paragraph_Temp"
23.      ActiveDocument.Bookmarks("Move_Paragraph_Temp").Delete
24.      With ActiveDocument.Bookmarks
```

```
25.           .DefaultSorting = wdSortByName
26.           .ShowHidden = False
27.      End With
28.  End Sub
```

You can probably read the macro easily enough by now:

♦ Line 1 starts the macro, and line 28 ends it. Lines 2 and 5 are blank comment lines around the comment lines showing the macro's name (line 3) and description (line 4).

♦ Lines 6 through 10 contain a With statement that adds the Move_Paragraph_Temp bookmark. Lines 7 and 8 are unnecessary here, but the Macro Recorder records all the settings in the Bookmark dialog box, including the setting for the Sort By option button and the Hidden Bookmarks check box.

♦ Lines 11 through 15 use the Extend Selection feature to select the current paragraph.

♦ Lines 17, 19, 20, and 21 record the syntax for moving the insertion point up and down, one paragraph and two paragraphs, respectively.

♦ Line 16 records the Cut command, and Line 18 the Paste command.

♦ Line 22 moves the insertion point to the Move_Paragraph_Temp bookmark, and line 23 deletes the bookmark. Lines 24 through 27 again record the settings in the Bookmark dialog box, which you don't need here either.

You can quickly delete the unnecessary lines, and collapse the first With structure, to give a more succinct version of the code:

```
1.  Sub Move_Paragraph()
2.      ActiveDocument.Bookmarks.Add Range:=Selection.Range, _
            Name:="Move_Paragraph_Temp"
3.      Selection.Extend
4.      Selection.Extend
5.      Selection.Extend
6.      Selection.Extend
7.      Selection.EscapeKey
8.      Selection.Cut
9.      Selection.MoveUp Unit:=wdParagraph, Count:=1
10.     Selection.PasteAndFormat (wdPasteDefault)
11.     Selection.MoveDown Unit:=wdParagraph, Count:=1
12.     Selection.MoveUp Unit:=wdParagraph, Count:=2
13.     Selection.MoveDown Unit:=wdParagraph, Count:=2
14.     Selection.GoTo What:=wdGoToBookmark, Name:="Move_Paragraph_Temp"
15. End Sub
```

CREATING THE DIALOG BOX

Next, create the dialog box for the procedure (see Figure 14.17).

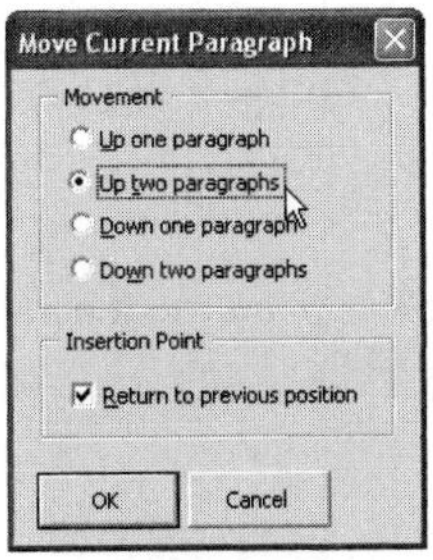

FIGURE 14.17
The Move Current Paragraph dialog box that you will connect to the Move_Paragraph macro

1. Start a user form by clicking the Insert button's drop-down list and choosing UserForm (or just click the Insert button if it's already showing the UserForm icon) or by choosing Insert ➤ UserForm.

2. Use the Properties window for the user form to set its `Name` and `Caption` properties. Click in the cell next to the `Name` cell and enter the `Name` property there, and then click in the cell next to the `Caption` cell and enter the `Caption` property. The example user form is named `frmMoveCurrentParagraph` and has the caption `Move Current Paragraph`, so that the name of the form is closely related to the text the user will see in the title bar of the dialog box but different from the procedure name (`Move_Current_Paragraph`).

3. Place two frames in the user form, as shown in Figure 14.18, to act as group boxes in the dialog box:

   A. Double-click the Frame tool in the Toolbox, and then click and drag in the user form to place each frame. Click the Select Objects button to restore the selection pointer.

   B. Align the frames by selecting them both and choosing Format ➤ Align ➤ Lefts.

   C. With the frames still selected, verify that the frames are the same width by choosing Format ➤ Make Same Size ➤ Width. (Don't choose Format ➤ Make Same Size ➤ Height or Format ➤ Make Same Size ➤ Both here—the top frame will need to be taller than the bottom frame.)

   D. Caption the top frame **Movement** and the bottom frame **Insertion Point** by selecting each in turn and then setting the Caption property in the Properties window. Then name the top frame **fraMovement** and the bottom frame **fraInsertionPoint**.

FIGURE 14.18
Start by placing two frames in the user form.

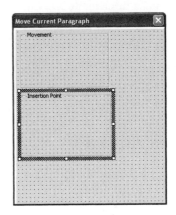

4. Place four option buttons in the Movement frame, as shown in Figure 14.19:

A. Double-click the OptionButton tool in the Toolbox, and then click in the Movement frame to place each option button. This time, don't click and drag—just click to place a normal-width option button.

B. When you've placed the four option buttons, click the Select Objects button in the Toolbox to restore the selection pointer. Then select the four option buttons and align them with each other by choosing Format ➢ Align ➢ Lefts. Even out any disparities in spacing by choosing Format ➢ Vertical Spacing ➢ Make Equal. If necessary, use the other items on the Format ➢ Vertical Spacing submenu—Increase, Decrease, and Remove—to adjust the amount of space between the option buttons.

C. Change the caption for each option button by setting the Caption property in the Properties window. Caption them as illustrated in Figure 14.19: **Up one paragraph**, **Up two paragraphs**, **Down one paragraph**, and **Down two paragraphs**. These option buttons will control the number of paragraphs the procedure moves the current paragraph.

D. If you need to resize the option buttons, select them and group them by right-clicking and choosing Group from the context menu, by choosing Format ➢ Group, or by clicking the Group button on the UserForm toolbar. Then select the group and drag one of the handles to resize all the option buttons evenly. For example, if you need to lengthen all the option buttons to accommodate the text you entered, drag the handle at the right midpoint of the group outward.

E. Name the option buttons **optUpOne**, **optUpTwo**, **optDownOne**, and **optDownTwo**, respectively, by changing the Name property of each in turn in the Properties window.

TIP By default, all the option buttons on a user form are part of the same option group. This means that only one of the option buttons can be selected at a time. If you want to provide multiple groups of option buttons on a user form, you need to specify the separate groups. The easiest way to do this is to position each group within a separate frame control. Alternatively, you can set the GroupName property for each option button.

F. Next, set the first option button's Value property to True by selecting the default False value in the Properties window and entering **True** instead. Doing so will select the option button in the user form you're designing, and when the dialog box is displayed, that option button will be selected as the default choice for the option group. Set its accelerator key to *U* by entering **U** as its Accelerator property. Set the Accelerator property of the second option button to **t**, the third to **D**, and the fourth to **w**.

NOTE The Accelerator property is case sensitive only when the caption for the control contains both the uppercase and lowercase versions of the same letter.

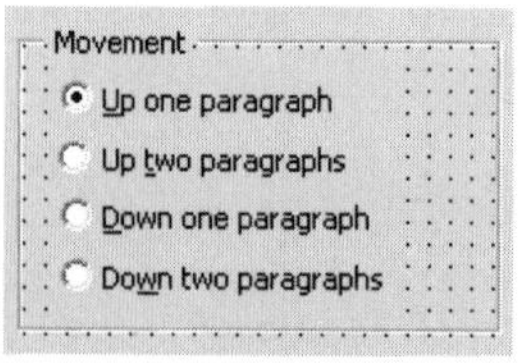

FIGURE 14.19
Place four option buttons in the Movement frame like this.

5. Place a check box in the Insertion Point frame, as shown in Figure 14.20:

   A. Click the CheckBox tool in the Toolbox and then click in the Insertion Point frame in the user form to place a check box of the default size.

   B. In the Properties window, set the name of the check box to **chkReturnToPreviousPosition** (a long name but a descriptive one). Then set its Caption property to **Return to previous position**. Set its accelerator key to *R* by entering **R** as its Accelerator property. Finally, set the check box to be selected by default by entering **True** as its Value property.

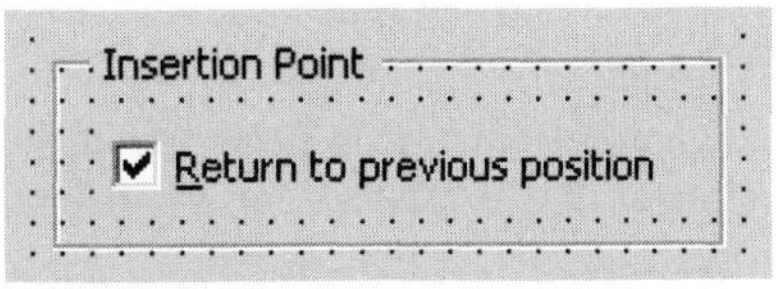

FIGURE 14.20

Place a check box in the Insertion Point frame.

6. Next, insert the command buttons for the form (see Figure 14.21):

   A. Double-click the CommandButton tool on the Toolbox and click to place the first command button at the bottom of the user form. Click to place the second command button, and then click the Select Objects button to restore the selection mouse pointer.

   B. Size and place the command buttons by using the commands on the Format menu. For example, group the buttons, and then use the Format ➢ Center In Form ➢ Horizontally command to center the pair horizontally. You must group the buttons before doing this—if you simply select both of them, VBA centers one button on top of the other so that only the uppermost button is visible.

   C. Set properties for the command buttons as follows: For the left-hand button (which will become the OK button), set the Name property to **cmdOK**, the Caption property to **OK**, the Accelerator property to **O** (that's *O* as in *OK*, not a zero), and the Default property to **True**. For the right-hand button (which will become the Cancel button), set the Name property to **cmdCancel**, the Accelerator property to **A**, the Caption property to **Cancel**, and the Cancel property to **True**. Leave the Default property set to **False**.

FIGURE 14.21

Add two command buttons and set their properties.

7. Double-click the Cancel button to display the code associated with it:

```
Private Sub cmdCancel_Click()

End Sub
```

Type an End statement between the lines:

```
Private Sub cmdCancel_Click()
    End
End Sub
```

This End statement removes the dialog box from the screen and ends the current procedure—in this case, the `Move_Current_Paragraph` procedure.

Now you'll set the OK button, which is where things get interesting. When the user clicks the OK button, the procedure needs to continue and do all of the following:

◆ Remove the dialog box from display by hiding it or by unloading it (or, preferably, both). As discussed earlier in the chapter, the choice is yours, but using both commands is usually clearest.

◆ Check the `Value` property of the checkbox to see whether it was selected or cleared.

◆ Check the `Value` property of each option button in turn to see which of them was selected when the OK button was clicked.

8. Double-click the OK button to display the code attached to it. (If you're still working in the code attached to the Cancel button, scroll up or down from the `Private Sub cmdCancel_Click()` code to find the `Private Sub cmdOK_Click()` code.)

```
Private Sub cmdOK_Click()

End Sub
```

First, enter the following two lines between the `Private Sub` and `End Sub` lines:

```
frmMoveParagraph.Hide
Unload frmMoveParagraph
```

The `frmMoveParagraph.Hide` line activates the `Hide` method for the `frmMoveParagraph` user form, hiding it from display on the screen. The `Unload frmMoveParagraph` line unloads the dialog box from memory.

NOTE It isn't necessary to hide or unload a dialog box to continue execution of a procedure, but if you don't, users may become confused. For example, if you click the OK button on a Print dialog box in a Windows application, you expect the dialog box to disappear and the Print command to be executed. If the dialog box didn't disappear (but it started printing the job in the background), you'd probably think it hadn't registered the click, so you'd click again and again until it went away.

9. Next, the procedure needs to check the `Value` property of the `chkReturnToPreviousPosition` check box to find out whether to insert a bookmark in the document to mark the current position of the insertion point. To do this, enter a straightforward `If… Then` statement:

```
If chkReturnToPreviousPosition = True Then
End If
```

If the `chkReturnToPreviousPosition` statement is set to `True`—that is, if the check box is selected—the code in the lines following the `Then` statement runs. The `Then` statement consists of the lines for inserting a bookmark that you recorded earlier. Cut these lines from the procedure and paste them into the `If`... `Then` statement like this:

```
If chkReturnToPreviousPosition = True Then
    With ActiveDocument.Bookmarks
        .Add Range:=Selection.Range, Name:=" Move_Paragraph_Temp"
    End With
End If
```

If the check box is selected, the procedure inserts a bookmark; if the check box is cleared, the procedure passes over these lines.

10. Next, paste in the code for selecting the current paragraph and cutting it to the Clipboard:

```
Selection.Extend
Selection.Extend
Selection.Extend
Selection.Extend
Selection.Cut
```

11. After this, you need to retrieve the `Value` properties from the option buttons to see which one was selected when the user chose the OK button in the dialog box. For this, you can again use an If condition—this time, an `If`... `Then` `ElseIf`... `Else` condition, with the relevant insertion-point–movement lines from the recorded procedure pasted in:

```
If optUpOne = True Then
    Selection.MoveUp Unit:=wdParagraph, Count:=1
ElseIf optUpTwo = True Then
    Selection.MoveUp Unit:=wdParagraph, Count:=2
ElseIf optDownOne = True Then
    Selection.MoveDown Unit:=wdParagraph, Count:=1
Else
    Selection.MoveDown Unit:=wdParagraph, Count:=2
End If
Selection.Paste
```

Here, `optUpOne`, `optUpTwo`, `optDownOne`, and `optDownTwo` (which uses the `Else` statement here and therefore isn't specified by name in the listing) are the four option buttons from the dialog box, representing the choice to move the current paragraph up one paragraph, up two paragraphs, down one paragraph, or down two paragraphs, respectively. The condition is straightforward: If `optUpOne` is `True` (that is, if the option button is selected), the first `Then` condition runs, moving the insertion point up one paragraph from its current position (after cutting the current paragraph, the insertion point will be at the beginning of the paragraph that was after the current one). If `optUpOne` is `False`, the first `ElseIf` condition is evaluated; if it is `True`, the second `Then` condition runs; and if it is `False`, the next `ElseIf` condition is evaluated. If that too is False, the Else code is run. In this case, the Else statement means that the optDownTwo option button was selected in the dialog box, so the Else code moves the insertion point down two paragraphs.

Wherever the insertion point ends up after the attentions of the option buttons, the next line of code (Selection.Paste) pastes in the cut paragraph from the Clipboard.

12. Finally, the procedure must return the insertion point to where it was originally if the chkReturnToPreviousPosition check box is selected. Again, you can test for this with a simple If… Then condition that incorporates the go-to-bookmark and delete-bookmark lines from the recorded procedure:

```
If chkReturnToPreviousPosition = True Then
    Selection.GoTo What:=wdGoToBookmark, _
        Name:=" Move_Paragraph_Temp"
    ActiveDocument.Bookmarks("Move_Paragraph_Temp").Delete
End If
```

If the chkReturnToPreviousPosition check box is selected, VBA moves the insertion point to the temporary bookmark and then deletes that bookmark.

Listing 14.1 shows the full listing for the cmdOK button.

LISTING 14.1:

```
 1.  Private Sub cmdOK_Click()
 2.      frmMoveCurrentParagraph.Hide
 3.      Unload frmMoveCurrentParagraph
 4.      If chkReturnToPreviousPosition = True Then
 5.          With ActiveDocument.Bookmarks
 6.              .Add Range:=Selection.Range, _
                     Name:=" Move_Paragraph_Temp"
 7.          End With
 8.      End If
 9.      Selection.Extend
10.      Selection.Extend
11.      Selection.Extend
12.      Selection.Extend
13.      Selection.Cut
14.      If optUpOne = True Then
15.          Selection.MoveUp Unit:=wdParagraph, Count:=1
16.      ElseIf optUpTwo = True Then
17.          Selection.MoveUp Unit:=wdParagraph, Count:=2
18.      ElseIf optDownOne = True Then
19.          Selection.MoveDown Unit:=wdParagraph, Count:=1
20.      Else
21.          Selection.MoveDown Unit:=wdParagraph, Count:=2
22.      End If
```

```
23.        Selection.Paste
24.        If chkReturnToPreviousPosition = True Then
25.            Selection.GoTo What:=wdGoToBookmark, _
                   Name:=" Move_Paragraph_Temp"
26.            ActiveDocument.Bookmarks("Move_Paragraph_Temp").Delete
27.        End If
28.    End Sub
```

General Example: Opening a File from a List Box

This example shows you a user form that uses a list box to let the user select a file to open. The user form is simple, as is its code, which uses a loop and an array to gather the names of the files in the folder and then displays the filenames in the list box. The user gets to select a file and click the Open button to open it. Figure 14.22 shows the user form in action for Excel files.

You can adapt this example to any of the applications discussed in this book by changing the filename to an appropriate type and changing a couple of the key statements. The example shows you how to create the code in Excel, but you can then adapt it for the application you want to use.

FIGURE 14.22
The user form you'll build in this example contains a list box that gives the user quick access to all current files.

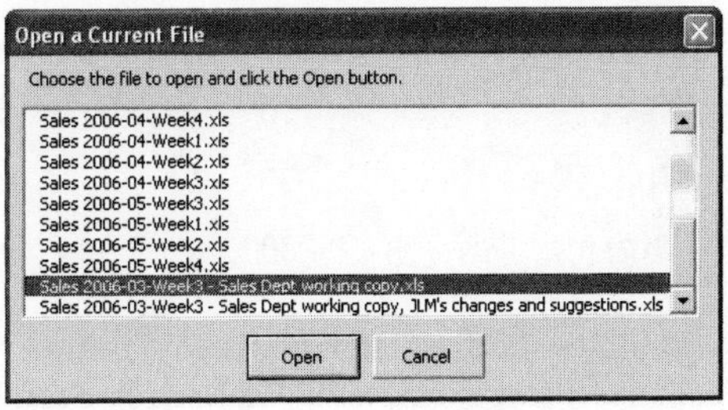

BUILDING THE USER FORM

Follow these steps to build the user form:

1. Start the application you want to work in. The example uses Excel.

2. Display the Visual Basic Editor by pressing the F11 key or choosing Tools ➢ Macro ➢ Visual Basic Editor.

3. In the Project Explorer, right-click the project to which you want to add the user form and choose Insert ➢ UserForm from the context menu to insert a default-size user form in the project.

4. Drag the handle at the lower-right corner of the user form to the right to make the user form a bit wider.

5. Set the name of the form to **frmOpen_a_Current_File** and its Caption to **Open a Current File**. Check the Width property: You want it to be about 350 pixels wide.

6. Click the Label button in the Toolbox, and then click in the upper-left corner of the user form to place a default-size label there. Activate the Properties window and set the properties for the label as shown in the following list:

Property	Value
(Name)	lblInfo
AutoSize	True
Caption	Choose the file to open and click the Open button.
Left	10
Top	6
WordWrap	False

7. Click the ListBox button in the Toolbox, and then click below the label in the user form to place a default-size list box there. Set its properties as follows:

Property	Value
(Name)	lstFiles
Height	100
Left	10
Top	25
Width	300

8. Double-click the CommandButton button in the Toolbox, and then click twice at the bottom of the user form to place two default-size command buttons there. Set their properties as follows:

Property	First Button Value	Second Button Value
(Name)	cmdOpen	cmdCancel
Cancel	False	True
Caption	Open	Cancel
Default	True	False
Height	21	21
Width	55	55

9. Arrange the command buttons as follows:

   A. Click the cmdCancel button to select it, and then drag it close to the cmdOK button.

   B. With the cmdCancel button still selected, Ctrl+click the cmdOK button to add it to the selection.

   C. Choose Format ➢ Group to group the buttons.

   D. Choose Format ➢ Center In Form ➢ Horizontally to center the buttons horizontally in the form.

   E. Drag the group up or down as necessary.

Creating the Code for the User Form

Follow these steps to create the code for the user form:

1. With the user form selected, press the F7 key to display the user form's code sheet.

2. In the declarations portion of the code sheet, enter an **Option Base 1** statement to make array numbering start at 1 instead of at 0:

```
Option Base 1
```

3. Make sure that UserForm is selected in the Object drop-down list, and then pull down the Procedure drop-down list and choose Initialize from it. The Visual Basic Editor enters the stub of an Initialize procedure in the code sheet, like this:

```
Private Sub UserForm_Initialize()

End Sub
```

4. Enter the statements for the Initialize procedure shown in Listing 14.2.

5. In the Object drop-down list, select cmdCancel. The Visual Basic Editor enters the stub of a Click procedure, as shown below. (Click is the default event for the CommandButton control, so the Visual Basic Editor assumes that you want to create a Click procedure.)

```
Private Sub cmdCancel_Click()

End Sub
```

6. Enter the statements for the cmdCancel_Click procedure shown in Listing 14.2.

7. In the Object drop-down list, select cmdOpen. The Visual Basic Editor enters the stub of a Click procedure.

8. Enter the statements for the cmdOpen_Click procedure shown in Listing 14.2.

9. Customize line 9 (in the Initialize procedure) and line 32 (in the cmdOpen_Click procedure) so that the code will work with the application you're using, as shown in the following list. The procedure as shown is set up to run for Excel, but you'll probably need to change the path to reflect where the target files are on your computer.

   For Word, change the Workbooks.Open statement to Documents.Open:

```
If lstFiles.Value <> "" Then Documents.Open _
    Filename:="z:\transfer\" & lstFiles.Value
```

   For PowerPoint, change the Workbooks.Open statement to Presentations.Open:

```
If lstFiles.Value <> "" Then Presentations.Open _
    Filename:="z:\transfer\" & lstFiles.Value
```

Listing 14.2 shows the full version of the code behind the user form.

LISTING 14.2:

```
1.   Option Base 1
2.
3.   Private Sub UserForm_Initialize()
4.
5.       Dim strFileArray() As String
6.       Dim strFFile As String
7.       Dim intCount As Integer
8.
9.       strFFile = Dir("z:\transfer\spreads\*.xls")
10.      intCount = 1
11.
12.      Do While strFFile <> ""
13.          If strFFile <> "." And strFFile <> ".." Then
14.              ReDim Preserve strFileArray(intCount)
15.              strFileArray(intCount) = strFFile
16.              intCount = intCount + 1
17.              strFFile = Dir()
18.          End If
19.      Loop
20.
21.      lstFiles.List() = strFileArray
22.
23.  End Sub
24.
25.  Private Sub cmdCancel_Click()
26.      Me.Hide
27.      Unload Me
28.  End Sub
29.
30.  Private Sub cmdOpen_Click()
31.      Me.Hide
32.      If lstFiles.Value <> "" Then Workbooks.Open _
             Name:="z:\transfer\spreads" & lstFiles.Value
33.      Unload Me
34.  End Sub
```

Listing 14.2 contains all the code that appears on the code sheet for the frmOpen_a_Current_File user form: a declarations section and three event procedures.

In the declarations section, line 1 contains the Option Base 1 statement, which makes any array used on the code sheet begin at 1 rather than at 0. Line 2 is a spacer.

Here's what happens in the UserForm_Initialize procedure (lines 3 to 23):

◆ Line 3 begins the Initialize procedure for the user form. Line 4 is a spacer.

◆ Line 5 declares the String array variable strFileArray. Line 6 declares the String variable strFFile. Line 7 declares the Integer variable intCount. Line 8 is a spacer.

◆ Line 9 assigns to strFFile the result of a directory operation on the designated folder (here, z:\transfer\spreads\) for files with an .xls extension.

◆ Line 10 sets the intCount counter to 1. Note that if you don't use the Option Base 1 declaration for this procedure, you need to set Count to 0 (or the corresponding value for a different option base that you use). The first call to Dir, which specifies the pathname in an argument, returns the first file it finds in the folder (assuming it finds at least one file). Each subsequent call without the argument returns the next file in the folder, until Dir finds no more files.

◆ Line 11 is a spacer. Lines 12 through 19 contain a Do While…Loop loop that runs while strFFile isn't an empty string (" "):

    ◆ Line 13 makes sure that strFFile isn't a folder by comparing it to the single period and double period used to denote folders (or directories, as they used to be in DOS). If strFFile isn't a folder, line 14 uses a ReDim Preserve statement to increase the dimensions of the strFileArray array to the number in intCount while retaining the current information in the array, thus building the list of files in the folder.

    ◆ Line 15 assigns to the intCount subscript of the strFileArray array the current contents of strFFile.

    ◆ Line 16 then adds 1 to intCount, and Line 17 sets strFFile to the result of the Dir function (the first filename matching the *.xls pattern in the designated folder).

    ◆ Line 18 ends the If condition. Line 19 contains the Loop keyword that will continue the loop as long as the Do While statement is True. Line 20 is a spacer.

◆ When the loop ends, line 21 sets the List property of the lstFiles list box in the dialog box to the contents of strFileArray, which now contains a list of all the files in the folder.

◆ Line 22 is a spacer, line 23 ends the procedure, and line 24 is another spacer.

Here's what happens in the cmdCancel_Click procedure (lines 25 through 28):

◆ Line 25 starts the cmdCancel_Click procedure, and line 28 ends it.

◆ Line 26 hides the user form, using the Me keyword to reference it.

◆ Line 27 unloads the user form from memory.

Here's what happens in the cmdOpen_Click procedure (lines 30 through 34):

◆ Line 30 starts the cmdOpen_Click procedure, and line 34 ends it.

◆ Line 31 hides the user form, again by using the Me keyword.

◆ Line 32 checks to make sure the `Value` property of the `lstFiles` list box is not an empty string (`""`) and, if it is not, uses the `Open` method of the `Documents` collection to open the file selected in the list box. The statement adds to the path (`z:\transfer\spreads\`) the `Value` property of the list box to produce the full filename.

◆ Line 33 unloads the user form from memory.

Using an Application's Built-in Dialog Boxes from VBA

Some applications, such as Word and Excel, let you use their built-in dialog boxes via VBA. If a built-in dialog box offers the functionality you need, using it can be a great solution: you don't have to build a custom dialog box, just link the built-in dialog box to your code; you shouldn't need to debug the dialog box; and users of your procedures will probably be familiar with the dialog box from their work in the application.

Displaying a Built-in Dialog Box

To display a built-in dialog box, you need to know its name and constant. You also must decide which method to use to display the dialog box.

FINDING THE DIALOG BOX NAME AND CONSTANT

Built-in Word dialog boxes are identified by constants starting with the letters *wdDialog* (as in Word Dialog), followed by the name of the dialog box. The name of the dialog box is derived from the menu commands required to display the dialog box: For example, to refer to the Open dialog box, you use the constant `wdDialogFileOpen`, because you'd choose File ➢ Open to display the dialog box. Likewise, to display the Print dialog box (File ➢ Print), you use the constant `wdDialogFilePrint`, and to display the Options dialog box (Tools ➢ Options), you use the constant `wdDialogToolsOptions`.

Excel follows a similar but less rigid convention. Built-in Excel dialog boxes are identified by constants starting with the letters xlDialog followed by the name of the dialog box. The name of the dialog box is derived either from the menu commands required to display it or from the dialog box's title. For example, to refer to the Open dialog box, you use the constant `xlDialogOpen` (rather than `xlDialogFileOpen`).

The easiest way to find the name for the built-in dialog box you need is to view the "Built-in Dialog Box Argument Lists" topic in VBA Help from Word or Excel. From the Visual Basic Editor, choose Help ➢ Microsoft Visual Basic Help, and then search for "built-in dialog argument." These lists include the arguments that you can set in the dialog boxes.

NOTE You can also view a list of built-in dialog boxes by displaying the Object Browser and typing **wddialog** or **xldialog** (as appropriate) in the Search Text box.

You use these constants with the `Dialogs` property, which returns the `Dialogs` collection object, which contains all the built-in dialog boxes in the host application. For example, to return Word's Save As dialog box and display it using the `Show` method, you'd use the following statement:

```
Dialogs(wdDialogFileSaveAs).Show
```

NOTE In Word, the `Dialogs` collection is a creatable object, so you can access it directly without going through the `Application` object. In Excel, the `Dialogs` collection is not creatable, so you must always use the Application object—for example, `Application.Dialogs (xlDialogOptionsGeneral).Show`.

Choosing Between the Show Method and the Display Method

VBA provides two methods of displaying built-in dialog boxes on-screen: Show and Display:

- The Show method displays the specified Dialog object and then executes the actions the user takes in the dialog box. For example, if you use the Show method to display the wdDialogFileSaveAs dialog box, and the user enters a name for the file in the File Name box and clicks the Save button, VBA saves the file with the given name in the specified folder (and with any options the user chose).

- The Display method displays the dialog box on-screen but does *not* execute the actions the user takes in the dialog box. Instead, it allows you to return the settings from the dialog box once the user dismisses it and use them for your own purposes.

Displaying a Particular Tab of a Word Dialog Box

If the dialog box you want to display has tabs, you can display the tab of your choice by specifying the DefaultTab property. You refer to a tab by the name of the dialog box plus the word *Tab* and the name of the tab. For example, the constant for the Bullets And Numbering dialog box is wdDialogFormatBulletsAndNumbering, and the constant for its Outline Numbered tab is wdDialogFormatBulletsAndNumberingTabOutlineNumbered. Likewise, the Font dialog box is referred to as wdDialogFormatFont, and its Character Spacing tab is referred to as wdDialogFormatFontTabCharacterSpacing. You could display this tab by using the following statements:

```
With Dialogs(wdDialogFormatFont)
    .DefaultTab = wdDialogFormatFontTabCharacterSpacing
    .Show
End With
```

To get a list of all the tab constants, search for wdWordDialogTab in the Object Browser.

Using the Show Method to Display and Execute a Dialog Box

The Show method displays the specified dialog box and executes the actions the user takes in it. Show is useful when you need to have the user perform a conventional interactive action while you're running a procedure. As a simple example, in a procedure that's supposed to perform certain formatting tasks on the current document, you could check to make sure that a document was open before attempting to perform the formatting; then, if no document was open, you could display the Open dialog box so that the user could open a file. (You might precede the Open dialog box with a message box explaining the problem.) Listing 14.3 shows the code for this part of the procedure.

Listing 14.3:

```
1.  If Documents.Count = 0 Then
2.      Proceed = MsgBox("There is no document open." _
            & vbCr & vbCr & _
```

```
                  "Please open a document for the procedure to work on.", _
                  vbOKCancel + vbExclamation, "Format Report")
3.       If Proceed = vbOK Then
4.            Dialogs(wdDialogFileOpen).Show
5.            If Documents.Count = 0 Then End
6.       Else
7.            End
8.       End If
9.   End If
10.  'rest of procedure here
```

Analysis

Here's how the code works:

◆ Line 1 checks the Count property of the Documents collection to see if no documents are open; if that's the case, the statements in lines 2 through 8 run.

◆ Line 2 displays a message box informing the user that no document is open and asking them to open one for the procedure to work on. The message box has OK and Cancel buttons, and stores the button chosen in the variable Proceed.

◆ Line 3 checks to see if the OK button was chosen; if it was, line 4 displays the Open dialog box so that the user can select the file, which VBA will open when they click the Open button in the Open dialog box.

◆ The user can cancel the procedure at this point by clicking the Cancel button in the Open dialog box, so line 5 checks the Count property of the Documents collection again and uses an End statement to terminate execution of the procedure if there is still no document open.

◆ If the OK button was not chosen, execution moves from line 3 to the Else statement in line 6, and the End statement in line 7 ends execution of the procedure.

◆ Line 8 contains the End If statement for the nested If statement, and line 9 contains the End If statement for the outer If statement.

◆ Line 10 contains a comment to indicate that the rest of the procedure would run from this point, which is reached only if a document is open.

USING THE DISPLAY METHOD TO DISPLAY A DIALOG BOX

Unlike the Show method, the Display method displays a built-in dialog box but doesn't execute the actions the user takes in the dialog box. Instead, you can return the settings that the user made in the dialog box and use whichever of them you want in your procedures. The user gets to work with familiar dialog boxes, but you use only the settings you actually need for the procedure.

For example, you'll often need to find out which folder a procedure should be working in, such as when you need the location of a number of documents that the user wants to manipulate. To get the folder, you *could* display a straightforward input box and prompt the user to type in the correct path to the folder—if the user knows the path and can type it correctly. A possible solution is to display a list box containing the tree of drives, folders, and files; but to do this you need to dimension an array and fill it with the folders and file names, *and* you need to refresh the display every time the user moves up or down the tree—quite a lot of work. You can achieve the same result much more easily by using a built-in dialog box that has the tree built in (for example, the Open dialog box) and retrieving the settings for your own purposes.

TIP If you need to execute the settings in a built-in dialog box that you've displayed using the Display method, use the Execute method. For example, you might want to check the user's selection in the dialog box before implementing them.

Setting and Restoring Options in a Built-in Dialog Box

Most of the built-in Word and Excel dialog boxes have arguments that you can use for retrieving or setting values in the dialog box. For example, the Open dialog box in Word has arguments for Name, ConfirmConversions, ReadOnly, LinkToSource, AddToMru (adding the document to the Most Recently Used document list at the foot of the File menu), PasswordDoc, and more. Some of these are options that you'll see in the Open dialog box itself; others are associated options that you'll find on the various tabs of the Options dialog box. You can guess some argument names from the names of the corresponding controls in the dialog box, but other names aren't directly related. Use the "Built-in Dialog Box Argument Lists" topic in VBA Help to learn the names.

For example, the following statements set the contents of the File Name text box in the Save As dialog box in Word and then display the dialog box:

```
With Dialogs(wdDialogFileSaveAs)
    .Name = "Yellow Paint Primer"
    .Show
End With
```

If you change the settings in a dialog box that uses sticky settings, it's a good idea to change the settings back so that the user doesn't get unexpected results the next time they use the dialog box.

Returning the Button the User Chose in a Dialog Box

To find out which button the user clicked in a dialog box, check the return value of the Show method or the Display method. The return values are as follows:

Return Value	Button Clicked
−2	Close
−1	OK
0	Cancel
1	The first command button
2	The second command button
>2	Subsequent command buttons

For example, you might cancel a procedure if the user clicked the Cancel button in a dialog box:

```
If Dialogs(wdDialogFileOpen).Show = 0 Then End
```

Specifying a Timeout for a Dialog Box

In some applications, including Word, you can display some built-in dialog boxes only for a specified time rather than having them stay open until the user dismisses them. To do so, you use the TimeOut Variant argument with the Show method or the Display method. You specify TimeOut as a number of units, each of which is approximately a thousandth of a second. (If the system is busy with many other tasks, the units may be longer.) So you could display the User Information tab of the Options dialog box for 10 seconds—long enough for the user to check the Name setting and change it if necessary—by using the following statements:

```
With Dialogs(wdDialogToolsOptions)
    .DefaultTab = wdDialogToolsOptionsTabUserInfo
    .Show (15000)
End With
```

WARNING TimeOut doesn't work for custom dialog boxes, only for built-in Word dialog boxes. Also, some built-in Word dialog boxes—such as the New dialog box (wdDialogFileNew) and the Customize dialog box (wdDialogToolsCustomize)—don't respond to TimeOut.

Timing out a dialog box is especially useful for noncritical information like the user name in this example, because it allows the procedure to continue even if the user has left the computer. Likewise, you might want to time out a Save As dialog box in which the procedure suggested a viable file name but allowed the user to override it if they were present. However, for a procedure in which the user's input is essential, you won't want to use the TimeOut argument.

Chapter 15

Creating Complex Dialog Boxes

◆ What is a complex dialog box?

◆ Updating a dialog box to reflect the user's choices

◆ Revealing and hiding parts of a dialog box

◆ Creating multipage dialog boxes

◆ Using a tab strip to drive a dialog box

◆ Creating modeless dialog boxes

◆ Working with user form events

While simple dialog boxes tend to be static, many complex dialog boxes are *dynamic*, in that they change when the user clicks certain elements in them. Such changes can include the following:

◆ The application changes the information in the dialog box to reflect choices that the user has made. For example, if they've selected a particular check box, the application may make another check box unavailable because the option controlled by the second check box isn't available or applicable when they use the option controlled by the first check box.

◆ The dialog box displays a hidden section of secondary options when the user clicks a button in the primary area of the dialog box.

◆ The application uses the dialog box to keep track of a procedure and to guide the user to the next step by displaying appropriate instructions and by activating the relevant control. In this chapter, you'll look at a simple example of this technique.

In this chapter, you'll start by investigating how to create dynamic dialog boxes. Dynamic dialog boxes cost you a little more work than static dialog boxes, but they're a great way both to present information and make choices in your procedures.

From dynamic dialog boxes you'll move on to multipage dialog boxes, which you use to present more information or options to the user than the eye and mind can comfortably compass at once. You'll then look at how create modeless dialog boxes.

The chapter ends by showing you how to work with the many events supported by the UserForm object and the controls you use on it. By using events, you can monitor what the user does and take action accordingly, or even prevent the user from doing something that doesn't seem like a good idea.

Creating and Working with Complex Dialog Boxes

You should never use a complex dialog box where a simple one would do the trick and be easier for users to work with. Where all a procedure needs is a pair of check boxes and a group of option buttons, there's no need to put in multiple pages of dynamically updating controls—nor is there any benefit from doing so. But often, you'll need to create complex dialog boxes (such as the examples given at the beginning of this chapter) to provide users with the flexibility that your procedures demand.

Updating a Dialog Box to Reflect the User's Choices

You'll find it relatively easy to update a dialog box to reflect the options the user chooses in it. Your primary tool for doing this is the Click event to which most controls in a dialog box react, and to which you can add a procedure on the code sheet attached to the dialog box. Some controls have different default events than Click; you'll meet the Change event as you work with complex dialog boxes, and you'll meet the full slew of other events in the second half of the chapter.

Listing 15.1 in the next section shows you an example of updating a dialog box.

Revealing an Extra Part of a Dialog Box

Hiding part of a complex dialog box is a great way to simplify the user's initial interaction with the dialog box. Consider the Find And Replace dialog box in Word: When you display it (by choosing Edit ➢ Replace or pressing Ctrl+H) for the first time in a Word session, you see only the part of the dialog box shown in the top picture of Figure 15.1. (If you choose Edit ➢ Find, you see an even smaller part of the dialog box.) If you need to use the more complex options than the Find And Replace dialog box offers, you can click the More button to display the bottom part of the dialog box, as shown in the lower picture of Figure 15.1.

FIGURE 15.1

Word's Find And Replace dialog box hides some of its options (above) until you click the More button to display its lower half (below).

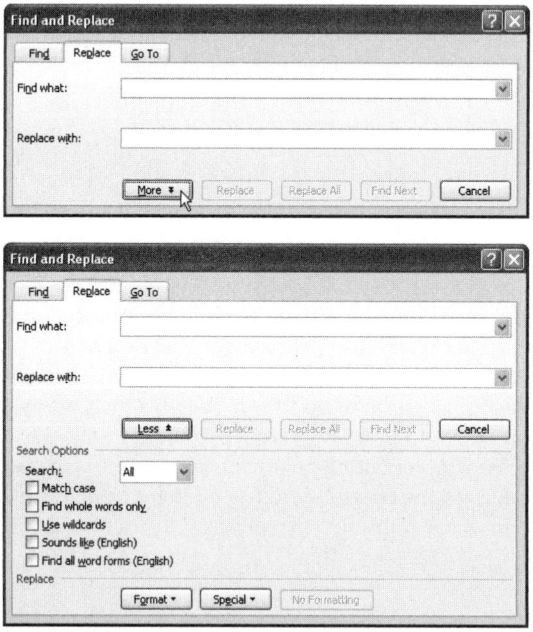

You may want to take a similar approach with complex dialog boxes that contain a subset of actions with which most users will be content most of the time. To do so, you can use two techniques, either separately or in tandem:

◆ Set the Visible property to False to hide a control that appears in a displayed part of the dialog box. Set the Visible property to True when you want to display the control.

◆ Increase the height or width (or both) of the dialog box to reveal an area containing further controls.

TIP With either of the above techniques, you'll typically want to set the Enabled property for hidden controls to False until you reveal them so that the user can't move to a control that they can't see.

As a simple example of the latter technique, consider the dialog box shown in Figure 15.2. When you display the dialog box, only the top part is visible; when you click the More button, the bottom half is displayed. Listing 15.1 contains the code behind the dialog box.

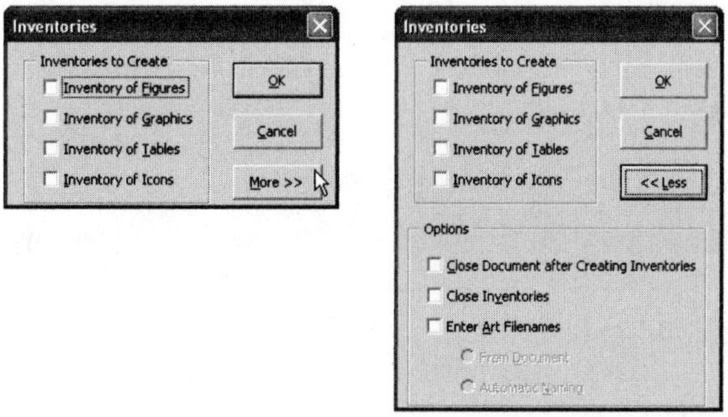

FIGURE 15.2

The top part of the Inventories dialog box (left) offers the most frequently used options. Clicking the More button reveals the rest of the dialog box (right), which contains less-used controls.

LISTING 15.1:

```
 1.   Private Sub UserForm_Initialize()
 2.       frmInventories.Height = 120
 3.   End Sub
 4.
 5.   Private Sub cmdMore_Click()
 6.       If cmdMore.Caption = "More >>" Then
 7.           cmdMore.Caption = "<< Less"
 8.           cmdMore.Accelerator = "L"
 9.           frmInventories.Height = 240
10.           fraOptions.Enabled = True
11.       Else
12.           frmInventories.Height = 120
13.           cmdMore.Caption = "More >>"
14.           cmdMore.Accelerator = "M"
15.       End If
16.   End Sub
```

```
17.
18.   Private Sub chkArtNames_Click()
19.       If chkArtNames = True Then
20.           optFromDocument.Enabled = True
21.           optFromDocument = True
22.           optAutoNames.Enabled = True
23.       Else
24.           optFromDocument.Enabled = False
25.           optFromDocument = False
26.           optAutoNames.Enabled = False
27.           optAutoNames = False
28.       End If
29.   End Sub
30.
31.   Private Sub cmdOK_Click()
32.       frmInventories.Hide
33.       Unload frmInventories
34.       'create inventories here
35.   End Sub
36.
37.   Private Sub cmdCancel_Click()
38.       End
39.   End Sub
```

Listing 15.1 contains five short procedures that control the behavior of the dialog box:

UserForm_Initialize Initializes the dialog box before it's displayed.

cmdMore_Click Runs when the cmdMore button is chosen. This button bears the caption "More" when only the top half of the dialog box is displayed and the caption "Less" when the full dialog box is displayed.

chkArtNames_Click Runs when the Enter Art Filenames check box is chosen.

cmdOK_Click Runs when the OK button is chosen.

cmdCancel_Click Runs when the Cancel button is chosen.

Here's what happens in the code:

The UserForm_Initialize procedure sets the Height property of the frmInventories user form to 120, which is enough to display only the top part of the dialog box. (To find the appropriate height for your dialog box, drag it to the depth that looks right and note the Height property in the Properties window.) This procedure is necessary only if the user form is set to its full height at design time: By setting the user form to a height of 120 at design time, you could avoid having to use a UserForm_Initialize procedure. However, for a user form that has three or more different sizes—or for a user form with two different sizes, one of which needs to be chosen at runtime depending on environmental conditions—you'll need to use a UserForm_Initialize procedure.

The cmdMore_Click procedure starts by checking in line 6 if the Caption property of the cmdMore command button is More >>. If so, that means that only the top half of the dialog box is displayed. Line 7 then sets the Caption property of the cmdMore command button to << Less, the button that will be used to hide the bottom part of the dialog box again if necessary. Line 8 sets the `Accelerator` property of the `cmdMore` command button to L (to make the *L* in *Less* the accelerator key for the button). Line 9 sets the `Height` property of `frmInventories` to 240, which is the depth required to show all the contents of the dialog box. Line 10 enables the `fraOptions` frame (identified as Options in the dialog box and disabled in the user form, as are the `optFromDocument` option button and the `optAutoNames` option button), making it and the controls it contains available to the user.

NOTE Checking the `Caption` property of the `cmdMore` button is an effective way of checking the current state of the dialog box, but it's not the most elegant of methods. Instead, you could maintain an internal state variable in which you store information about whether the dialog box is displayed in its full state or its partial state. Using the internal state variable would have the added benefit of not having to be patched if the dialog box were *localized*, adapted for a different language locale.

If the condition in line 6 is `False`, execution shifts from line 6 to the `Else` statement in line 11. This must mean that the `Caption` property of the `cmdMore` button is already set to << Less, so the dialog box is already at its expanded size, and the << Less button is being clicked to shrink the dialog box again. Line 12 sets the `Height` property of the user form back to 120, thus hiding the lower part of the dialog box. Line 13 restores the `Caption` property of the `cmdMore` command button to More >>. Line 14 sets the `Accelerator` property of the `cmdMore` command button back to M. Line 16 ends the `cmdMore_Click` procedure.

The `chkArtNames_Click` procedure (lines 18 to 29) runs when the Enter Art Filenames check box is clicked. This procedure enables and disables the option buttons below it as appropriate. Line 19 checks to see if the `chkArtNames` check box is selected. If it is, the statements in lines 20 through 22 run. Line 20 sets the `Enabled` property of the `optFromDocument` option button (identified as From Document in the dialog box) to `True`, thus making it available, and line 21 selects this option button as the default choice. Line 22 enables `optAutoNames`, the option button identified as Automatic Naming in the dialog box.

If the `chkArtNames` check box isn't selected, execution shifts to the `Else` statement in line 23, which directs execution to line 24. This line sets the `Enabled` property of the `optFromDocument` option button to `False`, disabling it. Line 25 then deselects this option button (whether it's selected or not). Line 26 disables the `optAutoNames` option button, and line 27 deselects it (again, whether it's selected or not). The `End If` statement in line 28 ends this `If` statement, and line 29 ends this procedure.

The `cmdOK_Click` procedure in lines 31 to 35 shows the beginning of the procedure that runs once the OK button is clicked. Line 32 hides the Inventories dialog box, and line 33 unloads it from memory. Line 34 contains a comment indicating that the instructions for creating the inventories appear here.

The `cmdCancel_Click` procedure contains only an `End` statement to end execution of the procedure if the user chooses the Cancel button.

Tracking a Procedure in a Dialog Box

The next stage of complexity in a dialog box is using it to track the different stages of a procedure and to guide the user as to how to continue.

Take a look at the Create New Employee Web Page dialog box shown in Figure 15.3. This dialog box guides the user through a four-stage procedure to create a web page for a new employee. The first step is to identify the employee deserving of this honor by using either the drop-down list or the Select Other Employee command button in the Step 1 frame. The second step is to enter suitable introductory or laudatory text about the employee. The third step is to select the most (or perhaps least) flattering photo of the employee to include in the web page. The fourth step is to save the web page to a folder on the company's intranet.

When the user first displays the Create New Employee Web Page dialog box, they will see the version of the dialog box shown in Figure 15.3, with Steps 2, 3, and 4 disabled, and instructions for Step 1 shown in the Instructions box at the top. When the user follows the instructions and selects the employee by using either the combo box drop-down list or the Select Other Employee command button, the code attached to the combo box drop-down list or the command button enables the Step 2 frame, making its text box available to the user, as shown in Figure 15.4. Following the figure is the code for the Change event of the cmbSelectEmployee combo box; the code for the Click event of the cmdSelectOtherEmployee command button is similar, although a little more complex.

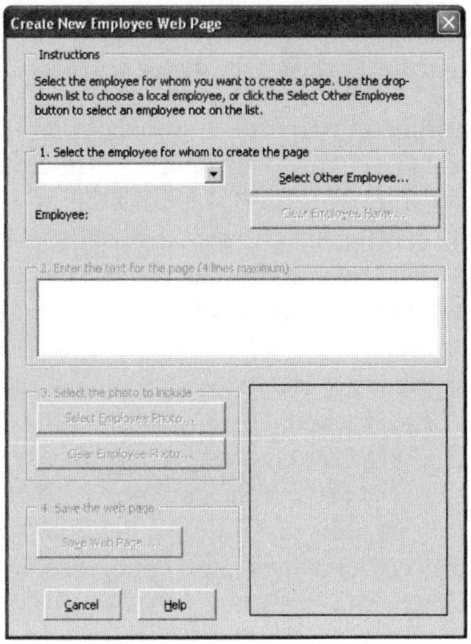

FIGURE 15.3

The Create New Employee Web Page dialog box provides the user with instructions that it updates as they work their way through the procedure.

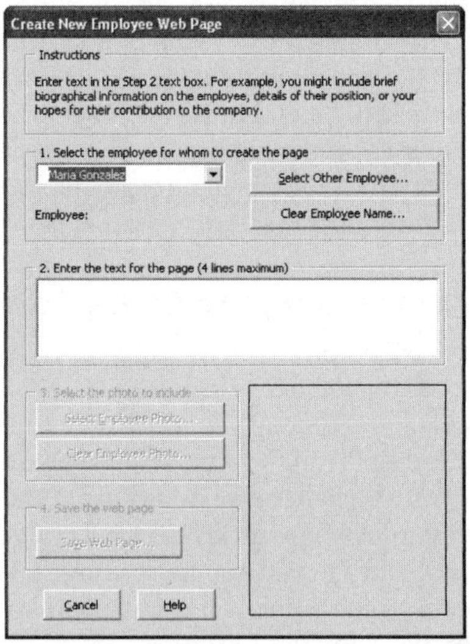

FIGURE 15.4

The second stage of the Create New Employee Web Page dialog box. Notice the changes from the first stage: The instructions in the Instructions frame have changed, and the use of the Step 1 combo box drop-down list has enabled the Step 2 frame.

```
Private Sub cmbSelectEmployee_Change()
  lblEmployeeName = cmbSelectEmployee.Text
  fraStep2.Enabled = True
  lblInstructions = "Enter text in the Step 2 text box. " & _
    "For example, you might include brief biographical " & _
    "information on the employee, details of their position, " & _
    "or your hopes for their contribution to the company."
  cmdClearEmployeeName.Enabled = True
End Sub
```

NOTE The Select Other Employee button in the Create New Employee Web Page dialog box bears an ellipsis (…), as do some of the other command buttons. The ellipsis is the Windows convention for indicating that the choice (here a command button, but often a menu item) results in a dialog box being displayed rather than an action being taken immediately.

These are the changes that occur when the user completes Step 1 of the dialog box:

◆ The text of the label in the Instructions box at the top of the dialog box is changed to contain information for Step 2 of the procedure.

◆ The name of the employee selected by the user is listed alongside the Employee label in the Step 1 frame.

◆ The frame for Step 2 is enabled (the text box it contains is enabled along with the frame).

Using Multipage Dialog Boxes and Tab Strip Controls

VBA includes the MultiPage control, which enables you to create multipage dialog boxes, and the TabStrip control, which lets you create dialog boxes driven by tab strips. You've almost certainly used multipage dialog boxes (if you're not sure, choose Tools ➢ Options in any of the Office applications or in the Visual Basic Editor to see an example of one). You can access any page (one at a time) by clicking the tab at the top of the page. Each page contains a different set of controls and can have a different layout appropriate to the controls.

NOTE The tab is the little thing that sticks out from the top of the page, not the whole page. Many people refer to the pages as "tabs," because the tab is the part you click to access the page. This discussion uses "tab" to mean only the tab component and "page" to refer to the page.

Multipage dialog boxes are great for packing a lot of information into a single dialog box without having it take up the whole screen and become visually bewildering. You'll need to divide the information into discrete sets of related information to fit it onto the pages. Each page can (and should) have a different layout of controls that govern the behavior of discrete items; the pages are normally separate in theme. Again, the Options dialog boxes in the Office applications and the Visual Basic Editor provide examples of this.

A dialog box that uses a tab strip differs from a multipage dialog box in that it contains a tab strip control containing multiple *tabs* but not multiple *pages*: The rest of the dialog box, apart from the tab strip, stays the same no matter which tab on the tab strip is selected. This means that the dialog box has only one layout, so the controls don't change. Instead, the tab strip acts as a control for accessing the set of data to display in the other controls: To change the set of data displayed in the controls in the dialog box, you select a different tab in the tab strip.

Tab strips are useful when you need to display consistent sets of information, such as the records you might maintain on your company's customers. Each customer has an account number, a name (perhaps several), an address, phone numbers, e-mail addresses, URLs, an order history, an account balance, and so on, so you can use the same set of controls (text boxes and labels, for example) to display the information and use a tab strip control to control which customer's set of information is displayed in them. Because few databases have a small and fixed number of records, you'll need to populate the tab strip on-the-fly with tabs and captions, but it works fine.

LIMIT THE NUMBER OF PAGES IN YOUR MULTIPAGE DIALOG BOXES

The Visual Basic Editor allows you to create dialog boxes with dozens of tabs or dozens of pages; if you run out of horizontal space to display the tabs, the Visual Basic Editor adds a scroll bar to enable you to scroll through the tabs. You'll probably want to avoid creating multipage dialog boxes with more than 10 or 12 pages, as the wealth of information such a dialog box will contain is likely to overwhelm the user.

If you need more than a dozen pages to organize the information in a dialog box, you're probably trying to present the user with too much data at once. Consider an alternative way of displaying it.

Tabs are a different matter. Because you use a tab strip to move through the records in a recordset, you may need to use many tabs in a given tab strip. Unless the number of tabs is absurdly large, this shouldn't normally be a problem.

NOTE Table 14.7 in Chapter 14 explains the properties unique to the TabStrip control and Multi-Page control.

MULTIPAGE DIALOG BOXES

To create a multipage dialog box, click the MultiPage button in the Toolbox, and then click in the user form where you want the control to appear. The Visual Basic Editor places a MultiPage control with two pages, whose tabs have the labels Page 1 and Page 2. You can then move and size the control as usual. In typical usage, you'll want to create a MultiPage control that's only a little smaller than the user form it inhabits (as in most of the multipage dialog boxes you'll see in Windows applications).

Once you've created a MultiPage control, you work with a page on it by right-clicking its tab and using the resulting context menu:

- To add a page, right-click the label and choose New Page from the context menu. VBA will add a new page of the default size and will name it Page*n*, where *n* is the next number after the current number of pages (even if the other pages have names other than Page1, Page2, and so on).

- To rename a page in a MultiPage control, right-click the label and choose Rename from the context menu. In the Rename dialog box (see Figure 15.5), enter the caption (the label text) for the page in the Caption text box, the accelerator key in the Accelerator Key text box, and any control-tip text (the tip the user sees when they move the mouse pointer over the tab for the page) in the Control Tip Text text box. Click the OK button to close the Rename dialog box.

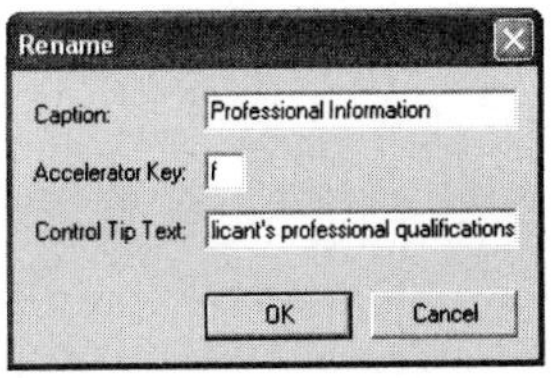

FIGURE 15.5
Use the Rename dialog
box to set the caption,
accelerator key, and
control-tip text for
a page.

- To delete a page from a MultiPage control, right-click the label and choose Delete Page from the context menu. The Visual Basic Editor will remove the page without prompting for confirmation.

- To move a page to a different place in the MultiPage control, right-click the label and choose Move from the context menu to display the Page Order dialog box (see Figure 15.6). In the Page Order list box, select the page or pages that you want to move (Shift+click to select multiple contiguous pages; Ctrl+click to select multiple noncontiguous pages) and then use the Move Up and Move Down buttons to rearrange the page or pages as desired. When you've finished, select the OK button to close the Page Order dialog box.

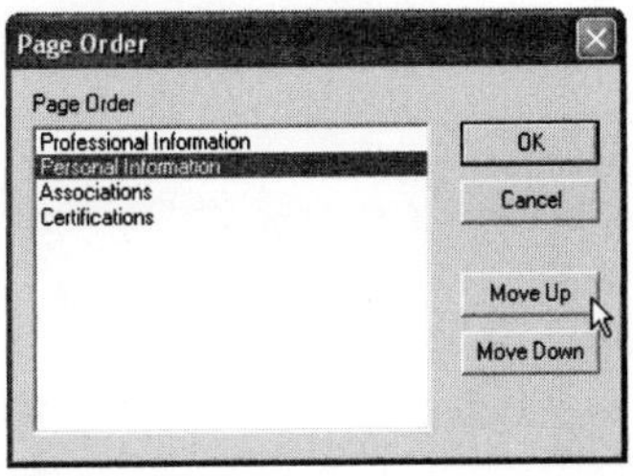

FIGURE 15.6
Use the Move Up and
Move Down buttons in
the Page Order dialog
box to change the order
of pages in a MultiPage
control.

- To specify which page of a multipage dialog box to display by default, use the Value property of the MultiPage control. You can set this property either at design time or at runtime. For example, you could use an initialization procedure such as the one shown here to display the third page (identified by the value 2, because the page numbering starts at 0) of a dialog box with a MultiPage control called MyMulti at runtime:

```
Sub UserForm_Initialize()
   MyMulti.Value = 2
End Sub
```

Once you've created a multipage dialog box, you can populate its pages with controls using the techniques you learned in Chapter 14. Each control must have a unique name within the dialog box (not just within the page on which it appears).

When designing a multipage dialog box, keep the following issues in mind:

- What's the best way to divide the information or options in the dialog box? What belongs on which page? Which information or options will the user expect to find grouped together?

- Which controls should appear on each page? Most dialog boxes need at least a pair of command buttons—such as OK and Cancel, or OK and Close—available from each page to allow the user to dismiss the dialog box from whichever page they happen to end up on. In rare instances, you may want to force the user to return to a particular page in order to close a dialog box. In these cases, make sure that each page that doesn't contain a command button to dismiss the dialog box gives the user an indication of where they will find such a command button.

♦ For settings, do you need to have an Apply button as well as an OK button to apply the changes on a particular page without closing the dialog box?

Because each control in a multipage dialog box has a unique name, when returning information from a multipage dialog box you need specify only the relevant object—you don't need to specify which page it's on.

Figure 15.7 shows an example of a multipage dialog box. The first page contains the customer's personal contact information, the second the customer's professional information, the third the associations the customer belongs to, and the fourth the certifications the customer holds.

FIGURE 15.7

By using multiple pages in a dialog box, you can present a clean and un-cluttered look that the user will be able to navigate easily.

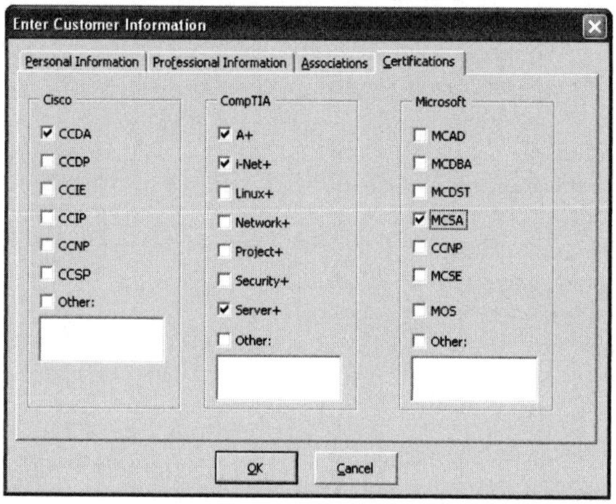

Most of the properties of the MultiPage control are straightforward, but a few deserve special mention:

♦ The `Style` property offers `fmStyleTabs` (the default setting, showing tabs for navigating between the pages), `fmStyleButtons` (which gives each page a rectangular button, with the button for the current page appearing pushed in), or `fmStyleNone` (which provides no means of navigating between the pages of the multipage dialog and no indication of the borders of the multipage dialog). `fmStyleNone` can be useful for creating user forms that have two or more alternate layouts of which the user will only ever need to see one at a time. By including one set of controls on one page of the multipage dialog and another set of controls on the other page, you can present two apparently different dialog boxes by doing nothing more than changing which page of the MultiPage control is displayed. For example, you can use this approach to create a wizard.

♦ The `TabOrientation` property controls where the tabs (or buttons) for the pages appear on the control. Your choices are `fmTabOrientationTop` (the default setting, placing the tabs at the top of the control), `fmTabOrientationBottom`, `fmTabOrientationLeft`, and `fmTabOrientationRight`. Experiment with the effects that the bottom, left, and right orientations offer, but unless they provide significant advantages over the more normal top orientation, use them sparingly if at all. Users won't thank you for confusing the interface unnecessarily.

◆ The `MultiRow` property controls whether a MultiPage control has one row of tabs for its pages (`False`) or multiple rows (`True`). When you have `MultiRow` set to `True`, the Visual Basic Editor adds the second or subsequent rows of tabs when you run out of space on the first or current row.

The MultiPage control doesn't have to take up the whole dialog box—in fact, most dialog boxes keep the key command buttons outside the multipage area so that they're available to the user no matter which page the user is on. That said, it isn't usually a good idea to use a MultiPage control as a less-than-dominant part of a dialog box. In a complex and busy dialog box, a small MultiPage control can appear to be little more than a group box, and the user may miss the tabs, particularly if they're taking only a cursory sweep of the controls presented to locate a specific option.

DIALOG BOXES THAT USE TAB STRIPS

Dialog boxes that use tab strips are substantially different from multipage dialog boxes: The TabStrip control is used not to arrange other controls but to control what appears in them, as the user moves from one set of data to another.

For instance, you might use a dialog box driven by a tab strip to view and update the records in a data source such as a Word table, an Excel spreadsheet, or an Access database. This example uses an Excel workbook in which information is stored on a number of worksheets. Figure 15.8 shows the DataSurfer dialog box, which is driven by a tab strip.

FIGURE 15.8
Using a TabStrip control to create a multitab dialog box. The tab strip is used to control which set of information is displayed in the other controls in the dialog box.

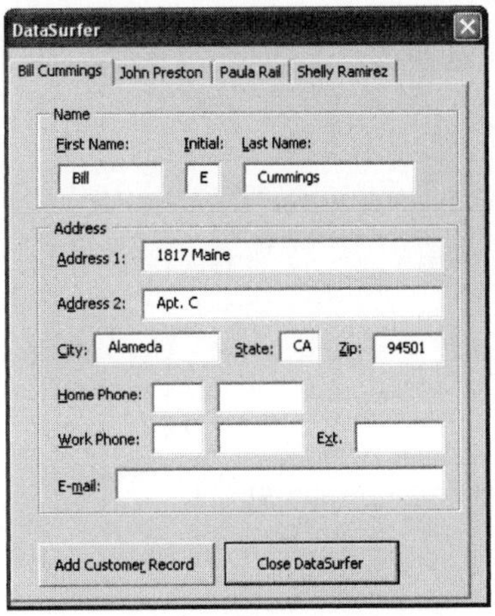

To create a multitab dialog box, you place a TabStrip control above, below, or beside the controls that it will help populate. Above is the conventional—and default—position, but vertical and bottom tabs are showing up increasingly in Windows applications these days. As with the MultiPage control, use the `TabOrientation` property of the TabStrip control to specify whether the tab strip should appear at the top, bottom, left, or right of its control.

The tab strip can contain zero, one, or more tabs. For most purposes, there's little point in having only one tab on a tab strip, and even less in having no tab at all. But if you dynamically populate the tab strip with tabs in your procedures (as you're about to do) and create one tab for each record found, you may run into situations with only one record and thus a dialog box with only one tab—or even a tab strip without any tabs at all.

Click the TabStrip button on the Toolbox, click in the user form to place the tab strip, and then drag it to an appropriate size. Depending on what the rest of the dialog box looks like, you may want to make the tab strip large enough to encompass all the controls it will affect, either in one dimension (as in Figure 15.8), or in both dimensions. Bear in mind that this is only a visual connection for the user's benefit, because you establish the logical connection between the tab strip and the other controls through code. You can then add, rename, move, and delete tabs in the same way as you can pages in a MultiPage control.

If you haven't placed the other controls for the dialog box, you would then do so.

Once everything's in place, you write the code that will enable the tab strip to control the contents of the other controls. Listing 15.2 shows the code for the tab strip in the DataSurfer dialog box. This tab strip is named `tabSurfer`, and the code works with its `Change` event—the event that fires when the user moves from one tab of the tab strip to another.

LISTING 15.2:

```
1.  Private Sub tabSurfer_Change()
2.      If blnInitializing = False Then
3.          With ActiveWorkbook.Sheets(tabSurfer.Value + 1)
4.              'load the contents of the worksheet that corresponds _
                to the tab chosen
5.              .Activate
6.              txtFirstName.Text = .Cells(1, 2).Text
7.              txtInitial.Text = .Cells(2, 2).Text
8.              txtLastName.Text = .Cells(3, 2).Text
9.              txtAddress1.Text = .Cells(4, 2).Text
10.             txtAddress2.Text = .Cells(5, 2).Text
11.             txtCity.Text = .Cells(6, 2).Text
12.             txtState.Text = .Cells(7, 2)
13.             txtZip.Text = .Cells(8, 2).Text
14.             txtHomeArea.Text = .Cells(9, 2).Text
15.             txtHomePhone.Text = .Cells(10, 2).Text
16.             txtWorkArea.Text = .Cells(11, 2).Text
17.             txtWorkPhone.Text = .Cells(12, 2).Text
18.             txtWorkExtension.Text = .Cells(13, 2).Text
19.             txtEmail.Text = .Cells(14, 2).Text
20.         End With
21.     End If
22. End Sub
```

After specifying the worksheet, the code in Listing 15.2 essentially repeats itself for each of the text boxes that appears in the DataSurfer dialog box. This dialog box works with a data source implemented as Excel spreadsheets in the active workbook.

Each worksheet in the workbook is one customer's record, with the name of the customer appearing on the worksheet's tab and the customer's data appearing in the second column: the first name in the first cell of the second column, the middle initial in the second cell, the last name in the third cell, and so on for the address, phone numbers (both home and work), and e-mail address. So to get at any piece of information, you need to know the sheet of the record in question and the appropriate cell in the second column.

Here's how the code works:

◆ Line 1 declares the private procedure `tabSurfer_Change`, which runs automatically whenever the `Change` event of the `tabSurfer` tab strip fires. The `Change` event fires each time the user changes the tab displayed, so you use this event to control the information displayed in the text boxes.

◆ The `Change` event also fires when a tab is added to (or removed from) the tab strip. Because the DataSurfer user form uses the `Initialize` event procedure to populate the tab strip with tabs (one per worksheet in the workbook), you need to stop the `Change` event procedure from running unnecessarily. So the user form declares a private Boolean variable named `blnInitializing` that the `Initialize` procedure sets to `True` while it's running and `False` just before it ends. Line 2 of the `Change` event procedure checks to make sure that `blnInitializing` is `False`. If it's not, the `Initialize` procedure has fired the event, and the `Change` procedure does not need to load the information into the cells—so execution continues at line 21, just before the end of the procedure. But once the `Initialize` procedure has finished running, `blnInitializing` will be set to `False`, and the `Change` event procedure will run each time the user changes tabs in the tab strip.

◆ Line 3 begins a `With` statement that works with the appropriate worksheet in the active workbook: `(ActiveWorkbook.Sheets(tabSurfer.Value + 1)`. The `Value` property of the `tabSurfer` tab strip tells us which tab in the tab strip is selected. Because the first tab in the tab strip is numbered 0 and the first worksheet in the workbook is numbered 1, you need to add 1 to the `Value` of the tab strip to even the numbers.

◆ Line 4 is a comment. Line 5 uses the `Activate` method to activate the worksheet in question.

◆ Lines 6 through 19 then set the `Text` property of each text box in the user form to the contents of the corresponding cell in the second column on the worksheet. For example, line 6 sets the `Text` property of the `txtFirstName` text box (which appears under the First Name label in the dialog box) to the contents of the first cell in the second column: `.Cells(1, 2).Text`.

◆ Line 20 ends the `With` statement, line 21 ends the `If` statement, and line 22 ends the procedure.

USING A PICTURE IN A DIALOG BOX

You can add a picture to a dialog box by using an Image control. Click the Image button in the Toolbox, and then click in the user form where you want the Image control to appear. Once you've placed the Image control, you can size and move the picture just like any other control.

WARNING Make sure the picture you choose is available to all computers that will display the dialog box. If the picture isn't available, it fails to appear in the dialog box, which spoils the effect.

To choose the picture that will appear in the Image control, select the `Picture` property in the Properties window and click the ellipsis button that then appears to the right of the entry. The Visual Basic Editor displays the Load Picture dialog box. Select the picture file and choose the Open button. The `Picture` property in the Properties window registers the type of picture you selected (such as (`Bitmap`)) but not its filename, and the picture appears in the Image control so that you can see if it's an appropriate size.

TIP You can also use a picture as the basis for a user form itself by setting the `Picture` property of the user form.

LOADING A PICTURE INTO AN IMAGE CONTROL PROGRAMMATICALLY

When specifying the picture for an Image control programmatically, you need to use a LoadPicture statement rather than simply assigning the picture to the Picture property of the Image control. LoadPicture takes the following syntax:

```
LoadPicture filename, [WidthDesired], [HeightDesired]
```

filename is a string argument specifying the name of the picture file to be loaded into the Image control. WidthDesired is an optional Long argument specifying the width of the picture in twips, and HeightDesired is an optional Long argument specifying the height of the picture.

For example, the following statement loads the picture Company Logo.jpg in f:\common\ images\:

```
LoadPicture "f:\common\images\Company Logo.jpg"
```

Once you've chosen the picture, you have various options for positioning it and formatting it:

◆ If necessary, set the alignment of the picture by using the PictureAlignment property. (If the picture fully fills the Image control—neither overlapping it nor leaving parts of it empty—you may not need to set the alignment for it.) Table 15.1 shows the constants and values for the PictureAlignment property.

TABLE 15.1:　Constants and Values for the *PictureAlignment* Property

CONSTANT	VALUE	PICTURE ALIGNMENT IN IMAGE CONTROL
fmPictureAlignmentTopLeft	0	Top left
fmPictureAlignmentTopRight	1	Top right
fmPictureAlignmentCenter	2	Centered
fmPictureAlignmentBottomLeft	3	Bottom left
fmPictureAlignmentBottomRight	4	Bottom right

◆ If necessary, clip, stretch, or zoom the picture by using the PictureSizeMode property: fmPictureSizeModeClip (0) clips the picture to fit the Image control; fmPictureSizeModeStretch (1) stretches or squeezes the picture so that it fits the Image control (this option often makes for strange effects); and fmPictureSizeModeZoom (2) enlarges or reduces the picture so that its nearest dimension exactly fits the width or height of the Image control without changing the picture's proportions (this option usually leaves an unfilled gap on the other side).

◆ If you need to tile the image to take up the remaining space in the control, set the PictureTiling property to True.

◆ If you need to adjust the position of the picture relative to its caption, set the PicturePosition property of the check box, command button, label, option button, or toggle button in question. Table 15.2 shows the constants and values for PicturePosition.

TABLE 15.2: Constants and Values for the *PicturePosition* Property

CONSTANT	VALUE	PICTURE POSITION	CAPTION ALIGNMENT
fmPicturePositionLeftTop	0	Left of the caption	With top of picture
fmPicturePositionLeftCenter	1	Left of the caption	Centered on picture
fmPicturePositionLeftBottom	2	Left of the caption	With bottom of picture
fmPicturePositionRightTop	3	Right of the caption	With top of picture
fmPicturePositionRightCenter	4	Right of the caption	Centered on picture
fmPicturePositionRightBottom	5	Right of the caption	With bottom of picture
fmPicturePositionAboveLeft	6	Above the caption	With left edge of picture
fmPicturePositionAboveCenter	7	Above the caption	Centered below picture (This is the default setting.)
fmPicturePositionAboveRight	8	Above the caption	With right edge of picture
fmPicturePositionBelowLeft	9	Below the caption	With left edge of picture
fmPicturePositionBelowCenter	10	Below the caption	Centered above picture
fmPicturePositionBelowRight	11	Below the caption	With right edge of picture
fmPicturePositionCenter	12	In center of control	Centered horizontally and vertically on top of picture

Once you've placed, sized, and formatted a picture, there are various possibilities for what you can do with it, such as using a picture's Click event to trigger an action. For example, if you present the user with a choice of two formats for a document, you could have them click the appropriate picture to make their choice instead of having them select the picture and then click a command button.

Creating a Modeless Dialog Box

VBA version 6 and later let you can create a *modeless* dialog box—one that the user can leave on-screen while they continue to work in their application. You're doubtless familiar with modeless dialog boxes from working with Office. For example, the Find And Replace dialog box in Word and Excel is modeless, as is the Replace dialog box in PowerPoint.

When you display a modeless dialog box, it takes the focus just as any modal dialog box does, and its title bar takes the color of the active title bar, but you can click in the application window to transfer the focus back to that window. When the modeless dialog box loses the focus, its title bar takes on the inactive title bar color. To restore the focus to the modeless dialog box, you click it again.

Creating a modeless dialog box is as simple as setting the ShowModal property of the user form to False from its default setting of True.

There are various reasons for creating a modeless dialog box rather than a modal dialog box. As a simple example, you might create a procedure and dialog box in Word that collects information from the user for a memo or a report. By making the dialog box modeless, you could allow the user to harvest information from an open document (or open other documents and gather information from them) and paste it into the dialog box, as illustrated in Figure 15.9—saving the user from having to copy the information before invoking the dialog box and allowing them to copy multiple separate items easily. Likewise, you could create a modeless user form (perhaps shaped like a toolbar) that the user could keep on-screen and use to automatically enter text into predefined sections of three or four other documents without losing their place in the current document.

FIGURE 15.9

If you make a dialog box modeless rather than modal, the user can continue to work in the application window while the dialog box is displayed.

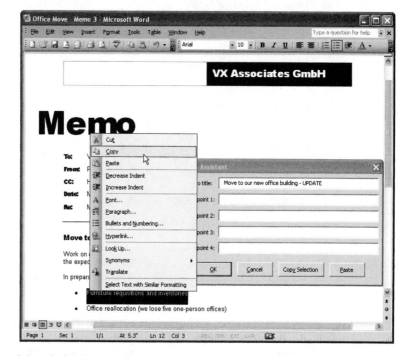

You can also use modeless dialog boxes to display complex sets of interrelated user forms in which the user needs to transfer information easily from one user form to another, or at least to access different areas of two or more displayed user forms at the same time. Displaying multiple forms at once can be confusing to the user, but you may sometimes find it necessary.

Most of the time, you'll probably want to use modal dialog boxes in your VBA procedures. With modal dialog boxes, the user must deal with the dialog box before they can continue to work in the application, and there's no risk that they'll end up with multiple dialog boxes scattered around the screen in assorted states of disuse.

NOTE You can't use both modal and modeless user forms at the same time, but you can display one modal dialog box from another modal dialog box. When the user closes the second modal dialog box, VBA returns them to the first modal dialog box by default. However, you can write code to make the second modal dialog box close the first dialog box after it closes itself.

Choosing the Position for the Dialog Box

By default, VBA centers a dialog box on the middle of the application window as far as possible, which is the normal behavior for Windows applications. If you need to use a different start-up position (for example, to avoid obscuring important data on-screen), set the StartUpPosition property for the user form. Table 15.3 explains the settings you can use.

TABLE 15.3: *StartUpPosition* Property Settings

StartUpPosition **PROPERTY**	**VALUE**	**EFFECT**
Manual	0	Displays the user form in the upper-left corner of the Windows Desktop.
CenterOwner	1	Centers the user form horizontally and vertically in the *owner* application—the application to which the user form belongs.
CenterScreen	2	Centers the user form horizontally and vertically on the Desktop. In a multi-monitor arrangement, this value centers the user form on the monitor containing the active window.
WindowsDefault	3	Displays the user form in the default position for Windows dialog boxes.

Using Events to Control Forms

This section discusses how to use the events that VBA supports for user forms and for the individual controls to give yourself fine control over how your user forms look and behave.

So far in this chapter, you've used three of the most useful events:

◆ You used the Initialize event to add items to list boxes just before a form is loaded and to adjust the number of tabs on a tab strip.

◆ You used the Click event to take action when the user clicks a particular control in a user form. So far you've been using Click mostly for command buttons, but you can use it for just about any control—including the user form itself.

◆ You used the Change event to control what happens when the user changes the tab displayed on a tab strip.

Table 15.4 lists the events that VBA supports and the objects and controls with which each can be used.

NOTE The ByVal keyword is used to pass arguments between procedures. When used with forms, it can return ReturnBoolean, ReturnEffect, ReturnInteger, and ReturnString objects.

As you can see, VBA's events fall into several categories, which are discussed in the following sections in descending order of usefulness:

TABLE 15.4:   Events that VBA Supports and the Objects and Controls Associated with Them

EVENT	OCCURS	APPLIES TO THESE CONTROLS AND OBJECTS
Activate	When the user form becomes the active window	UserForm
Deactivate	When the user form ceases to be the active window	UserForm
AddControl	When a control is added at runtime	Frame, MultiPage, UserForm
AfterUpdate	After the user has changed data in a control	CheckBox, ComboBox, CommandButton, Frame, Image, Label, ListBox, MultiPage, OptionButton, ScrollBar, SpinButton, TabStrip, TextBox, ToggleButton, UserForm
BeforeDragOver	When the user is performing a drag-and-drop operation	CheckBox, ComboBox, CommandButton, Frame, Image, Label, ListBox, MultiPage, OptionButton, ScrollBar, SpinButton, TabStrip, TextBox, ToggleButton, UserForm
BeforeDropOrPaste	When the user is about to release a dragged item or about to paste an item	CheckBox, ComboBox, CommandButton, Frame, Image, Label, ListBox, MultiPage, OptionButton, ScrollBar, SpinButton, TabStrip, TextBox, ToggleButton, UserForm
BeforeUpdate	When the user has changed data in the control before the new data appears in the control	CheckBox, ComboBox, ListBox, OptionButton, ScrollBar, SpinButton, TextBox, ToggleButton
Change	When the Value property of a control changes	CheckBox, ComboBox, ListBox, MultiPage, OptionButton, ScrollBar, SpinButton, TabStrip, TextBox, ToggleButton
Click	When the user clicks a control or object with the primary mouse button	CheckBox, ComboBox, CommandButton, Frame, Image, Label, ListBox, MultiPage, OptionButton, TabStrip, ToggleButton, UserForm
DblClick	When the user double-clicks a control or object with the primary mouse button	CheckBox, ComboBox, CommandButton, Frame, Image, Label, ListBox, MultiPage, OptionButton, TabStrip, TextBox, ToggleButton, UserForm
DropButtonClick	When the user displays or hides a drop-down list	ComboBox, TextBox

TABLE 15.4: Events that VBA Supports and the Objects and Controls Associated with Them *(CONTINUED)*

EVENT	OCCURS	APPLIES TO THESE CONTROLS AND OBJECTS
Enter	Just before one control on a user form receives the focus from another control	CheckBox, ComboBox, CommandButton, Frame, ListBox, MultiPage, OptionButton, ScrollBar, SpinButton, TabStrip, TextBox, ToggleButton
Exit	Just before one control on a user form loses the focus to another control	CheckBox, ComboBox, CommandButton, Frame, ListBox, MultiPage, OptionButton, ScrollBar, SpinButton, TabStrip, TextBox, ToggleButton
Error	When a control or object encounters an error	CheckBox, ComboBox, CommandButton, Frame, Image, Label, ListBox, MultiPage, OptionButton, ScrollBar, SpinButton, TabStrip, TextBox, ToggleButton, UserForm
Initialize	After a user form is loaded but before it's displayed	UserForm
KeyDown	When the user presses a key on the keyboard	CheckBox, ComboBox, CommandButton, Frame, ListBox, MultiPage, OptionButton, ScrollBar, SpinButton, TabStrip, TextBox, ToggleButton, UserForm
KeyUp	When the user releases a key they've pressed on the keyboard	CheckBox, ComboBox, CommandButton, Frame, ListBox, MultiPage, OptionButton, ScrollBar, SpinButton, TabStrip, TextBox, ToggleButton, UserForm
KeyPress	When the user presses an ANSI key on the keyboard	CheckBox, ComboBox, CommandButton, Frame, ListBox, MultiPage, OptionButton, ScrollBar, SpinButton, TabStrip, TextBox, ToggleButton, UserForm
Layout	When the size of a frame, multipage, or user form is changed	Frame, MultiPage, UserForm
MouseDown	When the user depresses the primary mouse button	CheckBox, ComboBox, CommandButton, Frame, Image, Label, ListBox, MultiPage, OptionButton, ScrollBar, SpinButton, TabStrip, TextBox, ToggleButton, UserForm

TABLE 15.4: Events that VBA Supports and the Objects and Controls Associated with Them *(CONTINUED)*

EVENT	OCCURS	APPLIES TO THESE CONTROLS AND OBJECTS
MouseUp	When the user releases the primary mouse button (after depressing it)	CheckBox, ComboBox, CommandButton, Frame, Image, Label, ListBox, MultiPage, OptionButton, ScrollBar, SpinButton, TabStrip, TextBox, ToggleButton, UserForm
MouseMove	When the user moves the mouse	CheckBox, ComboBox, CommandButton, Frame, Image, Label, ListBox, MultiPage, OptionButton, TabStrip, TextBox, ToggleButton, UserForm
QueryClose	When a user form is about to close	UserForm
RemoveControl	When a control is deleted	Frame, MultiPage, UserForm
Resize	When a user form is resized	UserForm
Scroll	When the user moves the scroll box	Frame, MultiPage, ScrollBar, UserForm
SpinDown	When the user clicks the down button on a SpinButton control	SpinButton
SpinUp	When the user clicks the up button on a SpinButton control	SpinButton
Terminate	When a user form has been unloaded from memory	UserForm
Zoom	When the Zoom property of the control or user form is changed	Frame, MultiPage, UserForm

◆ Events that apply only to the UserForm object

◆ Events that apply to the UserForm object and other container objects (such as the Frame control and the MultiPage control)

◆ Events that apply to many or most of the controls, sometimes including the UserForm object as well

TIP To make the maximum use of forms, you need to understand the order in which events take place. If you don't, you can confuse yourself by using events in ways that trigger each other or conflict with each other.

Events That Apply Only to the UserForm Object

This section discusses the events that apply only to the UserForm object. These are the Initialize, QueryClose, Activate, Deactivate, Resize, and Terminate events.

INITIALIZE EVENT

The Initialize event occurs when the user form is loaded but before it appears on-screen.

VBA's syntax for the Initialize event is as follows, where *userform* is a valid UserForm object:

```
Private Sub userform_Initialize()
```

Typical uses for the Initialize event include retrieving information that the user form or application needs and assigning information to the controls on the user form (especially ListBox and ComboBox controls, to which you need to add the information at runtime rather than at design time).

Depending on the style and complexity of your user forms, you may also want to use the Initialize event to resize the user form, resize controls on the user form, display or hide particular controls, and in general make sure the user form is as closely suited as possible to the user's needs before displaying it.

QUERYCLOSE EVENT

The QueryClose event applies to the UserForm object only. This event fires just before the user form closes.

The syntax for the QueryClose event is

```
Private Sub UserForm_QueryClose(Cancel As Integer, CloseMode As Integer)
```

Here, Cancel is an integer, typically 0 (zero). A nonzero value prevents the QueryClose event from firing and stops the user form (and the application) from closing.

CloseMode is a value or a constant giving the cause of the QueryClose event. Table 15.5 shows the values and constants for CloseMode.

TABLE 15.5:   Values and Constants for the *CloseMode* Argument

CONSTANT	VALUE	CAUSE OF THE QueryClose EVENT
vbFormControlMenu	0	The user has closed the user form by clicking its close button or by invoking the Close command from the user form's control menu (for example, by right-clicking the title bar of the user form and choosing Close from the context menu).
vbFormCode	1	An Unload statement in code has closed the user form.
vbAppWindows	2	Windows is closing down and is closing the user form.
vbAppTaskManager	3	The Task Manager is closing the application and so is closing the user form.

At first glance, QueryClose may appear to have few uses beyond double-checking that the user really wants to close a user form that they're attempting to close. For example, if you established that the user had entered a lot of data in the user form they were about to close, you might want to check that they hadn't clicked the user form's close button or Cancel button by mistake, as in the following code fragment for Word:

```
Private Sub UserForm_QueryClose(Cancel As Integer, _
    CloseMode As Integer)
    'make sure the user wants to close the user form
    'if they have entered information in it
    Select Case CloseMode
        Case 0
            'user has clicked the close button or invoked an Unload statement
            'if text box contains more than 5 characters, ask to save it
            If Len(txtDescription.Text) > 5 Then
                If MsgBox("The Description text box contains " & _
                    "a significant amount of text." & vbCr & _
                    "Do you want to save this text?", vbYesNo + _
                    vbQuestion, "Close Form") <> 0 Then
                    Documents.Add
                    Selection.TypeText txtDescription.Text
                    ActiveDocument.SaveAs _
                        "c:\temp\Temporary Description.doc"
                    MsgBox "The contents of the Description text " & _
                        "box have been saved in " & _
                        "c:\temp\Temporary Description.doc.", _
                        vbOKOnly + vbInformation, _
                        "Form Information Saved"
                End If
            End If
```

However, QueryClose really comes into its own when the application, rather than the user form, is closing. If the user form is modeless, the user may not be aware that it's still open and that they're about to lose data from it.

Sometimes you may be able to use QueryClose to save information from a user form when the application has stopped responding and is being closed by Windows or the Task Manager. Be warned that QueryClose's record isn't perfect on this—the code sometimes won't run.

To stop an application from closing, set the Cancel property of the QueryClose event to True.

ACTIVATE EVENT

The Activate event fires when the user form becomes the active window. Typically, this means the event fires when the user form is displayed, occurring just after the Initialize event if the user form is loaded by a Show statement rather than a Load statement.

NOTE   If the user form is loaded by using a Load statement before being displayed with the Show statement, the Initialize event fires after the Load statement. The Activate event, firing after the Show statement, fires later.

However, the `Activate` event also fires when the user form is reactivated after having been deactivated. For example, if you create a modeless user form with an `Activate` event procedure, the code is executed each time the user reactivates the user form after having deactivated it (for example, by working in the application window). Likewise, if you display one user form from another and then close the second user form, returning the focus to the first user form and reactivating it, the `Activate` event fires again.

The syntax for the `Activate` event is

```
Private Sub UserForm_Activate()
```

BUG ALERT: PROBLEMS USING *DEACTIVATE* AND *ACTIVATE* IN IMMEDIATE SUCCESSION

VBA can't always execute the event procedures for the `Deactivate` event of one user form and the `Activate` event of another user form in immediate succession. Sometimes things work as they should; more often, they don't.

For example, say you have two user forms, named One and Two, each with an `Activate` event procedure and a `Deactivate` event procedure. If you display Two from One, the `Deactivate` event code from One should run, followed by the `Activate` event code from Two. This doesn't usually happen: Often, the `Deactivate` code of One will run, but the `Activate` code of Two won't. Run it again, and you may get the `Activate` code of Two to run but not the `Deactivate` code of One. However, if you remove or comment out the `Deactivate` event procedure from One and try again, Two's `Activate` code will run consistently each time One displays Two, indicating that the `Activate` event is firing but the `Activate` event procedure's code isn't running when the `Deactivate` event procedure is present.

DEACTIVATE EVENT

The `Deactivate` event fires when the user form loses the focus after having been the active window, but it doesn't fire when the user form is hidden or unloaded. For example, if you display a user form that contains a `Deactivate` event procedure and then close the user form, the `Deactivate` event doesn't fire. However, if you display one user form from another, the `Deactivate` event for the first user form fires as the focus is transferred to the second user form. With modeless user forms, the `Deactivate` event is triggered each time you leave one user form by clicking on another.

The syntax for the `Deactivate` event is

```
Private Sub UserForm_Deactivate()
```

See the previous sidebar for details on a bug in using the `Deactivate` and `Activate` events in immediate succession.

RESIZE EVENT

The `Resize` event fires when a user form is resized either manually or programmatically.

The syntax for the `Resize` event is

```
Private Sub UserForm_Resize()
```

The main use for the `Resize` event is to move, resize, display, or hide controls to accommodate the new dimensions of the user form. For example, you might resize a text box so that it occupies most of the width of the user form it lives on (see Figure 15.10) by using code such as that shown in Listing 15.3.

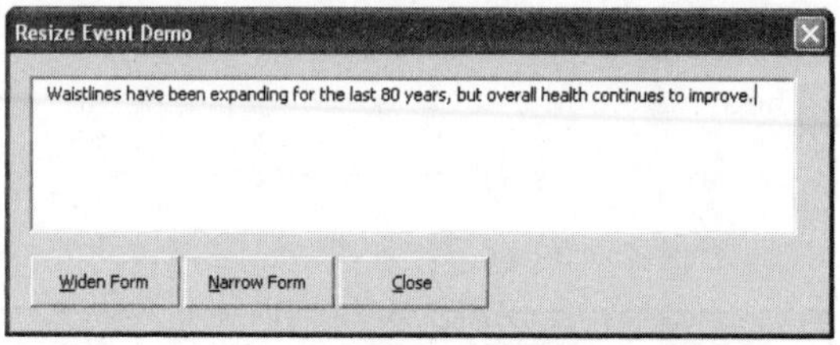

FIGURE 15.10
You can use the Resize event of a user form to re-size or reposition the controls it contains.

LISTING 15.3:

```
1.   Private Sub cmdWidenForm_Click()
2.       With frmResize
3.           If .Width < 451 Then
4.               .Width = .Width + 50
5.               If cmdNarrowForm.Enabled = False Then _
                     cmdNarrowForm.Enabled = True
6.               If .Width > 451 Then _
                     cmdWidenForm.Enabled = False
7.           End If
8.       End With
9.   End Sub
10.
11.  Private Sub cmdNarrowForm_Click()
12.      With frmResize
13.          If .Width > 240 Then
14.              .Width = .Width - 50
15.              If cmdWidenForm.Enabled = False Then _
                     cmdWidenForm.Enabled = True
16.              If .Width < 270 Then _
                     cmdNarrowForm.Enabled = False
17.          End If
18.      End With
19.  End Sub
20.
21.  Private Sub cmdClose_Click()
22.      Unload Me
23.  End Sub
24.
25.  Private Sub UserForm_Resize()
26.      txt1.Width = frmResize.Width - 30
27.  End Sub
```

Listing 15.3 contains four short procedures: one for the Click event of the cmdWidenForm command button, one for the Click event of the cmdNarrowForm command button, one for the Click event of the cmdClose command button, and one for the Resize event of the user form.

The cmdWidenForm_Click procedure shown in lines 1 through 9 increases the width of the user form by 50 points (1 point is ¹⁄₇₂ inch) when the user clicks the Widen Form button, as long as the Width property of the user form is less than 451 points. Line 5 enables the cmdNarrowForm command button if it isn't already enabled. (The cmdNarrowForm command button is disabled when the user form is displayed at its original narrow width.) Line 6 disables the cmdWidenForm command button if the Width property of the user form is more than 451 points.

The cmdNarrowForm_Click procedure shown in lines 11 through 19 narrows the user form by 50 points as long as the Width of the user form is greater than 240 points (its original width), re-enabling the cmdWidenForm button if it's disabled and disabling the cmdNarrowForm button if the Width of the user form is less than 270 points.

The cmdClose_Click procedure shown in lines 21 through 23 simply unloads the user form (which it refers to by the Me keyword).

The UserForm_Resize event procedure in lines 25 though 27 sets the Width property of txt1, the text box in the user form, to 30 points less than the Width of the user form. If you step through the code for the user form, you'll notice that the Resize event fires when the size of the user form changes. For example, when line 4 of the cmdWidenForm_Click procedure is executed, execution branches to the Resize event procedure in line 25, and this procedure is executed before the code in line 5.

TERMINATE EVENT

The Terminate event fires when the user form has been unloaded—or, more precisely, when all references to an instance of the user form have been removed from memory or have gone out of scope.

The syntax for the Terminate event is

```
Private Sub UserForm_Terminate()
```

Events That Apply to the UserForm Object and to Container Controls

This section discusses the events that apply to the UserForm object and to the container controls—the MultiPage control and the Frame control. (The Scroll event applies to the ScrollBar control as well as to MultiPage, Frame, and UserForm.) These events are Scroll, Zoom, Resize, Layout, AddControl, and RemoveControl.

SCROLL EVENT

The Scroll event applies to the Frame control, the MultiPage control, the ScrollBar control, and the UserForm object. This event occurs when the user moves the scroll box (the thumb) on a scroll bar on a frame, multipage control, scroll bar, or user form.

The syntax for the Scroll event varies for the three controls and the UserForm object. The syntax for the Scroll event with the UserForm object is

```
Private Sub UserForm_Scroll(ByVal ActionX As MSForms.fmScrollAction, ByVal ActionY
    As MSForms.fmScrollAction, ByVal RequestDx As Single, ByVal RequestDy As Single,
    ByVal ActualDx As MSForms.ReturnSingle, ByVal ActualDy As MSForms.ReturnSingle)
```

The syntax for the Scroll event with the ScrollBar control is

```
Private Sub scrollbar_Scroll()
```

The syntax for the Scroll event with the MultiPage control is

```
Private Sub multipage_Scroll(index As Long, ActionX As fmScrollAction, ActionY As
fmScrollAction, ByVal RequestDx As Single, ByVal RequestDy As Single, ByVal
ActualDx As MSForms.ReturnSingle, ByVal ActualDy As MSForms.ReturnSingle)
```

The syntax for the Scroll event with the Frame control is

```
Private Sub frame_Scroll(ActionX As fmScrollAction, ActionY As fmScrollAction,
ByVal RequestDx As Single, ByVal RequestDy As Single, ByVal ActualDx As
MSForms.ReturnSingle, ByVal ActualDy As MSForms.ReturnSingle)
```

In these last three syntax statements, *scrollbar* is a valid ScrollBar object, *multipage* is a valid MultiPage object, and *frame* is a valid Frame object.

Here are the arguments for the Scroll event:

index A required argument specifying the page of the MultiPage with which the event procedure is to be associated.

ActionX and ActionY Required arguments determining the user's horizontal and vertical actions (respectively), as shown in Table 15.6.

TABLE 15.6: *ActionX* and *ActionY* Constants and Values for the *Scroll* Event

CONSTANT	VALUE	SCROLL BOX MOVEMENT
fmScrollActionNoChange	0	There was no change or movement.
fmScrollActionLineUp	1	The user moved the scroll box a short way upward on a vertical scroll bar (equivalent to pressing the ↑ key) or a short way to the left on a horizontal scroll bar (equivalent to pressing the ← key).
fmScrollActionLineDown	2	The user moved the scroll box a short way downward on a vertical scroll bar (equivalent to pressing the ↓ key) or a short way to the right on a horizontal scroll bar (equivalent to pressing the → key).
fmScrollActionPageUp	3	The user moved the scroll box up one page on a vertical scroll bar (equivalent to pressing the Page Up key) or one page to the left on a horizontal scroll bar (also equivalent to pressing the Page Up key).
fmScrollActionPageDown	4	The user moved the scroll box down one page on a vertical scroll bar (equivalent to pressing the Page Down key) or one page to the right on a horizontal scroll bar (also equivalent to pressing the Page Down key).

TABLE 15.6:   *ActionX* and *ActionY* Constants and Values for the *Scroll* Event *(CONTINUED)*

CONSTANT	VALUE	SCROLL BOX MOVEMENT
fmScrollActionBegin	5	The user moved the scroll box to the top of a vertical scroll bar or to the left end of a horizontal scroll bar.
fmScrollActionEnd	6	The user moved the scroll box to the bottom of a vertical scroll bar or to the right end of a horizontal scroll bar.
fmScrollActionPropertyChange	8	The user moved the scroll box, changing the value of either the ScrollTop property or the ScrollLeft property.
fmScrollActionControlRequest	9	The scroll action was requested by a control in the container in question.
fmScrollActionFocusRequest	10	The user moved the focus to a different control. This movement scrolls the user form so that the selected control is fully displayed in the available area.

RequestDx   The distance to move the scroll box horizontally, specified in points.

RequestDy   The distance to move the scroll box vertically, specified in points.

ActualDx   The distance the scroll box moved horizontally, measured in points.

ActualDy   The distance the scroll box moved vertically, measured in points.

ZOOM EVENT

The Zoom event fires when the Zoom property of the object is changed at runtime. The Zoom property can be changed either automatically through code or by the user's manipulating a control that changes the property through code; the user can't change the Zoom property manually.

The Zoom property uses this syntax for the control and the UserForm object:

```
Private Sub object_Zoom(Percent As Integer)
```

Here, *object* is a Frame control or a UserForm object. Percent is an Integer argument used to specify the percentage (from 10 percent to 400 percent) the user form is to be zoomed to. By default, user forms and controls are displayed at 100 percent Zoom—full size.

The Zoom property uses this syntax for the MultiPage control:

```
Private Sub multipage_Zoom(ByVal Index As Long, Percent As Integer)
```

Here Index is the index (name or number) of the Page object in the MultiPage control with which the Zoom event procedure is associated.

Zooming a user form zooms all the controls that are on it. For example, say a user form named frmEventsDemo includes a combo box named cmbZoom that offers a selection of zoom percentages. When the user selects an item in the combo box, the Change event for cmbZoom applies the combo box's Value property to the Zoom property of the user form, zooming it to the percentage selected.

Zooming the user form triggers the Zoom event, whose procedure in this example sets the Width and Height of the user form to new values suited to the new zoom percentage:

```
Private Sub cmbZoom_Change()
    frmEventsDemo.Zoom = cmbZoom.Value
End Sub

Private Sub UserForm_Zoom(Percent As Integer)
    frmEventsDemo.Width = 300 * cmbZoom.Value / 100
    frmEventsDemo.Height = 350 * cmbZoom.Value / 100
End Sub
```

LAYOUT EVENT

The Layout event occurs when the size of the frame, multipage control, or user form is changed, either programmatically, automatically by an autosized control becoming resized, or by the user.

By default, the Layout event automatically calculates the new position for any control that has been moved and repaints the screen accordingly. However, you can also use the Layout event for your own purposes if you need to.

The syntax for the Layout event with a Frame control or a UserForm object is

```
Private Sub object_Layout()
```

Here, *object* is a Frame control or a UserForm object.

The syntax for using the Layout event with a MultiPage control is

```
Private Sub multipage_Layout(index As Long)
```

Here, *multipage* is a MultiPage control and index is the Page object in the multipage control.

NOTE When a control is resized, VBA stores its previous height and width in the OldHeight and OldWidth properties, while the Height and Width properties take on the new height and width. To restore a control to its previous size, use the OldHeight and OldWidth properties.

ADDCONTROL EVENT

The AddControl event is triggered when a control is added programmatically to the frame, the multipage control, or the user form at runtime; it isn't triggered when you add a control manually at design time. The event isn't triggered when the user form is initialized unless the Initialize event adds a control to the user form.

The syntax for the AddControl event varies depending on the object or control. The syntax for the UserForm object and the Frame control is

```
Private Sub object_AddControl(ByVal Control As MSForms.Control)
```

Here, *object* is a UserForm object or Frame control, and Control is the control that's being added.

The syntax for the MultiPage control is

```
Private Sub multipage_AddControl(ByVal Index As Long, ByVal Control As
MSForms.Control)
```

Here, Index is the index number or name of the Page object that will receive the control.

For example, the cmdAddControl_Click procedure shown below adds three option buttons (opt1, opt2, and opt3, respectively) to the frame fraOptions and sets properties for the first. (A comment indicates where the code would go on to set properties for the second and third option buttons.) The fraOptions_AddControl event procedure displays a message box giving the number of controls the frame now contains. Because the cmdAddControl_Click procedure adds three controls, the AddControl event fires three times, and the fraOptions_AddControl procedure runs thrice:

```
Private Sub cmdAddControl_click()
    Dim opt1 As OptionButton
    Dim opt2 As OptionButton
    Dim opt3 As OptionButton
    Set opt1 = fraOptions.Controls.Add("Forms.OptionButton.1")
    Set opt2 = fraOptions.Controls.Add("Forms.OptionButton.1")
    Set opt3 = fraOptions.Controls.Add("Forms.OptionButton.1")
    With opt1
        .Left = 10
        .Top = 10
        .Name = "optDomestic"
        .Caption = "Domestic"
        .AutoSize = True
        .Accelerator = "D"
    End With
    'set properties for opt2 and opt3 here
End Sub

Private Sub fraOptions_AddControl(ByVal Control As MSForms.Control)
    MsgBox "The frame now contains " & _
        fraOptions.Controls.Count & " controls."
End Sub
```

REMOVECONTROL EVENT

The RemoveControl event fires when a control is deleted from the frame, multipage control, or user form in question, either programmatically or manually at runtime. (To remove a control manually, the user would typically use a control built into the user form for that purpose.)

The syntax for the RemoveControl event is as follows for all controls but the MultiPage control:

```
Private Sub object_RemoveControl(ByVal Control As MSForms.Control)
```

Here, object is a valid object, and Control is a valid control.

The syntax for the RemoveControl event is as follows for the MultiPage control:

```
Private Sub multipage_RemoveControl(ByVal Index As Long, ByVal Control As
MSForms.Control)
```

Here, multipage is a valid MultiPage object. For a multipage, Index specifies the Page object in the MultiPage control that contains the control to be deleted.

Events That Apply to Many or Most Controls

This section discusses the events that apply to many, most, or all controls. Some of these events apply to the UserForm object as well. These events are Click; Change; Enter and Exit; BeforeUpdate and AfterUpdate; KeyDown, KeyUp, and KeyPress; MouseDown, MouseUp, and MouseMove; BeforeDragOver; BeforeDropOrPaste; DblClick; and Error.

CLICK EVENT

The Click event applies to the CheckBox, ComboBox, CommandButton, Frame, Image, Label, ListBox, MultiPage, OptionButton, TabStrip, and ToggleButton controls. It doesn't apply to the TextBox control, the ScrollBar control, or the SpinButton control, but it does apply to the UserForm object.

The Click event occurs both when the user clicks a control with the primary mouse button and when the user selects a value for a control that has more than one possible value. For most controls, this means that each time the user clicks the control, the event fires. But there are a few exceptions:

♦ Clicking a disabled control fires the Click event of the user form (as if the user were clicking the user form through the control).

♦ The Click event of an OptionButton control fires when the user clicks the option button to select it. If the option button is already selected, clicking it has no effect. (On the other hand, the Click event of a CheckBox control fires each time the user clicks the check box—either to select it or to clear it.)

♦ The Click event of a ListBox control or ComboBox control fires when the user clicks to select an item from the list (not when the user clicks on the drop-down arrow or in the undropped portion of the combo box). If the user clicks an already-selected item, the Click event doesn't fire again.

♦ The Click event of a ToggleButton control occurs whenever the toggle button is clicked and when its Value property is changed. This means that it isn't a good idea to use the Click event of the ToggleButton control to toggle its Value.

♦ The Click event of a selected CommandButton control fires when you press the spacebar.

♦ The Click event of the default command button (the button with its Default property set to True) fires when the user presses Enter with no other command button selected.

♦ The Click event of the command button with its Cancel property set to True fires when the user presses Esc. The Click event for a control with an accelerator key set also fires when the user presses the accelerator key.

For all controls except the TabStrip control and the MultiPage control, the Click event needs no arguments, as follows:

```
Private Sub object_Click()
```

For a TabStrip control or a MultiPage control, you react to the Index argument, a required Long argument that VBA passes to indicate the affected tab or page of the control:

```
Private Sub object_Click(ByVal Index As Long)
```

Here, *object* is a valid MultiPage control or TabStrip control.

Sequence of Events: What Happens When the User Clicks (and Clicks Again)

When the user clicks a command button, the Enter event for the button occurs before the Click event if the click transfers the focus to the command button. When the Enter event for the command button fires, it usually prevents the Click event from firing.

When the user clicks a control, the first event triggered is the MouseDown event, which fires when the user depresses the mouse button. Then the MouseUp event fires when the user releases the mouse button. The Click event occurs after the MouseUp event. If the user clicks again within the double-click timeframe set in Windows, the DblClick event fires, followed by another MouseUp event.

Change Event

The Change event applies to the CheckBox, ComboBox, ListBox, MultiPage, OptionButton, ScrollBar, SpinButton, TabStrip, TextBox, and ToggleButton controls. This event fires when the Value property of a control changes. This change can occur either through an action of the user's (such as selecting an option button, selecting or clearing a checkbox, clicking a toggle button, or changing the page displayed on a multipage control) or through an action taken programmatically at runtime. Bear in mind that when the Change event is fired by an action of the user's, that action may also trigger a Click event. (Even when this happens, Change is regarded as a better way of determining the new Value of the control than Click—though for many purposes Click will work satisfactorily as well.)

NOTE Changing the Value property of a control manually at design time doesn't fire a Change event.

The syntax for the Change event is

```
Private Sub object_Change()
```

The Change event is useful for updating other controls after the user changes a control. For example, if the user enters the name for a new report into a text box (here, txtReportName), you could use the Change event to build in another text box (here, txtFileName) the name of the file in which to save the report:

```
Private Sub txtReportName_Change()
    txtFileName.Text = txtReportName.Text & ".txt"
End Sub
```

Enter and *Exit* Events

The Enter and Exit events apply to CheckBox, ComboBox, CommandButton, Frame, ListBox, Multi-Page, OptionButton, ScrollBar, SpinButton, TabStrip, TextBox, and ToggleButton controls.

The Enter event fires when the focus is moved from one control on a user form to another control. The event fires just before the second control receives the focus.

Like the Enter event, the Exit event fires when the focus is moved from one control on a user form to another control. However, the Exit event fires just before the first event loses the focus.

The syntax for the Enter event is

```
Private Sub object_Enter()
```

The syntax for the `Exit` event is a little more complex:

```
Private Sub object_Exit(ByVal Cancel As MSForms.ReturnBoolean)
```

Here, `Cancel` is a required argument specifying event status. The default setting is `False`, which specifies that the control involved should handle the event and that the focus will pass to the next control; a setting of `True` specifies that the application handle the event, which keeps the focus at the current control.

By using the `Enter` and `Exit` events, you can track the user's progress through the controls on a user form.

The `Exit` event is useful for making sure that the user has made an appropriate selection in the control or has entered a suitable value. For example, you could check the user's entry in the control and, if you find it inappropriate, display a message box alerting the user to the problem, and then return the focus to the control so that the user might try again.

> **NOTE**   Other events that you might use for checking the contents of a control after the user has visited it include AfterUpdate and LostFocus. Similarly, you might use the BeforeUpdate and GotFocus events instead of the Enter event. A significant difference between Enter and GotFocus—and between Exit and LostFocus—is that GotFocus and LostFocus fire when the user form receives or loses the focus, respectively, but Enter and Exit don't fire.

BeforeUpdate Event

The `BeforeUpdate` event applies to the CheckBox, ComboBox, ListBox, OptionButton, ScrollBar, SpinButton, TextBox, and ToggleButton controls. This event occurs as the value of or data in the specified control is changed; you can use the event to evaluate the change and decide whether to implement it.

The syntax for the `BeforeUpdate` event is

```
Private Sub object_BeforeUpdate(ByVal Cancel As MSForms.ReturnBoolean)
```

Here, *object* is a valid object, and `Cancel` is a required argument indicating the status of the event. The default setting of `False` makes the control handle the event; `True` prevents the update from being executed and makes the application handle the event.

Here's the sequence in which events fire as you move to a control, update it, and move on:

◆ The `Enter` event for the control fires when you move the focus to the control.

◆ The `BeforeUpdate` event for the control fires after you've entered the information for the update (for example, after you've pressed a key in a text box) but before the update is executed. By setting `Cancel` to `True`, you can prevent the update from taking place. (If you don't set `Cancel` to `True`, the update occurs, and the `AfterUpdate` event can't prevent it from occurring.)

◆ The `AfterUpdate` event for the control fires after you've entered the information in the control and the update has been executed. If you set the `Cancel` argument for `BeforeUpdate` to `True`, the `AfterUpdate` event doesn't fire.

◆ The `Exit` event for the control fires when you move from this control to another control. (After the `Exit` event fires for the control you've left, the `Enter` event fires for the control to which you have moved the focus.)

AfterUpdate Event

The AfterUpdate event applies to the CheckBox, ComboBox, ListBox, OptionButton, ScrollBar, Spin-Button, TextBox, and ToggleButton controls. This event fires after the user changes information in a control and after that update has been executed.

The syntax for the AfterUpdate event is the same for all the controls and objects it applies to:

```
Private Sub object_AfterUpdate( )
```

KeyDown and *KeyUp* Events

The KeyDown event and KeyUp event apply to the CheckBox, ComboBox, CommandButton, Frame, ListBox, MultiPage, OptionButton, ScrollBar, SpinButton, TabStrip, TextBox, and ToggleButton controls, and to the UserForm object. These events don't apply to the Image and Label controls.

The KeyDown event fires when the user presses a key on the keyboard. The KeyUp event fires when the user lets the key up again. The KeyDown and KeyUp events also occur when a key is sent to the user form or control programmatically by using the SendKeys statement. These events don't occur when the user presses Enter when the user form contains a CommandButton control with its Default property set to True, nor when the user presses Esc when the user form contains a CommandButton control with its Cancel property set to True.

When the keystroke moves the focus to another control, the KeyDown event fires for the original control, while the KeyPress and KeyDown events fire for the control to which the focus is moved.

NOTE   The KeyPress event fires after the KeyDown event and before the KeyUp event.

The syntax for the KeyDown event is

```
Private Sub object_KeyDown(ByVal KeyCode As MSForms.ReturnInteger, ByVal Shift
As Integer)
```

The syntax for the KeyUp event is

```
Private Sub object_KeyUp(ByVal KeyCode As MSForms.ReturnInteger, ByVal Shift
As Integer)
```

Here, *object* is an object name and is required. KeyCode is a required Integer argument specifying the key code of the key pressed. For example, the key code for the letter *t* is 84. The key code isn't an ANSI value—it's a special number that identifies the key on the keyboard.

Shift is a required argument specifying whether the Shift key, the Ctrl key, or the Alt key was pressed. Use the constants or values shown in Table 15.7:

TABLE 15.7:   *Shift* Constants and Values

CONSTANT	VALUE	DESCRIPTION
fmShiftMask	1	Shift key pressed
fmCtrlMask	2	Ctrl key pressed
fmAltMask	4	Alt key pressed

KEYPRESS EVENT

The KeyPress event applies to the CheckBox, ComboBox, CommandButton, Frame, ListBox, Multi-Page, OptionButton, ScrollBar, SpinButton, TabStrip, TextBox, and ToggleButton controls. It also applies to the UserForm object. It doesn't apply to the Label control.

The KeyPress event fires when the user presses an ANSI key—a printable character, Ctrl plus an alphabet character, Ctrl plus a special character, the Esc key, or the Backspace key—while the control or object in question has the focus. Pressing the Tab key, the Enter key, or an arrow key doesn't cause the KeyPress event to fire, nor does a keystroke that moves the focus to another control from the current control.

The Delete key isn't an ANSI key, so pressing the Delete key to delete, say, text in a text box doesn't fire the KeyPress event. But deleting the same text in the same text box using the Backspace key does, because Backspace is an ANSI key.

NOTE   The KeyPress event fires after the KeyDown event and before the KeyUp event. It also fires when you use SendKeys to send keystrokes to a user form programmatically.

The syntax for the KeyPress event is

```
Private Sub object_KeyPress(ByVal KeyAscii As MSForms.ReturnInteger)
```

Here, *object* is a required argument specifying a valid object, and KeyAscii is a required Integer argument specifying an ANSI key code. To get the ANSI key code, use the Asc function. For example, Asc("t") returns the ANSI key code for the letter *t* (the code is 116).

By default, the KeyPress event processes the code for the key pressed—in humble terms, what you press is what you get. For example, if you press the *t* key, you get a *t*; if you press the Delete key, you get a Delete action; and so on. By using a KeyPress event procedure, you can perform checks such as filtering out all nonnumeric keys when the user must enter a numeric value.

MOUSEDOWN EVENT AND *MOUSEUP* EVENT

The MouseDown and MouseUp events apply to the CheckBox, ComboBox, CommandButton, Frame, Image, Label, ListBox, MultiPage, OptionButton, ScrollBar, SpinButton, TabStrip, TextBox, and Toggle-Button controls, and to the UserForm object. The MouseDown event fires when the user depresses a button on the mouse, and the MouseUp event occurs when they release that button. The Click event fires after the MouseUp event occurs.

The syntax for the MouseDown and MouseUp events is as follows for all controls except the Multi-Page control and the TabStrip control:

```
Private Sub object_MouseDown(ByVal Button As Integer, ByVal Shift As Integer, ByVal
X As Single, ByVal Y As Single)

Private Sub object_MouseUp(ByVal Button As Integer, ByVal Shift As Integer, ByVal X
As Single, ByVal Y As Single)
```

The syntax for the MouseDown and MouseUp events with the MultiPage control and the TabStrip control adds an Index argument to specify the index of the page or the tab involved:

```
Private Sub object_MouseUp(ByVal Index As Long, ByVal Button As Integer, ByVal
Shift As Integer, ByVal X As Single, ByVal Y As Single)

Private Sub object_MouseDown(ByVal Index As Long, ByVal Button As Integer, ByVal
Shift As Integer, ByVal X As Single, ByVal Y As Single)
```

Here, *object* is a valid object for the statement.

Index returns −1 if the user clicks outside the page or tab area of the control but still within the control (for example, to the right of the rightmost tab in a top-tab tab strip).

Button is a required Integer argument specifying the mouse button that perpetrated the event. Table 15.8 lists the possible values for Button.

TABLE 15.8: *Button* Values and Constants

CONSTANT	VALUE	DESCRIPTION
fmButtonLeft	1	Left (primary)
fmButtonRight	2	Right (non-primary)
fmButtonMiddle	4	Middle

Shift is a required argument specifying whether the Shift key, the Ctrl key, or the Alt key was pressed. Table 15.9 lists the values for Shift.

TABLE 15.9: *Shift* Values

SHIFT VALUE	KEY OR KEYS PRESSED
1	Shift
2	Ctrl
3	Shift+Ctrl
4	Alt
5	Alt+Shift
6	Alt+Ctrl
7	Alt+Shift+Ctrl

You can also detect a single key by using the key masks listed in Table 15.7, earlier in the chapter.

X is a required Single argument specifying the horizontal position in points from the left edge of the user form, frame, or page. Y is a required Single argument specifying the vertical position in points from the top edge of the user form, frame, or page.

MOUSEMOVE EVENT

The MouseMove event applies to the CheckBox, ComboBox, CommandButton, Frame, Image, Label, ListBox, MultiPage, OptionButton, TabStrip, TextBox, and ToggleButton controls, and to the UserForm object. This event fires when the user moves the mouse over the control or object in question.

The syntax for the MouseMove event is different for the MultiPage control and the TabStrip control than for the other controls and for the UserForm object. The syntax for the other controls is

```
Private Sub object_MouseMove(ByVal Button As Integer, ByVal Shift As Integer, ByVal
X As Single, ByVal Y As Single)
```

The syntax for the MultiPage control and the TabStrip control is

```
Private Sub object_MouseMove(ByVal Index As Long, ByVal Button As Integer, ByVal
Shift As Integer, ByVal X As Single, ByVal Y As Single)
```

Here, *object* is a required argument specifying a valid object.

For the MultiPage control and the TabStrip control, Index is a required argument that returns the index of the Page object in the MultiPage control or the Tab object in the TabStrip control associated with the event procedure.

Button is a required Integer argument that returns which mouse button (if any) the user is pressing. Table 15.10 lists the values for Button.

TABLE 15.10:   *Button* Values

BUTTON VALUE	BUTTON PRESSED
0	No button
1	Left
2	Right
3	Left and right
4	Middle
5	Left and middle
6	Middle and right
7	Left, middle, and right

Shift is a required Integer argument that returns a value indicating whether the user is pressing the Shift, Alt, and/or Ctrl keys. Refer back to Table 15.9 for the list of Shift values.

X is a required Single argument that returns a value specifying the horizontal position in points from the left edge of the user form, frame, or page. Y is a required Single argument specifying the vertical position in points from the top edge of the user form, frame, or page.

As with the MouseDown and MouseUp events, you can also detect a single key by using the key masks listed in Table 15.7 (earlier in the chapter).

Like Windows, user forms largely experience life as a nonstop sequence of mouse events. MouseMove events monitor where the mouse pointer is on the screen and which control has captured it. MouseMove events fire even if you use the keyboard to move a user form from under the mouse pointer, because the mouse pointer ends up in a different place in relation to the user form even though it hasn't moved in the conventional sense.

One use for the MouseMove event is to display appropriate text or an image for a control at which the user is pointing. For example, suppose a user form provides a list of available products, with each product's title appearing in a label. When the user positions the mouse pointer over a title in the label, you could use the MouseMove event to load a picture of the product into an Image control and a short description into another label.

NOTE   The user form traps MouseMove events when the mouse pointer isn't over any control. However, if the user moves the mouse pointer quickly from one control to another very close to it, the user form may fail to trap the movement over the short intervening space.

BEFOREDRAGOVER EVENT

The BeforeDragOver event applies to the UserForm object itself and to the following controls: Check-Box, ComboBox, CommandButton, Frame, Image, Label, ListBox, MultiPage, OptionButton, ScrollBar, SpinButton, TabStrip, TextBox, and ToggleButton. The BeforeDragOver event occurs when the user is performing a drag-and-drop operation.

The syntax for the BeforeDragOver event depends on the object or control in question. The basic syntax for the UserForm object and all controls except the Frame, TabStrip, and MultiPage is as follows, where *object* is a valid UserForm or control:

```
Private Sub object_BeforeDragOver(ByVal Cancel As MSForms.ReturnBoolean, ByVal
Control As MSForms.Control, ByVal Data As MSForms.DataObject, ByVal X As Single,
ByVal Y As Single, ByVal State As MSForms.fmDragState, ByVal Effect As
MSForms.ReturnEffect, ByVal Shift As Integer)
```

The syntax for the BeforeDragOver event with the Frame control is as follows, where *frame* is a valid Frame control:

```
Private Sub frame_BeforeDragOver(ByVal Cancel As MSForms.ReturnBoolean, ByVal
Control As MSForms.Control, ByVal Data As MSForms.DataObject, ByVal X As Single,
ByVal Y As Single, ByVal State As MSForms.fmDragState, ByVal Effect As
MSForms.ReturnEffect, ByVal Shift As Integer)
```

The syntax for the BeforeDragOver event with the MultiPage control is as follows, where *multipage* is a valid MultiPage control:

```
Private Sub multipage_BeforeDragOver(ByVal Index As Long, ByVal Cancel As
MSForms.ReturnBoolean, ByVal Control As MSForms.Control, ByVal Data As
MSForms.DataObject, ByVal X As Single, ByVal Y As Single, ByVal State As
MSForms.fmDragState, ByVal Effect As MSForms.ReturnEffect, ByVal Shift As Integer)
```

The syntax for the BeforeDragOver event with the TabStrip control is as follows, where tabstrip is a valid TabStrip control:

```
Private Sub tabstrip_BeforeDragOver(ByVal Index As Long, ByVal Cancel As
MSForms.ReturnBoolean, ByVal Data As MSForms.DataObject, ByVal X As Single, ByVal Y
As Single, ByVal DragState As MSForms.fmDragState, ByVal Effect As
MSForms.ReturnEffect, ByVal Shift As Integer)
```

These are the different parts of the statements:

◆ Index is the index of the Page object in a MultiPage control, or the Tab object in a TabStrip control, affected by the drag-and-drop.

◆ Cancel is a required argument giving the status of the BeforeDragOver event. The default setting is False, which makes the control handle the event. A setting of True makes the application handle the event.

◆ Control is a required argument specifying the control that is being dragged over.

◆ Data is a required argument specifying the data being dragged.

◆ X is a required argument specifying the horizontal distance in points from the left edge of the control. Y is a required argument specifying the vertical distance in points from the top of the control.

◆ DragState is a required argument specifying where the mouse pointer is in relation to a target (a location on which the data can be dropped). Table 15.11 lists the constants and values for DragState.

◆ Effect is a required argument specifying the operations the source of the drop is to support, as listed in Table 15.12.

◆ Shift is a required argument specifying whether the Shift, Ctrl, or Alt keys are held down during the drag-and-drop operation, as listed in Table 15.7 (earlier in the chapter).

TABLE 15.11: *DragState* Constants and Values

CONSTANT	VALUE	POSITION OF MOUSE POINTER
fmDragStateEnter	0	Within range of a target
fmDragStateLeave	1	Outside the range of a target
fmDragStateOver	2	At a new position, but remains within range of the same target

TABLE 15.12: *Effect* Constants and Values

CONSTANT	VALUE	DROP EFFECT
fmDropEffectNone	0	Doesn't copy or move the source to the target
fmDropEffectCopy	1	Copies the source to the target
fmDropEffectMove	2	Moves the source to the target
fmDropEffectCopyOrMove	3	Copies or moves the source to the target

You use the BeforeDragOver event to control drag-and-drop actions that the user performs. Use the DragState argument to make sure that the mouse pointer is within range of a target.

BeforeDropOrPaste Event

The BeforeDropOrPaste event applies to the CheckBox, ComboBox, CommandButton, Frame, Image, Label, ListBox, MultiPage, OptionButton, ScrollBar, SpinButton, TabStrip, TextBox, and ToggleButton controls, and to the UserForm object.

The BeforeDropOrPaste Event occurs just before the user drops or pastes data onto an object.

The syntax for the BeforeDropOrPaste event is different for the MultiPage control and the Tab-Strip control than for the UserForm object and for the other controls. The basic syntax is

```
Private Sub object_BeforeDropOrPaste(ByVal Cancel As MSForms.ReturnBoolean, ByVal
Control As MSForms.Control, ByVal Action As MSForms.fmAction, ByVal Data As
MSForms.DataObject, ByVal X As Single, ByVal Y As Single, ByVal Effect As
MSForms.ReturnEffect, ByVal Shift As Integer)
```

The syntax for the MultiPage control is as follows, where *multipage* is a valid MultiPage control:

```
Private Sub multipage_BeforeDropOrPaste(ByVal Index As Long, ByVal Cancel  As
MSForms.ReturnBoolean, ByVal Control As MSForms.Control, ByVal Action As
MSForms.fmAction, ByVal Data As MSForms.DataObject, ByVal X As Single, ByVal Y As
Single, ByVal Effect As MSForms.ReturnEffect, ByVal Shift As Integer)
```

The syntax for the TabStrip control is as follows, where *tabstrip* is a valid TabStrip control:

```
Private Sub tabstrip_BeforeDropOrPaste(ByVal Index As Long, ByVal Cancel  As
MSForms.ReturnBoolean, ByVal Action As MSForms.fmAction, ByVal Data As
MSForms.DataObject, ByVal X As Single, ByVal Y As Single, ByVal Effect  As
MSForms.ReturnEffect, ByVal Shift As Integer)
```

Here are the parts of the syntax:

◆ *object* is a required object specifying a valid object.

◆ For the MultiPage control, Index is a required argument specifying the Page object involved.

◆ Cancel is a required argument giving the status of the event. The default setting of False makes the control handle the event; True makes the application handle the event.

◆ Control is a required argument specifying the target control.

◆ Action is a required argument specifying the result of the drag-and-drop operation. Table 15.13 shows the constants and values for Action.

TABLE 15.13:   *Action* Constants and Values

Action CONSTANT	VALUE	ACTION TAKEN
fmActionPaste	2	Pastes the object into the target.
fmActionDragDrop	3	The user has dragged the object from its source and dropped it on the target.

◆ Data is a required argument specifying the data (contained in a DataObject) being dragged and dropped.

◆ X is a required argument specifying the horizontal distance in points from the left edge of the control for the drop. Y is a required argument specifying the vertical distance in points from the top of the control.

◆ Effect is a required argument specifying whether the drag-and-drop operation copies the data or moves it, as listed in Table 15.12 (earlier in the chapter).

Shift is a required argument specifying whether the user has pressed the Shift, Ctrl, and/or Alt keys, as listed in Table 15.7 (earlier in the chapter).

The BeforeDropOrPaste event fires when a data object is transferred to a MultiPage or TabStrip and just before the drop or paste operation occurs on other controls.

DBLCLICK EVENT

The DblClick event applies to the CheckBox, ComboBox, CommandButton, Frame, Image, Label, ListBox, MultiPage, OptionButton, TabStrip, TextBox, and ToggleButton controls. It also applies to the UserForm object. The DblClick event occurs when the user double-clicks a control or object with the primary mouse button. The double-click must be fast enough to register as a double-click in Windows (this speed is controlled by the setting in the Mouse Properties dialog box) and occurs after the MouseDown event, the MouseUp event, and the Click event (for controls that support the Click event).

The DblClick event takes different syntax for the MultiPage control and the TabStrip control than for the other controls and for the user form. For the MultiPage control and the TabStrip control, the syntax is

```
Private Sub object_DblClick(ByVal Index As Long, ByVal Cancel As
MSForms.ReturnBoolean)
```

The syntax for the DblClick event for other controls is

```
Private Sub object_DblClick(ByVal Cancel As MSForms.ReturnBoolean)
```

Here, *object* is a required argument specifying a valid object. For the MultiPage control and the TabStrip control, Index is a required argument specifying the Page object within a MultiPage control or the Tab object within a TabStrip control to be associated with the event procedure.

Cancel is a required argument specifying the status of the event. The default setting of False causes the control to handle the event; True causes the application to handle the event instead and causes the control to ignore the second click.

In controls that support both the Click event and the DblClick event, the Click event occurs before the DblClick event. If you take an interface action (such as displaying a message box) with the Click event procedure, it blocks the DblClick event procedure from running. In the following example, the DblClick event procedure doesn't run:

```
Private Sub CommandButton1_Click()
    MsgBox "Click event"
End Sub

Private Sub CommandButton1_DblClick _
    (ByVal Cancel As MSForms.ReturnBoolean)
    MsgBox "Double-click event"
End Sub
```

However, you can execute non-interface statements in the Click event procedure without blocking the DblClick event procedure. The following example declares a Private String variable named strMessage in the declarations portion of the code sheet for the user form. The Click event procedure for the CommandButton1 command button assigns text to strMessage. The DblClick event procedure assigns more text to strMess and then displays a message box containing strMessage so that you can see that both events have fired. Don't step into this code—run it, or it won't work:

```
Private strMess As String

Private Sub CommandButton1_Click()
    strMess = "Click event" & vbCr
End Sub

Private Sub CommandButton1_DblClick _
    (ByVal Cancel As MSForms.ReturnBoolean)
    strMessage = strMessage & "Double-click event"
    MsgBox strMessage
End Sub
```

For most controls you won't want to use both a Click event procedure and a DblClick event procedure—you'll choose one or the other as appropriate to the control's needs.

ERROR EVENT

The Error event applies to the CheckBox, ComboBox, CommandButton, Frame, Image, Label, ListBox, MultiPage, OptionButton, ScrollBar, SpinButton, TabStrip, TextBox, and ToggleButton controls. It also applies to the UserForm object. The Error event fires when a control encounters an error and is unable to return information about the error to the program that called the control.

The syntax for the Error event for the UserForm object and for all controls except the MultiPage control is

```
Private Sub object_Error(ByVal Number As Integer, ByVal Description As
MSForms.ReturnString, ByVal SCode As Long, ByVal Source As String, ByVal HelpFile
As String, ByVal HelpContext As Long, ByVal CancelDisplay As MSForms.ReturnBoolean)
```

The syntax for the Error event for the MultiPage control is as follows, where *multipage* is a valid MultiPage control:

```
Private Sub multipage_Error(ByVal Index As Long, ByVal Number As Integer, ByVal
Description As MSForms.ReturnString, ByVal SCode As Long, ByVal Source As String,
ByVal HelpFile As String, ByVal HelpContext As Long, ByVal CancelDisplay As
MSForms.ReturnBoolean)
```

These are the components of the syntax:

◆ *object* is the name of a valid object.

◆ For a MultiPage control, Index is the index of the Page object in the MultiPage control associated with the event.

◆ Number is a required argument that returns the value used by the control to identify the error.

- ◆ `Description` is a required String argument describing the error.

- ◆ `SCode` is a required argument giving the OLE status code for the error.

- ◆ `Source` is a required String argument containing the string identifying the control involved.

- ◆ `HelpFile` is a required String argument containing the full path to the Help file that contains the `Description`.

- ◆ `HelpContext` is a required Long argument containing the context ID for the `Description` within the Help file.

- ◆ `CancelDisplay` is a required Boolean argument that controls whether VBA displays the error message in a message box.

Events That Apply Only to a Few Controls

This section discusses the three events that apply only to one or two controls. The first of the three is the `DropButtonClick` event, which applies only to the ComboBox and TextBox controls; the second and third are the `SpinUp` and `SpinDown` events, which apply only to the SpinButton control.

DROPBUTTONCLICK EVENT

The `DropButtonClick` event fires when the user displays or hides a drop-down list on a ComboBox by clicking the drop-down button or by pressing the F4 key. `DropButtonClick` also fires when the user press the F4 key with a TextBox control selected, though this manifestation of the event is arcane enough to be singularly useless. It also fires when the `DropDown` method is executed in VBA to display the drop-down list, and it fires again when the `DropDown` method is executed again to hide the drop-down list.

The syntax for the `DropButtonClick` event is

```
Private Sub object_DropButtonClick( )
```

Here, *object* is a valid ComboBox or TextBox control.

One use for the `DropButtonClick` event is to add items to a ComboBox control rather than adding them at load time by using the `Initialize` event. By adding these items only on demand (I'm assuming the user might not use the ComboBox control at all or might type information into its text box area), you can cut down on load time for the user form. You can also load the ComboBox with data relevant to the other choices the user has made in the dialog box, allowing for more targeted information than you could have provided by loading the ComboBox with the `Initialize` event.

SPINDOWN AND *SPINUP* EVENTS

The `SpinDown` and `SpinUp` events apply only to the SpinButton control. `SpinDown` and `SpinUp` are used to control what happens when the user clicks either the down-arrow button and up-arrow button, respectively, of a vertical SpinButton control or the right-arrow button and left-arrow button, respectively, of a horizontal SpinButton control. The `SpinDown` event fires when the user clicks the down-arrow or right-arrow button, and the `SpinUp` event fires when the user clicks the up-arrow or left-arrow button.

The syntax for the SpinUp event and the SpinDown event is

```
Private Sub spinbutton_SpinDown( )
Private Sub spinbutton_SpinUp( )
```

Here, *spinbutton* is a SpinButton control.

By default, the SpinDown event decreases the Value property of the SpinButton by the SmallChange increment, and the SpinUp event increases it.

Part 5

Creating Effective Code

Chapter 16

Building Modular Code and Using Classes

- ◆ Modular code: What, where, and why?
- ◆ Arranging your code in modules
- ◆ Calling a procedure
- ◆ Making logical and visual improvements to your code
- ◆ Passing information from one procedure to another
- ◆ Understanding what classes are and what they're for
- ◆ Creating an object class
- ◆ Creating properties for the class
- ◆ Creating methods for the class
- ◆ Using the class

This chapter shows you how to start building modular code—code broken up into individual components rather than all built together into a monolithic lump. You'll also see how to approach creating reusable code that you can use in other procedures.

The second part of this chapter discusses how you can build and use your own classes in VBA to implement custom objects, store information in them, and return information from them.

Creating Modular Code

The code that you've created so far in this book has been effective, but much of it has been less concise and less elegant than it might be. This section shows you how to make some improvements in your code.

NOTE   *Elegant* in the context of computer code means not only that the code is bug-free and impeccably put together, and that the interface is well designed, but also that the code contains nothing extra—it has been stripped down to the minimum required to achieve the desired effect.

What Is Modular Code?

Modular code is code composed of different procedures that you can use in combination. The name doesn't specifically come from the fact that you store your VBA code in modules (although you do continue to do so).

For example, suppose you're working in Word. You could take a monolithic approach and create a single procedure that created a document based on the user's choice of template, performed certain operations on that document (for example, inserting text and formatting it), saved it in a particular folder under a name of the user's choice, printed it to a specific printer, and then closed it.

Alternatively, you could take a modular approach and create several separate procedures—one for creating a document based on the user's choice of template, another for performing the text and formatting operations, another for saving the document, another for printing the document to the correct printer, and another for closing the document. You could then create a procedure that runs these procedures to achieve the same effect as the monolithic procedure. You could also create other procedures that use the individual procedures in different combinations with other procedures to achieve different effects.

Advantages of Using Modular Code

Modular code has several advantages over code that lumps everything together in one long listing. For one thing, it's often easier to write modular code, because you create a number of short procedures, each of which performs a specific task. You can usually debug these procedures relatively easily too, because their shorter length makes it simpler to identify, locate, and eliminate bugs. The procedures will also be more readable because they're less complex, and you can more easily follow what they do.

Modular code also provides a more efficient approach to programming, for four reasons:

- By breaking your code into procedures, you can repeat actions at different points in a sequence of procedures without needing to repeat the lines of code. Having less code should make your procedures run faster.

- By reusing whole procedures, you can greatly reduce the amount of code you have to write. And by writing less code, you give yourself less chance to write new errors into it.

- If you need to change an item in the code, you can make a single change in the appropriate procedure instead of having to make changes at a number of locations in a long procedure (and perhaps missing some of them). This change then carries through to all procedures that call the procedure.

- You can call individual procedures from other procedures without having to assimilate them into another procedure. Just think how tedious it would be if you had to create each of VBA's many functions from scratch instead of being able to invoke them at will. You can do much the same with your code.

How to Approach Creating Modular Code

How much you worry about creating modular code will vary from project to project and from procedure to procedure. For example, if you record a macro to perform a one-time task on a number of presentations, there's no need to worry about breaking it down into its components and formalizing them as procedures. On the other hand, when you sit down to plan a procedure that's going to automate the creation of your company's budget-estimate spreadsheets, you can benefit greatly from planning the code as a set of procedures.

You can go about creating modular code in two main ways:

◆ Record (if the application you're using supports the VBA Macro Recorder) or write a procedure as usual and then examine it and break it into modules as necessary. This is a great way to start creating modular code, but it's usually less efficient: You'll end up spending a lot of time retrofitting your procedures as you break them into procedures.

◆ Plan the different actions that a procedure will take and create each action (or set of actions) as a separate procedure. This method requires more forethought but usually proves more efficient in the long run.

Arranging Your Code in Modules

Once you've created a set of procedures, you can move them to a different module within the same project, or even to a different project. By grouping your procedures in modules, you can easily distribute the procedures to your colleagues without including procedures they don't need. And by grouping your modules in projects, you give yourself an even easier way of distributing the modules and procedures. In addition, you can remove from your immediate working environment any modules of code that you don't need, thus avoiding slowing your computer.

TIP Give your modules descriptive names so that you can instantly identify them in the Organizer dialog box (in Microsoft applications) and other module-management tools. Avoid leaving modules named Module*n*, because it's all too easy to get them confused.

Calling a Procedure

When a procedure needs to use another procedure, it *calls* it in the same way that you learned to call a function in Chapter 9. To call a procedure in the same project, either enter the name of the procedure to be called as a statement in the calling procedure or use a Call statement with the name of the procedure. The syntax for the Call statement is the same for procedures as for functions:

```
[Call] name[, argumentlist]
```

Here, *name* is a required String argument giving the name of the procedure to call. Meanwhile, *argumentlist* is an optional argument providing a comma-delimited list of the variables, arrays, or expressions to pass to the procedure. You use *argumentlist* only for procedures that require arguments.

For example, the following CreateReceiptLetter procedure calls the procedure FormatDocument:

```
Sub CreateReceiptLetter()
    'other actions here
    Call FormatDocument
    'other actions here
End Sub
```

You can also omit the Call keyword, using just the name of the procedure:

```
Sub CreateReceiptLetter()
    'other actions here
    FormatDocument
    'other actions here
End Sub
```

In the following example, the `Calling` procedure calls the `CallMe` procedure, which takes the String argument `strFeedMe`. Note that when you use `Call`, you need to enclose the argument list in parentheses:

```
Sub Calling()
    Call CallMe("Hello")
End Sub

Sub CallMe(ByVal strFeedMe As String)
    Msgbox strFeedMe
End Sub
```

Again, you can omit the `Call` keyword:

```
Sub Calling2()
    CallMe "Hello"
End Sub
```

As with functions, using the `Call` keyword can make it clearer that your code is calling a procedure, and it enables you to search more easily for your calls.

As well as calling a procedure in the same project, you can call a procedure in another open project in the same host application (but usually not in another application). Typically, the syntax used to call a procedure in another project is

```
Project.Module.Procedure
```

although it may vary by application and version.

To call a procedure in another project, you need to add a reference to that project in the References dialog box. Choose Tools ➢ References, select the project (click the Browse button if you need to browse to it), and then click the OK button. Once this reference is in place, you can call the procedure.

WARNING   You can't add to the current project a reference to a project that itself contains a reference to the current project. When you add the reference and close the References dialog box, the Visual Basic Editor displays a message box with the warning "Cyclic reference of projects not allowed" and doesn't place the reference. (It does close the References dialog box, though.)

Besides writing modular code, you can refine your code and make it run faster by making logical improvements and visual improvements.

Making Logical Improvements to Your Code

Breaking a procedure into procedures can improve the logic of your code by forcing you to consider each set of actions the procedure takes as modular, which means they're separate from other sets of actions. But you can also improve the logic of your code by using explicit variable declarations, by simplifying any code you record, and by using `With` statements to reduce the number of object references.

DECLARING VARIABLES EXPLICITLY INSTEAD OF IMPLICITLY

Instead of declaring variables implicitly, declare all your variables explicitly. This allows VBA to allocate only as much memory as that variable type needs. When you specify the data type of a variable, VBA also doesn't have to spend time checking the data type of the variable each time it encounters it. Better still, you avoid the risk of your unintentionally storing the wrong type of data in the variable:

Because the variable is explicitly typed, VBA gives an error rather than storing the data and changing the variable type.

TIP   You can also specify a data type for an implicitly declared variable by using its type-declaration character, but your code is easier to read and to debug when you use explicit declarations rather than implicit declarations.

Table 16.1 shows the details on the amounts of memory that the different types of variables require.

TABLE 16.1:   Memory Consumed by the Different Types of Variables

VARIABLE	MEMORY NEEDED (BYTES)
Boolean	2
Byte	1
Currency	8
Date	8
Variant/Decimal	12
Double	8
Integer	2
Long	4
Object	4
Single	4
String	Variable-length strings: 10 bytes plus the storage required for the string, which can be up to about 2 billion characters
	Fixed-length strings: the number of bytes required to store the string, which can be from 1 to about 64,000 characters
Variant	Variants that contain numbers: 16 bytes
	Variants that contain characters: 22 bytes plus the storage required for the characters

How much memory you save by specifying data types, and how much difference choosing variable types makes to your procedures, depends on the type of work you're doing. For example, if you store a million characters in a variable, the 12 bytes you save by specifying that it's a String variable rather than a Variant variable make little difference. But if you use many variables on a computer with limited memory, specifying the appropriate data types for your variables may save enough memory to enable your procedure to run where it otherwise wouldn't have been able to, or enable it to run faster.

A second reason for declaring your variables explicitly rather than implicitly is to make your code easier to read and to debug.

A third reason for declaring your variables explicitly is that you can implement some runtime range checking. If you *know* something will be less than 32,768, and you declare it as being the Integer data type, you'll automatically get a helpful error when a Long creeps into it somehow at runtime.

SIMPLIFYING RECORDED CODE

The Macro Recorder (in the Microsoft applications that support it) provides a great way to kick-start creating code by letting you identify quickly the objects the procedure will need to work with and the methods and properties you'll need to use with them. But as you've seen, the drawback of the Macro Recorder is that it tends to record a lot of code that you don't actually need in your procedures, because it records all the commands and settings you might be trying to record. For example, when you record a procedure that changes one setting in a dialog box such as the Font dialog box in Word, the Macro Recorder records all the other settings on not only that page of the dialog box but on all the other pages as well, just in case you wanted them.

Once you've finished recording the procedure, you'll often want to open it to make minor adjustments; add loops, decisions, or UI items (message boxes, input boxes, or user forms); or even lift parts of the code for use in other procedures. When you do this, examine the code the Macro Recorder has recorded and, where possible, strip it down to leave only the pieces that you need.

Take this Word example. Compare the `Recorded_Macro_Applying_Arial_Font` procedure that follows with the `Stripped_Down_Procedure_Applying_Arial_Font` procedure that comes after it:

```
Sub Recorded_Macro_Applying_Arial_Font()
'
' Recorded_Macro_Applying_Arial_Font
' Macro recorded 7/07/06 by Peter Beier
'
    With Selection.Font
        .Name = "Arial"
        .Size = 10
        .Bold = False
        .Italic = False
        .Underline = wdUnderlineNone
        .StrikeThrough = False
        .DoubleStrikeThrough = False
        .Outline = False
        .Emboss = False
        .Shadow = False
        .Hidden = False
        .SmallCaps = False
        .AllCaps = False
        .Color = wdColorAutomatic
        .Engrave = False
        .Superscript = False
        .Subscript = False
        .Spacing = 0
        .Scaling = 100
        .Position = 0
        .Kerning = 0
```

```
            .Animation = wdAnimationNone
        End With
    End Sub

    Sub Stripped_Down_Procedure_Applying_Arial_Font()
        Selection.Font.Name = "Arial"
    End Sub
```

As you can see, the `Stripped_Down_Procedure_Applying_Arial_Font` code has the same effect as the recorded procedure, but it contains three lines to the recorded procedure's thirty.

USING *WITH* STATEMENTS TO SIMPLIFY YOUR CODE

When you're performing multiple actions with an object, you can often use `With` statements to reduce the number of object references involved. This simplifies your code and may make it run marginally faster. When you need to work with multiple objects in a single object, you can either use separate `With` statements or pick the lowest common denominator of the objects you want to work with and use a common `With` statement along with nested `With` statements.

For example, the following statements contain multiple references to the first `Paragraph` object—`Paragraphs(1)`—in the `ActiveDocument` object in Word:

```
ActiveDocument.Paragraphs(1).Range.Font.Bold = True
ActiveDocument.Paragraphs(1).Range.Font.Name = "Times New Roman"
ActiveDocument.Paragraphs(1).LineSpacingRule = wdLineSpaceSingle
ActiveDocument.Paragraphs(1).Borders(1).LineStyle = wdLineStyleDouble
ActiveDocument.Paragraphs(1).Borders(1).ColorIndex = wdBlue
```

Instead, however, you could use a `With` statement that references the `Paragraphs(1)` object in the `ActiveDocument` object to simplify the number of references involved:

```
With ActiveDocument.Paragraphs(1)
    .Range.Font.Bold = True
    .Range.Font.Name = "Times New Roman"
    .LineSpacingRule = wdLineSpaceSingle
    .Borders(1).LineStyle = wdLineStyleDouble
    .Borders(1).ColorIndex = wdBlue
End With
```

You can further reduce the number of object references here by using nested `With` statements for the `Font` object in the `Range` object and for the `Borders(1)` object:

```
With ActiveDocument.Paragraphs(1)
    With .Range.Font
        .Bold = True
        .Name = "Times New Roman"
    End With
    .LineSpacingRule = wdLineSpaceSingle
    With .Borders(1)
        .LineStyle = wdLineStyleDouble
        .ColorIndex = wdBlue
    End With
End With
```

DON'T USE *WITH* STATEMENTS POINTLESSLY

With statements are great for simplifying object references and making your code easier to read, but don't use them just because you can. If you have only one statement within a With statement, as in the following example (which again uses Word), you're probably wasting your time typing extra code:

```
With ActiveDocument.Sections(1).Headers(wdHeaderFooterPrimary) _
    .Range.Words(1)
    .Bold = True
End With
```

Likewise, don't nest With statements unless you need to:

```
With ActiveDocument
    With .Sections(1)
        With .Headers(wdHeaderFooterPrimary)
            With .Range
                With .Words(1)
                    With .Font
                        .Italic = True
                        .Bold = False
                        .Color = wdColorBlack
                    End With
                End With
            End With
        End With
    End With
End With
```

This code is better represented like this:

```
With ActiveDocument.Sections(1).Headers(wdHeaderFooterPrimary).Range. _
    Words(1).Font
    .Italic = True
    .Bold = False
    .Color = wdColorBlack
End With
```

OPTIMIZING YOUR *SELECT CASE* STATEMENTS

When you use a Select Case statement, arrange the Case statements so that the most likely ones appear first. This saves VBA some work and time—VBA goes through the Case statements until it finds a match, so the sooner the match, the quicker the execution of the statement.

DON'T CHECK THINGS POINTLESSLY

If you need to implement a setting (especially a Boolean one) every time a particular procedure runs, there's no point in checking the current value. For example, suppose you wanted to make sure the EnableAutoRecover property (a Boolean property that sets or returns whether the AutoRecover feature is on for the workbook) of the `ActiveWorkbook` object in Excel is set to `True`. You could check the current value of `EnableAutoRecover` and, if it is `False`, set it to `True` like this:

```
If ActiveWorkbook.EnableAutoRecover = False Then _
    ActiveWorkbook.EnableAutoRecover = True
```

But that wastes code. Instead, simply set the property to `True`:

```
ActiveWorkbook.EnableAutoRecover = True
```

REMOVING UNUSED ELEMENTS FROM YOUR CODE

To improve the efficiency of your code, try to remove all unused elements from it. When creating a complex project with many interrelated procedures, it's easy to end up with some procedures that are almost or entirely useless.

You'll find it easier to remove superfluous procedures if you've commented your code comprehensively while creating it so you can be sure that what you're removing is unused rather than used. If you're in doubt as to which procedure is calling which, display the Call Stack dialog box (see Figure 16.1); choose View ➢ Call Stack, or press Ctrl+L) to see what's happening.

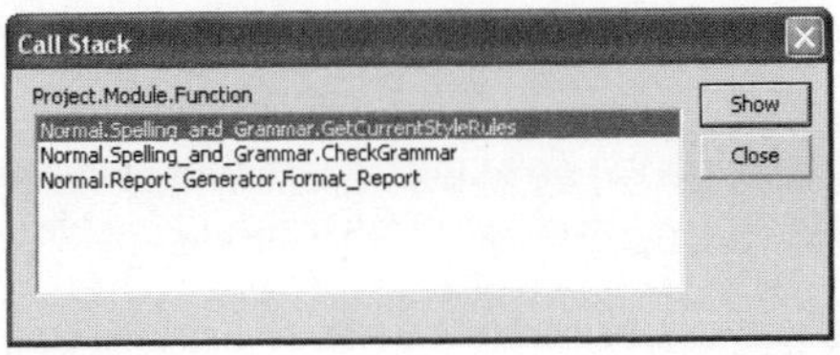

FIGURE 16.1

The Call Stack dialog box lets you see which procedure has called which.

Alternatively, try one of these techniques:

◆ Set a breakpoint at the beginning of a suspect procedure so that you'll be alerted when it's called.

◆ Display message boxes at decisive junctures in your code.

◆ Use a `Debug.Print` statement at an appropriate point (again, perhaps the beginning of a procedure) to implement temporary logging of information in the Immediate window.

Before you remove an apparently dead procedure from your code, make sure not only that it's unused in the way the procedure is currently being run, but also that it's not used in ways in which the procedure *might* be run were circumstances different. If you think that the procedure might still be used, try moving it to another project from which you can easily restore it, rather than deleting it outright.

Once you've removed the extra procedures, examine the variables in the procedures. Even if you're using the `Option Explicit` declaration and declaring every variable explicitly, check that you haven't declared variables that end up not being used. For simple projects, you'll be able to catch the unused variables by using the Locals window to see which of them never get assigned a value. For more complex projects, you may want to try some of the assorted third-party tools that help you remove unneeded elements from your code.

TIP Before removing an entire module, use the File ➢ Export File command to export a copy of the module to a `.BAS` file in a safe storage location in case the module contains anything you'll subsequently discover to be of value. Similarly, export your user forms to `.FRM` files and your classes to `.CLS` files.

If in doubt, comment out the declaration of the supposedly superfluous variable, make sure you're using Option Explicit, and run the code a few more times, exercising the different paths that it can take. If you don't get a "Variable not defined" compile error, you can probably eliminate the variable.

Making Visual Improvements to Your Code

The second category of improvements you can make to your code consists of visual improvements. These improvements are not about aesthetics, but about making your code as easy to read, maintain, and modify as possible.

INDENTING THE DIFFERENT LEVELS OF CODE

As you've seen in the examples so far in this book, you can make your code much easier to follow by indenting the lines of code with tabs or spaces to show their logical relation to each other. You can click the Indent and Outdent buttons on the Edit toolbar or press Tab and Shift+Tab to quickly indent or unindent a selected block of code, with the relative indentation of the lines within the block remaining the same.

NOTE   You can't indent labels. If you try to indent a label, the Visual Basic Editor removes all spaces to the left of the label as soon as you move the insertion point off the line containing the label. This lack of indentation makes labels easy to spot.

USING LINE-CONTINUATION CHARACTERS TO BREAK LONG LINES

Use the line-continuation character (an underscore after a space) to break long lines of code into two or more shorter lines. Breaking lines makes long statements fit within the Code window on an average-size monitor at a readable point size and enables you to break the code into more logical segments.

USING THE CONCATENATION CHARACTER TO BREAK LONG STRINGS

You can't use the line-continuation character to break a long string, so you must divide the string and then use the concatenation character (&) to attach the parts together again. You can separate the parts of the divided string with the line-continuation character. For example, consider a long string such as this:

```
strMessageText = "The macro has finished running. Please check your presentation
➡ to ensure that all blank slides have been removed."
```

Instead, you could divide the string into two, and then rejoin it like this:

```
strMessageText = "The macro has finished running. " & _
    "Please check your presentation to ensure that " & _
    "all blank slides have been removed."
```

NOTE   You can also use the addition character (+) to concatenate one string with another but not to concatenate a string and a numeric variable—VBA tries to add them instead of concatenating them. Your code is easier to read if you stick with the concatenation character for concatenating strings.

USING BLANK LINES TO BREAK UP YOUR CODE

To make your code more readable, use blank lines to separates statements into logical groups. For example, you might segregate all the variable declarations in a procedure as shown in the example below so that they stand out more clearly:

```
Sub Create_Rejection_Letter
```

```
Dim strApplicantFirst As String, strApplicantInitial As String, _
    strApplicantLast As String, strApplicantTitle As String
Dim strJobTitle As String
Dim dteDateApplied As Date, dteDateInterviewed As Date
Dim blnExperience As Boolean

'next statements in the procedure
```

USING VARIABLES TO SIMPLIFY COMPLEX SYNTAX

You can use variables to simplify and shorten complex syntax. For example, you could display a message box by using an awkwardly long statement such as this one:

```
If MsgBox("The document contains no text." & vbCr & vbCr _
    & "Click the Yes button to continue formatting the document." & _
    " Click the No button to cancel the procedure.", _
    vbYesNo & vbQuestion, _
    "Error Selecting Document: Cancel Procedure?") Then
```

Alternatively, you could use one String variable for building the message and another String variable for the title:

```
Dim strMsg As String
Dim strTBar As String
strMsg = "The document contains no text." & vbCr & vbCr
strMsg = strMsg & "Click the Yes button to continue formatting the document. "
strMsg = strMsg & "Click the No button to cancel the procedure."
strTBar = "Error Selecting Document: Cancel Procedure?"
If MsgBox(strMsg, vbYesNo & vbQuestion, strTBar) Then
```

At first sight, this code looks more complex than the straightforward message box statement, mostly because of the explicit variable declarations that increase the length of the code segment. But in the long run, this type of arrangement is much easier to read and modify.

NOTE In the previous example, you could also replace the vbYesNo & vbQuestion part of the MsgBox statement with a variable (preferably a Long rather than a Variant). But doing so makes the code harder to read and is seldom worthwhile.

PASSING INFORMATION FROM ONE PROCEDURE TO ANOTHER USING ARGUMENTS

Often when you call another procedure, you'll need to pass information to it from the calling procedure and, when the procedure has run, pass back either other information or a modified version of the same information.

The best way to pass information from one procedure to another is by using arguments. You declare the arguments to pass in the declaration line of the procedure that passes them. The arguments appear in the parentheses after the procedure's name. You can pass either a single argument (as the first of the following statements does) or multiple arguments separated by commas (as the second does):

```
Sub PassOneArgument(MyArg)
Sub PassTwoArguments(FirstArg, SecondArg)
```

As with functions (discussed in Chapter 9), you can pass an argument either *by reference* or *by value*. When a procedure passes an argument to another procedure by reference, the recipient procedure gets access to the memory location where the original variable is stored and can change the original variable. By contrast, when a procedure passes an argument to another procedure by value, the recipient procedure gets only a copy of the information in the variable and can't change the information in the original variable.

Passing an argument by reference is useful when you want to manipulate the variable in the recipient procedure and then return the variable to the procedure from which it originated. Passing an argument by value is useful when you want to use the information stored in the variable in the recipient procedure and at the same time make sure that the original information in the variable doesn't change.

By reference is the default way to pass an argument, but you can also use the ByRef keyword to state explicitly that you want to pass an argument by reference. Both of the following statements pass the argument MyArg by reference:

```
Sub PassByReference(MyArg)
Sub PassByReference(ByRef MyArg)
```

To pass an argument by value, you must use the ByVal keyword. The following statement passes the ValArg argument by value:

```
Sub PassByValue(ByVal ValArg)
```

If necessary, you can pass some arguments for a procedure by reference and others by value. The following statement passes the MyArg argument by reference and the ValArg argument by value:

```
Sub PassBoth(ByRef MyArg, ByVal ValArg)
```

You can explicitly declare the data type of arguments you pass in order to take up less memory and ensure that your procedures are passing the type of information you intend them to. But when passing an argument by reference, you need to make sure that the data type of the argument you're passing matches the data type expected in the procedure. For example, if you declare a string and try to pass it as an argument when the receiving procedure is expecting a variant, VBA gives an error.

To declare the data type of an argument, include a data-type declaration in the argument list. The following statement declares MyArg as a string to be passed by reference and ValArg as a variant to be passed by value:

```
Sub PassBoth(ByRef MyArg As String, ByVal ValArg As Variant)
```

You can specify an optional argument by using the Optional keyword. Place the Optional keyword before the ByRef or ByVal keyword if you need to use ByRef or ByVal:

```
Sub PassBoth(ByRef MyArg As String, ByVal ValArg As Variant, _
    Optional ByVal MyOptArg As Variant)
```

Listing 16.1 shows a segment of a procedure that uses arguments to pass information from one procedure to another.

LISTING 16.1:

```
1.  Sub GetCustomerInfo()
2.      Dim strCustName As String, strCustCity As String, _
            strCustPhone As String
```

```
3.        'Get strCustName, strCustCity, strCustPhone from sources
4.        CreateCustomer strCustName, strCustCity, strCustPhone
5.    End Sub
6.
7.    Sub CreateCustomer(ByRef strCName As String, _
          ByRef strCCity As String, ByVal strCPhone As String)
8.        Dim strCustomer As String
9.        strCustomer = strCName & vbTab & strCCity _
              & vbTab & strCPhone
10.       'take action with strCustomer string here
11.   End Sub
```

Listing 16.1 contains two minimalist procedures—GetCustomerInfo and CreateCustomer—that show how to use arguments to pass information between procedures:

◆ The first procedure, GetCustomerInfo, explicitly declares three String variables in line 2: strCustName, strCustCity, and strCustPhone.

◆ Line 3 contains a comment indicating where the procedure would assign information to the variables.

◆ Line 4 calls the CreateCustomer procedure and passes to it the variables strCustName, strCustCity, and strCustPhone as arguments. Because this statement doesn't use the Call keyword, the arguments aren't enclosed in parentheses.

◆ Execution then switches to line 7, which starts the CreateCustomer procedure by declaring the three String arguments it uses: strCName and strCCity are to be passed by reference, and strCPhone is to be passed by value.

◆ Line 8 declares the String variable strCustomer. Line 9 then assigns to strCustomer the information in strCName, a tab, the information in strCCity, another tab, and the information in strCPhone.

◆ Line 10 contains a comment indicating where the procedure would take action with the strCustomer string (for example, dumping it into some kind of primitive database), and line 11 ends the procedure.

PASSING INFORMATION FROM ONE PROCEDURE TO ANOTHER USING PRIVATE OR PUBLIC VARIABLES

Another way to pass information from one procedure to another is to use either private variables or public variables. You can use private variables if the procedures that need to share information are located in the same module. If the procedures are located in different modules, you'll need to use public variables to pass the information.

WARNING Using private or public variables to pass information from one procedure to another is widely considered poor programming practice. Doing so requires more memory than using arguments and makes it harder to track the flow of information between procedures, especially when several procedures are involved. However, you may sometimes find this method of passing information helpful—or you may be required to work with someone else's code that uses this method.

Listing 16.2 contains an example of passing information by using private variables.

LISTING 16.2:

```
1.   Private strPassMe As String
2.
3.   Sub PassingInfo()
4.       strPassMe = "Hello."
5.       PassingInfoBack
6.       MsgBox strPassMe
7.   End Sub
8.
9.   Sub PassingInfoBack()
10.      strPassMe = strPassMe & " How are you?"
11.  End Sub
```

Listing 16.2 begins by declaring the private String variable strPassMe at the beginning of the code sheet for the module. strPassMe is then available to all the procedures in the module.

The PassingInfo procedure (lines 3 to 7) assigns the text Hello. (with the period) to strPassMe in line 4 and then calls the PassingInfoBack procedure in line 5. Execution then shifts to line 9, which starts the PassingInfoBack procedure. Line 10 adds How are you? with a leading space to the strPassMe String variable. Line 11 ends the PassingInfoBack procedure, at which point execution returns to the PassingInfo procedure at line 6, which displays a message box containing the strPassMe string (now *Hello. How are you?*). Line 7 ends the procedure.

Creating and Using Classes

A *class* is the formal definition of an object—typically, a custom object. By defining classes, you can build your own custom objects. A class acts as a sort of template for an object: Once you've created the class, you can create objects based on it.

What Can You Do with Class Modules?

You can use classes to store information, to process information, and to make information accessible to the various objects in an application. For example, if you retrieve information from outside the host application you're using and need to make it available to your VBA procedures in that host application, you might encapsulate it in a class to simplify access to the information. Using a class is neater and more efficient than, say, using public variables to store information and make it available.

A Brief Overview

To create a class, you insert a class module in a project and give the class the name by which you'll access it. You then create on the class's code sheet the code (constant and variable declarations, procedures, and functions) that defines the properties and methods that the class will have. When you've finished, the class contains all the information that the custom object needs to perform its tasks and store data.

Instead of executing the code in your class module as you execute code in a code module, you declare an object variable of the class's type and then use the objects and properties of that method in your code.

Classes sometimes seem difficult to grasp, so this section presents a simple example of a class that relates to something physical—the book you're holding. The example describes a class named Book that contains the salient information about a book. After creating the class, the example adds this book's information to it so that you can see how the class works.

NOTE The example class works in any VBA host application.

Planning Your Class

Before you start creating a class, decide the following:

- What the object that the class describes does.

- What information the class needs to contain for the object to do what it's supposed to do. You use variables and properties to store this information. You use variables to store information inside the object and properties to make available pieces of that information that need to be accessed from outside the object. You can create both read-only and read/write properties.

- What actions the user will need to take with the class. You create procedures and functions to implement the methods that make these actions available—procedures for the methods that take an action and functions for the methods that return a value.

Each object based on the Book class contains information about a book project. The class requires properties for storing information such as the title, author, and price, and a method to display all the book information at the same time.

Creating the Class Module

The first step in creating your class is to insert a class module in the appropriate project. You create a class module in much the same way as you create a regular module.

In the Project Explorer, right-click the target project or one of the items it contains and choose Insert ➤ Class Module from the context menu. Alternatively, choose Insert ➤ Class Module from the menu bar, or click the Insert button on the Standard toolbar and choose Class Module from the drop-down list. The Visual Basic Editor creates a new class module named Class*n* (where *n* is the next-higher unused consecutive number) and opens a Code window for it. If the project doesn't already contain a Class Modules folder, VBA adds one, and it appears in the Project Explorer.

If you have the Require Variable Declarations check box selected (on the Editor page of the Options dialog box for the Visual Basic Editor), the Visual Basic Editor places an Option Explicit statement in the declarations area at the top of the code sheet for the class.

NOTE If you don't have Require Variable Declarations selected, it's a good idea to add the Option Explicit statement anyway to force yourself to declare variables explicitly in the class module.

Naming the Class

Now change the name of the class to something more descriptive than Class*n*. Display the Properties window (if it's not already displayed) and enter the new name in the (Name) text box. Make the name descriptive, because you'll be using it in your code and you'll need to grasp its function immediately. The example class is named Book. Press Enter or click elsewhere in the Visual Basic Editor window to make the change take effect.

Setting the *Instancing* Property

The Instancing property controls whether the class module is visible from a project that contains a reference to the project that the class module is in. The default setting, 1 - Private, prevents other projects from seeing the class module and from working with instances of that class. The other setting is 2 - PublicNonCreatable, which allows a project with a reference set to the class's project to see the class and work with instances of it created by the class's project. The project with the reference still can't create instances of the class by itself.

If you need other projects to be able to access instances of the class that were created by projects other than them, set the Instancing property to 2 – PublicNonCreatable. Otherwise, leave the default setting of 1 – Private intact.

Declaring Variables and Constants for the Class

Next, declare the variables and constants that the class will need for its internal operations. These declarations work just like the declarations you've met so far in the book, except that you'll probably want to use a naming convention to indicate that the variables and constants belong to the class. The example uses the prefix book on the constants and variables to denote that they're part of the Book class.

The Book class uses the declarations shown in the following snippet to declare one constant (bookName) and five variables (bookTitle, bookAuthor, bookPages, bookPrice, and bookPublicationDate) of assorted types:

```
Const bookName = "Book Project"

Dim bookTitle As String
Dim bookAuthor As String
Dim bookPages As Long
Dim bookPrice As Currency
Dim bookPublicationDate As Date
```

Adding Properties to the Class

Now add the properties to the class. Table 16.2 lists the properties that the Book class uses.

You can create properties for a class in either of two ways. The first way is less formal than the second but provides you with less control over the properties.

TABLE 16.2: Properties of the *Book* Class

PROPERTY	DESCRIPTION
ISBN	A read-only String property that contains the International Standard Book Number (ISBN) for the book. Creating a new object of the Book class prompts the user for the ISBN; after this, the property can't be changed.
Title	A read/write String property that sets or returns the formal title of the book.
Author	A read/write String property that sets or returns the author's name.
Pages	A read/write Long property that sets or returns the page count of the book.
Price	A read/write Currency property that sets or returns the price of the book.
PublicationDate	A read/write Date property that sets or returns the publication date of the book.
HardCover	A read/write Boolean property that specifies whether the book is hardcover (True) or softcover (False).
CD	A read/write Byte property that sets or returns the number of CDs included with the book.

CREATING A PROPERTY BY USING A PUBLIC VARIABLE

The first way to create a property is to declare a Public variable in the class module. Doing so creates a read/write property with the name of the variable. For example, the following statement (entered in a class module) creates a read/write Boolean property named HardCover:

```
Public HardCover As Boolean
```

Using a Public variable is an easy way to create a property, but it's a bit limited: You can't choose to make the property read-only (or write-only), and you can't execute any other code when you set or return the value of the property.

You can then set and return the property in the normal manner. For example, say we've created the Boolean property HardCover in an instance named MastVBA of the Book class. The following statements set the property and then display a message box returning it:

```
MastVBA.HardCover = False
MsgBox MastVBA.HardCover
```

CREATING A PROPERTY BY USING PROPERTY PROCEDURES

The second and more formal way to create a property is to use property procedures. There are three types of property procedures—Property Let, Property Get, and Property Set:

◆ A Property Let procedure assigns a value to a property.

◆ A Property Get procedure returns the value from a property.

◆ A Property Set procedure sets a reference to an object.

You typically use these procedures in pairs, pairing a Property Get procedure with a Property Let procedure or a Property Set procedure with a Property Let procedure. You can also use a Property Let procedure on its own to create a read-only property.

Assigning a Value to a Property with a Property Let Procedure

To assign a value to a property, you use a Property Let procedure. The syntax for a Property Let procedure is as follows:

```
Property Let name ([arglist,] value)
    [statements]
End Property
```

These are the components of the syntax:

◆ The Property keyword starts the procedure, and the End Property keywords end the procedure.

◆ *name* is a required argument specifying the name of the property procedure being created. If you're creating a Property Get procedure as well for this property, it will use the same name as the Property Let procedure.

◆ *arglist* is a required argument listing the arguments that are passed to the procedure. If *arglist* contains multiple arguments, you separate them with commas.

For example, the following `Property Let` procedure creates the String property `Title` for the class, assigning the argument `NewTitle` and passing its value to the variable `bookTitle`:

```
Property Let Title(NewTitle As String)
    bookTitle = NewTitle
End Property
```

At the end of that property procedure, you have a write-only property named `Title`. Write-only properties aren't widely useful, so the next step is to assign a method of writing to the property.

Returning a Value from a Property with a Property Get Procedure

To return a value from a property, you use a `Property Get` procedure. The syntax for a `Property Get` procedure is as follows:

```
Property Get name [(arglist)] [As type]
    [statements]
End Property
```

The components of the syntax are the same as for the `Property Let` procedure, except for two things:

◆ First, `Property Get` adds the optional *type* argument, which specifies the data type for the property.

◆ Second, for `Property Get`, the *arglist* argument is optional. You *can* have arguments for `Property Get` procedures, but you won't usually need to. If you do use arguments, their names and data types must match those in the corresponding `Property Let` procedure.

For example, the following `Property Get` procedure creates the String property `Title`, assigning to it the contents of the `bookTitle` variable:

```
Property Get Title() As String
    Title = bookTitle
End Property
```

As it stands, this `Property Get` procedure produces a read-only property. But when paired with the `Property Let Title` procedure shown in the previous section, it produces a read/write property—so with both procedures, the `Title` property is ready for use.

Assigning an Object to a Property with a Property Set Procedure

Instead of assigning a value to a property, you can assign an object to it. To do so, you use a `Property Set` procedure rather than a `Property Let` procedure. The syntax for a `Property Set` procedure is as follows:

```
Property Set name ([arglist,] reference)
    [statements]
End Property
```

The components of the syntax are the same as for the `Property Let` procedure, except that `Property Set` uses the *reference* argument rather than the `value` argument. *reference* is a required argument specifying the object to reference.

For example, the following `Property Set` procedure creates the object property `Where` that references a range:

```
Property Set Where(rngR As Range)
    bookRange = rngR
End Property
```

TIP   For an object variable, you can use both a `Property Set` procedure and a `Property Let` procedure, but in most cases it makes more sense to use only a `Property Set` procedure.

THE PROPERTIES FOR THE *BOOK* CLASS

Listing 16.3 shows the full listing of properties for the Book class.

LISTING 16.3:

```
1.   Public Property Let Title(strT As String)
2.       bookTitle = strT
3.   End Property
4.
5.   Public Property Get Title() As String
6.       Title = bookTitle
7.   End Property
8.
9.   Public Property Let Author(strA As String)
10.       bookAuthor = strA
11.  End Property
12.
13.  Public Property Get Author() As String
14.       Author = bookAuthor
15.  End Property
16.
17.  Public Property Let Pages(intPages As Integer)
18.       bookPages = intPages
19.  End Property
20.
21.  Public Property Get Pages() As Integer
22.       Pages = bookPages
23.  End Property
24.
25.  Public Property Let Price(curP As Currency)
26.       bookPrice = curP
27.  End Property
28.
29.  Public Property Get Price() As Currency
30.       Price = bookPrice
31.  End Property
32.
```

```
33.   Public Property Let PublicationDate(dtePD As Date)
34.       bookPublicationDate = dtePD
35.   End Property
36.
37.   Public Property Get PublicationDate() As Date
38.       PublicationDate = bookPublicationDate
39.   End Property
40.
41.   Public Property Get Available() As Boolean
42.       Available = Date >= bookPublicationDate
43.   End Property
```

In Listing 16.3, each property for the Book class is declared as Public so that it is publicly accessible.

The code puts each Property Let procedure next to the corresponding Property Get procedure: The Property Let Title procedure in lines 1 through 3 is matched by the Property Get Title procedure in lines 5 through 7, and so on for the Author, Pages, Price, and PublicationDate property procedures. Pairing the procedures makes it easy to read the code, to make sure that each procedure that should have a counterpart does have one, and to make sure that the arguments match. But you can separate your Property Let procedures and Property Get procedures if you prefer.

You'll notice that the Property Get Available property procedure in lines 41 through 43 doesn't have a corresponding Property Let procedure. The Available property is read-only, with its value being generated inside the object.

Adding Methods to the Class

Now add the methods to the class by adding procedures and functions as necessary. Aside from their code being located within the class module, which causes them to show up as methods in the list of properties and methods for the class, these procedures and functions are like the procedures and functions you use in code modules.

The Book class uses only one method, ShowInfo, which displays a message box showing the properties of the book. Listing 16.4 shows the ShowInfo procedure.

LISTING 16.4:

```
1.   Sub ShowInfo()
2.       Dim strM As String
3.       strM = "Title:" & vbTab & bookTitle & vbCr
4.       strM = strM & "Author:" & vbTab & bookAuthor & vbCr
5.       strM = strM & "Pages:" & vbTab & bookPages & vbCr
6.       strM = strM & "Price:" & vbTab & "$" & bookPrice & vbCr
7.       strM = strM & "Date:" & vbTab & Me.PublicationDate & vbCr
8.       If Me.Available Then strM = strM & vbCr & "AVAILABLE NOW"
9.       MsgBox strM, vbOKOnly + vbInformation, bookName _
               & " Information"
10.  End Sub
```

The ShowInfo procedure builds a string containing the information from the class and then displays the string in a message box. Here's what happens:

◆ Line 2 declares the String variable strM, which the procedure uses to store the information for the prompt argument in the message box.

◆ Line 3 adds to strM the text Title:, a tab, the contents of the bookTitle variable (which contains the title of the book in the object), and a carriage return.

◆ Line 4 builds on strM, adding the author information. Likewise, line 5 adds the information on the page count, and line 6 adds the price information (including a dollar sign for completeness).

◆ Line 7 also builds on strM, adding the date information. Instead of using the class's internal variable (bookPublicationDate) to return the date stored, however, it calls the PublicationDate property of the object (which is identified by the Me keyword). This is by way of an example—returning bookPublicationDate works fine too. But you'll see the difference when you retrieve information from the object: Instead of supplying the variable, VBA runs the Property Get PublicationDate procedure to return the information.

◆ Line 8 returns the Available property of the object (again referred to as Me). If Available is True, this statement adds a blank line (another vbCr) and the string AVAILABLE NOW to strM.

◆ Line 9 displays an OK message box containing strM. The message box title is set to bookName (the constant that contains the text Book Project) and Information, and the message box uses an Information icon.

Using Your Class

To use the class you created, you create a new instance of the object by using the New keyword in either a Dim statement or a Set statement. For example, the following statement creates a new Book-class object variable:

```
Dim myBook As New Book
```

The following statements declare an object variable named bookAnotherBook and then assign to it a new instance of the Book object:

```
Dim bookAnotherBook As Object
Set bookAnotherBook = New Book
```

You can then access the properties and methods of the Book object as you would any other VBA object's properties and methods. For example, the following statement sets the Price property of bookAnotherBook:

```
bookAnotherBook.Price = 54.99
```

Listing 16.5 contains a short procedure called Class_Test that shows the Book class in action.

LISTING 16.5:

```
1.   Sub Class_Test()
2.
3.       Dim myBook As New Book
4.
5.       myBook.Title = "Mastering VBA Second Edition"
6.       myBook.Price = 39.99
7.       myBook.Author = "Anonymous"
8.       myBook.Pages = 704
9.       myBook.PublicationDate = #9/23/2005#
10.
11.      myBook.ShowInfo
12.
13.  End Sub
```

The listing shows an example of using the new class. Here's what happens:

◆ Line 1 begins the Class_Test procedure, and line 13 ends it.

◆ Line 2 is a spacer. Line 3 declares a new object variable named myBook of the Book class. Line 4 is another spacer.

◆ Lines 5 through 9 set the five properties of the myBook object—Title, Price, Author, Pages, and PublicationDate—as you'd set the properties for any other object.

◆ Line 10 is a spacer. Line 11 invokes the ShowInfo method of the myBook object—again, as you'd invoke a method for any other object.

Here's one more thing to try. As you remember, the Available property is implemented as a read-only Boolean property. Try to set this property by entering the following statement in the Code window in the Class_Test procedure right after the declaration of myBook:

```
myBook.Available = True
```

When you press the . key after typing myBook, VBA displays Available on the list of properties and methods. But once you've entered it and an equal sign (myBook.Available =), VBA doesn't display the Auto List Members list with False and True as it would for a read/write Boolean property, because Available isn't available in this context. Second, when you try to run the code, you'll get a compile error, "Can't assign to read-only property."

Chapter 17

Debugging Your Code and Handling Errors

- ◆ Understanding the basic principles of debugging
- ◆ The four different types of errors you'll create
- ◆ Uncatchable bugs
- ◆ VBA's debugging tools
- ◆ Dealing with runtime errors
- ◆ Handling user interrupts

In this chapter, you'll learn some of the things that can go wrong in your VBA code and what you can do about them. You'll examine the types of errors that can occur, from simple typos to infinite loops to errors that occur only once in a while.

The chapter starts by quickly explaining the principles of debugging. Then you'll work with the tools that VBA offers for debugging VBA code and use them to get the bugs out of a few statements. The end of the chapter discusses the various methods of handling errors and when to use each one.

Principles of Debugging

A *bug* is an error in hardware or software that causes a program to execute incorrectly. *Debugging* means removing the bugs from hardware or software.

NOTE There are various explanations of the etymology of the word *bug* in this context, ranging from apocryphal stories of moths being found in the circuit boards of malfunctioning computers to musings that the word came from the mythological *bugbear*, an unwelcome beast. But in fact, this usage of *bug* seems to come from the early days of the telegraph rather than originating in the computer age. For more information, see "bug" entry in the Free Online Dictionary of Computing at a site such as http://foldoc.doc.ic.ac.uk/foldoc/.

Your goal in debugging should be to remove all detectable bugs from your code as quickly and efficiently as possible. Your order of business will probably go something like this:

1. First, test your code to see whether it works as it should. If you're confident that it will work, test it by simply running the procedure once or twice on suitable files or appropriate data. Even if it seems to work, continue testing for a reasonable period on sample documents before unleashing the procedure on the world (or your colleagues).

2. If your code doesn't work as you expected it to, you'll need to debug it. That means following the procedures in this chapter to locate the bugs and then remove them. Once you've removed all the bugs that you can identify, test the code as described in the first step.

3. When testing your code, try to anticipate the unorthodox uses that users will devise for your procedure. For example, you might write a sophisticated procedure for manipulating a Word document on the (perfectly reasonable) assumption that the document will be open when the user starts the procedure running. You can test it on sample documents until you're blue in the face, and it'll work fine every time. But if a user tries to run the procedure without first opening a document, it'll crash every time—guaranteed.

4. When you're ready to distribute your procedure, you may want to write instructions for its use. In these instructions, you may also need to document any bugs that you can't squash or circumstances under which the procedure shouldn't be run.

Debugging a procedure tends to be idiosyncratic work. There's no magic wand that you can wave over your code to banish bugs (although the Visual Basic Editor does its best to help you eliminate certain types of errors from your code as you create it). Moreover, such simple things as forgetting to initialize a variable can wreak havoc on your code. You'll probably develop your own approach to debugging your procedures, partly because they will inevitably be written in your own style. But when debugging, it helps to focus on understanding what the code is supposed to do. You then correlate this with your observations of what the code actually does. When you reconcile the two, you'll probably have worked out how to debug the procedure.

TIP   The more complex your code, the higher the probability that it will contain bugs. Keep your code as simple as possible by breaking it into separate procedures and modules, as discussed in Chapter 16.

The Different Types of Errors

You'll encounter four basic kinds of errors in your procedures:

- Language errors
- Compile errors
- Runtime errors
- Program logic errors

This section looks at these kinds of errors in turn and discusses how to prevent them. After that, you'll examine the tools VBA provides for fixing them.

Language Errors

The first type of error is a *language error* (also known as a *syntax error*). When you mistype a word in the Code window, omit a vital piece of punctuation, scramble a statement, or leave off the end of a construction, that's a language error. If you've worked your way through the book to this point, you've probably already made dozens of language errors as part of the learning process and through simple typos.

VBA helps you eliminate many language errors as you create them, as you'll see in the next section. Those language errors that the Visual Basic Editor doesn't catch as you create them usually show up as compile errors, so the next section shows you examples of both language errors and compile errors.

Compile Errors

Compile errors occur when VBA can't compile a statement correctly—that is, when VBA can't turn a statement that you've entered into viable code. For example, if you tell VBA to use a certain property for an object that doesn't have that property, a compile error results.

The good news about language errors and compile errors is that the Visual Basic Editor detects many language errors and some compile errors when you move the insertion point from the offending line. For example, try typing the following statement in the Code window and pressing Enter to create a new line (or pressing ↑ or ↓ to move to another line, or clicking in another line):

```
If X > Y
```

The Visual Basic Editor displays the compile error "Expected: Then or GoTo" (see Figure 17.1) to tell you that the statement is missing a vital element: It should say `If X > Y Then` or `If X > Y GoTo`. This vigilance on the part of the Visual Basic Editor prevents you from running into this type of error deep in the execution of your code.

FIGURE 17.1
The Visual Basic Editor helps debug your code by identifying many compile errors as it checks the statements you enter.

NOTE   This chapter assumes that you're keeping VBA's Auto Syntax Check feature and other features switched on. Some developers choose to turn off these features because they don't want to be nagged—but working without these features can prove a cure worse than the disease.

The Visual Basic Editor picks up the previous problem easily enough, but you can also make language errors that the Visual Basic Editor does *not* identify when you move the insertion point from the line in which you've inserted them. Instead, VBA identifies these errors as compile errors when it compiles the code. For example, if you enter the statement below in the Code window when working with Word, the Visual Basic Editor doesn't detect anything wrong. But when you run the procedure, VBA compiles the code, discovers the error, and objects to it (see Figure 17.2):

```
ActiveDocument.SaveAs FileMame:="My File.doc"
```

This error is a straightforward typo—`FileMame` instead of `FileName`—but VBA can't identify the problem until it runs the code.

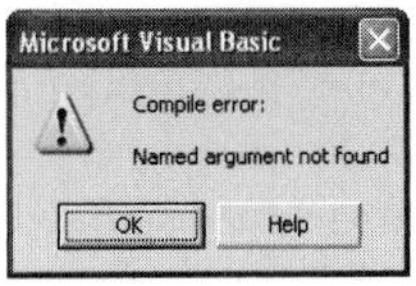

FIGURE 17.2
Other errors appear only when you try to run the code.

The Visual Basic Editor does help you pick up some errors of this type. Say you're trying to enter a `Documents.Close` statement in Word and mistype `Documents` as `Docments`. In this case, the Visual Basic Editor doesn't display the Properties/Methods list because you haven't entered a valid object (unless you've created a custom collection or object named `Docments` that has a `Close` method, which would be a poor idea). Not seeing the list should alert you that something is wrong. If you continue anyway and enter the `Docments.Close` statement, the Visual Basic Editor doesn't spot the mistake— it shows up as a "Run-time error 424: Object required" message (if you don't have `Option Explicit` on) when you try to run the procedure. (If you do have `Option Explicit` on, you get a "Variable not defined" compile error instead.)

Similarly, if you specify a property or method for an object to which that property or method doesn't apply, VBA gives a compile error. For example, say you forget the `Add` method and enter `Documents.Create` instead. VBA highlights the offending word and gives the compile error "Method or data member not found" (see Figure 17.3), which tells you there's no `Create` method for the `Documents` collection.

FIGURE 17.3

The "Method or data member not found" error tells you that you've used a method or property that isn't available for the object in question.

Runtime Errors

The third type of error is the *runtime error*, which occurs while code is executing. You create a runtime error when you write a statement that causes VBA to try to perform an impossible operation, such as opening a document that doesn't exist, closing a file when no file is open, or performing something mathematically impossible such as dividing by zero. An unhandled runtime error results in a crash that manifests itself as a Microsoft Visual Basic dialog box displaying a runtime error number, such as the one shown in Figure 17.4.

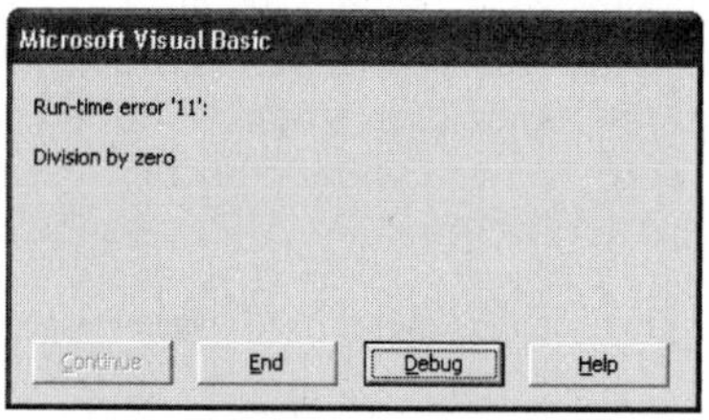

FIGURE 17.4

An unhandled runtime error causes VBA to display a message box such as this one.

As an example of an impossible operation, consider the archetypal division by zero. The following statements give a "Run-time error '11': Division by zero" message:

```
Dim DZ
DZ = 1 / 0
```

You're unlikely to enter anything as obviously wrong as this demonstration line in your code; this line will inevitably produce a division-by-zero error because the divisor is zero. But it's easy to enter a valid equation, such as `MonthlyPay = Salary/Months`, and forget to assign a value to `Months` (if a numeric variable is empty, it counts as a zero value) or to produce a zero value for Months by addition or subtraction.

To avoid runtime errors, track the values of your variables by using the Watch window (discussed in "The Watch Window," later in this chapter).

Program Logic Errors

The fourth type of error is the *program logic error*, which is an error that produces incorrect results. With program logic errors, the code has no syntactical problem, so VBA is able to compile and run it without generating any errors—but you get a different result than you intended. Program logic errors range in scope from the relatively obvious (such as performing detailed manipulations on the wrong workbook in Excel because your code doesn't check which window is active) to the subtle (such as extending a range to the wrong character or cell). In the first example, the manipulation procedure is likely to run perfectly, but the resulting workbook will bear little resemblance to what you were trying to produce. In the second example, you might get a result that is almost correct—or the error might cause you to get perfect results sometimes and slightly wrong results at other times.

Program logic errors tend to be the hardest errors to catch. To nail them down, you need to trace the execution of your code and pinpoint where things start to go wrong. To do so, you need the tools discussed in the next section.

NOTE   There are two other types of errors that you may well run into—even though you shouldn't. The first type is where Microsoft has documented a VBA item differently than it actually works. This shouldn't happen, but because of the complexity of VBA, it does. If you find that your code absolutely won't work even though it follows the Microsoft documentation to the letter, consider the possibility that the documentation may be incorrect. Search the Web using the VBA keywords to find if others have encountered this problem and learn how they've worked around it. The second type of error, a distant relation of the first type, is where VBA behaves differently in one version of VBA to another. For example, you might create a procedure that works perfectly in Word 2000 but that you have to change to make it work with Word 2003. In an ideal world, this shouldn't happen—but as you know, this world is far from ideal.

VBA's Debugging Tools

VBA provides a solid assortment of debugging tools to help you remove the bugs from your procedures. The main tools for debugging are the Immediate window, the Locals window, and the Watch window. You can access these tools in various ways, one of which is by using the Debug toolbar (shown in Figure 17.5). Three of the buttons—Run Sub/UserForm (Continue), Break, and Reset—are shared with the Standard toolbar. You'll meet most of the others later in this chapter.

FIGURE 17.5

The Debug toolbar provides 13 commands for debugging your procedures.

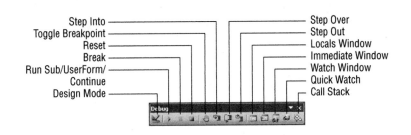

UNCATCHABLE BUGS

The more complex your code, the more likely you are to create bugs that are truly difficult to catch. Usually, with determination and ingenuity, you can track down the bugs in a procedure; but bugs that depend on several unforeseen and improbable circumstances occurring simultaneously can be tough to isolate. For example, an error that occurs in a procedure when the user makes a certain choice in a dialog box is relatively easy to catch. But if the error occurs only when the user has made two particular choices in the dialog box, it's much harder to locate—and if the error is contingent on three specific choices the user has made in the dialog box, or if it depends on an element in the file on which the procedure is being run, you'll have a much harder time pinpointing it.

Hacker folklore defines various kinds of bizarre bugs by assigning them quasi-jocular names derived from such disciplines as philosophy and quantum physics. For instance, a *heisenbug* is defined as "a bug that disappears or alters its behavior when one attempts to probe or isolate it." Heisenbugs are frustrating, as are Bohr bugs and mandelbugs (search online for details if you're curious). But the worst kind of bug is the *schroedingbug*, which is a design or implementation bug that remains quiescent until someone reads the code and notices that it shouldn't work, whereupon it stops working until the code is made logically consistent.

These bugs are, of course, ridiculous—until you start to discover bit rot at work on your code and have to explain the problem to your superiors.

Break Mode

Break mode is a vital tool for debugging your procedures because it lets you watch your code execute step-by-step in the Code window. For example, if an If… Then… ElseIf… Else statement appears to be executing incorrectly, you can step through it in Break mode and watch exactly which statements are executing to produce the result.

These are the easiest ways to enter Break mode:

♦ Place the insertion point in the procedure you want to run in the Code window and press the F8 key (or click the Step Into button on the Debug toolbar, or choose Debug ➢ Step Into) to start stepping through it.

♦ Set one or more breakpoints in the procedure to cause VBA to enter Break mode when it reaches one of the marked lines. A breakpoint allows you to stop execution of code at a particular point in a procedure. The easiest way to set a breakpoint is to click in the Margin Indicator Bar to the left of the Code window beside the line you want to affect. (You can also right-click in the line and choose Toggle ➢ Breakpoint from the context menu.) You can set any number of breakpoints. They're especially useful when you need to track down a bug in a procedure, because they let you run the parts of a procedure that have no problems at full speed and then stop the procedure where you think there might be problems. From there, you can step through the statements that might be problematic and watch how they execute.

You can also enter Break mode in a couple of other ways:

♦ Interrupt your code by pressing Ctrl+Break and then click the Debug button in the resulting dialog box (see Figure 17.6). Normally, the only reason to enter Break mode this way is if your code gets stuck in an endless loop (which you'll typically realize when the code appears to be doing nothing for a long time or repeating itself when you think it shouldn't be). VBA highlights the statement that was executing when you pressed Ctrl+Break, but (depending on your timing) it's unlikely to be the statement that's causing the problem in your code—it'll just be one of the statements in the offending loop. You'll then need to step through the loop to identify the offending statement.

FIGURE 17.6

You can enter Break mode by pressing Ctrl+Break and then clicking the Debug button in this dialog box.

- ◆ Click the Debug button in a runtime error dialog box such as the one shown in Figure 17.7. In the Code window, VBA highlights the statement that caused the error. (You can also click the Help button in the runtime error dialog box to get an explanation of the error before clicking the Debug button.)

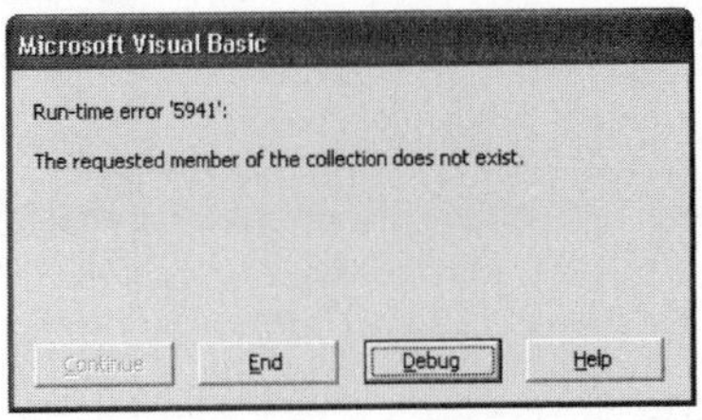

FIGURE 17.7

Entering Break mode from a runtime error dialog box like this one takes you straight to the offending statement in your code.

The Step Over and Step Out Commands

In Chapter 3, you learned how to step through a procedure by pressing the F8 key to issue the Step Into command. (You can also issue this command by clicking the Step Into button on the Debug toolbar or choosing Debug ➢ Step Into.) Stepping into lets you see exactly what each statement in your code does, but you'll often find that you need to get past sections of code that are working fine so that you can step through a section that may be problematic.

Break mode offers three features to speed up stepping through your code: the Step Over command, the Step Out command, and the Run To Cursor command.

NOTE   The Step Over and Step Out commands aren't available until you enter Break mode (for example, by using the Step Into command).

The Step Over command (which you can issue by pressing Shift+F8, clicking the Step Over button on the Debug toolbar, or choosing Debug ➢ Step Over) executes the whole procedure or function called from the current procedure, instead of stepping through the called procedure statement by statement, as the Step Into command would do. (It "steps over" that procedure or function.) Use the Step Over command when you're debugging a procedure that calls another procedure or function that you know to be error-free and that you don't need to test step-by-step.

The Step Out command (which you can issue by Ctrl+Shift+F8, clicking the Step Out button on the Debug toolbar, or choosing Debug ➢ Step Out) runs the rest of the current procedure at full speed.

Use the Step Out command to execute quickly the rest of the procedure once you've gotten through the part that you needed to watch step-by-step.

The Run To Cursor command (which you can issue by pressing Ctrl+F8 or choosing Debug ➢ Run To Cursor) runs the code at full speed until it reaches the statement the cursor is currently in, whereupon it enters Break mode. Position the cursor in the appropriate statement before invoking this command.

The Locals Window

The Locals window provides a quick readout of the value and type of all expressions in the active procedure via a collapsible tree view (see Figure 17.8). The Expression column displays the name of each expression, listed under the name of the procedure in which it appears. The Value column displays the current value of the expression (including Empty if the expression is empty, or Null or Nothing as appropriate). And the Type column displays the data type of the expression, with Variants listed as "Variant" along with their assigned data type (for example, "Variant/String" for a Variant assigned the String data type).

FIGURE 17.8
Use the Locals window to see at a glance all the expressions in the active procedure.

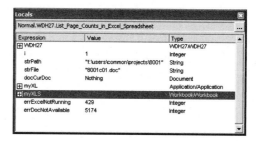

To display the Locals window, click the Locals Window button on the Debug toolbar or choose View ➢ Locals Window. To remove the Locals window, click its close button.

From the Locals window, you can also click the button marked with an ellipsis (…) to display the Call Stack dialog box, discussed in the section titled "The Call Stack Dialog Box," later in the chapter. This button is available only in Break mode.

The Watch Window

The Watch window (identified as Watches in Figure 17.9) is a separate window that you use to track the values of variables and expressions as your code executes. To display the Watch window, click the Watch Window button on the Debug toolbar or choose View ➢ Watch Window in the Visual Basic Editor. To hide the Watch window again, click its close button (clicking the Watch Window button or choosing View ➢ Watch Window again doesn't hide it).

FIGURE 17.9
Use the Watch window to track the values of variables and expressions in your code.

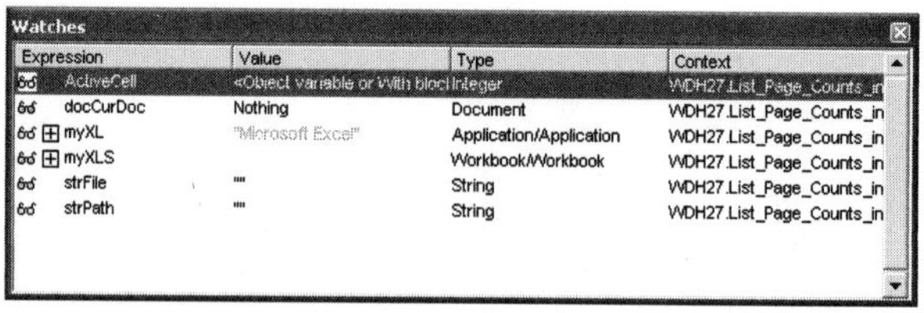

The Watch window displays *watch expressions*—expressions you set ahead of time to give you a running display of the value of a variable or an expression. This information allows you to pinpoint where an unexpected value for a variable or an expression occurs as your code executes. The Watch window lists the names of the watched expressions or variables in the Expression column, their values in the Value column, their type (Integer, Byte, String, Long, and so on) in the Type column, and their context (the module and procedure in which they're operating) in the Context column. So to track the value of a given variable, you need only look at the Watch window at any given point while in Break mode.

NOTE If a variable or expression listed in the Watch window hasn't been initialized, the Watch window displays "<Out of Context>" in the Value column and "Empty" (for a variable other than a Variant) or "Variant/Empty" (for a Variant) in the Type column.

The Visual Basic Editor updates all watch expressions in the Watch window whenever you enter Break mode and whenever you execute a statement in the Immediate window. So if you step through a procedure in the Code window by pressing the F8 key (which keeps you in Break mode), you can watch the value of a variable or an expression as each statement executes. This is a great way to pinpoint where an error or an unexpected value occurs—and much easier than moving the mouse over each variable or expression in question to check its value by using the Auto Data Tips feature.

Before you can display a variable in the Watch window, you must declare it (otherwise the Visual Basic Editor responds with a "Variable not created in this context" error). This is another good reason for declaring variables explicitly at the beginning of a procedure rather than declaring them implicitly in mid-procedure.

Because watch expressions slow down execution of your code, the Visual Basic Editor doesn't save them with the code—you need to place them separately for each editing session. The Visual Basic Editor stores watch expressions during the current editing session, so you can move from procedure to procedure without losing your watch expressions.

SETTING WATCH EXPRESSIONS

To set a watch expression, add it to the list in the Watch window:

1. Right-click the variable or expression in your code and choose Add Watch from the shortcut menu to display the Add Watch dialog box (see Figure 17.10). The variable or expression in which you right-clicked appears in the Expression text box.

FIGURE 17.10
In the Add Watch dialog box, specify the watch expression you want to add.

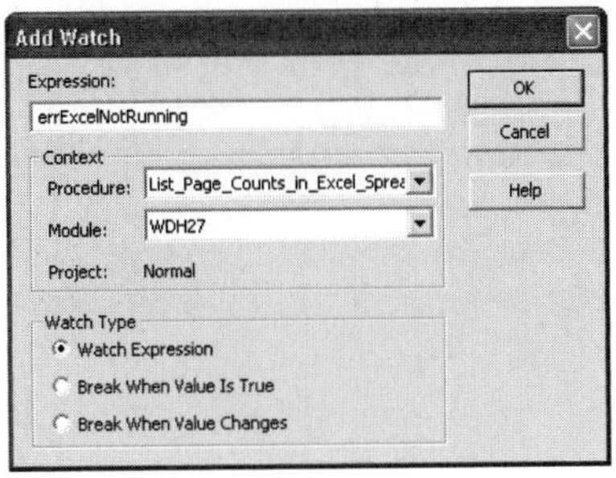

NOTE   You can also select the variable or expression in the Code window and choose Debug ➤ Add Watch to display the Add Watch dialog box. If you choose Debug ➤ Add Watch without selecting the variable or expression, you must enter it manually in the Expression text box, which is a waste of time.

2. If necessary, adjust the settings in the Context group box. The Procedure drop-down list is set to the current procedure, and the Module drop-down list is set to the current module.

3. In the Watch Type group box, adjust the option button setting if necessary:

   ◆ The default setting—Watch Expression—adds the variable or expression in the Expression text box to the list in the Watch window.

   ◆ Break When Value Is True causes VBA to enter Break mode whenever the value of the variable or expression changes to True.

   ◆ Break When Value Changes causes VBA to enter Break mode whenever the value of the watch expression changes. Use this setting when dealing either with a watch expression whose value you don't expect to change but that appears to be changing or with a watch expression whose every change you need to observe.

TIP   The Break When Value Is True option button allows you to run your code without stepping through each statement that doesn't change the value of the watch expression to True. The Break When Value Changes option button allows you to run your code and stop with each change of the value.

4. Click the OK button to add the watch expression to the Watch window.

TIP   You can also drag a variable or an expression from the Code window to the Watch window; doing so sets a default watch expression in the current context. To set Break When Value Is True or Break When Value Changes, edit the watch expression after dragging it to the Watch window.

EDITING WATCH EXPRESSIONS

To edit a watch expression, right-click it in the Watch window and choose Edit Watch from the context menu, or select it in the Watch window and choose Debug ➤ Edit Watch. Either action will display the Edit Watch dialog box with the watch expression selected in the Expression box, as shown in Figure 17.11. Change the context or watch type for the watch expression by using the settings in the Context group box and the Watch Type group box, and then click the OK button to apply your changes.

FIGURE 17.11
You can edit your watch expressions in the Edit Watch dialog box.

DELETING WATCH EXPRESSIONS

To delete a watch expression, right-click it in the Watch window and choose Delete Watch from the context menu. You can also delete the current watch expression by clicking the Delete button in the Edit Watch dialog box.

USING THE QUICK WATCH FEATURE

For times when you don't want to create a watch expression for an expression or a variable, you can use the Quick Watch feature, which displays the Quick Watch dialog box (see Figure 17.12) containing the context and value of the selected expression. To use Quick Watch, select the expression or variable in the Code window and then either click the Quick Watch button on the Debug toolbar, choose Debug ➢ Quick Watch, or press Shift+F9. (If you're already working in the Quick Watch dialog box, you can click the Add button to add the expression to the Watch window.)

FIGURE 17.12
Use the Quick Watch dialog box to get quick information on a variable or expression for which you don't want to set a watch expression in the Watch window.

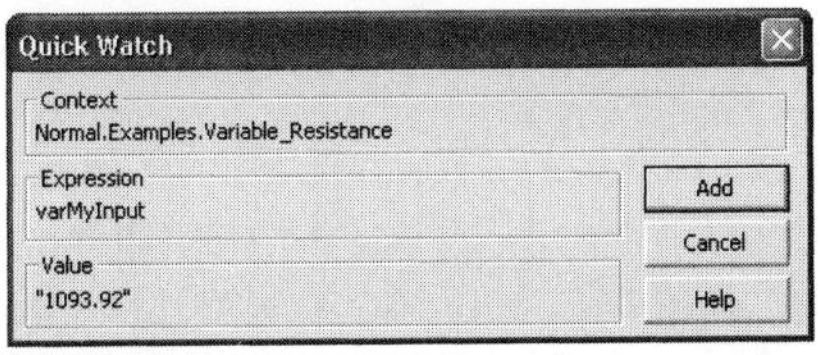

The Immediate Window

You can use the Immediate window as a virtual scratchpad to enter lines of code that you want to test without entering them in the procedure itself, or to display information to help you check the values of variables while a procedure is executing. In the first case, you enter code in the Immediate window; in the second, you use statements entered in the Code window to display information in the Immediate window, where you can easily view it.

To display the Immediate window, click the Immediate Window button on the Debug toolbar, choose View ➢ Immediate Window, or press Ctrl+G. To hide the Immediate window again, click its close button. (Clicking the Immediate Window button, choosing View ➢ Immediate Window, or pressing Ctrl+G when the Immediate window is displayed doesn't hide the Immediate window.)

You can execute code in the Immediate window in both Break mode and Design mode.

WHAT YOU CAN'T DO IN THE IMMEDIATE WINDOW

There are a number of restrictions on the code you can use in the Immediate window:

◆ You can't use declarative statements (such as `Dim`, `Private`, `Public`, `Option Explicit`, `Static`, or `Type`) or control-flow statements (such as `GoTo`, `Sub`, or `Function`). These statements cause VBA to return an "Invalid in Immediate Pane" error.

◆ You can't use multi-line statements (such as block `If` statements or block `For… Next` statements) because there's no logical connection between statements on different lines in the Immediate window: Each line is treated in isolation.

◆ You can't place breakpoints in the Immediate window.

ENTERING CODE IN THE IMMEDIATE WINDOW

The Immediate window supports a number of standard Windows key combinations, such as Ctrl+X (Cut), Ctrl+C (Copy), Ctrl+V (Paste), Ctrl+Home (move the insertion point to the start of the window), Ctrl+End (move the insertion point to the end of the window), Delete (delete the current selection), and Shift+F10 (display the context menu).

The Immediate window also supports the following Visual Basic Editor keystrokes and key combinations:

◆ F5 continues running a procedure.

◆ Alt+F5 runs the error-handler code for the current procedure.

◆ F8 single-steps through code (executing one statement at a time).

◆ Shift+F8 procedure-steps through code (executing one procedure at a time).

◆ Alt+F8 steps into the error handler for the current procedure.

◆ F2 displays the Object Browser.

Finally, the Immediate window has a couple of commands of its own:

◆ Pressing Enter runs the current line of code.

◆ Pressing Ctrl+Enter inserts a carriage return.

PRINTING INFORMATION TO THE IMMEDIATE WINDOW

As well as entering statements in the Immediate window for quick testing, you can include in your procedures statements to print information to the Immediate window by using the `Print` method of the `Debug` object. Printing like this provides you with a way of viewing information as a procedure runs without having to be in Break mode or having to display a message box or dialog box that stops execution of the procedure.

The syntax for the `Print` method is

```
Debug.Print [outputlist]
```

outputlist is an optional argument specifying the expression or expressions to print. You'll almost always want to include *outputlist*—if you don't, the `Print` method prints a blank line, which is of little use to anyone alive. Construct your *outputlist* using the following syntax:

```
[Spc(n) | Tab(n)] expression
```

Here, `Spc(n)` inserts space characters and `Tab(n)` inserts tab characters, with *n* being the number of spaces or tabs to insert. Both are optional arguments, and for simple output, you'll seldom need to use them.

expression is an optional argument specifying the numeric expression or String expression to print:

◆ To specify multiple expressions, separate them with either a space or a semicolon.

◆ A Boolean value prints as either `True` or `False` (as appropriate).

◆ If *outputlist* is Empty, `Print` doesn't print anything. If *outputlist* is Null, `Print` prints Null.

◆ If *outputlist* is an error, `Print` prints it as `Error errorcode`, where *errorcode* is the code specifying the error.

As an example, you could log the contents of the String expressions `CustName`, `Address1`, `Address2`, `City`, `State`, and `Zip` to the Immediate window in an address format by using the following statements:

```
Debug.Print CustName
Debug.Print Address1 & ", " & Address2
Debug.Print City & ", " & State & " " & Zip
```

As another example, the following procedure prints the names and paths of all open workbooks in Excel to the Immediate window:

```
Sub Debug_Print_All_Workbook_Names()
    Dim oBook As Workbook
    For Each oBook In Workbooks
        Debug.Print oBook.FullName
    Next
End Sub
```

The Call Stack Dialog Box

When working in Break mode, you can summon the Call Stack dialog box (see Figure 17.13) to display a list of the active *procedure calls*—the procedures being called by the current procedure. When you begin running a procedure, that procedure is added to the call stack list in the Call Stack dialog box. If that procedure then calls another procedure, the name of the second procedure is added to the call stack list for as long as the procedure takes to execute; it's then removed from the list. By using the Call Stack dialog box, you can find out what procedures are being called by another procedure; this can help you establish which parts of your code you need to check for errors.

FIGURE 17.13
Use the Call Stack dialog box to see a list of the procedures that are being called by the current procedure.

To display the Call Stack dialog box, click the Call Stack button on the Debug toolbar, press Ctrl+L, or select View ➢ Call Stack. To display one of the procedures listed in the Call Stack dialog box, select it in the Project.Module.Function list box and click the Show button. To close the Call Stack dialog box, click its Close button.

Dealing with Infinite Loops

You'll probably find it easy to tell when a procedure gets stuck in an infinite loop: You'll notice that the procedure simply doesn't stop executing. To interrupt an infinite loop, press Ctrl+Break. The Visual Basic Editor then displays a Code Execution Has Been Interrupted dialog box.

There are several ways to guarantee getting stuck in infinite loops, such as using `GoTo` statements without `If` conditions or `Do` loops without `While` or `Until` constraints. These are easy enough to avoid, but even if you do, it's still possible for infinite loops to occur in your code because of conditions you haven't been able to anticipate.

The best way to approach detecting and eliminating an infinite loop is to use breakpoints or a watch expression to pinpoint where the procedure enters the infinite loop. Once you've reached it, use the Step Into command to step into the procedure. Then use the Watch window or the Locals window to observe the variable and expressions in the loop, which should indicate when something is going wrong and causing the loop to be endless.

If your code contains a loop that should execute only a set number of times but that you suspect is running endlessly, you can use a counter in the loop with either an `Exit For` statement or an `Exit Do` statement (whichever is appropriate) to exit the loop if it runs more than a certain number of times.

Dealing with Runtime Errors

Despite the help that VBA provides in eliminating language errors and compile errors, runtime errors remain an unpleasant fact of life. Sooner or later, you will get errors in your code, but you don't have to take them lying down. VBA enables you to write *error handlers*, which are pieces of code that trap errors, analyze them, and take action if they match given error codes.

When Should You Write an Error Handler?

Consider writing an error handler in the following circumstances:

◆ When a runtime error can cause your code to fail disastrously. For a procedure that tweaks a couple of objects on a slide in PowerPoint, you're unlikely to need an error handler. By contrast, for a procedure that creates, deletes, or moves files, you'll probably want an error handler.

◆ When you can identify particular errors that are likely to occur and that can be trapped. For example, when the user tries to open a file, certain errors can occur—such as if the file doesn't exist; is currently in use by another computer; or is on a network drive, floppy drive, CD-ROM drive, or removable drive that isn't available at the time. You'll also run into errors if the user tries to use a printer or other remote device (say, a scanner or a digital camera) that's not present, connected, powered up, and configured correctly. Similarly, any procedure that deals with a particular object in a document (for example, a chart in Excel) will run into trouble if that object is not present or not available.

NOTE In some instances, you may find it simpler to trap a resulting error from a procedure than to anticipate and try to forestall the various conditions that might lead to the generation of the error. For example, instead of checking to make sure a file exists before you try to open or manipulate the file, trap any error that results if the file doesn't exist.

Trapping an Error

Trapping an error means catching it so that you can do something about it. Usually, you'll want to prevent an error from stopping your VBA code, but you can also anticipate particular errors and use them to determine a suitable course of action to follow from the point at which they occur.

To trap an error, you use the `On Error` statement. The usual syntax for `On Error` is

```
On Error GoTo line
```

Here, *line* is a label specifying the line to which execution is to branch when a runtime error occurs. For example, to branch to the label named `ErrorHandler`, you could use a structure like this:

```
Sub ErrorDemo()
    On Error GoTo ErrorHandler
    'statements here
    Exit Sub
ErrorHandler:
    'error-handler statements here
End Sub
```

The label you use to identify the error handler can be named with any valid label name—you don't have to call it `ErrorHandler` or anything similar. Some people find that a descriptive label (perhaps one that identifies the type or types of error expected, such as `HandleErrorNoFileOpen`) is clearer in the long run than a generic name; others prefer to go with a generic name (such as `HandleErr`) for most or all of their error handlers.

Usually, you'll want to place the error trap early in a procedure so that it's active and ready to trap errors for the rest of the procedure. If necessary, you can place several different error traps in a document by entering multiple `On Error` statements where they're needed—but only one can be enabled at a time. (*Enabled* means that an error trap has been switched on by an `On Error` statement. When an error occurs and execution branches to the error handler, that error handler is *active*.) Having multiple error handlers in a procedure can be useful when you're dealing with statements that require different types of action to be trapped. In the following example, the first `On Error` statement directs execution to `ErrorHandler1`, and the second `On Error` statement directs execution to `ErrorHandler2`:

```
Sub ErrorDemo2()
    On Error GoTo ErrorHandler1
    'statements here
    On Error GoTo ErrorHandler2
    Exit Sub
    'statements here
ErrorHandler1:
    'statements for first error handler here
ErrorHandler2:
    'statements for second error handler here
End Sub
```

Each error handler is limited to the procedure in which it appears, so you can create different error handlers for different procedures and have each enabled in turn as the procedures run.

Because the error handler appears as code in the procedure, you need to make sure that it doesn't run when no error has occurred. You can do this by using either an `Exit Sub` statement before the error handler statement (to end execution of the procedure) or a `GoTo` statement that directs execution to a label beyond the error-handling code. The `Exit Sub` statement is better if you choose to place your error handler at the end of its procedure, which is standard practice and usually makes sense. The `GoTo` statement may prove easier to use if you choose to place your error handler elsewhere in the procedure.

NOTE   For a function, use an `Exit Function` statement rather than an `Exit Sub` statement. For a property, use an `Exit Property` statement.

The following example uses an `Exit Sub` statement to cause execution to end before the error handler if no error occurs:

```
Sub ErrorDemo3()
    On Error GoTo ErrorHandler
    'statements
    Exit Sub
ErrorHandler:
    'statements for error handler
End Sub
```

This next example uses a `GoTo` statement to skip the error handler—which is placed within the code of the procedure—unless an error occurs. When execution reaches the `GoTo SkipErrorHandler` statement, it branches to the `SkipErrorHandler` label, thus bypassing the code in the error handler:

```
Sub ErrorDemo4()
    On Error GoTo ErrorHandler
    'statements
    GoTo SkipErrorHandler
ErrorHandler:
    'statements for error handler
SkipErrorHandler:
    'statements
End Sub
```

You read earlier than some people don't like `GoTo` statements for uses such as the second use here. Given that this `GoTo` statement makes the flow of the procedure a little harder to follow, you may be inclined to agree with them in this case. (The use of `GoTo` in the `On Error` statement is unavoidable.)

Disabling an Error Trap

An error trap works only for the procedure in which it appears, and VBA disables it when the code in the procedure has finished executing. You can also disable an error trap before the end of a procedure in which it appears by using the following statement:

```
On Error GoTo 0
```

You might want to disable an error trap while testing a procedure to enable yourself to pinpoint errors that occur after a certain point while retaining error-trapping for the first part of the procedure.

Resuming after an Error

You use the `Resume` statement to resume execution of a procedure after trapping an error or handling an error with an error-handling routine. The `Resume` statement takes three forms: `Resume`, `Resume Next`, and `Resume *line*`.

USING A *RESUME* STATEMENT

`Resume` itself causes execution to resume with the line that caused the error. Use `Resume` with an error-handling routine that detects and fixes the problem that caused the offending statement to fail. For example, look at the error handler in Listing 17.1, which runs when VBA is unable to apply a specified style in Word.

LISTING 17.1:

```
1.  Sub StyleError()
2.
3.      On Error GoTo Handler
4.
5.      Selection.Style = "Executive Summary"
6.
7.      'the rest of the procedure happens here
8.
9.      'exit the procedure once execution gets this far
10.     Exit Sub
11.
12. Handler:
13.
14.     If Err = 5834 Then
15.         ActiveDocument.Styles.Add _
                Name:="Executive Summary", Type:=wdStyleTypeParagraph
16.         Resume
17.     End If
18.
19. End Sub
```

Here's how the StyleError procedure in Listing 17.1 works:

◆ Line 1 starts the procedure, and line 19 ends it. Lines 2, 4, 6, 8, 11, 13, and 18 are spacers.

◆ Line 3 uses an On Error statement to enable the imaginatively named error handler Handler, which is identified by the Handler label in line 12.

◆ Line 5 applies the style named Executive Summary to the current selection. If this operation succeeds, execution will continue at line 7, which in this example contains only a comment indicating that this is where the rest of the procedure would take place.

◆ Line 9 is a comment introducing line 10, which holds the Exit Sub statement to end execution of the procedure before the error handler.

◆ If the Selection.Style statement in line 5 causes an error, execution branches to the Handler label in line 12, and the error handler is activated. Line 14 compares the error value to 5834, the error that occurs if the specified style doesn't exist. If it matches, line 15 then adds the missing style to the document, and the Resume statement in line 16 causes execution to resume where the error occurred, on line 5. Because the specified style is now available, the Selection.Style statement runs without an error.

TIP To find error numbers, search the VBA Help file for error numbers or cause the error yourself and note the number and description in the resulting dialog box.

USING A *RESUME NEXT* STATEMENT

Resume Next causes execution to resume with the next statement after the statement that caused the error. You can use Resume Next in either of the following circumstances:

◆ With an error-handling routine that ignores the error and allows execution to continue without executing the offending statement

◆ As a straightforward On Error Resume Next statement that causes execution to continue at the next statement after the statement that caused an error, without using an error handler to fix the error

As an example of the first circumstance, if the style specified in the previous example isn't available, you can use a Resume Next statement to skip applying it:

```
Sub StyleError2()

    On Error GoTo Handler

    Selection.Style = "Executive Summary"

    'the rest of the procedure happens here

    'exit the procedure once execution gets this far
    Exit Sub

Handler:
    Resume Next

End Sub
```

The descriptions of Resume and Resume Next apply if the error occurred in the procedure that contains the error handler. But if the error occurred in a different procedure from the procedure that contains the error handler, Resume causes execution to resume with the last statement to call out of the procedure that contains the error handler; Resume Next causes execution to resume with the statement *after* the last statement to call out of the procedure that contains the error handler.

USING A *RESUME LINE* STATEMENT

Resume *line* causes execution to resume at the specified line. Use a label to indicate the line, which must be in the same procedure as the error handler.

For example, if a procedure tried to open a particular file, you could create a simple error handler that uses a Resume *line* statement, as shown in Listing 17.2. This procedure works with Word. To make it work with other applications, substitute the appropriate error numbers in line 15.

LISTING 17.2:

```
1.  Sub Handle_Error_Opening_File()
2.
3.      Dim strFName As String
```

```
 4.
 5.  StartHere:
 6.
 7.      On Error GoTo ErrorHandler
 8.      strFName = InputBox("Enter the name of the file to open.", _
            "Open File")
 9.      If strFName = "" Then End
10.      Documents.Open strFName
11.      Exit Sub
12.
13.  ErrorHandler:
14.
15.      If Err = 5174 Or Err = 5273 Then MsgBox _
             "The file " & strFName & " does not exist." & vbCr & _
             "Please enter the name again.", _
             vbOKOnly + vbCritical, "File Error"
16.      Resume StartHere
17.
18.  End Sub
```

Here's how the Handle_Error_Opening_File procedure that comprises Listing 17.2 works:

◆ Line 1 starts the procedure, and line 18 ends it.

◆ Line 2 is a spacer. Line 3 declares the String variable strFName. Line 4 is another spacer.

◆ Line 5 contains the StartHere label, to which execution will return from the Resume statement in line 16. Line 6 is a spacer.

◆ Line 7 uses an On Error statement to enable the error handler ErrorHandler.

◆ Line 8 displays an input box prompting the user for the name of the file they want to open and stores the name in the variable strFName, which line 9 then tries to open. Line 10 checks strFName against an empty string and ends execution if it matches.

◆ If the file exists and can be opened, execution passes to line 11, where an Exit Sub statement exits the procedure, ending its execution. Otherwise, an error is generated, and execution branches to the ErrorHandler label in line 13, where the error handler becomes active.

◆ Line 14 is a spacer. Line 15 then compares the value of the error to 5174 (the error that occurs if VBA can't find the file) and to 5273 (the error that occurs if the document name or path isn't valid in Word). If either of these comparisons matches, line 15 displays a message box advising the user of the error and prompting them to enter the correct filename.

◆ The Resume statement in line 16 then returns execution to the StartHere label in line 5. Line 17 is a spacer.

TIP   For some procedures, you may want to build in a counter mechanism to prevent the user from repeating the same error endlessly because they don't grasp what's wrong. By incrementing the counter variable each time the error handler is invoked and checking the resulting number, you can choose to take a different action after a number of unsuccessful attempts to execute a particular action.

WARNING You can't use a Resume statement anywhere other than in an error-handling routine (or an On Error Resume Next statement). If you do, VBA gives an error.

Getting the Description of an Error

To see the description of the current error, return the Description property of the Err object:

```
MsgBox Err.Description
```

Error messages tend to be terse, cryptic, and of less help to the end user than to the people who built VBA and the application in question. Think twice before displaying one of these error messages to an end user. Usually, you'll get much better results by displaying a more verbose error message of your own devising that explains in more normal English what the problem is—and, preferably, what (if anything) the user can do to solve it.

Raising Your Own Errors

As part of your testing, you'll often need to cause errors so that you can see how well your error handler handles them.

To cause an error, use the Raise method of the Err object, specifying only the *number* argument. *number* is a Long argument giving the number of the error that you want to cause. For example, the following statement raises error 5121:

```
Err.Raise 5121
```

Suppressing Alerts

Many of the procedures you build will use message boxes or dialog boxes to allow the user to choose options for the procedure. In some applications—such as Word, Excel, and PowerPoint—you can use the DisplayAlerts property of the Application object to suppress the display of message boxes and errors while a procedure is running:

- In Word, DisplayAlerts can be set to wdAlertsNone (0) to suppress alerts and message boxes, wdAlertsMessageBox (-2) to suppress alerts but display message boxes, or wdAlertsAll (-1, the default) to display all alerts and message boxes. DisplayAlerts is a sticky setting. You need to set DisplayAlerts explicitly back to one of four things: to True or to wdAlertsAll when you want to see alerts again after setting it to False; to wdAlertsNone; or to wdAlertsMessageBox. VBA resets the default value when you restart Word.

- In Excel, DisplayAlerts is a read/write Boolean property that can be set to True to display alerts and False to suppress them. The setting sticks until you change it or restart Excel, at which point VBA resets it to True.

- In PowerPoint, DisplayAlerts is a read/write property that can be set to ppAlertsAll to display all alerts and ppAlertsNone to suppress all alerts. The setting sticks until you change it or until you restart PowerPoint, at which point VBA resets it to ppAlertsNone.

Handling User Interrupts in Word, Excel, and Project

Errors may seem quite enough of a problem, but you also need to decide what will happen if a user tries to interrupt your code by pressing Ctrl+Break while it's executing. Some VBA hosts, including Word and Excel, offer you three options:

◆ You can allow a user interrupt to stop your code. This is the easy way to proceed (and, as the default condition, needs no effort on your part), but in complex procedures, it may cause problems.

◆ You can prevent user interrupts by disabling user input while the procedure is running. This is simple to do, but you run the risk of creating unstoppable code if a procedure enters an endless loop.

◆ As a compromise between the first two options, you can allow user interrupts during certain parts of a procedure and prevent user interrupts during more critical parts of a procedure.

Disabling User Input while a Procedure Is Running

To disable user input while a procedure is executing, disable the Ctrl+Break key combination by setting the EnableCancelKey property of the Application object to wdCancelDisabled (in Word) or xlDisabled (in Excel):

```
Application.EnableCancelKey = wdCancelDisabled     'Word
Application.EnableCancelKey = xlDisabled           'Excel
```

VBA automatically enables user input again when the procedure stops executing. You can also reenable user input during a procedure by setting the EnableCancelKey property to wdCancelInterrupt (in Word) or xlInterrupt (in Excel):

```
Application.EnableCancelKey = wdCancelInterrupt    'Word
Application.EnableCancelKey = xlInterrupt          'Excel
```

Excel offers a third setting, xlErrorHandler, that traps the Ctrl+Break keystroke as error 18. You can deal with this error as you would any other error. Here's a quick example:

```
Sub CancelKey_Example()
    Dim i As Long
    On Error GoTo EH
    Application.EnableCancelKey = xlErrorHandler
    For i = 1 To 100000000
        Application.StatusBar = i
    Next i
EH:
    If Err.Number = 18 Then
        If MsgBox("Do you want to stop the procedure?" _
            & vbCr & vbCr & "If not, stop pressing Ctrl+Break!", _
            vbYesNo + vbCritical, "User Interrupt Detected") = vbYes Then End
    End If
End Sub
```

Disabling User Input while Part of a Procedure Is Running

You may want to temporarily disable user input while a procedure is executing a procedure that doesn't bear interruption and then reenable user input when it's safe for the user to stop the procedure again. For example, in a procedure whose actions include moving a number of files from one folder to another, you can prevent the code that executes the move operations from being interrupted so that the user can't stop the procedure with some files still in the source folder and some in the destination folder. Here's an example using Word:

```
'interruptible actions up to this point
Application.EnableCancelKey = wdCancelDisabled
For i = 1 to LastFile
    SourceFile = Source & "\Section" & i
    DestFile = Destination & "\Section" & i
    Name SourceFile As DestFile
Next i
Application.EnableCancelKey = wdCancelInterrupt
'interruptible actions after this point
```

WARNING Never disable user input for any code that may get stuck in an endless loop. If you do, you'll have to close down the program from Task Manager (right-click the notification area, choose Task Manager from the shortcut menu, select the application on the Applications page, and then click the End Task button). Doing so causes you to lose any unsaved work in the application.

Documenting Your Code

You can greatly simplify debugging your procedures by documenting your code. The best way to document your code is to add comments to it, either as you create the code or when you've finished creating it.

Document your code as you create it in any procedure in which you're exploring your way and trying different methods to reach your goal. Add comments to explain what action each group of statements is trying to achieve. Once you've gotten the procedure to work, go through the code and delete the statements you didn't use, using the comments to identify which sections are now useless and which are still worthwhile, and leaving only the comments that are relevant to how the remaining code functions.

NOTE You might also want to leave comment lines on any methods of achieving the same goal that you decided not to use. For example, if you think that you might be able to rewrite a procedure to run faster when you have a few hours and some brain cells to spare, you could make a note of that. You could also note other possible applications for parts of the code in this procedure to help you locate it if you need to reuse it in another procedure.

Likewise, add comments when you're changing an existing procedure so that you don't lose track of your changes. Once you have the procedure working to your liking, remove any unnecessary comments and reword any verbose or unclear comments.

Documenting your code when you've finished writing it allows you to enter only the comment lines that you want to be there permanently. This is the way to go when you're fairly sure of the direction of your code when you start writing the procedure, and the procedure needs only a few pointers to make its code clear once it's complete.

To document your code, use comments prefaced by either the apostrophe character (') or the Rem keyword (short for *remark*). You can comment out either a whole line or part of a line: Anything to the right of the apostrophe or the Rem keyword is commented out. For partial lines, the apostrophe is usually the better character to use; if you choose to use the Rem keyword, you'll need to add a colon before it to make it work consistently (some statements accept a Rem without a colon at their end; others generate a compile error):

```
Rem This is a comment line.
Documents.Add: Rem create a document based on Normal.dot
```

Generally, apostrophe-commented remarks separated by a few spaces or tabs from any statement the line contains (as in the second line below) are easier to read than comments using Rem:

```
'This is a comment line
Documents.Add      'create a document based on Normal.dot
```

It's tempting to think that you don't need to document your code because you'll be able to remember what it does. But once you've written a lot of code, you probably won't be able to remember. Coming back to a procedure six months after writing it, you'll find it as unfamiliar as if someone else had written it. And if you've advanced in your usage of VBA, you may even find it hard to think back down to the clumsy methods you were using at that time.

Most programmers have a distinct aversion to documenting their code; in some, the dislike for documenting is almost pathological. You can see why: When you're writing the code, documenting what it does slows you down and distracts you from your purpose; and when the code works, documenting it is tedious work. Besides, anyone competent should be able to read the code and see what it does… shouldn't they?

Maybe so, but consider this: First, it's likely that you won't always be the person working on your code—at times, others will work on it too, and they'll appreciate all the help they can get in understanding your code. Second, the code on which you work won't always be your own—you may at times have to debug code that others have written, and in this case *you'll* be the one in need of comments.

Chapter 18

Building Well-Behaved Code

◆ What is a well-behaved procedure?

◆ Retaining and restoring the user environment

◆ Letting the user know what's happening

◆ Checking that the procedure is running under suitable conditions

◆ Cleaning up after a procedure

Once you've built a procedure that's useful and that works consistently as intended, you'll probably want to distribute it to as many of your coworkers as might use it or even to a wider audience on the Internet. Before you distribute it, though, you should make sure that the procedure is as civilized as possible in its interaction with the user and with the settings the user may have chosen on their computer. It's all too easy to distribute an apparently successful procedure that runs roughshod over the user's preferences or one that fails unexpectedly under certain circumstances. In this chapter, you'll look at how to avoid such problems and how to construct your procedures so that the user will have no problem interacting with them.

This chapter concentrates on the principles of good behavior. The specifics of good behavior vary from application to application, and you will need to apply the principles to the application with which you're working. This chapter gives some examples.

What Is a Well-Behaved Procedure?

A well-behaved procedure is one that leaves no trace of its actions beyond those that the user expected it to perform. This means the following:

◆ Making no detectable changes to the user environment, or restoring the previous settings if the procedure needs to make changes (for example, in order to run successfully).

◆ Presenting the user with relevant choices for the procedure and relevant information once the procedure has finished running.

◆ Showing or telling the user what is happening while the procedure is running.

◆ Making sure (if possible) that conditions are appropriate for the procedure to run successfully—before the procedure takes any actions.

- Anticipating or trapping errors wherever possible so that the procedure doesn't crash; or if it does crash under exceptional circumstances, doing so as gracefully as possible and minimizing damage to the user's work.

- Leaving the user in the optimal position to continue their work after the procedure finishes executing.

- Cleaning up any scratch documents, folders, or other detritus that the procedure creates in order to perform its duties.

If you stop for a moment, you can probably think of a couple of examples in which applications you use don't exactly do this. For example, do you use Word? Then you're probably familiar with this less-than-inspiring behavior:

- If you press the Page Up key once and then the Page Down key once when working in a document, the insertion point doesn't always return to the same exact point in the document as it should. So if you page through your document and try to return to where you were last, you always need to check that the insertion point is in the right place before you start typing—otherwise, the characters may land in the wrong place.

- Similarly, if you're working in Print Preview in Word, and you choose View ➤ Header And Footer to work on a header, Word switches the view to Print Layout view. Most people can accept that Print Layout view is the view you use to work on headers and footers, even though earlier versions of Word used a Header and Footer pane instead or as well. But when you click the Close button on the Header And Footer toolbar to return to the main document, Word switches the view back to the view you were using before Print Preview rather than returning you to Print Preview.

Such weaknesses in commercial applications' interfaces provoke two main reactions among developers. First, that if the user is accustomed to such niggles as having to reposition the selection or change the view when they shouldn't need to, they're unlikely to have a problem with having to perform similar actions after running a procedure—particularly a procedure that saves them plenty of time and effort. The second reaction is an impressive (and sometimes overzealous) determination to restore the user environment absolutely perfectly even if major software corporations seem incapable of producing software that does so.

The first approach tends to be more economical in its code and the second more inventive. To get your work done and retain your sanity, you'll probably want to steer a course between the two extremes.

Retaining or Restoring the User Environment

In many cases, your procedures will run without needing to change the user environment—but if you do need to change the user environment, restore it as closely as possible to its previous state. What this means depends on the host application, but here are some examples of changes in Word, Excel, and PowerPoint:

- In Word: changing the revision-marking (Track Changes) setting, so that you could change the text without the changes being marked as revisions.

- In Word or PowerPoint: changing the view to a different view so that you could perform certain operations that cannot be performed in the original view.

◆ In Excel: creating a temporary worksheet on which you can manipulate data secure in the knowledge that you don't need to check whether any ranges are already occupied by user data.

◆ In any application that lets you manipulate its Find and Replace features: using the Find and Replace features to identify and/or manipulate parts of a document, then restoring the user's last search (and replace, if necessary) so that they can perform it again seamlessly. The problem here is that most applications have "sticky" Find and Replace settings to allow the user to perform the same search or replacement operation again quickly without reentering the parameters. If you've replaced the user's search and replacement parameters, they'll get a rude shock the next time they try to search or replace.

To store such information, you can use private variables, public variables, or custom objects as appropriate.

Leaving the User in the Best Position to Continue Working

After your procedure finishes running, the user needs to be in the best possible position to continue their work. What exactly the best possible position entails depends on the situation, but here are three simple suggestions:

◆ Usually, you'll want to leave the user facing the same document they were working on when they started running the procedure. There are some obvious exceptions to this, such as when the procedure creates a new file for the user and the user is expecting to work in that file, but the general principle is sound.

◆ If the file is essentially untouched (at least from the user's point of view), the selection should probably be back where it was when the user started running the procedure. To restore the selection, you may want to define a range at the beginning of the procedure and then move the selection back to it at the end of the procedure. In some applications, you could also use a bookmark or a named range—but if you do, be sure to remove it afterward.

◆ If the procedure has created a new object in the file, and the user will be expecting to work with it, you may want to have that object selected at the end of the procedure.

Keeping the User Informed during the Procedure

A key component of a well-behaved procedure is keeping the user adequately informed throughout the process. In a macro that performs a basic if tedious task, adequate information may require only a clear description in the macro's Description field to assure the user that they're choosing the right procedure from the Macros dialog box. In a more complex procedure that takes wider ranging actions, adequate information will probably be more extensive: You may need to display a starting message box or dialog box, show information on the status bar during the procedure, display an ending message box, or create a log file of information so that the user has a record of what took place during execution of the procedure.

First, decide whether to disable user input during the procedure. In Word and Excel, you can disable user input to protect sensitive sections of your procedures by setting the `EnableCancelKey` property of the `Application` object (as discussed in "Disabling User Input while a Procedure Is Running" in Chapter 17). When you do so, it's a good idea to indicate to the user at the beginning of the procedure that input will be disabled and explain why. Otherwise, a user may respond to a procedure that seems not to be responding in the same way as if the application had hung—by trying to close the application forcibly via Microsoft Office Application Recovery or Task Manager.

To keep the user informed about other aspects of the procedure, you have several options, which are discussed in the following sections. But first, the next section examines how you can *hide* information from the user (and the reasons for doing so) by disabling screen updating in Word and Excel.

Disabling Screen Updating

Word and Excel let you disable screen updating—that is, stop the redrawing of the information in the document area. The other parts of the application window—the title bar, command bars, status bar, scroll bars, and so on—continue to update, but these items are usually relatively static compared to the document area and so don't take much updating. Still, if you change the size of the application window or the document window, you'll see that change even with screen updating disabled.

There are two advantages to disabling screen updating:

◆ First, you can speed up the running of your procedures somewhat. This improvement was marked in the last century, but it is still noticeable for underpowered computers that have slow graphics cards. Most computers built since 2003 or so have relatively fast graphics cards, so turning off screen updating makes less difference. Any speed improvement from disabling screen updating applies especially to procedures that cause a lot of changes to the on-screen display. For example, suppose a procedure in Word strips a certain type of information out of the current document, pastes it into a new document, creates a table out of it, and applies assorted formatting to the table. The computer will expend a fair amount of effort updating what's appearing on the monitor. This is wasted effort if the user isn't hanging on every operation, so you might as well turn off screen updating.

◆ Second, you can hide from the user any parts of the procedure that you don't want them to see. This sounds totalitarian, but it's usually more like a cross between benevolent dictatorship and public television: People shouldn't see certain things that might really upset them, and there's a lot that most people don't *really* need to know about. So with VBA: If the user doesn't know about the operations that a procedure will routinely perform to achieve certain effects, they may be surprised or dismayed by what they see on-screen. For example, in a procedure that moves an open file, you might want to hide from the user the fact that the procedure closes the open file, moves it, and then reopens the file from its new location. By disabling screen updating, you can achieve this effect.

The major disadvantage to disabling screen updating is that doing so prevents the user from seeing information that might be useful to them. In the worst case, the user may assume from the lack of activity on-screen that either the procedure has entered an endless loop or the computer has hung; and so they may try to stop the procedure by pressing Ctrl+Break or press Ctrl+Alt+Delete so that they can use Task Manager to close the application. (Task Manager typically lists the host application as "Not responding" for much of the time VBA code is running, which doesn't help.)

To forestall users from disrupting a procedure or an application with a two- or three-finger salute, warn them in advance that a procedure will disable screen updating. For instance, you might mention the fact in a message box at the beginning of the procedure, or you might display a dialog box that allows the user to choose whether to disable screen updating and have the procedure run faster or to leave screen updating on and have the procedure run at its normal speed and give a show possibly worth watching.

If you don't display a message box or dialog box at the beginning of a procedure, you may want to display information on the status bar to tell the reader what's going during the procedure. Word and Excel update the status bar and the title bar of the application even if screen updating is turned off—provided that the status bar and the title bar are visible. To display information on the status bar, assign a suitable string to the `StatusBar` property of the `Application` object:

```
Application.StatusBar = _
    "Word is creating 308 new documents for you to edit. Please wait..."
```

Alternatively, you can disable screen updating for parts of a procedure and turn it back on, or refresh it, for other parts. Consider a procedure that creates and formats a number of documents from an existing document. If you turn off screen updating at the beginning of the procedure and then refresh it once each document has been created and formatted, the user will see each document in turn (which conveys the progress the procedure is making) without seeing the details of the formatting. What's more, the procedure will run faster than if the screen were showing all of the formatting taking place.

To turn off screen updating, set the `ScreenUpdating` property of the `Application` object to `False`:

```
Application.ScreenUpdating = False
```

To turn screen updating back on, set `ScreenUpdating` to `True` again:

```
Application.ScreenUpdating = True
```

In Word, to refresh the screen with the current contents of the video memory buffer, use the `ScreenRefresh` method of the `Application` object:

```
Application.ScreenRefresh
```

Manipulating the Cursor

When you're using Word or Excel as the host application, you may want to manipulate the cursor (the mouse pointer). You may need to do this for many procedures, because VBA automatically displays the busy (hourglass) cursor while a procedure is running and then restores a normal cursor when it has finished. Sometimes, however, you may need or want to set the cursor manually.

WARNING   After using computers for even a few months, users tend to develop almost Pavlovian reactions to the cursor, with the busy cursor signifying (in ascending order) a momentary breather (or a slow computer), a chance to grab a cup of coffee or chat with a colleague, or the onset of panic that the computer has hung before they've saved the last three hours of work. You usually won't want to mess with these reactions. So it's a mistake to display an I-beam cursor or "normal" cursor when the system is in fact busy—or to display a busy cursor after the procedure has in fact finished running.

MANIPULATING THE CURSOR IN WORD

Word implements the cursor via the `System` object. To manipulate the cursor, you set the `Cursor` property. This is a read/write Long property that can be set to the following values: `wdCursorIBeam` (1) for an I-beam cursor, `wdCursorNormal` (2) for a normal cursor, `wdCursorNorthWestArrow` (3) for a left-angled resizing arrow (pointing up), and `wdCursorWait` (0) for the busy cursor. The exact appearance of the cursor depends on the cursor scheme the user has selected.

For example, the following statement displays a busy cursor:

```
System.Cursor = wdCursorWait
```

MANIPULATING THE CURSOR IN EXCEL

Excel lets you manipulate the cursor through the Cursor property of the Application object. Cursor is a read/write Long property that can be set to the following values: xlDefault (-4143) for a default cursor, xlWait (2) for an hourglass cursor, xlNorthwestArrow (1) for the arrow pointing up and to the left, and xlIBeam (3) for an I-beam cursor.

For example, the following statement displays the hourglass cursor:

```
Application.Cursor = xlWait
```

NOTE   When you explicitly set the Cursor property of the Application object in Excel, remember to reset it to something appropriate before your code stops executing, because otherwise the cursor stays as you left it.

Displaying Information at the Beginning of a Procedure

At the beginning of many procedures, you'll probably want to display a message box or a dialog box. For this purpose, you'll typically use a Yes/No or OK/Cancel message box that tells the user what the procedure will do and gives them the chance to cancel the procedure without running it any further.

A dialog box will usually present options for the procedure (for example, mutually exclusive options via option buttons or non-exclusive options via check boxes), allowing the user to enter information (via text boxes, list boxes, or combo boxes) and of course letting them cancel the procedure if they've cued it by accident. If you have time to create a Help file to accompany the procedures and user forms you create, you might add a Help button to each message box or dialog box, linking it to the relevant topic in the Help file.

TIP   As mentioned earlier, you can also use a message box or dialog box to warn the user that the procedure is going to turn off screen updating. Likewise, if the procedure will disable user interrupts for part or all of its duration, warn the user about that, too.

Displaying Information in a Message Box or Dialog Box at the End of a Procedure

With some procedures, you'll find it useful to collect information on what the procedure is doing so that you can display that information to the user in a message box or dialog box when the procedure stops running. As you saw in Chapter 13, message boxes are easier to use but are severely limited in their capabilities for laying out text—you're limited to the effects you can achieve with spaces, tabs, carriage returns, and bullets. With dialog boxes, on the other hand, you can lay out text however you need to (by using labels or text boxes) and include images if necessary.

The easiest way to collect information while running a procedure is to build one or more strings containing the information you want to display. For an example of this, look back to Listing 12.2 in Chapter 12, in which the cmdOK_Click procedure collects information while creating a series of folders and then displays a message box telling the user what it has done.

Creating a Log File

If you need to collect a lot of information during the course of running a procedure and either present it to the user once the procedure has finished or just have it available for reference if needed, consider using a log file rather than a message box or dialog box. Log files are useful for lengthy procedures involving critical data: By writing information periodically to a log file (and by saving it frequently), you can keep a record of what the procedure achieves before any crash it suffers.

NOTE   If you want the log file to be useful to normal users as well as to the technically inclined, make its entries readable and helpful while including any more technical information required for advanced troubleshooting. For example, a message such as *The data files for the "Madrid" office (madrid060430.xls) and the "Taos" office (taos060430.xls) were not found in the expected location, "\\server2\data\dayfiles\", so the information could not be included* is usually more widely helpful than a cryptic *Error code 44E: Required Data Missing.*

For example, say you wrote a procedure for Word that collects information from a variety of sources each day and writes it into a report. You might want to keep a log file that tracks whether information from each source is successfully transferred and at what time. Listing 18.1 provides an example of such a procedure. At the end of the procedure, you could leave the log file open so that the user could check whether the procedure was successful in creating the report or leave the summary file open so that the user could read the report itself.

LISTING 18.1:

```
1.    Sub Create_Log_File()
2.
3.        Dim strDate As String
4.        Dim strPath As String
5.        Dim strCity(10) As String
6.        Dim strLogText As String
7.        Dim strLogName As String
8.        Dim strSummary As String
9.        Dim strFile As String
10.       Dim i As Integer
11.
12.       On Error GoTo Crash
13.
14.       strCity(1) = "Chicago"
15.       strCity(2) = "Toronto"
16.       strCity(3) = "New York"
17.       strCity(4) = "London"
18.       strCity(5) = "Lyons"
19.       strCity(6) = "Antwerp"
20.       strCity(7) = "Copenhagen"
21.       strCity(8) = "Krakow"
22.       strCity(9) = "Pinsk"
23.       strCity(10) = "Belgrade"
24.
25.       strDate = Month(Date) & "-" & Day(Date) & "-" _
              & Year(Date)
26.       strPath = "f:\Daily Data\"
27.       strLogName = strPath & "Reports\Log for " _
              & strDate & ".doc"
28.       strSummary = strPath & "Reports\Summary for " _
              & strDate & ".doc"
```

```
29.        Documents.Add
30.        ActiveDocument.SaveAs strSummary
31.
32.        For i = 1 To 10
33.            strFile = strPath & strCity(i) & " " & strDate & ".doc"
34.            If Dir(strFile) <> "" Then
35.                Documents.Open strFile
36.                Documents(strFile).Paragraphs(1).Range.Copy
37.                Documents(strFile).Close _
38.                    SaveChanges:=wdDoNotSaveChanges
39.                With Documents(strSummary)
40.                    Selection.EndKey Unit:=wdStory
41.                    Selection.Paste
42.                    .Save
43.                End With
44.                strLogText = strLogText & strCity(i) _
                        & vbTab & "OK" & vbCr
45.            Else
46.                strLogText = strLogText & strCity(i) _
                        & vbTab & "No file" & vbCr
47.            End If
48.        Next i
49.
50.    Crash:
51.
52.        Documents.Add
53.        Selection.TypeText strLogText
54.        ActiveDocument.SaveAs strLogName
55.        Documents(strLogName).Close
56.        Documents(strSummary).Close
57.
58.    End Sub
```

The procedure in Listing 18.1 creates a new document to contain a summary, opens a number of files in turn, copies the first paragraph out of each and pastes it into the summary document, and then closes the file. As it does this, it maintains a string of log information from which it creates a log file at the end of the procedure or if an error occurs during the procedure. Here's what happens in the code:

◆ Lines 3 through 9 declare six String variables—strDate, strPath, strLogText, strLogName, strSummary, and strFile—and one String array, strCity, containing 10 items. (The procedure uses an Option Base 1 statement that doesn't appear in the listing, so strCity(10) produces 10 items in the array rather than 11.) Line 10 declares the Integer variable i, which the procedure will use as a counter.

◆ Line 11 is a spacer. Line 12 uses an On Error GoTo statement to start error handling and direct execution to the label Crash: in the event of an error. Line 13 is a spacer.

◆ Lines 14 through 23 assign the names of the putative company's 10 mythical offices to the strCity array. Line 24 is a spacer.

◆ Line 25 assigns to `strDate` a string created by concatenating the month, the day, and the year for the current date (with a hyphen between each part) by using the `Month`, `Day`, and `Year` functions, respectively. For example, January 21, 2006 will produce a date string of `1-21-2006`. (The reason for creating a string like this is that Windows can't handle slashes in filenames—slashes are reserved for indicating folders.)

◆ Line 26 sets `strPath` to the `f:\Daily Data\` folder. Line 27 then builds a filename for the log file in the `\Reports\` subfolder, and line 28 creates a filename for the summary file, also in the `\Reports\` subfolder.

◆ Line 29 creates a new document based on `Normal.dot`, and line 30 saves this document under the name stored in the `strSummary` variable. Line 31 is a spacer.

◆ Line 32 begins a `For...Next` loop that runs from `i = 1` to `i = 10`. Line 33 assigns to the String variable `strFile` the filename for the first of the cities stored in the `strCity` array: `strPath & strCity(i) & " " & strDate & ".doc"`.

◆ Line 34 then begins an `If` statement that checks whether `Dir(strFile)` returns an empty string. If not, line 35 opens the document specified by `strFile`, line 36 copies its first paragraph, and line 37 closes it without saving changes. The procedure doesn't make any changes to the document, but if the document contains hot fields (such as date fields or links) that update themselves when the document is opened, it may have become dirty. Including the `SaveChanges` argument ensures the user doesn't get an unexpected message box prompting them to save a document they know they haven't changed. (An alternative would be to set the `Saved` property of the document to `True` and then close it without using the `SaveChanges` argument.)

◆ Lines 39 through 43 contain a `With` statement that works with the `Document` object specified by `strSummary`. Line 40 uses the `EndKey` method with the `Unit` argument `wdStory` to move the selection to the end of the document. Line 41 pastes in the material copied from the document just opened, and line 42 saves the document. Line 43 ends the `With` statement.

◆ Line 44 adds to `strLogText` the contents of `strCity(i)`, a tab, the text `OK`, and a carriage return, which will produce a simple tabbed list of the cities and the status of their reports.

◆ If the condition posed in line 34 isn't met, execution branches to the `Else` statement in line 45, and line 46 adds to `strLogText` the contents of `strCity(i)`, a tab, `No file`, and a carriage return. Line 47 ends the `If` statement, and line 48 ends the `For...Next` loop, returning execution to line 32.

◆ Line 49 is a spacer. Line 50 contains the `Crash:` label and marks the start of the error handler. Unlike in many procedures, you don't want to stop execution before entering the error handler—as it happens, you want to execute these statements (to create the log file) even if an error occurs. Line 51 is a spacer.

◆ Line 52 creates a new document based on the default template, into which line 53 types the contents of `strLogText` and which line 54 saves under the name `strLogName`. Line 55 closes this new document (alternatively, you could leave the document open so that the user could view it). Line 56 closes the summary document (which has remained open since it was created; again, you might want to leave this open so that the user might view it or offer the user the option of keeping it open). Line 57 is a spacer, and line 58 ends the procedure.

Making Sure the Procedure Is Running under Suitable Conditions

Another important element of creating a well-behaved procedure is to check that it's running under suitable conditions. This ideal is nearly impossible to achieve under all circumstances, but you should take some basic steps, such as the following:

◆ Make sure that a file is open in a procedure that needs a file to be open—otherwise, you'll get an error every time. For example, in Excel, you might check the Count property of the Workbooks collection to make sure that at least one workbook is open:

```
If Workbooks.Count = 0 Then _
    MsgBox "This procedure will not run without a " _
    & "workbook open.", vbOKOnly + vbExclamation, _
    "No Workbook Is Open"
```

◆ Check that the procedure is running on an appropriate item, if the procedure has definable requirements. For example, in an Excel procedure that applies intricate formatting to a chart the user has selected, make sure that the user has selected a chart. Trying to manipulate another object with chart-related commands is likely to cause an error.

◆ Make sure the file contains the element required by the procedure. (If it doesn't, an error will likely result.) Alternatively, trap the error that will result from the item's not being present.

Cleaning Up after a Procedure

Like your children or housemates, your procedures should learn to clean up after themselves. Cleaning up involves the following:

◆ Undoing any changes that the procedure had to make to enable itself to run

◆ Closing any files that no longer need to be open

◆ Removing any scratch files or folders that the procedure has created to achieve its effects

Undoing Changes the Procedure Has Made

In some cases, you'll need to make changes to a document in order to run a procedure successfully. Here are a couple of examples:

◆ In Word, you might need to apply some formatting to half of a table but not to the rest of it. In this case, it may be easier to split the table into two tables so that you can select columns in the relevant part and format or change them without affecting the columns in the other half of the original table. If you perform a procedure like this, you'll want to join the tables together again afterward by removing the break you've inserted between the original table's two halves. The easiest way to do this is to bookmark the break that you insert; you can then go back to the bookmark and delete it and the break at the same time. Alternatively, you could use a Set statement to define a range for the break and then return to the range and remove the break.

◆ In Excel, you may need to define named ranges in a workbook so that you can easily reference them from the code. (Usually, you'll do better to use ranges via VBA, which won't leave unwanted named ranges in the workbook.) Delete these named ranges when you're finished with them.

Removing Scratch Files and Folders

During a complex procedure, you may need to create scratch files in which to temporarily store or manipulate information or scratch folders in which to store files. For example, if you need to perform complex formatting on a few paragraphs of a long document in Word, you may find it easier to copy and paste those paragraphs into a new blank document and manipulate them there than to continue working in the same document and risk unintentionally affecting other paragraphs as well. Likewise, in PowerPoint, you might need to create a new presentation that you could use for temporary or backup storage of intricate objects.

Creating scratch files, while often necessary for the safe and successful operation of a procedure, is antisocial toward the user of the computer: You're cluttering up their drive with information that's probably of no use to them. Creating scratch folders in which to save the scratch files is even worse. Always go the extra distance to clean up any mess that you've made on the drive, and remove both scratch files and scratch folders that you've created. Before you ask—no, commercial applications don't always do this, not even Microsoft's applications; and no, that doesn't mean you should follow their poor example.

If your procedure is going to remove any scratch files it creates, you may be tempted to conceal from the user their creation and subsequent deletion. This usually isn't a good idea—in most cases, the best thing is to warn the user that the procedure will create scratch files. You might even let the user specify or create a suitable folder for the scratch files, or present the user with a list that logs the files created and whether they were successfully deleted. Doing so will allow the user to safely remove any scratch files left on their computer if a procedure goes wrong or is interrupted during execution.

Another possibility is to use the API (application programming interface) commands `GetTempDir` and `GetTempFileName` to return the computer's temporary folder and a temporary filename that you can use. API calls are outside the scope of this book—but even if you use the temporary folder, you should delete any files that you create in it when you've finished using them. Again, a disappointing number of commercial software developers fail to do this.

BUILDING A SCRATCH FOLDER

You can use a `MkDir` statement to create a folder. For example, the following statement creates a folder named `Scratch Folder` on the `C:` drive:

```
MkDir "c:\Scratch Folder"
```

Before creating a folder, use a `Dir` statement to check to see that the name isn't already in use. (If a folder with that name already exists, an error results.)

TIP For temporary storage, you may want to build a folder name based on the date and time to lessen the chance that a folder with that name already exists. You might also use the `Rnd` function to generate a random number to use as part of the folder name.

DELETING THE SCRATCH FOLDER

You can use the RmDir statement to remove an empty folder. (Make sure that the folder is empty first—otherwise RmDir will fail.) For example, the following statement removes the scratch folder named Scratch Folder on the C: drive:

```
RmDir "c:\Scratch Folder"
```

Chapter 19

Securing Your Code with VBA's Security Features

♦ Understanding how VBA implements security

♦ Signing a macro project with a digital signature

♦ Getting a digital certificate

♦ Choosing the appropriate security level

♦ Designating trusted publishers or trusted sources

♦ Locking your code

This chapter discusses how to use the security tools that VBA provides for distributing and implementing macros and VBA code. VBA security falls into three parts: securing your applications against rogue VBA code; establishing that your VBA code isn't itself rogue so that it can be run; and securing your code against theft, alteration, or snooping.

Understanding How VBA Implements Security

To secure an application against rogue VBA code, you choose the level of security that you want the application to use when running VBA code so that it will run only code from a trusted source (also called a *trusted publisher*). You can specify which sources to trust and how well to trust them. A trusted source might be someone who works for the same company as you or someone who has a digital certificate from a third party you trust, such as the VeriSign certification authority. Because you (in this example) trust VeriSign, you trust the third party to whom VeriSign has issued a digital certificate.

To establish that your own code is okay for the applications to trust, you sign a document or template project that contains customizations or macro project items (code modules, class modules, or user forms) with a digital signature generated by a digital certificate that uniquely identifies you or your company. This chapter shows you this technique first, because it sets the stage for specifying the level of security to use.

To secure your code, you can lock a macro project with a password so that nobody can open the code. Doing so serves both to prevent anyone from tinkering with your code and either stopping it from working or rendering it harmful, and to protect your intellectual property: If nobody can see your code, they can't steal your ideas. The end of the chapter shows you how to do this.

NOTE Not every VBA host supports VBA's security features—so this chapter may not apply to what you're doing. In particular, applications that use VBA 5 rather than VBA 6 do not support the security features.

Signing Your Macro Projects with Digital Signatures

VBA provides a security mechanism for securing macro projects with digital signatures. The digital signatures provide a means of establishing the provenance of the projects, which should help you to decide whether to trust the code or not. If you trust the source of the code to produce benevolent code, you can open the project and run the code. If you suspect the source or the information of being malignant, you can either avoid opening the project or open the project with the code disabled.

The same goes for other people: You'll need to sign your projects so that other people know where they come from and who created them. Once you've signed the projects, the code is available to any application that has specified you as a trusted source for macro projects. (This assumes they're using a Medium, High, or Very High level of security in the application. You'll see how you set the security level later in this chapter.)

This section discusses what digital certificates are, what they mean in practical terms, how you get hold of them, and how you use them to create digital signatures.

NOTE   VBA's security mechanism, and the list of certificates and trusted sources, is shared across the range of VBA-enabled applications on your computer. So if you designate a trusted source from one application, all the other applications that support VBA security will trust that source as well. For example, if you open a document that contains code in Word and choose to trust the source of the code, Excel and Outlook also gain that trust and open projects from that source without prompting you.

What Is a Digital Certificate?

A *digital certificate* is a piece of code that uniquely identifies its holder. You use your digital certificate to create a digital signature for a project. This project can be a document project, a template project, or an add-in. The project doesn't have to contain macros, procedures, user forms, classes, or VBA code for you to sign it, although these contents are the usual reason for signing a project.

A digital signature applies to a whole macro project—typically, a document project or a template project. You can't apply a digital signature to just part of a project—say, just to one module of code or to one user form. Each macro project item in that macro project—each module, user form, class, and reference—is covered by the digital certificate.

Getting a Digital Certificate

There are several types of digital certificates: those you create yourself, those you get from your company or organization, and those you get from a commercial certification authority, or certificate authority (CA).

A digital certificate you create yourself is of little use to people beyond you and those who trust you, whereas a certificate from a commercial certification authority should be good enough for general use in the wide world. A certificate issued by your company falls in the middle: In many cases, the company will have obtained the certificate from the commercial certification authority, which means the commercial certification authority has established to its satisfaction that the company is trustworthy. Whom the company chooses to trust with the certificate is another matter and introduces another link of complication into the chain of trust. However, server software such as Windows 2003 Server include independent certification-authority services that do not require a certificate from a commercial certification authority, so you should be careful which certificates you trust. See "Whose Certificate Is It, and What Does It Mean?" later in this chapter, for a discussion of how to discern a certificate's provenance and meaning.

CREATING A DIGITAL CERTIFICATE OF YOUR OWN

The quickest and easiest way of getting a digital certificate is to create one yourself. Microsoft Office 2003, XP, and 2000 all ship with a tool for creating your own digital certificates.

To understand how digital certificates work, you'll probably want to create several of your own and practice with them on sample files. By designating some of your digital certificates as trusted sources and leaving others untrusted, you can get a clear idea of how digital certificates work without having to use suspect code on your system.

To open the Create Digital Certificate dialog box (see Figure 19.1), take one of the following actions:

◆ On Office 2003, choose Start ➤ All Programs ➤ Microsoft Office ➤ Microsoft Office Tools ➤ Digital Certificate For VBA Projects.

◆ On Office XP, choose Start ➤ Run, type **%programfiles%**, and press Enter to open a Windows Explorer window to your Program Files folder. Open the Microsoft Office\Office10 folder and double-click the SELFCERT.EXE file.

◆ On Office 2000, choose Start ➤ Run, type **%programfiles%**, and press Enter to open a Windows Explorer window to your Program Files folder. Open the Microsoft Office\Office folder and double-click the SELFCERT.EXE file. Alternatively, you can run the SELFCERT.EXE file from the PFiles\MSOffice\Office\ folder on the Office CD.

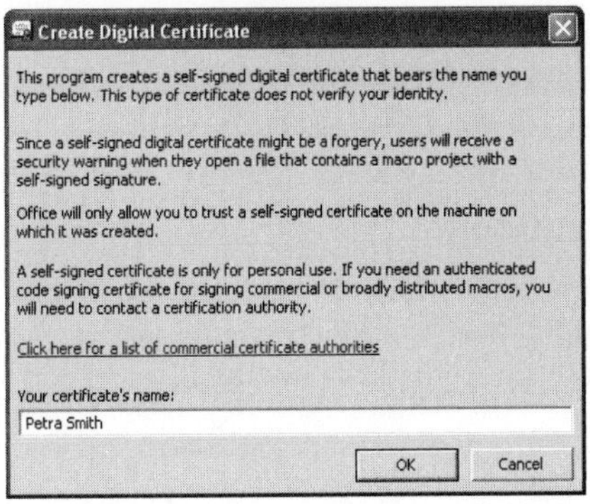

FIGURE 19.1
In the Create Digital Certificate dialog box, enter the name that you want the digital certificate to bear.

Type the name for the certificate in the text box, and then click the OK button. The SelfCert application creates the certificate, installs it automatically, and displays the SelfCert Success dialog box (see Figure 19.2).

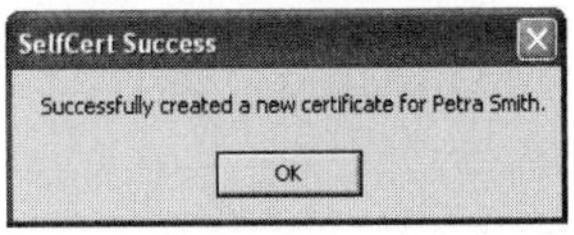

FIGURE 19.2
The SelfCert Success dialog box confirms that the certificate has been created.

GETTING A DIGITAL CERTIFICATE FROM YOUR COMPANY

Your second option is to get a digital certificate from a digital certificate server that your company has. The details of this procedure vary from company to company. The certificates the company provides via its digital certificate server are generated in the same fashion as the digital certificates distributed by the commercial certification authorities discussed in the next section, except that the company distributes the certificates from a pool that it has been allocated, without needing to apply to the certification authority for each certificate as it's needed, or creates the certificates of its own accord without getting them from a certification authority.

GETTING A DIGITAL CERTIFICATE FROM A COMMERCIAL CERTIFICATION AUTHORITY

Your third choice is to get a digital certificate from a commercial certification authority, such as VeriSign (www.verisign.com), Thawte, Inc. (www.thawte.com, a VeriSign company), or GlobalSign NV-AS (www.globalsign.net).

Several different types of certificate are available, depending on what you want to do. If you're creating and distributing software, you'll probably want to consider one of the certificates targeted at developers.

The procedure for proving your identity varies depending on the CA and the type of certificate you want. Generally speaking, the greater the degree of trust that the certificate is intended to inspire, the more proof you'll need to supply. For example, you can get a basic certificate on the strength of nothing more than a verifiable e-mail address, but this type of certificate is unlikely to make people trust you. Other certificate types require you to appear in person before a registration authority with full documentation (such as a passport, driver's license, or other identity documents). Such certificates carry more trust.

INSTALLING A DIGITAL CERTIFICATE

Once you have a digital certificate, you need to install it so that Windows and the applications that will use it know where it's located.

NOTE The Office SelfCert program automatically registers the certificates it creates on the computer on which it creates them. If you created a digital certificate for yourself, you shouldn't need to install it on the same computer. If you want to practice installing it, you'll need to use a different computer.

To install a digital certificate, follow these steps:

1. Choose Start ➢ Control Panel to open a Control Panel window. In Category View, click the Network And Internet Connections link, and then click the Internet Options icon. In Classic View, double-click the Internet Options icon. Windows displays the Internet Properties dialog box.

2. Click the Content tab to display the Content page.

3. In the Certificates group box, click the Certificates button to display the Certificates dialog box, shown in Figure 19.3.

4. Click the Import button to start the Certificate Import Wizard, and then click the Next button to display the File To Import stage of the Certificate Import Wizard dialog box.

FIGURE 19.3
Windows provides
the Certificates dialog
box to manage digital
certificates.

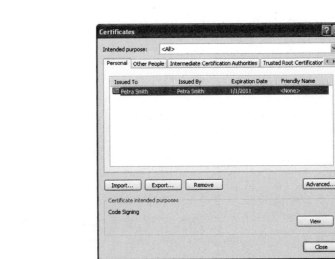

5. In the File Name text box, enter the name of the certificate file you want to import:

♦ Either type the name of the certificate by hand (or paste it in, if you have copied it), or click the Browse button to display the Open dialog box, locate the certificate as usual, and then click the Open button. Make sure the Files Of Type drop-down list in the Open dialog box is set to the appropriate type of certificate, so that the certificate's file shows up in the dialog box. For example, if your certificate is stored in a .CER file, choose the X.509 Certificate filter in the Files Of Type drop-down list so that the .CER and .CRT files are listed.

♦ Click the Next button to display the Certificate Store stage of the Certificate Import Wizard dialog box, shown in Figure 19.4.

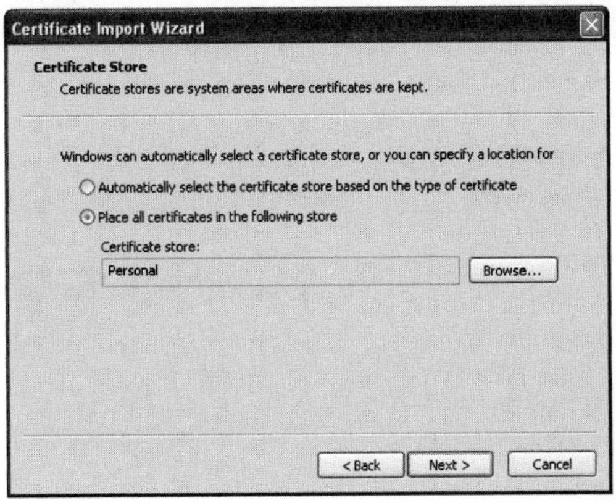

FIGURE 19.4
On the Certificate Store
page of the Certificate
Import Wizard, choose
the certificate store in
which to store the certificate you're importing.

6. Choose how to store the certificate:

◆ To have Windows store each certificate automatically in the default certificate store for the certificate's type, select the Automatically Select The Certificate Store Based On The Type Of Certificate option button.

◆ To control where Windows stores the certificates, select the Place All Certificates In The Following Store option button. To specify the store, click the Browse button to display the Select Certificate Store dialog box, shown in Figure 19.5. Choose the certificate store (for example, Personal) and click the OK button. To specify a particular location within a certificate store, select the Show Physical Stores check box, and then click the plus (+) sign next to the store in question to display its subfolders. Select the folder you want, and then click the OK button.

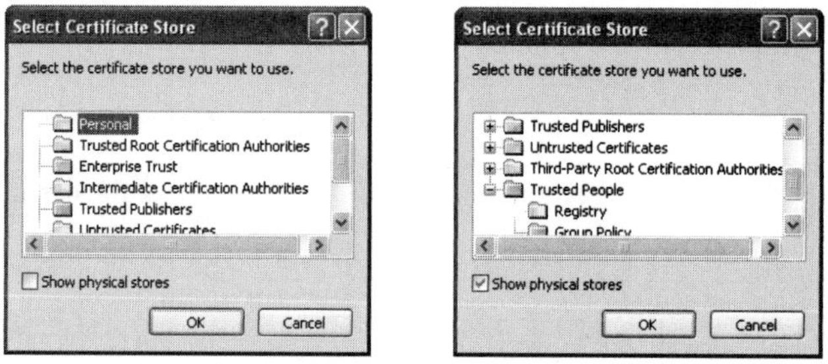

FIGURE 19.5
Use the Select Certificate Store dialog box to specify the certificate store in which you want to store the certificate. The screen on the left shows the categories of stores; the screen on the right shows the physical stores displayed.

7. Click the Next button to finish setting up the import procedure. The Completing The Certificate Import Wizard dialog box is displayed to confirm the choices you've made.

8. Check your choices, and then click the Finish button. The Certificate Import Wizard imports the certificate and then confirms that the operation was successful.

If you decide to import the certificate into the root certificate store rather than one of the other stores, Windows displays a Security Warning dialog box (see Figure 19.6) to make sure you understand that placing the certificate in the root store will make Windows automatically trust any certificate issued by the CA. Double-check the certificate, as it probably belongs in another store.

Now that you've imported the certificate, it appears in the Certificates dialog box on the appropriate page.

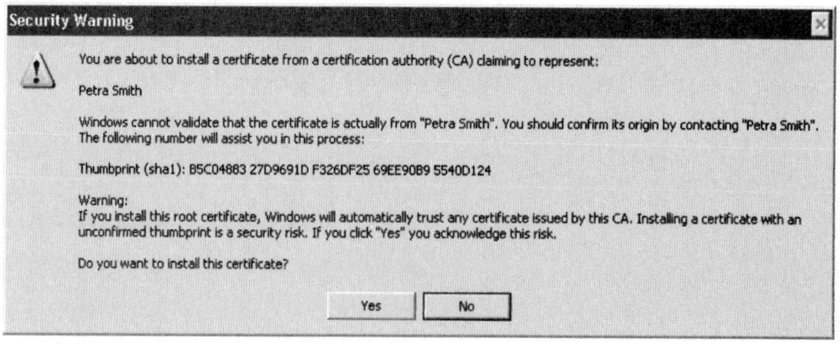

FIGURE 19.6
Windows displays a Security Warning dialog box when you're about to import a certificate into the root certificate store.

EXPORTING A DIGITAL CERTIFICATE

You may need to export a certificate for backup (so that you can keep it safely on removable media away from your computer) or so that you can install it on another computer. For security, you should not store the digital certificate on your hard drive after you install it, because storing it there is a security risk.

To export a certificate, select it in the Certificates dialog box and click the Export button. Windows starts the Certificate Export Wizard, which walks you through the process of exporting the certificate. If you choose to export the private key with the certificate, be sure to protect it with a password.

REMOVING A DIGITAL CERTIFICATE

To remove a digital certificate from Windows' digital certificate store, follow these steps:

1. Display the Certificates dialog box.

2. Click the tab of the page that contains the digital certificate in question, and then select the certificate you want to remove.

3. Click the Remove button. Windows displays a dialog box warning you of the consequences of deleting the digital certificate and asking you to confirm the deletion. Figure 19.7 shows the warning you get when removing a certification authority (above) or a personal certificate (below). Click the Yes button to delete the certificate.

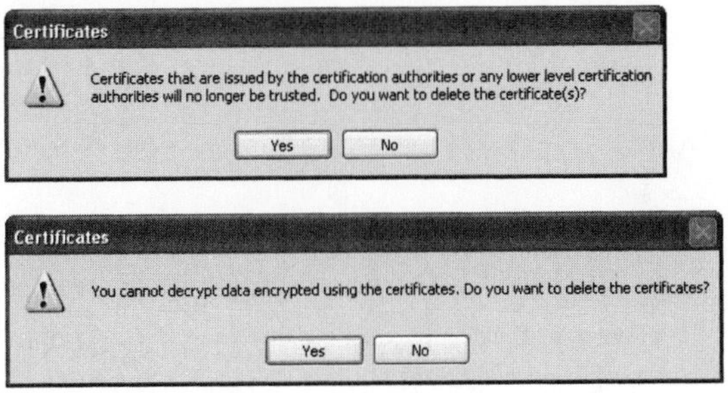

FIGURE 19.7
Two of the warnings the Certificate Manager displays when you're about to remove a digital certificate

SIGNING A MACRO PROJECT WITH A DIGITAL SIGNATURE

Once you've completed a macro project and have it ready for distribution, you sign it with a digital signature so that applications that use a high or very high level of security can use it.

To sign a macro project digitally, follow these steps:

1. In the Visual Basic Editor, navigate to the document or template project that contains the macro project.

2. Select the project in the Project Explorer.

3. Choose Tools ➢ Digital Signature to display the Digital Signature dialog box (see Figure 19.8).

FIGURE 19.8
Use the Digital Signature dialog box to specify the digital signature for a macro project.

NOTE If the Digital Signature dialog box lists the certificate you want in the Sign As area, simply click the OK button to use that certificate.

4. Click the Choose button to display the Select Certificate dialog box (see Figure 19.9).

FIGURE 19.9
Use the Select Certificate dialog box to specify the certificate with which to sign the macro project.

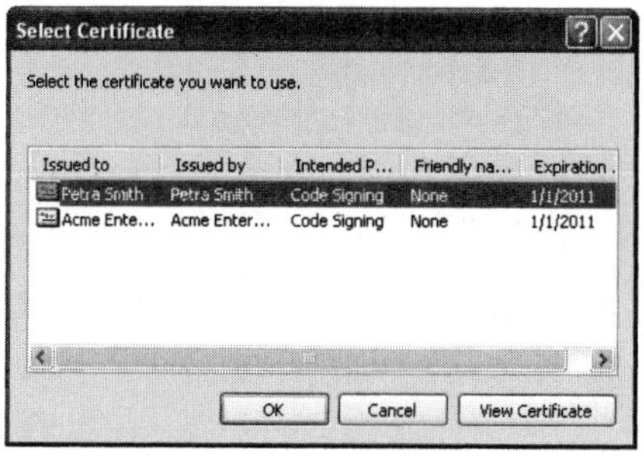

5. Click the certificate you want to use for the macro project.

6. Click the OK button to apply the selected certificate and close the Select Certificate dialog box.

7. Click the OK button to close the Digital Signature dialog box.

8. Click the Save button on the Standard toolbar, press Ctrl+S, or choose File ➢ Save to save the document or template project with the digital signature applied to it.

REMOVING A DIGITAL SIGNATURE FROM A MACRO PROJECT

To remove a digital signature from a macro project, follow these steps:

1. In the Visual Basic Editor, navigate to the document or template project that contains the macro project.

2. Select the project in the Project Explorer.

3. Choose Tools ➢ Digital Signatures to display the Digital Signature dialog box.

4. Click the Remove button. Both the Certificate Name readout in the The VBA Project Is Currently Signed As area and the Certificate Name in the Sign As area of the Digital Signature dialog box will display [No Certificate] to indicate that the project currently has no digital certificate assigned to it.

5. Click the OK button to close the Digital Signature dialog box.

Once you have the macro project back into shape for distribution, you can reapply the digital signature to the project as before.

WHOSE CERTIFICATE IS IT, AND WHAT DOES IT MEAN?

When you receive a digitally signed project, you'll want to find out who has signed it and what type of digital certificate they used. To view the details of a digital certificate, follow these steps:

1. In the Visual Basic Editor, navigate to the document or template project that contains the macro project.

2. Select the project in the Project Explorer.

3. Choose Tools ➢ Digital Signature to display the Digital Signature dialog box.

4. Click the Details button to display the Certificate dialog box (see Figure 19.10).

NOTE   If you want to view the details of one of your own certificates, click the Choose button in the Digital Signature dialog box, choose the certificate in the Select Certificate dialog box, and then click the View Certificate button to display the Certificate dialog box.

TIP   You can also view a certificate by double-clicking its entry in the Certificates dialog box.

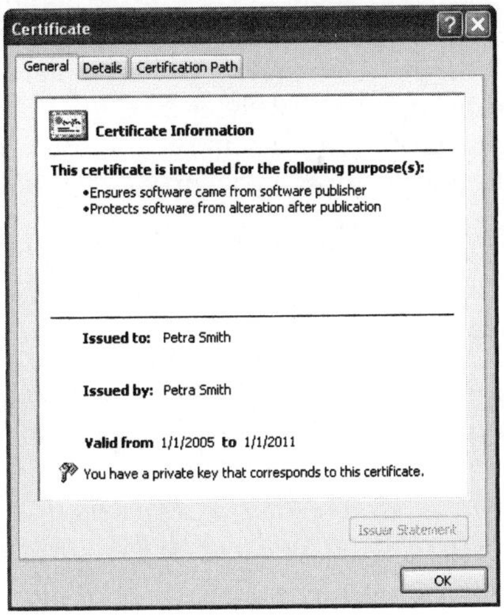

FIGURE 19.10
Use the Certificate dialog box to examine the properties of a certificate.

The Certificate dialog box has three pages:

◆ The General page displays basic information about the certificate: for what purpose the certificate is intended, to whom the certificate is issued, by whom it's issued, and the period for which it's valid.

◆ The Details page of the Certificate dialog box, shown in Figure 19.11, contains about a score of specifics on the certificate. Click one of the fields in the list box to display its value in the text box below.

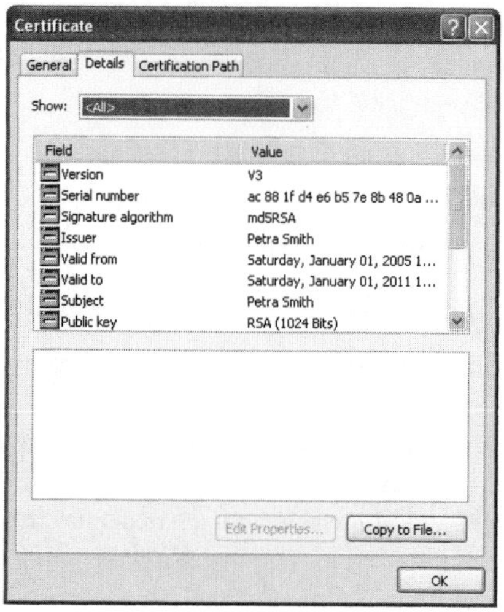

FIGURE 19.11
The Details page of the Certificate dialog box contains a host of details about the certificate.

◆ The Certification Path page of the Certificate dialog box shows the path by which the certificate has been issued from the issuing authority to the current holder. To check one of the links in the chain, select it in the Certification Path list box and click the View Certificate button (if it's available). You'll then see the Certificate dialog box for the certificate in question. You can then pursue the certification path for that certificate if you choose or click the OK button to dismiss the second (or subsequent) Certificate dialog box and return to the previous one.

When you finish exploring the certificate, click the OK button to close the Certificate dialog box.

Choosing a Suitable Level of Security

To work effectively with VBA, you must choose a suitable level of security—high enough to protect you from the threats posed by malicious or incompetent code, but low enough that it doesn't prevent you from running code that you need to run.

Understanding the Security Threats Posed by VBA

As macro languages have grown in power and sophistication over the years, so has the threat they pose when misused. Using relatively simple VBA commands, you can create files, delete files, manipulate existing data, and control other applications.

Even code developed with the best of intentions can damage a computer when run under unsuitable circumstances—for example, a procedure might delete valuable data or delete critical files, making the computer crash. Such unintentional damage happens frequently enough, but what tends to make the headlines is damage caused intentionally by malicious code in macro viruses and other malicious software (or *malware*).

NOTE A *macro virus* is a computer virus written in a macro language such as VBA. A *computer virus* is malicious code that spreads itself automatically from one computer to another.

Protecting against Macro Viruses

Protecting your computer (and computers connected to it) against macro viruses requires three main steps:

1. Install and run antivirus software, such as Norton Antivirus (`www.symantec.com`) or McAfee VirusScan (`http://www.mcafee.com`), on your computer. Update the antivirus software frequently and regularly with the latest virus definitions. (Most antivirus software offers automatic checking for updates.)

2. Configure suitable security settings in the applications you use, especially in those applications that host VBA or other programming languages or scripting languages. For example, configure VBA security settings as described in the next section.

3. Be careful when opening any file that might contain code. Most modern applications warn you when there might be a problem with a file. Many macro viruses attempt to outwit such warnings by *social engineering*—conning the user—rather than by sophisticated programming. For example, a macro virus may transmit itself as an e-mail attachment to the addresses in an e-mail application. The message and attachment suggest that the contents of the attachment are interesting or amusing—for example, jokes or compromising pictures. Because the file comes from someone known and trusted, and because the contents seem compelling, many users will open the file and ignore any security warnings. The action of opening the file can cause the code within the file to execute.

Specifying a Suitable Security Setting

First, set a suitable level of security for your purposes. Choose Tools ➢ Macro ➢ Security to display the Security dialog box (see Figure 19.12).

Depending on the application you're using, VBA offers three or four levels of protection: Very High (in some applications only), High, Medium, and Low. Here's what those settings mean:

Very High security The application runs only code that is installed in trusted locations. (The next section shows you how to specify which locations to trust.) It doesn't matter whether the code is signed or not—it's the trusted location that counts. This setting is good for developing code, because as long as the code is in a trusted location, you don't have to sign it.

High security The application runs only procedures that are signed by trusted sources (more about designating trusted sources in just a moment). High security is a good choice for most corporate environments and many home users. By specifying High security, signing any code you distribute, and keeping as strict control as possible over the list of trusted sources on each computer, you can provide users with known procedures (for example, those developed in-house) without encountering any problems, while at the same time preventing them from running any unapproved code.

FIGURE 19.12
On the Security Level page of the Security dialog box, choose the level of security you want to use when running macros.

Medium security The application offers the user the choice of running procedures that aren't signed by trusted sources, without trusting everything that comes from this source. Medium security is the best security choice for home users who need to use macros developed by others who do not sign their code. If the application you're using doesn't offer the Very High security setting, you will probably need to use Medium security to give yourself the flexibility you need to perform your work.

Low security The application doesn't prevent you from running—or even warn you about the dangers of—any code not signed by a trusted source. Under most circumstances, it isn't a good idea to choose the Low security setting on any computer that contains information you value, unless the computer isn't connected to a network (or the Internet) *and* you never receive files from other people.

Specifying Whom to Trust

VBA provides two ways of designating trusted sources: by trusting sources identified in templates and add-ins already installed on the computer and by adding to them trusted sources that crop up in documents you open that contain code or customizations.

NOTE The Office 2003 applications use the term "trusted publishers," while the Office XP and Office 2000 applications use the term "trusted source."

WHOM DOES THE COMPUTER TRUST ALREADY?

To find out whom the computer trusts already, choose Tools ➤ Macro ➤ Security to display the Security dialog box, and then click the Trusted Publishers tab or the Trusted Sources tab to display the Trusted Publishers page or Trusted Sources page. Figure 19.13 shows the Trusted Publishers page of the Security dialog box for Excel 2003.

TRUSTING THE SOURCES ALREADY ON THE COMPUTER

In a Microsoft Office application, you can choose to trust the sources already on the computer by selecting the Trust All Installed Add-Ins And Templates check box on the Trusted Publishers page or the Trusted Sources page of the Security dialog box.

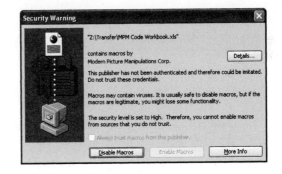

Trusting installed add-ins and templates is handy, provided you know the provenance of what's on your computer. For example, in a corporate environment in which the administrator installs approved templates and add-ins with each new installation of Word and PowerPoint, it makes sense to select this check box and snap all the implied trusts into place. The individual user, on the other hand, needs to make sure their installation of Office won't be compromised by unquestioning acceptance of what's already on the computer.

ADDING A TRUSTED SOURCE

To add a trusted source, open a document or template that contains VBA code from the source you want to add. The application will detect the untrusted code and will display a Security Warning dialog box (see Figure 19.14).

FIGURE 19.14
When you open a file (or
load an add-in) that con-
tains code from a source
that isn't currently specified as trusted, the application displays the Security
Warning dialog box. To
add the source to your list
of trusted sources, select
the Always Trust Macros
From This Publisher check
box and choose the Enable
Macros button.

The Security Warning dialog box tells you several things:

◆ The name and location of the file containing the untrusted code.

◆ The name of the person or company that created the code.

◆ Whether the digital signature on the certificate is trustworthy. (In the figure, it isn't.)

◆ Whether you're using the High level of security, as in the figure. (If you're using the Very High level, VBA opens the file but disables the code automatically. If you're using the Medium level, the Security Warning dialog box won't mention it. If you're using the Low level, you won't see the Security Warning dialog box.)

From the Security Warning dialog box, you have from three to five choices:

◆ You can click the Details button to display the Certificate dialog box and then inspect the certificate as discussed earlier in the chapter. You'll probably want to take this step first with a file you're not sure about. Examining the certificate may help you decide on one of the next two choices.

◆ You can click the Disable Macros button to open the file with the code disabled. Disabling the code prevents it from running. Any functionality that the code provides will not be available in the file.

◆ If the Enable Macros button is available, you can click it to open the file with the procedures and customizations enabled. If you have the Medium level of security set, you can choose whether to select the Always Trust Macros From This Source check box when doing so. If you have the High level of security set, you must select this check box in order to enable the Enable Macros button. The Enable Macros button is not available if the publisher can't be authenticated.

◆ You can click the close button (the × button) on the Security Warning dialog box to close the dialog box without opening the file. Doing so is useful both when you don't want to deal with the question and when you want to set a different level of security before opening the file. For example, if you have the High level of security set and you encounter the Security Warning dialog box, you might want to duck the decision so that you can set the Medium level of security instead. That setting will allow you to enable the procedures in the document or template without adding their creator to your list of trusted sources.

◆ Select the Always Trust Macros From This Publisher check box to add the source to your list of trusted sources, but then click the Disable Macros button rather than the Enable Macros button to disable the macros in this particular file. You'll seldom need to do this.

NOTE   Once you've specified a source as trusted, any of the VBA-enabled applications will open files containing procedures from that source.

REMOVING A PREVIOUSLY TRUSTED SOURCE

To remove a previously trusted source from your list of trusted sources, follow these steps:

1. Choose Tools ➢ Macro ➢ Security to display the Security dialog box.

2. Click the Trusted Publishers tab or the Trusted Sources tab to display the Trusted Publishers page or Trusted Sources page.

3. In the list box, select the trusted source that you want to remove.

4. Click the Remove button to remove the trusted source from the list.

Locking Your Code

To prevent anyone from viewing the contents of a project, you can lock it with a password. Typically, you'll want to do this before distributing a project to your colleagues. If your workplace is particularly volatile, you might want to lock projects under development on your own desktop as well. The argument against locking a project on which you're still actively working is that the lock adds a tedious step to accessing the modules and forms in the project—but if you need the security, it's well worth the small amount of effort involved.

Follow these steps to lock a document or template project:

1. Open the document or template project in the application, and then display the Visual Basic Editor.

2. In the Project Explorer, right-click the project that you want to lock, and choose VBAProject Properties from the context menu to display the Project Properties dialog box. Alternatively, select the project in the Project Explorer and choose Tools ➤ VBAProject Properties.

3. Click the Protection tab to display the Protection page (see Figure 19.15).

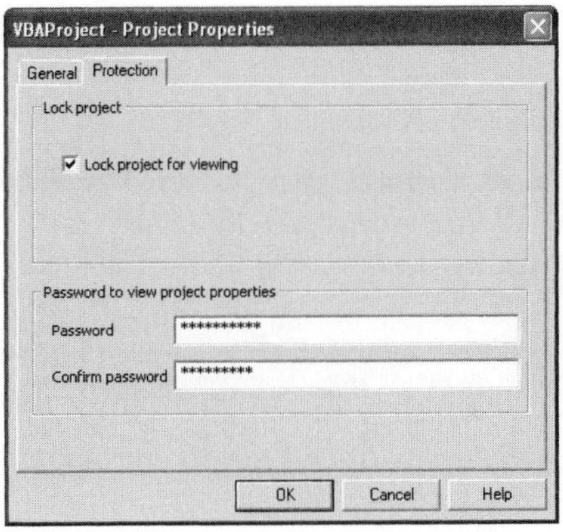

FIGURE 19.15
Use the Protection page of the Project Properties dialog box to lock the project.

4. Select the Lock Project For Viewing check box in the Lock Project group box.

5. In the Password To View Project Properties group box, type a password in the Password text box and the same password in the Confirm Password text box. Setting a password is compulsory: You can't lock a project without specifying a password.

6. Click the OK button to apply the locking to the project. The Visual Basic Editor closes the Project Properties dialog box but leaves the contents of the project open for you to view and work with.

7. Switch back to the application, save the project, and close it.

Once you've done that, the project is locked and can't be viewed or edited without the password (unless someone breaks the password; see the sidebar titled, "How Hard Is It to Break the Password Protection on a Project?" later in the chapter). When you choose to edit a procedure in the project from the application or try to expand the project in the Project Explorer in the Visual Basic Editor, the VBAProject Password dialog box appears (see Figure 19.16). Type the password in the Password text

---

CHOOSING A STRONG ENOUGH PASSWORD FOR LOCKING YOUR CODE

The longer and the more complex your locking password is, the harder it will be for anyone to crack. In practice, this means using passwords 8 to 15 characters in length; passwords longer than 15 characters tend to be difficult to remember and laborious to type in.

As usual, don't use real words for passwords, even real words in other languages: Crackers (malicious hackers) can run foreign dictionary attacks just as easily as native-language ones. Concatenate words or phrases into one password, mixing in numbers and symbols (&, !, #, and so on) to make the password more complex. And memorize your passwords relentlessly.

---

box and click the OK button to display the contents of the project. (If you enter the wrong password, the application or the Visual Basic Editor displays the Project Locked message box followed by the Project Password dialog box for you to try again.)

FIGURE 19.16
When you open a locked project, you need to enter the password for the project in the VBAProject Password dialog box.

To unlock a project, open it in the Visual Basic Editor (supplying the password), display the VBAProject Properties dialog box, clear the Lock Project For Viewing check box on the Protection page, and click the OK button. Save the file that contains the project.

HOW HARD IS IT TO BREAK THE PASSWORD PROTECTION ON A PROJECT?

No password is unbreakable. You can create unguessable passwords by using enough characters, including numbers and symbols, and avoiding real words in any language, but any password protection can eventually be broken by brute force or by decryption. If an infinite number of monkeys with an infinite number of keyboards were to hammer away at the password you set on a VBA project, chances are they'd happen upon it sooner or later.

Nobody has yet marshaled those monkeys, but they don't need to, because people have built any number of password-cracking programs that can try to identify a password. Some cracking programs use brute force, trying different words as passwords until they find the one that works, but more sophisticated programs can unwrap the security of the password in question: To find the password for the VBA project in a file, they read the file and decipher the password.

To find password-cracking programs, search for "Microsoft Office password recovery" or similar terms.

Given that anyone can get password-cracking software either free or for a pittance, plan to use passwords as only your first line of defense (seen from the inside). To keep your secrets safe, you'll need to secure your files so that nobody gets to run password crackers on them.

Part 6

Programming the Office Applications

Chapter 20

Understanding the Word Object Model and Key Objects

◆ Examining the Word object model

◆ Understanding Word's creatable objects

◆ Working with the Documents collection and the Document object

◆ Working with the Selection object

◆ Creating and using ranges

◆ Setting options

This chapter shows you how to start getting to grips with the Word object model, the theoretical architecture underlying Word, and shows you how to perform common actions with the most immediately useful Word objects. These objects include the Documents collection and the Document object, the Selection object, Range objects, and the Options object.

Examining the Word Object Model

You don't need to understand how the Word object model fits together in order to work with VBA in Word, but most people find having a general idea of the object model helpful. To see the object model, follow these steps:

1. Launch or activate Word, and then press Alt+F11 to launch or activate the Visual Basic Editor.

2. Choose Help ➢ Microsoft Visual Basic Help to display the Visual Basic Help task pane.

3. Type **word object model** in the Search text box, and then press Enter or click the Go button.

4. In the Search Results pane, click the Word Object Model entry—the one without parentheses and another object name after it. You'll see a Help screen (see Figure 20.1).

When you look at the Word Object Model entry on your screen, you'll see that some of the boxes are shaded yellow, while the others are shaded blue. The yellow boxes are objects that are organized into collections, while the blue objects are ones that do not have collections. Click a box to see the help screen for the object, including a schematic of the related objects in the object model. Figure 20.2 shows part of the Help screen for the RecentFiles collection, which contains details of the files in the Most Recently Used list (the list that appears by default at the bottom of the File menu).

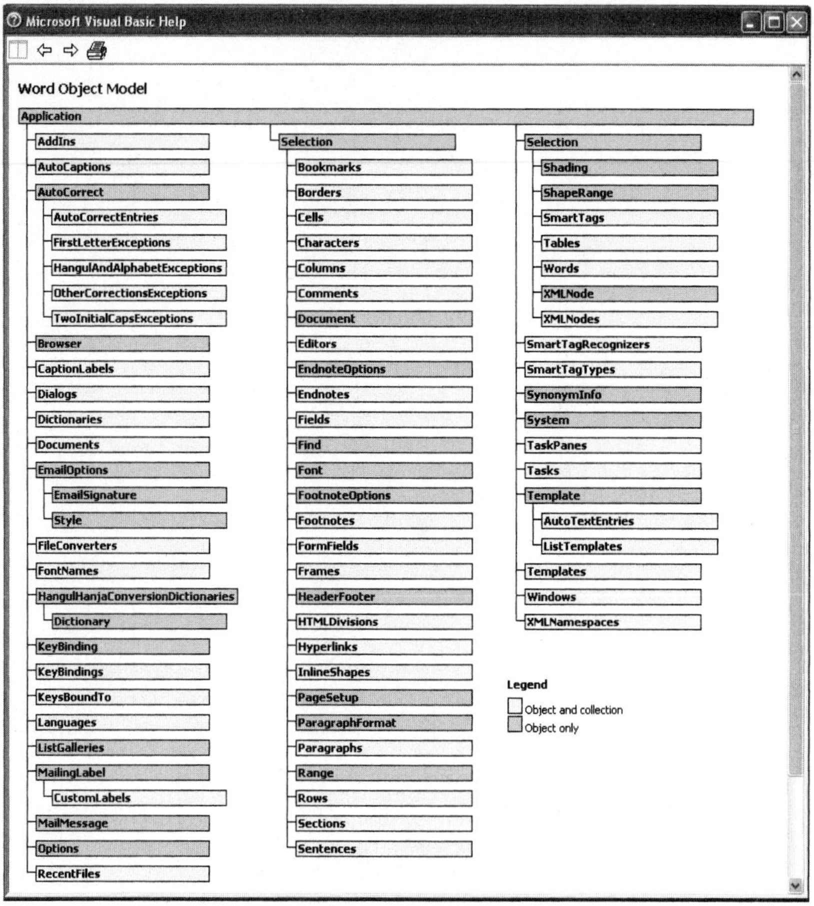

FIGURE 20.1
Microsoft Visual Basic Help provides a schematic of the Word object model. (This is the object model for Word 2003.) You can click an object to see details about it.

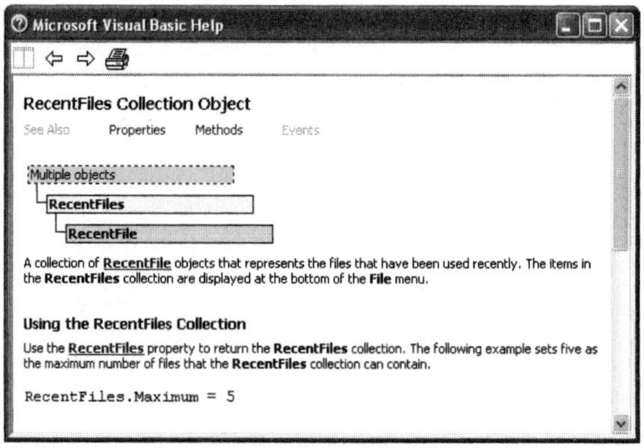

FIGURE 20.2
The Help screen for an individual object or collection includes a diagram showing the objects to which it's related.

Understanding Word's Creatable Objects

Like most VBA-enabled applications, Word has a number of creatable objects, allowing you to access the commonly used objects without having to go through the Application object. The following are typically the most useful of these creatable objects:

◆ The ActiveDocument object returns a document object that represents the active document.

◆ The ActiveWindow object returns a Window object that represents the active window.

◆ The Documents collection contains the Document objects, each of which represents an open document.

◆ The Options object represents Word options and document options, including most of the options that appear in the Options dialog box.

◆ The Selection object represents the selection in the active document. Selection represents the selection (containing text or other objects) or collapsed selection (containing nothing—an insertion point) in the document.

◆ The Windows collection contains the Window objects that represent all open windows.

The following sections show you how to work with some of these objects, starting with the Documents collection and the Document object. You'll see how to use the ActiveWindow object and the Windows collection in the next chapter.

Working with the *Documents* Collection and the *Document* Object

In many of your Word procedures, you'll need to work with documents: creating new documents, saving documents, opening existing documents, closing documents, and printing documents. To do so, you work with the Documents collection, which contains a Document object for each open document in Word.

Creating a Document

To create a new file, use the Add method of the Documents collection. The syntax is

```
expression.Add Template, NewTemplate, DocumentType, Visible
```

Here, *expression* is a required expression that returns a Documents collection. Typically, you'll want to use the Documents collection itself.

Template is an optional Variant argument that specifies the template on which to base the new document. If you omit Template, Word uses the Normal template (as if you'd clicked the New Blank Document button on the Standard toolbar). So you need specify a Template argument only when you need to base the new document on a template other than Normal.

NewTemplate is an optional Variant argument that you can set to True to create a template rather than a document. NewTemplate is set to False by default, so you can safely omit this argument unless you're creating a template.

DocumentType is an optional Variant argument that you can use to specify the type of document to create: wdNewBlankDocument (the default), wdNewEmailMessage, wdNewFrameset (for a frameset), or wdNewWebPage.

Visible is an optional Variant argument that you can set to False to have the document created in a window that isn't visible. The default setting is True, making the document window visible.

CREATING A DOCUMENT BASED ON *NORMAL.DOT*

The following statement creates a new document based on the Normal.dot global template:

```
Documents.Add
```

CREATING A DOCUMENT BASED ON A TEMPLATE

The following statement creates a new document based on the template named Company Report.dot stored in the network folder designated \\server\public\templates:

```
Documents.Add Template:= "\\server\public\templates\Company Report.dot"
```

CREATING A TEMPLATE

The following statements declare a new object variable named myTemplate of the Template class, create a new template based on the template named Overhead.dot stored in one of the default template folders, assign it to myTemplate, and hide the window:

```
Dim myTemplate As Template
Set myTemplate = Documents.Add(Template:="Overhead.dot", _
    NewTemplate:=True, Visible:=False)
```

In this example, the path to the template isn't specified because the template is in one of the template folders.

NOTE   Word has two templates folders: the user templates folder and the workgroup templates folder. You can change the locations of these folders by choosing Tools ➢ Options and working on the File Locations tab of the Options dialog box.

Saving a Document

As when working interactively, when working with VBA you must specify a filename and path the first time you save a document. After that, you can save it under the same name or specify a different name or format.

SAVING A FILE FOR THE FIRST TIME OR AS A DIFFERENT FILE

To save a file for the first time, or to save a file under a different name or in a different format, use the SaveAs method. The syntax is

```
expression.SaveAs(FileName, FileFormat, LockComments, Password, AddToRecentFiles,
WritePassword, ReadOnlyRecommended, EmbedTrueTypeFonts, SaveNativePictureFormat,
SaveFormsData, SaveAsAOCELetter, Encoding, InsertLineBreaks, AllowSubstitutions,
LineEnding, AddBiDiMarks)
```

Here, *expression* is an expression that returns a Document object. For example, you might use the ActiveDocument object or an object in the Documents collection.

FileName is an optional Variant argument that specifies the name for the document. If you omit FileName, VBA uses the current folder and the default filename of Doc*n*.doc for a document and Dot*n*.dot for a template, where *n* is the next available number (for example, Doc5.doc for a document or Dot2.dot for a template).

WARNING   When saving a document, you should check whether a document with this name and location already exists. If it does, VBA overwrites it without warning, causing data loss.

FileFormat is an optional Variant argument that specifies the format in which to save the document. Table 20.1 lists the wdSaveFormat constants for specifying commonly used formats.

TABLE 20.1:   WdSaveFormat Constants

CONSTANT	SAVES DOCUMENT AS
wdFormatDocument	A Word document
wdFormatDOSText	A DOS text file
wdFormatDOSTextLineBreaks	A DOS text file with layout
wdFormatEncodedText	A text file with encoding
wdFormatFilteredHTML	A filtered HTML file (Word 2003 and XP only)
wdFormatHTML	An HTML file
wdFormatRTF	A Rich Text Format file
wdFormatTemplate	A Word template
wdFormatText	A text file (plain ASCII)
wdFormatTextLineBreaks	A text file with line breaks
wdFormatUnicodeText	A text file with Unicode characters
wdFormatWebArchive	A Web archive file
wdFormatXML	An XML file (Word 2003 only)

For example, the following statement saves the active document as a filtered HTML file under the name Example.html in the current folder:

```
ActiveDocument.SaveAs FileName:="Example.html", _
    FileFormat:=wdFormatFilteredHTML
```

TIP Apart from these constants, you can save documents in other formats for which you have file converters installed by specifying the appropriate value for the SaveFormat property of the FileConverter object—for example, ActiveDocument.SaveAs FileFormat:=FileConverters (15).SaveFormat. See the FileConverters entry in the VBA Help file for more information.

AddToRecentFiles is an optional Variant argument that you can set to True to have Word add the document to the list of recently used files on the File menu. (Often, when working with documents in procedures, you'll want to avoid listing them on the Most Recently Used list, leaving the user's previous list of recent files undisturbed.)

To protect the document as you save it, you can use four different protection features:

◆ LockComments is an optional Variant argument that you can set to True to lock the document so that reviewers can enter comments but can't change the text of the document.

◆ Password is an optional Variant argument that you can use to set a password for opening the document.

◆ WritePassword is an optional Variant argument that you can use to set a password for saving changes to the document.

◆ ReadOnlyRecommended is an optional Variant argument that you can set to True to have Word recommend that the user open the document as read-only.

Finally, there are the following optional arguments you'll want to use infrequently:

◆ EmbedTrueTypeFonts is an optional Variant argument that you can set to True to save TrueType fonts with the document. (This is a good idea only if you're distributing the document to someone whom you know doesn't have the TrueType fonts installed to view the document correctly.)

◆ SaveNativePictureFormat is an optional Variant argument that you can set to True to have graphics imported from another platform saved as Windows graphics.

◆ SaveFormsData is an optional Variant argument that you can set to True to save the data entered in a form as a data record (as opposed to saving the whole form, including its static text).

◆ SaveAsAOCELetter is an optional Variant argument that you can set to True to save the document as an AOCE letter (a mailing format for routing documents).

◆ Encoding is an optional Variant argument for using a different code page than the system code page. For example, you might need to save a document using a Cyrillic code page.

◆ InsertLineBreaks is an optional Variant argument that you can set to True when saving a document as a text file to make Word insert a line break at the end of each line of text.

◆ AllowSubstitutions is an optional Variant argument that you can set to True when saving a document as a text file to make Word substitute some symbol characters with similar text. For example, Word substitutes (TM) for a trademark symbol (™).

◆ LineEnding is an optional Variant argument that you can use when saving a document as a text file to control how Word marks line breaks and paragraph breaks.

◆ AddBiDiMarks is an optional Variant argument that you can set to True to make Word add control characters to the file to maintain bidirectional layout.

Usually, when saving a file for the first time, you'll need to specify only its name and path; if you want to save it in a format other than Word document, specify that, too. The following statement saves the active document under the name Beehives.doc in the folder \\server\Products\Field\:

```
ActiveDocument.SaveAs _
    "\\server\Products\Field\Beehives.doc"
```

SAVING A DOCUMENT THAT HAS ALREADY BEEN SAVED

Once a document has been saved, you can save it under the same name by using the Save method. For a Document object, the Save method takes no arguments. For example, the following statement saves the document named Recipe01.doc:

```
Documents("Recipe01.doc").Save
```

SAVING ALL OPEN DOCUMENTS

To save all open documents, use the Save method with the Documents collection. The syntax is

```
expression.Save(NoPrompt, OriginalFormat)
```

Here, *expression* is an expression that returns a Documents collection. Often, you'll use the Documents collection itself.

NoPrompt is an optional Variant argument that you can set to True to make Word save all open documents containing unsaved changes and any attached templates containing unsaved changes without prompting the user. The default setting is False, which causes Word to prompt the user whether to save each document and template. Even if you set NoPrompt to True, Word will prompt you to save changes to Normal.dot if the Prompt To Save Normal Template check box on the Save tab of the Options dialog box is selected.

OriginalFormat is an optional Variant argument that you can set to wdOriginalDocumentFormat to save the documents in their original formats, wdWordDocument to force each document to be saved as a Word document, or wdPromptUserX to prompt the user about which format to use.

For example, the following statement saves all open documents and templates without prompting the user:

```
Documents.Save NoPrompt:=True
```

CHECKING WHETHER A DOCUMENT CONTAINS UNSAVED CHANGES

To find out whether a document contains unsaved changes, check its Saved property. Saved is a read/write Boolean property that returns False if the document contains unsaved changes and True if it does not. A new document contains no unsaved changes, even though it has never been saved.

Opening a Document

To open a document, use the Open method with the appropriate Document object. The syntax for the Open method is

```
expression.Open FileName, ConfirmConversions, ReadOnly, AddToRecentFiles,
PasswordDocument, PasswordTemplate, Revert, WritePasswordDocument,
WritePasswordTemplate, Format, Encoding, Visible
```

The arguments are as follows:

♦ *expression* is a required expression that returns a `Documents` collection. Usually, you'll want to use the `Documents` collection itself.

♦ `FileName` is a required Variant argument specifying the name (and path, if necessary) of the document to open.

♦ `ConfirmConversions` is an optional Variant argument that you can set to `True` to have Word display the Convert File dialog box if the file is in a format other than Word.

♦ `ReadOnly` is an optional Variant argument that you can set to `True` to open the document as read-only.

♦ `AddToRecentFiles` is an optional Variant argument that you can set to `True` to have Word add the filename to the list of recently used files at the foot of the File menu.

♦ `PasswordDocument` is an optional Variant argument that you can use to set a password for opening the document.

♦ `PasswordTemplate` is an optional Variant argument that you can use to set a password for opening the template.

♦ `Revert` is an optional Variant argument that specifies what Word should do if the `FileName` supplied matches a file that's already open. By default (that is, if you don't include the `Revert` argument), `Revert` is set to `False`, which means that Word activates the open instance of the document and doesn't open the saved instance. You can set `Revert` to `True` to have Word open the saved instance of the document and discard any changes to the open instance.

♦ `WritePasswordDocument` is an optional Variant argument that indicates the password for saving changes to the document.

♦ `WritePasswordTemplate` is an optional Variant argument that indicates the password for saving changes to the template.

♦ `Format` is an optional Variant argument that you can use to specify the file converter with which to open the document. Table 20.2 lists the `WdOpenFormat` constants you can use specify the file converter.

TABLE 20.2: WdOpenFormat Constants for Opening a Document

CONSTANT	EFFECT
wdOpenFormatAllWord	Word opens the document in any recognized Word format as a Word document.
wdOpenFormatAuto	Word chooses a converter automatically. This is the default setting.
wdOpenFormatDocument	Word opens the document as a Word document.
wdOpenFormatEncodedText	Word opens the document as a text file with encoding.

TABLE 20.2: WdOpenFormat Constants for Opening a Document *(CONTINUED)*

CONSTANT	EFFECT
wdOpenFormatRTF	Word opens the document as a Rich Text Format file.
wdOpenFormatTemplate	Word opens the document as a template.
wdOpenFormatText	Word opens the document as a text file.
wdOpenFormatUnicodeText	Word opens the document as a Unicode text file.
wdOpenFormatWebPages	Word opens the document as a web page.

◆ Encoding is an optional Variant argument specifying the document encoding (the code page or the character set) for Word to use when opening the document.

◆ Visible is an optional Variant argument that you can set to False to have Word open the document in a window that isn't visible. (The default setting is True, specifying a visible window.)

The following statement opens the document Times.doc in the C:\My Documents\ folder:

```
Documents.Open "C:\My Documents\Times.doc"
```

The following statement opens the file Statistics.doc in the D:\Temp\ folder as read-only and adds it to the list of most recently used files:

```
Documents.Open "D:\Temp\Statistics.doc", ReadOnly:=True, _
    AddToRecentFiles:=True
```

Closing a Document

To close a document, use the Close method with the application Document object. The syntax is

```
expression.Close(SaveChanges, OriginalFormat, RouteDocument)
```

Here, *expression* is a required expression that returns a Document object or a Documents collection.

SaveChanges is an optional Variant argument you can use to specify how to handle unsaved changes. Use wdDoNotSaveChanges to discard changes, wdPromptToSaveChanges to have Word prompt the user to save changes, or wdSaveChanges to save changes without prompting.

OriginalFormat is an optional Variant argument you can use to specify the save format for the document. Use wdOriginalDocumentFormat to have Word use the original document format, wdPromptUser to have Word prompt the user to choose a format, or wdWordDocument to use the Word document format.

RouteDocument is an optional Variant argument that you can set to True to route a document that has a routing slip attached.

For example, the following statement closes the active document without saving changes:

```
ActiveDocument.Close SaveChanges:=wdDoNotSaveChanges
```

The following statement closes all open documents (but not the Word application itself) and saves changes automatically:

```
Documents.Close SaveChanges:=wdSaveChanges
```

Changing a Document's Template

To change the template attached to a document, set the `AttachedTemplate` property of the `Document` object you want to affect to the path and name of the appropriate template. For example, the following statement attaches the template named `SalesMarket02.dot` to the active document. The template is assumed to be in one of the Word templates folders, so the path is not specified.

```
ActiveDocument.AttachedTemplate = "SalesMarket02.dot"
```

Printing a Document

To print a document, use the `PrintOut` method for the appropriate `Document` object. The syntax for the `PrintOut` method is

```
expression.PrintOut(Background, Append, Range, OutputFileName, From, To, Item,
Copies, Pages, PageType, PrintToFile, Collate, FileName, ActivePrinterMacGX,
ManualDuplexPrint, PrintZoomColumn, PrintZoomRow, PrintZoomPaperWidth,
PrintZoomPaperHeight)
```

These are the components of the `PrintOut` method:

♦ *expression* is a required expression specifying an `Application`, `Document`, or `Window` object. Usually, you'll print a `Document` object.

♦ `Background` is an optional Variant argument that you can set to `True` to have Word print the document in the background, allowing the procedure to continue running.

♦ `Append` is an optional Variant argument that you can set to `True` to append the document being printed to file to the print file specified.

♦ `Range` is an optional Variant argument specifying the selection or range of pages to print: `wdPrintAllDocument` (0, the default), `wdPrintCurrentPage` (2), `wdPrintFromTo` (3; use the `From` and `To` arguments to specify the pages), `wdPrintRangeOfPages` (4), or `wdPrintSelection` (1).

♦ `OutputFileName` is an optional Variant argument used to specify the name for the output file when printing to file.

♦ `From` is an optional Variant argument used to specify the starting page number when printing a range of pages.

♦ `To` is an optional Variant argument used to specify the ending page number when printing a range of pages.

♦ `Item` is an optional Variant argument used to specify the item to print: `wdPrintAutoTextEntries` (4), `wdPrintComments` (2), `wdPrintDocumentContent` (0, the default), `wdPrintKeyAssignments` (5, shortcut key assignments for the document or its template), `wdPrintProperties` (1), or `wdPrintStyles` (3).

- ◆ Copies is an optional Variant argument used to specify the number of copies to print. (If you omit Copies, Word prints one copy.)

- ◆ Pages is an optional Variant argument used to specify the pages to print—for example, 1, 11-21, 31.

- ◆ PageType is an optional Variant argument used to specify whether to print all pages (wdPrintAllPages, 0, the default), odd pages (wdPrintOddPagesOnly, 1), or even pages (wdPrintEvenPagesOnly, 2).

- ◆ PrintToFile is an optional Variant argument that you can set to True to direct the output of the print operation to a file.

- ◆ Collate is an optional Variant argument used when printing multiple copies of a document to specify whether to collate the pages (True) or not (False).

- ◆ FileName is an optional Variant argument used to specify the filename and path of the document to print. (If you omit FileName, VBA prints the active document.)

- ◆ ActivePrinterMacGX is an optional Variant argument used on the Macintosh to specify the printer if QuickDraw GX is installed.

- ◆ ManualDuplexPrint is an optional Variant argument that you set to True for two-sided printing on a printer that doesn't have duplex capabilities. When ManualDuplexPrint is True, you can use the PrintOddPagesInAscendingOrder property or the PrintEvenPagesInAscendingOrder property of the Options object to print odd or even pages in ascending order to create a manual duplex effect (reloading the odd-page–printed paper into the printer the other way up to print the even pages). The ManualDuplexPrint argument is available only in some languages.

- ◆ PrintZoomColumn and PrintZoomRow are optional Variant arguments that you use to specify the number of pages to print on a page horizontally (PrintZoomColumn) and vertically (PrintZoomRow). Each property can be 1, 2, or 4.

- ◆ PrintZoomPaperWidth is an optional Variant argument that you can use to specify the width (measured in twips) to which to scale printed pages.

- ◆ PrintZoomPaperHeight is an optional Variant argument that you can use to specify the height (measured in twips) to which to scale printed pages.

For example, the following statement prints three collated copies of the active document in the background:

```
ActiveDocument.PrintOut Background:=True, Copies:=3, Collate:=True
```

The following statement prints pages 2 through 5 of the active document:

```
ActiveDocument.PrintOut Range:=wdPrintFromTo, From:=2, To:=5
```

The following statement prints the active document at two pages per sheet of paper:

```
ActiveDocument.PrintOut PrintZoomColumn:=2, PrintZoomRow:=1
```

Working with the *ActiveDocument* Object

The ActiveDocument object returns a Document object that represents the active document—whichever document has the focus in the Word window. The ActiveDocument object behaves like a Document object, but watch out for two possible problems when working with it.

The first problem is that if there's no document open in Word, there's no ActiveDocument object, and any code that tries to work with the ActiveDocument object returns an error. You can check the Count property of the Documents collection to make sure there's a document open—for example:

```
If Documents.Count = 0 Then
    If MsgBox("No document is open." & vbCr & vbCr & _
        "Do you want to create a new blank document?", _
        vbYesNo + vbExclamation, "No Document Is Open") = vbYes Then
        Documents.Add
    Else
        End
    End If
End If
```

The second problem is that a different document may be active than your code assumes is active. This problem tends to occur when a procedure starts with the active document and then creates a new document to work in; the new document becomes the active document, and from this point on, confusion may result. If you know the name of the document that should be active, you can check that the name of the document that's actually active matches it to verify that you've got the right document.

If there's any doubt about which document you're working with, declare a Document object variable and work with that object variable rather than the ActiveDocument object. For example, the following statements declare a Document object and assign the ActiveDocument object to it, so that subsequent code can work with the Document object:

```
Dim myDocument As Document
Set myDocument = ActiveDocument
With myDocument
    'actions here
End With
```

Working with the *Selection* Object

To perform actions on part of a document using VBA, you can work in any of several ways: by using the Selection object, by directly accessing the object that you want to affect, or by defining a range that encompasses the object. Using the Selection object is analogous to working interactively with Word and is good for procedures that require the user to select an object or position the insertion point to denote what the procedure should affect.

NOTE   Using the Selection object is also good when you're learning to use VBA with Word, as many actions that you record using the Macro Recorder use the Selection object.

The Selection object represents the current selection in the active document in Word. The selection can be collapsed to an insertion point, in which case nothing is selected, or it can contain one or more objects—one or more characters, one or more words, one or more paragraphs, a graphic, a table, and so on.

Even if the selection is collapsed to an insertion point, you can use it to refer to objects outside the selection. For example, `Selection.Paragraphs(1).Range.Words(10).Text` returns the tenth word in the paragraph in which the insertion point is positioned or the tenth word in the first paragraph of the one or more paragraphs that are selected.

Checking the Type of Selection

When you're working in the active document, you'll often need to check what type of selection is active, so that you know whether you're dealing with a block of selected text, no selection, or a special type of selection such as a table or a graphic. Depending on the current selection, you may not be able to take certain actions in a procedure, and you may not want to take others.

Table 20.3 lists the types of selections that Word differentiates.

TABLE 20.3:   Selection Types in Word

WDSELECTIONTYPE CONSTANT	VALUE	MEANING
wdNoSelection	0	There's no selection. (This state seems impossible to achieve. You'd think it'd be when no document is open, but then Selection statements return runtime error 91. Stay tuned…)
wdSelectionIP	1	The selection is collapsed to a plain insertion point—nothing is selected.
wdSelectionNormal	2	A "normal" selection, such as a selected word or sentence.
wdSelectionFrame	3	A frame is selected.
wdSelectionColumn	4	A column or part of a column (two or more cells in a column, or one cell in each of two or more columns) is selected.
wdSelectionRow	5	A full row in a table is selected.
wdSelectionBlock	6	A block is selected (a vertical part of one or more paragraphs, selected by holding down the Alt key and dragging with the mouse or by using column-extend mode).
wdSelectionInlineShape	7	An inline shape or graphic (a shape or graphic that's in the text layer rather than floating over it) is selected.
wdSelectionShape	8	A Shape object is selected. (A text box counts as a Shape object.)

To find out what type of selection you currently have, return the Type property of the Selection object. The following statements check that the current selection is an insertion point before inserting a text string strMyString:

```
If Selection.Type = wdSelectionIP Then
    Selection.TypeText strMyString
End If
```

Checking the Story Type of the Selection

Beyond the type of selection, you'll often need to find out which story the selection is in—the main text story, the comments story, the text frame story, and so on. Checking the story can help you avoid problems, such as trying to perform actions in a header or footer that Word supports only in a main text story.

Table 20.4 lists the wdStoryType constants and the stories to which they correspond.

TABLE 20.4: Word Story Types

WDSTORYTYPE CONSTANT	VALUE	MEANING
wdMainTextStory	1	Main text of the document
wdCommentsStory	4	Comments section
wdEndnotesStory	3	Endnotes section
wdFootnotesStory	2	Footnotes section
wdTextFrameStory	5	Text in frames
wdPrimaryFooterStory	9	Main footer
wdEvenPagesFooterStory	8	Even-page footer
wdFirstPageFooterStory	11	First-page footer
wdPrimaryHeaderStory	7	Main header
wdEvenPagesHeaderStory	6	Even-page header
wdFirstPageHeaderStory	10	First-page header

For example, the following statements display a message box if the selection isn't in the main text of a document:

```
If Selection.StoryType <> wdMainTextStory Then
    MsgBox "This range is not in the main text."
End If
```

Getting Other Information about the Current Selection

To work effectively with the current selection, you'll often need to know what it contains and where it's positioned. To find out, use the Information property to return the details you need. Table 20.5 lists the information available in the Information property.

TABLE 20.5:   Information Available in the Information Property

WDINFORMATION CONSTANT	RETURNS THIS INFORMATION
Environment Information	
wdCapsLock	True if Caps Lock is on.
wdNumLock	True if Num Lock is on.
wdOverType	True if Overtype mode is on. (You can turn Overtype mode on and off by changing the Overtype property.)
wdRevisionMarking	True if change tracking is on.
wdSelectionMode	A value that specifies the current selection mode: 0 indicates a normal selection, 1 indicates an extended selection (Extend mode is on), and 2 indicates a column selection.
wdZoomPercentage	The current zoom percentage.
Selection and Insertion Point Information	
wdActiveEndAdjustedPageNumber	The number of the page containing the active end of the selection or range. This number reflects any change you make to the starting page number; wdActiveEndPageNumber doesn't.
wdActiveEndPageNumber	The number of the page containing the active end of the selection or range.
wdActiveEndSectionNumber	The number of the section containing the active end of the selection or range.
wdFirstCharacterColumnNumber	The character position of the first character in the selection or range. If the selection or range is collapsed to an insertion point, this constant returns the character number immediately to the right of the insertion point. (Note that this "column" is relative to the currently active left margin and doesn't have to be inside a table. This is the number that appears in the Col readout in the status bar.)

TABLE 20.5: Information Available in the Information Property *(CONTINUED)*

WDINFORMATION CONSTANT	RETURNS THIS INFORMATION
wdFirstCharacterLineNumber	In Print Layout view and Print Preview, this constant returns the line number of the first character in the selection. In non-layout views (e.g., Normal view), it returns −1.
wdFrameIsSelected	True if the selection or range is a whole frame or text box.
wdHeaderFooterType	A value that specifies the type of header or footer containing the selection or range: −1 indicates that the selection or range isn't in a header or footer; 0 indicates an even page header; 1 indicates an odd page header in a document that has odd and even headers, and the only header in a document that doesn't have odd and even headers; 2 indicates an even page footer; 3 indicates an odd page footer in a document that has odd and even footers, and the only footer in a document that doesn't have odd and even headers; 4 indicates a first-page header; and 5 indicates a first-page footer.
wdHorizontalPositionRelativeToPage	The horizontal position of the selection or range—the distance from the left edge of the selection or range to the left edge of the page, measured in twips.
wdHorizontalPositionRelativeToTextBoundary	The horizontal position of the selection or range—the distance from the left edge of the selection or range to the text boundary enclosing it, measured in twips.
wdInCommentPane	True if the selection or range is in a comment pane.
wdInEndnote	True if the selection or range is an endnote (defined as appearing in the endnote pane in Normal view or in the endnote area in Print Layout view).
wdInFootnote	True if the selection or range is in a footnote (defined as appearing in the footnote pane in Normal view or in the footnote area in Print Layout view).
wdInFootnoteEndnotePane	True if the selection or range is in a footnote or endnote.
wdInHeaderFooter	True if the selection or range is in a header or footer (defined as appearing in the header or footer pane in Normal view or in the header or footer area in Print Layout view).

TABLE 20.5:   Information Available in the Information Property *(CONTINUED)*

WDINFORMATION CONSTANT	RETURNS THIS INFORMATION
wdInMasterDocument	True if the selection or range is in a master document (a document containing at least one subdocument).
wdInWordMail	A value that specifies the WordMail location of the selection or range: 0 indicates that the selection or range isn't in a WordMail message; 1 indicates that it's in a WordMail message you're sending; and 2 indicates that it's in a WordMail you've received.
wdNumberOfPagesInDocument	The number of pages in the document in which the selection or range appears.
wdReferenceOfType	A value that specifies where the selection is in relation to a footnote reference, endnote reference, or comment reference. −1 indicates the selection or range includes a reference. 0 indicates the selection or range isn't before a reference. 1 indicates the selection or range is before a footnote reference, 2 that it's before an endnote reference, and 3 that it's before a comment reference.
wdVerticalPositionRelativeToPage	The vertical position of the selection or range— the distance from the top edge of the selection to the top edge of the page, measured in twips.
wdVerticalPositionRelativeToTextBoundary	The vertical position of the selection or range— the distance from the top edge of the selection to the text boundary enclosing it, measured in twips.
Table Information	
wdWithInTable	True if the selection is in a table.
wdStartOfRangeColumnNumber	The number of the table column containing the beginning of the selection or range.
wdEndOfRangeColumnNumber	The number of the table column containing the end of the selection or range.
wdStartOfRangeRowNumber	The number of the table row containing the beginning of the selection or range.
wdEndOfRangeRowNumber	The number of the table row number containing the end of the selection or range.

TABLE 20.5: Information Available in the Information Property *(CONTINUED)*

WDINFORMATION CONSTANT	RETURNS THIS INFORMATION
wdAtEndOfRowMarker	True if the selection or range is at the end-of-row marker in a table (not the end-of-cell marker).
wdMaximumNumberOfColumns	The largest number of table columns in any row in the selection or range.
wdMaximumNumberOfRows	The largest number of table rows in the table in the selection or range.

Inserting Text at, after, or before the Selection

You can insert text at the selection by using the TypeText method of the Selection object, insert text after the selection by using the InsertAfter method, or insert text before the selection by using the InsertBefore method. The syntax is

```
Selection.TypeText string
Selection.InsertAfter string
Selection.InsertBefore string
```

Here, *string* is a required String expression containing the text you want to insert in double quotation marks. For example:

```
Selection.TypeText "Please come to the meeting next Friday at 9:00 A.M."
Selection.InsertBefore "Dr. "
Selection.InsertAfter vbCr & Address
```

When you use the InsertAfter method or the InsertBefore method, VBA extends the selection to include the text you inserted.

NOTE   When you have a whole paragraph selected, the selection includes the paragraph mark at the end of the paragraph. So any text you add to the end of the selection appears at the beginning of the next paragraph rather than at the end of the selected paragraph.

Inserting a Paragraph in a Selection

To lay out text suitably, you can insert a paragraph:

◆ To insert a paragraph at the current selection, use the InsertParagraph method.

◆ To insert a paragraph after the current selection, use the InsertParagraphAfter method.

◆ To insert a paragraph before the current selection, use the InsertParagraphBefore method.

You can also have VBA type a paragraph by using the Selection.TypeParagraph command.

Applying a Style

To apply a style to a paragraph, set the `Style` property of the `Paragraph` object:

```
Selection.Style = "Heading 3"
```

Similarly, you can apply a character style to the current selection or (as in the following example) to a specific range of words or characters:

```
myDocument.Paragraphs(1).Range.Words(3).Style = "Emphasis"
```

WARNING   A character style must always be applied to a range, rather than directly to a paragraph.

Extending a Selection

To extend a selection, use the `EndOf` method for a `Range` or `Selection` object. The syntax for the `EndOf` method is as follows:

```
expression.EndOf(Unit, Extend)
```

Here, *expression* is a required expression that returns a `Range` or `Selection` object, such as an object in the `Characters`, `Words`, `Sentences`, or `Paragraphs` collection. `Unit` is an optional Variant specifying the unit of movement (see Table 20.6).

TABLE 20.6:   Units of Movement for the EndOf Method

UNIT	MEANING
wdCharacter	A character.
wdWord	A word. (This is the default setting if you omit the argument.)
wdSentence	A sentence.
wdLine	A line. (This unit can be used only with `Selection` objects, not with ranges.)
wdParagraph	A paragraph.
wdSection	A section of a document.
wdStory	The current story—for example, the document story or the header and footer story.
wdCell	A cell in a table.
wdColumn	A column in a table.
wdRow	A row in a table.
wdTable	A whole table.

Extend is an optional Variant specifying whether to move or extend the selection or range. wdMove moves the selection or range and is the default setting; wdExtend extends the selection or range. For example, the following statement extends the current selection to the end of the paragraph:

```
Selection.EndOf Unit:=wdParagraph, Extend:=wdExtend
```

The following statement moves the selection to the end of the paragraph:

```
Selection.EndOf Unit:=wdParagraph, Extend:=wdMove
```

The following statement selects from the current selection to the end of the current Word story:

```
Selection.EndOf Unit:=wdStory, Extend:=wdExtend
```

To select the whole active document, use ActiveDocument.Content.Select. This command has the same effect as choosing Edit ➢ Select All when working interactively.

Collapsing a Selection

When you've finished working with a selection that that isn't collapsed to an insertion point, you may need to deselect it, so that the selection is collapsed when the procedure ends. The easiest way to do so is to use the Collapse method of the Selection object to collapse the selection to its start or its end:

```
Selection.Collapse Direction:=wdCollapseStart
Selection.Collapse Direction:=wdCollapseEnd
```

Alternatively, you can reduce the selection to just one point by setting the selection's end selection equal to its start (collapsing the selection to its start) or by setting the selection's start equal to its end (collapsing the selection to its end):

```
Selection.End = Selection.Start
Selection.Start = Selection.End
```

Creating and Using Ranges

In Word, a *range* is a contiguous area of a document with a defined starting point and ending point. For example, if you define a range that consists of the first two paragraphs in a specified document, the range's starting point is at the beginning of the first paragraph, and its ending point is at the end of the second paragraph (after the paragraph mark).

The typical use of ranges in Word VBA is similar to how you use bookmarks when working interactively with Word: to mark a location in a document that you want to be able to access quickly or manipulate easily. Like a bookmark, a range can contain any amount of text in a document, from a single character to all the contents of the document. A range can even have the same starting point and ending point, which gives it no contents and makes it in effect an invisible mark in the document that you can use to insert text. Once you've created a range, you can refer to it, access its contents or insert new contents in it, or format it, all by using the properties of the range and the methods that apply to it.

TIP   The main difference between a range and a bookmark is that the lifetime of a range is limited to the VBA procedure that defines it, whereas a bookmark is saved with the document or template that contains it and can be accessed at any point (whether or not a procedure is running).

Defining a Named Range

To create a Range object, you use a Set statement and either the Range method on a Document object or the Range property for an object—for example, the Selection object, the Paragraphs collection, or a Paragraph object. The syntax for using the Range method is

```
Set RangeName = Document.Range(Start, End)
```

Here, RangeName is the name you are assigning to the range, and Start and End are optional arguments specifying the starting and ending points of the range.

The syntax for using the Range property on an object is

```
Set RangeName = object.Range
```

For example, the following statement uses the Range property of the Paragraphs collection to define a range named FirstPara that consists of the first paragraph of the active document. This statement doesn't use Start and End arguments because the starting point and ending point of the paragraph are clearly defined:

```
Set FirstPara = ActiveDocument.Paragraphs(1).Range
```

The following statements uppercase the first three words at the start of a document:

```
Dim InitialCaps As Range
Set InitialCaps = ActiveDocument.Range(Start:=ActiveDocument. Words(1).Start, _
    End:=ActiveDocument.Words(3).End)
InitialCaps.Case = wdUpperCase
```

The first statement defines a Range object named InitialCaps. The second statement assigns InitialCaps to a range in the active document, from the beginning of the first word to the end of the third word. The third statement changes the case of the InitialCaps Range object to uppercase.

Because InitialCaps is now defined as a Range object for the duration of the procedure that declares it, you can return to InitialCaps and manipulate it later in the procedure if you want to.

Redefining a Range

To redefine a range to make it refer to another part of a document, use the SetRange method. The syntax is

```
expression.SetRange(Start, End)
```

Here, expression is a required expression that returns a Range or Selection object, and Start and End are optional arguments specifying the starting and ending points of the range.

For example, the following statement redefines the range InitialCaps to refer to the first two characters of the document:

```
InitialCaps.SetRange Start:=0, End:=2
```

You can also redefine a range by using the Set method again, creating the range again from scratch.

Using the Duplicate Property to Store or Copy Formatting

You can use the Duplicate property to store or copy a range so that you can apply it to another range. For example, the following statements declare two ranges, Range1 and Range2, store the duplicate of the current selection's range in Range1, assign to Range2 the Range of the first bookmark in the active document, and then apply to Range2 the contents of Range1:

```
Dim Range1 As Range, Range2 As Range
Set Range1 = Selection.Range.Duplicate
Set Range2 = ActiveDocument.Bookmarks(1).Range
Range2.Paragraphs(1).Range = Range2
```

Setting Options

In your procedures, you'll often need to check the status of options in the Word application or in a particular document. In VBA, many of the options are controlled by the Options object, which has dozens of properties but only one method (SetWPHelpOptions, which sets options for Word's Word-Perfect help features).

This section shows four brief examples of setting options, three examples using the Options object and one using a property of the Document object. To see the full list of properties available for the Options object, search for "options object" in the Word VBA help file.

Making Sure Hyperlinks Require Ctrl+Clicking

Hyperlinks in Word documents have proved a mixed blessing—especially since Microsoft's changes to the way Word handles hyperlinks tend to leave users unsure whether to click or Ctrl+click the hyperlink to follow it. You can set the CtrlClickHyperlinkToOpen property of the Options object to True to ensure that hyperlinks require Ctrl+clicking:

```
Options.CtrlClickHyperlinkToOpen = True
```

Turning Off Overtype

To make sure your procedures behave as expected, you may need to check that Word is using Insert mode rather than Overtype mode. (In Insert mode, Word inserts the characters you type at the insertion point, moving any text to the right of the characters along. In Overtype mode, each character you type replaces the character to the right of the insertion point.)

Overtype mode is controlled by the Overtype property of the Options object. When OverType is True, Overtype mode is on; when Overtype is False, Insert mode is on. The following statements store the Overtype setting in a Boolean variable named blnOvertypeOn, set Overtype to False, perform its actions, and then restore the user's Overtype setting:

```
Dim blnOvertypeOn As Boolean
blnOvertypeOn = Options.Overtype
Options.Overtype = False
'take actions here
Options.Overtype = blnOvertypeOn
```

Setting a Default File Path

When configuring Word on a computer, you may need to make sure that its default file paths are set to the correct folders. You can do so by working with the `DefaultFilePath` property of the `Options` object. The syntax is

```
expression.DefaultFilePath(Path)
```

Here, *expression* is a required expression that returns an `Options` object. Often, it's easiest to use the `Options` object itself. `Path` is one of the self-explanatory enumerated constants shown in the following list:

wdAutoRecoverPath	wdStyleGalleryPath
wdBorderArtPath	wdTempFilePath
wdCurrentFolderPath	wdTextConvertersPath
wdDocumentsPath	wdToolsPath
wdGraphicsFiltersPath	wdTutorialPath
wdPicturesPath	wdUserOptionsPath
wdProgramPath	wdUserTemplatesPath
wdProofingToolsPath	wdWorkgroupTemplatesPath
wdStartupPath	

For example, the following statements set the user templates path and workgroup templates path:

```
Options.DefaultFilePath(wdUserTemplatesPath) = "c:\user\templates"
Options.DefaultFilePath(wdWorkgroupTemplatesPath) = "\\server\users\templates"
```

Turning Off Track Changes

Before running a procedure that adds, deletes, or formats text, you may need to turn off the Track Changes feature so that the changes the procedure makes are not marked. If the user had Track Changes on, you should turn it back on at the end of the procedure so that changes the user makes are tracked again. The following example stores the `TrackRevisions` setting for the `ActiveDocument` object in a Boolean variable named `blnTrackChangesOn`, sets `TrackRevisions` to `False`, performs its actions, and then restores the user's `TrackRevisions` setting:

```
Dim blnTrackChangesOn As Boolean
blnTrackChangesOn = ActiveDocument.TrackRevisions
ActiveDocument.TrackRevisions = False
'take actions here
ActiveDocument.TrackRevisions = blnTrackChangesOn
```

Chapter 21

Working with Widely Used Objects in Word

◆ Using Find and Replace via VBA

◆ Working with headers, footers, and page numbers

◆ Working with sections, page setup, windows, and views

◆ Working with tables

In the previous chapter, you learned how to work with some of the main objects in the Word object model, such as Document objects, the Selection object, Range objects, and the Options object. This chapter shows you how to go further with VBA in Word by working with Find and Replace; with headers, footers, and page numbers; with sections, page setup, windows, and views; and with tables.

Using Find and Replace via VBA

Word's Find and Replace features can be very useful in your procedures. To access these features via VBA, you use the Find and Replacement objects. This section shows you the easiest way to use the Find object, which is by using its Execute method. When you do this, you usually specify the parameters for the Find operation as arguments in the Execute statement, but you can also set them beforehand using properties.

Table 21.1 describes the Find properties you'll find most useful for common search operations.

TABLE 21.1:   Properties of the Find Object

FIND PROPERTY	MEANING
Font	Font formatting you're searching for (on either specified text or an empty string).
Forward	A Boolean argument specifying whether to search forward (True) or backward (False) through the document.
Found	A Boolean property that's True if the search finds a match and False if it doesn't.
Highlight	A Long argument controlling whether highlighting is included in the formatting for the replacement text (True) or not (False).

TABLE 21.1:   Properties of the Find Object *(CONTINUED)*

FIND PROPERTY	MEANING
MatchAllWordForms	A Boolean property—True or False—corresponding to the Find All Word Forms check box.
MatchCase	A Boolean property corresponding to the Match Case check box.
MatchSoundsLike	A Boolean property corresponding to the Sounds Like check box.
MatchWholeWord	A Boolean property corresponding to the Find Whole Words Only check box.
MatchWildcards	A Boolean property corresponding to the Use Wildcards check box.
ParagraphFormat	Paragraph formatting you're searching for (on either specified text or an empty string).
Replacement	Returns a Replacement object containing the criteria for a replace operation.
Style	The style for the search text. Usually, you'll want to use the name of a style in the current template, but you can also use one of the built-in Word constant style names, such as wdStyleHeading1 (Heading 1 style).
Text	The text you're searching for (what you'd enter in the Find What box in the Find and Replace dialog box). Use an empty string (" ") to search only for formatting.
Wrap	A Long property that governs whether a search that starts anywhere other than the beginning of a document (for a forward search) or the end of a document (for a backward search), or a search that takes place in a range, *wraps* (continues) when it reaches the end or beginning of the document or the end or beginning of the selection.

You use the Replacement object to specify the replace criteria in a replacement operation. The Replacement object has the following properties, which correspond to the properties of the Find object (but pertain to the replacement operation instead): Font, Highlight, ParagraphFormat, Style, and Text.

Understanding the Syntax for the *Execute* Method

The syntax for the Execute method is as follows:

```
expression.Execute(FindText, MatchCase, MatchWholeWord, MatchWildcards,
    ➡MatchSoundsLike, MatchAllWordForms, Forward, Wrap, ReplaceWith, Replace)
```

The parts of this statement are explained here:

◆ *expression* is a required expression that returns a Find object. Usually, it's easiest to use the Find object itself.

◆ `FindText` is an optional Variant specifying the text for which to search. Although this argument is optional, you'll almost always want to specify it, even if you specify only an empty string (`" "`) to allow you to search for formatting. (If you don't specify `FindText`, you run the risk of searching inadvertently for the previous item searched for.) You can search for special characters by using special characters you use when working interactively (for example, `^p` for a paragraph mark or `^a` for an annotation), and for wildcards by using the regular wildcards. For wildcards to work, you need to set `MatchWildcards` to `True`. You can search for a symbol by entering a caret and a zero followed by its character code. For example, to search for a smart double closing quote, you'd specify **^0148**, because its character code is 148.

◆ `MatchCase` is an optional Variant that you can set to `True` to make the search case-sensitive.

◆ `MatchWholeWord` is an optional Variant that you can set to `True` to restrict the search to finding whole words rather than words contained in other words.

◆ `MatchWildcards` is an optional Variant that you can set to `True` to use wildcards in the search.

◆ `MatchSoundsLike` is an optional Variant that you can set to `True` to have Word find words that it thinks sound similar to the Find item specified.

◆ `MatchAllWordForms` is an optional Variant that you can set to `True` to have Word find all forms of the Find item specified (for example, different forms of the same verb or noun).

◆ `Forward` is an optional Variant that you can set to `True` to have Word search forward (from the beginning of the document toward the end) or `False` to have Word search backward.

◆ `Wrap` is an optional Variant that governs whether a search that begins anywhere other than the beginning of a document (for a forward search) or at the end of a document (for a backward search), or a search that takes place in a range, *wraps* (continues) when it reaches the end or beginning of the document. Word offers the following options for `Wrap`:

Constant	Value	Meaning
`wdFindAsk`	2	Word searches the selection or range—or from the insertion point to the end or beginning of the document—and then displays a message box prompting the user to decide whether to search the rest of the document.
`wdFindContinue`	1	Word continues to search after reaching the end or beginning of the search range or the end or beginning of the document.
`wdFindStop`	0	Word stops the Find operation upon reaching the end or beginning of the search range or the end or beginning of the document.

◆ `Format` is an optional Variant that you can set to `True` to have the search operation find formatting as well as (or instead of) any Find text you've specified.

◆ `ReplaceWith` is an optional Variant specifying the replacement text. You can use an empty string for `ReplaceWith` to simply remove the `FindText` text; you can also use special characters for `ReplaceWith` as you can for the `FindText` argument. To use a graphic object, copy it to the Clipboard and then specify **^c** (the contents of the Clipboard).

NOTE To use a graphic object as described in the previous paragraph, it needs to be in the text layer (not floating over text). If the graphic was floating over text, ^c pastes in the previous text contents of the Clipboard.

◆ Replace is an optional Variant that controls how many replacements the Find operation makes: one (wdReplaceOne), all (wdReplaceAll), or none (wdReplaceNone).

Using the *ClearFormatting* Method

When you use the Find object and the Replacement object, you'll often need to use the ClearFormatting method, which clears any formatting specified under the Find What box or the Replace With box. Using the ClearFormatting method has the same effect as clicking the No Formatting button with the focus on the Find What box or the Replace With box. The following statements (which appear within a With structure) clear formatting from the Find and Replacement objects, respectively:

```
With ActiveDocument.Content.Find
    .ClearFormatting
    .Replacement.ClearFormatting
End With
```

Putting Find and Replace to Work

The simplest way to use Find and Replace is to specify as many parameters as you need in an Execute statement, leaving out any optional parameters that you don't need to specify. For example, to replace all pairs of paragraph marks in the active document, you could search for **^p^p** and replace it with **^p** with the following statement:

```
ActiveDocument.Content.Find.Execute FindText:="^p^p", ReplaceWith:="^p", _
    Replace:=wdReplaceAll
```

By running this statement in a loop, you could replace all extra paragraph marks in the document.

You can also use a With statement to specify the properties for a Find and Replace operation. Listing 21.1 shows an example of this. The code changes all bold formatting in the open document named Example.doc to italic formatting.

LISTING 21.1:

```
1.   With Documents("Example.doc").Content.Find
2.       .ClearFormatting
3.       .Font.Bold = True
4.       With .Replacement
5.           .ClearFormatting
6.           .Font.Bold = False
7.           .Font.Italic = True
8.       End With
9.       .Execute FindText:="", ReplaceWith:="", _
             Format:=True, Replace:=wdReplaceAll
10.  End With
```

Here, line 1 identifies the Document object (Example.doc in the Documents collection) with which to work and begins a With statement with its Find object. Line 2 uses the ClearFormatting method to clear any formatting from the Find object, and line 3 then sets the Bold property of its Font object to True.

Lines 4 through 8 contain a nested With statement for the Replacement object. Line 5 uses the ClearFormatting method to clear formatting from the Replacement object; line 6 sets its Bold property to False; and line 7 sets its Italic property to True.

Line 9 then uses the Execute method to execute the replacement operation. Both FindText and ReplaceWith here are specified as empty strings to cause Word to work with formatting only; Format is set to True to activate the formatting set in the Find and Replacement objects; and Replace is set to wdReplaceAll to replace all instances of the bold formatting with the italic formatting.

Line 10 ends the outer With statement.

Working with Headers, Footers, and Page Numbers

This section shows you how to work with headers and footers in Word documents. You'll also learn how to use VBA to manipulate page numbers, which many headers and footers need to include.

Understanding How VBA Implements Headers and Footers

A Word document can contain six types of headers and footers you can create—the primary header and footer, different first-page headers and footers, different even-page headers and footers—and different sets of headers and footers for each of the sections in a document if need be. Every document that you create gets a primary header and a primary footer, even if you don't put anything in them. You can then create different first-page and even-page headers by changing the Page Setup options for the section.

VBA uses the following objects for headers and footers:

◆ Both headers and footers are contained in HeaderFooter objects. You access headers through the Headers property and footers through the Footers property.

◆ The HeadersFooters collection contains all the HeaderFooter objects in a given section of a document. Because each section of a document can have different headers and footers than the other sections, you reach any given header or footer by going through the section.

◆ To return the HeadersFooters collection, you use the Headers property or the Footers property of the appropriate Section object in the appropriate Document object. Alternatively, you can use the HeaderFooter property of the Selection object to return a single HeaderFooter object, but this approach tends to be more limited in its use.

◆ The HeaderFooter object gives access to the Range object, the Shapes collection, and the PageNumbers collection.

Getting to the Header or Footer

You access a header or footer through the appropriate section within the document. For example, the following statement displays a message box containing the text in the first-page footer in the second section of the open document Transfer.doc:

```
MsgBox Documents("Transfer.doc").Sections(2). _
    Footers(wdHeaderFooterFirstPage).Range.Text
```

The following statements declare the HeaderFooter object variable myHeader and assign to it the primary header in the first section in the active document:

```
Dim myHeader As HeaderFooter
Set myHeader = ActiveDocument.Sections(1).Headers _
    (wdHeaderFooterPrimary)
```

Checking to See if a Header or Footer Exists

Word creates a primary header and primary footer in each document you create, so these objects always exist. To find out whether other headers or footers exist, check the Exists property of the application HeaderFooter object. The following statements check if the even-pages footer exists in each section in turn in the active document and create a generic header (containing the section number and the full name of the document) formatted with the style named Footer (which exists by default in most Word documents).

```
Dim cSection As Section
With ActiveDocument
    For Each cSection In .Sections
        cHeader = cSection.Headers(wdHeaderFooterEvenPages)
        If Not cSection.Headers(wdHeaderFooterEvenPages).Exists Then
            cSection.PageSetup.OddAndEvenPagesHeaderFooter = True
            cSection.Headers(wdHeaderFooterEvenPages).Range.Text _
                = "Section " & cSection.Index & " of " & .FullName
            cSection.Headers(wdHeaderFooterEvenPages).Range. _
                Style = "Even Footer"
        End If
    Next cSection
End With
```

Linking to the Header or Footer in the Previous Section

By default, Word links the header and footer in each section after the first to the header and footer in the previous section. To break the link, set the LinkToPrevious property of the header or footer to False; to create the link, set this property to True. The following statement unlinks the primary footer in the third section of the active document from the corresponding footer in the second section:

```
ActiveDocument.Sections(3).Footers(wdHeaderFooterPrimary).LinkToPrevious = False
```

Creating a Different First-Page Header

To create a different header on the first page of a section, set the DifferentFirstPageHeaderFooter property of the PageSetup object for the section to True. The following statements check to see if the tenth section of the active document contains a first-page header and create one if it doesn't:

```
With ActiveDocument.Sections(10)
    If .Headers(wdHeaderFooterFirstPage).Exists = False Then _
        .PageSetup.DifferentFirstPageHeaderFooter = True
End With
```

Creating Different Odd- and Even-Page Headers

To produce different headers for odd and even pages of your document (other than the first page), you create an even-page header. The primary header by default appears on both odd and even pages until you create an even-page header, at which point the primary header becomes the odd-page header.

As with the first-page header, you work through the PageSetup object to create a different even-page header, setting the OddAndEvenPagesHeaderFooter property to True, as in the following statement:

```
ActiveDocument.Sections(1).PageSetup.OddAndEvenPagesHeaderFooter = True
```

TIP   If you write procedures to format documents, you'll often need to check or change all the headers and footers in a document. The easiest way to do so is to use two For Each... Next loops, the outer loop working through each Section object in the Sections collection and the inner loop working through each HeaderFooter object in the HeaderFooters collection within that section.

Adding Page Numbers to Your Headers and Footers

The header or footer of a document often contains a page number: either a simple number in a straightforward format (1, 2, 3, and so on) or a more complex number denoting the chapter and page within it, separated by a separator character.

VBA implements page numbers through a PageNumbers collection that you return by using the PageNumbers property of the appropriate HeaderFooter object within the appropriate section of the document.

ADDING PAGE NUMBERS TO ONE OR MORE SECTIONS OF A DOCUMENT

To add page numbers to a document, use the Add method with the PageNumbers collection for the appropriate section of the document.

The syntax for the Add method is as follows:

```
expression.Add PageNumberAlignment, FirstPage
```

Here, *expression* is a required expression that returns a PageNumbers collection. Usually, you'll use the PageNumbers collection itself.

PageNumberAlignment is an optional Variant argument specifying the alignment for the page numbers being added. Table 21.2 lists the constants and values you can use.

TABLE 21.2:   PageNumberAlignment Constants and Values

CONSTANT	VALUE	RESULTING ALIGNMENT
wdAlignPageNumberLeft	0	Left
wdAlignPageNumberCenter	1	Centered
wdAlignPageNumberRight	2	Right (default)
wdAlignPageNumberInside	3	Inside margin (right on left-hand pages, left on right-hand pages)
wdAlignPageNumberOutside	4	Outside margin (left on left-hand pages, right on right-hand pages)

FirstPage is an optional Variant argument that you can set to False to make the header and footer on the first page suppress the page number. If you omit the FirstPage argument, the DifferentFirstPageHeaderFooter property of the PageSetup object controls whether the header and footer on the first page are the same as or different than the other pages in the section.

Both the PageNumberAlignment argument and the FirstPage argument are optional, but you'll usually want to specify at least the PageNumberAlignment argument.

The following subprocedure adds page numbers to all the headers in each section of a document by using two For Each... Next loops:

```
Sub AddPageNumbersToAllHeadersAndSections()
    Dim cHeader As HeaderFooter, cSection As Section
    With Documents("Headers and Footers.doc")
        For Each cSection In .Sections
            For Each cHeader In cSection.Headers
                cSection.Headers(wdHeaderFooterPrimary).PageNumbers _
                    .Add.PageNumberAlignment:= _
                    wdAlignPageNumberRight, FirstPage:=True
            Next cHeader
        Next cSection
    End With
End Sub
```

REMOVING PAGE NUMBERS FROM ONE OR MORE SECTIONS OF A DOCUMENT

To remove a page number from a page, specify the PageNumber object and use the Delete method. The following subprocedure removes each PageNumber object from the current section of the active document:

```
Sub RemovePageNumbersFromCurrentSection()
    Dim ThisHeader As HeaderFooter
    Dim ThisPageNumber As PageNumber
    With Selection.Sections(1)
        For Each ThisHeader In .Headers
            For Each ThisPageNumber In ThisHeader.PageNumbers
                ThisPageNumber.Delete
            Next ThisPageNumber
        Next ThisHeader
    End With
End Sub
```

FINDING OUT IF A SECTION OF A DOCUMENT HAS PAGE NUMBERS

The easiest way to find out if any given page number exists is to check the Count property for the PageNumbers collection for the appropriate section. For example, the following statement adds centered page numbers to the even-pages header in the current section if the header doesn't already have them:

```
If Selection.Sections(1).Headers(wdHeaderFooterEvenPages) _
    .PageNumbers.Count = 0 Then Selection.Sections(1) _
    .Headers(wdHeaderFooterEvenPages).PageNumbers.Add _
    PageNumberAlignment:=wdAlignPageNumberCenter
```

CHANGING THE PAGE NUMBERING FOR A SECTION

To change the page numbering for a section, you work with the StartingNumber property, using the RestartNumberingAtSection property, the IncludeChapterNumber property, and the ChapterPageSeparator property as necessary.

The StartingNumber property is a Long property that contains the starting page number for the section when the RestartNumberingAtSection property is set to True. When the RestartNumberingAtSection property is set to False, StartingNumber returns 0 (zero). The following statements set the page numbering for the primary header in the fourth section of the active document to start at 55 if it doesn't currently have a starting number assigned:

```
With ActiveDocument.Sections(4).Headers(wdHeaderFooterPrimary)
    If .PageNumbers.StartingNumber = 0 Then
        .PageNumbers.RestartNumberingAtSection = True
        .PageNumbers.StartingNumber = 55
    End If
End With
```

To add the chapter number to the page numbers, use heading numbering in your document, set the IncludeChapterNumber property to True, and specify the separator to use (for example, wdSeparatorEnDash for an en dash):

```
With ActiveDocument.Sections(4).Headers(wdHeaderFooterPrimary) _
    .PageNumbers
    .IncludeChapterNumber = True
    .ChapterPageSeparator = wdSeparatorEnDash
End With
```

SUPPRESSING THE PAGE NUMBER FOR THE FIRST PAGE

To suppress the page number for the first page in a section, set the ShowFirstPageNumber property for the appropriate HeaderFooter object in the appropriate section to False:

```
ActiveDocument.Sections(1).Footers(wdHeaderFooterPrimary).PageNumbers_
    .ShowFirstPageNumber = False
```

FORMATTING PAGE NUMBERS

You can format page numbers in two ways: by setting the format in which they're displayed (for instance, as regular Arabic numbers or as lowercase Roman numerals) and by formatting the font in which that format is displayed.

To choose the format in which the page numbers are displayed, set the NumberStyle property of the PageNumbers collection in question. For example, the following statement formats the page numbers in the primary header in the fourth section of the active document as lowercase letters:

```
ActiveDocument.Sections(4).Headers(wdHeaderFooterPrimary) _
    .PageNumbers.NumberStyle = wdPageNumberStyleLowercaseLetter
```

Once the page numbers are in the header or footer, you can format them in any of several ways. One easy way to set the font in which a given page number is formatted is to use the Select method to select the PageNumber object and then apply formatting to it as you would any other selection, as in the following statements:

```
ActiveDocument.Sections(4).Headers(wdHeaderFooterPrimary) _
    .PageNumbers(1).Select
With Selection.Font
    .Name = "Impact"
    .Size = 22
    .Bold = True
End With
```

CREATING "PAGE X OF Y" PAGE NUMBERS

You can also implement page numbering by using Word's field codes in the header or footer. This technique is especially useful when you want to number the pages with an "X of Y" numbering scheme—"Page 168 of 192" and so on. The following statements select the primary header for the final section of the active document, apply center alignment, and enter the text and fields to produce this type of numbering:

```
ActiveDocument.Sections(ActiveDocument.Sections.Count) _
    .Headers(wdHeaderFooterPrimary).Range.Select
With Selection
    .Paragraphs(1).Alignment = wdAlignParagraphCenter
    .TypeText Text:="Page "
    .Fields.Add Range:=Selection.Range, Type:=wdFieldEmpty, Text:= _
        "PAGE ", PreserveFormatting:=True
    .TypeText Text:=" of "
    .Fields.Add Range:=Selection.Range, Type:=wdFieldEmpty, Text:= _
        "NUMPAGES ", PreserveFormatting:=True
End With
```

If you insert a page number by using a field in this way, you can still access the page number by using the appropriate PageNumber object. (In this case, the PageNumber object consists of the PAGE field, not of the NUMPAGES field.)

Working with Sections, Page Setup, Windows, and Views

Each Word document contains at least one section by default and can contain multiple sections as needed for its contents and layout. The section of the document controls the page layout so that different sections of a document can use different page layouts if necessary.

Adding a Section to a Document

You can add a section to a document either by using the Add method with the Sections collection or by using the InsertBreak method with a Range or Selection object.

The Add method takes the following syntax:

expression.Add Range, Start

Here, *expression* is a required expression that returns a Sections collection. Range is an optional Variant argument specifying the range at the beginning of which to insert the break. (If you omit Range, VBA inserts the break at the end of the document.) Start is an optional Variant argument used to specify the type of section break to insert:

- ◆ wdSectionContinuous (0) for a continuous break

- ◆ wdSectionEvenPage (3) for an even-page break

- ◆ wdSectionOddPage (4) for an odd-page break

- ◆ wdSectionNewColumn (1) for a new-column break

- ◆ wdSectionNewPage (2, the default) for a new-page break

The following statement adds a new-page section to the active document, placing it before the second paragraph:

```
ActiveDocument.Sections.Add Range:=.Range(Start:=.Paragraphs(2).Range.Start, _
        End:=.Paragraphs(2).Range.Start), Start:=wdSectionNewPage
```

The InsertBreak method takes the following syntax:

```
expression.InsertBreak Type
```

Here, *expression* is a required expression that returns a Selection or Range object. Type is an optional Variant argument specifying the type of section break to be inserted:

- ◆ wdSectionBreakNextPage (2) for a new-page break

- ◆ wdSectionBreakContinuous (3) for a continuous break

- ◆ wdSectionBreakEvenPage (4) for an even-page break

- ◆ wdSectionBreakOddPage (5) for an odd-page break

- ◆ wdColumnBreak (8) for a new-column break

The following statement inserts a continuous section break before the second paragraph in the active document:

```
ActiveDocument.Paragraphs(2).Range.InsertBreak Type:=wdSectionBreakContinuous
```

Changing the Page Setup

To change the page setup of a document or a section, you work with the PageSetup object of the application Document object or Section object. For example, the following statements work with the PageSetup object of the document named Planning.doc, setting letter-size paper, portrait orientation, mirror margins, and margin measurements (in points):

```
With Documents("Planning.doc").PageSetup
    .PaperSize = wdPaperLetter
    .Orientation = wdOrientPortrait
    .TopMargin = 1
    .BottomMargin = 1
```

```
        .LeftMargin = 1
        .RightMargin = 1.5
        .MirrorMargins = True
End With
```

Opening a New Window Containing an Open Document

To open a new window containing an open document, use the Add method. Its syntax is straightforward:

```
expression.Add window
```

Here, *expression* is an expression that returns a `Windows` collection, and *window* is an optional Variant argument specifying the window containing the document for which you want to open a new window. If you omit *window*, VBA opens a new window for the active document.

NOTE There are two `Windows` collections: one for the application and one for the windows displaying the document with which you're working. The `Windows` collection for the `Document` object can be useful if you have multiple windows open for the same document (as you can do with the Window ➢ New Window command), but usually you'll want to use the `Windows` collection for the `Application` object. `Windows` is a creatable object, so you don't need to specify the `Application` object.

For example, the following statements open a new window for the first window open for the active document, assigning the window to the variable `myWindow`:

```
Dim myWindow As Window
Set myWindow = Windows.Add(Window:=ActiveDocument.Windows(1))
```

Closing All Windows but the First for a Document

Occasionally, it's useful to open one or more new windows for a document. If you do so, sooner or later you'll need to close all the secondary windows to give yourself more room to maneuver. The following statements close all windows for the active document except the first window:

```
Dim myWin As Window, myDoc As String
myDoc = ActiveDocument.Name
For Each myWin In Windows
    If myWin.Document = myDoc Then _
        If myWin.WindowNumber <> 1 Then myWin.Close
Next myWin
```

Splitting a Window

To split a window in two parts horizontally, set its `Split` property to `True`. To specify the split percentage (which controls how far down the window, measuring vertically, the split is placed), set the `SplitVertical` property. The following statements split the active window 70 percent of the way down the window:

```
With ActiveWindow
    .Split = True
```

```
    .SplitVertical = 70
End With
```

To remove the split from the window, set the `Split` property to `False`:

```
ActiveWindow.Split = False
```

Displaying the Document Map for a Window

To display the Document Map for a window at the Document Map's previous width percentage (of the document's window), set the `DocumentMap` property to `True`:

```
ActiveWindow.DocumentMap = True
```

To display the Document Map at a different width, or to change the width of the Document Map, set the `DocumentMapPercentWidth` property to a suitable percentage of the window's width:

```
ActiveWindow.DocumentMapPercentWidth = 25
```

To hide the Document Map again, set the `DocumentMap` property to `False` or set the `DocumentMapPercentWidth` property to 0.

Scrolling a Window

To scroll a window up, down, left, or right, use either the `LargeScroll` method or the `SmallScroll` method.

The `LargeScroll` method is analogous to clicking before or after the thumb (the scroll box) on the horizontal or vertical scroll bar of a window; it scrolls the contents of the window by one "screen" (or multiple screens) in the specified direction. The `SmallScroll` method is analogous to clicking the scroll buttons on a scroll bar; it scrolls the contents of the window up or down by one line and left or right by a small scroll increment.

The syntax for the `LargeScroll` method is as follows:

```
expression.LargeScroll(Down, Up, ToRight, ToLeft)
```

The syntax for the `SmallScroll` method is almost identical:

```
expression.SmallScroll(Down, Up, ToRight, ToLeft)
```

Here, *expression* is a required expression that returns a `Window` object. *Down, Up, ToRight*, and *ToLeft* are optional Variant arguments that specify the number of screens (for `LargeScroll`) or lines or horizontal movement units (for `SmallScroll`) to scroll the contents of the window in the directions their names indicate.

The following statement scrolls the active window up two screens:

```
ActiveWindow.LargeScroll Up:=2
```

Arranging Windows

To arrange a number of windows, use the `Arrange` method. The syntax for the `Arrange` method is as follows:

```
expression.Arrange ArrangeStyle
```

Here, *expression* is an expression that returns a `Windows` collection, and `ArrangeStyle` is an optional Variant argument that specifies how to arrange the windows: as icons (`wdIcons`, 1) or tiled (`wdTiled`, 0). The default is `wdTiled`.

For example, the following statement tiles the open windows:

```
Windows.Arrange ArrangeStyle:=wdTiled
```

Positioning and Sizing a Window

To position a window, set its `Left` and `Top` properties. For example:

```
ActiveWindow.Left = 100
ActiveWindow.Top = 200
```

To size a window, set its `Height` and `Width` properties:

```
With ActiveWindow
    .Height = 300
    .Width = 400
End With
```

To maximize, minimize, or "restore" a window, set its `WindowState` property to `wdWindowStateMaximize`, `wdWindowStateMinimize`, or `wdWindowStateNormal`, respectively. The following statements maximize the window containing the document named `Example.doc` if the window is minimized:

```
With Documents("Example.doc").Windows(1)
    If .WindowState = wdWindowStateMinimize Then _
        .WindowState = wdWindowStateMaximize
End With
```

Making Sure an Item Is Displayed in the Window

After opening or arranging windows, you'll often need to make sure that an item you want the user to see—a range, some text, a graphic or other shape, or a field—is displayed in the window. The easiest way to do so is to use the `ScrollIntoView` method of the `Window` object. This method moves the view but not the selection, so if you need the selection to move to the range, you'll need to move it there separately.

The `ScrollIntoView` method takes the following syntax:

```
expression.ScrollIntoView(Obj, Start)
```

Here, *expression* is a required expression that returns a `Window` object. `Obj` is a required argument specifying a `Range` or `Shape` object. `Start` is an optional Boolean argument that you can set to `True` (the default) to have the upper-left corner of the range or shape displayed or `False` to have the lower-right corner displayed. Specify `False` for `Start` when you need to make sure the end of a range or shape that may be larger than the window is displayed.

The following statements position the selection at the end of the last paragraph in the first list in the active document, ready to add a new paragraph to the list:

```
Dim rngFirstList As Range
Set rngFirstList = ActiveDocument.Lists(1).Range
```

```
ActiveDocument.Windows(1).ScrollIntoView Obj:=rngFirstList, Start:=False
rngFirstList.Select
Selection.Collapse Direction:=wdCollapseEnd
Selection.MoveLeft Unit:=wdCharacter, Count:=1, Extend:=wdMove
```

Changing a Document's View

To change a document's view, set the Type property of the View object for the appropriate window to wdMasterView, wdNormalView, wdOutlineView, wdPrintPreview, wdPrintView, wdReadingView, or wdWebView. For example, the following statement changes the view for Sample.doc to Print Layout view:

```
Documents("Sample.doc").Windows(1).View.Type = wdPrintView
```

Zooming the View to Display Multiple Pages

To zoom Print Layout view or Print Preview to display multiple pages, set the PageColumns and PageRows properties of the appropriate View object. (Change the view first if necessary.) The following statement displays Sample.doc in Print Layout view with six pages displayed (three across by two deep):

```
With Documents("Sample.doc").Windows(1).View
    .Type = wdPrintView
    With .Zoom
        .PageColumns = 3
        .PageRows = 2
    End With
End With
```

Working with Tables

You'll often need to work with tables in your Word documents, either creating them from scratch or manipulating existing tables. VBA uses the Table object to represent a table, and the Table objects are gathered together into the Tables collection. To work with tables, you use the Tables property to return the Tables collection for the Document, Range, or Selection object in question.

The Tables collection and the Table object contain the following collections and objects:

♦ The Rows collection contains the rows in the table. Each row is represented by a Row object.

♦ The Columns collection contains the columns in the table. Each column is represented by a Column object.

♦ The Cell object provides access to a specified cell directly from the Table object. You can also reach the cells in the table by going through the row or column in which they reside.

♦ The Range object provides access to ranges within the table.

♦ The Borders collection contains all the borders for the table.

♦ The Shading object contains all the shading for the table.

Creating a Table

To create a new table from scratch (rather than converting existing text to a table), use the Add method with the Tables collection. The Add method takes the following syntax for the Tables collection:

```
expression.Add(Range, NumRows, NumColumns, DefaultTableBehavior, AutoFitBehavior)
```

The arguments are as follows:

◆ *expression* is a required expression that returns a Tables collection. Typically, you'll want to use the Tables collection for the appropriate document.

◆ Range is a required argument supplying the range where you want to insert the table. If the range is a selection (rather than being collapsed), the table replaces the range.

◆ NumRows is a required Long argument specifying the number of rows the table is to have.

◆ NumColumns is a required Long argument specifying the number of columns the table is to have.

◆ DefaultTableBehavior is an optional Variant argument specifying whether the table autofits its columns to their contents or to the window when you change the contents or the window width. Use wdWord9TableBehavior to have the table autofit its columns or wdWord8TableBehavior (the default) to have the columns retain their width.

◆ AutoFitBehavior is an optional Variant argument specifying the AutoFit behavior for the table. This argument applies only when DefaultTableBehavior is wdWord9TableBehavior. Use wdAutoFitContent to resize the columns to their contents, wddAutoFitWindow to resize the columns to the window width, or wdAutoFitFixed to use a fixed column width.

For example, the following statement inserts a new, blank, non-autofitting table containing 10 rows and 5 columns at the current position of the insertion point in the active document:

```
ActiveDocument.Tables.Add Range:=Selection.Range, NumRows:=10, _
    NumColumns:=5, DefaultTableBehavior:=wdWord8TableBehavior
```

Selecting a Table

To select a table, specify the Document, Range, or Selection object involved, and then identify the Table object and use the Select method. This method takes no arguments.

The following statement selects the first table in the active document:

```
ActiveDocument.Tables(1).Select
```

The following statements declare the variable tempTable and then select the first table in the document named Log.doc and assign its Range object to tempTable:

```
Dim tempTable
Documents("Log.doc").Tables(1).Select
Set tempTable = Selection.Tables(1).Range
```

The following statement selects the second table in the range named tempRange:

```
tempRange.Tables(2).Select
```

The following statement selects the first table in the current selection:

```
Selection.Tables(1).Select
```

Converting Text to a Table

To convert text to a table (as opposed to inserting a new table from scratch), use the `ConvertToTable` method with an appropriate `Range` or `Selection` object. The `ConvertToTable` method takes the following syntax:

```
expression.ConvertToTable(Separator, NumRows, NumColumns, InitialColumnWidth,
Format, ApplyBorders, ApplyShading, ApplyFont, ApplyColor, ApplyHeadingRows,
ApplyLastRow, ApplyFirstColumn, ApplyLastColumn, AutoFit, AutoFitBehavior,
DefaultTableBehavior)
```

The arguments are as follows:

- *expression* is a required argument specifying an expression that returns a `Range` object or a `Selection` object.

- `Separator` is an optional Variant argument specifying the separator character (also known as the *delimiter* character) to use to mark where the column divisions were. You can use these values for `Separator`:

  - `wdSeparateByCommas` separates column information at commas.

  - `wdSeparateByDefaultListSeparator` separates column information at the currently specified Other list separator character (the character shown in the text box alongside the Other option button in the Convert Table To Text dialog box).

  - `wdSeparateByParagraphs` separates column information at the paragraph marks.

  - `wdSeparateByTabs` (the default separator if you don't specify one) separates column information at tabs.

  - Alternatively, you can specify a single separator character of your choice as a string or between double quotation marks. For example, enter **Separator:="|"** to use a vertical bar [|] as the separator.

- `NumRows` is an optional Variant argument specifying the number of rows the table should have. If you omit the `NumRows` argument, Word decides the number of rows in the table based on the number of columns specified and/or the number of the chosen separator characters it finds.

- `NumColumns` is an optional Variant argument specifying the number of columns the table should have. As with `NumRows`, if you omit the `NumColumns` argument, Word decides the number of columns in the table based on the number of rows specified and/or the number of the chosen separator characters it finds.

- `InitialColumnWidth` is an optional Variant argument that you can use to specify the initial width (in points) of each column in the table. If you omit the `InitialColumnWidth` argument, Word uses the full width of the page—from margin to margin—and allocates an equal width to each column, regardless of the relative widths of the contents of the columns. The `InitialColumnWidth` argument is useful primarily for restraining tables from using the full width of the page automatically. In many cases, autofitting the columns provides a better solution.

◆ Format is an optional Variant argument that you can use to specify one of Word's built-in auto-format styles for tables. To use the Format argument, specify the appropriate WdTableFormat constant (such as wdTableFormatElegant to specify the Elegant autoformat style). If you choose to apply a format, you can specify which properties of the autoformat style to apply to the table by using the following optional Variant arguments:

   ◆ Set ApplyBorders to True to apply the border formatting, or to False not to apply it.

   ◆ Set ApplyShading to True to apply the shading, or to False not to apply it.

   ◆ Set ApplyFont to True to apply the font formatting, or to False not to apply it.

   ◆ Set ApplyColor to True to apply the color formatting, or to False not to apply it.

   ◆ Set ApplyHeadingRows to True to apply any heading-row formatting, or to False not to apply it.

   ◆ Set ApplyLastRow to True to apply any last-row formatting, or to False not to apply it.

   ◆ Set ApplyFirstColumn to True to apply any first-column formatting, or to False not to apply it.

   ◆ Set ApplyLastColumn to True to apply any last-column formatting, or to False not to apply it.

◆ AutoFit is an optional Variant argument you can set to True to have Word adjust the column width to best fit the contents of the cells. When autofitting, Word doesn't increase the overall width of the table—it either reduces the table or keeps it the same width.

◆ AutoFitBehavior and DefaultTableBehavior are as described in the section "Creating a Table," earlier in the chapter.

The following statement converts the current selection to a five-column table, separating the information at commas. It applies autofitting to the table based on cell content and sets the cells to resize automatically:

```
Set myTable = Selection.ConvertToTable(wdSeparateByCommas, _
    Selection.Paragraphs.Count, 5, , , , , , , , , , , True, _
    wdAutoFitContent, wdWord9TableBehavior)
```

Making Sure the Selection Is within a Table

Before running any procedure that expects it will take place within a table, it's a good idea to make sure that the current selection is suitable. To check whether the selection is currently within a table, use the wdWithInTable argument of the Information property for the selection. wdWithInTable is Boolean, returning True if the selection is in a table and False if it isn't. For example:

```
If Selection.Information(wdWithInTable) = True Then
    'take actions here
End If
```

Finding Out Where the Selection Is in the Table

Apart from establishing whether the selection is in a table, you can use the Information property to find out other information that can be useful when working with tables via a Range object or Selection object.

Once you've established that the selection is within a table (probably by using the wdWithinTable argument), check whether the selection is at an end-of-row marker rather than being in a cell. If the selection is at an end-of-row marker, certain actions fail. For example, attempting to select the current cell or column fails because the selection is outside any cell or column, but attempting to select the current row succeeds.

To check whether the selection is at the end-of-row marker, use the AtEndOfRowMarker argument for the Information property. The following statement moves the selection left one character (into the last cell in the same row) if the selection is at the end-of-row marker:

```
If Selection.Information(wdAtEndOfRowMarker) = True Then _
    Selection.MoveLeft Unit:=wdCharacter, Count:=1
```

If the selection contains the end-of-row marker, rather than being a collapsed selection (an insertion point) before the marker, the wdAtEndOfRowMarker argument returns False. To avoid a selected end-of-row marker causing problems in your procedures, collapse the selection if it isn't collapsed before checking whether it's at the end-of-row marker. The following statements do this, using a variable named curSel to restore the selection it collapses, unless collapsing the selection leaves the selection at an end-of-row marker:

```
Dim curSel
With Documents("Communications.doc")
    If Selection.Type <> wdSelectionIP Then
        Set curSel = Selection.Range
        Selection.Collapse Direction:=wdCollapseStart
    End If
    If Selection.Information(wdAtEndOfRowMarker) = True Then
        Selection.MoveLeft Unit:=wdCharacter, Count:=1, Extend:=wdMove
    Else
        If curSel <> "" Then curSel.Select
        Set curSel = Nothing
    End If
End With
```

After establishing that the selection is safely in a table, you can retrieve six useful pieces of information about the table:

♦ wdStartOfRangeColumnNumber returns the number of the column in which the beginning of the selection or range falls. The following statement selects the column in which the current selection begins:

```
Selection.Tables(1).Columns(Selection.Information _
    (wdStartOfRangeColumnNumber)).Select
```

◆ wdEndOfRangeColumnNumber returns the number of the column in which the end of the selection or range falls. The following statements delete the column in which the range testRange ends if the range is more than one column wide:

```
With testRange
    If .Information(wdStartOfRangeColumnNumber) <> _
        .Information(wdEndOfRangeColumnNumber) Then _
        .Tables(1).Columns(.Information _
        (wdEndOfRangeColumnNumber)).Delete
End With
```

◆ wdStartOfRangeRowNumber returns the number of the row in which the beginning of the selection or range falls.

◆ wdEndOfRangeRowNumber returns the number of the row in which the end of the selection or range falls.

◆ wdMaximumNumberOfColumns returns the highest number of columns in any row in the selection or range.

◆ wdMaximumNumberOfRows returns the highest number of rows in the specified selection or range in the table.

Sorting a Table

To sort a table, identify the table and use the Sort method. Sort takes the following syntax with the Table object:

```
expression.Sort(ExcludeHeader, FieldNumber, SortFieldType, SortOrder, FieldNumber2,
SortFieldType2, SortOrder2, FieldNumber3, SortFieldType3, SortOrder3, CaseSensitive,
BidiSort, IgnoreThe, IgnoreKashida, IgnoreDiacritics, IgnoreHe, LanguageID)
```

The arguments are as follows:

◆ *expression* is an expression that returns a Table object.

◆ ExcludeHeader is an optional Variant argument that you can set to True to exclude the first row in the table (which is often the table header row) from the sort or to False to include the first row in the table.

◆ FieldNumber, FieldNumber2, and FieldNumber3 are optional Variant arguments specifying the first, second, and third fields by which to sort (respectively). Usually you'll want to specify at least FieldNumber; if you don't, Word performs an alphanumeric sort on the table.

◆ SortFieldType, SortFieldType2, and SortFieldType3 are optional Variant arguments specifying the type of sorting you want to use for FieldNumber, FieldNumber2, and FieldNumber3, respectively. For U.S. English, the options are alphanumeric sorting (wdSortFieldAlphanumeric, the default), numeric sorting (wdSortFieldNumeric), or date sorting (wdSortFieldDate).

◆ SortOrder, SortOrder2, and SortOrder3 are optional Variant arguments specifying the sorting order for FieldNumber, FieldNumber2, and FieldNumber3. Use wdSortOrderAscending to specify an ascending sort (the default) or wdSortOrderDescending to specify a descending sort.

◆ `CaseSensitive` is an optional Variant argument that you can set to `True` to specify case-sensitive sorting. The default setting is `False`.

◆ The next five arguments (`BidiSort`, `IgnoreThe`, `IgnoreDiacritics`, `IgnoreKashida`, and `IgnoreHe`) are for specialized sorting (such as right-to-left languages, Arabic, and Hebrew).

◆ `LanguageID` is an optional Variant argument that you can use to specify the language in which to sort. For example, to sort in Lithuanian, you could specify `wdLithuanian` for `LanguageID`. For sorting in your default language, you can omit this argument.

Adding a Column to a Table

To add a column to a table, use the `Add` method with the `Columns` collection for the appropriate `Table` object. The `Add` method takes the following syntax for the `Columns` collection:

```
expression.Add [BeforeColumn]
```

Here, *expression* is a required expression that returns a `Columns` collection, and `BeforeColumn` is an optional Variant argument specifying the column to the left of which you want to insert the new column.

The following statements use the `Count` property to check the number of columns in the first table in the active document and, if the table contains fewer than five columns, add one or more columns to bring the number of columns up to five. Each new column is added before the existing last column in the table:

```
With ActiveDocument.Tables(1)
    .Select
    If .Columns.Count < 5 Then
        Do Until .Columns.Count = 5
            .Columns.Add BeforeColumn:=.Columns(.Columns.Count)
        Loop
    End If
End With
```

Deleting a Column from a Table

To delete a column, identify it and use the `Delete` method. `Delete` takes no arguments. The following statement deletes the first column in the table referenced by the object variable `myTable`:

```
myTable.Columns(1).Delete
```

Setting the Width of a Column

You can set the width of a column by using the `AutoFit` method, by using the `SetWidth` method, or by specifying the `Width` property for the column.

The `AutoFit` method resizes each column automatically to a width suitable to its contents. `AutoFit` takes no arguments. The following statement uses the `AutoFit` method to resize each column in the first table in the active document:

```
ActiveDocument.Tables(1).Columns.AutoFit
```

The `SetWidth` method allows you to set the width of one or more columns and specify how the other columns in the table should change as a result. The syntax for the `SetWidth` method is as follows:

```
expression.SetWidth ColumnWidth, RulerStyle
```

Here, *expression* is an expression that returns the `Columns` collection or `Column` object whose width you want to set. `ColumnWidth` is a required Single argument specifying the width of the column or columns, measured in points. `RulerStyle` is a required Long argument that specifies how Word should adjust the width of the columns:

◆ The default value, `wdAdjustNone`, sets all the specified columns to the specified width, moving other columns to the left or right as necessary. This argument is analogous to Shift+dragging a column border when working interactively.

◆ `wdAdjustFirstColumn` applies the specified width to the first specified column, adjusting only as many columns to the right of this column as necessary. For example, widening the first column in a table slightly causes Word to narrow the second column but leave the third and subsequent columns unchanged; widening the first column significantly causes Word to narrow the second and third columns, leaving the fourth and subsequent columns unchanged. This argument is analogous to dragging a column border when working interactively.

◆ `wdAdjustProportional` applies the specified width to the first specified column, keeping the right edge of the table in its previous position and adjusting all non-specified columns proportionally to accommodate the change.

◆ `wdAdjustSameWidth` applies the specified width to the first specified column, keeping the right edge of the table in its previous position and adjusting all the other columns to an identical width to accommodate the change. This argument is analogous to Ctrl+dragging a column border when working interactively.

The following statement sets the width of the second column in the first table in the active document to 50 points, adjusting the columns to the right of the second column proportionally:

```
ActiveDocument.Tables(1).Columns(2).SetWidth ColumnWidth:=50, _
    RulerStyle:=wdAdjustProportional
```

The `Width` property lets you change the width of a column without worrying about the effect on the other columns. Specify the width you want in points—for example:

```
ActiveDocument.Tables(11).Columns(44).Width = 100
```

Selecting a Column

To select a column, use the `Select` method with the appropriate `Column` object. `Select` takes no arguments. The following statement selects the second column in the third table in the document named `Originals.doc`:

```
Documents("Originals.doc").Tables(3).Columns(2).Select
```

Adding a Row to a Table

To add a row, use the Add method with the Rows collection for the table. The Add method takes the following syntax for the Rows collection:

```
expression.Add [BeforeRow]
```

Here, *expression* is a required expression that returns a Rows object, and BeforeRow is an optional Variant argument specifying the row before which you want to add the new row. If you omit BeforeRow, VBA adds the new row after the last existing row in the table.

The following statement adds a new first row to the table referenced by the object variable myTable:

```
myTable.Rows.Add BeforeRow:=1
```

Deleting a Row from a Table

To delete a row, use the Delete method with the appropriate Row object. The Delete method takes no arguments. The following statement deletes the first row in the table referenced by the object variable myTable:

```
myTable.Rows(1).Delete
```

Setting the Height of One or More Rows

You can set the height of rows by letting Word set the row height automatically, by using the SetHeight method to specify an exact height or a minimum height, or by setting the Height property of the row or rows directly.

To have Word set the height of a row automatically, set the row's HeightRule property to wdRowHeightAuto. Word then adjusts the height of the row to accommodate the cell with the tallest contents. The following statement sets the HeightRule property for the second row in the fourth table in the active document to wdRowHeightAuto:

```
ActiveDocument.Tables(4).Rows(2).HeightRule = wdRowHeightAuto
```

To specify an exact height or a minimum height for one or more rows, use the SetHeight method with the row or rows. The syntax for the SetHeight property is as follows:

```
expression.SetHeight RowHeight, [HeightRule]
```

Here, *expression* is an expression that returns a Row object or a Rows collection. HeightRule is a required Variant argument specifying the rule for setting the row height: Use wdRowHeightAtLeast to specify a minimum height or wdRowHeightExactly to specify an exact height. (The third setting for HeightRule is wdRowHeightAuto, which specifies automatic row height and which you won't want to use in this case.)

Instead of using the SetHeight method, you can set the Height property of the row or rows in question by specifying the height in points:

```
Documents("Tables.doc").Tables(3).Rows(3).Height = 33
```

Selecting a Row

To select a row, use the `Select` method for the appropriate Row object. The `Select` method takes no arguments. The following statement selects the last row in the last table in the document named `Tables.doc`:

```
Documents("Tables.doc").Tables(.Tables.Count).Rows.Last.Select
```

Inserting a Cell

To insert a cell, use the `Add` method with the `Cells` collection. The `Add` method takes the following syntax for the `Cells` collection:

```
expression.Add [BeforeCell]
```

Here, *expression* is an expression that returns a `Cells` collection, and `BeforeCell` is an optional Variant argument that specifies the cell to the left of which the new cell should be inserted. (If you omit the `BeforeCell` argument, VBA adds a new row of cells to the end of the table if you're using the `Cells` collection of the `Columns` collection or a new cell to the first row in the table if you're using the `Cells` collection of the `Rows` collection.)

The following statement inserts a cell before the second cell in the first row of the first table in the document named `Tables.doc`:

```
Documents("Tables.doc").Tables(1).Rows(1).Cells.Add _
    BeforeCell:=Documents("Tables.doc").Tables(1).Rows(1).Cells(2)
```

Returning the Text within a Cell

To return the contents of a cell, use the `Text` property of the `Range` object for the cell. The following statement returns the text in the first cell in the second row of the third table in the active document and assigns it to the variable `strCellText`:

```
strCellText = ActiveDocument.Tables(3).Rows(2).Cells(1).Range.Text
```

Because the `Text` property includes the end-of-cell marker (which takes up two characters), you'll usually want to strip off the last two characters when assigning the `Text` property to a string:

```
strCellText = ActiveDocument.Tables(3).Rows(2).Cells(1).Range.Text
strCellText = Left(strCellText, Len(strCellText) - 2)
```

Through the `Range` object, you can work with any of the objects and collections it contains. For example, to work with the paragraphs in a cell, use the `Paragraphs` collection.

Entering Text in a Cell

To enter text in a cell, assign the text to the `Text` property of the `Range` object for the cell. The following statements enter text in the first three cells in the first row of the current selection:

```
With Selection.Tables(1).Rows(1)
    .Cells(1).Range.Text = "Sample text in first cell."
    .Cells(2).Range.Text = "Sample text in second cell."
    .Cells(3).Range.Text = "Sample text in third cell."
End With
```

Deleting Cells

To delete cells, use the `Delete` method with the appropriate `Cell` object or `Cells` collection. When you delete one or more cells, you must specify what happens to the rest of the table—whether the cells to the right of those you deleted move to the left or whether the cells below those you deleted move up.

The syntax for the `Delete` method for the `Cells` collection and the `Cell` object is as follows:

```
expression.Delete [ShiftCells]
```

Here, *expression* is an expression that returns a `Cells` collection or a `Cell` object. `ShiftCells` is an optional Variant argument that specifies how the cells below or to the right of the deleted cell or cells should move. Use these values:

◆ `wdDeleteCellsEntireColumn` deletes the whole column the specified cell or cells is in.

◆ `wdDeleteCellsEntireRow` deletes the whole row.

◆ `wdDeleteCellsShiftLeft` moves cells across to the left to fill the gap.

◆ `wdDeleteCellsShiftUp` moves cells up to fill the gap.

The following statement deletes the first cell in the first row of the first table in the active document and shifts the other cells in the first row to the left to fill the gap:

```
ActiveDocument.Tables(1).Rows(1).Cells(1).Delete _
    ShiftCells:=wdDeleteCellsShiftLeft
```

For procedures that rely on the user to make a selection within a table, you may want to determine how many rows or columns are in the selection before deciding how to shift the cells. The following example checks the number of rows and columns in the selection. If the selection is only one cell, or if the selection is all in one column, the code deletes the cell or cells and moves the other cells in the row to the left. If the selection is multiple cells in one column, the code deletes the cells and moves the other cells in the column up. If the selection spans columns and rows, the code displays a message box asking the user to make a selection in only one row or only one column:

```
With Selection
    If .Columns.Count > 1 And .Rows.Count > 1 Then
        MsgBox "Please select cells in only one row " _
            & "or only one column."
        End
    Else
        If .Cells.Count > 1 Then
            If .Columns.Count > 1 Then
                .Cells.Delete ShiftCells:=wdDeleteCellsShiftUp
            Else
                .Cells.Delete ShiftCells:=wdDeleteCellsShiftLeft
            End If
        Else
            .Cells.Delete ShiftCells:=wdDeleteCellsShiftLeft
        End If
    End If
End With
```

Selecting a Range of Cells

To select a range of cells within a table, declare a Range variable, assign to it the cells you want to select, and then select the range. The following example declares the Range variable myCells, assigns to it the first four cells in the first table in the active document, and then selects the range:

```
Dim myCells As Range
With ActiveDocument
    Set myCells = .Range(Start:=.Tables(1).Cell(1, 1).Range.Start, _
        End:=.Tables(1).Cell(1, 4).Range.End)
    myCells.Select
End With
```

Converting a Table or Rows to Text

To convert a table, a row, or a number of rows to text, specify the table, row, or rows and use the ConvertToText method. The ConvertToText method takes the following syntax:

```
expression.ConvertTotext(Separator, Nested Tables)
```

Here, *expression* is a required expression that returns a Table object, a Row object, or a Rows collection. Separator is an optional Variant argument specifying the separator character (also known as the *delimiter* character) to use to mark where the column divisions were. The possible values are as follows:

◆ wdSeparateByCommas separates column information by commas.

◆ wdSeparateByDefaultListSeparator separates column information by the currently specified Other list separator character (the character shown in the text box alongside the Other option button in the Convert Table To Text dialog box).

◆ wdSeparateByParagraphs separates column information with paragraph marks.

◆ wdSeparateByTabs (the default separator if you don't specify one) separates column information by tabs.

◆ Alternatively, you can specify a separator character of your choice as a string or between double quotation marks. For example, enter **Separator:="|"** to use a vertical bar [|] as the separator. (You can supply more than one separator character here, but Word uses only the first character.)

The following statement converts the first table in the current selection to text using an asterisk (*) as the separator character:

```
Selection.Tables(1).ConvertToText Separator:="*"
```

You can use the ConvertToText method with a Table object, a Row object, or a Rows collection. The following statement converts only the first row of the selected table to tab-delimited text:

```
Selection.Tables(1).Rows(1).ConvertToText Separator:=wdSeparateByTabs
```

If you need to continue working with the contents of the table once you've converted it, assign a range to the table as you convert it. You can then work with the Range object afterward to manipulate the information. For example, the following statements convert the first table in the document named Cleveland Report.doc to text separated by paragraphs and assign the range exTable to the converted information, and then copy the range, create a new document, and paste in the information:

```
Dim exTable As Range
Set exTable = Documents("Cleveland Report.doc").Tables(1). _
    ConvertToText(Separator:=wdSeparateByParagraphs)
exTable.Copy
Documents.Add
Selection.Paste
```

Chapter 22

Understanding the Excel Object Model and Key Objects

◆ Getting an overview of the Excel object model

◆ Understanding Excel's creatable objects

◆ Working with workbooks

◆ Working with worksheets

◆ Working with the active cell or selection

◆ Working with ranges

◆ Setting options

This chapter shows you how to start working with the Excel object model, the theoretical architecture underlying Excel. It also shows you how to perform common actions with the most immediately useful Excel objects. These objects include the `Workbooks` collection and the `Workbook` object, the `ActiveCell` object, and `Range` objects. You'll also learn how to set options in Excel.

Getting an Overview of the Excel Object Model

It's not crucial to understand how the Excel object model fits together in order to work with VBA in Excel, but most people find that knowing the main objects in the object model is helpful. To see the Excel object model, follow these steps:

1. Launch or activate Excel, and then press Alt+F11 to launch or activate the Visual Basic Editor.

2. Choose Help ➢ Microsoft Visual Basic Help to display the Visual Basic Help task pane.

3. Type **excel object model** in the Search text box, and then press Enter or click the Go button.

4. In the Search Results pane, click the Microsoft Excel Object Model entry. You'll see a Help screen (see Figure 22.1).

When you look at the Microsoft Excel Object Model entry on your screen, you'll see that some of the boxes are shaded yellow, while the others are shaded blue. The yellow boxes are objects that are organized into collections, while the blue objects are ones that do not have collections. Click a box to see the help screen for the object, including a schematic of the related objects in the object model. Figure 22.2 shows part of the Help screen for the `Workbooks` collection, which contains details of the open workbooks in Excel.

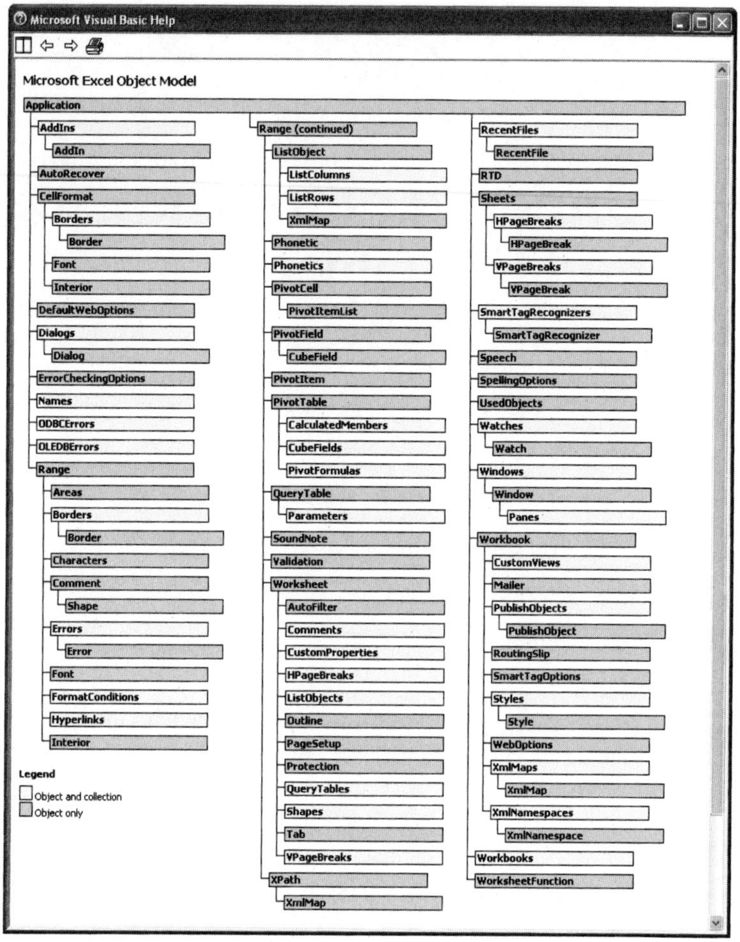

FIGURE 22.1
Microsoft Visual Basic Help provides a diagram of the Excel object model. This is the object model for Excel 2003. You can click an object to see details about it.

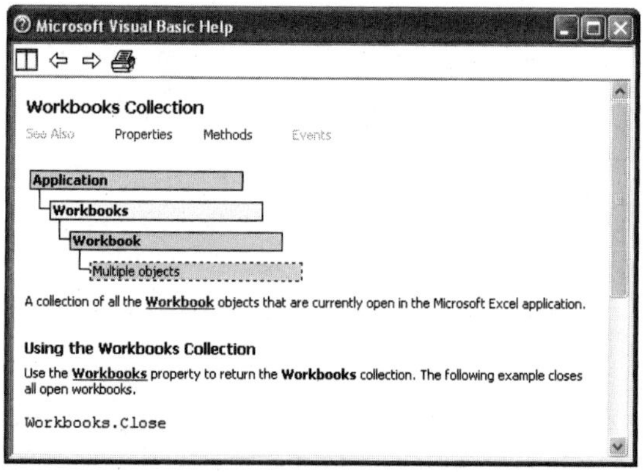

FIGURE 22.2
The Help screen for an individual object or collection includes a diagram showing the objects to which it's related.

Understanding Excel's Creatable Objects

Excel exposes various creatable objects, allowing you to reach most of the interesting objects in its object model without explicitly going through the `Application` object. For most purposes, these are the key objects:

- The `Workbooks` collection contains the `Workbook` objects that represent all the open workbooks. Within a workbook, the `Sheets` collection contains the `Worksheet` objects that represent the worksheets and the `Chart` objects that represent chart sheets. On a sheet, the `Range` object gives you access to ranges, which can be anything from an individual cell to a complete worksheet.

- The `ActiveWorkbook` object represents the active workbook.

- The `ActiveSheet` object represents the active worksheet.

- The `Windows` collection contains the `Window` objects that represent all the open windows.

- The `ActiveWindow` object represents the active window. When using this object, be sure to check that the window it represents is the type of window you want to manipulate, as the object returns whatever window currently has the focus.

- The `ActiveCell` object represents the active cell. This object is especially valuable for simple procedures (for example, those that compute values or correct formatting) that work on a cell selected by the user.

Working with Workbooks

In many of your Excel procedures, you'll need to work with workbooks: creating new workbooks, saving workbooks in various locations and formats, opening existing workbooks, closing workbooks, and printing workbooks. To do so, you work with the `Workbooks` collection, which contains a `Workbook` object for each open workbook in Excel.

Creating a Workbook

To create a workbook, use the `Add` method with the `Workbooks` collection. The syntax is

```
Workbooks.Add(Template)
```

Here, `Template` is an optional Variant argument that specifies how to create the workbook. The following subsections discuss the options.

CREATING A NEW BLANK WORKBOOK

To create a blank workbook (as if you'd clicked the New button on the Standard toolbar when working interactively), omit the `Template` argument:

```
Workbooks.Add
```

The new workbook receives the amount of sheets set in the Sheets In New Workbook text box on the General tab of the Options dialog box. You can get or set this value in VBA by using the `SheetsInNewWorkbook` property of the `Application` object. For example, the following macro declares an Integer variable named `mySiNW`, stores the current `SheetsInNewWorkbook` property in it, sets the SheetsInNewWorkbook property to 12, creates a new workbook (with those 12 work-sheets), and then restores the SheetsInNewWorkbook setting to its previous value:

```
Sub MVBA_New_Workbook_with_12_Sheets()
    Dim mySiNW As Integer
    mySiNW = Application.SheetsInNewWorkbook
    Application.SheetsInNewWorkbook = 12
    Workbooks.Add
    Application.SheetsInNewWorkbook = mySiNW
End Sub
```

CREATING A NEW WORKBOOK BASED ON A TEMPLATE

To create a workbook based on a template, specify the full path and name of the template file. For example, the following statement creates a new workbook based on the template Balance Sheet.xlt in the network folder \\server\template\excel:

```
Workbooks.Add Template:= "\\server\template\excel\Balance Sheet.xlt"
```

CREATING A NEW WORKBOOK BASED ON AN EXISTING WORKBOOK

To create a workbook based on an existing workbook, specify the full name and path of the workbook file. For example, the following statement creates a new workbook based on the existing workbook named Personnel.xls in the C:\Business folder:

```
Workbooks.Add Template:= "C:\Business\Personnel.xls"
```

CREATING A CHART WORKBOOK, A MACRO SHEET, OR A WORKSHEET

You can also create a workbook that contains a single chart, macro sheet, or worksheet by using the constants shown in Table 22.1 with the Template argument.

TABLE 22.1: Constants for Creating a Chart Workbook, Macro Sheet, or Worksheet

CONSTANT	CREATES A WORKBOOK CONTAINING
xlWBATChart	A chart sheet
xlWBATExcel4IntlMacroSheet	An international macro sheet
xlWBATExcel4MacroSheet	A macro sheet
xlWBATWorksheet	A worksheet

For example, the following statement creates a workbook containing a single chart sheet:

```
Workbooks.Add Template:=xlWBATChart
```

Saving a Workbook

The first time you save a workbook, you must specify the path and filename to use. After that, you can save the workbook under the same name or specify a different path, name, format, or all three.

SAVING A WORKBOOK FOR THE FIRST TIME OR AS A DIFFERENT FILE

To save a workbook for the first time, or to save a workbook using a different path, name, or format, use the SaveAs method. The syntax is

```
expression.SaveAs(FileName, FileFormat, Password, WriteResPassword,
ReadOnlyRecommended, CreateBackup, AccessMode, ConflictResolution, AddToMru,
TextCodepage, TextVisualLayout, Local)
```

The components of the syntax are as follows:

◆ *expression* is a required expression that returns a Workbook object.

◆ FileName is an optional Variant argument that specifies the name for the workbook. If you omit FileName, VBA uses the current folder and the default filename of Book*n*.xls for a workbook, where *n* is the next available number (for example, Book5.xls). VBA uses the default file format, which is set in the Save Excel Files As drop-down list on the Transition tab of the Options dialog box (Tools ➢ Options). You can get and set the default save format by using the DefaultSaveFormat property of the Application object. For example, the following statement sets the default save format to xlNormal, the "Microsoft Office Excel Workbook" or "Microsoft Excel Workbook" format (depending on the version of Excel you're using):

```
Application.DefaultSaveFormat = xlNormal
```

WARNING　When saving a workbook, you should check whether a workbook with this name already exists in that folder. If it does, VBA overwrites it without warning, causing data loss. See "Using the *Dir* Function to Check Whether a File Exists" in Chapter 9 for instructions on how to check whether a file with a particular name already exists.

◆ FileFormat is an optional Variant argument that specifies the format in which to save the workbook. Table 22.2 lists the XlFileFormat constants for specifying commonly used formats.

TABLE 22.2:　*XlFileFormat* Constants for Widely Used Formats

CONSTANT	SAVES DOCUMENT AS
xlNormal	A normal workbook
xlXMLSpreadsheet	An XML spreadsheet
xlWebArchive	A single file web page
xlHtml	A web page
xlTemplate	A template
xlExcel9795	An Excel workbook for Excel versions 95 and later

◆ `Password` is an optional Variant argument that you can use to supply the password that is to be required to open the workbook (the "password to open"). `Password` is case sensitive. If the user can't provide the password, Excel won't open the workbook.

◆ `WriteResPassword` is an optional Variant argument that you can use to supply the password that is required to open the workbook in a writable form (the "password to modify"). `WriteResPassword` is case sensitive. If the user can't provide the password, Excel will open the workbook as read-only.

◆ `ReadOnlyRecommended` is an optional Variant argument that you can set to `True` to have Excel recommend that the user open the document as read-only. Such recommendations typically carry little force, and you'll do better to protect the workbook with a "password to modify."

◆ `CreateBackup` is an optional Variant argument that you can set to `True` to make Excel automatically create a backup of the workbook. The default setting is `False`.

◆ `AccessMode` is an optional argument that you can use to specify whether the workbook is shared or is in exclusive mode. Specify `xlExclusive` for exclusive mode, `xlShared` for shared mode, and `xlNoChange` to leave the access mode unchanged (this is the default setting).

◆ `ConflictResolution` is an optional argument that you can use to specify how to resolve any conflicting changes to the workbook. Use `xlLocalSessionChanges` to accept the changes in the current Excel session, `xlOtherSessionChanges` to accept the other user's or users' changes, and `xlUserResolution` to display the Resolve Conflicts dialog box so that the user can choose how to resolve the conflicts.

◆ `AddToMru` is an optional Variant argument that you can set to `True` to add the workbook to the list of recently used files at the bottom of the File menu. The default setting is `False`.

◆ `TextCodePage` and `TextVisualLayout` are optional Variant arguments used in international versions of Excel (not in U.S. English Excel). `Local` is an optional Variant that controls whether the language used is that of Excel (`True`) or of VBA (`False`). (You'll seldom need to use `Local`.)

For example, the following statement saves the active workbook in the current folder under the name `Salaries.xls` and using the default save format:

```
ActiveWorkbook.SaveAs FileName:="Salaries.xls"
```

The following statement saves the open workbook named `Schedule.xls` under the name `Building Schedule.xls` in the folder named `\\server2\Public` using the "Microsoft Excel 97–2003 & 5.0/95" format (from Excel 2003):

```
ActiveWorkbook.SaveAs Filename:="\\server2\Public\Building Schedule.xls", _
    FileFormat:=xlExcel9795
```

NOTE The `xlExcel9795` format has a different name in the Excel user interface depending on the version of Excel you're using. Excel 2003 calls it the "Microsoft Excel 97–2003 & 5.0/95" format, Excel XP calls it the "Microsoft Excel 97–2002 & 5.0/95" format, and Excel 2000 calls it the "Microsoft Excel 97–2000 & 5.0/95 Workbook" format. Whichever name it uses, the format is backward compatible with Excel 95 and later versions.

SAVING A WORKBOOK THAT HAS ALREADY BEEN SAVED

Once a workbook has been saved, you can save it under the same name by using the Save method. For a Workbook object, the Save method takes no arguments. For example, the following statement saves the workbook named Data Book.xls:

```
Workbooks("Data Book.doc").Save
```

SAVING ALL OPEN WORKBOOKS

The Workbooks collection doesn't have a Save method, but you can save all open workbooks by using a loop such as that shown in the following subprocedure:

```
Sub Save_All_Workbooks()
    Dim myWorkbook As Workbook
    For Each myWorkbook In Workbooks
        myWorkbook.Save
    Next myWorkbook
End Sub
```

Opening a Workbook

To open a workbook, use the Open method with the Workbooks collection. The syntax is

```
expression.Open(FileName, UpdateLinks, ReadOnly, Format, Password, WriteResPassword,
IgnoreReadOnlyRecommended, Origin, Delimiter, Editable, Notify, Converter, AddToMru,
Local, CorruptLoad)
```

The components of the syntax are as follows:

◆ *expression* is a required expression that returns a Workbooks collection. Often, you'll want to use the Workbooks collection itself.

◆ FileName is a required String argument that supplies the path and name of the workbook to open.

◆ UpdateLinks is an optional Variant that controls how Excel updates any links in the workbook. Table 22.3 shows the values and their effects.

TABLE 22.3:   Values for the UpdateLinks Argument

VALUE	EFFECT
(omitted)	Excel prompts the user to decide how to update links.
0	Excel doesn't update links.
1	Excel updates external links but not remote links.
2	Excel updates remote links but not external links.
3	Excel updates all links.

♦ `ReadOnly` is an optional Variant that you can set to `True` to open the workbook as read-only. The default is `False`.

♦ `Format` is an optional Variant that you can use to specify the delimiter character when opening a text file. Use 1 for tabs, 2 for commas, 3 for spaces, 4 for semicolons, 5 for no delimiter character, and 6 for a delimiter you specify using the `Delimiter` argument.

♦ `Password` is an optional Variant argument that you can use to provide the password required to open the workbook (the "password to open"). `Password` is case sensitive. If you omit `Password`, and a password is required, Excel prompts the user for it.

WARNING If possible, avoid placing passwords in your code, as it may be possible for other people to read them.

♦ `WriteResPassword` is an optional Variant argument that you can use to provide the password required to open the workbook in a writable form (the "password to modify"). `WriteResPassword` is case sensitive. If you omit `WriteResPassword`, and a password is required, Excel prompts the user for it.

♦ `IgnoreReadOnlyRecommended` is an optional Variant argument that you can set to `True` to have Excel ignore a read-only recommendation on the workbook.

♦ `Origin` is an optional Variant argument that you can use when opening a text file to specify the operating system used to encode it and thus how to treat carriage-return/line-feed characters and character encoding. Use `xlWindows` to indicate Windows, `xlMacintosh` to indicate Mac OS, or `xlMSDOS` to indicate DOS.

♦ `Delimiter` is an optional Variant argument you can use with a `Format` value of 6 to specify one delimiter character to use when opening a text file.

♦ `Editable` is an optional Variant argument that you can set to `True` when `FileName` specifies a template to open the template itself rather than start a workbook based on the template (`False`). `Editable` also applies to Excel 4.0 add-ins: `True` opens the add-in in a visible window, while `False` opens the add-in hidden.

♦ `Notify` is an optional Variant argument that you can set to `True` to have Excel add the workbook to the notification list when someone else has the workbook open for editing when VBA requests the workbook. Excel then notifies the user when the workbook becomes available. If you specify `Notify:=False`, opening the workbook fails if someone else has the workbook open.

♦ `Converter` is an optional Variant argument that you can use to specify the first file converter to use when opening a file.

♦ `AddToMru` is an optional Variant argument that you can set to `True` to add the workbook to the list of recently used files at the bottom of the File menu. The default setting is `False`.

♦ `Local` is an optional Variant that controls whether the language used is that of Excel (`True`) or of VBA (`False`). (You'll seldom need to use `Local`.)

♦ `CorruptLoad` is an optional Variant that you can use to control how Excel handles corruption it encounters when opening the workbook. Use `xlNormalLoad` to use normal behavior—first, opening the workbook as usual; second, repairing the file if there's a problem; and third, recovering the data from the workbook. Use `xrRepairFile` to go straight to the repair stage or `xlExtractData` to go straight to the recovery stage.

For example, the following statement opens the workbook named `Expenses.xls` stored in the `C:\Business` folder without updating links:

```
Workbooks.Open Filename:= "C:\Business\Expenses.xls", UpdateLinks:=0
```

The following statement opens the workbook named `Plan.xls` stored in the `D:\Planning` folder, providing the password for opening the workbook:

```
Workbooks.Open Filename:="D:\Planning\Plan.xls", Password:="s@cur1ng!"
```

The following statement opens the text file named `Data13.txt` in the folder `z:\transfer` using an exclamation point (!) as the delimiter character:

```
Workbooks.Open Filename:="z:\transfer\Data13.txt", Format:=6, Delimiter:="!"
```

Closing a Workbook

To close a workbook, use the `Close` method with the appropriate `Workbook` object. The syntax is

```
expression.Close(SaveChanges, Filename, RouteWorkbook)
```

The components of the syntax are as follows:

- ◆ *expression* is a required expression that returns a `Workbook` object or the `Workbooks` collection.

- ◆ `SaveChanges` is an optional Variant argument that lets you specify whether to save any unsaved changes in the workbook (`True`) or not (`False`). If you omit the `SaveChanges` argument, Excel prompts the user to save any workbook that contains unsaved changes.

- ◆ `Filename` is an optional Variant that you can use to specify the filename under which to save the workbook if it contains changes. In most cases, it's best to use the `SaveAs` method to save the workbook under a different name before you use the `Close` method to close it.

- ◆ `RouteWorkbook` is an optional Variant argument that you can set to `True` to route the workbook to the next recipient on its routing slip or `False` to refrain from routing the workbook. If the workbook has no routing slip attached, `RouteWorkbook` has no effect.

For example, the following statement closes the active workbook without saving changes:

```
ActiveWorkbook.Close SaveChanges:=False
```

CLOSING ALL OPEN WORKBOOKS

To close all open workbooks, use the `Close` method with the `Workbooks` collection:

```
Workbooks.Close
```

The `Close` method takes no arguments. Excel prompts you to save any workbook that contains unsaved changes. If such prompts will be inconvenient in a procedure, use a loop (for example, a `For Each... Next` loop with the `Workbooks` collection) to close each open workbook individually, using the `SaveChanges` argument to control whether Excel saves or discards any unsaved changes.

Sharing a Workbook

To determine whether a workbook is shared, check its `MultiUserEditing` property. This is a read-only Boolean property.

To share a workbook, use the `SaveAs` method (discussed in "Saving a Workbook for the First Time or as a Different File," earlier in this chapter) to save the file using the `xlShared` value for the `AccessMode` argument.

For example, the following statements share the workbook named `Brainstorming.xls` if it is not already shared:

```
With Workbooks("Brainstorming.xls")
    If MultiUserEditing = False Then
        .SaveAs Filename:=.FullName, AccessMode:=xlShared
    End If
End With
```

Protecting a Workbook

To protect a workbook, use the `Protect` method with the appropriate `Workbook` object. The syntax is

```
expression.Protect(Password, Structure, Windows)
```

The components of the syntax are as follows:

- ◆ *expression* is a required expression that returns a `Workbook` object.

- ◆ `Password` is an optional Variant argument that specifies the password for unprotecting the workbook. `Password` is case sensitive. You'll almost always want to supply `Password`—if you don't, anybody who can open your workbook can unprotect it.

- ◆ `Structure` is an optional Variant argument that you can set to `True` to protect the workbook's structure (how the worksheets are positioned relative to each other) or leave at its default setting, `False`.

- ◆ `Windows` is an optional Variant argument that you can set to `True` to protect the workbook windows or omit to leave the windows unprotected.

For example, the following statement protects the structure and windows of the active workbook with the password `011securd`:

```
ActiveWorkbook.Protect Password:="011securd", Structure:=True, Windows:=True
```

NOTE In addition to protecting a workbook against modifications, you can protect it against being opened. See "Setting Passwords and Read-Only Recommendation for a Workbook," later in this chapter, for details.

Working with the *ActiveWorkbook* Object

The `ActiveWorkbook` object returns a `Workbook` object that represents the active workbook—whichever workbook has the focus in the Excel window. The `ActiveWorkbook` object behaves like a `Workbook` object and is very useful in procedures that the user calls after opening the workbook that they want to affect.

If no workbook is open, there is no `ActiveWorkbook` object, and any code that tries to use the `ActiveWorkbook` object returns an error. The user can run a macro when no workbook is open in Excel, so it's a good idea to verify that at least one workbook is open before trying to execute code that assumes there is an active workbook. One option is to check that the `ActiveWorkbook` object is not `Nothing` before running the code, as in the following example:

```
If ActiveWorkbook Is Nothing Then
    MsgBox "Please open a workbook and click in it before running this macro." _
        & vbCr & vbCr & "This macro will now end.", _
        vbOKOnly + vbExclamation, "No Workbook Is Open"
    End
End If
```

It's also a good idea to check that the workbook your code assumes is the active workbook actually *is* the active workbook. This problem can easily occur when a procedure starts with the active workbook and then creates a new workbook to work in; the new workbook becomes the active workbook, and from this point on, the code may start running on the wrong workbook.

If there's any doubt about which workbook you're working with, declare a `Workbook` object variable and work with that object variable rather than the `ActiveWorkbook` object. For example, the following statements declare a `Workbook` object variable and assign the `ActiveWorkbook` object to it, so that subsequent code can work with the object variable:

```
Dim myWorkbook As Workbooks
Set myWorkbook = ActiveWorkbook
With myWorkbook
    'actions here
End With
```

Working with Worksheets

Most workbooks you need to manipulate via VBA will contain one or more worksheets, so most procedures will need to work with worksheets —inserting them, deleting them, copying or moving them, or simply printing the appropriate range from them.

Each worksheet is represented by a `Sheet` object. The `Sheet` objects are gathered in the `Sheets` collection.

Inserting a Worksheet

To insert a worksheet into a workbook, use the `Add` method with the `Sheets` collection. The syntax is

```
expression.Add(Before, After, Count, Type)
```

The components of the syntax are as follows:

◆ *expression* is a required expression that returns a `Sheets` collection. Often, you'll want to use the `Sheets` collection itself.

◆ `Before` is an optional Variant argument that specifies the sheet before which to add the new sheet. `After` is an optional Variant argument that specifies the sheet after which to add the new sheet. Typically, you'll want to specify either Before or After, but not both. You can also omit both arguments to make Excel insert the new sheet before the active worksheet.

◆ Count is an optional Variant argument that specifies how many sheets to add. If you omit Count, VBA uses the default value, 1.

◆ Type is an optional Variant that specifies the type of sheet to insert. The default is xlWorksheet, a standard worksheet. You can also insert a chart sheet (xlChart), an Excel 4 macro sheet (xlExcel4MacroSheet), or an Excel 4 international macro sheet (xlExcel4IntlMacroSheet).

For example, the following statements declare a Worksheet object variable named mySheet, insert a worksheet before the first sheet in the first open workbook and assign the new sheet to mySheet, and then set the Name property of mySheet to Summary. (The Name property controls the text that appears on the worksheet's tab.)

```
Dim mySheet As Worksheet
Set mySheet = Workbooks(1).Sheets.Add(before:=Sheets(1))
mySheet.Name = "Summary"
```

The following statements insert two chart sheets after the last worksheet in the active workbook. The chart sheets receive default names, such as Chart1 and Chart2:

```
ActiveWorkbook.Sheets.Add After:=Sheets(Sheets.Count), Count:=2, Type:=xlChart
```

Deleting a Worksheet

To delete a worksheet, use the Delete method of the appropriate Sheet object. The Delete method takes no arguments. For example, the following statement deletes the worksheet named Summary from the workbook referenced by the myWorkbook object variable:

```
myWorkbook.Sheets("Summary").Delete
```

Deleting a worksheet loses any data stored on that worksheet, so Excel confirms the deletion with the user by default (see Figure 22.3). If you need to avoid this user interaction—for example, in a procedure that adds a worksheet without the user's knowledge, uses it to manipulate data, and then deletes it—you can turn off alerts in Excel by setting the DisplayAlerts property of the Application object to False before deleting the worksheet and then turning alerts back on again:

```
Application.DisplayAlerts = False
myWorkbook.Sheets("Summary").Delete
Application.DisplayAlerts = True
```

FIGURE 22.3
When deleting a worksheet, you must either suppress alerts in Excel or have the user confirm the deletion in this dialog box.

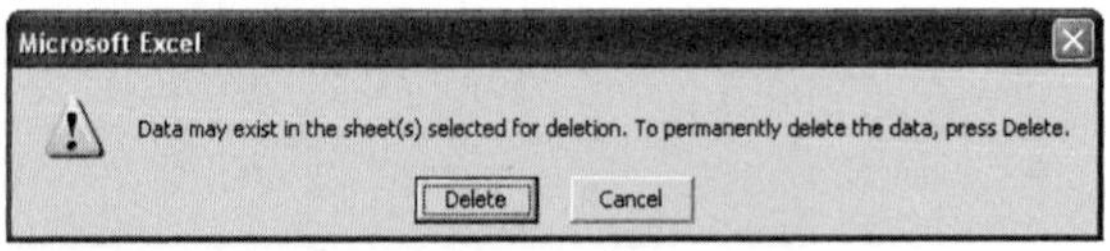

Microsoft Excel

⚠ Data may exist in the sheet(s) selected for deletion. To permanently delete the data, press Delete.

[Delete]   [Cancel]

Copying or Moving a Worksheet

To copy a worksheet, use the Copy method of the appropriate Sheet object. To move a worksheet, use the Move method. The syntax is

```
expression.Copy(Before, After)
expression.Move(Before, After)
```

Here, *expression* is a required expression that returns a Worksheet object. Before is an optional Variant argument that specifies the sheet before which to place the copy or the moved sheet. After is an optional Variant argument that specifies the sheet after which to place it:

◆ Typically, you'll want to specify either Before or After, but not both.

◆ You can specify another workbook by name to copy or move the worksheet to another workbook.

◆ You can also omit both arguments to make Excel create a new workbook containing the copied or moved sheet. The new workbook becomes the active workbook, so you can use the ActiveWorkbook object to start working with it or to assign it to an object variable.

For example, the following statement copies the worksheet named Costs – Materials in the workbook named Building Schedule.xls, placing the copy after the last of the current worksheets in the workbook:

```
Workbooks("Building Schedule.xls").Sheets("Costs - Materials").Copy, _
    After:=Sheets(Sheets.Count)
```

The following statement moves the worksheet named Homes from the workbook named Planning.xls to the workbook named Building Schedule.xls, inserting the worksheet before the first existing worksheet in the workbook:

```
Workbooks("Planning.xls").Sheets("Homes").Move , _
    Before:=Workbooks("Building Schedule.xls").Sheets(1)
```

Printing a Worksheet

To print a worksheet, use the PrintOut method with the appropriate Worksheet object.

TIP The PrintOut method also applies to other objects, including the Worksheets collection, the Chart object and the Charts collection, the Workbook object, the Window object, and the Range object.

The syntax for the PrintOut method is

```
expression.PrintOut(From, To, Copies, Preview, ActivePrinter, PrintToFile, Collate,
PrToFileName)
```

The components of the syntax are as follows:

◆ *expression* is a required expression that returns the appropriate Worksheet object or other object to which the PrintOut method applies.

◆ From is an optional Variant argument that specifies the number of the page at which to start printing. Omit From to start printing at the beginning of the object.

NOTE From and To refer to the pages in the printout, not the overall number of pages that the object would take up.

◆ To is an optional Variant argument that specifies the number of the page at which to stop printing. Omit To to print to the end of the object.

◆ Copies is an optional Variant argument that specifies the number of copies to print. If you omit Copies, Excel prints one copy.

◆ Preview is an optional Variant argument that you can set to True to display the object in Print Preview before printing it. Set Preview to False, or simply omit this argument, to print the object without previewing it.

TIP Use the PrintPreview method to display an object in Print Preview without printing it.

◆ ActivePrinter is an optional Variant argument that you can use to specify on which printer to print.

◆ PrintToFile is an optional Variant argument that you can set to True to make Excel print to a print file rather than a printer. When printing to a file, you can use the PrToFileName property to specify the filename or omit it and have Excel prompt the user for the filename.

◆ Collate is an optional Variant argument that you can set to True to have Excel print multiple copies for collation rather than printing all the copies of one page, all the copies of the next, and so on.

◆ PrToFileName is an optional Variant argument that you can use with PrintToFile:=True to specify the filename of the print file.

For example, the following statement prints two copies of each page of the first worksheet in the active workbook, collating the pages:

```
ActiveWorkbook.Sheets(1).Printout Copies:=2, Collate:=True
```

The following statement prints the first two pages of the worksheet named Summary in the workbook named Planning.xls to a file named Planning Summary.prn in the network folder \\server\to_print:

```
Workbooks("Planning.xls").Sheets("Summary").PrintOut From:=1, To:=2, _
    PrintToFile:=True, PrToFileName:="\\server\to_print\Planning Summary.prn"
```

Protecting a Worksheet

To protect a worksheet, use the Protect method with the appropriate Worksheet object. The syntax is

```
expression.Protect(Password, DrawingObjects, Contents, Scenarios,
UserInterfaceOnly, AllowFormattingCells, AllowFormattingColumns,
AllowFormattingRows, AllowInsertingColumns, AllowInsertingRows,
AllowInsertingHyperlinks, AllowDeletingColumns, AllowDeletingRows, AllowSorting,
AllowFiltering, AllowUsingPivotTables)
```

The components of the syntax are as follows:

◆ *expression* is a required expression that returns a `Worksheet` object.

◆ `Password` is an optional Variant argument that specifies the password for unprotecting the worksheet. `Password` is case sensitive. You'll almost always want to supply `Password` to prevent unauthorized people from unprotecting the workbook.

◆ `DrawingObjects` is an optional Variant argument that you can set to `True` to protect shapes in the worksheet. The default setting is `False`.

◆ `Contents` is an optional Variant argument that protects the locked cells when set to `True`, its default value. Set `Contents` to `False` to leave the locked cells unprotected.

◆ `Scenarios` is an optional Variant argument that protects scenarios when set to `True`, its default value.

◆ `UserInterfaceOnly` is an optional Variant argument that you can set to `True` to leave macros unprotected while protecting the user interface. The default value is `False`.

◆ `AllowFormattingCells`, `AllowFormattingColumns`, and `AllowFormattingRows` are optional Variant arguments that you can set to `True` to allow the formatting of cells, columns, and rows, respectively. The default value for each argument is `False`.

◆ `AllowInsertingColumns`, `AllowInsertingRows`, and `AllowInsertingHyperlinks` are optional Variant arguments that you can set to `True` to allow the user to insert columns, rows, and hyperlinks, respectively. The default value for each argument is `False`.

◆ `AllowDeletingColumns` and `AllowDeletingRows` are optional Variant arguments that you can set to `True` to allow the user to delete columns or rows, respectively, where every cell in the column or row is unlocked. The default setting is `False`.

◆ `AllowSorting` is an optional Variant argument that you can set to `True` to allow the user to sort unlocked cells on the protected worksheet. The default setting is `False`.

◆ `AllowFiltering` is an optional Variant argument that you can set to `True` to allow the user to set filters or change filter criteria (but not enable or disable an autofilter) on a protected worksheet. The default setting is `False`.

◆ `AllowUsingPivotTables` is an optional Variant argument that you can set to True to allow the user to work with PivotTables on the protected worksheet. The default value is `False`.

For example, the following statement protects the worksheet referenced by the object variable `myWorksheet` using the password `no1getsln`:

```
myWorksheet.Protect Password:="no1getsln"
```

The following statement protects the `myWorksheet` worksheet with the same password but allows the formatting of cells and allows the sorting of unlocked cells:

```
myWorksheet.Protect Password:="no1getsln", AllowFormattingCells:=True, _
    AllowSorting:=True
```

Working with the *ActiveSheet* Object

The ActiveSheet object returns the active worksheet in the specified workbook or (if you don't specify a workbook) the active worksheet in Excel.

If no sheet is active, ActiveSheet returns Nothing. Before executing code that depends on there being an active sheet, it's a good idea to check—for example:

```
If ActiveSheet Is Nothing Then End
```

Working with the Active Cell or Selection

In a procedure that manipulates a selection that the user has made, you'll typically work with either the active cell or the selection. The active cell is always a single cell, but the selection can encompass multiple cells or other objects.

Working with the Active Cell

The ActiveCell property of the Application object or the Window object returns a Range object that represents the active cell in the Excel application or in the specified window. If you use ActiveCell without specifying the window, VBA returns the active cell in the active window.

For example, the following statement returns the address of the active cell in the active workbook:

```
ActiveCell.Address
```

The following statement returns the text in the active cell in the first window open on the workbook named Planning.xls:

```
MsgBox Workbooks("Planning.xls").Windows(1).ActiveCell.Text
```

If no worksheet is active, or if a chart sheet is active, there is no active cell. If you try to access ActiveCell, VBA returns an error. So before using code that assumes there is an active cell, check that ActiveCell is not Nothing:

```
If ActiveCell Is Nothing Then End
```

GETTING AND SETTING THE VALUE OF THE ACTIVE CELL

To return the value of the active cell, use the Value property. For example, the following statement sets the value of the active cell to 25:

```
ActiveCell.Value = 25
```

MOVING THE ACTIVE CELL TO ANOTHER ADDRESS

The active cell is often convenient to work with, so sometimes you'll want to make a different cell the active cell in order to work with it via the ActiveCell object. To make a cell the active cell, use the Activate method with the appropriate Range object. For example, the following statement makes cell L7 the active cell in the worksheet identified by the object variable myWorksheet:

```
myWorksheet.Range("B5").Activate
```

Often, you'll need to move the active cell to a different range a specified number of rows or columns away. To do so, use the `Offset` property of the active cell object, specifying the number of rows with the `RowOffset` argument and the number of columns with the `ColumnOffset` argument. Use a positive offset to move the active cell right or down and a negative offset to move the active cell left or up. For example, the following statement moves the active cell up two rows (`RowOffset:=-2`) and four columns to the right (`ColumnOffset:=4`):

```
ActiveCell.Offset(RowOffset:=-2, ColumnOffset:=4).Activate
```

In procedures that the user triggers, it's often a good idea to return the active cell to where it was when the user started the procedure. To do so, you can store the location of the active cell and then return it to the stored location. For example:

```
Set myActiveCell = ActiveCell
Set myActiveWorksheet = ActiveSheet
Set myActiveWorkbook = ActiveWorkbook

'take actions here

myActiveWorkbook.Activate
myActiveWorksheet.Activate
myActiveCell.Activate
```

WARNING   Always test your procedures carefully with various types of data. Errors can sometimes occur when you move cells that contain equations that use relative cell addresses.

WORKING WITH THE REGION AROUND THE ACTIVE CELL

You can work with the range of cells around the active cell by using the `CurrentRegion` property to return the `CurrentRegion` object. The current region extends from the active cell to the first blank row above and below and to the first blank column to the left and right. For example, the following statements use the `Font` property of the `CurrentRegion` object to set the font of the current region to 12-point Times New Roman with no bold or italics:

```
With ActiveCell.CurrentRegion.Font
    .Name = "Times New Roman"
    .Size = 12
    .Bold = False
    .Italic = False
End With
```

Working with the User's Selection

In macros designed to be run by a user, you will often need to work with cells that the user has selected. For example, a user might select a range of cells and then run a macro to manipulate the contents of the range.

To work with the range the user has selected, use the `RangeSelection` property of the appropriate `Window` object. For example, you might assign the `RangeSelection` property to a range so that you could work with it in a macro and then select in again at the end of the macro, leaving the user ready to work with the selection again.

```
Dim myMacroRange As Range
Set myMacroRange = ActiveWindow.RangeSelection
With myMacroRange
    'take actions on the range here
End With
myMacroRange.Activate
```

Working with Ranges

Within a worksheet, you'll often need to manipulate ranges of cells. You can work with absolute ranges (ranges for which you specify the absolute addresses of the cells you want to affect) or ranges relative to the active cell.

You can either specify a range by using the Range property or create a named range by using the Names collection. Excel also provides the UsedRange property for working with the used range on a worksheet, and the SpecialCells method of the Range object for working with cells that meet specific criteria.

Working with a Range of Cells

To work with a range of cells, use the Range property of the appropriate Worksheet object to specify the cells. For example, the following statement sets the value of cell C12 on the active worksheet to 44:

```
ActiveSheet.Range("C12").Value = "44"
```

Creating a Named Range

To create a named range, use the Add method with the Names collection. The syntax is

```
expression.Add(Name, RefersTo, Visible, MacroType, ShortcutKey, Category,
NameLocal, RefersToLocal, CategoryLocal, RefersToR1C1, RefersToR1C1Local)
```

The components of the syntax are as follows:

- *expression* is a required expression that returns a Names object.

- Name is an optional Variant argument that specifies the name to assign to the named range. Name is required if you don't specify the NameLocal argument (see below). The name cannot be a cell reference, nor can it contain spaces.

- RefersTo is an optional Variant argument that specifies the range for the named range. You need to specify RefersTo unless you use the RefersToLocal argument, the RefersToR1C1 argument, or the RefersToR1C1Local argument.

- Visible is an optional Variant argument that you can omit or set to True to have Excel make the name visible in the user interface (in the Go To dialog box, the Paste Name dialog box, and other locations) or set to False to make the name hidden.

- ◆ MacroType is an optional Variant argument that you can use to assign a macro type to the range: 1 for a user-defined Function procedure, 2 for a Sub procedure, and 3 or omitted for no macro.

- ◆ ShortcutKey is an optional Variant argument that specifies the shortcut key for a command macro assigned to the named range.

- ◆ Category is an optional Variant argument that specifies the category of the macro or function specified by MacroType. You can specify one of the categories used by the Function Wizard or specify another name to have Excel create a new category with that name.

- ◆ NameLocal is an optional Variant argument that specifies the name for the range in the local language. Use NameLocal when you omit Name.

- ◆ RefersToLocal is an optional Variant argument that specifies the range for the named range. Use RefersToLocal when you omit RefersTo, RefersToR1C1, and RefersToR1C1Local.

- ◆ CategoryLocal is an optional Variant argument that you use to specify the category of the macro or function specified by MacroType. Use CategoryLocal when you omit Category.

- ◆ RefersToR1C1 is an optional Variant argument that specifies the range for the named range using R1C1 notation. Use RefersToR1C1 when you omit RefersTo, RefersToLocal, and RefersToR1C1Local.

- ◆ RefersToR1C1Local is an optional Variant argument that specifies the range for the named range using R1C1 notation in the local language. Use RefersToR1C1Local when you omit RefersTo, RefersToLocal, and RefersToR1C1.

For example, the following statement defines a range named myRange that refers to the range A1:G22 on the worksheet named Materials in the workbook named Building Schedule.xls:

```
Workbooks("Building Schedule.xls").Names.Add Name:="myRange", _
    RefersTo:="=Materials!$A$1:$G$22"
```

Deleting a Named Range

To delete a named range, use the Delete method with the appropriate Name object. For example, the following statement deletes the range named myRange in the workbook named Building Schedule.xls:

```
Workbooks("Building Schedule.xls").Names("myRange").Delete
```

Working with a Named Range

To work with a named range, specify the name with the Range object. For example, the following statements set the row height of the rows in the named range myRange to 20 points and applies 16-point Arial font to the cells:

```
With Range("myRange")
    .RowHeight = 20
    .Font.Name = "Arial"
    .Font.Size = "16"
End With
```

Working with the Used Range

If you need to work with all the cells on a worksheet, but not with any unoccupied areas of the worksheet, use the UsedRange property. For example, the following statement autofits all the columns in the used range in the active worksheet:

```
ActiveSheet.UsedRange.Columns.AutoFit
```

Working with the Special Cells

If you need to work with only some types of cells on a worksheet or in a range, use the SpecialCells method of the Range object to return the cells you need. The syntax is

```
expression.SpecialCells(Type, Value)
```

These are the components of the syntax:

◆ *expression* is a required expression that returns a Range object.

◆ Type is a required argument that specifies which cells you want. Table 22.4 lists the constants you can use.

◆ Value is an optional Variant argument that you can use when Type is xlCellTypeConstants or xlCellTypeFormulas to control which cells Excel includes. Table 22.5 shows the constants and what they return.

TABLE 22.4: Constants for the Type Argument for the SpecialCells Method

CONSTANT	RETURNS THIS KIND OF CELLS
xlCellTypeAllFormatConditions	All formats
xlCellTypeAllValidation	That use validation
xlCellTypeBlanks	Empty
xlCellTypeComments	Containing notes
xlCellTypeConstants	Containing constants
xlCellTypeFormulas	Containing formulas
xlCellTypeLastCell	The last cell in the used range
xlCellTypeSameFormatConditions	That have the same format
xlCellTypeSameValidation	That contain the same validation criteria
xlCellTypeVisible	All visible

TABLE 22.5:   Constants for the `Value` Argument for the `SpecialCells` Method

CONSTANT	RETURNS CELLS CONTAINING
xlErrors	Errors
xlLogical	Logical values
xlNumbers	Numbers
xlTextValues	Text formulas

For example, the following statement activates the last cell in the worksheet referenced by the object variable `myWorksheet`:

```
myWorksheet.Cell.SpecialCells(Type:=xlCellTypeLastCell).Activate
```

The following statement identifies all the cells that contain formulas resulting in errors in the active worksheet:

```
ActiveSheet.Cells.SpecialCells(Type:=xlCellTypeFormulas, _
    Value:=xlErrors).Activate
```

Entering a Formula in a Cell

To enter a formula in a cell, set the `Formula` property of the appropriate `Cell` object. For example, the following statement enters the formula =SUM($G$12:$G$22) in the active cell:

```
ActiveCell.Formula = "=SUM($G$12:$G$22)"
```

Setting Options

Unlike Word, in which most of the options that you find in the Options dialog box are available through the `Options` object, Excel keeps most of the options from the Options dialog box in the `Application` object. You can access the workbook-specific properties that appear in the Options dialog box through the appropriate `Workbook` object.

Setting Options in the *Application* Object

This section shows three examples of setting widely useful options in the `Application` object.

CONTROLLING EXCEL'S CALCULATION

In complex worksheets that perform many calculations, you may need to turn off automatic calculation so that a procedure can enter data quickly without the calculations taking place. To do so, set the `Calculation` property of the `Application` object to `xlCalculationManual`, enter the data, and then set the `Calculation` property back to its previous value. For example:

```
Dim varAutoCalculation As Variant
varAutoCalculation = Application.Calculation
```

```
Application.Calculation = xlCalculationManual
'enter the data here
Application.Calculation = xlCalculationAutomatic
```

CLEARING THE RECENTLY USED FILES LIST

Sometimes you may find it useful to clear all the entries from the recently used files list at the bottom of the File menu in Excel. You can do so by setting the Maximum property of the RecentFiles object to 0. After doing so, you may want to restore the previous setting, as in the following example:

```
Dim myMax As Long
With Application.RecentFiles
    myMax = .Maximum
    .Maximum = 0
    .Maximum = myMax
End With
```

SETTING A DEFAULT FILE LOCATION

To set the default location for saving and opening files, use the DefaultFilePath property of the Application object. For example:

```
Application.DefaultFilePath = "\\server3\users\mjones\files"
```

Setting Options in a Workbook

Workbook-specific options include the following:

◆ Security options (such as those shown in the following two subsections)

◆ Whether to update remote references in the workbook (the Boolean UpdateRemoteReferences property) and whether to save external link values (the Boolean SaveLinkValues property)

◆ Whether to use AutoRecover (the Boolean EnableAutoRecover property)

◆ Whether to accept labels in formulas (the Boolean AcceptLabelsInFormulas property) and whether to use the 1904 date system (the Boolean Date1904 property).

SETTING EXCEL TO REMOVE PERSONAL INFORMATION FROM THE FILE PROPERTIES WHEN YOU SAVE

To make Excel remove personal information from a workbook's properties when you save it, set the RemovePersonalInformation property of the workbook to True:

```
ActiveWorkbook.RemovePersonalInformation = True
```

SETTING PASSWORDS AND READ-ONLY RECOMMENDATION FOR A WORKBOOK

To protect a workbook against an unauthorized user opening it or modifying it, you can set a "password to open" or a "password to modify" on the workbook. Office's protection is relatively weak, but it works well enough in a typical office situation. You can also specify that, when anyone opens a workbook, Excel recommend that they open it as read-only rather than read/write. This protection is almost useless but may give considerate colleagues pause for thought.

To set a "password to open," set the `Password` property of the `Workbook` object. For example, the following statement sets the active workbook to use the "password to open" `1mpass4`:

```
ActiveWorkbook.Password = "1mpass4"
```

To set a "password to modify," set the `WritePassword` property of the `Workbook` object. For example, the following statement sets the active workbook to use the "password to modify" `n0mods`:

```
ActiveWorkbook.WritePassword = "n0mods"
```

To apply a read-only recommendation to a workbook, set its `ReadOnlyRecommended` property to `True`. For example:

```
Workbooks("Strategy.xls").ReadOnlyRecommended = True
```

Chapter 23

Working with Widely Used Objects in Excel

- ◆ Working with charts
- ◆ Working with windows
- ◆ Working with Find and Replace

In the previous chapter, you learned to work with some of the main objects in the Excel object model, such as `Workbook` objects, the `ActiveCell` object, `Range` objects, and the `Options` object. This chapter shows you how to take further actions with VBA in Excel by working with charts, windows, and Find and Replace.

Working with Charts

This section shows you how to use VBA to create and format charts, either as chart sheets in a workbook or as objects on an existing worksheet.

Creating a Chart

You can create a new chart either on a new chart sheet or as an object in an existing worksheet. VBA uses the `Chart` object to represent a chart on a chart sheet and a `ChartObject` object to represent an embedded chart on a worksheet. The `ChartObject` object contains a `Chart` object, which you can manipulate by accessing it through the `ChartObject`.

Whichever method you use, you create the chart or chart object in a different order than when working manually:

- ◆ First, you add the chart or chart object.
- ◆ Second, you specify the source range for its data.
- ◆ Third, you specify the chart type.
- ◆ Fourth, you specify any other items you want to add.

CREATING A CHART ON A NEW CHART SHEET

To create a chart on a new chart sheet, use the `Add` method with the `Charts` collection. The syntax is

```
expression.Add(Before, After, Count)
```

The components of the syntax are as follows:

◆ *expression* is a required expression that returns a Charts collection.

◆ Before is an optional Variant argument that you can use to specify the sheet before which to add the new chart sheet. After is an optional Variant argument that you can use to specify the sheet after which to add the new sheet. Typically, you'll use either Before or After. If you omit both arguments, VBA adds the new chart sheet before the active sheet.

◆ Count is an optional Variant argument that you can use to specify how many chart sheets to add. The default is one.

For example, the following statements declare an object variable named myChartSheet as being of the Chart type (a chart worksheet) and then assign to myChartSheet a new chart sheet added after the last existing sheet in the active workbook:

```
Dim myChartSheet As Chart
Set myChartSheet = ActiveWorkbook.Sheets.Add _
    (After:=ActiveWorkbook.Sheets(ActiveWorkbook.Sheets.Count), _
    Type:=xlChart)
```

CREATING A CHART ON AN EXISTING WORKSHEET

To create a chart on an existing worksheet, use the Add method with the ChartObjects collection. The syntax is

```
expression.Add(Left, Top, Width, Height)
```

The components of the syntax are as follows:

◆ *expression* is a required expression that returns a ChartObjects collection.

◆ Left is a required Double argument that specifies the position of the upper-left corner of the chart in points from the left edge of cell A1.

◆ Top is a required Double argument that specifies the position of the upper-left corner of the chart in points from the top edge of cell A1.

◆ Width is a required Double argument that specifies the width of the chart in points.

◆ Height is a required Double argument that specifies the height of the chart in points.

For example, the following statements declare a new ChartObject object named myChartObject and assign to it a new chart object 400 points wide by 300 points deep, positioned 200 points from the left edge and 200 points from the top of the worksheet:

```
Dim myChartObject As ChartObject
Set myChartObject = ActiveSheet.ChartObjects.Add(Left:=200, Top:=200, _
    Width:=400, Height:=300)
```

To work with the chart inside the ChartObject, return the Chart property of the ChartObject object.

Specifying the Source Data for the Chart

So far, the chart (on the chart sheet or in the chart object) is blank. To give it contents, specify the chart's source data by using the SetSourceData method of the Chart object. For example, the following statement specifies the range A1:E5 on the worksheet named Chart Data in the active workbook as the source data of the Chart object in the ChartObject object named myChartObject:

```
myChartObject.Chart.SetSourceData Source:= _
    ActiveWorkbook.Sheets("Chart Data").Range("A1:E5")
```

Specifying the Chart Type

To specify the chart type, set the ChartType property of the Chart object. Excel offers too wide a variety of charts to list here, but you can easily identify the chart types from their constants. For example, the constant xl3DArea represents the 3-D Area chart type, xlColumnStacked represents the Stacked Column chart type, and xlDoughnutExploded represents the Exploded Doughnut chart type.

The following statement sets the type of the chart represented by the object variable myChart to the Stacked Column type:

```
myChart.ChartType = xlColumnStacked
```

Working with Series in the Chart

To work with the series in a chart, you use the SeriesCollection collection, which contains all the series in the specified chart.

ADDING A NEW SERIES

To add a new series to a SeriesCollection collection, use the Add method with the appropriate SeriesCollection object. The syntax is

```
expression.Add(Source, Rowcol, SeriesLabels, CategoryLabels, Replace
```

The components of the syntax are as follows:

◆ *expression* is a required expression that returns a SeriesCollection collection.

◆ Source is a required Variant argument that specifies the source of the data for the new series. You can supply the data either as a range or as an array of data points.

◆ Rowcol is an optional argument that you can set to xlRows to specify that the new values are in rows in the specified range or use the default setting, xlColumns, to specify that the new values are in columns. If you omit this argument, Excel uses xlColumns.

◆ SeriesLabels is an optional Variant argument that you can set to True to specify that the first row or column in the source area contains the series labels or False to specify that the first row or column in the source area contains the first data point for the series. If you omit this argument, Excel tries to work out whether the first row or column contains a series label. It's best to specify this argument to avoid confusion. If Source is an array, VBA ignores this argument.

◆ CategoryLabels is an optional Variant argument that you can set to True to specify that the first row or column contains the name for the category labels or set to False to specify that it does not contain them. If you omit this argument, Excel tries to work out whether the first row or column contains a category label. It's best to specify this argument to avoid confusion. If Source is an array, VBA ignores this argument.

◆ Replace is an optional Variant argument that you can set to True when CategoryLabels is True to make the categories replace the existing categories for the series or set to False (the default value) to prevent the existing categories from being replaced.

For example, the following statement adds a new series to the chart identified by the object variable myChart, drawing the data from the range C4:K4 on the active worksheet in the active workbook, using rows:

```
myChart.SeriesCollection.Add Source:=ActiveSheet.Range("C4:K4"), Rowcol:=xlRows
```

EXTENDING AN EXISTING SERIES

To extend an existing series, use the Extend method with the appropriate SeriesCollection object. The syntax is

```
expression.Extend(Source, Rowcol, CategoryLabels)
```

The components of the syntax are as follows:

◆ expression is a required expression that returns a SeriesCollection object.

◆ Source is a required Variant argument that specifies the source of the data for the new series. You can supply the data either as a range or as an array of data points.

◆ Rowcol is an optional argument that you can set to xlRows to specify that the new values are in rows in the specified range or use the default setting, xlColumns, to specify that the new values are in columns. If you omit this argument, Excel uses xlColumns.

◆ CategoryLabels is an optional Variant argument that you can set to True to specify that the first row or column contains the name for the category labels or set to False to specify that it does not contain them. If you omit this argument, Excel tries to work out whether the first row or column contains a category label. It's best to specify this argument to avoid confusion. If Source is an array, VBA ignores this argument.

For example, the following statement extends the series in the chart identified by the object variable myChart using the data in the cells P3:P8 on the worksheet named Chart Data:

```
myChart.SeriesCollection.Extend Source:=Worksheets("Chart Data").Range("P3:P8")
```

CREATING A NEW SERIES

To create a new series, use the NewSeries method with the SeriesCollection collection. For example, the following statement adds a new series to the chart represented by the object variable myChart:

```
myChart.SeriesCollection.NewSeries
```

Adding a Legend to the Chart

To add a legend to the chart, set its `HasLegend` property to `True`. To manipulate the legend, work with the properties of the `Legend` object. Key properties include these:

- The `Position` property controls where the legend appears: `xlLegendPositionBottom`, `xlLegendPositionCorner`, `xlLegendPositionLeft`, `xlLegendPositionRight`, or `xlLegendPositionTop`.

- The `Height` property and the `Width` property control the height and width of the legend, respectively, in points.

- The `Font` property returns the `Font` object, whose properties you can set to specify the font size, name, and effects.

For example, the following statements add the legend to the chart represented by the object variable `myChart` and apply 16-point Arial font to it:

```
With myChart.Legend
    .HasLegend = True
    .Font.Size = 16
    .Font.Name = "Arial"
End With
```

Adding a Chart Title

To add a title to the chart, set its `HasTitle` property to `True`—for example:

```
myChart.HasTitle = True
```

Excel adds the title with the default text `Chart Title`. To change the text, set the `Text` property of the `ChartTitle` object, which represents the chart title. For example:

```
myChart.ChartTitle.Text = "Industrial Disease in North Dakota"
```

To position the title, set its `Top` property (specifying the number of points from the top edge of the worksheet) and its `Left` property (specifying the number of points from the left edge of the worksheet). For example:

```
With myChart.ChartTitle
    .Top = 100
    .Left = 150
End With
```

To format the text of the title, work with its `Font` object—for example:

```
myChart.ChartTitle.Font.Name = "Elephant"
```

Working with a Chart Axis

To work with an axis of a chart, use the `Axes` method to access the appropriate axis. The syntax is

```
expression.Axes(Type, Group)
```

Here, *expression* is a required expression that returns a Chart object. Type is an optional Variant argument that specifies the axis to return. Use xlValue to return the value axis, xlCategory to return the category axis, or xlSeriesAxis to return the series axis (on 3-D charts only). Group is an optional argument that you can set to xlSecondary to specify the second axis group instead of xlPrimary (the default setting), which specifies the first axis group.

For example, the following statements work with the category axis in the primary group of the chart, applying its title, adding text, setting the font and font size, and turning major gridlines on and minor gridlines off:

```
With .Axes(Type:=xlCategory, AxisGroup:=xlPrimary)
    .HasTitle = True
    .AxisTitle.Text = "Years"
    .AxisTitle.Font.Name = "Times New Roman"
    .AxisTitle.Font.Size = 12
    .HasMajorGridlines = True
    .HasMinorGridlines = False
End With
```

Working with Windows

The Windows collection contains a Window object for every open window in the Excel application. Normally, when you open a workbook, Excel opens a window so that you can see it. You can also open further windows as necessary—for example, by choosing Window ➢ New Window in the user interface.

In most cases, windows aren't a very useful way to access data via VBA, because you can access it more easily using objects such as the ActiveSheet object or the ActiveCell object. However, you may want to open, close, activate, or arrange windows programmatically to display data to the user in a particular way.

Opening a New Window on a Workbook

To open a new window on a workbook, use the NewWindow method of the appropriate Window object. This method takes no arguments. For example, the following statement opens a new window showing the contents of the first window open on the workbook identified by the object variable myWorkbook:

```
myWorkbook.Windows(1).NewWindow
```

Closing a Window

To close a window, use the Close method with the appropriate Window object. The syntax is

```
expression.Close(SaveChanges, Filename, RouteWorkbook)
```

Here, *expression* is a required expression that returns a Window object. This syntax is the same as for closing a workbook (see "Closing a Workbook" in the previous chapter). The difference is that if two or more windows are open on the same workbook, closing the second or subsequent window does not close the workbook, so the arguments are not relevant. (If the window you're closing is the workbook's last window, however, you do need to specify the windows—otherwise, Excel prompts the user to save any unsaved changes.) For example, the following statement closes all windows open on the workbook referenced by the object variable myWorkbook except for one window:

```
Do While myWorkbook.Windows.Count > 1
    myWorkbook.Windows(myWorkbook.Windows.Count).Close
Loop
```

Activating a Window

To activate a window, use the Activate method of the appropriate Window object. For example, the following statement activates the first window open on the workbook Planning.xls:

```
Workbooks("Planning.xls").Windows(1).Activate
```

Similarly, you can activate the previous window by using the ActivatePrevious method or the next window by using the ActivateNext method.

Arranging and Resizing Windows

To arrange windows, use the Arrange method with the appropriate Windows collection. The syntax is

```
expression.Arrange(ArrangeStyle, ActiveWorkbook, SyncHorizontal, SyncVertical)
```

The components of this syntax are as follows:

- *expression* is a required expression that returns a Windows collection.

- ArrangeStyle is an optional argument that you can set to xlArrangeStyleTiled to tile the windows (the default setting), xlArrangeStyleHorizontal to arrange the windows horizontally, xlArrangeStyleVertical to arrange the windows vertically, or xlArrangeStyleCascade to cascade the windows in an overlapping arrangement that lets you see the title bar of each window but the contents of only the front window.

- ActiveWorkbook is an optional Variant argument that you can set to True to make VBA arrange only the windows of the active workbook. The default value is False, which arranges all open windows.

- SyncHorizontal and SyncVertical are optional Variant arguments that you can set to True when you use ActiveWorkbook:=True to make the windows of the active workbook scroll horizontally or vertically in sync (when you scroll one window, the other windows scroll by the same amount in the same direction). The default is False.

For example, the following statement arranges the windows in the workbook Budget.xls vertically and sets synchronized scrolling on them:

```
Workbooks("Budget.xls").Windows.Arrange ArrangeStyle:=xlArrangeStyleVertical, _
    ActiveWorkbook:=True, SyncVertical:=True
```

You can maximize, minimize, or restore the application window by setting the WindowState property of the Application object to xlMaximized, xlMinimized, or xlNormal. Similarly, within the application window, you can maximize, minimize, or restore a document by setting its WindowState property.

When a window is in a "normal" state (xlNormal; not maximized or minimized), you can position it by using the Top and Left properties to specify the position of the upper-left corner of the window and size it by setting its Height and Width properties. Check the UsableWidth property and the UsableHeight property of the Application object to find the amount of space available in the Application window. (Similarly, you can check the UsableWidth property and the UsableHeight of the Window object to see how much space is available in the window—for example, so that you can size or position an object correctly.)

The following example declares two Window object variables, myWindow1 and myWindow2, assigns myWindow1 to the active window and myWindow2 to a new window showing the same worksheet as myWindow1. The example then sizes and positions the two windows so that each is the full height available in the application window, with myWindow1 taking one-quarter of the available width and myWindow2 taking the remaining three-quarters of the available width.

```
Dim myWindow1 As Window, myWindow2 As Window
Set myWindow1 = ActiveWindow
Set myWindow2 = myWindow1.NewWindow
With myWindow1
    .WindowState = xlNormal
    .Top = 0
    .Left = 0
    .Height = Application.UsableHeight
    .Width = Application.UsableWidth * 0.25
End With
With myWindow2
    .WindowState = xlNormal
    .Top = 0
    .Left = (Application.UsableWidth * 0.25) + 1
    .Height = Application.UsableHeight
    .Width = Application.UsableWidth * 0.75
End With
```

Zooming a Window and Setting Display Options

To change the zoom, set the Zoom property of the appropriate Window object. For example, the following statement zooms the active window to 150 percent:

```
ActiveWindow.Zoom = 150
```

In some procedures, you may need to change the display of the Excel window to ensure that certain features are (or are not) available to the user. Use the Boolean properties DisplayScrollBars, DisplayStatusBar, and DisplayFormulaBar to control whether Excel displays the scroll bars, status bar, and formula bar. Use the DisplayFullScreen property to toggle full-screen view on and off.

For example, the following statements make sure that the scroll bars and status bar are hidden and that the formula bar is displayed:

```
With Application
    .DisplayScrollBars = False
    .DisplayStatusBar = False
    .DisplayFormulaBar = True
End With
```

Working with Find and Replace

Excel's Find and Replace features can be useful for locating data in your procedures. In Excel, Find and Replace are implemented through methods rather than through a Find object (as in Word).

The Find method and Replace method apply (with different syntax) to the Range object and the WorksheetFunction object. For most find and replace operations, you'll want to use these methods with the Range object—for example, to replace the contents of specific cells on a worksheet.

Searching with the *Find* Method

The syntax for the Find method for the Range object is

```
expression.Find(What, After, LookIn, LookAt, SearchOrder, SearchDirection,
MatchCase, MatchByte, SearchFormat)
```

The components of the syntax are as follows:

- *expression* is a required expression that returns a Range object.

- What is a required Variant argument that specifies the data to find. This data can be a string of text or any Excel data type.

- After is an optional Variant argument that you can use to specify the cell after which to begin searching. After must be a cell in the range that's being searched. If you omit After, Excel begins the search at the upper-left cell in the range.

- LookIn is an optional Variant argument that you can use to specify whether to search in formulas (xlFormulas), values (xlValues), or comments (xlComments).

- LookAt is an optional Variant argument that you can set to xlWhole to search for the entire contents of a cell or xlPart to search for the match within the contents of cells. (This setting corresponds to the Match Entire Cell Contents check box in the Find And Replace dialog box.)

- SearchOrder is an optional Variant argument that you can set to xlByRows to search by rows or xlByColumns to search by columns.

- SearchDirection is an optional Variant argument that you can set to xlNext to search downward or xlPrevious to search upward.

- MatchCase is an optional Variant argument that you can set to True to use case-sensitive searching. The default setting is False.

- MatchByte is an optional Variant argument used only if you've installed double-byte language support.

- SearchFormat is an optional Variant argument that controls whether Excel searches for specified formatting (True) or not (False).

WARNING   The LookIn, LookAt, SearchOrder, and MatchByte arguments are *sticky*—Excel retains them from one search to the next. Unless you know that the settings used in the last search are suitable for your needs, you should set these arguments explicitly in each search to avoid getting unexpected results.

For example, the following statement searches for 2008 in formulas in cells after the active cell, without searching for formatting:

```
Cells.Find(What:="2008", After:=ActiveCell, LookIn:=xlFormulas, LookAt _
    :=xlWhole, SearchOrder:=xlByRows, SearchDirection:=xlNext, MatchCase:= _
    True, SearchFormat:=False).Activate
```

Continuing a Search with the *FindNext* Method and *FindPrevious* Method

After you have executed a search using the Find method, you can use the FindNext method to find the next instance of the search item or the FindPrevious method to find the previous instance. The syntax is

```
expression.FindNext(After)
expression.FindPrevious(After)
```

Here, *expression* is a required expression that returns a Range object, and After is an optional Variant argument that specifies the cell after which you want to search (for the FindNext method) or before which you want to search (for the FindPrevious method). After must be a single cell.

For example, the following statement finds the next instance of the search item:

```
Cells.FindNext
```

Replacing with the *Replace* Method

To replace using VBA, use the Replace method with the Range object. The syntax is

```
expression.Replace(What, Replacement, LookAt, SearchOrder, MatchCase, MatchByte,
SearchFormat, ReplaceFormat)
```

The components of the syntax are the same as for the Search method except for the following:

◆ Replacement is a required Variant argument that specifies the replacement string for the search.

◆ ReplaceFormat is an optional Variant argument that controls whether Excel replaces formatting in the search (True) or not (False).

For example, the following statement replaces the instances of the word Sales in column B of the active worksheet with the words Sales & Marketing, using case-sensitive matching:

```
ActiveSheet.Columns("B").Replace What:="Sales", _
    Replacement:="Sales & Marketing", SearchOrder:=xlByColumns, _
    MatchCase:=True
```

Searching for and Replacing Formatting

To search for formatting, use the FindFormat property of the Application object to define the formatting, and then set the SearchFormat argument of the Find method to True. Similarly, use the ReplaceFormat property of the Application object to define the replacement formatting, and then set the ReplaceFormat property of the Replace method to True.

For example, the following statements use a `With` structure to set the `Application.FindFormat.Font` properties for which to search, a `With` structure to set the `Application.ReplaceFormat.Font` with which to replace them, and the `Replace` method of the `Cells` collection to effect the replacement:

```
With Application.FindFormat.Font
    .Name = "Arial"
    .Size = "12"
    .Bold = True
End With
With Application.ReplaceFormat.Font
    .Name = "Arial Black"
    .Bold = False
End With
Cells.Replace What:="5", Replacement:="5", LookAt:=xlPart, SearchOrder _
    :=xlByColumns, MatchCase:=False, SearchFormat:=True, ReplaceFormat:=True
```

Chapter 24

Understanding the PowerPoint Object Model and Key Objects

- ◆ Getting an overview of the PowerPoint object model
- ◆ Understanding PowerPoint's creatable objects
- ◆ Working with presentations
- ◆ Working with windows and views
- ◆ Working with slides
- ◆ Working with masters

This chapter shows you how to start working with the PowerPoint object model, the theoretical architecture underlying PowerPoint. The chapter demonstrates how to perform common actions with the most immediately useful PowerPoint objects. These objects include the `Presentations` collection and the `Presentation` object, the `ActivePresentation` object, the `Slides` collection and `Slide` objects, `Window` objects, and `Master` objects.

Getting an Overview of the PowerPoint Object Model

To begin exploring the PowerPoint object model, start the Microsoft Visual Basic Help application and display the PowerPoint Object Model topic. Launch the Visual Basic Editor if it's not already displayed, then choose Help ➢ Microsoft Visual Basic Help, type **PowerPoint object model** and press Enter, and then click the PowerPoint Object Model topic.

Figure 24.1 shows the PowerPoint Object Model topic. The topic is too long to fit on most screens, so the figure shows the top part of the topic on the left and the remainder of the topic on the right.

Understanding PowerPoint's Creatable Objects

In PowerPoint, the `Application` object gives you access to all the objects in the PowerPoint application. But for many operations, you can go directly through one of the creatable objects that Power-Point exposes. The five most useful exposed creatable objects are as follows:

- ◆ The `ActivePresentation` object represents the active presentation.

- ◆ The `Presentations` collection contains the `Presentation` objects, each of which represents one of the open presentations.

FIGURE 24.1
The PowerPoint Object Model screen in VBA Help is a good place to start your exploration of the PowerPoint object model.

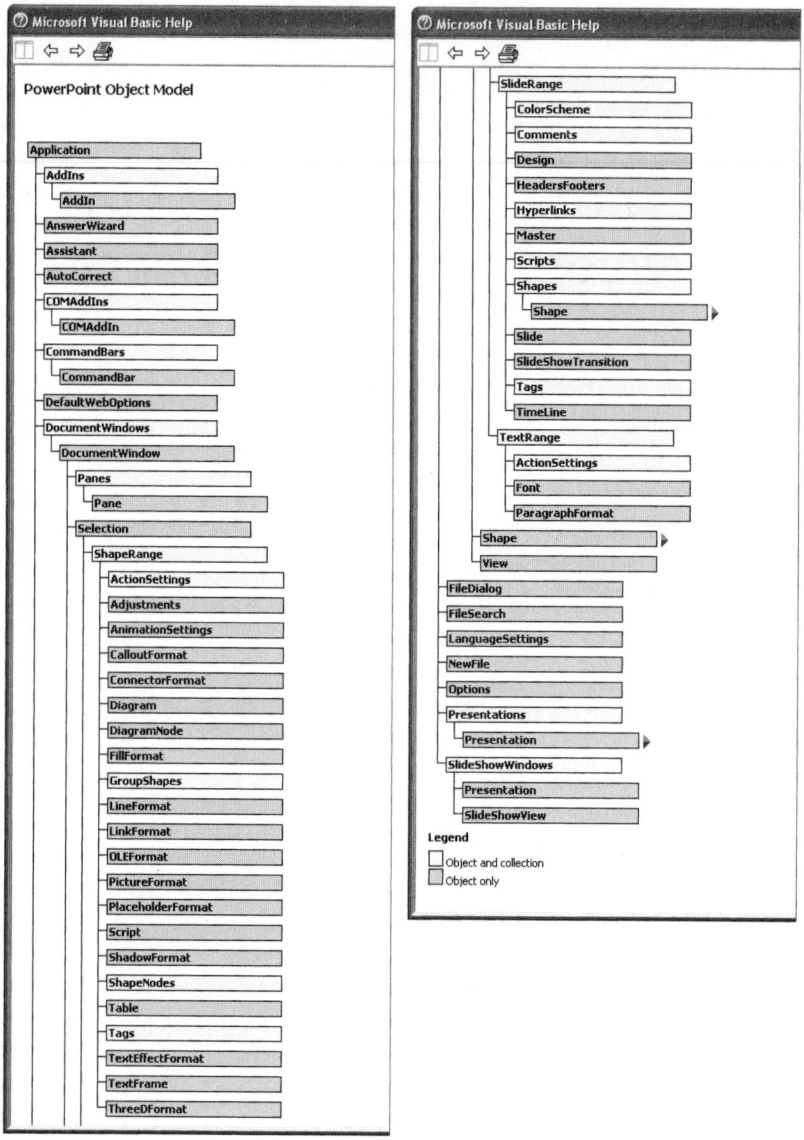

- The ActiveWindow object represents the active window in the application.

- The CommandBars collection contains the CommandBar objects, each of which represents a command bar (the toolbars, menu bar, and context menus) in the PowerPoint application. By manipulating the assorted CommandBar objects, you can change the PowerPoint interface programmatically.

- The SlideShowWindows collection contains the SlideShowWindow objects, each of which represents an open slide show window. This collection is useful for manipulating a slide show that's currently displayed.

Within a presentation, you'll typically find yourself working with the Slides collection, which contains all the Slide objects that represent the slides. On a slide, most items are represented by Shape objects gathered into the Shapes collection. For example, the text in a typical placeholder is contained in the Text property of the TextRange object in the TextFrame object within a Shape object on a slide.

Working with Presentations

To get any work done in PowerPoint, you'll usually need to work with one or more presentations. VBA uses the Presentation object to represent a presentation and organizes the open Presentation objects into the Presentations collection.

Creating a New Presentation Based on the Default Template

To create a new presentation based on the default template (the equivalent of clicking the New button on the Standard toolbar in PowerPoint), use the Add method with the Presentations collection. The syntax is

```
expression.Add(WithWindow)
```

The components of the syntax are as follows:

◆ *expression* is a required expression that returns a Presentations object. Often, it's easiest to use the Presentations object itself.

◆ WithWindow is an optional Long argument. Set WithWindow to msoFalse to prevent the new presentation from being visible—for example, so that you can create and manipulate it without the user seeing the details. (You may want to hide the presentation so that the user doesn't have to endure the irritating flickering effect that PowerPoint tends to exhibit while creating presentation objects programmatically.) The default value is msoTrue, making the new presentation visible.

For example, the following statements declare an object variable of the Presentation type named myPresentation, create a new presentation, assign the new presentation to myPresentation, and make it invisible to the user:

```
Dim myPresentation As Presentation
Set myPresentation = Presentations.Add(WithWindow:=msoFalse)
```

UNDERSTANDING TRI-STATE VALUES

PowerPoint makes extensive use of MsoTriState values, which are a kind of super-Boolean value: Instead of being set to True or False, and always having to be set to one value or the other, a tri-state value can be set to msoTrue (which represents True), msoFalse (which represents False), or another value (such as msoTriStateMixed, which indicates a mixture of values). In most cases, you'll want to set a tri-state value to either msoTrue or msoFalse. You wouldn't set msoTriStateMixed; rather, you would check for the value to find out if the property you were getting contained a mixture of msoTrue and msoFalse values.

Creating a New Presentation Based on a Template

To create a new presentation based on a template, use the `Open` method of the `Presentations` collection. The syntax is

```
expression.Open(FileName, ReadOnly, Untitled, WithWindow, OpenConflictDocument)
```

The components of the syntax are explained here:

◆ `expression` is a required expression that returns a `Presentations` object. Often, it's easiest to use the `Presentations` object itself.

◆ `FileName` is a required String argument that specifies the path and name of the file to use as a template for the new presentation. This file can be either a template in the conventional sense or a presentation that you want to use as a template.

◆ `ReadOnly` is an optional argument that specifies whether the file is opened with read-only status (`msoTrue`) or with read/write status (`msoFalse`). When creating a new presentation based on a template, you don't need to specify `ReadOnly`.

◆ `Untitled` is an optional argument that specifies whether to open the file as itself (`msoFalse`) or as a copy (`msoTrue`). When creating a new presentation based on a template, set `Untitled` to `msoTrue`.

◆ `WithWindow` is an optional argument that you can set to `msoFalse` to prevent the new presentation from being visible. The default value is `msoTrue`, making the new presentation visible.

◆ `OpenConflictDocument` is an optional argument that controls whether PowerPoint opens any existing conflict file for a presentation that has an offline conflict (`msoTrue`) or ignores the conflict document (`msoFalse`). (A conflict document is a file created when two versions of the same base file contain different changes that have not been synchronized.) This argument is not relevant when creating a new presentation based on the template, only when you're opening an existing file (see the next subsection).

For example, the following statement creates a new presentation based on the template named `Capsules.pot` in the `C:\Program Files\Microsoft Office\Templates\Presentation Designs\` folder:

```
Presentations.Open FileName:="C:\Program Files\Microsoft
Office\Templates\Presentation Designs\Capsules.pot", Untitled:=msoTrue
```

Opening a Presentation

To open an existing presentation, use the `Open` method of the `Presentations` collection. The syntax is as shown in the previous section. The difference is that you use the `FileName` argument to specify the presentation you want to open (as opposed to the file that you want to use as the template for the new presentation) and either omit the `Untitled` argument or set it to `msoFalse`. You may also need to use the `OpenConflictDocument` argument to specify how to handle any conflict file that exists for the presentation you're opening.

For example, the following statement opens the existing presentation named `Train Time.ppt` stored in the folder `Z:\Public`, opening the presentation for editing rather than opening it as read-only:

```
Presentations.Open FileName:="Z:\Public\Train Time.ppt", ReadOnly:=msoFalse
```

Saving a Presentation

The first time you save a presentation, you must specify the path and filename to use. After that, you can save the presentation under the same name or specify a different path, name, format, or all three.

SAVING A PRESENTATION FOR THE FIRST TIME OR UNDER A DIFFERENT NAME

To save a presentation for the first time, or to save a presentation using a different path, name, or format, use the SaveAs method. The syntax is

```
expression.SaveAs(Filename, FileFormat, EmbedFonts)
```

The components of the syntax are as follows:

◆ *expression* is a required expression that returns a Presentation object.

◆ Filename is a required String argument that specifies the filename under which to save the presentation. Normally, you include the path in Filename; if you omit the path, PowerPoint uses the current folder.

◆ FileFormat is an optional argument that specifies the file format to use. Table 24.1 lists the most widely useful formats.

TABLE 24.1: *FileFormat* Constants for Saving PowerPoint Files

FORMAT NAME	CONSTANT
PowerPoint format	ppSaveAsPresentation
Default format (set on the Save tab of the Options dialog box)	ppSaveAsDefault
Single File Web Page	ppSaveAsWebArchive
Web Page	ppSaveAsHTML
PowerPoint 95	ppSaveAsPowerPoint7
Presentation for Review	ppSaveAsPresForReview
Design Template	ppSaveAsTemplate
PowerPoint Show	ppSaveAsShow

◆ EmbedFonts is an optional argument that you can set to msoTrue to embed TrueType fonts in the presentation or False (the default) to not embed them.

For example, the following statement saves the presentation identified by the object variable myPresentation under the name HR.ppt in the folder Z:\Shared\Presentations, using the Power-Point 95 format and not embedding fonts:

```
myPresentation.SaveAs FileName:="Z:\Shared\Presentations\HR.ppt", _
    FileFormat:=ppSaveAsPowerPoint7, EmbedTrueTypeFonts:=msoFalse
```

SAVING A PRESENTATION UNDER ITS EXISTING NAME

To save a presentation under its existing name, use the Save method. This method takes no arguments. For example, the following statement saves the active presentation:

```
ActivePresentation.Save
```

If the presentation on which you use the Save method has never been saved, PowerPoint doesn't prompt the user to specify the filename and location. Instead, PowerPoint saves the presentation using the default name assigned to its window (for example, a presentation whose window is called Presentation11 will be saved as Presentation11.ppt) and in the current folder. To avoid this default name and location, check the Path property of the Presentation object before using the Save method if you need to determine whether the presentation has been saved. For example:

```
If ActivePresentation.Path = "" Then
    ActivePresentation.SaveAs FileName:="z:\public\presentations\Corporate.ppt"
Else
    ActivePresentation.Save
End If
```

SAVING A COPY OF A PRESENTATION

Instead of using the SaveAs method to save an open presentation under a different name, you can use the SaveCopyAs method to save a copy of the open presentation without affecting the open presentation (the presentation remains open, and any unsaved changes remain unsaved). The syntax and arguments for the SaveCopyAs method are the same as for the SaveAs method:

```
expression.SaveAs(Filename, FileFormat, EmbedFonts)
```

For example, the following statement saves a copy of the active presentation under the name Copy 1.ppt in the folder Z:\Public\Presentations, using the same file format as the presentation currently uses:

```
ActivePresentation.SaveCopyAs FileName:="Z:\Public\Presentations\Copy 1.ppt"
```

SAVING ALL OPEN PRESENTATIONS

The Presentations collection doesn't have a Save method, but you can save all open presentations by using a loop such as that shown in the following subprocedure. This subprocedure leaves unsaved any presentation that doesn't yet have a filename assigned.

```
Sub Save_All_Presentations()
    Dim myPresentation As Presentation
    For Each myPresentation In Presentations
        If myPresentation.Path <> "" Then myPresentation.Save
    Next myPresentation
End Sub
```

Closing a Presentation

To close a presentation, use the Close method of the appropriate Presentation object. The Close method takes no arguments. For example, the following statement closes the active presentation:

```
ActivePresentation.Close
```

If the presentation you're closing contains unsaved changes, PowerPoint prompts the user to save them. To avoid the user being prompted, set the `Saved` property of the `Presentation` object to `True` before using the `Close` method—for example:

```
With Presentations("Karelia Industry.ppt")
    .Saved = True
    .Close
End With
```

Exporting a Presentation or Some Slides to Graphics

You can export either an entire presentation, a single slide, or a range of slides by using the `Export` method of the `Presentation` object, the `Slide` object, or a `SlideRange` object. The syntax for the `Export` method with a `Presentation` object is

```
expression.Export(Path, FilterName, ScaleWidth, ScaleHeight)
```

The syntax for the `Export` method with a `Slide` object or a `SlideRange` object is almost the same:

```
expression.Export(FileName, FilterName, ScaleWidth, ScaleHeight)
```

The components of the syntax are as follows:

◆ *expression* is a required expression that returns a `Presentation` object, a `Slide` object, or a `SlideRange` object, as appropriate.

◆ `Path` (for a `Presentation` object) is a required String argument that specifies the path of the folder in which to save the graphics files of the slides.

◆ `FileName` (for a `Slide` object or a `SlideRange` object) is a required String argument that specifies the filename to use for the exported graphic. Include the path in `FileName` unless you want PowerPoint to use the current folder.

◆ `FilterName` is a required String argument that specifies the filter to use. Use the registered file extension (JPG, TIF, BMP, or PNG) for `FilterName`.

◆ `ScaleWidth` is an optional Long argument that you can include to specify the width of the graphic in pixels.

◆ `ScaleHeight` is an optional Long argument that you can include to specify the height of the graphic in pixels.

For example, the following statement exports all the slides in the active presentation to 800×600 JPG graphics in the `Z:\Public\Presentations` folder. PowerPoint names the graphics `Slide1`, `Slide2`, and so on.

```
ActivePresentation.Export Path:="Z:\Public\Presentations", _
    FilterName:="JPG", ScaleWidth:=800, ScaleHeight:=600
```

The following statement exports the sixth slide in the active presentation to the file named `Slide6.png` in the `Z:\Public\Presentations` folder, using the PNG format:

```
ActivePresentation.Slides(6).Export _
    FileName:="Z:\Public\Presentations\Slide6.png", FilterName:="PNG"
```

Printing a Presentation

To print a presentation, use the `PrintOut` method of the appropriate `Presentation` object. The syntax is

```
expression.PrintOut(From, To, PrintToFile, Copies, Collate)
```

The components of the syntax are as follows:

◆ `expression` is a required expression that returns a `Presentation` object.

◆ `From` and `To` are optional Integer arguments that specify the first slide and last slide to print. If you omit `From`, PowerPoint prints from the first slide; if you omit `To`, PowerPoint prints through the last slide.

◆ `PrintToFile` is an optional String argument that you can include to make PowerPoint print to the specified file rather than to the printer.

◆ `Copies` is an optional Integer argument that specifies how many copies of the presentation or slides to print. Omit `Copies` to use the default value, 1.

◆ `Collate` is an optional argument that you can set to `msoFalse` to prevent PowerPoint from collating multiple copies (which is the default setting).

For example, the following statement prints all the slides in the active presentation:

```
ActivePresentation.PrintOut
```

The following example prints slides 5 through 12 of the presentation identified by the object variable `myPresentation`:

```
myPresentation.PrintOut From:=5, To:=12
```

Applying a Template to a Presentation, to a Slide, or to a Range of Slides

You can apply a design template to a presentation, to a single slide within a presentation, or to a range of slides by using the `ApplyTemplate` method with the `Presentation` object, the `Slide` object, or the `SlideRange` object. The syntax is

```
expression.ApplyTemplate(FileName)
```

Here, `expression` is a required expression that returns a `Presentation` object, a `Slide` object, or a `SlideRange` object. `FileName` is a required String argument that specifies the path and name of the design template.

For example, the following statement applies the design template named `Clouds.pot` stored in the `C:\Program Files\Microsoft Office\Templates\Presentation Designs` folder to the active presentation:

```
ActivePresentation.Slides(1).ApplyTemplate FileName:= _
"C:\Program Files\Microsoft Office\Templates\Presentation Designs\Clouds.pot"
```

The following statement applies the design template named `Mountain Top.pot` stored in the `Z:\Public\Template` folder to the first slide in the presentation named `Success.ppt`:

```
Presentations("Success.ppt").Slides(1).ApplyTemplate FileName:= _
    "Z:\Public\Template\Mountain Top.pot"
```

The following example applies the design template named `Disaster.pot` stored in the `Z:\Public\Template` folder to a range of slides consisting of the first, fourth, and sixth slides in the active presentation:

```
ActivePresentation.Slides.Range(Array(1, 4, 6)).ApplyTemplate _
    FileName:="Z:\Public\Template \Disaster.pot"
```

Working with the Active Presentation

The `ActivePresentation` property of the `Application` object returns a `Presentation` object that represents the active presentation (the presentation in the active window). The `ActivePresentation` object can be very useful for procedures that the user starts.

If no window is open, trying to use the `ActivePresentation` object returns an error. Unless you're sure that there is an active presentation, it's a good idea to check that a window is open before you access the `ActivePresentation` object. For example:

```
If Windows.Count = 0 Then
    MsgBox "Please open a presentation before running this macro."
    End
End If
```

Working with Windows and Views

To get the PowerPoint window into the state you want, you'll often need to work with the window and with the view. PowerPoint uses two types of windows: document windows and slide show windows:

◆ Document windows are windows that contain documents (presentation files) rather than slide shows. VBA considers document windows to be `DocumentWindow` objects organized into the `DocumentWindows` collection but represents them with `Window` objects organized into the `Windows` collection.

◆ Slide show windows are windows that contain open slide shows. VBA uses `SlideShowWindow` objects and the `SlideShowWindows` collection to represent slide show windows.

This section shows you how to work with document windows. You'll learn how to work with slide show windows in "Setting Up and Running a Slide Show" in Chapter 25.

The `Windows` collection contains a `Window` object for every open window in the PowerPoint application. When you open a presentation while working interactively, PowerPoint opens a window so that you can see the presentation. When you open a presentation via VBA, you can set the `WithWindow` argument of the `Add` method to `msoFalse` to prevent PowerPoint from displaying a window for the presentation. You can also open further windows as necessary—for example, by choosing Window ➢ New Window in the user interface.

Working with the Active Window

PowerPoint uses the `ActiveWindow` object to represent the window that is active (the window that has the focus). Only one window is active at a time. The active window is always the first `Window` object in the `Windows` collection—`Windows(1)`.

If no window is open at all, or all open windows are hidden, there is no active window, and using the `ActiveWindow` object causes VBA to return an error. To make sure that a window is open, check whether the `Count` property of the `Windows` collection is 0—for example:

```
If Windows.Count = 0 Then MsgBox "There is no active window.", vbOkOnly + _
    vbExclamation, "No Window Is Open"
```

When you're working with presentations using VBA, you may sometimes find that the `ActiveWindow` object is a handy way to access a presentation, especially for a macro that the user runs after choosing the presentation, slide, or other object that they want to affect. In other cases, you may find that the `ActivePresentation` object is a more convenient way to access the presentation you need to work with, or you may prefer to access the presentation via the `Presentations` collection.

Opening a New Window on a Presentation

To open a new window, use the `NewWindow` method of the appropriate `Window` object. This method takes no arguments. For example, the following statement opens a new window showing the contents of the active window:

```
ActiveWindow.NewWindow
```

Closing a Window

To close a window, use the `Close` method with the appropriate `Window` object. In PowerPoint, the `Close` method takes no arguments.

WARNING If the window you're closing is the last window open for the presentation, PowerPoint simply closes the window without prompting the user to save any unsaved changes. For this reason, be careful when closing windows.

For example, you might close all windows but one on a presentation:

```
Do While ActivePresentation.Windows.Count > 1
    ActivePresentation.Windows(ActivePresentation.Windows.Count).Close
Loop
```

Alternatively, you might use the `Save` method to save a presentation before closing its last window, as in the next example. (More simply, you could use the `Close` method to close the presentation itself after saving it.)

```
With ActivePresentation
    If .Path = "" Then
        MsgBox "Please save this presentation.", vbOKOnly
    Else
        .Save
        For Each myWindow In Windows
            .Close
        Next myWindow
    End If
End With
```

Activating a Window

To activate a window or one of its panes, use the `Activate` method of the appropriate `Window` object. For example, the following statement activates the first window open on the presentation `Benefits.ppt`:

```
Presentations("Benefits.ppt").Windows(1).Activate
```

Arranging and Resizing Windows

To arrange windows, use the `Arrange` method with the appropriate `Windows` collection. The syntax is

```
expression.Arrange(ArrangeStyle)
```

Here, *expression* is a required expression that returns a `Windows` collection. `ArrangeStyle` is a required argument that specifies how to arrange the windows, `ppArrangeCascade` (cascade the windows in an overlapping arrangement that lets you see the title bar of each window but the contents of only the front window) or `ppArrangeTiled` (tile the windows; the default setting).

You can maximize, minimize, or restore the application window by setting the `WindowState` property of the `Application` object to `ppWindowMaximized`, `ppWindowMinimized`, or `ppWindowNormal`. Similarly, within the application window, you can maximize, minimize, or restore a document by setting its `WindowState` property.

When a window is in a "normal" state (`ppWindowNormal`; not maximized or minimized), you can position it by using the `Top` and `Left` properties to specify the position of the upper-left corner of the window and size it by setting its `Height` and `Width` properties.

The following example maximizes the application window and cascades the document windows within it:

```
Application.WindowState = ppWindowMaximized
Windows.Arrange ArrangeStyle:=ppArrangeCascade
```

Changing the View

To change the view in a window, set the `ViewType` property of the appropriate `Window` object to the appropriate constant: `ppViewHandoutMaster`, `ppViewMasterThumbnails`, `ppViewNormal`, `ppViewNotesMaster`, `ppViewNotesPage`, `ppViewOutline`, `ppViewPrintPreview`, `ppViewSlide`, `ppViewSlideMaster`, `ppViewSlideSorter`, `ppViewThumbnails`, or `ppViewTitleMaster`. For example, the following statement switches the active window into Slide Sorter view:

```
ActiveWindow.ViewType=ppViewSlideSorter
```

To zoom the view, specify a value from 10 to 400 for the `Zoom` property of the `View` object for the appropriate window. The value represents the zoom percentage, but you do not include the percent sign. For example, the following statement zooms the active window to 150 percent:

```
ActiveWindow.View.Zoom = 150
```

Working with Panes

The Pane object represents a pane of the PowerPoint window in Slide view. The Outline pane is represented by index number 1, the Slide pane by index number 2, and the Notes pane by index number 3. You can activate a pane by using the Activate method with the appropriate Pane object. The following example switches the view in the active window to Slide view and activates the Outline pane:

```
With ActiveWindow
    .ViewType = ppViewSlide
    .Panes(1).Activate
End With
```

To change the setup of the PowerPoint window in Slide view, use the SplitHorizontal property and the SplitVertical property of the Window object. The SplitHorizontal property controls the percentage of the document window's width that the Outline pane occupies, and the SplitVertical property controls the percentage of the document window's height that the Slide pane occupies. The following example sets the Outline pane to take 25 percent of the width of the document window (leaving 75 percent to the Slide pane) and the Slide pane to take 75 percent of the height of the window (leaving 25 percent to the Notes pane).

```
With ActiveWindow
    .SplitHorizontal = 25
    .SplitVertical = 75
End With
```

Working with Slides

Once you have created or opened the presentation you want to affect, you can access the slides it contains by using the Slides collection, which contains a Slide object for each slide in the presentation. Each slide is identified by its index number, but you can also use object variables to refer to slides or assign names to slides. These techniques are especially useful when you add slides to or delete slides from the presentation, making the index numbers of the slides change.

Adding a Slide to a Presentation

To add a slide to a presentation, use the Add method with the Slides collection. The syntax is

```
expression.Add(Index, Layout)
```

The components of the syntax are as follows:

- ◆ *expression* is a required expression that returns a Slides collection. In many cases, it's easiest to use the Slides collection itself.

- ◆ Index is a required Long argument that specifies the index number for positioning the slide in the presentation. For example, the number 2 makes the new slide the second slide in the presentation.

- ◆ Layout is a required Long argument that specifies the layout for the new slide. The layout names correspond closely to the names you'll see in the Insert Slide dialog box or the Slide Layout task pane. For example, ppLayoutBlank specifies a blank slide, ppLayoutTitleOnly a title-only slide, and ppLayoutChartAndText a chart-and-text slide.

For example, the following statements declare an object variable named mySlide and assign to it a new title slide added at the beginning of the active presentation:

```
Dim mySlide As Slide
Set mySlide = ActivePresentation.Slides.Add(Index:=1, _
    Layout:=ppLayoutTitle)
```

UNDERSTANDING THE "MIXED" CONSTANTS

If you look at the list of constants for the Layout property, you'll notice one is called ppLayoutMixed. There's no "Mixed" layout in the list of slide layouts, and if you try to apply ppLayoutMixed to a slide, VBA returns an error. This is because ppLayoutMixed is the value VBA returns for the Layout property of a slide range that contains multiple slides with different designs.

Other properties have similar Mixed values to indicate that the objects use different values. For example, ppTransitionSpeedMixed means that the slides or shapes used different transition speeds. Don't try to set a property to a Mixed value, because doing so always gives an error.

Inserting Slides from an Existing Presentation

When creating presentations automatically, it's often useful to insert slides from an existing presentation. To do so, use the InsertFromFile method of the Slides collection. The syntax is

```
expression.InsertFromFile(FileName, Index, SlideStart, SlideEnd)
```

The components of the syntax are as follows:

- *expression* is a required expression that returns a Slides collection. Often, you'll want to use the Slides collection itself.

- FileName is a required String argument that specifies the file from which to insert the slides.

- Index is a required Long argument that specifies the slide position in the open presentation at which to insert the slides.

- SlideStart is an optional Long argument that specifies the first slide to insert. If you omit SlideStart, PowerPoint starts at the first slide.

- SlideEnd is an optional Long argument that specifies the last slide to insert. If you omit SlideEnd, PowerPoint goes up to the last slide.

For example, the following statement inserts slides 2 through 8 from the presentation named Handbook.ppt stored in the folder Z:\Transfer\Presentations, placing the slides starting at the fifth slide in the open presentation Corporate.ppt:

```
Presentations("Corporate.ppt").Slides.InsertFromFile _
    FileName:="Z:\Transfer\Presentations\Handbook.ppt", Index:=5, _
    SlideStart:=2, SlideEnd:=8
```

Finding a Slide by Its ID Number

When working programmatically with a presentation, it can be difficult to track which slide is which, especially when you add, delete, insert, copy, or move slides. To help you, PowerPoint assigns a slide ID number to each slide when it's created. The slide ID number doesn't change when you move a slide to a different position in the presentation, unlike the index number, which always reflects the slide's position in the presentation. You can check a slide's ID number by returning the `SlideID` property of the appropriate `Slide` object.

To find a slide by its ID number, use the `FindBySlideID` method of the `Slides` collection. The syntax is

```
expression.FindBySlideID(SlideID)
```

Here, *expression* is a required expression that returns that returns a `Slides` collection. `SlideID` is a required Long argument that specifies the ID number of the slide you want to return.

The following example declares a Long variable named `TargetSlide` and assigns to it a new slide added at the fifth index position in the active presentation, inserts a full presentation at the third index position, and then uses the `FindBySlideID` method to return the slide identified by `TargetSlide` and apply a different design template to it.

```
Dim TargetSlide As Long
TargetSlide = ActivePresentation.Slides.Add(Index:=5, _
    Layout:=ppLayoutFourObjects).SlideID
Presentations("Corporate.ppt").Slides.InsertFromFile _
    FileName:="Z:\Transfer\Presentations\Handbook.ppt", Index:=3
ActivePresentation.Slides.FindBySlideID(TargetSlide).ApplyTemplate _
    FileName:="C:\Program Files\Microsoft Office\Templates\Presentation
➡Designs\Brain Blitz.pot"
```

Changing the Layout of an Existing Slide

To change the layout of an existing slide, set its `Layout` property. For example, the following statement changes the layout of the first slide in the active presentation to the clip-art-and-vertical-text layout:

```
ActivePresentation.Slides(1).Layout = ppLayoutClipArtAndVerticalText
```

NOTE   When you change the layout of a slide, PowerPoint moves its existing contents to allow any new objects needed to be added to the slide.

Deleting an Existing Slide

To delete an existing slide, use the `Delete` method with the appropriate `Slide` object. For example, the following statement deletes the first slide in the active presentation:

```
ActivePresentation.Slides(1).Delete
```

WARNING   PowerPoint doesn't confirm the deletion of a slide via VBA.

Copying and Pasting a Slide

To copy a slide, use the Copy method of the appropriate Slide object. The Copy method takes no arguments. (You can also cut a slide by using the Cut method, which also takes no arguments.)

To paste a slide, use the Paste method of the Slides collection. The Paste method takes an Index argument that specifies the slide position at which to paste in the slide.

For example, the following statements copy the first slide in the active presentation and paste it in so that it is the fifth slide.

```
ActivePresentation.Slides(1).Copy
ActivePresentation.Slides.Paste Index:=5
```

Duplicating a Slide

Instead of copying and pasting, you can duplicate a slide by using the Duplicate method of the Slide object. This method takes no arguments and places the duplicate of the slide immediately after the original. For example, the following statement duplicates the fourth slide in the active presentation, placing the copy at the fifth index position:

```
ActivePresentation.Slides(4).Duplicate
```

Moving a Slide

Instead of cutting and pasting a slide, you can move it by using the MoveTo method with the appropriate Slide object. Moving a slide has the same net effect as cutting and pasting it but has the advantage of not changing the contents of the Clipboard (which you might need to preserve for the user or for other purposes). The syntax for the MoveTo method is

```
expression.MoveTo(ToPos)
```

Here, *expression* is a required expression that returns a Slide object, and ToPos is a required Long argument that specifies the index position to which you want to move the slide.

For example, the following statement moves the third slide in the presentation identified by the object variable myPresentation to the beginning of the presentation:

```
myPresentation.Slides(3).MoveTo ToPos:=1
```

Accessing a Slide by Name

Instead of accessing a slide by its index number, you can assign a name to it by using the Name property of the Slide object. For example, the following statements assign the name Chairman's Introduction to the fifth slide in the active presentation and then use the Select method of the Slide object to select that slide by name:

```
ActivePresentation.Slides(1).Name = "Chairman's Introduction"
ActivePresentation.Slides("Chairman's Introduction").Select
```

Working with a Range of Slides

To work with a range of slides, use the Range method of the Slides collection to return a SlideRange object that represents the slides. The SlideRange object can represent a single slide, but you're usually better off using it to represent a range of slides. (You can access a single slide more easily by its index number or by a name you assign to it than through a SlideRange object.)

To return a SlideRange object that encompasses two or more slides, use the Array function with a comma-delimited list of the slides. The list can use either the index numbers or the names of the slides. For example, the following statements declare the SlideRange object variable mySlideRange and assign to it the first five slides in the open presentation named HR.ppt:

```
Dim mySlideRange As SlideRange
Set mySlideRange = Presentations("HR.ppt").Slides.Range(Array(1, 2, 3, 4, 5))
```

The following statement assigns to the SlideRange object variable mySlideRange the slides named Intro and Outro in the active presentation:

```
Set mySlideRange = ActivePresentation.Slides.Range(Array("Intro", "Outro"))
```

Formatting a Slide

You can apply a design template to a slide by using the ApplyTemplate method, as discussed in "Applying a Template to a Presentation, to a Slide, or to a Range of Slides," earlier in this chapter. You can also apply a background or a color scheme, as discussed in this section.

APPLYING A BACKGROUND TO ONE OR MORE SLIDES

To apply a background to a slide or several slides, use the Background property of the appropriate Slide object or SlideRange object to return the ShapeRange object representing the background of the slide or slides. You can then use the Fill object to set a color, fill, gradient, or picture in the background.

The following example applies the picture Winter.jpg from the folder C:\Sample Pictures to the fourth slide in the presentation named Corporate.ppt. The example sets the FollowMasterBackground property to msoFalse, making the slide use a different background than the slide master, and also sets the DisplayMasterShapes property to msoFalse, making the slide not display the shapes on the slide master.

```
With Presentations("Corporate.ppt").Slides(4)
    .FollowMasterBackground = msoFalse
    .DisplayMasterShapes = msoFalse
    With .Background
        .Fill.ForeColor.RGB = RGB(255, 255, 255)
        .Fill.BackColor.SchemeColor = ppAccent1
        .Fill.UserPicture "C:\Sample Pictures\Winter.jpg"
    End With
End With
```

APPLYING A COLOR SCHEME TO A SLIDE

A *color scheme* is a group of eight colors that are used to create the look of the title, background, and other elements of a slide, handout, or notes page. VBA uses an RGBColor object to represent each color and a ColorScheme object to represent each color scheme. The ColorScheme objects are gathered in a ColorSchemes collection for the entire presentation.

To change the color scheme of a slide or several slides, use the ColorScheme property of the appropriate Slide object or SlideRange object to return the ColorScheme object, and then work with the Colors method to specify the color. The syntax is

```
expression.Colors(SchemeColor)
```

Here, *expression* is a required expression that returns a ColorScheme object. SchemeColor is a required argument that specifies which color in the color scheme to set—for example, ppAccent1 (for the first accent in the color scheme), ppBackground (the background color), or ppTitle (the title color).

The following statement sets the background color of the color scheme for the first three slides in the active presentation to black (RGB(0, 0, 0)):

```
ActivePresentation.Slides.Range(Array(1, 2, 3)) _
    .ColorScheme.Colors(ppBackground).RGB = RGB(0, 0, 0)
```

Setting a Transition for a Slide, a Range of Slides, or a Master

To set a transition for a slide, a range of slides, or a master, use the SlideShowTransition property of the Slide object, the SlideRange object, or the Master object to return the SlideShowTransition object.

To specify the effect to use, set the EntryEffect property to the constant for the effect. There are too many constants to list here, but their names are easy to decipher. For example, the ppEffectBlindsHorizontal constant represents the Blinds Horizontal transition, the ppEffectDissolve constant represents the Dissolve effect, and the ppEffectNone constant represents the No Transition setting.

To specify the speed at which the transition runs, set its Speed property to ppTransitionSpeedFast, ppTransitionSpeedMedium, or ppTransitionSpeedSlow.

To control how the slide advances, set the AdvanceOnTime property to msoTrue (for automatic advancing) or msoFalse (for manual advancing). If you use automatic advancing, use the AdvanceTime property to specify the number of seconds. If you want the slide to advance when the user clicks, set the AdvanceOnClick property to msoTrue. (You can set both AdvanceOnTime and AdvanceOnClick to msoTrue. The slide advances manually if the user clicks before the AdvanceTime interval has elapsed.)

To play a preset sound effect with the transition, use the SoundEffect property of the SlideShowTransition object to return the SoundEffect object, use the Name property to specify the name of the sound effect, and then use the Play method to play the sound effect. You can also play a separate sound file by using the ImportFromFile method of the SoundEffect object and using the FullName argument to specify the path and filename of the sound file.

If you want the sound to loop until the next sound, set the LoopSoundUntilNext property of the SlideShowTransition object to msoTrue. The default value is msoFalse.

The following example sets up a transition for the second slide in the active presentation. The transition uses the Dissolve effect running at Medium speed, sets advancing either on click or after a delay of 30 seconds, and plays a sound file from an external source without looping:

```
With ActivePresentation.Slides(2)
    With .SlideShowTransition
        .EntryEffect = ppEffectDissolve
        .Speed = ppTransitionSpeedMedium
```

```
            .AdvanceOnClick = msoTrue
            .AdvanceOnTime = msoTrue
            .AdvanceTime = 30
            .SoundEffect.ImportFromFile _
                FileName:="d:\Sounds\Crescendo.wav"
            .LoopSoundUntilNext = msoFalse
        End With
End With
```

Working with Masters

VBA uses the `Master` object to represent the various masters that PowerPoint uses: the slide master, title master, handout master, and notes master.

Working with the Slide Master

To work with the slide master for a presentation, use the `SlideMaster` property of the `Presentation` object

To return the slide master for a slide, use the `Master` property of the appropriate `Slide` object. For example, the following statement adds a title to the slide master for the active presentation. (If the slide master already has a title, VBA returns an error.)

```
ActivePresentation.SlideMaster.Shapes.AddTitle.TextFrame.TextRange.Text = _
    "Orientation"
```

Working with the Title Master

To find out whether a presentation has a title master, check the `HasTitleMaster` property. If it doesn't, you can use the `AddTitleMaster` method of the `Presentation` object to add a title master, as in the following example. If the presentation already has a title master, VBA returns an error when you try to add a title master.

```
If Not ActivePresentation.HasTitleMaster Then ActivePresentation.AddTitleMaster
```

To return the title master for the presentation, use the `TitleMaster` property of the `Presentation` object. The following example checks that the title master exists and, if it does, formats the date and time to be visible and to use the dMMMyy format with automatic updating:

```
With myPresentation
    If .HasTitleMaster Then
        With .TitleMaster.HeadersFooters.DateAndTime
            .Visible = msoTrue
            .Format = ppDateTimedMMMyy
            .UseFormat = msoTrue
        End With
    End If
End With
```

Working with the Handout Master

To work with the handout master, use the HandoutMaster property of the Presentation object to return the Master object. The following example uses the HandoutMaster property of the ActivePresentation object to fill the background of the handout master with a picture:

```
With ActivePresentation.HandoutMaster.Background
    .Fill.ForeColor.RGB = RGB(255, 255, 255)
    .Fill.BackColor.SchemeColor = ppAccent1
    .Fill.UserPicture "d:\igrafx\dawn.jpg"
End With
```

Working with the Notes Master

To work with the notes master, use the NotesMaster property of the Presentation object to return the Master object. For example, the following statement clears the HeaderFooter objects in the notes master in the first open presentation:

```
Presentations(1).NotesMaster.HeadersFooters.Clear
```

Deleting a Master

You can delete the title master or handout master, but not the slide master or notes master. To delete the title master or handout master, use the Delete method of the Master object. The following example checks that the active presentation has a title master and then deletes it:

```
If ActivePresentation.HasTitleMaster Then ActivePresentation.TitleMaster.Delete
```

Chapter 25

Working with Shapes and Running Slide Shows

◆ Working with shapes

◆ Working with headers and footers

◆ Setting up and running a slide show

In the previous chapter, you learned to work with Presentation objects, Slide objects, and Master objects. In this chapter, you'll learn to work with Shape objects to manipulate the contents of slides and with HeaderFooter objects to control the contents of headers and footers. You'll also learn how to set up and run a slide show using VBA

Working with Shapes

Most of the objects on a typical PowerPoint slide are Shape objects. For example, a title box is a Shape object, as is a picture or a Word table that you've pasted in. You access the Shape objects through the Shapes collection of a Slide object, a SlideRange object, or a Master object.

Adding Shapes to Slides

The Shapes collection uses different methods for adding the different types of shapes. Table 25.1 lists the Shape objects you can add and the methods and arguments for adding them. This section explains the arguments.

TABLE 25.1:   Shapes and the Methods for Adding Them to Slides

TO ADD THIS SHAPE	USE THIS METHOD AND ARGUMENTS
Callout	AddCallout(Type, Left, Top, Width, Height)
Comment	AddComment(Left, Top, Width, Height)
Connector	AddConnector(Type, BeginX, BeginY, EndX, EndY)
Curve	AddCurve(SafeArrayOfPoints)
Diagram	AddDiagram(Type, Left, Top, Width, Height)

TABLE 25.1:   Shapes and the Methods for Adding Them to Slides *(CONTINUED)*

TO ADD THIS SHAPE	USE THIS METHOD AND ARGUMENTS
Label	AddLabel(Orientation, Left, Top, Width, Height)
Line	AddLine(BeginX, BeginY, EndX, EndY)
Media object	AddMediaObject(FileName, Left, Top, Width, Height)
OLE object	AddOLEObject(Left, Top, Width, Height, ClassName, FileName, DisplayAsIcon, IconFileName, IconIndex, IconLabel, Link)
Picture	AddPicture(FileName, LinkToFile, SaveWithDocument, Left, Top, Width, Height)
Placeholder	AddPlaceholder(Type, Left, Top, Width, Height)
Polyline	AddPolyline(SafeArrayOfPoints)
Shape	AddShape(Type, Left, Top, Width, Height)
Table	AddTable(NumRows, NumColumns, Left, Top, Width, Height)
Textbox	AddTextbox(Orientation, Left, Top, Width, Height)
Title	AddTitle
WordArt object	AddTextEffect(PresetTextEffect, Text, FontName, FontSize, FontBold, FontItalic, Left, Top)

SHARED ARGUMENTS FOR ADDING SHAPES

These are the arguments that are shared among various Shape-adding methods:

◆ BeginX and EndX are required Single arguments (arguments of the Single type) that specify the horizontal starting position and ending position of the connector or line, measured in points from the left edge of the slide.

◆ BeginY and EndY are required Single arguments that specify the vertical starting point and ending point of the connector or line, measured in points from the top of the slide.

◆ FileName is a required String argument used to specify the file to be used for creating the object (for example, the media file for creating a media object).

◆ Left is a required Single argument that specifies the position of the left edge of the shape from the left edge of the slide, measured in points. Top is a required Single argument that specifies the position of the top edge of the shape from the top edge of the slide, measured in points.

◆ Height is a required Single argument that specifies the height of the shape, measured in points. Width is a required Single argument that specifies the width of the shape, measured in points.

- `LinkToFile` is on optional argument that you can set to `msoTrue` to link the picture to its source file.

- `NumColumns` and `NumRows` are required Long arguments that specify the number of columns and rows in the table you're adding.

- `Orientation` is a required argument that specifies the orientation: `msoTextOrientationHorizontal` (horizontal) or `msoTextOrientationVerticalFarEast` (vertical).

- `SafeArrayOfPoints` is a required Variant argument that supplies an array of coordinate pairs that give the vertices and control points of a curve or polyline. The line begins at the first pair of coordinates and ends at the last pair.

- `SaveWithDocument` is a required argument that controls whether PowerPoint saves the linked picture in the presentation (`msoTrue`) or not (`msoFalse`). If you set `LinkToFile:=msoFalse`, you must set `SaveWithDocument:=msoTrue`.

TYPE ARGUMENT FOR ADDING SHAPES

The Type argument is different for the various methods that use it:

- `Type` for the `AddPlaceholder` method is a required argument that specifies the type of placeholder to add. The names are self-explanatory: `ppPlaceholderBitmap`, `ppPlaceholderBody`, `ppPlaceholderCenterTitle`, `ppPlaceholderChart`, `ppPlaceholderDate`, `ppPlaceholderFooter`, `ppPlaceholderHeader`, `ppPlaceholderMediaClip`, `ppPlaceholderObject`, `ppPlaceholderOrgChart`, `ppPlaceholderSlideNumber`, `ppPlaceholderSubtitle`, `ppPlaceholderTable`, `ppPlaceholderTitle`, `ppPlaceholderVerticalBody`, or `ppPlaceholderVerticalTitle`.

WARNING   You can use the `ppPlaceholderVerticalBody` and `ppPlaceholderVerticalTitle` placeholders only on slides that use vertical text—the slide layouts `ppLayoutVerticalText`, `ppLayoutClipArtAndVerticalText`, `ppLayoutVerticalTitleAndText`, and `ppLayoutVerticalTitleAndTextOverChart`.

- `Type` for the `AddCallout` method is a required argument that specifies the type of callout line to add: `msoCalloutOne` (a one-segment line that can be vertical or horizontal), `msoCalloutTwo` (a one-segment line that rotates freely), `msoCalloutThree` (a two-segment line), or `msoCalloutFour` (a three-segment line).

- `Type` for the `AddShape` method is a required argument that specifies the type of AutoShape to add. There are too many constants to list here, but most are easy to identify from their names. For example, `msoShapeHeart` is a heart shape, and `msoShapeLightningBolt` gives a lightning bolt. To see a list of the constants, search for the `AddShape` method in the Help file, and then click the link in the Type entry.

- `Type` for the `AddDiagram` method is a required argument that specifies the diagram type: `msoDiagramCycle` (a cycle diagram), `msoDiagramOrgChart` (an org chart), `msoDiagramPyramid` (a pyramid diagram), `msoDiagramRadial` (a radial diagram), `msoDiagramTarget` (a target diagram), or `msoDiagramVenn` (a Venn diagram).

ARGUMENTS SPECIFIC TO THE *ADDTEXTEFFECT* METHOD

The following arguments apply only to the AddTextEffect method:

◆ PresetTextEffect is a required argument that specifies the preset text effect to use. These preset text effects are identified by the constants msoTextEffect1 through msoTextEffect30, which correspond to the order in which the samples appear in the WordArt Gallery dialog box (1 through 6 are the first row, 7 through 12 the second row, and so on).

◆ Text is a required String argument that specifies the text to use in the WordArt object.

◆ FontBold is a required argument that you set to msoTrue to make the font bold or msoFalse to make it not bold.

◆ FontItalic is a required argument that you set to msoTrue to make the font italic and msoFalse to make it not italic.

◆ FontName is a required String argument that specifies the font name to use.

◆ FontSize is a required Single argument that specifies the font size to use.

ARGUMENTS SPECIFIC TO THE *ADDOLEOBJECT* METHOD

The following arguments apply only to the AddOLEObject method:

◆ ClassName is an optional String argument that specifies the program ID (the ProgID) or OLE long class name for the object. You must use either ClassName or FileName, but not both. In most cases, it's easiest to use FileName.

◆ DisplayAsIcon is an optional argument that you can set to msoTrue to display the OLE object as an icon rather than as itself (the default).

◆ IconFileName is an optional String argument that you can use with DisplayAsIcon:=True to specify the filename of the icon you want to display for the object.

◆ IconIndex is an optional Integer argument that specifies the index of the icon to use within the icon file specified by IconFileName. If you omit the IconIndex argument, VBA uses the second icon in the icon file, the icon at position 1 (the first icon in the file is at position 0).

◆ IconLabel is an optional String argument that you can use to specify the caption (or label) to display under the icon.

◆ Link is an optional argument that you can set to msoTrue to link the OLE object to its source file when you use the FileName argument. Link must be msoFalse when you use ClassName to specify a class name.

AN EXAMPLE OF USING THE *ADDSHAPE* METHOD

The following statement uses the AddShape method to add a bent-up arrow to the upper-right corner of the penultimate slide in the active presentation:

```
ActivePresentation.Slides(ActivePresentation.Slides.Count - 1) _
    .Shapes.AddShape Type:=msoShapeBentUpArrow, Left:=575, Top:=10, _
    Width:=150, Height:=75
```

An Example of Using the *AddTextEffect* Method

The following example inserts a blank slide after the last slide in the presentation and then uses the AddTextEffect method to add a WordArt item with the text Questions and Answers (on three lines) on it. The WordArt item uses 54-point bold ITC Avant Garde Gothic.

```
Dim QASlide As Slide
With myPresentation
    Set QASlide = .Slides.Add(Index:=.Slides.Count + 1, Layout:=ppLayoutBlank)
    QASlide.Shapes.AddTextEffect PresetTextEffect:=msoTextEffect28, _
        Text:="Questions" + Chr$(CharCode:=13) + _
        "and" + Chr$(CharCode:=13) + "Answers", _
        FontName:="ITC Avant Garde Gothic", FontSize:=54, FontBold:=msoTrue, _
        FontItalic:=msoFalse, Left:=230, Top:=125
End With
```

An Example of Using the *AddTextbox* Method

The following example adds a text box to the eighth slide in the presentation identified by the object variable myPresentation and assigns text to it:

```
Dim myTextBox As Shape
With myPresentation.Slides(8)
    Set myTextBox = .Shapes.AddTextbox _
        (Orientation:=msoTextOrientationHorizontal, Left:=100, Top:=50, _
        Width:=400, Height:=100)
    myTextBox.TextFrame.TextRange.Text = "Corrective Lenses"
End With
```

Deleting a Shape

To delete a shape, use the Delete method with the appropriate Shape object. For example, the following statement deletes the first Shape object on the second slide in the active presentation:

```
ActivePresentation.Slides(2).Shapes(1).Delete
```

Selecting All Shapes

To select all the shapes on a slide, use the SelectAll method of the appropriate Shapes collection. For example, the following statement selects all the Shape objects on the last slide in the presentation identified by the object variable myPresentation:

```
myPresentation.Slides(myPresentation.Slides.Count).Shapes.SelectAll
```

Repositioning and Resizing a Shape

To reposition a shape, set its Left property (to specify the distance in points from the left edge of the slide to the left edge of the shape) and its Top property (to specify the distance in points from the top edge of the slide to the top edge of the shape).

To change the size of a shape, set its `Width` and `Height` properties to the appropriate number of points.

For example, the following statements position the first shape on the first slide in the active presentation 200 points from the left of the slide and 100 points from its top and make the shape 300 points wide by 200 points high:

```
With ActivePresentation.Slides(1).Shapes(1)
    .Left = 200
    .Top = 100
    .Width = 300
    .Height = 200
End With
```

You can also move a shape by using the `IncrementLeft` method and the `IncrementTop` method and rotate the shape by using the `IncrementRotation` method. Each of these methods takes an `Increment` argument:

◆ For the `IncrementLeft` and `IncrementTop` methods, the `Increment` argument specifies the number of points to move the shape. A negative number moves the shape to the left or upward, while a positive number moves the shape to the right or downward.

◆ For the `IncrementRotation` method, the `Increment` argument specifies the number of degrees to rotate the shape. A positive number rotates the shape clockwise; a negative number rotates the shape counterclockwise.

The following example works with the first shape on the third slide of the presentation identified by the object variable `myPresentation`, moving it 100 points to the left and 200 points down, and rotating it 90 degrees counterclockwise:

```
With myPresentation.Slides(3).Shapes(1)
    .IncrementLeft Increment:=-100
    .IncrementTop Increment:=200
    .IncrementRotation Increment:=-90
End With
```

Copying Formatting from One Shape to Another

Often, it's useful to be able to apply the same formatting to multiple shapes. When one shape has the formatting you need, you can use the `PickUp` method of the `Shape` object to pick up the formatting from that shape and then use the `Apply` method to apply that formatting to another shape.

Neither the `PickUp` method nor the `Apply` method uses any arguments. The following example copies the formatting from the first shape on the second slide in the active presentation and applies it to the third shape on the fourth slide:

```
With ActivePresentation
    .Slides(2).Shapes(1).PickUp
    .Slides(4).Shapes(3).Apply
End With
```

Working with Text in a Shape

The text within a shape is contained in a TextRange object, which itself is contained in a TextFrame object. To work with the text in a shape, you use the TextFrame property of the Shape object to return the TextFrame object and then use the TextRange property of the TextFrame object to return the TextRange object. Within the TextRange object, the Text property contains the text, the Font object contains the font formatting, the ParagraphFormat object contains the paragraph formatting, and the ActionSettings collection contains the action settings for the text range.

FINDING OUT WHETHER A SHAPE HAS A TEXT FRAME

Not every shape has a text frame, so it's a good idea to check that the shape in which you're intending to manipulate text has a text frame. To do so, check that the HasTextFrame property of the Shape object is msoTrue—for example:

```
If ActivePresentation.Slides(1).Shapes(1).HasTextFrame = msoTrue Then
    MsgBox "The shape contains a text frame."
End If
```

You may also need to check whether the text frame contains text. To do so, check that the HasText property of the TextFrame object is msoTrue. For example:

```
With ActivePresentation.Slides(1).Shapes(1).TextFrame
    If .HasText = msoTrue Then MsgBox .TextRange.Text
End With
```

RETURNING AND SETTING THE TEXT IN A TEXT RANGE

To return or set the text in a text range, you can simply use the Text property of the TextRange object. For example, the following statement sets the text in the first shape on the first slide in the presentation identified by the object variable myPresentation to Strategic Planning Meeting:

```
myPresentation.Slides(1).Shapes(1).TextFrame.TextRange.Text _
    = "Strategic Planning Meeting"
```

You can also return parts of the text by using the Paragraphs method, the Sentences method, the Lines method, the Words method, the Characters method, or the Runs method. The syntax for these methods is shown here, using the Paragraphs method as the example:

```
expression.Paragraphs(Start, Length)
```

The components of the syntax are as follows:

◆ *expression* is a required expression that returns a TextRange object.

◆ Start is an optional Long argument that specifies the first item (paragraph, sentence, line, word, character, or text run) to return.

◆ Length is an optional Long argument that specifies how many items to return—for example, two paragraphs, three sentences, or four words.

NOTE A *text run* is a sequence of characters that have the same font formatting. Text runs can be useful for picking out parts of text ranges that are formatted in a particular way.

For example, the following statement returns the second through fifth words (the four words starting with the second word) from the first shape on the first slide in the active presentation:

```
MsgBox ActivePresentation.Slides(1).Shapes(1).TextFrame _
    .TextRange.Words(Start:=2, Length:=4)
```

The following statement sets the text of the second paragraph in the second shape on the sixth slide in the presentation identified by the object variable myPresentation to VP of Business Development:

```
myPresentation.Slides(6).Shapes(2).TextFrame.TextRange _
    .Paragraphs(Start:=2, Length:=1).Text = "VP of Business Development"
```

FORMATTING THE TEXT IN A TEXT RANGE

To format the text in a text range, use the ParagraphFormat object to control the paragraph formatting (including the alignment and the space before and after) and the Font object to control the font formatting.

The most useful properties of the ParagraphFormat object are these:

◆ The Alignment property controls the alignment. Use ppAlignLeft for left alignment, ppAlignCenter for centering, ppAlignJustify for justified alignment, ppAlignDistribute for distributed alignment (justified using all available space), or ppAlignRight for right alignment.

◆ The Bullet property returns the BulletFormat object, which represents the bullet formatting. See the next section for details.

◆ The LineRuleBefore property, the LineRuleAfter property, and the LineRuleWithin property determine whether the measurements set by the SpaceBefore property, the SpaceAfter property, and the SpaceWithin property use lines (msoTrue) or points (msoFalse).

◆ The SpaceBefore property and the SpaceAfter property control the amount of space before and after each paragraph. The SpaceWithin property controls the amount of space between base lines in a paragraph. All measurements are in points.

The following example sets left alignment, 18 points of spacing before and after paragraphs, and 12 points of spacing between lines, for the second shape on the slide identified by the object variable mySlide:

```
With mySlide.Shapes(2).TextFrame.TextRange.ParagraphFormat
    .Alignment = ppAlignLeft
    .LineRuleAfter = msoFalse
    .SpaceAfter = 18
    .LineRuleBefore = msoFalse
    .SpaceBefore = 18
    .LineRuleWithin = msoFalse
    .SpaceWithin = 12
End With
```

FORMATTING THE BULLETS FOR A TEXT RANGE

Bullets and numbers are vital to many PowerPoint slides. To control whether and how bullets and numbers appear, use the `Bullet` property of the `TextRange` object to return the `BulletFormat` object, and then work with the `BulletFormat` object's properties and methods.

To make bullets and numbers visible, set the `Visible` property of the `BulletFormat` object to `msoTrue`; to hide bullets and numbers, set `Visible` to `msoFalse`.

To specify which type of bullet or numbering to use, set the `Type` property of the `BulletFormat` object to `ppBulletUnnumbered` (for a bullet), `ppBulletNumbered` (numbers), `ppBulletPicture` (for a picture), or `ppBulletNone` (no bullet).

NOTE   The `Type` property of the `BulletFormat` object returns the value `ppBulletMixed` when the selection includes multiple types of bullets. You can't set `Type` to `ppBulletMixed`.

To specify the bullet character, use the `Character` property and the character number (you can learn the character number from the Symbol dialog box or the Character Map applet, which you can run by choosing Start ➢ All Programs ➢ Accessories ➢ System Tools ➢ Character Map). Use the `Font` property to specify the font name, size, and color. The following example sets the bullet for the first shape on the slide identified by the object variable `mySlide` to Wingdings character 254, a check box, using the color white (`RGB(255, 255, 255)`) and 44-point size:

```
With mySlide.Shapes(1).TextFrame.TextRange.ParagraphFormat.Bullet
    .Type = ppBulletUnnumbered
    .Character = 254
    With .Font
        .Name = "Wingdings"
        .Size = 44
        .Color = RGB(255, 255, 255)
    End With
End With
```

To use a picture as a bullet, set the `Type` property of the `BulletFormat` object to `ppBulletPicture` and then use the `Picture` method with the `Picture` argument, a required String argument that specifies the path and filename of the file to use as the bullet. You can use most types of graphics files, including BMP, EPS, GIF, JPG, JPEG, PCX, PNG, TIFF, and WMF files. The following example uses the file `Face1.jpg` stored in the folder `Z:\Public\Pictures` as the bullet for the first shape on the slide identified by the object variable `mySlide`:

```
With mySlide.Shapes(1).TextFrame.TextRange.ParagraphFormat.Bullet
    .Type = ppBulletPicture
    .Picture Picture:="z:\Public\Pictures\Face1.jpg"
End With
```

Setting an Animation for a Shape or a Range of Shapes

To set an animation for a shape or a range of shapes, use the `AnimationSettings` property of the `Shape` object or the `ShapeRange` object to return the `AnimationSettings` object.

To specify the animation effect to use, set the `EntryEffect` property to the constant for the effect. There are too many constants to list here, but their names are easy to work out from the names in the

Custom Animation pane in PowerPoint. For example, the `ppEffectFlyFromRight` constant represents the Fly In animation with the From Right direction.

To make the animation occur, set the `Animate` property to `msoTrue`. (To turn off an animation, set `Animate` to `msoFalse`.)

To control how the text in a shape is animated, set the `TextLevelEffect` property to `ppAnimateLevelNone` (no animation), `ppAnimateByFirstLevel`, `ppAnimateBySecondLevel`, `ppAnimateByThirdLevel`, `ppAnimateByFourthLevel`, `ppAnimateByFifthLevel`, or `ppAnimateByAllLevels`.

If you set `TextLevelEffect` to any value other than `ppAnimateByAllLevels` or `ppAnimateLevelNone`, you can use the `TextUnitEffect` property to specify how to animate the text. Use `ppAnimateByParagraph` to animate by paragraph, `ppAnimateByWord` to animate by word, or `ppAnimateByCharacter`.

To reverse the order of the animation, set the `AnimateTextInReverse` property to `msoTrue`. (The default is `msoFalse`.)

To control how the animation advances, set the `AdvanceMode` property to `ppAdvanceOnTime` (for automatic advancing using a timing) or `ppAdvanceOnClick` (for manual advancing). If you use automatic advancing, use the `AdvanceTime` property to specify the number of seconds to wait before advancing.

To play a preset sound effect with the transition, use the `SoundEffect` property of the `AnimationSettings` object to return the `SoundEffect` object, use the `Name` property to specify the name of the sound effect, and then use the `Play` method to play the sound effect. You can also play a separate sound file by using the `ImportFromFile` method of the `SoundEffect` object and using the `FullName` argument to specify the path and filename of the sound file.

To control how a media clip is played, use the `PlaySettings` property of the `AnimationSettings` object to return the `PlaySettings` object. For example, if you want the sound to loop until the next sound, set the `LoopSoundUntilNext` property of the `PlaySettings` object within the `AnimationSettings` object to `msoTrue`. The default value is `msoFalse`.

The following example applies a custom animation to the first shape on the slide identified by the object variable `mySlide`. The animation uses the entry effect Fly In from the right, plays a sound effect from a file, animates the text by first-level paragraphs and by whole paragraphs, and advances when the user clicks.

```
With mySlide.Shapes(1).AnimationSettings
    .EntryEffect = ppEffectFlyFromRight
    .AdvanceMode = ppAdvanceOnClick
    .SoundEffect.ImportFromFile FileName:="D:\Media\Whistle4.wav"
    .TextLevelEffect = ppAnimateByFirstLevel
    .TextUnitEffect = ppAnimateByParagraph
End With
```

Working with Headers and Footers

PowerPoint uses `HeaderFooter` objects to represent the headers, footers, slide numbers, and date and time on slides. The `HeaderFooter` objects are organized into the `HeadersFooters` collection, which you access through the `HeaderFooters` property of the `Master` object, a `Slide` object, or a `SlideRange` collection.

NOTE Notes pages have no HeaderFooter objects. Notes masters and handout masters have headers, but the other objects do not.

Returning the Header or Footer Object You Want

To return the object you want, use the appropriate property of the HeaderFooter object:

◆ Use the DateAndTime property to return the date and time.

◆ Use the Footer property to return the footer.

◆ Use the Header property to return the header on a notes page or handout.

◆ Use the SlideNumber property to return the slide number on a slide or the page number on a notes page or a handout.

The following example uses the Footer property to set the text of the HeaderFooter object of the SlideMaster object. Making a change to the slide master effects that change on all slides that use the master.

```
myPresentation.SlideMaster.HeadersFooters.Footer.Text = "Sentience 102"
```

Displaying or Hiding a Header or Footer Object

To display the HeaderFooter object, set its Visible property to msoTrue. To hide the HeaderFooter object, set its Visible property to msoFalse. For example, the following statement hides the footer on the fifth slide in the active presentation:

```
ActivePresentation.Slides(5).HeadersFooters.Footer.Visible = msoFalse
```

Setting the Text in a Header or Footer

To set the text that you want in a HeaderFooter object, assign a string containing the text to the object's Text property. For example, the following statement sets the text of the footer of the fifth slide in the active presentation to Confidential:

```
ActivePresentation.Slides(5).HeadersFooters.Footer.Text = "Confidential"
```

Setting the Format for Date and Time Headers and Footers

If your slides, notes pages, or handouts use dates and times in their footers or headers, use the Format property to specify how the dates and times should appear. Table 25.2 lists the constants you can use.

TABLE 25.2: Format Property Constants for Date and Time Headers and Footers

FORMAT	EXAMPLE
ppDateTimedddddMMMMddyyyy	Thursday, October 05, 2006
ppDateTimedMMMMyyyy	5 October 2006

TABLE 25.2: Format Property Constants for Date and Time Headers and Footers *(CONTINUED)*

FORMAT	EXAMPLE
ppDateTimedMMMyy	5-Oct-06
ppDateTimeHmm	10:17
ppDateTimehmmAMPM	10:17 AM
ppDateTimeHmmss	10:17:16
ppDateTimehmmssAMPM	10:17:16 AM
ppDateTimeMdyy	10/5/2006
ppDateTimeMMddyyHmm	10/5/2006 10:17 AM
ppDateTimeMMddyyhmmAMPM	10/5/2006 10:17:16 AM
ppDateTimeMMMMdyyyy	October 5, 2006
ppDateTimeMMMMyy	October 06
ppDateTimeMMyy	Oct-06

Set the UseFormat property of the HeaderFooter to msoTrue if you want the date and time to be updated automatically. Set UseFormat to msoFalse if you want the date and time to remain unchanged.

The following section shows an example of using the UseFormat property and the format property of a HeaderFooter object.

Standardizing All the Headers and Footers in a Presentation

If you write procedures that assemble presentations by taking slides from various existing presentations, or if your colleagues are prone to using inconsistent headers and footers in their presentations, you may need to standardize all the headers and footers in a presentation. The following example clears the existing headers and footers, ensures that all slides display the shapes that are on the slide master, and applies a header and footer to all the slides in the presentation:

```
Sub Standardize_Headers_and_Footers()

    Dim myPresentation As Presentation, mySlide As Slide
    Set myPresentation = ActivePresentation

    For Each mySlide In myPresentation.Slides
        mySlide.HeadersFooters.Clear
        mySlide.DisplayMasterShapes = msoTrue
    Next mySlide
    With myPresentation.SlideMaster.HeadersFooters
```

```
        With .Footer
            .Visible
            .Text = "Company Confidential"
        End With
        With .DateAndTime
            .Visible = True
            .UseFormat = True
            .Format = ppDateTimeMMMMYy
        End With
    End With

End Sub
```

Setting Up and Running a Slide Show

Not only can you assemble and format a slide show using VBA, but you can also run it using VBA. To set up a slide show, use the `SlideShowSettings` property of the `Presentation` object to return the `SlideShowSettings` object. When you run the slide show, VBA creates a `SlideShowWindow` object, which you can then manipulate to control the slide show.

Controlling the Show Type

To specify the type of show, set the `ShowType` property of the `SlideShowSettings` object to `ppShowTypeSpeaker` (for a standard full-screen presentation presented by a speaker), `ppShowTypeKiosk` (for a kiosk presentation), or `ppShowTypeWindow` (for a "browsed by an individual" presentation that appears in a window). For a show in a window, you can use the `Left` and `Top` properties to specify the position of the upper-left corner of the window and the `Height` and `Width` properties to specify its size.

To control whether animation and narration are used, set the `ShowWithAnimation` property and the `ShowWithNarration` property of the `SlideShowSettings` object to `msoTrue` or `msoFalse`.

To control whether the presentation loops until stopped, set the `LoopUntilStopped` property of the `SlideShowSettings` object to `msoTrue` or `msoFalse`.

To control how the presentation advances, set the `AdvanceMode` property to `ppSlideShowManualAdvance` (for manual advancing), `ppSlideShowUseSlideTimings` (for automatic advancing using timings already set), or `ppSlideShowRehearseNewTimings` (to rehearse new timings while the show plays).

The following example sets the active presentation running as a kiosk presentation that will advance automatically using its timings and loop until it is stopped:

```
With ActivePresentation.SlideShowSettings
    .LoopUntilStopped = msoCTrue
    .AdvanceMode = ppSlideShowUseSlideTimings
    .ShowType = ppShowTypeKiosk
    .Run
End With
```

The following example sets the presentation named Corporate.ppt running in speaker (full-screen) mode, sizing the image to 800×600 pixels and positioning it at the upper-left corner of the screen. The show uses manual advancing:

```
With Presentations("Corporate.ppt").SlideShowSettings
    .LoopUntilStopped = msoFalse
    .ShowType = ppShowTypeSpeaker
    .AdvanceMode = ppSlideShowManualAdvance
    With .Run
        .Height = 600
        .Width = 800
        .Left = 0
        .Top = 0
    End With
End With
```

Creating a Custom Show

Custom shows within a presentation are represented by the NamedSlideShows collection within the SlideShowSettings object. Use the NamedSlideShows property of the SlideShowSettings object to return the NamedSlideShows collection.

To create a custom show, use the Add method of the NamedSlideShows collection. The syntax is

```
expression.Add(Name, SafeArrayOfSlideIDs)
```

Here, *expression* is a required expression that returns a NamedSlideShows object. Name is a required String argument that specifies the name to assign to the new custom show. SafeArrayOfSlideIDs is a required Variant that specifies the numbers or names of the slides to include in the custom show.

For example, the following statements declare an array of the Long data type, assign to it slides 2, 4, 5, and 10 from the open presentation named Corporate.ppt, and create a new custom show named Short Show using the array:

```
Dim myArray(4) As Long
With Presentations("Corporate.ppt")
    myArray(1) = .Slides(2).SlideID
    myArray(2) = .Slides(4).SlideID
    myArray(3) = .Slides(5).SlideID
    myArray(4) = .Slides(10).SlideID
    .SlideShowSettings.NamedSlideShows.Add Name:"Short Show", _
        safeArrayOfSlideIDs:=myArray
End With
```

Deleting a Custom Show

To delete a custom show, use the Delete method with the appropriate NamedSlideShow object. For example, the following statement deletes the custom show named Overview from the active presentation:

```
ActivePresentation.SlideShowSettings.NamedSlideShows("Overview").Delete
```

Starting a Slide Show

To start a slide show using the whole presentation, use the `Run` method of the `SlideShowSettings` object. For example, the following statement starts the slide show running in the presentation identified by the object variable `myPresentation`:

```
myPresentation.SlideShowSettings.Run
```

To show only a range of slides from a presentation, set the `RangeType` property of the `SlideShowSettings` object to `ppShowSlideRange`, use the `StartingSlide` property of the `SlideShowSettings` object to specify the first slide and the `EndingSlide` property to specify the last slide, and then use the `Run` method to run the presentation. The following example shows slides 4 through 8 in the presentation named `Corporate.ppt`:

```
With Presentations("Corporate.ppt").SlideShowSettings
    .RangeType = ppShowSlideRange
    .StartingSlide = 4
    .EndingSlide = 8
    .Run
End With
```

To start running a custom show, set the `RangeType` property of the `SlideShowSettings` object to `ppShowNamedSlideShow`, use the `SlideShowName` property to specify the name of the custom show, and then use the `Run` method to run the custom show. The following example shows the custom show named `Short Show` in the active presentation:

```
With ActivePresentation.SlideShowSettings
    .RangeType = ppShowNamedSlideShow
    .SlideShowName = "Short Show"
    .Run
End With
```

When you start a slide show, VBA creates a `SlideShowWindow` object representing the object. You can access the `SlideShowWindow` object either through the `SlideShowWindows` collection (a creatable object that contains a `SlideShowWindow` object for each open slide show) or through the `SlideShowWindow` property of the `Presentation` object. If you know which presentation is running, it's easier to go through the appropriate `Presentation` object.

Changing the Size and Position of the Slide Show

To find out whether a slide show is displayed full screen or in a window, check the `IsFullScreen` property of the `SlideShowWindow` object. If the `IsFullScreen` property returns -1, the presentation is full screen; if the property returns 0, the presentation is a window.

To set the height and width of the slide show window in pixels, use the `Height` property and the `Width` property. To set its position, use the `Top` property to specify the distance in pixels of the top edge of the presentation from the top of the window or screen and the `Left` property to specify the distance in pixels of the left edge of the presentation from the left edge of the window or the screen.

Moving from Slide to Slide

Apart from controlling the position and size of the presentation, most of the actions you can take with it involve the View object. To find out which slide is displayed, return the CurrentShowPosition property:

```
MsgBox ActivePresentation.SlideShowWindow.View.CurrentShowPosition
```

To display the first slide in the presentation, use the First method. To display the last slide, use the Last method:

```
ActivePresentation.SlideShowWindow.View.First
ActivePresentation.SlideShowWindow.View.Last
```

To display the next slide, use the Next method. To display the previous slide, use the Previous method. For example:

```
ActivePresentation.SlideShowWindow.View.Previous
```

To display a particular slide in the slide show, use the GotoSlide method of the View object, using the Index argument to specify the slide number. For example, the following statement displays slide 5 in the first open slide show window:

```
Application.SlideShowWindows(1).View.GotoSlide Index:=5
```

Pausing the Show and Using White and Black Screens

To show a black screen, set the State property of the View object to ppSlideShowBlackScreen. To show a white screen, set the State property to ppSlideShowWhiteScreen.

```
ActivePresentation.SlideShowWindow.View.State = ppSlideShowBlackScreen
ActivePresentation.SlideShowWindow.View.State = ppSlideShowWhiteScreen
```

To toggle the black screen or white screen off and start the show running again, set the State property to ppSlideShowRunning.

To pause the presentation, set the State property of the View object to ppSlideShowPaused. To start the show again, set the State property to ppSlideShowRunning. For example:

```
With ActivePresentation.SlideShowWindow.View
    .State = ppSlideShowPaused
    .State = ppSlideShowRunning
End With
```

Starting and Stopping Custom Shows

To start a custom show running, use the GotoNamedShow method and use the SlideShowName argument to specify the name of the custom show. For example, the following statement starts the custom show named New Show running:

```
SlideShowWindows(1).GotoNamedShow SlideShowName:="New Show"
```

To exit a custom show, use the EndNamedShow method and then use the Next method to advance the presentation. PowerPoint then displays the first slide in the full presentation. For example:

```
With ActivePresentation.SlideShowWindow.View
    .EndNamedShow
    .Next
End With
```

Exiting the Slide Show

To exit the slide show, use the Exit method of the View property of the SlideShowWindow object. For example, the following statement exits the slide show in the active presentation:

```
ActivePresentation.SlideShowWindow.View.Exit
```

Chapter 26

Understanding the Outlook Object Model and Key Objects

◆ Getting an overview of the Outlook object model

◆ Understanding where Outlook stores VBA items

◆ Understanding Outlook's creatable objects and main user interface items

◆ Working with the Application object

◆ Understanding general methods for working with Outlook objects

◆ Working with messages

◆ Working with calendar items

◆ Working with tasks and task requests

◆ Searching for items

In this chapter, you'll start to get to grips with the Outlook object model and using VBA to manipulate Outlook. You'll learn where Outlook stores VBA items, meet the VBA objects for Outlook's creatable objects and main user interface items, and work with some of the main Outlook objects, from the Application object that represents the object through the objects that represent individual messages, calendar items, and tasks. You'll also learn how to search for items programmatically.

Getting an Overview of the Outlook Object Model

Many people find Outlook harder to get to grips with using VBA than other applications, and it's helpful to look at the Outlook object model to see which objects Outlook uses and how they're related. To see the Outlook object model, follow these steps:

1. Launch or activate Outlook, and then press Alt+F11 to launch or activate the Visual Basic Editor.

2. Choose Help ➢ Microsoft Visual Basic Help to display the Visual Basic Help task pane.

3. Type **outlook object model** in the Search text box, and then press Enter or click the Go button.

4. In the Search Results pane, click the Outlook Object Model entry. You'll see a Help screen (see Figure 26.1).

When you look at the Outlook Object Model entry on your screen (rather than in the figure), you'll see that some of the boxes are shaded yellow, while the others are shaded blue. The yellow boxes are objects that are organized into collections, while the blue objects are ones that do not have collections.

Click a box to see the help screen for the object, including a schematic of the related objects in the object model. Figure 26.2 shows the Help screen for the Inspectors collection, which contains details of the Inspector objects available in Outlook.

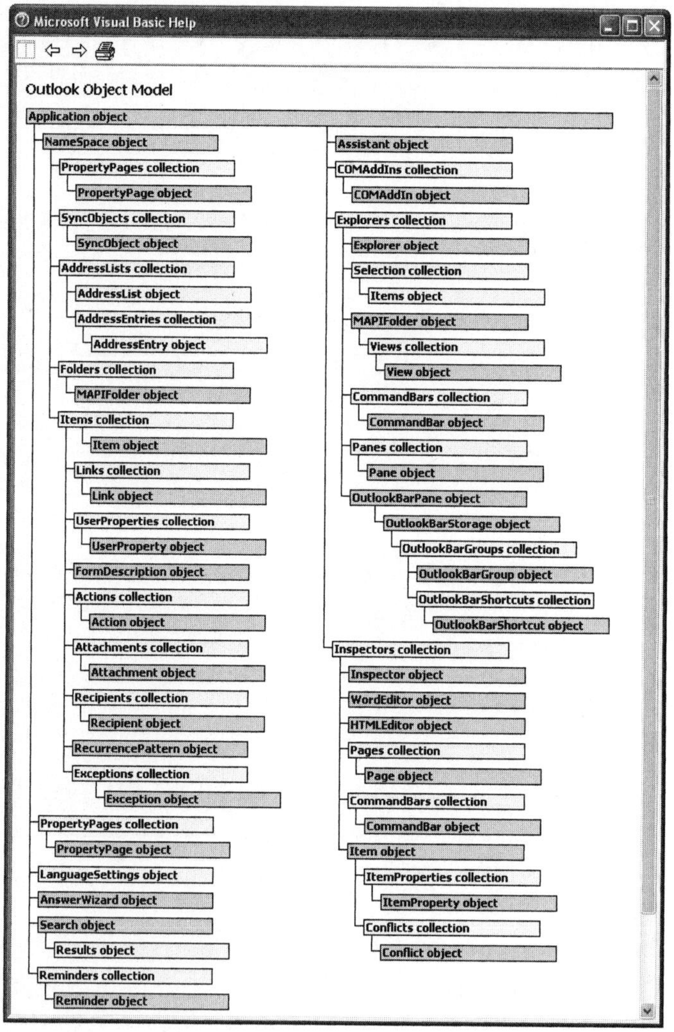

FIGURE 26.1
The Outlook Object Model screen in the Help file shows you how the Outlook objects are related to each other. This is the object model for Outlook 2003. You can click an object to see details about it.

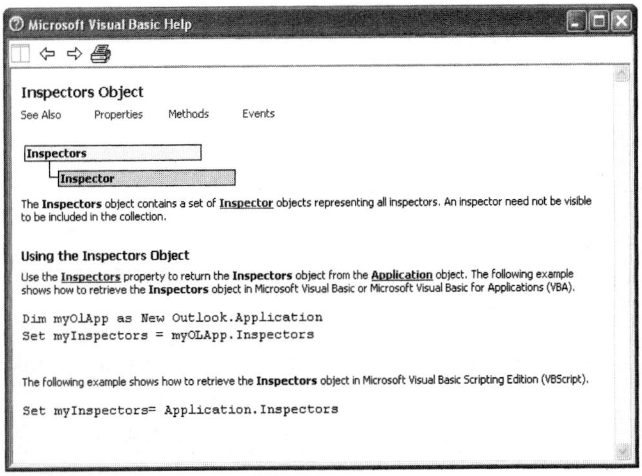

FIGURE 26.2
The Help screen for an individual object or collection includes a diagram showing the objects to which it's related.

FIGURE 26.2
The Help screen for an individual object or collection includes a diagram showing the objects to which it's related.

Understanding Where Outlook Stores VBA Items

As you've seen earlier in this book, Word and Excel let you store VBA projects either in a global location (the `Normal.dot` template in Word or the Personal Macro Workbook in Excel) or in individual templates or document files, while PowerPoint lets you store VBA projects in presentation files and templates. Outlook, by contrast, doesn't let you store VBA projects in individual items (such as e-mail messages or contacts). Instead, Outlook uses a single VBA project called `VbaProject.OTM`, which is stored in the `%userprofile%\Application Data\Microsoft\Outlook` folder.

NOTE   `%userprofile%` is a Windows environment variable that stores the path to the folder that contains your user profile—folders and files with details of your preferences and settings for Windows and your applications.

Understanding Outlook's Creatable Objects and Main User Interface Items

The `Application` object represents the entire Outlook application, so you can access any Outlook object by going through the `Application` object. However, Outlook also exposes various creatable objects, allowing you to reach some of the objects in its object model without explicitly going through the `Application` object. These are the main creatable objects; you'll meet most of them in more detail later in this chapter and in the next chapter:

- The `Explorers` collection contains an `Explorer` object for each window that displays the contents of a folder.

- The `Inspectors` collection contains an `Inspector` object for each window that's open displaying an Outlook item.

- The `COMAddIns` collection contains a `COMAddIn` object for each COM (Component Object Model) add-in loaded in Outlook.

- The `Reminders` collection contains a `Reminder` object for each reminder.

The most prominent objects in the Outlook user interface are represented in VBA by items whose names reflect the object types. For example:

◆ The MailItem object represents a mail item.

◆ The ContactItem object represents a contact.

◆ The TaskItem object represents a task.

◆ The AppointmentItem object represents an appointment.

◆ The JournalItem object represents a journal entry.

◆ The NoteItem object represents a note.

You'll learn how to work with these objects later in this chapter and in the next chapter.

Working with the *Application* Object

You can have only one instance of Outlook running at a time. (By contrast, you can run multiple instances of Word or Excel at the same time.) You probably won't find this a limitation when you're working within Outlook, but when you create a procedure to automate Outlook from another application, you will need to check whether there is an instance of Outlook before you create an instance programmatically. (See Chapter 30 for instructions on accessing one application programmatically from another application.)

Working with the *NameSpace* Object

In order to perform many actions with Outlook items such as e-mail messages, tasks, or contacts programmatically, you use the GetNameSpace method of the Application object to return the NameSpace object that represents the root object of the data source. The syntax is

```
expression.GetNameSpace(Type)
```

Here, *expression* is a required expression that returns an Application object. Type is a required String argument that specifies the type of namespace you want to return. Outlook supports only the MAPI data source, so you always use Type:="MAPI" with the GetNameSpace method. For example, the following statement returns the NameSpace and uses the CurrentUser property to display the name of the current user in a message box:

```
MsgBox Application.GetNamespace("MAPI").CurrentUser
```

ACCESSING DEFAULT FOLDERS WITHIN THE *NAMESPACE* OBJECT

The NameSpace object contains the folders that Outlook uses—both the default folders used to store items such as e-mail messages, tasks, and contacts, and other folders created by the user or by custom procedures. These folders are represented in VBA by MAPIFolder objects that are organized into a Folders collection.

To access the default folders within the NameSpace object, you use the GetDefaultFolder method of the NameSpace object. The syntax is

```
expression.GetDefaultFolder(FolderType)
```

Here, *expression* is a required expression that returns a NameSpace object. FolderType is a required argument that specifies which default folder you want to return. The constants are self-explanatory: olFolderCalendar, olFolderContacts, olFolderDeletedItems, olFolderDrafts, olFolderInbox, olFolderJournal, olFolderNotes, olFolderOutbox, olFolderSentMail, olFolderTasks, or olPublicFoldersAllPublicFolders.

The following example creates the object variable myCal and assigns the default calendar folder to it:

```
Dim myCal As MAPIFolder
Set myCal = Application.GetNamespace("MAPI") _
    .GetDefaultFolder(FolderType:=olFolderCalendar)
```

ACCESSING OTHER FOLDERS WITHIN THE *NAMESPACE* OBJECT

Accessing the default folders in the NameSpace object via the GetDefaultFolder method is easy, but often you'll need to access other folders. To do so, use the Folders collection to access a folder.

The following example displays a message box (see Figure 26.3) containing a list of all the folders contained in the namespace:

```
Sub List_All_NameSpace_Folders()
    Dim myNS As NameSpace
    Dim myFolder As MAPIFolder
    Dim mySubfolder As MAPIFolder
    Dim strFolderList As String

    strFolderList = "Your Outlook NameSpace contains these folders:" _
        & vbCr & vbCr

    Set myNS = Application.GetNamespace("MAPI")
    With myNS
        For Each myFolder In myNS.Folders
            strFolderList = strFolderList & myFolder.Name & vbCr
            For Each mySubfolder In myFolder.Folders
                strFolderList = strFolderList & "*   " & mySubfolder.Name & vbCr
            Next mySubfolder
        Next myFolder

    End With
    MsgBox strFolderList, vbOKOnly + vbInformation, "Folders in NameSpace"

End Sub
```

CREATING A NEW FOLDER

To create a new folder, use the Add method with the Folders collection. The syntax is

```
expression.Add(Name, Type)
```

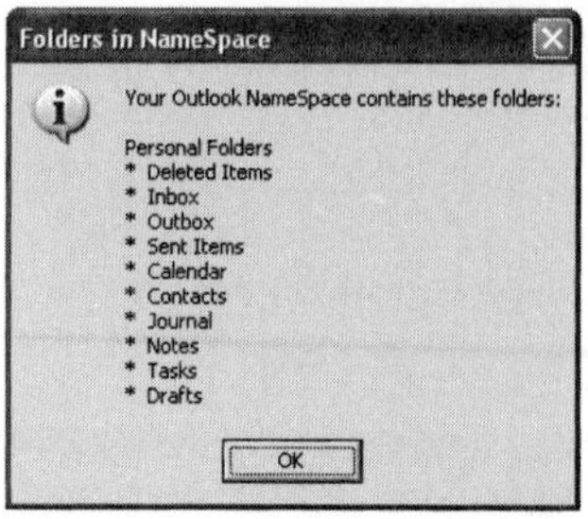

FIGURE 26.3

Listing the folders
contained in the
NameSpace object

Here, *expression* is a required expression that returns a `Folders` collection. `Name` is a required String argument that specifies the display name to assign to the new folder. `Type` is an optional Long argument that you can use to specify the type of folder to create: `olFolderCalendar`, `olFolderContacts`, `olFolderDrafts`, `olFolderInbox`, `olFolderJournal`, `olFolderNotes`, or `olFolderTasks`. If you omit `Type`, Outlook assigns the new folder the same type as its parent folder (the folder in which you create the new folder).

The following statement creates a new folder named `Personal Tasks` in the `Tasks` folder, assigning the new folder the `olFolderTasks` folder type explicitly for clarity:

```
Application.GetNamespace("MAPI").GetDefaultFolder(olFolderTasks) _
    .Folders.Add Name:="Personal Tasks", Type:=olFolderTasks
```

DELETING A FOLDER

To delete a folder, use the `Delete` method with the appropriate `MAPIFolder` object. This method takes no arguments. The following example deletes the folder named `Personal Tasks` in the `Tasks` folder:

```
Application.GetNamespace("MAPI").GetDefaultFolder(olFolderTasks) _
    .Folders("Personal Tasks").Delete
```

WARNING   Be careful when deleting objects with Outlook. First, Outlook doesn't request any confirmation before deleting an object. Second, the deletion is permanent.

Working with Inspectors and Explorers

VBA uses two major Outlook objects that most users wouldn't recognize from working with the Outlook user interface:

◆ An `Inspector` is an object that represents a window displaying an Outlook item, such as an e-mail message or an appointment.

◆ An `Explorer` object represents a window that displays the contents of a folder.

NOTE   Unlike with many collections, an `Explorer` object is included in the `Explorers` collection even if it is not visible.

OPENING AN INSPECTOR WINDOW

To open an inspector window for an object, use the `Display` method of the `Inspector` object. For example, the following statement displays an inspector window for the object referenced by the object variable `myItem`:

```
myItem.Display
```

RETURNING THE INSPECTOR ASSOCIATED WITH AN ITEM

To return the inspector associated with an item, use the `GetInspector` property of the appropriate object. The following example returns the inspector for the item identified by the object variable `myItem`:

```
myItem.GetInspector
```

RETURNING THE ACTIVE WINDOW, INSPECTOR, OR EXPLORER

Unlike Word, Excel, and PowerPoint, Outlook doesn't have an `ActiveWindow` object that represents the active window. However, Outlook's `Application` object does have an `ActiveWindow` method, which returns the topmost Outlook window. (If there is no window, `ActiveWindow` returns `Nothing`.) This window is either an `Inspector` object or an `Explorer` object. Similarly, the `ActiveExplorer` method of the `Application` object returns the active explorer, and the `ActiveInspector` method of the `Application` object returns the active inspector.

You can use the `TypeName` function to determine which type of window is active. The following example displays a message box that states which window type is active, as long as there is an active window:

```
If Not TypeName(ActiveWindow) = "Nothing" Then
    MsgBox "An " & TypeName(ActiveWindow) & " window is active."
End If
```

WORKING WITH THE ACTIVE INSPECTOR

In many procedures, you'll need to determine what the topmost inspector in the Outlook application is, either so that you can work with that inspector or so that you can restore this inspector to the topmost position at the end of a procedure that uses other inspectors. To return the topmost inspector, use the `ActiveInspector` method of the `Application` object. For example, the following statement maximizes the window of the topmost inspector:

```
Application.ActiveInspector.WindowState = olMaximized
```

There isn't always an active inspector in Outlook, so it's a good idea to make sure that there is an active inspector before you try to manipulate it. To do so, check that the `TypeName` function does not return `Nothing` when run on the `ActiveInspector` method of the `Application` object:

```
If TypeName(Application.ActiveInspector) = "Nothing" Then
    MsgBox "No item is open."
    End
End If
```

Creating Items

To create new items in Outlook, you use the `CreateItem` method or the `CreateItemFromTemplate` method of the `Application` object. The `CreateItem` method creates default items, while the `CreateItemFromTemplate` method creates items based on the templates you specify.

NOTE   You can also create new objects using a custom form. To do so, use the Add method with the `Items` collection.

USING THE *CREATEITEM* METHOD TO CREATE DEFAULT ITEMS

The syntax for the `CreateItem` method is

```
expression.CreateItem(ItemType)
```

Here, *expression* is a required expression that returns an `Application` object. `ItemType` is a required argument that specifies the type of item to create: `olAppointmentItem`, `olContactItem`, `olDistributionListItem`, `olJournalItem`, `olMailItem`, `olNoteItem`, `olPostItem`, or `olTaskItem`.

   The following example creates a new e-mail message; assigns a recipient (by setting the To property), a subject (by setting the `Subject` property), and body text (by setting the Body property); and then displays the message window:

```
Dim myMessage As MailItem
Set myMessage = Application.CreateItem(ItemType:=olMailItem)
With myMessage
    .To = "test@example.com"
    .Subject = "Test message"
    .Body = "This is a test message."
    .Display
End With
```

USING THE *CREATEITEMFROMTEMPLATE* METHOD TO CREATE ITEMS BASED ON TEMPLATES

Instead of creating a default item by using the `CreateItem` method, you can use the `CreateItemFromTemplate` method of the `Application` object to create a new item based on a template. The syntax for the `CreateItemFromTemplate` method is

```
expression.CreateItemFromTemplate(TemplatePath, InFolder)
```

Here, *expression* is a required expression that returns an `Application` object. `TemplatePath` is a required String argument that specifies the path and filename of the template on which to base the new item. `InFolder` is an optional Variant argument that you can use to specify the folder in which to create the item. If you omit the `InFolder` argument, Outlook creates the item in the default folder for that item type.

   The following example creates a new note item based on the custom template `Quick Note.oft` stored in the `\Application Data\Microsoft\Templates` folder within the user's user profile. The example then displays the new note item:

```
Dim myNoteItem As NoteItem
Set myNoteItem = Application.CreateItemFromTemplate _
    ("C:\Documents and Settings\Jana Cook\Application Data\" & _
    "Microsoft\Templates\Quick Note.oft")
myNoteItem.Display
```

Quitting Outlook

To quit Outlook, use the `Quit` method of the `Application` object. This method takes no arguments:

```
Application.Quit
```

NOTE You may also want to work with the events available to the `Application` object. See Chapter 27 for a discussion of how to work with these application-level events and with item-level events.

Understanding General Methods for Working with Outlook Objects

Many of the objects in Outlook use the following methods, which this section discusses in a communal section to save space. This section shows you brief examples of using the methods. You'll see further examples in the sections on the individual types of objects—e-mail messages, appointments, contacts, tasks, and so on—later in this chapter and in the next chapter.

Using the *Display* Method

To open an item in an inspector window, use the `Display` method. The syntax is

```
expression.Display(Modal)
```

Here, *expression* is a required expression that returns the type of object you want to display—for example, a `ContactItem` object or a `MailItem` object. `Modal` is an optional Variant argument that you can set to `True` to make the window modal instead of having it be modeless as it is by default or if you set `Modal` to `False`. Making the window modal means that the user must close the window before they can work with another window.

NOTE The `Modal` argument doesn't apply to the `Explorer` and `MAPIFolder` objects.

For example, the following statement uses the `Display` method to display the Inbox:

```
Application.GetNamespace("MAPI").GetDefaultFolder(olFolderInbox).Display
```

Using the *Close* Method

To close a window, use the `Close` method. The syntax is

```
expression.Close(SaveMode)
```

Here, *expression* is a required expression that returns the object you want to close. `SaveMode` is a required argument that specifies whether to save changes (`olSave`), discard the changes (`olDiscard`), or prompt the user to decide whether to save the changes (`olPromptForSave`).

The following example closes the active inspector and saves changes to its contents:

```
ActiveInspector.Close SaveMode:=olSave
```

Using the *Delete* Method

To delete an item, use the `Delete` method. This method takes no arguments. The following example deletes the item with the index number 1 in the Contacts folder:

```
Application.GetNamespace("MAPI").GetDefaultFolder(olFolderContacts) _
    .Items(1).Delete
```

Using the *PrintOut* Method

To print an item, use the `PrintOut` method. This method takes no arguments. The following example prints the item with the index number 1 in the Inbox:

```
Application.GetNamespace("MAPI").GetDefaultFolder(olFolderInbox) _
    .Items(1).PrintOut
```

Using the *Save* Method

To save an item, use the `Save` method. This method takes no arguments. The following example creates a new task; assigns it a subject, start date, and due date; turns off the reminder for the task; and then saves it:

```
Dim myTask As TaskItem
Set myTask = Application.CreateItem(ItemType:=olTaskItem)
With myTask
    .Subject = "Arrange Review Meeting"
    .StartDate = Date
    .DueDate = Date + 7
    .ReminderSet = False
    .Save
End With
```

Using the *SaveAs* Method

To save an item as a separate file, use the `SaveAs` method. The syntax is

```
expression.SaveAs(Path, Type)
```

Here, *expression* is a required expression that returns the object to be saved. `Path` is a required String argument that specifies the path and filename under which to save the file. `Type` is an optional Variant argument that you can use to control the file type used for the file, as shown in the following list:

Argument	Type of File
olHTML	HTML file
olMSG	Outlook message format (.msg file)
olRTF	Rich text format

Argument	Type of File
olTemplate	Template
olDoc	Word document format (e-mail messages using WordMail)
olTXT	Text file
olVCal	vCal file
olVCard	vCard file
olICal	iCal file
olMSGUnicode	Outlook Unicode message format (.msg file)

The following example saves the message open in the active inspector. If the IsWordMail property of the ActiveInspector object returns True, the example saves the message as a .doc file; if the IsWordMail property returns False, the example saves the message as an .rtf file. If no inspector window is active, the example displays a message box pointing out the problem to the user.

```
If TypeName(ActiveInspector) = "Nothing" Then
    MsgBox "This macro cannot run because " & _
        "there is no active window.", vbOKOnly, "Macro Cannot Run"
    End
Else
    If ActiveInspector.IsWordMail Then
        ActiveInspector.CurrentItem.SaveAs "c:\keep\message.doc"
    Else
        ActiveInspector.CurrentItem.SaveAs "c:\keep\message.rtf"
    End If
End If
```

Working with Messages

If you or your colleagues use Outlook's e-mail capabilities extensively, you may be able to save time by programming Outlook to create or process messages automatically. This section shows you how to create a new message, work with its contents, add an attachment, and send the message.

Creating a New Message

To create a new message, use the CreateItem method of the Application object and specify olMailItem for the ItemType argument. The following example creates a MailItem object variable named myMessage and assigns to it a new message:

```
Dim myMessage As MailItem
Set myMessage = Application.CreateItem(ItemType:=olMailItem)
```

Working with the Contents of a Message

To work with the contents of a message, set or get the appropriate properties. These are the most widely useful properties:

Property	Explanation
To	The recipient or recipients of the message.
CC	The recipient or recipients of carbon copies of the message.
BCC	The recipient or recipients of blind carbon copies of the message.
Subject	The subject line of the message.
Body	The body text of the message.
BodyFormat	The message's formatting type: olFormatPlain for text-only, olFormatRichText for text with formatting, and olFormatHTML for HTML formatting.
Importance	The importance of the message. Set it to olImportanceHigh, olImportanceNormal, or olImportanceLow.

The following example creates a new message item and assigns it to the object variable myMessage. It then adds an addressee, a subject, and body text; applies the HTML format; sets the importance to high; and sends the message:

```
Dim myMessage As MailItem
Set myMessage = Application.CreateItem(ItemType:=olMailItem)
With myMessage
    .To = "petra_smith@ourbigcompany.com"
    .Subject = "Preparation for Review"
    .Body = "Please drop by tomorrow and spend a few minutes" _
        & " discussing the materials we need for the review."
    .BodyFormat = olFormatHTML
    .Importance = olImportanceHigh
    .Send
End With
```

Adding an Attachment to a Message

To add an attachment to a message, use the Add method with the Attachments collection, which you return by using the Attachments property of the MailItem object. The syntax is

```
expression.Add(Source, Type, Position, DisplayName)
```

The components of the syntax are as follows:

◆ *expression* is a required expression that returns an Attachments collection.

◆ Source is a required String argument that specifies the path and filename of the attachment.

◆ Type is an optional String argument that you can use to specify the type of attachment.

◆ Position is an optional String argument that you can use with rich-text messages to specify the character at which the attachment is positioned in the text. Use character 0 to hide the attachment, 1 to position the attachment at the beginning of the message, or a higher value to position the attachment at the specified character position. To position the attachment at the end of the message, use a number higher than the number of characters in the message.

◆ DisplayName is an optional String argument that you can specify to control the name displayed for the attachment in the message.

The following example attaches to the message referenced by the object variable myMessage the file Corporate Downsizing.ppt stored in the folder Y:\Sample Documents, positioning the attachment at the beginning of the message and setting its display name to Downsizing Presentation:

```
myMessage.Attachments.Add _
    Source:="Y:\Sample Documents\Corporate Downsizing.ppt", _
    Position:=1, DisplayName:="Downsizing Presentation"
```

Sending a Message

To send a message, use the Send method. This method takes no arguments. The following example sends the message referenced by the object variable myMessage:

```
myMessage.Send
```

NOTE   The Send method applies to the AppointmentItem object, the MeetingItem object, and the TaskItem object as well as to the MailItem object.

To check whether a message has been sent, check its Sent property. This Boolean property returns True if the message has been sent and False if it has not.

Working with Calendar Items

If you create or receive many calendar items, you may be able to save time or streamline your scheduling by using VBA. This section shows you how to create a calendar item and work with its contents.

Creating a New Calendar Item

To create a new calendar item, use the CreateItem method of the Application object and specify olAppointmentItem for the ItemType argument. The following example creates an AppointmentItem object variable named myAppointment and assigns to it a new appointment item:

```
Dim myAppointment As AppointmentItem
Set myAppointment = Application.CreateItem(ItemType:=olAppointmentItem)
```

Working with the Contents of a Calendar Item

To work with the contents of a calendar item, set or get the appropriate properties. These are the most widely useful properties:

Property	Explanation
Subject	Subject of the appointment
Body	Body text of the appointment
Start	Start time of the appointment
End	End time of the appointment
BusyStatus	Your status during the appointment: olBusy, olFree, olOutOfOffice, or olTentative
Categories	The category or categories assigned to the item
ReminderSet	Whether the appointment has a reminder (True) or not (False)
ReminderMinutesBeforeStart	The number of minutes before the event that the reminder should occur

The following example creates a new AppointmentItem object and assigns it to the object variable myAppointment. It then sets the subject, body, start date (2:30 PM on the day seven days after the present date), end date (one hour after the start), marks the time as busy, assigns the Personal category, sets a reminder 30 minutes before the appointment, and saves the appointment:

```
Dim myAppointment As AppointmentItem
Set myAppointment = Application.CreateItem(ItemType:=olAppointmentItem)
With myAppointment
    .Subject = "Dentist"
    .Body = "Dr. Schmitt " & vbCr & "4436 Acacia Blvd."
    .Start = Str(Date + 7) & " 2.30 PM"
    .End = Str(Date + 7) & " 3.30 PM"
    .BusyStatus = olBusy
    .Categories = "Personal"
    .ReminderMinutesBeforeStart = 30
    .ReminderSet = True
    .Save
End With
```

TIP Assigning categories to an item programmatically can be difficult, especially because many users create custom categories or assign categories in an idiosyncratic manner. In many cases, it's better to allow the user to assign categories manually to an item by displaying the Categories dialog box at the appropriate point in the procedure. You can do so by using the ShowCategoriesDialog method of the item—for example, myAppointment.ShowCategoriesDialog for an item referenced by the object variable myAppointment.

Working with Tasks and Task Requests

You may also be able to save time and effort by using VBA to automate tasks and task requests. This section shows you how to create a task, work with the contents of a task item, and send a task request.

Creating a Task

To create a new task item, use the `CreateItem` method of the `Application` object and specify `olTaskItem` for the `ItemType` argument. The following example creates a `TaskItem` object variable named `myTask` and assigns to it a new task item:

```
Dim myTask As TaskItem
Set myTask = Application.CreateItem(ItemType:=olTaskItem)
```

Working with the Contents of a Task Item

To work with the contents of a task item, set or get the appropriate properties. These are the most widely useful properties:

Property	Explanation
Subject	Subject of the task.
Body	Body text of the task.
Start	Start time of the task.
DueDate	The due date of the task.
Importance	The importance of the task. Set it to `olImportanceHigh`, `olImportanceNormal`, or `olImportanceLow`.
Status	The status of the task: `olTaskNotStarted`, `olTaskWaiting`, `olTaskDeferred`, `olTaskInProgress`, or `olTaskComplete`.
PercentComplete	The percentage of the task completed.
Companies	The companies associated with the task.
BillingInformation	The company or department to bill for the task.

The following example creates a `TaskItem` object variable named `myTask` and assigns to it a new task item. It then sets the subject and body of the task, specifies a due date, sets the status to `olTaskInProgress` and the percentage complete to 10, specifies the company involved and who to bill, sets the importance to High, and then saves the task:

```
Dim myTask As TaskItem
Set myTask = Application.CreateItem(ItemType:=olTaskItem)
With myTask
    .Subject = "Create a business plan"
    .Body = "The business plan must cover the next four years." & _
        vbCr & vbCr & "It must provide a detailed budget, " & _
        "staffing projections, and a cost/benefit analysis."
    .DueDate = Str(Date + 28)
```

```
        .Status = olTaskInProgress
        .PercentComplete = 10
        .Companies = "Acme Polyglot Industrialists"
        .BillingInformation = "Sales & Marketing"
        .Importance = olImportanceHigh
        .Save
    End With
```

Assigning a Task to a Colleague

To assign a task to a colleague, use the `Assign` method of the `TaskItem` object, and then use the `Add` method of the `Recipients` collection to add one or more recipients. You can then use the `Send` method to send the task to your colleague.

The following example creates a task, uses the `Assign` method to indicate that it will be assigned, specifies a recipient, and sends the task:

```
Dim myTaskAssignment As TaskItem
Set myTaskAssignment = Application.CreateItem(ItemType:=olTaskItem)
With myTaskAssignment
    .Assign
    .Recipients.Add Name:="Peter Nagel"
    .Subject = "Buy Bagels for Dress-Down/Eat-Up Day"
    .Body = "It's your turn to get the bagels on Friday."
    .Body = .Body & vbCr & vbCr & "Remember: No donuts AT ALL."
    .DueDate = Str(Date + 3)
    .Send
End With
```

Searching for Items

To search for items, use the `AdvancedSearch` method of the `Application` object. The syntax is

expression`.AdvancedSearch(Scope, Filter, SearchSubFolders, Tag)`

The components of the syntax are as follows:

◆ *expression* is a required expression that returns an `Application` object.

◆ `Scope` is a required String argument that specifies the scope of the search (which items to search). Usually you'll search a particular folder. For example, you might search the Inbox for messages that match certain criteria, or you might search the `Tasks` folder for particular tasks.

◆ `Filter` is an optional Variant argument that specifies the search filter. While this argument is optional, you will need to use it unless you want to return all the items within the scope you've specified.

◆ `SearchSubFolders` is an optional Variant argument that you can set to `True` to search through any subfolders of the folder specified by the `Scope` argument or `False` to search only the specified folder. The default is `False`.

◆ `Tag` is an optional Variant argument that you can use to specify a name for the search you're defining. If you create a name, you can call the search again.

NOTE DASL is the abbreviation for DAV Search and Locating. DAV is the acronym for Distributed Authoring and Versioning. For more detail, see http://www.webdav.org/dasl/.

The complex part of performing an advanced search is creating the search filter, which needs to be in DASL format. If you have Outlook 2003 or a later version, you can have Outlook put together the filter for you. To do so, first put the Filter button on a toolbar:

1. In Outlook, choose Tools ➤ Customize to display the Customize dialog box. Click the Commands tab if it isn't already displayed.

2. In the Categories list box, click the View item.

3. In the Command list box, scroll down to the Filter command, and then drag it to a toolbar.

NOTE If you prefer, you can put the Filter command on a menu rather than on a toolbar.

4. Click the Close button to close the Customize dialog box.

Now you can display the Filter dialog box and put the filter together:

1. Click the Filter button on the toolbar to display the Filter dialog box (see Figure 26.4).

2. Use the controls on the Messages page, the More Choices page, and the Advanced page to specify the filter you want.

3. Click the SQL tab to display the SQL page, which contains the filter that you've created.

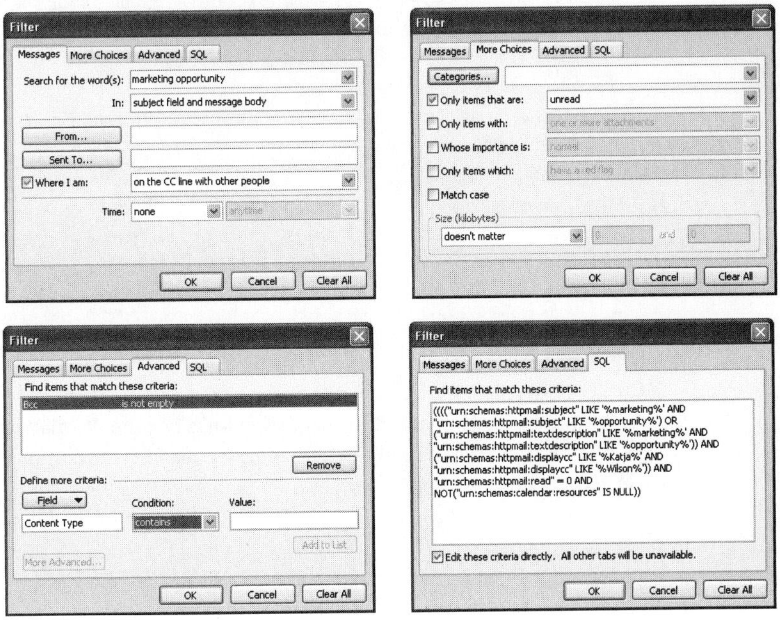

FIGURE 26.4

Use the Messages, More Choices, and Advanced pages of the Filter dialog box to put together the DASL filter needed for an advanced search. On the SQL tab, select the Edit These Criteria Directly. All Other Tabs Will Be Unavailable check box, select the filter, and then press Ctrl+C to copy it to the Clipboard so that you can paste it into the Visual Basic Editor.

4. Select the Edit These Criteria Directly. All Other Tabs Will Be Unavailable check box to make the Find Items That Meet These Criteria text box available.

5. Drag with the mouse to select the filter, and then press Ctrl+C to copy it to the Clipboard.

6. Click the Cancel button to close the Filter dialog box.

7. Press Alt+F11 to switch to the Visual Basic Editor, and then paste the filter into your code.

The following example searches the Inbox (Scope:="Inbox") for messages with the subject line Dam Project (Filter:="urn:schemas:mailheader:subject = 'Dam Project'"). If any messages are found, the procedure produces a list of sender names, which it assigns to the String variable strMessages. If no messages are found, the procedure assigns to strMessages text to let the user know this. The procedure then displays strMessages in a message box with the caption Search Results.

```
Sub Sample_Advanced_Search()

    Dim mySearch As Search
    Dim myResults As Results
    Dim intCounter As Integer
    Dim strMessages As String

    Set mySearch = AdvancedSearch(Scope:="Inbox", _
        Filter:="urn:schemas:mailheader:subject = 'Dam Project'")
    Set myResults = mySearch.Results
    If myResults.Count > 0 Then
        strMessages = "The Inbox contains messages that match " & _
            "the search criteria from these senders:" & vbCr & vbCr
    For intCounter = 1 To myResults.Count
        strMessages = strMessages & _
            myResults.Item(intCounter).SenderName & vbCr
    Next intCounter
    Else
        strMessages = "The Inbox contains no messages " & _
            "that match the search criteria."
    End If
    MsgBox strMessages, vbOKOnly, "Search Results"
End Sub
```

NOTE If necessary, you can run two or more searches at the same time. To do so, use the AdvancedSearch method in successive lines of code. While you can run up to 100 searches at the same time, doing so puts a considerable load on the computer and may make it run slowly or appear to stop responding.

Chapter 27

Working with Events in Outlook

- ◆ Working with application-level events
- ◆ Working with item-level events

If you want to automate the way that Outlook works, you may need to write code that responds to Outlook events. Outlook has two classes of events, application-level events and item-level events, which between them enable you to write code that responds to most occurrences in Outlook. In this chapter, you will learn how to work with both types of events, and you will see examples of some of the events.

NOTE In addition to the events discussed in this chapter, Outlook supports form events such as those discussed in "Using Events to Control Forms" in Chapter 15.

Working with Application-Level Events

An application-level event is an event that occurs to the Outlook application rather than to an individual item within it. For example, the Startup event is an application-level event that occurs when Outlook starts, and the Quit event is an application-level event that occurs when Outlook closes. By contrast, item-level events represent things that occur to individual items—for example, the opening of an e-mail message or a contact record, or a user's switching from one folder to another.

The application-level events are easier to access than the item-level events, because the Application object is the topmost object and is always available when Outlook is running. This means that you don't have to use an event handler to create the Application object in the way that you have to create objects for the item-level events.

To access the application-level events, you use the ThisOutlookSession class module. In the Visual Basic Editor, expand the Project1 item that represents the Outlook VBA project, expand the Microsoft Office Outlook item (in Office 2003) or the Microsoft Outlook Objects item (in Office XP or Office 2000), and then double-click the ThisOutlookSession item to open a Code window showing its contents. (If this is the first time you've opened the ThisOutlookSession class module, it will have no contents.)

Outlook 2003 supports the application-level events discussed in the following subsections. Outlook 2000 supports only the Startup, Quit, Reminder, ItemSend, NewMail, and OptionsPagesAdd application-level events. Outlook XP supports all the application-level events except the NewMailEx event.

NOTE Each of the events works with an Application object. For simplicity, most of the following examples use the Outlook Application object itself. You can also use an object variable that returns an Application object.

Using the *Startup* Event

The Startup event occurs when Outlook starts and takes no arguments. The Startup event is useful for making sure that Outlook is correctly configured for the user to start work. The following example creates a new NoteItem object (a note), assigns text to its Body property, and uses the Display item to display it:

```
Private Sub Application_Startup()
    Dim myNoteItem As NoteItem
    Set myNoteItem = Application.CreateItem(ItemType:=olNoteItem)
    myNoteItem.Body = "Please start a new time card for the day."
    myNoteItem.Display
End Sub
```

Using the *Quit* Event

The Quit event occurs when Outlook is closed, either by the user (for example, by choosing File ➤ Exit) or by using the Quit method of the Application object in VBA. When this event fires, all windows have been closed and all global variables have been released, so there's little left to do with this event. One possibility is to display a parting message to the user, as in the following example, which displays a message on the workday that precedes a national holiday to remind the user of the holiday:

```
Private Sub Application_Quit()

    Dim strMessage As String
    Select Case Format(Date, "MM/DD/YYYY")
        Case "01/13/2006"
            strMessage = "Next Monday is Martin Luther King Day."
        Case "02/17/2006"
            strMessage = "Next Monday is Presidents Day."
        Case "05/26/2006"
            strMessage = "Next Monday is Memorial Day."
        Case "06/30/2006"
            strMessage = "Next Tuesday is Independence Day." & _
                " Monday is a company holiday."
        Case "09/01/2006"
            strMessage = "Next Monday is Labor Day."
        'other National Holidays here
    End Select
    MsgBox strMessage, vbOKCancel + vbExclamation, "Don't Forget..."

End Sub
```

Using the *ItemSend* Event

The ItemSend event occurs when an item is sent, either by the user issuing a Send command (for example, by clicking the Send button in a message window) or by the Send method in VBA. The syntax for the ItemSend event is

```
Sub expression_ItemSend(ByVal Item As Object, Cancel As Boolean)
```

Here, *expression* is a required expression that returns an Application object. Item is a required argument that specifies the item that's being sent. Cancel is an optional Boolean argument that you can set to False to prevent the item from being sent.

The following example compares the Subject property of the Item object being sent. If the Subject property is an empty string, the message box prompts the user to add a subject line, and the Cancel = True statement cancels the sending of the item.

```
Private Sub Application_ItemSend(ByVal Item As Object, Cancel As Boolean)
    If Item.Subject = "" Then
        MsgBox "Please add a subject line to this message."
        Cancel = True
    End If
End Sub
```

Using the *NewMail* Event and *NewMailEx* Event

The NewMail event occurs when one or more new mail items arrives in the Inbox. The NewMail event can be useful for sorting messages automatically. (You can also use rules to sort messages automatically.) The NewMail event takes no arguments.

When new mail arrives and the NewMail event is triggered, the following example displays a message box that offers to show the Inbox:

```
Private Sub Application_NewMail()
    If MsgBox("You have new mail. Do you want to see your Inbox?", _
        vbYesNo + vbInformation, "New Mail Alert") = vbYes Then
        Application.GetNamespace("MAPI").GetDefaultFolder(olFolderInbox).Display
    End If
End Sub
```

The NewMailEx event is a more complex version of the NewMail event that passes a list of the items received in the Inbox since the event last fired. The NewMailEx event passes this list only for Exchange Server and other mailboxes that provide notification of messages received. The syntax is

```
Sub expression.NewMailEx(EntryIDCollection As String)
```

Here, *expression* is a required expression that returns an Application object. EntryIDCollection is a string that contains the entry IDs of the messages that have been received. Each entry ID is separated from the next by a comma; if there is a single entry ID, there is no comma in the EntryID Collection string.

The following example of a NewMailEx event procedure uses a Do While... Loop loop to separate the individual message IDs (by using the InStr function to identify each section of the EntryIDCollection string, up to the next comma, in turn) and then builds a string that contains introductory text followed by the subject line of each message, one message to a line. The procedure then displays the string in a message box, so that when Outlook receives new mail, the user receives an executive summary of the subject lines.

```
Private Sub Application_NewMailEx(ByVal EntryIDCollection As String)

    Dim myMailItem As Object
    Dim intMsgIDStart As Integer, intMsgIDEnd As Integer
    Dim intCutPoint As String, strMailItemID As String, strMailList As String

    intMsgIDStart = 1
    intCutPoint = Len(EntryIDCollection)

    intMsgIDEnd = InStr(intMsgIDStart, EntryIDCollection, ",")
    strMailList = "You have the following messages:"

    Do While intMsgIDEnd <> 0
        strMailItemID = Strings.Mid(EntryIDCollection, intMsgIDStart, _
            (intMsgIDEnd - intMsgIDStart))
        Set myMailItem = Application.Session.GetItemFromID(strMailItemID)
        strMailList = strMailList & vbCr & myMailItem.Subject
        intMsgIDStart = intMsgIDEnd + 1
        intMsgIDEnd = InStr(intMsgIDStart, EntryIDCollection, ",")
    Loop

    MsgBox strMailList, vbOKOnly + vbInformation, "Mail Alert"

End Sub
```

TIP   Instead of using the NewMail event and the NewMailEx event, you can use the ItemAdd event with the items in the Inbox to process each new message that arrives.

Using the *AdvancedSearchComplete* Event and the *AdvancedSearchStopped* Event

Outlook provides two events for working with advanced searches created using the AdvancedSearch method. The AdvancedSearchComplete event fires when the AdvancedSearch method is run via VBA and finishes searching. The AdvancedSearchStopped event fires when the AdvancedSearch method is run via VBA and is stopped by using the Stop method of the search.

The syntax for the AdvancedSearchComplete event is

```
Private Sub expression_ AdvancedSearchComplete(ByVal SearchObject As Object)
```

Here, *expression* is a required expression that returns an Application-type object variable that has been declared with events in a class module. SearchObject is the Search object that the AdvancedSearch method returns.

The following example uses the AdvancedSearchComplete event to return the number of search results that were found by the AdvancedSearch method:

```
Private Sub Application_AdvancedSearchComplete(ByVal SearchObject As Search)
    MsgBox "The search has finished running and found " & _
```

```
        SearchObject.Results.Count & " results.", vbOKOnly + vbInformation, _
        "Advanced Search Complete Event"
End Sub
```

The following example uses the AdvancedSearchStopped event to inform the user that the search has been stopped:

```
Private Sub Application_AdvancedSearchStopped(ByVal SearchObject As Search)
    MsgBox "The search was stopped by a Stop command.", vbOKOnly
End Sub
```

Using the *MAPILogonComplete* Event

The MAPILogonComplete event occurs when the user has successfully logged on to Outlook. You can use the MAPILogonComplete event to ensure that Outlook is configured correctly for the user or simply to display an informational message. The MAPILogonComplete event takes no arguments.

The following example of a MAPILogonComplete procedure displays an informational message about current trading conditions when the user has successfully logged on to Outlook. The code includes a comment indicating where the String variables strPubDownBegin and strPubForecast would be declared and assigned data in a full implementation.

```
Private Sub Application_MAPILogonComplete()

    Dim strMsg As String
    'strPubDowBegin and strPubForecast declared and assigned strings here
    strMsg = "Welcome to the UltraBroker Trading System!" & vbCr & vbCr
    strMsg = strMsg & "Today's starting value is " & strPubDowBegin & "." _
        & vbCr & vbCr
    strMsg = strMsg & "Today's trading forecast is " & strPubForecast & "."
    MsgBox strMsg, vbOKOnly + vbInformation, _
        "UltraBroker Trading System Logon Greeting"
End Sub
```

Using the *Reminder* Event

The Reminder event fires immediately before the reminder for a meeting, task, or appointment is displayed. You can use the Reminder event to take an action related to the reminder. Because the reminder itself is usually adequate for reminding the user of the meeting, task, or appointment, the Reminder event tends to be more useful when accessing Outlook programmatically than when working interactively with Outlook. The syntax is

```
Sub expression_Reminder(ByVal Item As Object)
```

Here, *expression* is a required expression that returns an Application object, and Item is the AppointmentItem object, MailItem object, ContactItem object, or TaskItem object associated with the reminder.

Using the *OptionsPagesAdd* Event

The `OptionsPagesAdd` event occurs when either the Options dialog box (Tools ➢ Options) or the Properties dialog box for a folder is opened. (To open the Properties dialog box for a folder, right-click the folder, and then choose Properties from the context menu.) You can use this event to add a custom page, which is contained in a COM (Component Object Model) add-in that you have created, to the Options dialog box or the Properties dialog box. The syntax for the `OptionsPagesAdd` event is

```
Sub expression_OptionsPagesAdd(ByVal Pages As PropertyPages, _
    ByVal Folder As MAPIFolder)
```

Here, *expression* is a required expression that returns an `Application` object or a `NameSpace` object. `Pages` is a required argument that gives the collection of custom property pages added to the dialog box. `Folder` is a required argument used when *expression* returns a `MAPIFolder` object. `Folder` returns the `MAPIFolder` object for which the Properties dialog box is being opened.

Working with Item-Level Events

As well as application-level events, Outlook also supports a wide variety of *item-level events*—events that fire when items are manipulated rather than the application as a whole being affected.

You can handle item-level events in Outlook in two ways:

◆ By declaring an event in a class module and running an initialization procedure, so that VBA then traps the event when it fires. This chapter takes this approach.

◆ By creating Visual Basic Script (VBScript) code and placing it in the form used by the item. This approach is especially useful for custom forms, but it is more limited than the previous approach, because some of the events that Outlook supports are not available in VBScript.

Declaring an Object Variable and Initializing an Event

Follow these steps to declare an object variable and initialize an event:

1. Decide which class module to use for the declaration by using one of the following three methods:

   ◆ To use the `ThisOutlookSession` module, double-click the `Project1` item that represents the Outlook VBA project, double-click the `Microsoft Office Outlook` item (in Office 2003) or the `Microsoft Outlook Objects` item (in Office XP or Office 2000), and then double-click the `ThisOutlookSession` item.

   ◆ Create a class module by right-clicking in the Project Explorer and choosing Insert ➢ Class Module from the shortcut menu. The Visual Basic Editor automatically opens a Code window for the class.

   ◆ Open an existing class module by double-clicking it in the Project Explorer.

2. In the declarations area at the beginning of the class module, declare a variable to represent the object to which the event applies. Use the `WithEvents` keyword to denote that the object has events. The following example creates a public variable named `myPublicContactItem`:

```
Public WithEvents myPublicContactItem As ContactItem
```

3. Initialize the object variable by setting it to represent the appropriate object. The following example sets the myPublicContactItem variable to represent the first item in the default contacts folder:

```
Set myPublicContactItem = Application.GetNamespace("MAPI") _
    .GetDefaultFolder(olFolderContacts).Items(1)
```

Once you've initialized the object variable, the procedure will run after the event fires.

You can initialize the object variable manually if necessary, and you may find it convenient to do so when you're writing code to handle events. But if you need to handle the event each time Outlook runs, it's better to run the code to initialize the object variable automatically. For example, you might use the Startup event of the Application object (discussed in "Using the *Startup* Event," earlier in this chapter) to run the code automatically each time Outlook starts.

Understanding the Events That Apply to All Message Items

Many of the item-level events apply to all the message items: the AppointmentItem, ContactItem, DistListItem, DocumentItem, Explorer, Inspector, JournalItem, MailItem, MeetingItem, PostItem, RemoteItem, ReportItem, TaskItem, TaskRequestAcceptItem, TaskRequestDeclineItem, TaskRequestItem, and TaskRequestUpdateItem items. Table 27.1 lists these events.

NOTE The Close event applies to the Inspector object and the Explorer object as well as to the objects mentioned above.

TABLE 27.1:   Item-Level Events That Apply to All Message Items

EVENT	EVENT OCCURS	AVAILABLE IN VBSCRIPT
AttachmentAdd	After an attachment is added to the item	Yes
AttachmentRead	When the user opens an e-mail attachment for reading	Yes
BeforeAttachmentSave	When the user chooses to save an attachment, but before the command is executed	Yes
BeforeCheckNames	Before Outlook checks the names of the recipients of an item being sent	Yes
BeforeDelete	Before an item is deleted	Yes
Close	When an inspector is being closed, but before the closing occurs	Yes
CustomAction	When the custom action of an item is executed	Yes
CustomPropertyChange	When a custom property of an item is changed	Yes
Forward	When the user forwards an item	Yes
Open	When an item is opened in an inspector	Yes

TABLE 27.1: Item-Level Events That Apply to All Message Items *(CONTINUED)*

EVENT	EVENT OCCURS	AVAILABLE IN VBSCRIPT
PropertyChange	When a standard property (as opposed to a custom property) in the item is changed	Yes
Read	When an item is opened for editing in an inspector window or is selected for editing in-cell	Yes
Reply	When the user issues a Reply command for an item	Yes
ReplyAll	When the user issues a Reply All command	Yes
Send	When a Send command has been issued, but before the item is sent	Yes
Write	When an item is saved, either explicitly by the user or implicitly by Outlook	Yes

The events that fire before an action occurs allow you to cancel the action so that it doesn't take place. The syntax for these events uses a Boolean argument named Cancel that you can set to True to prevent the action from taking place. For example, the syntax for the BeforeDelete event is

```
Sub expression_BeforeDelete(ByVal Item As Object, Cancel As Boolean)
```

Here, *expression* is a required expression that returns that returns one of the message items to which the event applies (for example, a TaskItem object). The following example uses the BeforeDelete event to check that the TaskItem object open in an inspector is marked as complete when the user tries to delete it. If the task is not marked as complete, a message box prompts the user to complete the task, and the example then sets the Cancel argument to True to prevent the deletion from occurring.

```
Private Sub myTaskItem_BeforeDelete(ByVal Item As Object, Cancel As Boolean)
    If myTaskItem.Complete = False Then
        MsgBox "Please complete the task before deleting it.", _
            vbOKOnly + vbExclamation, "Task Is Incomplete"
        Cancel = True
    End If
End Sub
```

NOTE The Read event and the Open event both occur when the user opens an existing item for editing. The difference between the two events is that the Open event occurs only when the item is being opened in an inspector window, whereas the Read event occurs both when the item is being opened in an inspector window and when it is being selected for editing in a cell.

Understanding the Events That Apply to Explorers, Inspectors, and Views

Table 27.2 lists the events that apply to explorers, inspectors, or views. Some events apply to both explorers and inspectors.

TABLE 27.2:   Events That Apply to Explorers, Inspectors, or Views

EVENT	APPLIES TO	EVENT OCCURS	AVAILABLE IN VBSCRIPT
BeforeFolderSwitch	Explorer	Before the explorer displays a new folder	No
BeforeItemCopy	Explorer	When the user issues a Copy command, but before the Copy operation takes place	Yes
BeforeItemCut	Explorer	When an item is cut from a folder	Yes
BeforeItemPaste	Explorer	Before an item is pasted	Yes
BeforeViewSwitch	Explorer	Before the view changes in the Outlook window	
FolderSwitch	Explorer	After an explorer displays a new folder	No
SelectionChange	Explorer	When the focus is moved to a different item in a folder, or Outlook select the first item in a folder when the user selects that folder	No
ViewSwitch	Explorer	When the view changes in the explorer window	No
Activate	Explorer, Inspector	An explorer window or an inspector window is activated (becomes the active window)	No
Deactivate	Explorer, Inspector	When an explorer window or an inspector window is deactivated (stops being the active window)	No
BeforeMaximize	Explorer, Inspector	When the user maximizes the explorer or inspector, but before maximization takes place	Yes
BeforeMinimize	Explorer, Inspector	When the user minimizes the explorer or inspector, but before minimization takes place	Yes
BeforeMove	Explorer, Inspector	When the user moves an explorer window or an inspector window but before the action takes place	Yes
BeforeSize	Explorer, Inspector	When the user resizes the explorer or inspector, but before the resizing takes place	Yes
NewExplorer	Explorers	When a new explorer window is opened	No
NewInspector	Inspectors	When a new inspector window is opened	No
ViewAdd	Views	When a view is added to the Views collection	Yes
ViewRemove	Views	When a view in removed from the Views collection	Yes

If you work on a small screen (for example, a laptop screen), you might prefer to use the NewInspector event to maximize each inspector window you open and to hide any toolbars you don't need. The first procedure in the following example (which includes the declarations) uses the NewInspector event to make sure the Standard toolbar is displayed, hide the Formatting toolbar, and assign the Inspector object representing the new inspector to the Public object variable myInspector. The second procedure uses the Activate event of the myInspector object to maximize its window by setting the WindowState property to olMaximized.

The net effect of these two event procedures is to configure the toolbars as described above and maximize the inspector window. The Activate event procedure is necessary because the NewInspector event runs before the inspector window is displayed, which means the NewInspector event procedure cannot maximize the inspector window.

```
Public WithEvents myInspectors As Inspectors
Public WithEvents myInspector As Inspector

Private Sub myInspectors_NewInspector(ByVal Inspector As Outlook.Inspector)
    With Inspector
        With .CommandBars
            .Item("Standard").Visible = True
            .Item("Formatting").Visible = False
        End With
        Set myInspector = Inspector
    End With
End Sub


Private Sub myInspector_Activate()
    myInspector.WindowState = olMaximized
End Sub
```

Understanding the Events That Apply to Folders

Outlook provides three events (see Table 27.3) that apply to folders.

TABLE 27.3:   Events That Apply to Folders

EVENT	EVENT OCCURS	AVAILABLE IN VBSCRIPT
FolderAdd	When a folder is added to the specified Folders collection	No
FolderChange	When a folder in the specified Folders collection is changed	No
FolderRemove	When a folder is removed from the specified Folders collection	No

Understanding the Events That Apply to Items and Results

Table 27.4 lists the events that apply to items and results.

TABLE 27.4: Events That Apply to Items and Results

EVENT	EVENT OCCURS	AVAILABLE IN VBSCRIPT
ItemAdd	When one or more items are added to the collection, but not when many items are added all at once	No
ItemChange	When an item in the Items collection or the Results collection is changed	No
ItemRemove	When an item is deleted from the Items collection or the Results collection, but not when 16 or more items are deleted at once from a Personal Folders file, an Exchange mailbox, or an Exchange public folder; also not when the last item in a Personal Folders file is deleted	No

The following example uses the ItemChange event to monitor when any contact is changed in the Contacts folder. After a change, the event procedure displays a message box asking if the user wants to inform their colleagues of the change to the contact. If the user clicks the Yes button, the example creates and sends a message containing the vCard for the contact. The message goes to the Marketing Associates distribution list and has the subject Contact details change: and the name of the contact.

```
Public WithEvents myContacts As Items

Public Sub Initialize_myContacts
    Set myContacts = Application.GetNamespace("MAPI") _
        .GetDefaultFolder(olFolderContacts).Items
End Sub

Private Sub myContacts_ItemChange(ByVal Item As Object)

    Dim ContactUpdateMessage As MailItem

    If MsgBox("Notify your colleagues of the contact change?", _
        vbYesNo + vbQuestion, "Contact Data Changed") = vbYes Then
        Set ContactUpdateMessage = Application.CreateItem(ItemType:=olMailItem)
        With ContactUpdateMessage
            .To = "Marketing Associates"
            .Subject = "Contact details change: " & Item.Subject
            .Body = "The following contact has changed: " & vbCr & vbCr _
                & Item.Subject
            .Attachments.Add Source:=Item, Position:=50
            .Send
        End With
    End If

End Sub
```

Understanding the Events That Apply to the Outlook Bar

Outlook supports various events that apply to the Outlook bar (see Table 27.5). You may find these events useful if you need to customize the Outlook bar or constrain the user's navigation capabilities. For example, you can use the BeforeNavigate event to check the shortcut to which the user is attempting to navigate. If the user is not permitted to access the folder associated with the shortcut, you can cancel the navigation.

TABLE 27.5:   Events That Apply to Outlook Bar Objects

EVENT	APPLIES TO	EVENT OCCURS	AVAILABLE IN VBSCRIPT
GroupAdd	OutlookBarGroup	After a new group is added to the Shortcuts pane.	No
BeforeGroupAdd	OutlookBarGroups	Before a new group is added to the Shortcuts pane.	No
BeforeGroupRemove	OutlookBarGroups	Before a group is removed from the Shortcuts pane.	No
BeforeGroupSwitch	OutlookBarPane	When a new group is opened in the Outlook Bar. Does not fire in Outlook 2003 because Outlook 2003 has a different Navigation pane and Shortcuts pane.	No
BeforeNavigate	OutlookBarPane	After the user clicks a shortcut in the Shortcuts pane but before Outlook displays the folder represented by the shortcut.	No
BeforeShortcutAdd	OutlookBarShortcuts	Before a new shortcut is added to a group in the Shortcuts pane.	No
BeforeShortcutRemove	OutlookBarShortcuts	Before a shortcut is removed from a group in the Shortcuts pane.	No
ShortcutAdd	OutlookBarShortcuts	After a new shortcut is added to a Shortcuts pane group.	No

Understanding the Events That Apply to Reminders

Table 27.6 explains the events that Outlook provides for reminders. You can use these events to take actions when a reminder fires, before the Reminder dialog box appears, when the user clicks the Snooze button to dismiss a reminder, or when reminders are added, changed, or removed.

TABLE 27.6:   Events That Apply to Reminders

EVENT	EVENT OCCURS	AVAILABLE IN VBSCRIPT
BeforeReminderShow	Before Outlook displays the Reminder dialog box	Yes
ReminderAdd	When a reminder is added	Yes
ReminderChange	After a reminder has been changed	Yes
ReminderFire	Before a reminder is executed	Yes
ReminderRemove	When a reminder is removed from the Reminders collection	Yes
Snooze	When the user dismisses a reminder by clicking the Snooze button	Yes

Understanding the Events That Apply to Synchronization

If you write procedures to synchronize Outlook, you may need to use the three events that apply to the SyncObject object, which represents a Send/Receive group for a user. (You can access the SyncObject object by using the SyncObjects property of the NameSpace object to return the SyncObjects collection.) Table 27.7 explains the events that apply to the SyncObject object.

TABLE 27.7:   Events That Apply to the SyncObject Object

EVENT	EVENT OCCURS	AVAILABLE IN VBSCRIPT
SyncStart	When Outlook starts synchronizing a user's folders	No
SyncEnd	After synchronization ends	No
OnError	When an error occurs during synchronization	No

The following example uses the `OnError` event with the object variable `mySyncObject`. If an error occurs during synchronization of the `SyncObject` represented by `mySyncObject`, the procedure displays an error message giving the error code and description.

```
Private Sub mySyncObject_OnError(ByVal Code As Long, _
    ByVal Description As String)

    Dim strMessage As String
    strMessage = "An error occurred during synchronization:" & vbCr & vbCr
    strMessage = strMessage & "Error code: " & Code & vbCr
    strMessage = strMessage & "Error description: " & Description
    MsgBox strMessage, vbOKOnly + vbExclamation, "Synchronization Error"

End Sub
```

Chapter 28

Understanding the Access Object Model and Key Objects

- ◆ Getting started with VBA in Access
- ◆ Getting an overview of the Access object model
- ◆ Understanding Access' creatable objects
- ◆ Opening and closing databases
- ◆ Working with the Screen object
- ◆ Setting startup properties for a database
- ◆ Using the DoCmd object to run commands

If you develop Access databases, forms, or reports, you'll find many opportunities for customizing Access using VBA to streamline your work and that of your colleagues. Depending on the purposes for which you use Access, you might program Access to automatically extract data sets you need or to create custom reports on a regular schedule.

Even if your work in Access consists simply of entering data into databases and checking that it is correct, you may be able to program VBA to make mundane tasks less onerous. For example, you might use VBA to simplify the process of data entry or to validate the data that the user enters, so as to avoid problems further down the line.

This chapter first shows you how to get started with VBA in Access, because Access implements VBA in a different way from the other applications this book has discussed. You then come to grips with the Access object model and learn about its most important creatable objects. After that, the chapter shows you how to open and close databases, set startup properties for a database, work with the Screen object, and use the DoCmd object to run commands.

The next chapter discusses how to manipulate the data in an Access database via VBA.

Getting Started with VBA in Access

Access implements VBA using a different model than most other VBA hosts. These are the main differences:

- ◆ Collections in Access are zero-based—the first item in a collection is numbered 0 (zero) rather than 1. For example, Forms(0).Name returns the Name property of the first Form object in the Forms collection.

◆ Macros are different in Access than in the other Office applications. A macro is a list of actions that you want to perform. Instead of keeping macros together with VBA, Access keeps them separate. You create macros by using the Macros category in the Access database window rather than by using VBA in the Visual Basic Editor.

◆ You can access a module directly from the Access user interface instead of having to go through the Visual Basic Editor. You can also go through the Visual Basic Editor, as in the other applications discussed in this book.

◆ To perform most tasks using VBA in Access, you write functions (`Function` procedures) rather than the subprocedures (`Sub` procedures) you mostly use in other VBA hosts such as Word and Excel.

◆ You can execute a function by using the `RunCode` action to run a macro that calls the function.

◆ To execute a subprocedure, create a function that calls the subprocedure. While you are working in the Visual Basic Editor, you can debug and run the subprocedure by using the Visual Basic Editor's usual commands (for example, press F5 to run the subprocedure), but you will not be able to run it directly from the Access user interface.

The following sections provide a straightforward example of working with VBA in Access.

Creating a Module

To create a module, open your database and follow these steps:

1. Display the database window. For example, open the Window menu and click the entry for the database window.

2. Click the Modules button in the Objects column to display the list of modules (if there are any). Figure 28.1 shows an example.

3. Click the New button. Access launches or activates the Visual Basic Editor and adds a new module named `Module1` (or the next unused name—for example, `Module2`). Access automatically enters the `Option Compare Database` statement. See "Understanding the *Option Compare Database* Statement" section, later in this chapter, for an explanation of this statement and the alternative means of comparison that you can use.

FIGURE 28.1
You can create a module or a macro from the database window in Access.

> **NOTE**   You can also create a module by using the Insert ➢ Module command in the Visual Basic Editor or by right-clicking the project's entry in the Project Explorer and choosing Insert ➢ Module from the shortcut menu.

4. Press Ctrl+S or choose File ➢ Save (the Save command also shows the database's name). Access displays the Save As dialog box (see Figure 28.2).

FIGURE 28.2

Type the name for the new module in the Save As dialog box.

5. Type the name for the module, and then press Enter or click the OK button to apply the name. Access saves the module.

> **NOTE**   You can also name the module by pressing F4 to activate the Properties window, typing the name you want to give the new module, and then pressing Enter. When you then display the Save As dialog box, the module already has the name, and you do not need to change it.

Creating a Function

After creating a module, you can create a function within it as described earlier in the book. The following example creates a function named Standard_Setup that simply displays a message box to indicate that it is running. The next section uses this macro as an example.

```
Public Function Standard_Setup()
    'put your choice of commands here
    MsgBox "The Standard_Setup macro is running."
End Function
```

After creating the function, switch back to Access by pressing Alt+F11 or clicking the View Microsoft Access button on the Standard toolbar in the Visual Basic Editor. (Alternatively, click the Access window or its button on the taskbar.)

Creating a Macro to Run a Function

To run the function, create a macro from the Access user interface. Follow these steps:

1. Display the database window if it's not already displayed. For example, open the Window menu and click the entry for the database window.

2. Click the Macros button in the Objects column to display the list of macros (if there are any).

3. Click the New button to open a new Macro window (see Figure 28.3).

FIGURE 28.3
Use the Macro window to create a new macro in Access.

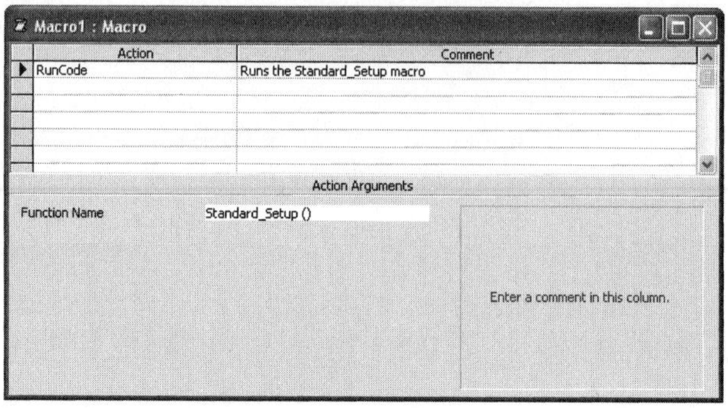

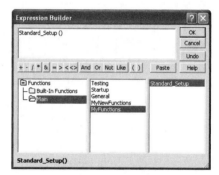

4. In the Action drop-down list, choose the RunCode item.

5. Type a description for the macro in the Comment text box.

6. In the Action Arguments area, click in the Function Name box, and then click the button with the ellipsis (the three dots: …) that appears at its right end. The Expression Builder window opens (see Figure 28.4).

FIGURE 28.4
Use the Expression Builder window to specify the function that you want the macro to run.

7. Double-click the Functions item to expand it, then select the entry for your database (which is called Main in the example), the module, and then the function. Click the Paste button to paste the function's name into the text box at the top of the Expression Builder dialog box.

8. Click the OK button to close the Expression Builder dialog box. Access enters the function name in the Function Name text box.

9. Press Ctrl+S or choose File ➢ Save to display the Save As dialog box.

10. Type the name for the macro, and then press Enter or click the OK button to apply the name.

11. Click the Close button to close the macro window.

12. If you want to test your macro, double-click its entry in the Macros list in the database window.

Using an AutoExec Macro to Set Up the Access Session

To set up your Access session, you can use an AutoExec macro. AutoExec is a special name for a macro that runs (executes) automatically when Access opens. For example, you might choose to maximize the application window, open a particular item (for example, a table), or display a particular record.

TIP To prevent an AutoExec macro from running when you open a database, hold down Shift as the database opens.

To create an AutoExec macro, start a new macro as described in the previous section, add to it the actions that you want the macro to perform, and save it with the name AutoExec. The macro then runs the next time you open the database.

NOTE You can also use macros to perform many other actions in Access. For example, you can create a macro that opens a form and performs a series of actions with it or a macro that prints out a report.

Running a Subprocedure

There's no good reason to create Access VBA code in a subprocedure rather than in a function, and if you do so, you must create a function that runs the subprocedure. This is clumsy, but it works. Here is a simple example:

1. In the Visual Basic Editor, create a subprocedure that performs the actions you want:

```
Sub SampleProcedure()
    MsgBox "The subprocedure named Sample Procedure is running."
End Sub
```

2. Still in the Visual Basic Editor, create a function that runs the subprocedure:

```
Public Function Run_SampleProcedure()
    Call SampleProcedure
End Function
```

3. Switch to Access and create a macro that uses the RunCode action to run the function that runs the subprocedure. (See the previous subsection for details on creating a macro to run a function.)

Understanding the *Option Compare Database* Statement

When you launch the Visual Basic Editor in Access (by pressing Alt+F11 or choosing Tools ➢ Macro ➢ Visual Basic Editor, as from any of the other Office applications) and open a code module, you'll notice that Access automatically enters an Option Compare Database statement in the declarations area. If you've selected the Require Variable Declaration check box on the Editor tab of the Options dialog box (Tools ➢ Options) to make the Visual Basic Editor force you to declare all variables explicitly, you'll see an Option Explicit statement in the declarations area as well.

Access supports three different ways of comparing strings: Option Compare Database, Option Compare Binary, and Option Compare Text:

◆ `Option Compare Database` is the default comparison type for Access databases and performs comparisons using the sort order for the locale Windows is using (for example, U.S. English). Sorting is not case sensitive. Access automatically inserts an `Option Compare Database` statement in the declarations section of each module that you insert. You can delete the `Option Compare Database` statement to make Access use `Option Compare Binary` instead.

◆ `Option Compare Binary` performs case-sensitive sorting. To use `Option Compare Binary`, either delete the `Option Compare Database` statement in the declarations section or change it to an `Option Compare Binary` statement.

◆ `Option Compare Text` performs case-insensitive sorting. To use `Option Compare Text`, change the `Option Compare Database` or `Option Compare Binary` statement to an `Option Compare Text` statement.

Getting an Overview of the Access Object Model

To start exploring the Access object model, start the Microsoft Visual Basic Help application and display the Microsoft Access Object Model topic. Launch the Visual Basic Editor if it's not already displayed, then choose Help ➢ Microsoft Visual Basic Help, type **Access object model** and press Enter, and then click the Microsoft Access Object Model topic. Figure 28.5 shows the main diagram in the Microsoft Access Object Model topic.

Understanding Access' Creatable Objects

The `Application` object gives you access to all the objects in the Access application. But for many operations, you can go directly through one of the creatable objects that Access exposes. The main creatable objects in Access are as follows:

◆ The `Forms` collection contains all the `Form` objects, which represent the open forms in a database.

◆ The `Reports` collection contains all the `Report` objects, which represent the open reports in a database.

◆ The `DataAccessPages` collection contains all the `DataAccessPage` objects, which represent the open data access pages in a project or a database.

NOTE An Access *project* is a file that connects to a SQL Server database.

◆ The `CurrentProject` object represents the active project or database in Access.

◆ The `CurrentData` object represents the objects stored in the current database.

◆ The `CodeProject` object represents the project containing the code database of a project or database.

◆ The `CodeData` object represents the objects stored in the code database.

◆ The `Screen` object represents the screen object that currently has the focus (the object that is receiving input or ready to receive input). The object can be a form, a report, or a control.

◆ The `DoCmd` object enables you to run Access commands using VBA.

◆ The Modules collection contains the Module objects, which represent the code modules and class modules in a database.

◆ The References collection contains the Reference objects, which represent the references set in the Access application.

FIGURE 28.5

The Microsoft Access Object Model screen in VBA Help is a good place to start exploring the Access object model. This screen also has several smaller diagrams that are not shown here.

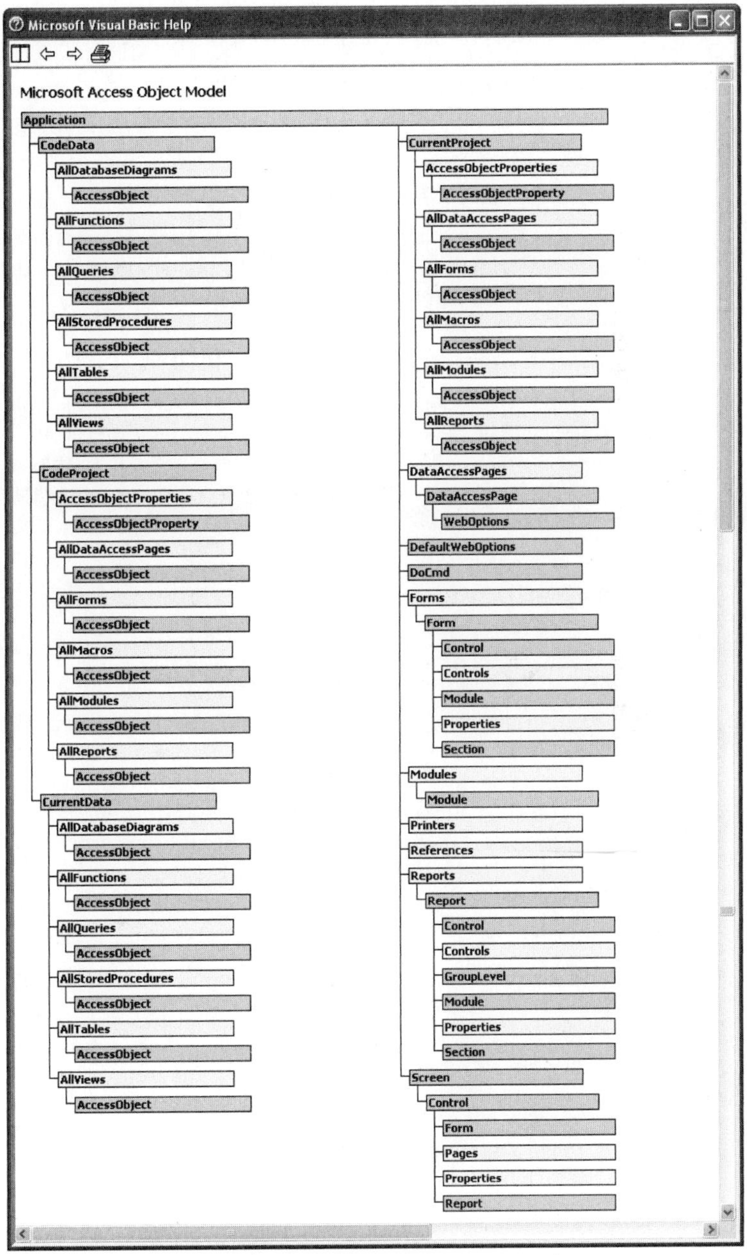

- The DBEngine object represents the Microsoft Jet database engine and is the topmost object in the Data Access Objects (DAO) hierarchy. The DBEngine object provides access to the Workspaces collection, which contains all the Workspace objects available to Access, and to the Errors collection, which contains an Error object for each operation involving DAO.

- The Workspace object contains a named session for a user. When you open a database, Access creates a workspace by default and assigns the open database to it. You can work with the current workspace or create further workspaces as needed.

- The Error object contains information about the data access errors that have occurred in a DAO operation.

Opening and Closing Databases

This section shows you how to open and close databases so that you can work with them. You can use the CurrentDb method to return the current database, open a database and treat it as the current database, or even open multiple databases at once. You can also create and remove workspaces.

Using the *CurrentDb* Method to Return the Current Database

To work with the database that's currently open in Access, use the CurrentDb method on the Application object or an object variable representing the Application object. The CurrentDb method returns a Database object variable representing the open database.

The following example declares an object variable of the Database type named myDatabase and then uses the CurrentDb method to assign the active database to it:

```
Dim myDatabase As Database
Set myDatabase = Application.CurrentDb
```

Opening a Database as the Current Database and Closing the Current Database

In Access, you can choose among several different ways of opening and closing a database. This section discusses the simplest method of opening and closing a database: by treating it as the current database. This method is similar to opening and closing a database when working interactively in Access. You can have only one database open at a time, so when you open another database, Access closes the database that was open before. See the next section for another method of opening and closing databases that lets you have two or more databases open at the same time.

To open a database as the current database, use the OpenCurrentDatabase method of the Application object. The syntax is

```
expression.OpenCurrentDatabase(Filepath, Exclusive, bstrPassword)
```

The components of the syntax are as follows:

- *expression* is a required expression that returns an Application object.

- Filepath is a required String argument that specifies the path and filename of the database to open. You should specify the file extension; if you omit it, Access assumes the extension is .mdb.

◆ Exclusive is an optional Boolean argument that you can set to True to open the database in exclusive mode rather than in shared mode (the default, or the result of an explicit False setting).

◆ bstrPassword is an optional String argument that specifies the password required to open the database.

To close the current database, use the CloseCurrentDatabase method with the Application object. This method takes no arguments.

You can run the CloseCurrentDatabase method from the current database, but you can't do anything after that, because the code stops after VBA executes the CloseCurrentDatabase method and the database containing the code closes. To close the current database and open another by using the OpenCurrentDatabase method, you must run the code from outside the databases involved—for example, by using Automation from another application.

The following example runs from another VBA host—for example, from Excel or from Word. The example declares the object variable myAccess as being of the Access.Application type and the object variable myDatabase as being of the Object type. The example uses the GetObject method to assign to myAccess the copy of Access that's running, uses the CloseCurrentDatabase method to close the open database, and then uses the OpenCurrentDatabase method to open another database in exclusive mode. The final statement uses the CurrentDb method to assign the open database to the myDatabase object variable.

```
Dim myAccess As Access.Application
Dim myDatabase As Object

Set myAccess = GetObject(, "Access.Application")
myAccess.CloseCurrentDatabase
myAccess.OpenCurrentDatabase _
    filepath:="Z:\Database\Current\Region1.mdb", Exclusive:=True
Set myDatabase = myAccess.CurrentDb
```

CREATING NEW DATABASES, FORMS, AND REPORTS IN ACCESS

The discussions of the other applications in this part of the book have emphasized creating and saving new files—for example, creating new documents in Word or new workbooks in Excel and saving them under suitable names and in the appropriate formats.

Access includes VBA commands for creating new databases, forms, reports, and other objects programmatically. For example:

◆ To create a new database, use the NewCurrentDatabase method of the Application object.

◆ To create a new form, use the CreateForm method. To place controls on the form, use the CreateControl method.

◆ To create a new report, use the CreateReport method. To place controls on the report, use the CreateReportControl method.

While creating a new database programmatically is quite feasible, it is not only complex but also something that you probably won't need to do often. In most cases, the goal of your Access VBA programming will be to manipulate the databases and objects that you have built manually.

Opening Multiple Databases at Once

Instead of using the `OpenCurrentDatabase` method to open a database as the current database, you can use the `OpenDatabase` method of the `Workspace` object to open another database and return a reference to the `Database` object representing it. The syntax for the `OpenDatabase` method is

```
Set database = workspace.OpenDatabase (Name, Options, ReadOnly, Connect)
```

The components of the syntax are as follows:

◆ *database* is an object variable that will represent the database you open.

◆ *workspace* is an optional object variable that specifies the workspace in which you want to open the database. If you omit *workspace*, Access opens the database in the default workspace. While you can open the database in the default workspace without problems, you may find it more convenient to create another workspace and use it to keep the database separate. See "Creating and Removing Workspaces," later in this chapter, for details.

◆ `Name` is a required String argument that specifies the name of the database to open. An error results if the database doesn't exist or isn't available, or if another user has opened the database for exclusive access.

◆ `Options` is an optional Variant argument that specifies any options you want to set for the database. For an Access database, you can specify `True` to open the database in exclusive mode or `False` (the default) to open it in shared mode. For ODBCDirect workspaces, you can use other options; see the Access Visual Basic Help file for details.

◆ `ReadOnly` is an optional Variant argument that you can set to `True` to open the database in read-only mode. The default value is `False`, which opens the database in read/write mode.

◆ `Connect` is an optional Variant that you can use to pass any necessary connection information, such as a password for opening the database.

The following example declares a `Workspace` object variable named myWorkspace and a `Database` object variable named myDatabase, assigns to myWorkspace the first `Workspace` object in the `Workspaces` collection (the default workspace), and assigns to myDatabase the database `Testing.mdb`, which it opens in exclusive mode with read/write access:

```
Dim myWorkspace As Workspace
Dim myDatabase As Database

Set myWorkspace = DBEngine.Workspaces(0)
Set myDatabase = myWorkspace.OpenDatabase _
    (Name:= "\\server\database\Testing.mdb", _
    Options:=True, ReadOnly:=False)
```

Closing a Database

To close a database that you've opened by using the `OpenDatabase` method, use the `Close` method of the object variable to which you've assigned the database. For example, the following statement closes the database assigned to the object variable myDatabase:

```
myDatabase.Close
```

Creating and Removing Workspaces

To keep different databases in separate sessions, you can create a new workspace as needed and remove it when you have finished working with it.

CREATING A NEW WORKSPACE

To create a new workspace, use the `CreateWorkspace` method of the `DBEngine` object. The syntax is

```
Set workspace = CreateWorkspace(Name, UserName, Password, UseType)
```

The components of the syntax are as follows:

◆ *workspace* is the object variable to which you want to assign the workspace you're creating.

◆ `Name` is a required String argument that specifies the name to assign to the new workspace.

◆ `UserName` is a required String argument that specifies the owner of the new workspace.

◆ `Password` is a required String argument that specifies the password for the new workspace. The password can be up to 14 characters long. Use an empty string if you need to set a blank password.

◆ `UseType` is an optional argument that indicates the type of workspace to create. Use `dbUseJet` to create a Microsoft Jet workspace. Use `dbUseODBC` to create an ODBCDirect workspace. Omit this argument if you want the `DefaultType` property of the `DBEngine` object to determine the type of data source connected to the workspace.

The following example declares an object variable named `myWorkspace` of the `Workspace` type and assigns to it a new Jet workspace named `Workspace2`. The example makes the `admin` account the owner of the new workspace.

```
Dim myWorkspace As Workspace
Set myWorkspace = CreateWorkspace(Name:="Workspace2", _
    UserName:="admin", Password:="", UseType:=dbUseJet)
```

After creating a new workspace, you can use it to open a new database. See the previous section for an example.

REMOVING A WORKSPACE

Before removing a workspace from the `Workspaces` collection, you must close all the open connections and databases. You can then use the `Close` method to close the `Workspace` object. For example, the following statement closes the `Workspace` object identified by the object variable `myWorkspace`:

```
myWorkspace.Close
```

Setting Startup Properties for a Database

You can use Access' startup properties to control the way in which a database opens and the interface it presents to the user. For example, you might open a specific form in a database so that the user can work with it immediately after opening the database.

When setting startup properties via VBA, you must be careful not to cause errors. If the database is new, the startup properties don't exist until the user has changed the default startup settings—for example, by choosing Tools ➤ Startup and using the options in the Startup dialog box (see Figure 28.6). Because the properties may not exist, you must write code to handle any error that results from a property not existing and to create the property if necessary.

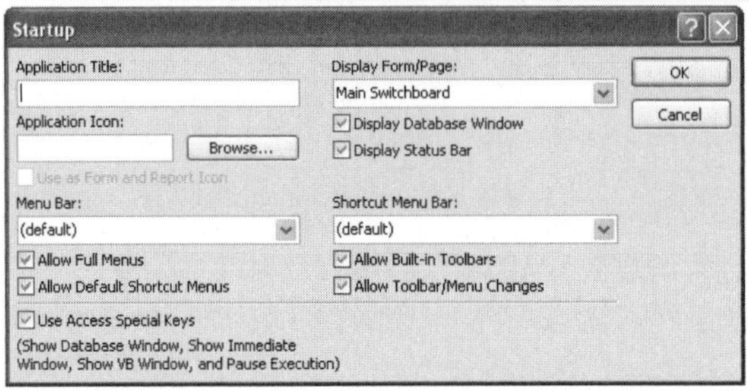

FIGURE 28.6
The Startup dialog box lets you manually set startup properties for an Access database or project. When you work with startup properties via VBA, you must make sure that they exist to avoid errors.

To set startup properties via VBA, use the properties listed in Table 28.1, which shows them alongside the corresponding options in the Startup dialog box.

TABLE 28.1: Startup Properties for Access Databases

PROPERTY NAME	CORRESPONDING OPTION IN THE STARTUP DIALOG BOX	CONTROLS
AllowBreakIntoCode		Whether the user can view code in the Visual Basic Editor after a run-time error occurs.
AllowBuiltInToolbars	Allow Built-In Toolbars	Whether the user can display Access' built-in toolbars.
AllowFullMenus	Allow Full Menus	Whether to make the full versions of Access' built-in menus available (True or –1) or not (False or 0); use False to display a custom subset of the built-in menus (for example, to prevent the user from taking certain actions).
AllowShortcutMenus	Allow Default Shortcut Menus	Whether the user can use shortcut menus.
AllowSpecialKeys	Use Access Special Keys	Whether the user can use special keys.
AllowToolbarChanges	Allow Toolbar/Menu Changes	Whether the user can change the toolbars and menus.
AppIcon	Application Icon	The icon displayed instead of the default Access icon; can be a bitmap (.bmp) or icon (.ico) file.

TABLE 28.1: Startup Properties for Access Databases *(CONTINUED)*

PROPERTY NAME	CORRESPONDING OPTION IN THE STARTUP DIALOG BOX	CONTROLS
AppTitle	Application Title	The title displayed in the application's title bar.
StartupForm	Display Form/Page	Which form is displayed when the database opens.
StartupMenuBar	Menu Bar	Which custom menu bar (if any) to display instead of the regular Access menu bar.
StartupShortcutMenuBar	Shortcut Menu Bar	Which custom shortcut menu (if any) to display instead of the regular Access shortcut menu
StartupShowDBWindow	Display Database Window	Whether to display the database window (True or -1) or hide it (False or 0) when the database opens.
StartupShowStatusBar	Display Status Bar	Whether to display the status bar (True or -1) or hide it (False or 0) when the database opens.

NOTE Startup properties are implemented differently in an Access project (an .adp file) than in an Access database (an .mdb file). In a project, startup properties are implemented through the AccessObjectProperties collection in the CurrentProject object rather than in the Properties collection.

Listing 28.1 sets startup properties for the current database, which it accesses by using the CurrentDb object.

LISTING 28.1:

```
1.  Public Function Set_Up_Database()
2.
3.      Call Set_Startup_Property(strName:="StartupShowDbWindow", _
            varType:=dbBoolean, varValue:=False)
4.      Call Set_Startup_Property(strName:="AllowSpecialKeys", _
            varType:=dbBoolean, varValue:=False)
5.      Call Set_Startup_Property(strName:="StartupShowStatusBar", _
            varType:=dbBoolean, varValue:=False)
6.
```

```
 7.  End Function
 8.
 9.
10.  Function Set_Startup_Property(strName As String, varType As Variant, _
         varValue As Variant)
11.
12.      Dim myProperty As Property
13.      Const conPropertyNotFound = 3270
14.
15.      On Error GoTo ErrorHandler
16.      CurrentDb.Properties(Item:=strName) = varValue
17.      Exit Function
18.  ErrorHandler:
19.      If Err = conPropertyNotFound Then
20.          Set myProperty = CurrentDb.CreateProperty _
                 (Name:=strName, Type:=varType, Value:=varValue)
21.          CurrentDb.Properties.Append myProperty
22.      Else
23.          MsgBox "An error occurred: " & vbCr & vbCr & _
                 "Error number: " & Err.Number & vbCr & _
                 "Error description: " & Err.Description, vbOKOnly + _
                 vbCritical, "Set_Up_Database Function"
24.      End If
25.  End Function
```

The two functions in Listing 28.1 work as follows:

◆ Lines 1 through 7 contain the Public function named Set_Up_Database, which is run to set up the database. Lines 10 through 25 contain the Set_Startup_Property function, which performs the actual setting of the startup properties and creates any necessary properties that do not already exist.

◆ Line 1 declares the Set_Up_Database function, and line 7 ends it. In between, lines 2 and 6 are spacers, and lines 3, 4, and 5 each call the Set_Startup_Property function, with each line passing a different string: line 3 passes StartupShowDbWindow, line 4 passes AllowSpecialKeys, and line 5 passes StartupShowStausBar. Each of these strings is the name of a property to set, and each is specified as being of the type dbBoolean (a database Boolean type) and is set to False.

◆ Line 10 declares the function Set_Startup_Property, declaring its arguments to be the String argument strName, the Variant argument varType, and the Variant argument varValue. Line 11 is a spacer.

◆ Line 12 declares the variable myProperty as being of the Property type. Line 13 declares the constant conPropertyNotFound and assigns to it the number 3270, the number of the error that VBA returns when you try to set a property that does not yet exist. Line 14 is a spacer.

◆ Line 15 uses an On Error GoTo statement to direct execution to the error handler, which is named ErrorHandler, when an error occurs. The ErrorHandler: label appears in line 18.

◆ Line 16 attempts to use set the property whose name is passed by strName to the value passed by varValue. If the property exists, this statement is executed without problem, and line 17 uses an Exit Function statement to exit the function. If the property doesn't exist, the error occurs, and execution moves to the error handler.

◆ Line 18 starts the error handler, which consists of an If… Then… Else statement. Line 19 checks whether the error matches conPropertyNotFound, the error for the property not existing. If it does, line 20 creates the property and assigns it to the myProperty object variable. If not, execution moves to the Else statement in line 22, line 23 displays a message box giving details of the error that has occurred. Line 24 ends the If… Then… Else statement, and line 25 ends the function.

Working with the *Screen* Object

If you've used VBA in the other Office applications, you've probably written code that works with whichever object is currently active. For example, in Word you can use the ActiveDocument object to work with the active document or the Selection object to work with the current selection, and in PowerPoint you can work with the ActivePresentation object to work with whichever presentation happens to be active.

In Access, you can use the Screen object to work with the form, report, or control that has the focus. The Screen object has various properties, including the following:

◆ The ActiveForm property returns the active form. If there is no active form, trying to use the ActiveForm property returns the error 2475.

◆ The ActiveDatasheet property returns the active datasheet. If there is no active datasheet, trying to use the ActiveDatasheet property returns the error 2484.

◆ The ActiveReport property returns the active report. If there is no active report, trying to use the ActiveReport property returns the error 2476.

◆ The ActiveDataAccessPage property returns the active data access page. If there is no active data access page, trying to use the ActiveDataAccessPage property returns the error 2022.

◆ The ActiveControl property returns the active control. If there is no active control, trying to use the ActiveControl property returns the error 2474.

◆ The PreviousControl property lets you access the control that previously had the focus.

To avoid errors, you should check which object is active before trying to manipulate it by using the Screen object. The following example uses the errors listed above to determine whether a form, report, datasheet, or data access page is active, and then displays a message box identifying the item and giving its name:

```
On Error Resume Next

Dim strName As String
Dim strType As String
strType = "Form"
strName = Screen.ActiveForm.Name
If Err = 2475 Then
```

```
        Err = 0
        strType = "Report"
        strName = Screen.ActiveReport.Name
        If Err = 2476 Then
            Err = 0
            strType = "Data access page"
            strName = Screen.ActiveDataAccessPage.Name
            If Err = 2022 Then
                Err = 0
                strType = "Datasheet"
                strName = Screen.ActiveDatasheet.Name
            End If
        End If
    End If
End If

MsgBox "The current Screen object is a " & strType & vbCr _
    & vbCr & "Screen object name: " & strName, _
    vbOKOnly + vbInformation, "Current Screen Object"
```

Using the *DoCmd* Object to Run Commands

The DoCmd object enables you to run Access commands by using VBA. You can return the DoCmd object by using the DoCmd property of the Application object, but since DoCmd is a creatable object, you do not need to go through the Application object. To run a command, you use the corresponding method of the DoCmd object. Table 28.2 lists the methods and explains briefly what they do.

TABLE 28.2:   Methods of the DoCmd Object

METHOD	EXPLANATION
AddMenu	Adds a menu to the global menu bar or to a custom menu bar.
ApplyFilter	Applies a filter so that only records that match certain criteria are displayed.
Beep	Makes the computer beep—for example, to attract the user's attention when an error has occurred.
CancelEvent	Cancels the event that has occurred.
Close	Closes the specified object—for example, a form or a report.
CopyDatabaseFile	Copies the database connected to the current project to a SQL Server file.
CopyObject	Copies the specified object (for example, a query or a table) into the specified database (or to a new table in the current database).
DeleteObject	Deletes the specified object from the database.
DoMenuItem	Performs a command from a menu or toolbar. This is an older command that has been replaced by the RunCommand method (see below).

TABLE 28.2:   Methods of the DoCmd Object *(CONTINUED)*

METHOD	EXPLANATION
Echo	Provides backward compatibility for running the Echo action in earlier versions of VBA. It's better to use Application.Echo now.
FindNext	Finds the next record matching the search criteria specified by the FindRecord method.
FindRecord	Performs a search for a record that matches the specified criteria.
GoToControl	Moves the focus to the specified control or field in a form or datasheet.
GoToPage	Moves the focus to the specified page of a form.
GoToRecord	Makes the specified record the current record.
Hourglass	Changes the mouse pointer to an hourglass (a wait pointer) or back to a normal pointer.
Maximize	Maximizes the active window.
Minimize	Minimizes the active window.
MoveSize	Moves or resizes (or both) the active window.
OpenDataAccessPage	Opens the specified data access page in the specified view.
OpenDiagram	Opens the specified database diagram.
OpenForm	Opens the specified form and optionally applies filtering.
OpenFunction	Opens the specified user-defined function in the specified view (for example, datasheet view) and mode (for example, for data entry).
OpenModule	Opens the specified VBA module at the specified procedure.
OpenQuery	Opens the specified query in the specified view and mode.
OpenStoredProcedure	Opens the specified stored procedure in the specified view and mode.
OpenTable	Opens the specified table in the specified view and mode.
OpenView	Opens the specified view in the specified view and mode.
OutputTo	Outputs the data in the specified object (for example, a report or a data access page) in the specified format.
PrintOut	Prints the specified object.
Quit	Provides backward compatibility with Access 95. With later versions of Access, use Application.Quit instead.

TABLE 28.2: Methods of the DoCmd Object *(CONTINUED)*

METHOD	EXPLANATION
Rename	Renames the specified object with the name given.
RepaintObject	Repaints the specified object, completing any screen updates that are pending.
Requery	Updates the data in the specified control by querying the data source again.
Restore	Restores the active window to its nonmaximized and nonminimized size.
RunCommand	Runs the specified built-in menu command or toolbar command.
RunMacro	Runs the specified macro.
RunSQL	Runs an Access action query using the specified SQL statement.
Save	Saves the specified object or (if no object is specified) the active object.
SelectObject	Selects the specified object in the database window or in an object that's already open.
SendObject	Sends the specified object (for example, a form or a report) in an e-mail message.
SetMenuItem	Sets the state of a menu item—for example, enabling or disabling a menu item.
SetWarnings	Turns system messages on or off.
ShowAllRecords	Removes any existing filters from the current form, query, or table.
ShowToolbar	Displays or hides the specified toolbar.
TransferDatabase	Imports data into or exports data from the current database or project.
TransferSQLDatabase	Transfers the specified SQL Server database to another SQL Server database.
TransferSpreadsheet	Imports data from or exports data to a spreadsheet.
TransferText	Imports data from or exports data to a text file.

The following sections show examples of using some of the methods detailed in Table 28.2.

Using the *OpenForm* Method to Open a Form

To open a form, use the OpenForm method of the DoCmd object. The syntax is

```
expression.OpenForm(FormName, View, FilterName, WhereCondition, DataMode,
WindowMode, OpenArgs)
```

The components of the syntax are as follows:

◆ *expression* is a required expression that returns a DoCmd object. In many cases, it's easiest to use the DoCmd object itself.

◆ FormName is a required Variant argument that specifies the name of the form you want to open. The form must be in the current database.

◆ View is an optional argument that specifies the view to use: acNormal (the default), acDesign, acFormDS, acFormPivotChart, acFormPivotTable, or acPreview.

◆ FilterName is an optional Variant argument that you can use to specify the name of a query. The query must be stored in the current database.

◆ WhereCondition is an optional Variant that you can use to specify a SQL WHERE clause. Omit the word WHERE from the clause.

◆ DataMode is an optional argument for specifying the mode in which to open the form: acFormPropertySettings, acFormAdd, acFormEdit, or acFormReadOnly. acFormPropertySettings is the default setting and opens the form using the mode set in the form.

◆ WindowMode is an optional argument for specifying how to open the form. The default is acWindowNormal, a normal window. You can also open the form as a dialog (acDialog) or as an icon (acIcon) or keep it hidden (acHidden).

◆ OpenArgs is an optional Variant that you can use to specify arguments for opening the form— for example, to move the focus to a particular record.

The following example uses the DoCmd object to open a form and display the first record for which the Country field matches France:

```
DoCmd.OpenForm FormName:="Customers", View:=acNormal, _
    WhereCondition:="Country ='France'"
```

Using the *PrintOut* Method to Print an Object

To print an object, use the PrintOut method. The syntax is

```
expression.PrintOut(PrintRange, PageFrom, PageTo, PrintQuality, Copies,
CollateCopies)
```

The components of the syntax are as follows:

◆ *expression* is a required expression that returns a DoCmd object.

◆ PrintRange is an optional argument that specifies what to print: all of the object (acPrintAll, the default), specific pages (acPages), or the selection (acSelection).

◆ PageFrom and PageTo are optional Variant arguments that you use with PrintRange:=acPages to specify the starting and ending page numbers of the print range.

◆ PrintQuality is an optional argument that you can use to specify the print quality. The default setting is acHigh, but you can also specify acLow, acMedium, or acDraft (draft quality, to save ink and time).

◆ Copies is an optional Variant argument that you can use to specify how many copies to print. The default is 1.

◆ CollateCopies is an optional Variant argument that you can set to True to collate the copies and False not to collate them. The default setting is True.

The following example prints three copies of each page in the active object at full quality without collating the copies:

```
DoCmd.PrintOut PrintRange:=acPrintAll, Copies:=3, CollateCopies:=False
```

Using the *RunMacro* Method to Run a Macro

To run a macro, use the RunMacro method. The syntax is

```
expression.RunMacro(MacroName, RepeatCount, RepeatExpression)
```

The components of the syntax are as follows:

◆ *expression* is a required expression that returns a DoCmd object.

◆ MacroName is a required Variant argument that specifies the macro name.

◆ RepeatCount is an optional Variant argument that you can use to specify an expression to control the number of times that the macro should run. The default is 1.

◆ RepeatExpression is an optional Variant argument that contains a numeric expression to be evaluated each time the macro runs. The macro stops when this expression evaluates to 0 (False).

The following example runs the macro named RemoveDuplicates:

```
DoCmd.RunMacro "RemoveDuplicates"
```

Chapter 29

Manipulating the Data in an Access Database via VBA

- ◆ Understanding how to proceed
- ◆ Preparing to access the data in the database
- ◆ Opening a recordset
- ◆ Accessing a particular record in a recordset
- ◆ Searching for a record
- ◆ Returning the fields in a record
- ◆ Editing a record
- ◆ Inserting and deleting records
- ◆ Closing a recordset

This chapter shows you how to begin manipulating the data in an Access database. You can do so either from Access or from another VBA-enabled application—for example, from Excel or from Word. This chapter shows you how to work from another application.

There are two main ways to access data in an Access database: via Data Access Objects (DAO) or via ActiveX Data Objects (ADO). DAO is the older method of accessing data, and it works for both Microsoft Jet databases (Microsoft Jet is the Access database engine) and ODBC-compliant data sources. (ODBC is Open Database Connectivity, a long-existing standard for accessing databases. ODBC is also useful for accessing open-source solutions, such as MySQL.) ADO is a high-level programming interface that provides access to a wide range of data sources.

If your software and database offer you the choice of access methods, you will probably find it easier to use ADO than DAO. If you cannot use ADO, use DAO.

Understanding How to Proceed

Once you've chosen between ADO and DAO, you take the following steps to manipulate the data in the database.

1. Add a reference to the object library you'll be using.

2. Establish a connection to the database that contains the data.

3. Create a recordset that contains the records with which you want to work.

4. Work with the records in the recordset.

5. Close the recordset.

All the steps work in more or less the same way for ADO and DAO, except that you create the recordset in different ways. The following sections take you through these steps, splitting the path where necessary to cover the differences in ADO and DAO.

Preparing to Access the Data in the Database

Before you can access the data in a database, you must create a reference to the appropriate object library. After that, you must establish a connection to the data source—the ActiveX Data Objects object library for an ADO connection or the Data Access Objects object library for a DAO connection.

Adding a Reference to the Appropriate Object Library

To create a reference to the object library you need, follow these steps:

1. Launch or switch to the application from which you will access the data. For example, open Excel or Word.

2. Launch or activate the Visual Basic Editor by pressing Alt+F11 or choosing Tools ➤ Macro ➤ Visual Basic Editor.

3. Choose Tools ➤ References to display the References dialog box.

4. Scroll down the Available References list box to the appropriate object library item, and then select its check box:

- For an ADO connection, select the check box for the Microsoft ActiveX Data Objects Library item.

- For a Data Access Objects connection, select the check box for the Microsoft DAO Object Library item.

NOTE The version number of the ActiveX Data Objects Library item or the Microsoft DAO Object Library item depends on the version of Access you're using. If multiple versions are available, use the newest.

5. Click the OK button to close the References dialog box.

Establishing a Connection to the Database

Before you can access the data in a database, you must establish a connection to the database. The easiest way to establish a connection is to create a data source by using the Data Sources applet in Control Panel.

NOTE You can also create a connection programmatically. This chapter doesn't cover this topic.

To establish a connection to a database by using the Data Sources applet, follow these steps:

1. Choose Start ➢ Control Panel to open a Control Panel window:

    ◆ If Control Panel is in Category View, click the Performance And Maintenance link, click the Administrative Tools link, and then double-click the Data Sources (ODBC) icon.

    ◆ If Control Panel is in Classic View, double-click the Data Sources (ODBC) icon.

2. In the ODBC Data Source Administrator dialog box, click the System DSN tab to display its page (see Figure 29.1).

FIGURE 29.1
To establish a connection
to a database, use the
ODBC Data Source Ad-
ministrator dialog box.

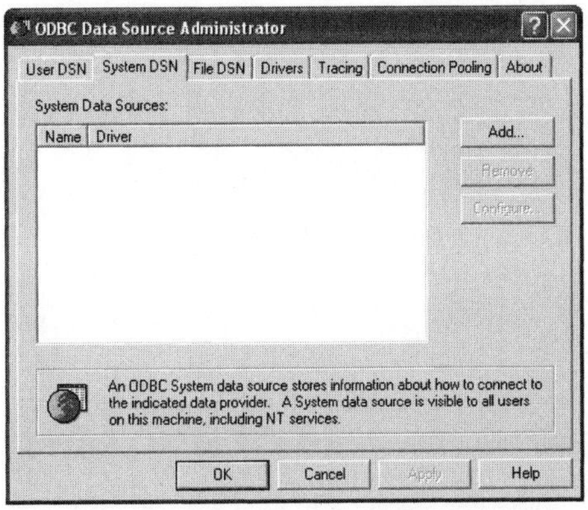

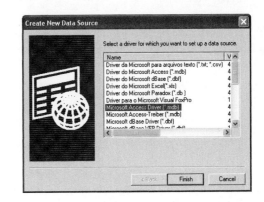

3. Click the Add button to display the Create New Data Source dialog box (see Figure 29.2).

FIGURE 29.2
To create a connection
to an Access database,
select the Microsoft
Access Driver (*.mdb)
item in the Create New
Data Source dialog box.

4. Select the Microsoft Access Driver (*.mdb) item in the list box.

5. Click the Finish button to display the ODBC Microsoft Access Setup dialog box (shown in Figure 29.3 with choices made).

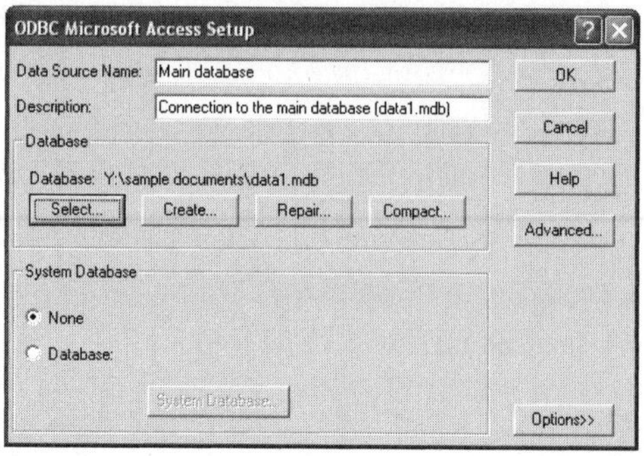

FIGURE 29.3
Use the ODBC Microsoft
Access Setup dialog box
to specify the details for
the connection.

6. In the Data Source Name text box, type the name you want to assign to the data source. This doesn't have to be the actual name of the data source, just the name that you want to use to refer to it.

7. In the Description text box, type a description for the connection. This is optional, but if you create multiple connections that have similar names, it's helpful to be able to use the description to distinguish them. (It's also helpful when someone else has to deal with connections you've created.)

8. Click the Select button to display the Select Database dialog box. Navigate to and select the database.

9. Select the Read Only check box if you need to open the database in read-only mode.

10. Select the Exclusive check box if you need to open the database in exclusive mode rather than in shared mode.

TIP   You can also specify exclusive mode or read-only mode from the ODBC Microsoft Access Setup dialog box. Click the Options button, and then select the Exclusive check box or the Read Only check box, as appropriate.

11. Click the OK button to close the Select Database dialog box and enter the details of the database in the ODBC Microsoft Access Setup dialog box.

12. Click the OK button to close the ODBC Microsoft Access Setup dialog box and display the ODBC Data Source Administrator dialog box.

13. Click the OK button to close the ODBC Data Source Administrator dialog box.

Opening a Recordset

To get to the records in the database to which you're establishing the connection, you must open a recordset. ADO and DAO use different procedures for opening a recordset. The following subsections give you the details.

Opening a Recordset Using ADO

To open a recordset using ADO, you use the Open method of the RecordSet object. The syntax for the Open method is

```
recordset.Open Source, ActiveConnection, CursorType, LockType, Options
```

The components of the syntax are as follows:

◆ *recordset* is the RecordSet object that you want to open. Often, you'll use an object variable that references the RecordSet object.

◆ Source is an optional Variant argument that specifies the table, command, SQL statement, or file that contains the recordset.

◆ ActiveConnection is an optional Variant argument. This can be either an object variable of the Connection type or a Variant/String containing parameters for the connection.

◆ CursorType is an optional argument for specifying the type of cursor to use in the recordset. Table 29.1 explains the cursor types.

◆ LockType is an optional argument for specifying how to lock the recordset while it is open. Table 29.2 explains the lock options.

◆ Options is an optional Long argument that you can use to control how the Source value is evaluated if it is not a Command object. Table 29.3 explains the available constants, which fall into two categories: command-type options and execute options. You can use two or more constants for the Options argument.

TIP Instead of specifying the arguments with the Open method, you can set the Source, ActiveConnection, CursorType, and LockType properties of the RecordSet object you're opening and then use the Open method without arguments. You may find that this approach makes your code easier to read. You'll see an example of this approach in "Using a SQL SELECT Statement to Access the Data in an ADO Recordset," later in this chapter.

TABLE 29.1:   Cursor-Type Constants for Opening a Recordset

CONSTANT	CURSOR TYPE AND EXPLANATION
adOpenForwardOnly	Forward-only cursor. You can scroll through the recordset only forward. This is the default cursor and provides the best performance when you need to go through the records only once.
adOpenDynamic	Dynamic cursor. You can move freely through the recordset, and you can see changes that other users make to records.
adOpenKeyset	Keyset cursor. You can move freely through the recordset and see changes that other users make to records. You cannot see records that other users add, and records that other users delete are inaccessible.
adOpenStatic	Static cursor. You can't see changes that other users make. Use a static cursor when you need only search for data or create reports from the data that exists when you open the recordset.

TABLE 29.2:   Lock Options for Opening a Recordset via ADO

CONSTANT	OPENS THE RECORDSET WITH
adLockReadOnly	The data is in read-only mode, so you cannot alter it. Use this constant if you need to search or analyze the data but not manipulate it.
adLockOptimistic	Optimistic locking, which locks a record only when you run the Update method to update it explicitly.
adLockBatchOptimistic	Optimistic batch locking, which enables you to perform a simultaneous update on several records that you've changed.
adLockPessimistic	Pessimistic locking, which locks a record immediately after you change it.

TABLE 29.3:   Choices for the Options Argument When Opening a Recordset

CONSTANT	EXPLANATION
Command-Type Options	
adCmdText	Evaluates Source as text specifying a command or stored procedure call.
acCmdTable	Evaluates Source as the name of a table consisting of columns returned by an internally generated SQL query.
acCmdStoredProc	Evaluates Source as the name of a stored procedure.
acCmdFile	Evaluates Source as the filename of a stored recordset.
acCmdTableDirect	Evaluates Source as a table name and returns all columns of the table. Do not use with adAsyncExecute.
Execute Options	
adAsyncExecute	Executes the command asynchronously. Does not work with acCmdTableDirect.
adAsyncFetch	Retrieves the rows specified by the CacheSize property synchronously and the remaining rows asynchronously.
adAsyncFetchNonBlocking	Prevents the main thread from blocking other data access while retrieving data.
adExecuteRecord	Treats the data returned by Source as a single row that becomes a record.

You'll see examples of opening a recordset a little later in this chapter. First, you must decide how to access the data in the recordset. The easiest methods are to use an existing table or a SQL SELECT statement.

Choosing How to Access the Data in an ADO Recordset

How you actually get to the data in the recordset you open depends on whether you want all the data in a table or just part of it. If you want all the data in a table, you can use a table to access the data. If you want to return only particular records, you can use a SQL SELECT statement.

USING A TABLE TO ACCESS THE DATA IN AN ADO RECORDSET

To open a whole table from the database in a recordset, specify the table name as the Source argument in the Open statement. The following example declares a RecordSet object variable, uses a CreateObject statement to assign the appropriate recordset to it, and then uses the Open method to open the Customers table in the Main database:

```
Dim myRecordset As Recordset
Set myRecordset = CreateObject("ADODB.Recordset")
myRecordset.Open Source:="Customers", ActiveConnection:="Main"
```

USING A SQL *SELECT* STATEMENT TO ACCESS THE DATA IN AN ADO RECORDSET

If you want to add to your recordset only those records that match criteria you specify, use a SQL SELECT statement. SELECT statements can be complex, but you can create straightforward statements with a little practice using this syntax:

```
SELECT [DISTINCT] fields FROM table WHERE criteria ORDER BY fields [DESC]
```

The words in capitals are the SQL keywords, and the words in lowercase italics are placeholders for the information you supply. Here are the details:

◆ The SELECT keyword indicates that you're creating a statement to select records (as opposed to, say, delete records).

◆ You can include the optional DISTINCT keyword (the brackets indicate that it is optional) to make the statement return only unique records, discarding any duplicates that the statement would otherwise return. If you omit DISTINCT, you get any duplicates as well.

◆ *fields* is a list of the fields that you want to have appear in the recordset. If you use two or more field names, separate them with commas—for example, contact, company, address. To return all field names, enter an asterisk (*).

◆ FROM *table* specifies the name of the table from which to draw the data.

◆ WHERE *criteria* specifies the criteria for filtering the records. Enter the field name, an equal sign, a single straight quote, the value you're looking for, and another single straight quote. For example, WHERE City='Taos' returns only the results where Taos appears in the City field.

◆ ORDER BY *fields* specifies the field or fields on which to sort the results. If you use two or more fields, put them in the order you want (the first sort field first, the second sort field second, and so on) and separate them with commas. The default sort order is ascending, but you can force a descending sort by adding the DESC keyword. For example, ORDER BY Zip DESC produces a descending sort by the Zip field, while ORDER BY State, City produces an ascending sort by the State field and, within that, by City.

Because SQL SELECT statements contain so many elements, putting a SELECT statement as an argument in an Open statement tends to create uncomfortably long lines of code. You can break the lines of code as usual, but you may find it easier to use the properties of the RecordSet object to specify the details of the recordset, as in the following example, rather than using the Open arguments. (Alternatively, you can assign the SELECT statement to a String variable and then use that to supply the argument.) The following example uses the SELECT statement to create a recordset containing the records for which the Country is Mexico, Brazil, or Argentina. The example sorts the recordset by country and then by city.

```
With myRecordset
    .Source = "SELECT * FROM Suppliers WHERE Country='Mexico'" & _
        "OR Country='Brazil' OR Country='Argentina'" & _
        "ORDER BY Country, City;"
    .ActiveConnection = "Main"
    .CursorType = adOpenStatic
    .Open
    If myRecordset.RecordCount = 0 Then
        MsgBox "There are no records that match the specified criteria."
    Else
        MsgBox myRecordset.Fields("CompanyName") & ": " & _
            myRecordset.Fields("Country")
    End If
End With
```

Because there may be no records that match the specified criteria, this example checks the RecordCount property of the RecordSet object to see how many matching records there are. If there are none (myRecordset.RecordCount = 0), the example displays a message box to inform the reader. If there are some matches, the example displays a message box containing the company name and country of the first matching record.

Opening a Recordset Using DAO

When working with DAO, you use the OpenRecordset method of the Database object to create a new recordset and add it to the Recordsets collection.

The syntax for the OpenRecordset method is

```
Set recordset = object.OpenRecordset (Name, Type, Options, LockEdit)
```

The components of the syntax are as follows:

◆ recordset is an object variable representing the RecordSet object you're opening.

◆ object is an object variable representing the database from which to create the new RecordSet object.

◆ Name is a required String argument that specifies the table, query, or SQL statement that provides the records for the recordset. If you're using a Jet database and returning a table-type recordset, you can use only a table name for the Name argument.

♦ Type is an optional argument that you can use to specify the type of recordset you're opening. Table 29.4 explains the constants you can use for Type.

♦ Options is an optional argument that you can use to specify constants that control how Access opens the recordset. Table 29.5 explains the constants you can use for Options.

♦ LockEdit is an optional constant that you can use to specify how the recordset is locked. Table 29.6 explains the constants you can use for LockEdit.

TABLE 29.4:　Constants for the Type Argument for the OpenRecordSet Method

CONSTANT	OPENS THIS TYPE OF RECORDSET
dbOpenTable	Table-type. This works only in Microsoft Jet workspaces. This is the default setting if you open a recordset in a Jet workspace.
dbOpenDynamic	Dynamic-type. This works only in ODBCDirect workspaces. The recordset is similar to an ODBC dynamic cursor and enables you to add, remove, or edit rows from a database table.
dbOpenDynaset	Dynaset-type. This recordset is similar to an ODBC keyset cursor and enables you to add, remove, or edit rows from a database table. You can also move freely through the rows in the dynaset.
dbOpenSnapshot	Snapshot-type. This recordset is similar to an ODBC static cursor. It opens a snapshot of the records but does not update them when other users make changes. To update the snapshot, you must close the recordset and reopen it.
dbOpenForwardOnly	Forward-only. You can move only forward through the recordset.

TABLE 29.5:　Constants for the Options Argument

CONSTANT	EXPLANATION	LIMITATIONS
dbAppendOnly	Users can add new records but cannot edit or delete existing records.	Jet dynaset-type recordsets only
dbSQLPassThrough	Passes a SQL statement to an ODBC data source connected via Jet.	Jet snapshot-type recordsets only
dbSeeChanges	Causes a runtime error if a user attempts to change data that another user is already editing.	Jet dynaset-type recordsets only
dbDenyWrite	Prevents other users from adding or modifying records.	Jet recordsets only
dbDenyRead	Prevents other users from reading data.	Jet table-type recordsets only

TABLE 29.5: Constants for the Options Argument *(CONTINUED)*

CONSTANT	EXPLANATION	LIMITATIONS
dbForwardOnly	Forces a forward-only recordset. This is an older option included for backward compatibility. Use Type:=dbOpenForwardOnly instead.	Jet snapshot-type recordsets only
dbReadOnly	Prevents users from changing the recordset. This in an older option included for backward compatibility. Use LockEdits:=dbReadOnly instead. If you must use Options:=dbReadOnly, do not include the LockEdits argument.	Jet recordsets only
dbRunAsync	Runs a query asynchronously (so that some results are returned while others are still pending).	ODBCDirect workspaces only
dbExecDirect	Runs a query by calling SQLExecDirect.	ODBCDirect workspaces only
dbInconsistent	Permits inconsistent updates, enabling you to update a field in one table of a multitable recordset without updating another table in the recordset. You can use either this constant or dbConsistent, but not both.	Jet dynaset-type and snapshot-type recordsets only
dbConsistent	Permits only consistent updates, so that shared fields in tables underlying a multitable recordset must be updated together. You can use either this constant or dbInconsistent, but not both.	Jet dynaset-type and snapshot-type recordsets only

TABLE 29.6: Constants for the LockEdits Argument

CONSTANT	EXPLANATION	DEFAULT OR LIMITATIONS
dbReadOnly	Prevents users from changing the recordset. Use this instead of Options:=dbReadOnly; do not use both.	Default for ODBCDirect workspaces
dbPessimistic	Uses pessimistic locking, which locks a record immediately after you change it.	Default for Jet workspaces
dbOptimistic	Uses optimistic locking, which locks a record only when you run the Update method to update it explicitly.	

TABLE 29.6: Constants for the LockEdits Argument *(CONTINUED)*

CONSTANT	EXPLANATION	DEFAULT OR LIMITATIONS
dbOptimisticValue	Uses optimistic concurrency, comparing the data values in old and new records to find out if changes have been made since the record was last accessed. The concurrency is based on row values.	ODBCDirect workspaces only
dbOptimisticBatch	Uses optimistic batch locking, which enables you to perform a simultaneous update on several records that you've changed.	ODBCDirect workspaces only

OPENING A DAO RECORDSET USING A TABLE

The easiest way to open a DAO recordset is to open an entire table by specifying the table name for the Name argument and using Type:=dbOpenTable to explicitly state that you're opening a table. The following example declares the object variable myRecordset as a DAO.Recordset object and then assigns to it the records from the Customers table in the database identified by the myDatabase object variable:

```
Dim myRecordset As DAO.Recordset
Set myRecordset = myDatabase.OpenRecordset(Name:="Customers", _
    Type:=dbOpenTable)
```

OPENING A DAO RECORDSET USING A SQL *SELECT* STATEMENT

If you want to return only particular records, use a SQL SELECT statement to open the DAO record-set. (See "Using a SQL *SELECT* Statement to Access the Data in an ADO Recordset," earlier in this chapter, for an explanation of the essentials of a SQL SELECT statement.) Specify the statement as the Name argument for the OpenRecordset method, as in the following example, which declares a Database object variable, assigns a database to it, declares a RecordSet object variable, and then assigns to the object variable the results of a SELECT statement run on the database:

```
Dim myDatabase As DAO.Database
Set myDatabase = OpenDatabase("Z:\Database\Main.mdb")

Dim myRecordset As DAO.Recordset
Set myRecordset = myDatabase.OpenRecordset _
    (Name:="SELECT * FROM Customers WHERE Country='Germany'", _
    Type:=dbOpenDynaset)
```

Accessing a Particular Record in a Recordset

To access a particular record in a recordset, you can either move through the records to find the one you want or search for the record. The RecordSet object includes these methods for moving about the records in the recordset:

Method	Moves to Record
MoveFirst	First
MoveNext	Next
MovePrevious	Previous
MoveLast	Last
Move	The specified record

Using the *MoveFirst, MoveNext, MovePrevious,* and *MoveLast* Methods

The MoveFirst method and MoveLast method are always safe to use, because as long as the recordset contains one or more records, there's always a first record and a last record. (If the recordset contains only one record, that record is both the first record and the last record.) But if you use the MovePrevious method from the first record in the recordset or the MoveNext method from the last record, you move beyond the recordset, accessing what is sometimes called a "phantom record"—one that isn't there. When you try to access the contents of the record, VBA gives the runtime error 3021 ("Either BOF or EOF is True, or the current record has been deleted. Requested operation requires a current record."). Figure 29.4 shows this error.

FIGURE 29.4

The run-time error "Either BOF or EOF is True..." usually means that you've moved outside the recordset by using the MoveLast method from the last record or the Move-Previous record from the first record in the recordset.

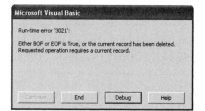

BOF is the beginning of the file, and EOF is the end of the file. To check whether you're at the beginning or end of the recordset, use the BOF property or the EOF property of the RecordSet object. The BOF property returns True when the current record is at the beginning of the file, and the EOF property returns True when the current record is at the end of the file. To avoid errors, check after using the MovePrevious method whether the beginning of the file has been reached—for example:

```
With myRecordset
    .MovePrevious
    If .BOF = True Then .MoveNext
End ith
```

Similarly, check after using the MoveNext method whether the end of the file has been reached—for example:

```
myRecordset.MoveNext
If myRecordset.EOF Then myRecordset.MovePrevious
```

Using the *Move* Method to Move by Multiple Records

To move by several records at once, but not to the first record or last record in the recordset, use the Move method. The syntax is different for ADO and for DAO.

The syntax for the Move method with ADO is

```
recordset.Move NumRecords, Start
```

The syntax for the Move method with DAO is

```
recordset.Move Rows, StartBookmark
```

Here, *recordset* is the RecordSet involved, NumRecords or Rows is the number of records by which to move (use a positive number to move forward or a negative number to move back), and Start or StartBookmark is an optional argument that you can use to specify the bookmark from which you want to start the movement. If you omit Start or StartBookmark, movement starts from the current record.

For example, the following statement moves 10 records forward from the current record in an ADO recordset:

```
myRecordset.Move NumRecords:=10
```

The following statement moves 5 records backward from the current record in a DAO recordset:

```
myRecordset.Move Rows:=-5
```

To create a bookmark, move to the record that you want to mark, and then use the Bookmark property of the RecordSet object. The following example declares a Variant variable named myBookmark and then assigns to it a bookmark representing the current record in an ADO recordset:

```
Dim myBookmark As Variant
myBookmark = myRecordset.Bookmark
```

After setting a bookmark, you can use it as the starting point of a move. For example, the following statement moves to the eighth record after the bookmark myBookmark in an ADO recordset:

```
myRecordset.Move NumRecords:=8, Start:=myBookmark
```

Searching for a Record

The process of searching for a record in a recordset is different in ADO and in DAO. The following subsections show you how to search.

TIP   Both ADO recordsets and DAO recordsets include a method called Seek, which is more complex and more powerful than the Find method for ADO and the four Find methods for DAO discussed here. Consult the Access VBA Help file for details on the Seek method.

Searching for a Record in an ADO Recordset

To search for a record in an ADO recordset, use the Find method of the RecordSet object. The syntax is

```
recordset.Find Criteria, SkipRows, SearchDirection, Start
```

The components of the syntax are as follows:

- *recordset* is the recordset involved.

- Criteria is a required String argument that specifies the column name, type of comparison, and value to use. For example, you might specify that the State column is equal (=) to CA.

- SkipRows is an optional Long value that you can use to specify an offset from the current row (or from the bookmark specified by the Start argument) at which to start searching instead of starting from the current row. For example, an offset of 3 starts the search three rows later than the current row.

- SearchDirection is an optional argument for specifying whether to search forward or backward. The default is adSearchForward; specify adSearchBackward to search backward instead.

- Start is an optional Variant argument that specifies the bookmark from which to start the search or the offset. If you omit Start, the search starts from the current row.

When you run the search, it stops at the first matching record. If no record matches, and you're searching forward, it stops at the end of the recordset; if you're searching backward, it stops at the beginning of the recordset. If the end or beginning of the recordset is reached, you know that there was no match for the search.

The following example moves to the first record in the recordset represented by the object variable myRecordset and then searches for the first record that matches the criterion "State='CA'". The example checks the EOF property to ensure that the end of the recordset has not been reached. If it has not, the example displays a message box with the name of the company for the record. If the end of the recordset has been reached, the example displays a message box stating that no match was found.

```
With myRecordset
    .MoveFirst
    .Find Criteria:="State='CA'"
    If Not .EOF Then
        MsgBox .Fields("CompanyName")
    Else
        MsgBox "No matching record was found."
    End If
End With
```

To search again for the same criteria, use the SkipRows argument to specify an offset so that you don't find the current record again. For example:

```
myRecordset.Find Criteria="State='CA'", SkipRows:=1
```

Searching for a Record in a DAO Recordset

To search for a record in a DAO recordset, you can use these four methods:

◆ The FindFirst method starts searching at the beginning of the recordset and searches forward.

◆ The FindNext method starts searching at the current record and searches forward.

◆ The FindPrevious method starts searching at the current record and searches backward.

◆ The FindLast method starts searching at the end of the recordset and searches backward.

The syntax for these four methods is

```
recordset.FindFirst Criteria
recordset.FindNext Criteria
recordset.FindPrevious Criteria
recordset.FindLast Criteria
```

Here, *recordset* is a required object variable that represents the RecordSet object involved. *Criteria* is a required String argument that specifies the criteria for the search. *Criteria* works in the same way as the WHERE clause in a SQL statement, except that it does not use the word WHERE.

The following example uses the FindFirst method to search from the beginning of the recordset for the first record that matches the criterion Country = 'Mexico':

```
myRecordset.FindFirst "Country = 'Mexico'"
```

When you start a search in a DAO recordset using one of the four Find methods, the NoMatch property of the RecordSet object is set to True. If the method finds a match, the NoMatch property is set to False. So you can use the NoMatch property to tell whether the search found a match or not. For example:

```
If .NoMatch = False Then
    MsgBox myRecordset.Fields("CompanyName").Value
End If
```

Returning the Fields in a Record

Once you've moved to the record, you can return the fields it contains by using the appropriate Field object from the Fields collection. Field is the default property for the RecordSet object, so you can omit it if you choose. For example, both the following statements return the WorkPhone field from the current record:

```
myRecordset.Fields("WorkPhone")
myRecordset("WorkPhone")
```

Editing a Record

To change the data in a record, specify the value to which you want to set the field, and then use the Update method of the RecordSet object to update the data in the underlying table. The following example changes the value in the ContactName field to `Pieter Schmidt` and then uses the Update method to update it:

```
With myRecordset
    .Fields("ContactName").Value = "Pieter Schmidt"
    .Update
End With
```

Inserting and Deleting Records

To insert a record, use the AddNew method of the RecordSet object. You can then assign data to the fields in the record. After that, use the Update method to add the data to the table in the database. The following example uses a With statement to perform these actions:

```
With myRecordset
    .AddNew
    .Fields("CustomerID").Value = "MURP04"
    .Fields("ContactName").Value = "Andrea Murphy"
    .Fields("CompanyName").Value = "Murphy's Chipping Services"
    .Fields("City").Value = "City of Industry"
    'add data for the other fields here
    .Update
End With
```

To delete a record, identify it by either moving to it or by searching for it, and then use the Delete method followed by the Update method. The following example deletes the current record and then updates the table:

```
myRecordset.Delete
myRecordset.Update
```

Closing a Recordset

After working with an object, you should close it. To close a recordset, use the Close method with the appropriate RecordSet object or the object variable that represents the RecordSet object. The following example closes the recordset represented by the object variable myRecordset:

```
myRecordset.Close
```

After closing the recordset, set its object variable to Nothing to release the memory it occupied.

```
Set myRecordset = Nothing
```

Chapter 30

Accessing One Application from Another Application

- ◆ Understanding the tools for communicating with other applications
- ◆ Using Automation to transfer information
- ◆ Using the Shell function to run an application
- ◆ Using data objects to store and retrieve information
- ◆ Communicating via DDE
- ◆ Communicating via SendKeys

So far, this book has shown you how to work with VBA to perform actions in the VBA host application. But you'll sometimes (perhaps often) need to work with other applications as well. This chapter shows you the tools for working with other applications: Automation, data objects, Dynamic Data Exchange (DDE), and SendKeys.

Understanding the Tools for Communicating with Other Applications

Most VBA host applications (such as the Office applications that this chapter uses as examples) offer several tools for communicating with other applications:

Automation Formerly known as Object Linking and Embedding (OLE); the newest and usually most effective method for transferring information from one Windows application to another. If the applications you're using support Automation, use it in preference to DDE and SendKeys.

Dynamic Data Exchange (DDE) An older method of transferring information between applications that remains a good fallback when Automation isn't available. DDE is available only in some applications.

SendKeys An older method of communicating with another application. SendKeys relies on sending keystroke equivalents to the other application rather than manipulating it in the more sophisticated ways that Automation and DDE use. While crude by comparison with Automation and DDE, SendKeys can still be effective.

Beyond these three communications tools, this chapter also discusses the DataObject object, which you can use to store information and to transfer information to and from the Windows Clipboard.

TIP If an application doesn't offer any of the control methods discussed in this chapter, you may be able to control it through the command line. For example, you can use the /p command line switch in many applications to print a file without any user interaction. Search the web for **"command line"**, **vba**, and the application's name to find relevant pages.

Using Automation to Transfer Information

Automation is the most powerful and efficient way to communicate with another application. Each application that supports Automation offers one or more Component Object Model (COM) objects that you can access programmatically—usually an object representing the application, an object representing the various types of files the application produces, objects representing its major components, and so on.

For any Automation transaction, there's a *server application* that provides the information and a *client application* that receives it. (There's also another pair of terms for the two applications: the server application is also sometimes known as the *object application*, and the client application is known as the *controlling application*.)

Automation lets the client application harness the capabilities of the server application. For example, Excel has far better calculation features than Word and can create charts, data maps, and so on. By using Automation, Word can use Excel's calculation engine to perform calculations and insert the results into a Word document, or it can use Excel to create a chart that it inserts into the document as well. Word can also take more limited actions, such as causing Excel to open a workbook, copy a group of cells from a spreadsheet in it, and paste-link them into a document.

To use Automation through VBA, you create an object in VBA that references the application you want to work with. You use the `CreateObject` function to create a new object in another application and the `GetObject` function to retrieve an existing object in another application.

When using Automation, you can choose whether to display the server application or keep it hidden from the user. For some procedures, you'll need to display it—for example, so that the user can choose a file or a folder or make another choice that requires live intervention. For other procedures, it can be best to keep the server application hidden so that the user isn't distracted by the application having apparently launched itself spontaneously.

Even if you decide to hide the server application when the procedure runs, in most cases it's helpful to display the server application while you're creating the procedure—doing so makes it much easier to see what's going wrong when your code doesn't work as expected.

Understanding Early and Late Binding

When you use Automation to access another application, you can choose which type of *binding* to use—that is, how to establish the reference between the client application and the server application.

Early binding involves adding a reference to the application's object library by using the References dialog box (Tools ➢ References) at design time and then declaring the object at the start of the code by using a `Dim` statement that declares the specific object class type rather than declaring the object `As Object`. For example, the following statements connect to a slide within a PowerPoint presentation by using early binding:

```
Dim myPowerPoint As PowerPoint.Application
Dim myPresentation As Presentation
Dim mySlide As Slide
```

```
Set myPowerPoint = CreateObject("PowerPoint.Application")
Set myPresentation = myPowerPoint.Presentations.Add
Set mySlide = myPresentation.Slides.Add(Index:=1, Layout:=ppLayoutTitleOnly)
```

In late binding, you create the object that references the other application when you run the code. If you declare the object explicitly, you declare it as an object—As Object—rather than declaring it as a specific object class type.

For example, the following statements declare the object variable myOutlook and then assign to it a reference to an Outlook.Application object:

```
Dim myOutlook As Object
Set myOutlook = CreateObject("Outlook.Application")
```

NOTE   Not all applications that support Automation support early binding. Some applications cannot provide direct access to their functions at design time, as is required for early binding, and can provide access to their functions only at runtime. With such applications, you must use late binding.

If the server application you're using supports early binding, use it in preference to late binding. There are three advantages:

♦   Once you've added to the project the reference to the application's object library, you can access the application's objects, properties, and methods through the Visual Basic Editor session from the host application. This makes it much easier to find the objects, properties, and methods you need in the application you're referring to and to avoid mistakes such as typos and missing arguments.

♦   Because you specify the type of the object variable when you declare it, you're less likely to get the wrong object by mistake.

♦   Because VBA has more information about the object when you're using early binding, references to methods and properties of the object should be faster.

Creating an Object with the *CreateObject* Function

The CreateObject function creates and returns a reference to an Automation object exposed to other applications. The syntax is

```
CreateObject(class [,servername])
```

Here, *class* is a required argument specifying the class (the formal definition) of the object to create. The *class* argument consists of the name of the library that will provide the object and the type of object to be provided, so it looks like this:

```
applicationname.objecttype
```

For example, to specify the Excel Application object as a class, use a *class* argument of Excel.Application. Here, Excel is the name of the application that provides the object, and Application is the type of object that Excel provides. Likewise, use Excel.Sheet to specify a worksheet object in Excel.

servername is an optional Variant argument of the String subtype used to specify the name of the network server on which to create the object. To use the local machine, omit *servername* or specify an empty string. To use a remote server, you must have DCOM (the Distributed Component Object Model) installed, and the object on the server computer must be configured to allow remote creation.

Typically, you'll use a `CreateObject` function with a `Set` statement to assign to an object variable the object that you create. For example, the following statements declare an object variable named `myNewSheet` and assign an Excel worksheet object to it:

```
Dim myNewSheet As Object
Set myNewSheet = CreateObject("Excel.Sheet")
```

TIP   You can use the `CreateObject` function with any COM object on your computer system, not just with application objects.

Returning an Object with the *GetObject* Function

The `GetObject` function returns a reference to an existing Automation object. The syntax is

```
GetObject([pathname] [, class])
```

Here, *pathname* is an optional Variant argument of the String subtype specifying the full path and name of the file that contains the object you want to retrieve. *pathname* is optional, but if you don't specify it, you must specify the *class* argument. *class*, which is optional if you specify *pathname* but required if you don't, is a Variant argument of the String subtype specifying the class of the object you want to return.

As with `CreateObject`, typically you'll use a `GetObject` function with a `Set` statement to assign to an object variable the object that you return with the `GetObject` function. For example, in the second of the following statements, the `GetObject` function returns an object consisting of the workbook `z:\Finance\Revenue.xls`. The `Set` statement assigns this object to the object variable named `Revenue` declared in the first statement:

```
Dim Revenue As Object
Set Revenue = GetObject("Z:\Finance\Revenue.xls")
```

Here, the workbook is associated with Excel. When this code runs, VBA starts Excel if it isn't already running and activates the workbook. You can then reference the object by referring to its object variable; in this example, you could manipulate the `Revenue` object to affect the workbook `Z:\Finance\Revenue.xls`.

Examples of Using Automation with the Office Applications

This section shows three examples of using Automation with the Office applications.

TRANSFERRING INFORMATION FROM AN EXCEL SPREADSHEET TO A WORD DOCUMENT

This example transfers information from an Excel spreadsheet to a Word document.

First, add to the target Word project (the project that will contain the code that accesses Excel) a reference to the Excel object library. For example:

1. Start or activate Word, and then launch the Visual Basic Editor (press Alt+F11 or choose Tools ➢ Macro ➢ Visual Basic Editor).

2. In the Project Explorer, click the project to which you want to add the reference. For example, if the procedure or procedures will reside in the `Normal.dot` template, select the Normal project in the Project Explorer before adding the reference.

3. Choose Tools ➢ References to display the References dialog box.

4. Select the check box for the Microsoft Excel Object Library item. The exact name of this check box depends on the version of Excel you're using—for example, Microsoft Excel 11.0 Object Library for Excel 2003, Microsoft Excel 10.0 Object Library for Excel XP, or Microsoft Excel 9.0 Object Library for Excel 2000.

5. Click the OK button to close the References dialog box.

Once you've added the reference, you can use the Object Browser to browse Excel objects. Display the Object Browser as usual by pressing F2 or choosing View ➢ Object Browser, and then choose Excel in the Project/Library drop-down list. The Object Browser will display the contents of the Excel object library, as shown in Figure 30.1. You can display the help for a selected Excel object by clicking the Help button in the Object Browser.

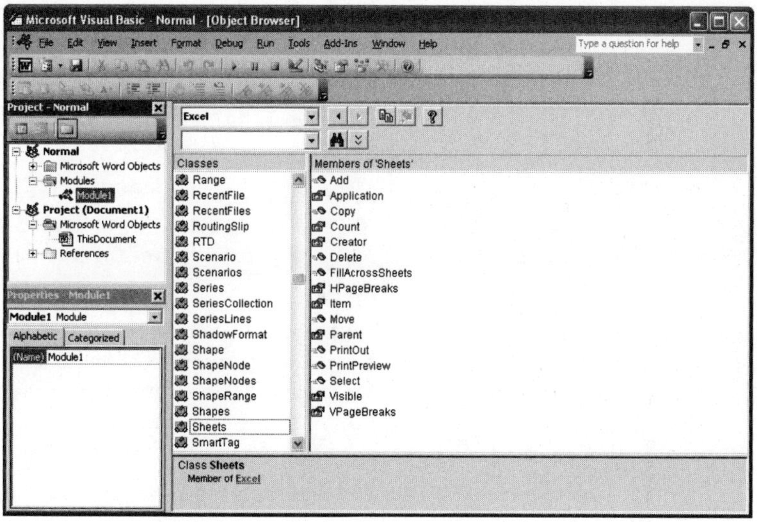

FIGURE 30.1
Once you've loaded the Excel object library, you can view its contents in the Object Browser from the Visual Basic Editor session launched from the host application (in this case, Microsoft Word).

Using the Visual Basic Editor's assistance and code-completion features, create the procedure shown in Listing 30.1. This procedure uses the `GetObject` function to retrieve the information from a cell in an Excel spreadsheet and insert it in the active Word document at the current selection.

LISTING 30.1:

```
1.   Sub Return_a_Value_from_Excel()
2.
3.       Dim mySpreadsheet As Excel.Workbook
4.       Dim strSalesTotal As String
5.
6.       Set mySpreadsheet = _
             GetObject("Y:\Users\Corporate\Sales Forecast.xls")
7.       strSalesTotal = mySpreadsheet.Application.Range("SalesTotal").Value
```

```
 8.        Set mySpreadsheet = Nothing
 9.
10.        Selection.TypeText "Current sales total: $" & strSalesTotal & "."
11.        Selection.TypeParagraph
12.
13.   End Sub
```

This subprocedure retrieves one piece of information from an Excel spreadsheet that's already open to give a simplified example of accessing information from another application. Here's what happens in the subprocedure:

◆ Line 3 declares the object variable mySpreadsheet of the type Excel.Workbook. Line 4 declares the String variable strSalesTotal.

◆ Line 6 uses a Set statement and the GetObject function to make mySpreadsheet reference the spreadsheet Y:\Users\Corporate\Sales Forecast.xls.

◆ Line 7 assigns to the String variable strSalesTotal the Value property of the Range object named SalesTotal in the Excel Application object. The SalesTotal range is a single cell, so strSalesTotal receives the value of the cell.

◆ Line 8 assigns to the mySpreadsheet object the special value Nothing, releasing the memory it occupied. (Because the procedure ends almost immediately afterward, this statement isn't necessary here—but it's good practice to free the memory assigned to an object when you no longer need to use the object.)

◆ Line 10 uses the TypeText method on the Selection object in Word to enter a string of text and the strSalesTotal string at the current selection. Line 11 uses the TypeParagraph method to insert a paragraph after the text. Line 13 ends the subprocedure.

TRANSFERRING INFORMATION FROM WORD DOCUMENTS TO AN EXCEL WORKBOOK

The previous example assumes that Excel is already running; if it is not, the GetObject function returns an error, and the subprocedure stops (unless you've built in an error handler). To avoid errors like this, check that your target application is running before you try to access it.

The procedure in Listing 30.2 performs this check. It also creates an Excel workbook from Word, transfers information to it, and saves the result.

As before, you'll find creating this procedure easier if you add to the current Word project a reference to the Excel object library. (See the previous section for instructions.)

LISTING 30.2:

```
1.   Sub List_Page_Counts_in_Excel_Spreadsheet()
2.
3.        Dim intCounter As Integer
4.        Dim strPath As String
5.        Dim strFile As String
6.        Dim docCurDoc As Document
```

```
 7.      Dim myXL As Excel.Application
 8.      Dim myXLS As Excel.Workbook
 9.      Const errExcelNotRunning = 429
10.      Const errDocNotAvailable = 5174
11.
12.      On Error GoTo Handle
13.
14.      Set myXL = GetObject(, "Excel.application")
15.      myXL.Visible = True
16.
17.      Set myXLS = myXL.Workbooks.Add
18.      myXL.ActiveCell = "Current Page Counts"
19.      strPath = "Y:\Sample Documents\Users\Projects\8001"
20.
21.      For intCounter = 1 To 20
22.          strFile = "8001c" & Format(intCounter, "00") & ".doc"
23.          Set docCurDoc = Documents.Open(strPath & "\" _
                  & strFile, AddToRecentFiles:=False)
24.          myXL.ActiveCell.Offset(1, 0).Range("A1").Select
25.          myXL.ActiveCell = docCurDoc.Name
26.          myXL.ActiveCell.Offset(0, 1).Range("A1").Select
27.          myXL.ActiveCell = docCurDoc _
                  .BuiltInDocumentProperties(wdPropertyPages)
28.          myXL.ActiveCell.Offset(0, -1).Range("A1").Select
29.          docCurDoc.Close SaveChanges:=wdDoNotSaveChanges
30.  SkipLoop:
31.      Next intCounter
32.      myXLS.SaveAs strPath & "\" & "8001stats.xls"
33.      myXLS.Close
34.      myXL.Quit
35.      Set myXL = Nothing
36.      Set myXLS = Nothing
37.      Exit Sub
38.
39.  Handle:
40.       If Err.Number = errExcelNotRunning Then
41.          Set myXL = CreateObject("Excel.Application")
42.          Err.Clear
43.          Resume Next
44.      ElseIf Err.Number = errDocNotAvailable Then
45.          myXL.ActiveCell.Offset(1, 0).Range("A1").Select
46.          myXL.ActiveCell = strFile
47.          myXL.ActiveCell.Offset(0, 1).Range("A1").Select
48.          myXL.ActiveCell = "Not available"
49.          myXL.ActiveCell.Offset(0, -1).Range("A1").Select
50.          Err.Clear
51.          GoTo SkipLoop
52.      Else
```

```
53.          Resume Next
54.      End If
55.
56.  End Sub
```

Here's what happens in Listing 30.2:

- Line 2 is a spacer. Line 3 declares the Integer variable `intCounter`. Line 4 declares the String variable `strPath`, and line 5 declares the String variable `strFile`. Line 6 declares the `Document` variable `docCurDoc`; line 7 declares the `Excel.Application` object variable `myXL`; and line 8 declares the `Excel.Workbook` object variable `myXLS`.

- Line 9 declares the constant `errExcelNotRunning`, setting its value to 429. Line 10 declares the constant `errDocNotAvailable`, setting its value to 5194. Line 11 is a spacer.

- Line 12 starts error handling for the procedure, directing execution to the label `Handle` in the event of an error. Line 13 is a spacer.

- Line 14 assigns to `myXL` the current instance of Excel, which it returns using the `GetObject` function. If Excel isn't running at this point, error 429 ("ActiveX component cannot create object") occurs, so line 40 in the error handler checks for this error by using the constant `errExcelNotRunning`. If it matches, line 41 assigns to `myXL` a new instance of Excel that it creates by using the `CreateObject` function. Line 42 then uses an `Err.Clear` statement to clear the error, and line 43 contains a `Resume Next` statement to cause VBA to resume execution at the statement after the offending statement.

- One way or another, by the time line 15 is run, `myXL` refers to a running instance of Excel. Line 15 sets the `Visible` property of `myXL` to `True`, so that it appears on screen. Line 16 is a spacer.

- Line 17 assigns to `myXLS` a new workbook created by using the `Add` method of the `Workbooks` object in `myXL`.

- Line 18 assigns to the active cell in `myXL` the text `Current Page Counts`. Line 19 assigns to `strPath` the path to the folder that contains the documents. Line 20 is a spacer.

- Lines 21 through 31 contain a `For...Next` loop that runs from 1 to 30, opening the document files for a project in their numbered sequence and inserting their names and page counts in the first two columns of the active worksheet in the workbook. Here's what happens:

  - Line 22 assigns to `strFile` a string specifying the name of the document. This string consists of the text 8001c, a two-digit representation of `intCounter` (returned by using the `Format` function), and `.doc`—8001c01.doc through 8001c20.doc.

  - Line 23 opens the document specified by `strPath`, a backslash, and `strFile`, assigning it to `docCurDoc`. If the document isn't available, an error occurs. You'll see how to handle this error in a moment.

  - Line 24 selects the Excel worksheet cell offset from the active cell by one row and zero columns (`Offset(1, 0)`).

  - Line 25 assigns the `Name` property of `docCurDoc` to the active cell in the worksheet.

- Line 26 uses the `Offset` property again, this time to select the cell one column to the right of the active cell.

- Line 27 enters in this cell the `wdPropertyPages` property from the `BuiltInDocumentProperties` collection of `docCurDoc`.

- Line 28 uses the `Offset` property a third time, this time selecting the cell one column to the left of the active cell. This move positions the active cell suitably for the next pass through the loop.

- Line 29 closes `docCurDoc` without saving changes.

- Line 30 contains a label named `SkipLoop`. If the document summoned in line 23 isn't available, an error results, and execution returns to this label. Line 23 causes the error, and the `ElseIf Err.Number = errDocNotAvailable` statement in line 44 of the error handler picks it up. The statements in lines 45 through 49 then mimic those in lines 24 through 28, except that they enter `strFile` in the left column rather than the `Name` property of `docCurDoc` and `Not available` in the right column rather than the page count. Line 50 then uses an `Err.Clear` statement to clear the error, and Line 51 hen uses a `GoTo` statement to direct execution to the `SkipLoop` label.

- Line 31 ends the `For... Next` loop.

- Line 32 saves myXLS under the name `8001stats.xls` in the `strPath` folder. Line 33 then closes myXLS, and line 34 uses the `Quit` method to close myXL.

- Lines 36 and 37 set myXL and myXLS to `Nothing`, reclaiming the memory they took up.

- Line 37 uses an `Exit Sub` statement to exit the procedure to avoid reaching the error-handling statements.

PLACING A POWERPOINT SLIDE IN AN OUTLOOK MESSAGE

The next procedure provides an example of establishing communication between PowerPoint and Outlook. The procedure, run from PowerPoint, returns the existing instance of Outlook or (if there is none) creates a new instance. The procedure then uses PowerPoint to send a message that gives details drawn from the presentation.

Listing 30.3 shows the procedure. There's one complication: Because PowerPoint doesn't have a central macro-storage project like Word's `Normal.dot` or Excel's Personal Macro Workbook, the code must be stored in an open presentation. This could be the presentation that is the subject of the e-mail, but it is much more convenient to maintain a code-only presentation that you open at the beginning of each PowerPoint session that requires the use of code.

First, add to the target PowerPoint project (the project that will contain the code that accesses Outlook) a reference to the Outlook object library. For example:

1. Start or activate PowerPoint, and then launch the Visual Basic Editor (press Alt+F11 or choose Tools ➢ Macro ➢ Visual Basic Editor).

2. In the Project Explorer, click the project to which you want to add the reference. For example, if you've designated a code presentation, click it in the Project Explorer before you add the reference.

3. Choose Tools ➢ References to display the References dialog box.

4. Select the check box for the Microsoft Outlook Object Library item. The exact name of this check box depends on the version of Outlook you're using—for example, Microsoft Outlook 11.0 Object Library for Outlook 2003, Microsoft Outlook 10.0 Object Library for Outlook XP, or Microsoft Outlook 9.0 Object Library for Outlook 2000.

5. Click the OK button to close the References dialog box.

LISTING 30.3:

```
1.   Sub Notify_of_New_Presentation()
2.
3.       Dim myPresentation As Presentation
4.       Dim strPresentationFilename As String
5.       Dim strPresentationTitle As String
6.       Dim strPresentationPresenter As String
7.       Dim myOutlook As Outlook.Application
8.       Dim myMessage As Outlook.MailItem
9.       Const errOutlookNotRunning = 429
10.
11.      On Error GoTo ErrorHandler
12.
13.      Set myPresentation = ActivePresentation
14.      With myPresentation
15.          strPresentationFilename = .FullName
16.          strPresentationTitle = _
                 .Slides(1).Shapes(1).TextFrame.TextRange.Text
17.          strPresentationPresenter = _
                 .Slides(1).Shapes(2).TextFrame.TextRange.Text
18.      End With
19.
20.      Set myOutlook = GetObject(, "Outlook.Application")
21.      Set myMessage = myOutlook.CreateItem(ItemType:=olMailItem)
22.      With myMessage
23.          .To = "Review Group"
24.          .CC = "Presentation Archive"
25.          .Subject = "Presentation for review: " & strPresentationTitle
26.          .BodyFormat = olFormatHTML
27.          .Body = "Please review the following presentation:" & _
                 vbCr & vbCr & "Title: " & strPresentationTitle & vbCr & _
                 "Presenter: " & strPresentationPresenter & vbCr & vbCr & _
                 "The presentation is in the file: " & _
                 strPresentationFilename
28.          .Send
29.      End With
30.
31.      myOutlook.Quit
32.
```

```
33.        Set myMessage = Nothing
34.        Set myOutlook = Nothing
35.        Exit Sub
36.   ErrorHandler:
37.        If Err.Number = errOutlookNotRunning Then
38.            Set myOutlook = CreateObject("Outlook.Application")
39.            Err.Clear
40.            Resume Next
41.        Else
42.            MsgBox Err.Number & vbCr & Err.Description, vbOKOnly + _
                   Critical, "An Error Has Occurred"
43.        End If
44.
45.   End Sub
```

Here's what happens in the procedure:

♦ Line 2 is a spacer. Line 3 declares a `Presentation` object variable named `myPresentation`. Line 4 declares a String variable named `strPresentationFilename`, which is used for storing the path and filename of the presentation. Line 5 declares a String variable named `strPresentationTitle`, which is used to store the title of the presentation. Line 6 declares a String variable named `strPresentationPresenter`, which is used to store the name of the presenter of the presentation.

♦ Line 7 declares an `Outlook.Application` object variable named `myOutlook` that is used to represent the Outlook application. Line 8 declares an `Outlook.MailItem` object variable named `myMessage` that is used to represent the message that the procedure creates. Line 9 declares a constant named `errOutlookNotRunning` and assigns to it the number 429, the number of the error returned if no instance of Outlook is available when the `GetObject` function tries to access it. Line 10 is a spacer.

♦ Line 11 starts error handling for the procedure, directing execution to the label `ErrorHandler` (in line 36) in the event of an error. Line 12 is a spacer.

♦ Line 13 assigns the active presentation to the `myPresentation` object variable. Lines 14 through 18 contain a `With` structure that works with `myPresentation`. Line 15 assigns the `FullName` property of `myPresentation` to `strPresentationFilename`. Line 16 assigns to `strPresentationTitle` the Text property of the `TextRange` object in the `TextFrame` object in the first `Shape` object on the first `Slide` object—in other words, the text from the first placeholder shape on the first slide in the presentation. Similarly, line 17 assigns to `strPresentationPresenter` the text from the second shape on the first slide. (The first slide in this presentation has two placeholder shapes, the first for the title and the second for the presenter's name.)

♦ Line 20 assigns to `myOutlook` the current instance of Outlook, which it returns using the `GetObject` function. If Outlook isn't running at this point, error 429 ("ActiveX component cannot create object") occurs, so line 37 in the error handler checks for this error by using the constant `errOutlookNotRunning`. If it matches, line 38 assigns to `myOutlook` a new instance of

Outlook that it creates by using the CreateObject function. Line 39 then uses an Err.Clear statement to clear the error, and line 40 contains a Resume Next statement to cause VBA to resume execution at the statement after the offending statement.

◆ Line 21 uses the CreateItem method of the Outlook Application object (represented by myOutlook) to create a new mail item, which it assigns to myMessage. Lines 22 through 29 contain a With structure that work with myMessage. Line 23 assigns recipients by setting the To property, line 24 adds a CC recipient by setting the CC property, and line 25 enters text for the Subject property. Line 26 specifies that the message use HTML formatting (.BodyFormat = olFormatHTML). Line 27 assigns text to the body of the message by using the Body property. Line 28 then uses the Send method to send the message. Line 30 is a spacer.

◆ Line 31 uses the Quit method to close myOutlook. Line 32 is a spacer.

◆ Line 33 sets myMessage to Nothing, releasing the memory it occupied. Similarly, line 34 sets myOutlook to Nothing. Line 35 then exits the procedure.

◆ As discussed earlier in this list, the primary function of the error handler is to launch an instance of Outlook if none is currently running. If any other error than error 429 occurs, execution branches to the Else statement in line 41, and line 42 displays a message box that gives the error number and description.

Using the *Shell* Function to Run an Application

Instead of using CreateObject to start an application and return a reference to it, you can use the Shell function to run another application. Shell can run any executable program, and its syntax is straightforward:

```
Shell(pathname[,windowstyle])
```

Here, pathname is the name of the program you want Shell to run, together with a path and any necessary command-line switches or arguments. If the program is in the computer's path, you don't need to specify the full path of the program, but it's usually safest to do so.

NOTE   Shell can also run a file whose extension is associated with a known program. For example, Shell "testfile.txt" usually starts Notepad, because Notepad is usually associated with .txt files. If Shell can't find the specified application or file, it returns a runtime error.

windowstyle is an optional Variant argument of the Integer subtype that you use to specify the type of window in which to run the application. Table 30.1 lists the constants and values for windowstyle.

TABLE 30.1:   Constants and Values for the windowstyle Argument

CONSTANT	VALUE	WINDOW STYLE
vbHide	0	Minimized and hidden, but with focus
vbNormalFocus	1	Normal ("restored") with focus
vbMinimizedFocus	2	Minimized with focus (the default)

TABLE 30.1:   Constants and Values for the `windowstyle` Argument *(CONTINUED)*

CONSTANT	VALUE	WINDOW STYLE
vbMaximizedFocus	3	Maximized with focus
vbNormalNoFocus	4	Normal ("restored") without focus
vbMinimizedNoFocus	6	Minimized without focus

USING THE *SLEEP* FUNCTION TO AVOID PROBLEMS WITH SHELL'S ASYNCHRONY

The `Shell` function runs other programs *asynchronously* rather than *synchronously*. So when VBA executes a `Shell` statement, it registers the statement as an action to be performed—but the action may not necessarily be finished before the next statement in the procedure executes.

This asynchrony can cause errors in your procedures if subsequent commands depend on the `Shell` statement having executed. If you run into this type of problem, a crude but often effective fix is to allow extra time for the `Shell` function to execute before taking any dependent action. For example, you might run the `Shell` function earlier in the process than you otherwise would have done rather than running it right before the dependent actions. A better solution is to use an API call (such as `Sleep`) to delay the execution of further statements for a few seconds so that the `Shell` function can finish executing. Place this declaration in the declarations section at the beginning of the code sheet:

```
Public Declare Sub Sleep Lib "kernel32" (ByVal dwMilliseconds As Long)
```

Then call the `Sleep` function at the appropriate point in your code, specifying the number of milliseconds you want the code to wait. The following statement uses `Sleep` to implement a two-second delay:

```
Sleep (2000)
```

Returning the Task ID of the Started Application

The `Shell` function returns a unique task identification number (*task ID*) that identifies the application it has just started. You can use this task ID to quickly access the application without having to list all the applications that are running.

To return the task ID of an application, assign the task ID to a variable when you run the `Shell` statement. The following example runs Lotus 1-2-3 and assigns the task ID to the `MyTaskID` variable:

```
Dim myTaskID As Long
myTaskID = Shell("c:\lotus\123\programs\123w.exe")
```

Activating an Application

To activate an application, use the `AppActivate` statement. `AppActivate` activates the other application but doesn't maximize or restore it—so if the application is minimized, focus will be shifted to its Taskbar icon, but the application won't be displayed. (To maximize, minimize, or restore an application window, use the `Shell` statement as discussed earlier in this chapter.)

The syntax for `AppActivate` is as follows:

```
AppActivate title[, wait]
```

Here, `title` is a required String specifying the title contained in the title bar of the application window to be activated. For example, to activate Excel, you'd specify **Microsoft Excel** for `title`, because Excel displays "Microsoft Excel" in its title bar:

```
AppActivate "Microsoft Excel"
```

TIP   If you have two or more sessions of Excel running, VBA arbitrarily picks one. To avoid this random choice, you can specify the full title in the title bar—for example, **Microsoft Excel - Book2**.

You can also activate an application by using the task ID for the application that you return with the `Shell` function. Using the task ID eliminates the possibility of confusing multiple sessions of the same application.

`wait` is an optional Boolean value that you can use to specify whether the application that calls the other application needs to have the focus before it can call the other application. The default `wait` setting is `False`, which specifies that the calling application doesn't need to have the focus before it can call the other application. You can set `wait` to `True` to have the calling application wait until it has the focus before it can call the other application. You might want to set `wait` to `True` to avoid having the calling application interrupt a sensitive process that had the focus.

For example, the following statement activates PowerPoint:

```
AppActivate "Microsoft PowerPoint"
```

The following statements start Lotus 1-2-3 and assign its task ID to a variable, and then use the variable to activate 1-2-3:

```
Dim myTaskID As Long
myTaskID = Shell("c:\lotus\123\programs\123w.exe")
AppActivate MyTaskID
```

Using Data Objects to Store and Retrieve Information

A data object is logically attached to a `UserForm` object in the Microsoft Forms object model, but you can use a data object without using a user form. A data object, which is represented in VBA by the `DataObject` object, is an object in which you store data. Each data object can hold multiple pieces of textual information, and each piece must be in a different, defined format. You can create and use multiple data objects to store multiple pieces of data in the same format, or you can cheat and tell VBA that information is in a different format when really it's not.

As you've seen so far in this book, you can store information in many other places using VBA. But what you may find useful about the data object is its ability to return information from and write information to the Clipboard.

The Clipboard can contain one text item and one item in another format, such as a graphical object. If you copy another text item to the Clipboard, that item will overwrite the previous text item, but any graphical item on the Clipboard will remain unscathed. Likewise, if you copy a graphical item to the Clipboard, it will overwrite any previous graphical item (or indeed any item in a non-text format) stored on the Clipboard, but any text item on the Clipboard won't be affected.

The data object works in a similar but different way: It can't store graphical information, but it can store multiple pieces of textual information, each defined as being in a different format. (The pieces of data don't actually have to be in different formats.)

Creating a Data Object

To create a data object, declare an object variable of the `DataObject` type and then use a `Set` statement to assign a new `DataObject` object to it. For example, the following statements declare a `DataObject` variable named `myDObj` and assign a new `DataObject` to it:

```
Dim myDObj As DataObject
Set myDObj = New DataObject
```

Storing Information in a Data Object

To store information in a data object, use the `SetText` method. The `SetText` method takes the following syntax:

```
object.SetText(StoreData [, format])
```

The components of the syntax are as follows:

◆ *object* is a required argument specifying a valid object.

◆ `StoreData` is a required argument specifying the data to store in the data object.

◆ `format` is an optional argument containing an Integer value or a String specifying the format of the information in `StoreData`. A value of 1 indicates text format; a value other than 1 or a String indicates a user-defined format.

For example, the following statement stores the text `Sample text string` in the `DataObject` named `myDObj`:

```
myDObj.SetText "Sample text string"
```

The following statement stores the text `Sample formatted text string` in the `DataObject` named `myDObj`, defining and using the custom format `myFormat`:

```
myDObj.SetText "Sample formatted text string", "myFormat"
```

Once the custom format has been defined and stored in the data object, you can access the data stored in that format by specifying the format. In this case, no formatting actually involved—the code simply uses the *format* argument to create and identify a different data slot in the data object so that the new string doesn't overwrite the existing text string.

Returning Information from a Data Object

To return information from a data object, use the `GetText` method of the `DataObject` object. The `GetText` method takes the following syntax:

```
object.GetText([format])
```

The components of the syntax are as follows:

◆ *object* is a required argument specifying a valid object.

◆ `format` is an optional argument containing a String or an Integer specifying the format of the data to retrieve.

For example, the following statement displays a message box containing the plain-text string stored in the `DataObject` named `myDObj`:

```
MsgBox myDObj.GetText
```

The following statement assigns to the String variable `strTemp` the text stored with the `myFormat` format in the `DataObject` named `myDObj`:

```
strTemp = myDObj.GetText("myFormat")
```

Assigning Information to the Clipboard

To assign text to the Clipboard from a data object, use the `PutInClipboard` method of the appropriate `DataObject` object. For example, the following statements create a new data object named `myDO`, assign to it the text `Atlanta Industrial Pharmaceuticals`, and then assign that text to the Clipboard:

```
Dim myDO As DataObject
Set myDO = New DataObject
myDO.SetText "Atlanta Industrial Pharmaceuticals"
myDO.PutInClipboard
```

Returning Information from the Clipboard to a Data Object

To return text information from the Clipboard and store it in a data object, use the `GetFromClipboard` method of the `DataObject` object. For example, the following statements create a data object referenced by the variable `aDO` and assign to it the text from the Clipboard:

```
Dim aDO As DataObject
Set aDO = New DataObject
aDO.GetFromClipboard
```

To return formatted information from the Clipboard and store it in a data object, use the `GetFormat` method of the `DataObject` object.

Finding Out Whether a Data Object Contains a Given Format

To find out whether a data object contains a given format, use the `GetFormat` method of the `DataObject` object. The syntax for the `GetFormat` method is as follows:

```
object.GetFormat(format)
```

The components of the syntax are as follows:

◆ *object* is a required argument that returns a valid `DataObject` object.

◆ `format` is an Integer or String specifying the format you're looking for. If the `DataObject` contains the format, `GetFormat` returns `True`; if not, `GetFormat` returns `False`.

For example, the following statement checks to see if the `DataObject` named `myDO` contains the format `myHTML` and assigns the format's contents to the string `strHTMLText` if it does:

```
If myDO.GetFormat("myHTML") = True Then _
    strHTMLText = myDO.GetText(Format:="myHTML")
```

Communicating via DDE

If the application with which you want to communicate doesn't support Automation, you can try Dynamic Data Exchange (DDE). DDE is a protocol that establishes a channel between two applications through which they can automatically exchange data. DDE can be tricky to set up, but once you get it working, it is usually reliable.

NOTE   Not all applications support DDE. Among the Office applications, Word, Excel, and Access support DDE, but PowerPoint and Outlook do not.

A typical DDE conversation can contain the following actions:

◆ Using the `DDEInitiate` method to start a DDE connection and establish the channel on which the connection operates

◆ Using the `DDERequest` method to return text from the other application or the `DDEPoke` method to send text to the other application

◆ Using the `DDEExecute` method to execute a command in the other application

◆ Using the `DDETerminate` method to close the current DDE channel or using the `DDETerminateAll` method to close all the DDE channels

Using *DDEInitiate* to Start a DDE Connection

To start a DDE connection, you use the `DDEInitiate` method. The `DDEInitiate` method takes the following syntax:

```
expression.DDEInitiate(App, Topic)
```

The components of the syntax are as follows:

◆ *expression* is an optional expression specifying an `Application` object.

◆ App is a required String argument specifying the name of the application with which the DDE connection is to be started.

◆ Topic is a required String argument specifying the DDE topic (such as an open file) in the application. To discover the list of topics available for an application, you send a DDE request (via the `DDERequest` method, discussed in the next section) to the `System` object in the application.

`DDEInitiate` returns the number of the DDE channel established. You then use this number for subsequent DDE calls.

For example, the following statements declare the Long variable `lngDDEChannel1` and assign to it a DDE channel established with the workbook `Sales Results.xls` in Excel:

```
Dim lngDDEChannel1 As Long
lngDDEChannel1 = DDEInitiate("Excel", "Sales Results.xls")
```

Using *DDERequest* to Return Text from Another Application

To return a string of text from another application, you use the DDERequest method. The DDERequest method takes the following syntax:

```
expression.DDERequest(Channel, Item)
```

The components of the syntax are as follows:

- *expression* is an optional expression than returns an Application object.
- *Channel* is a required Long argument specifying the DDE channel to use for the request.
- *Item* is a required String argument specifying the item requested.

To get the list of topics available via DDE, request the Topics item from the System topic. For example, the following statements establish a DDE channel to FrontPage (by using DDEInitiate) and return the list of DDE topics, assigning the list to the String variable strDDETopics:

```
Dim lngDDE1 As Long
Dim strDDETopics As String
lngDDE1 = DDEInitiate(App:="FrontPage", Topic:="System")
strDDETopics = DDERequest(Channel:=lngDDE1, Item:="Topics")
```

The following statements establish a DDE channel to the workbook Sales Results.xls in Excel and return the contents of cell C7 (R7C3) in the String variable strResult:

```
Dim lngDDEChannel1 As Long, strResult As String
lngDDEChannel1 = DDEInitiate("Excel", "Sales Results.xls")
strResult = DDERequest(lngDDEChannel1, "R7C3")
```

Using *DDEPoke* to Send Text to Another Application

To send text to another application, use the DDEPoke method. The DDEPoke method takes the following syntax:

```
expression.DDEPoke(Channel, Item, Data)
```

The components of the syntax are as follows:

- *expression* is an optional expression that returns an Application object.
- Channel is a required Long argument specifying the DDE channel to use.
- Item is a required String argument specifying the item to which to send the data.
- Data is a required String argument specifying the data to be sent.

Continuing the previous example, the following statements use the DDEPoke method to assign the data 2000 to cell C7 in the worksheet if the value of the result returned is less than 2000:

```
Dim lngDDEChannel1 As Long, strResult As String
lngDDEChannel1 = DDEInitiate("Excel", "Sales Results.xls")
strResult = DDERequest(lngDDEChannel1, "R7C3")
If Val(strResult) < 2000 Then
    DDEPoke Channel:=lngDDEChannel1, Item:="R7C3", Data:="2000"
End If
```

Using *DDEExecute* to Execute a Command in Another Application

To execute a command in another application, use the DDEExecute method. The DDEExecute method takes the following syntax:

```
expression.DDEExecute(Channel, Command)
```

The components of the syntax are as follows:

◆ *expression* is an optional expression that returns an Application object.

◆ Channel is a required Long argument specifying the DDE channel to use.

◆ Command is a required String argument specifying the command or series of commands to execute.

For example, the following statements establish a DDE channel to Excel and issue a Close command to close the active workbook:

```
Dim lngMyChannel
lngMyChannel = DDEInitiate(App:="Excel", Topic:="System")
DDEExecute lngMyChannel, Command:="[Close]"
```

Using *DDETerminate* to Close a DDE Channel

When you've finished a DDE communication, use the DDETerminate method to close the DDE channel you opened. The syntax for the DDETerminate method is as follows:

```
expression.DDETerminate(Channel)
```

The components of the syntax are as follows:

◆ *expression* is an optional expression that returns an Application object.

◆ Channel is a required Long argument specifying the DDE channel to close.

The following statements continue the previous example, closing the DDE channel that was opened:

```
Dim lngMyChannel
lngMyChannel = DDEInitiate(App:="Excel", Topic:="System")
DDEExecute lngMyChannel, Command:="[Close]"
DDETerminate lngMyChannel
```

Using *DDETerminateAll* to Close All Open DDE Channels

To close all open DDE channels, use the DDETerminateAll method:

```
DDETerminateAll
```

Because VBA doesn't automatically close DDE channels when a procedure ends, it's a good idea to use a DDETerminateAll statement to make sure you haven't inadvertently left any DDE channels open.

Communicating via *SendKeys*

The SendKeys statement is a basic and limited form of communication with other applications. You may find SendKeys useful if neither Automation nor DDE works with the target application.

SendKeys sends the specified keystrokes to the destination application. For example, to use SendKeys to send the command to create a new file in Notepad, you send the keystrokes for **Alt+F** and **N** (to execute the File ➢ New command), and Notepad reacts as if you had pressed the keys manually.

SendKeys works only with currently running Windows applications: You can't use SendKeys to start another application (for that you need to use Shell, as discussed earlier in this chapter), nor can you use SendKeys to communicate with DOS applications running in virtual DOS machines under Windows.

The syntax for the SendKeys statement is

```
SendKeys string[, wait]
```

Here, string is a required String expression specifying the keystrokes to be sent to the destination application. wait is an optional Boolean value specifying whether to wait after sending the keystrokes until the application has executed them (True) or to immediately return control to the procedure sending the keystrokes (False, the default setting).

Typically, string consists of a series of keystrokes (rather than a single keystroke). All alphanumeric characters that appear on the regular keyboard are represented by the characters themselves: To send the letter *H*, you specify **H** in the string, and to send the word *Hello*, you specify **Hello** in the string. To denote the movement and editing keys, SendKeys uses keywords enclosed within braces ({ }), as described in Table 30.2.

TABLE 30.2: SendKeys Keywords for Movement and Editing Keys

KEY	CODE
,	{DOWN}
fl	{LEFT}
‡	{RIGHT}
.	{UP}
Backspace	{BACKSPACE}, {BS}, or {BKSP}
Break	{BREAK}
Caps Lock	{CAPSLOCK}
Delete	{DELETE} or {DEL}
End	{END}
Enter	{ENTER}

TABLE 30.2:   SendKeys Keywords for Movement and Editing Keys *(CONTINUED)*

KEY	CODE
Esc	{ESC}
F1, F2, etc.	{F1}, {F2}, etc. (up to {F16})
Help	{HELP}
Home	{HOME}
Insert	{INSERT} or {INS}
Num Lock	{NUMLOCK}
Page Down	{PGDN}
Page Up	{PGUP}
Print Screen	{PRTSC}
Scroll Lock	{SCROLLLOCK}
Tab	{TAB}

To send meta keys, use the symbols shown in Table 30.3.

TABLE 30.3:   SendKeys Symbols for Meta Keys

KEY	CODE
Shift	+
Ctrl	^
Alt	%

SendKeys automatically assigns the keystroke after the meta key to the meta key. For example, to send a Ctrl+O keystroke, you specify **^O**, and SendKeys assigns the *O* to the Ctrl keystroke; the next keystroke after the *O* is considered to be struck separately. If you need to assign multiple keystrokes to the meta key, enter the keystrokes in parentheses after the meta key. For example, to send Alt+F, Alt+I, Alt+I, you'd specify **%(FII)** rather than **%FII**.

SendKeys has special meanings for the plus sign (+), caret (^), percent sign (%), and parentheses (); the tilde (~) gets special treatment as well. To use these characters to represent themselves, enter them within braces: {+} sends a regular + sign, {^} a regular caret, {%} a percent sign, {~} a tilde, and {()} parentheses. Likewise, you must enclose brackets (which have a special meaning in DDE in some applications) within braces; braces themselves also go within braces.

Using SendKeys is much less complex than these details initially make it appear—and with that reassurance, there's one more trick you should know: To repeat a key, enter the key and the number of repetitions in braces. For example, to send 5 ↑ keystrokes, you'd specify {**UP 5**}; to send 10 zeroes, you'd specify {**0 10**}.

Listing 30.4 shows an example of using SendKeys to start Notepad and send log-file information to it.

WARNING   Because SendKeys needs to activate the target application, you can't step into the code in the Visual Basic Editor—the Visual Basic Editor grabs the focus back at the wrong point, directing the keystrokes toward itself rather than the target application. Instead, you must run the procedure, either from the Visual Basic Editor or from the host app.

LISTING 30.4:

```
1.  Sub Send_to_Notepad()
2.      Dim strLogDate As String
3.      Dim strSaveLog As String
4.      Dim strMsg As String
5.      Dim appNotepad As Variant
6.      strMsg = "Sample log text here."
7.      strLogDate = Month(Now) & "-" & Day(Now) & "-" & Year(Now)
8.      strSaveLog = "Log file for " & strLogDate & ".txt"
9.      appNotepad = Shell("notepad.exe", vbNormalFocus)
10.     AppActivate appNotepad
11.     SendKeys strMsg & "%FS" & strSaveLog & "{Enter}" & "%{F4}", True
12.  End Sub
```

Here's how the code works:

◆ The Send_to_Notepad procedure starts by declaring (in lines 2, 3, and 4) three String variables—strLogDate, strSaveLog, and strMsg—and (in line 5) one Variant variable, appNotepad.

◆ Line 6 then assigns to strMsg a sample string of text.

◆ Line 7 assigns to strLogDate a date built of the Day, Month, and Year values for Now (which returns the current date and time). For example, if the date is July 11, 2006, Month(Now) will return 7, Day(Now) will return 11, and Year(Now) will return 2006, so the strLogDate string will contain 7-11-2006.

◆ Line 8 then assigns to the strSaveLog string (which will be used to supply the filename for the log file) text describing the file, the strLogDate string, and the .txt extension (to continue our example, Log file for 7-11-2006.txt).

◆ In line 9, the procedure finally gets down to business, using the Shell statement to run Notepad in a "normal" (not maximized or minimized) window with focus and storing the task ID of the Notepad session in the variable appNotepad.

- Line 10 then uses an `AppActivate` statement to activate Notepad.

- Line 11 uses a `SendKeys` statement to send to Notepad the following:

  - The information contained in the String variable `strMsg`.

  - An Alt+F keystroke (to pull down the File menu), followed by an S keypress to choose the Save item on the menu. This keypress displays the Save As dialog box with the File Name text box selected.

  - The `strSaveLog` String variable, which is entered in the File Name text box.

  - An Enter keypress to choose the Save button in the Save As dialog box.

  - An Alt+F4 keystroke to quit Notepad.

- Line 12 ends the procedure.

When you run this procedure (again, you need to run the procedure rather than stepping into it), you'll see the following:

1. Notepad springs to life.

2. The contents of the `Msg` string appear in the Notepad window.

3. The Save As dialog box displays itself, enters the filename in the File Name text box, and then dismisses itself.

4. Notepad closes.

Glossary

Boldface indicates that a term is defined elsewhere in the Glossary.

& operator

See **concatenation operator**.

A

access key

Another term for **accelerator key**.

active

(Of an **error handler**) Execution has branched to the **error handler**, and the error handler is in action.

adaptive menu

A menu that changes its items to reflect the user's usage, promoting the most-used items and hiding never-used items.

ANSI

American National Standards Institute

application-modal

(Of a message box) Prevents the user from taking further actions in the application until the message box is dismissed.

argument

A piece of information that you pass to a **procedure** or **function**.

arithmetic operators

Operators such as + and −, used for performing mathematical calculations.

array

A **variable** that can contain a number of values that have the same **data type**. VBA supports **fixed-size arrays** and **dynamic arrays**.

array subscript

The number declaring the number of items in an **array** or the number that identifies a particular item in the array.

assignment operator

The equal sign, used to assign a value to a **property** or a **variable**.

B

binary comparison

A case-sensitive comparison.

binary search

An efficient means of searching a sorted **array**.

block If

A multiple-line If… Then **statement**.

Boolean

(Of a **variable**) Has two possible values—True and False.

Break mode

When **code** is running but execution is temporarily suspended. Break mode lets you step through your **code** one command or one **procedure** at a time (rather than running all the commands at once). You use it to **debug** your **code**.

bug

An error in hardware or software that causes a program to execute incorrectly.

by reference

One way of passing an **argument** (the other is **by value**). When a **procedure** passes an **argument** to another **procedure** by reference, the recipient **procedure** gets access to the memory location where the original **variable** is stored and can change the original **variable**.

by value

One way of passing an **argument** (the other is **by reference**). When a **procedure** passes an **argument** to another **procedure** by value, the recipient **procedure** gets only a copy of the information in the **variable** and can't change the information in the original **variable**.

C

call

To invoke a **function** or **procedure**.

character code

The numbers by which computers refer to letters. For example, the **ANSI** character code for a capital *A* is 65 and for a capital *B* is 66; a lowercase *a* is 97, and a lowercase *b* is 98.

class instance

A custom **object**—an instance of a class defined in a **class module.**

class module

A module that contains the definition of a **class**.

clean

(Of a file) Contains no unsaved changes. Opposite of **dirty**.

code

Instructions in a programming language.

code module

A storage **module** that may contain **subprocedures** or **functions**.

collection

An **object** that contains several other **objects**, typically of the same type as one another. (For example, the `Workbooks` collection in Excel contains `Workbook` objects.) .

combination box

A **control** that combines a list box and a text box, allowing the user to select an existing entry from a list or type a new entry.

combo box

A diminutive for **combination box**.

COM

The acronym for Component Object Model.

comment

An explanatory line of text explaining what the **code** is doing (or trying to do). Comments are not executed.

comment out

To apply a **comment** to a line of code, so that it will not be executed.

comparison operators

Operators such as < and > (less-than and greater-than, respectively) used for values.

compile error

An error than occurs when VBA can't compile a statement correctly.

Component Object Model

Microsoft's standard for defining the programming interfaces that **objects** expose so that other **objects** can communicate with them.

concatenate

To join together (literally, "chain together"). For example, if you concatenate the **strings** `contra` and `diction`, you get `contradiction`.

concatenation operators

The operators & and +, used for joining two **strings** together.

constant

A named item that keeps a constant value while a program is executing. VBA uses **intrinsic constants** and **user-defined constants**.

context menu

A menu that displays items relevant to the current context. To display a context menu, you right-click an object with the mouse (click with the non-primary button).

control

An visual **object** on a **user form**.

coolswitch

To switch between applications by using the Alt+Tab keystroke.

D

data type

The type of data assigned to a **variable**.

data-typing

Assigning a **data type** to a **variable**.

data-typing error

An error that occurs when you assign to a strongly typed **variable** (a variable that has a defined data type) some information of the wrong **data type**.

debug

To test a **procedure** and (try to) remove every **bug** from it.

Design mode

Any time you're working in the Visual Basic Editor on your **code**, except when you're running **code**.

Design time

Another term for **Design mode**.

digital certificate

Encrypted digital information that uniquely identifies its holder. You use your digital certificate to create a digital signature for a **project**.

dirty

(Of a file) Contains unsaved changes. Opposite of **clean**.

Double

(Of a **variable**) A double-precision floating point number.

dynamic array

An **array** with a changeable number of **subscripts**.

dynamic dialog box

A dialog box that changes and updates itself when the user clicks a **control** within it.

E

edit box

Another term for **text box**.

elegant

(Of **code**) Stripped down to the minimum required to achieve the desired effect.

enabled

(Of an **error handler**) Has been switched on by an On Error **statement**.

error handler

A section of **code** designed to **trap** errors, analyze them, and take action if they match given error codes.

event

An occurrence that VBA recognizes as having happened. For example, the opening of a file (by the user or by a **procedure**) typically generates an event.

event procedure

Code that runs directly in response to an **event**.

expression

A combination of **keywords**, **operators**, **variables**, and **constants** that produces a **string**, number, or **object**.

F

fixed-iteration loop

A **loop** that repeats a set number of times.

fixed-size array

An **array** with a fixed number of **subscripts**.

folder contents view

A view in the Project Explorer that displays the **objects** within the **projects** that contain them.

folder view

A view in the Project Explorer that shows the **objects** separated into their folders beneath the **projects** that contain them.

form

Another term for **user form**.

function

A unit of **code** that begins with the declaration Function, ends with the **keywords** End Function, and returns a result.

G

get

To **return** the current value of a **property**.

group box

Another term for frame.

H

hard-coding

Writing fixed **code** as opposed to variable **code**.

I

indefinite loop

A **loop** that repeats a flexible number of times.

Integer variable

A type of **variable** used for storing whole numbers (numbers without fractions).

intrinsic constant

A **constant** that is built into an application. Each intrinsic **constant** is mapped to a numeric value in the group of **constants** in which it belongs.

iteration

One cycle through a **loop**.

K

keyword

A word defined as part of the VBA language—for example, the name of a **statement** or of a **function**.

L

language error

An error caused by misuse of the programming language—for example, mistyping a word, omitting punctuation, or omitting part of a construction.

lifetime

The period during which VBA remembers the value of a **variable**. A variable's lifetime is tied to its **scope**.

linear search

A simple form of search, starting at the beginning of the **array** and continuing until the target item is found or the end of the **array** is reached.

local scope

Another name for **procedure scope**.

logical operators

Operators such as And, Not, and Or, used for building logical structures.

loop

A programming structure that repeats one or more actions.

loop determinant

Another term for **loop invariant**.

loop invariant

A numeric **expression** or a logical **expression** that controls the running of a **loop**.

M

macro

A type of **subprocedure**, often recorded (by using an automatic tool, such as the Macro Recorder in some of the Microsoft Office applications), rather than written from scratch.

method

An action that an object can perform.

mnemonic

Another term for **accelerator key**.

modal

(Of a **user form**) Prevents the user from continuing work in the application while the **user form** remains on screen.

modeless

(Of a **user form**) Not **modal**—allows the user to continue work in the application while the **user form** remains on screen.

modular

(Of **code**) Composed of different components (for example, **procedures**) that you can use in combination. By designing code to be modular, you can easily replace individual components or add extra components.

module

A storage container for **code**.

O

object

A distinct unit of **code** and data, bound together. Most objects have **methods** and **properties** and recognize **events**.

object library

A reference file containing information on a **collection** of **objects** available to programs.

object model

The logical hierarchy in which the **objects** in an **object-oriented** application are considered to be arranged.

object variable

A type of **variable** used for storing references to **objects**.

object-oriented programming

Building an application out of **objects**.

operator

An item used to compare, combine, or otherwise work with values in an **expression**. VBA uses **arithmetic operators**, **comparison operators**, **concatenation operators**, and **logical operators**.

option button

A button that forms part of a group (or set) of options. Only one option button in the group can be selected at any one time. Selecting one option button deselects the option button that is currently selected.

owner application

The application that has created an **object** (such as a **user form**).

P

page

One of the tabbed items in a multipage dialog box (for example, the Options dialog box in many applications).

point

A unit of measurement, $1/72$ inch.

procedure

A unit of **code** that performs a particular task. There are two types of **procedures**: **subprocedures** and **functions**.

procedure calls

The **procedures** being called by the current **procedure**. You can display procedure calls in the Call Stack dialog box.

procedure scope

Scope that makes a **variable** available only to the **procedure** that declares it.

procedure-level scope

Another name for **procedure scope**.

program logic error

An error that produces incorrect results, although there are no syntactical problems and the **code** compiles and runs successfully.

property

An attribute of an **object**.

R

radio button

Another term for **option button**.

read-only property

A **property** whose value you can **return** but which you cannot **set**.

read-write property

A **property** whose value you can both **return** and **set**.

redimension

To resize a **dynamic array**.

remark line

Another name for **comment**.

return

(Of a **property's** value) To get the current value of a **property**.

Run mode

When **code** is running.

runtime

Another term for **Run mode**.

S

scalar variable

A **variable** that isn't an **array** or an object.

scope

The area in VBA within which a **variable** or **procedure** can operate.

set

To assign a value to a **property**.

shadow

To assign to a **variable** a name that VBA already uses as the name of a **function**, a **statement**, a **method**, or another **keyword**. Shadowing an item can cause confusion and is not recommended.

short-circuit evaluation

A logical technique used when evaluating conditions: If the first of two or more complementary conditions is false, you do not evaluate any other conditions contingent upon it. VBA does not perform short-circuit evaluation.

signed

(Of a number) Carries a plus or minus designation. Opposite of **unsigned**.

Single

(Of a **variable**) Single-precision floating point number.

statement

A unit of **code** that describes an action, defines an item, or gives the value of a **variable**.

static variable

A **variable** whose values you want to preserve between calls to the **procedure** in which it is declared.

step

To execute a **procedure** one command at a time (**step into**) or in groups of commands (**step over**, **step out**).

step into

To start to **step** into a **procedure** in **Break mode**.

step out

To execute without stepping the remaining commands in a **procedure** you've started to **step** through. When you step out of a **procedure**, VBA then reenters **Break mode** for any subsequent **procedure**.

step over

To run without stepping a **procedure** called from a **procedure** you're stepping through in **Break mode**. After running the called **procedure**, VBA reenters **Break mode** for the rest of the calling **procedure**.

String

A type of **variable** used for storing text characters or groups of characters.

subprocedure

A unit of code that begins with the declaration Sub and ends with the **keywords** End Sub. A subprocedure does not return a result.

subroutine

Another name for a **subprocedure**.

subscript

See **array subscript**.

syntax error

Another term for **language error**.

system modal

(Of a message box) Prevents the user from taking further actions on their computer until the message box is dismissed.

T

tab *or* **page tab**

The protruding item you click at the top of a **page** in a dialog box to display the page. Often confused with the **page** itself.

tab order

The order in which VBA selects **controls** in a **user form** or **frame** when you move through them by pressing the Tab key (to move forward) or the Shift+Tab key combination (to move backward).

test case

A **variable** or **expression** used to evaluate a Select Case statement.

textual comparison

A non–case-sensitive comparison.

trap

To catch an error with **code** (typically so that you can handle it with an **error handler**).

twip

A unit of measurement used for positioning **user forms** and message boxes. One twip is $1/1440$ inch.

type-declaration character

A character that you add to the end of a **variable's** name in an implicit declaration to tell VBA which **data type** to use for the **variable**.

U

unsigned

(Of a number) Carries no plus or minus designation. Opposite of **signed**.

user form

A custom dialog box and its associated **code**.

user-defined constant

A **constant** created by the user.

V

variable

A location in memory set aside for storing a piece of information that can be changed while a **procedure** is running.

Variant variable

A type of **variable** that can store any type of data. Variant is the default type of **variable**.

W

watch expression

An expression you designate to give you a running display of the value of a **variable** or an **expression**.

Index

Note to the reader: Throughout this index **boldfaced** page numbers indicate primary discussions of a topic. *Italicized* page numbers indicate illustrations.